THE *POETRY* ANTHOLOGY

THE
POETRY
ANTHOLOGY

*Ninety Years of America's Most
Distinguished Verse Magazine*

EDITED BY

Joseph Parisi & Stephen Young

WITH AN INTRODUCTION BY

JOSEPH PARISI

IVAN R. DEE
CHICAGO

THE *POETRY* ANTHOLOGY. Copyright © 2002, 2004 by
The Poetry Foundation. Introduction © 2002 by Joseph Parisi. All rights
reserved, including the right to reproduce this book or portions thereof
in any form. For information, address: Ivan R. Dee, Publisher,
1332 North Halsted Street, Chicago 60622. Manufactured in the United
States of America and printed on acid-free paper.

The permissions and credits beginning on page 491 are part of
this copyright page.

The paperback edition of this book carries the ISBN 1-56663-604-3.

Library of Congress Cataloging-in-Publication Data:
The poetry anthology, 1912–2002 : ninety years of America's most
distinguished verse magazine / edited by Joseph Parisi and Stephen
Young.
    p. cm.
  Includes index.
  ISBN 1-56663-468-7
  1. American poetry — 20th century. I. Parisi, Joseph, 1944–.
II. Young, Stephen. III. Poetry.

PS613.P643 2002
811'.508—dc21

                                            2002031178

CONTENTS

INTRODUCTION • xxiii

CONTENTS

CONTENTS

CONTENTS

CONTENTS

CONTENTS

CONTENTS

CONTENTS

CONTENTS

CONTENTS

xix

CONTENTS

CONTENTS

INTRODUCTION

"There is nothing quite like it anywhere else: *Poetry* has had its imitators, but has so far survived them all. It is an American Institution," T. S. Eliot wrote in 1954, almost forty years after it presented "The Love Song of J. Alfred Prufrock," his first publication. By the time Eliot debuted, in June 1915, the magazine was already famous for giving dozens of other experimentalists their earliest professional appearances. Soon after Harriet Monroe launched it in Chicago in 1912, *Poetry* became notorious, in fact, for promoting iconoclasts and their unorthodox techniques. Featuring Ezra Pound, William Carlos Williams, Carl Sandburg, Marianne Moore, and Wallace Stevens among the then obscure, now standard authors, it became the showcase for what was dubbed (and decried) as the New Poetry.

Poetry offered work by such recognized masters as William Butler Yeats and Edwin Arlington Robinson as well, and it gave the Bengali sage Rabindranath Tagore his first U.S. credit in 1912, the year before he was awarded the Nobel Prize. The magazine also printed many poets who wrote in conventional modes, including Sara Teasdale, Rupert Brooke, and Edna St. Vincent Millay. But the upstart authors of free verse provoked the strongest reactions, especially from irate readers and satirical newspaper columnists.

Vachel Lindsay's thumping rhythms and novel theatrics in "General William Booth Enters into Heaven" proved oddly entertaining in the January 1913 issue, which included the austere first efforts of the mysterious "H.D., *Imagiste*." "Prufrock," on the other hand, was deemed pathological. Carl Sandburg's brawny "Chicago Poems" (March 1914) were dismissed as simply incompetent. To most readers, sentimental versifying like "I think that I shall never see / A poem lovely as a tree" — now, *that* was the genuine article. *Poetry* first printed Joyce Kilmer's "Trees" in August 1913, and it became the most popular piece, by far, that Harriet Monroe printed.

Along with an eclectic mix of styles, the magazine also gave spirited defenses of the daringly different. Particularly for younger poets, widely scattered and struggling to find their own ways of expressing the rapidly changing modern world, the monthly issues validated a wide range of original talents. Within its first months, manuscripts flooded into the *Poetry* office. The "Poetry Renaissance" was rushing forward, forcing radical revisions in the practice and very perception of poetry.

Since that revolution and the seminal decade of the Modernist movement, usually dated from *Poetry*'s founding, the magazine has continued to introduce and promote several generations of New Poets and a remarkable profusion of poetic styles. Through wars and economic slumps, amid social crises and cultural upheavals, and even while teetering, repeatedly, on the brink of bankruptcy, *Poetry* has managed to come out every month, without interruption—an achievement still unmatched in the field. Now in its tenth decade, *Poetry* has presented, often for the first time, virtually every poet of note in the twentieth century. Surveying the record, one of those notables, A. R. Ammons (first appearance: 1959), was moved to write: "The histories of modern poetry in America and of *Poetry* in America are almost interchangeable, certainly inseparable."

Just how closely intertwined the relationship has been may be estimated in this anthology. Besides many groundbreaking works that premiered in *Poetry* and have since joined the canon, we have gathered less familiar pieces, particularly from the early decades, that still repay attention. But given the sheer quantity of work presented in the magazine since 1912, our selections can only suggest the richness of its history.

Volumes 1 through 180, comprising 1,080 issues, hold over 29,000 poems by 4,725 authors. Limited space prevents selections from the many foreign numbers and over 2,000 translations *Poetry* has offered from classical and modern Greek, Latin, Egyptian hieroglyphs, Hebrew, Chinese, Japanese, Gaelic, Indian dialects, German, French, Spanish, Italian, and Portuguese, as well as Russian and other Slavic languages. Nor is it possible to reprint long poems, except in a few excerpts, although the magazine provided first showings for many ambitious works: Pound's "Ur-" and later Cantos, segments of Williams's *Paterson*, John Ashbery's "Self-Portrait in a Convex Mirror," Joseph Brodsky's "A Part of Speech," Robert Pinsky's "An Explanation of

America," Anthony Hecht's "The Venetian Vespers," and "O," the opening section of James Merrill's *Mirabell*, to name but a few. Still, we hope this collection—both the poems that have entered cultural consciousness and the overlooked "gems," as Miss Monroe called her favorites—will offer a fair sample of the range of styles, creative personalities, and poetics that the magazine has played host to over its ninety-year history.

Poetry owes its longevity to this diversity, and to the devotion of generations of poets, editorial staff, readers, and supporters—but, above all, to the first principles and abiding spirit of the Founder, whose generosity, as much as her receptivity to talents of many kinds, set the magazine's standards. Beginning work in a very bleak period for poets, she was as surprised as anyone when her "experiment" turned into a Cinderella story in American letters.

Monroe did not foresee what was to follow from her initiative. She was neither a theorist nor a revolutionary. She had no narrow literary or social agenda: a major reason (along with shaky financing) that so many little magazines quickly fold. The Editor didn't issue a "mission statement" until her second issue, and then only to declare her lack of allegiance to any one aesthetic viewpoint. Rather, she declared, *Poetry* intended to be inclusive, not restrictive:

> The Open Door will be the policy of the magazine—may the great poet we are looking for never find it shut, or half-shut, against his ample genius! To this end the editors hope to keep free of entangling alliances with any single class or school. They desire to print the best English verse which is being written today, regardless of where, by whom, or under what theory of art it is written. Nor will the magazine promise to limit its editorial comments to one set of opinions.

Following these guidelines has been *Poetry*'s practice ever since, and the main source of the staying power that has made it an "Institution."

If Eliot's term is appropriate, *Poetry* is rather unusual for an institution, because of the affection it has elicited. But from the outset, Miss Monroe made the poet-editor relationship extremely personal. Besides detailed comments on manuscripts, a discerning place of publication, and a paycheck—all rarities for emerging poets in her time—she provided a sympathetic ear, "career counseling," and cash in emergencies. She also helped arrange first-book contracts, wrote recommendations, made introductions, and, in the case of Lindsay and Teasdale, even attempted to play matchmaker. *Poetry*'s "Open Door" was taken literally, and streams of poets visited the office and were offered hospitality there and in Miss Monroe's home. These innumerable acts of kindness inspired lifelong loyalties.

During the magazine's formative first decade, as Ezra Pound, Amy Lowell, and other aggressive types tried to sway her toward their particular theories, the Editor was often caught between warring factions. But though she was bullied, Monroe was not easily cowed. Those who didn't get their way considered her woefully misguided, and many told her so, and very bluntly, too. Since she let them rant, without retaliation, the disgruntled continued to argue with her, send manuscripts to her "rotten" magazine—and get printed there—some for decades. Just how candid (and often comical) the give-and-take could be between Monroe, as well as her successors, and hundreds of writers is evidenced in the transcriptions from the voluminous archives that Stephen Young and I have compiled in *Dear Editor: A History of* Poetry *in Letters* (Norton, 2002), which chronicles the politicking and backstage practicalities during its first fifty years.

Monroe's initial motivation for starting the magazine was, to put it frankly, frustration. After twenty-odd years of scant success herself in the literary world, the Editor was determined her own enterprise would be different. Major magazines had printed her poems, but only sporadically, since 1888. By 1910, she recalled in her autobiography, *A Poet's Life*, she had received so many rejections, she "well-nigh ceased sending poems to periodicals." Monroe's unhappy experiences were typical for poets who wrote longer works or dared to deviate from commercial norms. Journals of her time preferred short, generally "uplifting" verses, mainly to fill out columns at the ends of articles and stories.

Monroe's one great success came when she won a commission to write an inaugural poem for the World's Columbian Exposition in Chicago. But about a month before a chorus of five thousand was to perform her "Columbian Ode" on 21 October 1892, the *New York World* pirated the text. She sued for copyright violation, and eventually won a judgment of $5,000.

The episode made her a lifelong defender of poets' rights. The settlement also helped sustain her in the lean years that followed.

Monroe was an art critic for the *Chicago Tribune* from 1909 to 1914, which she realized was "a period of revolutionary change in the arts of painting and sculpture." She lauded Gaugulu, Van Gogh, Cézanne, James McNeill Whistler, and Matisse, and she tracked the latest movements. In *A Poet's Life*, she said the high point of her time as a reviewer was the famous New York Armory Show. At the 1913 exhibition, she enjoyed the puzzled and angry reactions to the dissident artists. Monroe herself didn't appreciate some of their works, but she approved: "They throw a bomb into the entrenched camps, give to American art a much needed shaking-up."

Modern architecture was Monroe's allied interest. She championed Louis Sullivan, the creator of the Chicago Stock Exchange and Auditorium Theater; her brother-in-law, John Wellborn Root, and Daniel H. Burnham designed Chicago's pioneering Monadnock and Rookery buildings. By 1910, cityscapes were transformed by skyscrapers their prototypes had defined. Architects, painters, novelists, dramatists — all had entered the new age created by science and technology. Surveying their progress in the first decade of the twentieth century, Monroe concluded that only poetry seemed stuck in the nineteenth.

Returning from a trip to China early in 1911, Monroe found Chicago "surging with art activities and aspirations," as she counted its cultural assets: the Chicago Symphony Orchestra, the Little Theatre, the new dance troupes, the high-rises, and the Art Institute, which was amply funded and gave large prizes to painters and sculptors. Monroe couldn't help making comparisons with her own neglected art and resenting the inequities. In *A Poet's Life*, she recalled: "I became convinced that something must be done; and since nobody else was doing anything, it might be 'up to me' to try to stir up the sluggish situation. But what could I do?" Instead of envying the Art Institute and the other successful Chicago cultural organizations, she decided to create one herself.

Monroe discussed her "harebrained project" of a poetry monthly with several confidantes, including Hobart C. Chatfield-Taylor, a trustee of several Chicago institutions. He suggested a financial plan. Get 100 people to underwrite the magazine at $50 a year for five years. The $5,000 annual budget would cover expenses; with subscription income, the Editor could even pay the poets. Both agreed the magazine should also offer annual prizes. Though not rich herself, Monroe had friends among Chicago's most prominent citizens, and she began knocking on their doors. By the spring of 1912, the aging entrepreneur (she was fifty-one) had seventy patrons. She then printed up a brochure stating her case. Perhaps even more persuasive than her plea for support was her list of Guarantors to the Fund, a Who's Who of Chicago commerce and society: Chauncey and Cyrus McCormick (McCormick Harvester Company), Mrs. George M. Pullman (railroad cars), Mrs. Julius Rosenwald and Albert H. Loeb (Sears, Roebuck), Edward L. and Martin A. Ryerson (steel), Charles H. Swift (meat packing), as well as newspaper editors, bankers, architects, and attorneys, including Clarence Darrow.

By June 1912, Monroe had 108 people signed up, and stopped soliciting—a decision she later regretted. She then chose her associate editor. Alice Corbin Henderson was witty and very well liked in Chicago artistic circles. Monroe outlined her project, and Mrs. Henderson agreed to join it as first reader. Her eye for talent and sharp critical sense would prove crucial to the magazine's early success.

Monroe then set about finding customers and authors. She spent several weeks in the Chicago Public Library reading recent poetry books, scanning verse in magazines, and making a list. To solicit subscribers and prospective contributors, she printed up two new flyers. The "poets' circular" carried the complete title: *Poetry: A Magazine of Verse,* and a motto from Whitman that would appear on each issue: "To have great poets, there must be great audiences too." Informing the poets of the backing for "this experiment" and of the first $250 prize, Monroe offered them "a chance to be heard in their own place, without the limitations imposed by the popular magazine," payment, and a promise: "We shall read with special interest poems of modern significance, but the most classic subject will not be declined if it reaches a high standard of quality." In early August she sent out the leaflets, with letters to the fifty poets she was most keen on having.

One of the first to respond was Ezra Pound, then a twenty-seven-year-old expatriate living in London. (There in 1910, Monroe had been alerted to his first two books, and read them on the Trans-Siberian Railroad en route to Peking.) Pound not only promised her exclusive U.S. rights to his poems but offered to gather material from "other sources." He enclosed "Middle-Aged" and "To Whistler, American" — in which he referred to his compatriots as "that mass of dolts" — and predicted that a Renaissance in American poetry was "inevitable." By return post, Monroe accepted both poems for her inaugural issue and asked Pound to be *Poetry*'s first foreign agent. So began one of the most productive and turbulent alliances in literary history.

Pound began sending a steady stream of long letters, filled with advice, exhortations, and diatribes against American publishers. In due course, he forwarded poems by Yeats and Tagore, as well as by his unknown "protégés," Richard Aldington and Hilda Doolittle, all of which he took the liberty of "correcting." After editing Doolittle's manuscript, Pound scrawled "H.D., Imagiste" at the bottom and informed her she was now a follower of Imagism, a "movement" he had just invented. Under that banner, he later herded, most uneasily, D. H. Lawrence, James Joyce, John Gould Fletcher, and T. S. Eliot, who, E.P. told H.M. with some surprise, had "actually trained himself AND modernized himself ON HIS OWN." But nearly all rebelled at such labeling. Several eventually allied themselves with the ambitious Amy Lowell, whose watered-down version of Imagism was dismissed by Pound as "Amygisme."

Pound's contributions to *Poetry* were perhaps fifty poems in all, his own and by others he sent. Yet, with the passing years, he claimed more and more credit for Monroe's enterprise, while deprecating her substantial labors. But aside from Eliot and Robert Frost (who already had a book in print), most of Pound's "finds" proved to be minor figures. (As poets, Lawrence and Joyce were great novelists.) E.P. himself became disenchanted with his younger "discoveries" within a few years. More important, to the art in general, were his dictates for radical reform. Pound's checklist, "A Few Don'ts by an Imagiste" (March 1913), and his practical criticism helped strip away the murky abstractions, ornate diction, artificial devices, and obsolete notions of nineteenth-century verse, while fostering precision, concrete language, and direct presentation: foundations of literary modernism.

At the same time, Monroe and Henderson were making their own choices, of course, and promoting Lindsay, Sandburg, Edgar Lee Masters, and Wallace Stevens, in particular. Monroe tore up the November 1914 "War Poem" issue as it was going to press, to make room for the unknown Stevens's "Phases." In 1915, she eagerly accepted "Sunday Morning"—provided he drop three of the original eight sections and allow her to rearrange the order of the sequence. Unlike several prima donnas the Editor dealt with, Stevens was exceedingly modest about his work, and he complied. (When he reprinted the poem in *Harmonium*, in 1923, he quietly restored his original text.) Monroe became his biggest booster. She printed his verse plays, *Three Travelers Watch a Sunrise* and *Carlos Among the Candles*, though both flopped on the stage. While most readers found Stevens hard to fathom, she continued to feature large groups of his poems and give him awards, and repeatedly chided him, in private and in *Poetry*, for not publishing a book. (Despite her enthusiastic support, his first royalties for *Harmonium*, he reported to H.M., came to $6.70.)

Both Pound and Monroe had mixed feelings about William Carlos Williams, and attempted to "improve" his distinctively American work. Dr. Williams did not always appreciate their assistance. H.M. had to pick carefully from among his copious but uneven submissions, and demanded many revisions, to his great irritation. But after venting his spleen, he usually acquiesced to the Editor's changes; sometimes he even admitted she was right. Though Williams could be testy, his self-deprecatory humor made him irresistible, and his several charms offered a sharp contrast to the acerbic and always dogmatic character of his old friend Ezra.

While supportive, Pound was skeptical about Monroe's project from the start. In his very first letter, he wondered: "But? Can you teach the American poet that poetry *is* an *art*? . . . Maybe." He was disappointed by the first numbers, and his faith wavered from issue to issue, especially as the Editor persisted in placing old-style lyrics beside the "advanced" pieces he sent. He was unimpressed by her own more adventurous selections. He ignored Stevens. Of Sandburg he wrote in 1914, "I don't think he is very important but that's the sort of stuff we ought to print." He loathed Lindsay, and predicted (correctly) that he was "set to follow Bret Harte and Field and all that lot."

As he grew less than confident about Monroe's judgment, he prodded her to be more restrictive. His own standards were exceedingly high, and he found even his disciples often fell short. Grateful at first, many he aided quarreled and finally broke with him—a pattern throughout his career—and sent directly to

Monroe. But she wasn't always pleased with them, either, and became more picky about "imports." When she had the temerity to start rejecting or demanding changes in Pound's own work, his little patience was tried, friction increased, and his letters took on a belligerent tone.

Pound was dissatisfied with the prose, as well, and wanted to enlarge the back of the magazine, particularly with his criticism. In 1913, he proposed it be edited entirely by him and his mentor, Ford Madox Hueffer (Ford, after World War I). Monroe told him it would not be "expedient." She had no intention of favoring his, or anyone else's, special agendas. E.P. warned about being "provincial." "If we are provincial," she shot back, "we shall always be so until we cease to take our art and art opinions ready-made from abroad, and begin to respect ourselves."

When the Editor refused to let him run *Poetry* his way, Pound became increasingly hostile, and his letters to Monroe bristled with contempt for her selections and policies. (Writing to others, he belittled "'Arriet" as a "bloody fool" and "silly old she-ass.") By 1914, their mutual endeavor was an undisputed success, but relations between Editor and Foreign Correspondent steadily deteriorated. And despite his promises, E.P. started sending work by himself and "his" authors elsewhere. Then, without telling her, in 1917 he joined Margaret Anderson's rival *Little Review*, also as foreign editor. Worse, in his first article there he declared:

> *Poetry* has done numerous things to which I could never
> have given my personal sanction, and which could not
> have occurred in any magazine which had constituted
> my "instrument." *Poetry* has shown an unflagging cour-
> tesy to a lot of old fools and fogies whom I would have
> told to go to hell tout pleinment and bonnement.

Alice Henderson, his staunchest ally, was shocked, especially since Monroe had not only promoted Pound and his ideas but steadfastly defended him from his many enemies. Instead of asking Pound to resign, Monroe accepted his "Draft of Three Cantos" (following A.C.H.'s encomiums) and paid him £21 in advance—and apologized that she couldn't offer more. Pound kept his affiliation with both magazines, though he groused about his shrinking paychecks from *Poetry*.

In March 1919, Monroe presented four sections from Pound's "Homage to Sextus Propertius." In the next issue, William Gardner Hale, a classicist at the University of Chicago, pointed out dozens of "school-boy" errors in Pound's "translation." "The result of his ignorance is that much of what he makes his author say is unintelligible," Hale concluded. "If Mr. Pound were a professor of Latin, there would be nothing left for him but suicide." Furious, Pound sent a short letter of protest, signing off: "In final commiseration." He did not offer poems again until 1933, though he continued to heckle Monroe and offer helpful hints for freshening up her "established family magazine."

But by 1917, the reform campaign they waged in *Poetry* was accomplished. Had it closed down then, its place in American letters still would have been secure. In some ways, the revolution was *too* successful. In 1918, Mrs. Henderson observed that Imagism (often mistakenly conflated with free verse) had become "a staple of the market": "Nowadays everyone is writing imagist *vers libre*, or what the writers conceive as such, particularly those who at the beginning made the most outcry against it. Free verse is now accepted in good society, where rhymed verse is even considered a little shabby and old-fashioned."

For all that, the Editor was disillusioned when the "great audience" she envisioned didn't materialize. Monroe had hoped that, after five years, the magazine would be self-sustaining; within the first year, in fact, she ran a deficit. Her dream of financial security turned out to be wildly unrealistic. For her successors, that happy state would prove equally elusive. Monroe and later Editors regularly faced major shortfalls, most of them on the eve of a ten-year anniversary, with several minor crises in between. (Although in its most precarious days rates had to be cut, *Poetry* has always found a way to pay its contributors.)

Poetry had other problems on the editorial side, as well. Alice Henderson contracted tuberculosis in 1916, and moved to Santa Fe. She was replaced by Eunice Tietjens, who was enthusiastic but had neither Henderson's rigorous standards nor the authority A.C.H. could apply when she felt H.M. was faltering. Like Pound, Henderson continued to scold when *Poetry* printed weak items, and steered poets Monroe's way, Sherwood Anderson among them. They also collaborated on *The New Poetry*, an often reprinted anthology that became a textbook for the younger generation.

Meanwhile, the Editor faced new competition. Following her pioneering work, and perhaps inspired by *Poetry's* success, several other little magazines had entered the field, the *Little Review* (1914), *Others* (1915), and the *Egoist* (1916) chief among them. At the same time, the big commercial journals, which had shunned the kind of avant-garde work that *Poetry* had gambled on, were beginning to welcome it. "Her" more accessible authors could now get better pay elsewhere. But most continued to send work to Monroe, and she remained loyal to them, as well.

Unfortunately, their later offerings were not always strong. Masters soon went into decline. By the twenties Lindsay became a huge success with the "Higher Vaudeville" of his dramatic readings—America's first "performance poet"—but he wrote less, and worse. Sandburg did not really "progress." The intellectual "high" Modernists thought his work wasn't much to begin with. Monroe's extravagant reviews of Lindsay and Masters, and the scores of pages she gave their later work, ultimately did not elevate their stature. The Editor also gave ample space to Amy Lowell's knock-offs of her betters, but she was seldom satisfied. In hundreds of letters, she nagged, wheedled, and tried to bribe for preferment. (A.C.H. told H.M. in 1918: "There is only one way to handle Amy, and that is with a pair of tongs.") Even in her own day, Lowell's artifices were never quite convincing. After she died, in 1925, and her formidable promotional machinery with her, her reputation faded.

Of course, the great bulk of creative work is middling or worse, whatever the medium or age, and doesn't survive its period of production. Like every other literary journal, *Poetry* devoted much space over the years to material that proved ephemeral. Many of Monroe's choices seem very dull indeed, at this remove—and not just the traditional effusions. "Make it new," Pound commanded, famously. But the majority of the trendy experimental pieces of the teens, in *Poetry* as elsewhere, now seem embarrassing failures. So do the much-heralded novelties of later decades, following an ageless principle of fashion: the more up-to-the-minute today, the more dated tomorrow. Pound likewise defined art as news that stays news. But artists like Yeats, Pound, Stevens, Marianne Moore, and Elizabeth Bishop are always rare. Many contributors over the years, including skillful hacks and celebrated mediocrities that *Poetry* presented in quantity, had their day. Their offerings are not without sociological interest, but (to quote Miss Moore) they can "detain" us no further.

Besides availability of talent, historical circumstances also affect artistic enterprises. World War I had a major impact, as most of *Poetry*'s best English writers went to the trenches and many Americans joined them Over There. Monroe tried to support the effort by printing war poems that dozens of soldiers sent from the front. Rupert Brooke, Joyce Kilmer, and Isaac Rosenberg died on duty, and poets who survived the horrors were slow to recover. After the war, many of the most talented in the new generation went to Paris — where the living was cheaper and easier than in puritanical, Prohibition-era America — and *Poetry* received submissions from several expatriates, including Ernest Hemingway and Kay Boyle. Monroe herself visited Paris in 1923, where she met Pound for the first time, as well as several of the leading writers, artists, and musicians.

But Monroe's stance after the war turned homeward. In several editorials she stated her belief that English tradition, reinforced by Eastern universities and magazines, had imposed a cultural "colonialism" on American artists, instilling a sense of inferiority that stifled their originality. After dealing with feuding theorists for years, Monroe became disenchanted with experiments, as well. As early as June 1916, Mrs. Henderson told her: "What we need to do is to forget schools, forget Imagism, forget *vers libre* (now that that's back history) and talk poetry." In "The Great Renewal" (September 1918), H.M. advised a return to Nature; and downplaying modernist theory, she suggested Americans look to Whitman, Emerson, and Thoreau for inspiration.

Standard-issue "nature" poems were always plentiful in *Poetry*, but Monroe tried to enliven the mix with regional topics. A Southern Number appeared in April 1922. (Allen Tate later edited a superior Southern Number for *Poetry*, in 1932.) On Henderson's recommendation, Monroe featured many cowboy ballads and "Western poems." She also printed A.C.H.'s articles on "New Mexico Folk-songs" and "The Folk Poetry of These States," as well as Helen Hoyt on "Negro Poets" and Fenton Johnson's "Negro Spirituals."

Monroe was a multiculturalist before the word was coined, and anxious to preserve the indigenous cultures of the places she visited. In a long article on Native American arts in the Southwest (September 1920), she worried that many would be destroyed by "Indian schools." She also highlighted Lew Sarett's transcriptions of Chippewa chants and Janet Lewis's renderings of Ojibway songs. These excursions may have come as a relief to readers who had grown weary of the rigors of Modernism and its ascetic tone. In the 10th Anniversary issue (October 1922), Monroe herself turned from foreign avant-gardes: "If America is ever to have a rich spiritual life and to express that life in art, this art must come, not from super-civilized coteries, but from the vital strength of the nation."

Much of what *Poetry* printed in the twenties was undistinguished. But against this drab backdrop, Monroe's displays of the truly first-rate shone all the more brightly, especially poems by Frost, Yeats, Williams, and, above all, Stevens. Meanwhile, another generation was emerging. To these aspiring authors, *Poetry's* reputation made it *the* place to be seen in print. But for them, the battles over formalism and free verse were history and the principles of Modernism simply givens. In their diverse manuscripts, the brightest pledged allegiance to no "schools." Among them were Malcolm Cowley, Glenway Wescott, Louise Bogan, Langston Hughes, Emanuel Carnevali (briefly an assistant at *Poetry*), Laura Riding, Archibald MacLeish, John Dos Passos, Richard Eberhart, and Robert McAlmon, the future founder of Contact Editions (and husband of H.D.'s friend Winifred Bryher). Most visible was the glamorous Edna St. Vincent Millay, whose conventional lyrics and unconventional lifestyle personified the liberated new era. She first appeared in *Poetry* in 1917, and in 1918 it presented "First Fig," which came to epitomize the Jazz Age.

Monroe welcomed the younger poets, even when she didn't accept their postwar attitudes. Of the many students who visited the Editor, the most precocious was Yvor Winters, a nineteen-year-old freshman when they met in 1918. In 1919, he contracted tuberculosis and went to Santa Fe, where he and Mrs. Henderson became friends. The same year, H.M. asked Janet Lewis, a schoolmate of Hemingway's, to tea, then offered her a summer job. Lewis and Hemingway made their first appearances in *Poetry* in January 1923. Lewis also caught TB and moved to New Mexico. She met Winters in 1921, and they married in 1926.

Winters freely offered Monroe his tart assessments of noted practitioners, and *Poetry*. (In 1920, he told her "ninety-five percent of the stuff" she printed was "damnable.") He recommended

Glenway Wescott, extolled Tate, and urged H.M. to print Hart Crane, although she was perplexed by his highly allusive, compressed style. When Crane submitted "At Melville's Tomb" in 1926, she queried him on his puzzling metaphors, and he explicated at length. Though still not convinced, Monroe printed the poem — and their correspondence, six pages of very small print — in the October 1926 issue. In 1927, *Poetry* published "O Caribe Isle!" and "Cutty Sark," section III of *The Bridge,* as well as "Eldorado" in 1930. After Crane's suicide, his mother gave Monroe his final poems, which *Poetry* published in 1933.

Winters's relations with Monroe soured when he became frustrated, like Pound, in his attempts to "enlighten" the Editor. "Believe me, then, for I speak it as a great critic," he notified her, "Edna sounds like a sack full of old kitchen utensils, and Lindsay sounds worse." After H.M. questioned his use of the word "greatest" in a review of Tate in October 1930, he turned nasty. As usual, H.M. took the abuse calmly, then tried, unsuccessfully, for a reconciliation.

By 1930, all of *Poetry*'s first competitors were out of business, including the erratic *Little Review.* As the Depression deepened, *Poetry*'s days appeared to be numbered, too. The Editor prepared for the end. In 1931, she bequeathed *Poetry*'s library, manuscripts, and correspondence files to the University of Chicago. Monroe managed to hold on, but in an April 1932 editorial, "Volume Forty," she doubted "whether there will be a *Volume XLI.*"

Letters poured in from anxious poets and readers, while newspapers across the country decried the possible loss of such a cultural "asset." A Hearst columnist declared: "If POETRY: A MAGAZINE OF VERSE perishes in Chicago, its death will be something in the nature of a national calamity." Many small donations trickled in, subscriptions increased, and some poets requested "no payment" for their work. Then, in 1933, an "emergency grant" from the Carnegie Corporation was received — "the most surprising thing that ever happened to us," Monroe wrote Pound. Even more surprising, the grant was renewed for three years. And so the magazine survived.

Despite *Poetry*'s own difficulties during the Depression, the editors went to great lengths to answer calls for help; the archives are filled with poignant pleas and thank-you letters, especially from younger poets, who were frequently desperate. Their work had a new urgency, too: the self-absorption of the Roaring

Twenties was less acceptable amid social upheaval. Jobless or barely getting by, many were drawn to socialist politics. H.M. was unimpressed by most of their material—she considered Muriel Rukeyser's early submissions "propaganda"—but she did print many leftists. H.M.'s associate editor, Morton Dauwen Zabel, was blunter in his opinion of "proletarian" verse: "The large majority of it reduces serious experience and banal sentiment to a level of equal mediocrity and slipshod craft." Even so, Monroe had Horace Gregory edit a Social Poets Number (May 1936), with work by Rukeyser, Edwin Rolfe, Kenneth Fearing, Hildegarde Flanner, Harold Rosenberg, and Delmore Schwartz.

Among the scores of other emerging writers that *Poetry* presented in the thirties were Theodore Roethke, Paul Engle, May Sarton, Paul Bowles, Robert Fitzgerald, Ruth Lechlitner, J. V. Cunningham, Robert Penn Warren, Lorine Niedecker, Kenneth Patchen, Josephine Miles, Mary Barnard, Richmond Lattimore, Stanley Kunitz, and Elizabeth Bishop. Many contributed reviews, as well, joining Tate, Moore, F. R. Leavis, and Kenneth Burke. The criticism in *Poetry* was often more interesting than the poetry, and reached a new level of incisiveness, thanks to Morton Zabel. An undergraduate at the University of Chicago when he came on in 1929, he was a sharp critic with a low tolerance for poetic claptrap. He corresponded with many authors, including Pound, who hoped to influence H.M. through her assistant. But Zabel thought E.P. was becoming increasingly unsound, disliked his latest protégés (H.M., too, found Basil Bunting and Louis Zukofsky hard to take), and referred to him, in *Poetry*, as "the perpetual undergraduate of Rapallo."

Nonetheless, Monroe printed Cantos XXXIV and XXXVII in 1933 and 1934, with great reluctance and after barbed exchanges. While Pound was denouncing her "ROTTEN EDITING" and praising Mussolini in his letters to Monroe, Winifred Bryher was sending her extremely disturbing reports from Europe detailing the growing violence by the Nazis. Bryher also warned of another war. Monroe did not live to see it.

Returning from a P.E.N. Congress in Buenos Aires in the fall of 1936, the Editor decided to see the Andes and visit the Inca ruins. When she reached Arequipa (or "place of rest"), she was exhausted, but determined to push on to Machu Picchu. On 25 September, she had a massive stroke, and died the next day. Cables flashed the news to Chicago, and papers nationwide ran obituaries praising Monroe's many efforts on behalf of American poets. In a special Memorial Issue for December, Zabel printed several remembrances. Leading them was a tribute from Ezra Pound:

> No one in our time or in any time has ever served the cause of an art with greater devotion, patience, and unflagging kindness. The greater and more frequent one's differences of view about that art, the greater opportunity one had for weighing these qualities in her. . . . It is to Miss Monroe's credit that POETRY never degenerated into a factional organ. . . . [N]o other publication has existed in America where any writer of poetry could more honorably place his writings. This was true in 1911. It is true as I write this.

Harriet Monroe was buried in Peru. Monroe's family, the *Poetry* staff, and many poet-friends resolved to keep the magazine alive as the most fitting monument. Zabel kept *Poetry* afloat for another year, during which he printed an English Number, co-edited by W. H. Auden (January 1937). Besides Auden's "Journey to Iceland," it held Dylan Thomas's "We Lying by Seasand" and work by Stephen Spender, George Barker, and Edwin Muir. After the 25th Anniversary and eight years of highly capable service, Zabel turned over the duties, and mounting deficits, to George Dillon in November 1937.

Like Zabel, Dillon had served as Monroe's right hand while still in college at the University of Chicago. Upon graduation, in 1927, he gained a reputation as a lyric poet with his first book, issued when he was twenty-one, and won the Pulitzer Prize for his second in 1932. In 1936, he and his sometime lover, Edna Millay, collaborated on a translation of Baudelaire's *Flowers of Evil*. Dillon had the unenviable task of preserving *Poetry* as war was about to break out. At this unpromising juncture, a young humorist, Peter De Vries, submitted poems, and Dillon asked him to become first reader in April 1938.

Dillon often edited at long distance, while looking after his aged parents in Virginia. De Vries eased his burdens by handling book reviews. A very witty impromptu speaker, he was soon called upon to help with fund-raising, as well. While *Poetry*'s finances remained shaky, on the editorial side operations ran smoothly, although the new man was more liberal than Dillon. In July 1938, with De Vries's hearty concurrence, he published a special issue devoted to poets in the Federal Writers' Project. Other issues featured longtime *Poetry* contributors Stevens, Williams, Walter de la Mare, Robinson Jeffers, Robert Penn Warren, and Langston Hughes. The best of the younger English poets—Auden, Spender, Bunting, Louis MacNeice—shared the pages with Bishop, Roethke, Gertrude Stein, E. E. Cummings, and Weldon Kees.

In 1941, the Modern Poetry Association was chartered to publish and to support *Poetry*. But by the spring of 1942, there was considerable doubt whether the magazine would last to celebrate the 30th Anniversary. Dillon had tried, twice, to get the Carnegie Corporation to renew its support; both requests were denied. "Beginning the sixtieth volume of POETRY," News Notes for April 1942 began, "we have much the sensation of starting to walk a plank." There was only enough cash to go on for one more week. A special committee hastily gathered donations. In Washington, a benefit was held, co-sponsored by Mrs. Franklin D. Roosevelt. By June the latest emergency was over.

Despite the constant financial worries, Dillon and De Vries maintained quality, as well as *Poetry*'s international perspective. The March 1942 issue featured *Exil* by St.-John Perse (diplomat Alexis Saint-Léger Léger), who eventually won the Nobel Prize in 1960. In May 1943, *Poetry* published its second Latin American issue, which included avant-garde and Marxist authors such as Pablo Neruda of Chile and Nicolas Guillén of Cuba. Not all readers were pleased with what was perceived as a leftist bent.

But *Poetry* continued to welcome a wide range of philosophical viewpoints and poetic styles, from the formal to the surreal. Among those who found very early (and sometimes very first) publication under Dillon and De Vries were Randall Jarrell, John Ciardi, Nelson Algren, Robert Duncan, Robert Lowell, Howard Moss, Howard Nemerov, William Meredith, John Frederick Nims, and Karl Shapiro. The editors were particularly helpful in promoting Shapiro and Nims, both future editors of the magazine—in Nims's case, at three different periods.

After war was declared, many were sending manuscripts from military bases or battle zones. In July 1942, Dillon himself was inducted. Trained for the Signal Corps, he served in West Africa through most of the war. Early in 1943, De Vries also was drafted, but left boot camp in March with a medical discharge and returned to the magazine. That month, he hired Katinka Loeser as associate editor; they were married in October. His predecessors, Jessica Nelson North and Marion Strobel, came back to lend a hand; late in 1944, John Nims joined them as a part-time reader. Amid his several duties at *Poetry*, De Vries completed his second novel and printed his essay, "James Thurber: The Comic Prufrock" (December 1943), with a drawing by the cartoonist— the first appearance of his whimsical Pegasus, which has become the magazine's logo.

Soldier-poets passing through Chicago during the war frequently stopped by the offices on Erie Street and were entertained by the staff and the Association's board members. However straitened its circumstances, *Poetry* maintained its tradition of hospitality. *Poetry*'s August 1943 issue was devoted to "Poets in the Service," including Shapiro, Kunitz, Jarrell, Nemerov, Roy Fuller, and Louis Aragon. As in the Great War, the prose section featured letters from soldiers and news from the battlefields (so far as the censors allowed), and listed deaths in combat. A January 1944 News Note reported that a Liberty ship had been christened the *Harriet Monroe*—probably the first (and only) time a piece of military equipment has been named after a poet or editor. Throughout the war years, the staff had to devote more and more time to fund-raising. Squadrons of volunteers were mobilized to put on additional programs—readings, lectures, musicales, anything but rummage sales—to raise money. Beginning in 1943, four lecture series were also held; among the first speakers were Frank Lloyd Wright, the pianist Rudolf Ganz, and Robert Penn Warren. James Thurber was gratified by De Vries's article (the first serious essay on his work), and agreed to appear in the second lecture series.

Thurber's "impromptu" speech was a great success, and De Vries's introduction itself was a brilliant performance. (Among his many puns, he said Thurber "hit the male on the head." Several in the audience thought *he* was Thurber.) De Vries's wit convinced Thurber that he would make a fine addition to Harold Ross's eccentric staff at *The New Yorker*. At their first meeting, when Ross asked if he could handle the Race Track column, De Vries replied: "No, but I can imitate a wounded gorilla." Ross knew he had the right man. The De Vrieses moved to New York in July 1944, and Peter divided his efforts between the two magazines. While he continued to handle submissions, book reviews, and proofreading from Manhattan, he also hunted for speakers for *Poetry*'s benefit programs.

Meanwhile, *Poetry* continued to make "discoveries." Gwendolyn Brooks, who began sending poems while in high school, first appeared in November 1944. James Merrill was nineteen when he was accepted, and in 1946 the magazine gave him his first professional credit. Kenneth Koch and John Ashbery were also about the same age when both debuted in November 1945 — Ashbery inadvertently, after a prep school classmate stole some of his poems and submitted them under a pseudonym. When Ashbery submitted poems himself, they were rejected. He feared the editors thought *he* was the plagiarist, and waited ten years before sending again.

Sgt. George Dillon was with the vanguard during the Liberation of Paris, and announced the news to the world on 25 August 1944 from his radio post in the Eiffel Tower. He then served in Paris as a translator while awaiting his discharge late in 1945. *Poetry*'s October 1945 issue was devoted to "Poets of the French Occupation and Resistance." Dillon wrote De Vries that he did most of the translations "while waiting around in jeeps." He returned to the States and, rather reluctantly, to the editorship in April 1946.

Editorially and financially, the postwar period was difficult. As costs escalated, the magazine approached over three dozen foundations for support. Every application was rejected. One more attempt was made, to the Bollingen Foundation, which awarded $15,000 for 1947, much to everyone's relief. It later renewed the grant for two years, with the proviso that "the educational benefits resulting from your program justify the expenditure." As part of the "program," between 1947 and 1950 *Poetry* published a series of "Critical Supplements" for classroom use, written by John Nims, Hayden Carruth, and John Berryman. *Poetry* also issued William Elton's *Guide to the New Criticism*, which ran to five editions. The magazine previewed MacLeish's *Notebooks, 1924–1938* in 1948, and three sections of Williams's autobiography-in-progress in 1948–49, as well. Not all readers were pleased with the new emphasis on prose.

Dillon and Nims were not happy about most of the poems coming in, either, although first appearances by David Wagoner, John Berryman, W. S. Merwin, William Stafford, Margaret Avison, Richard Wilbur, and Donald Justice did enliven the front of the magazine. After much debate, in September 1946 *Poetry* printed a section of Canto LXXX from Pound's *Pisan Cantos*, with commentaries by Dillon, T. S. Eliot, and R. P. Blackmur. (The issue led off with Robert Lowell's first appearance, "The Ghost: After Sextus Propertius.") Pound had been indicted for treason in 1943 for his infamous radio broadcasts from Rome. In 1945, he had been arrested, held near Pisa, then brought to the United States. Judged incompetent to stand trial, he was incarcerated in St. Elizabeths, a mental hospital in Washington. Sentiment against Pound ran high. Dillon felt the new Canto deserved to be judged "as a poem," he wrote John Nims, "and not for its academic interest, or topical interest, or anything else."

Constant money worries finally took their toll, and in March 1949 Dillon resigned. He recommended that Hayden Carruth take over. After service in Italy, Carruth had entered graduate school at the University of Chicago, and joined *Poetry* in the spring of 1948. But in naming him editor, the board felt that, at twenty-eight, Carruth was too inexperienced to have total authority. He was given control over prose, but Nims or Marion Strobel had to approve all decisions on poems. The situation soon proved untenable.

Meanwhile, the Library of Congress had awarded Pound the first Bollingen Prize, for the *Pisan Cantos*, early in 1949. Protests erupted, fueled by insinuations in the *Saturday Review of Literature* that the foundation and the judges had sinister intentions. Carruth refuted the smears, and defended freedom of expression, in "The Anti-Poet All Told" (August 1949). He then reprinted it in a pamphlet, "The Case Against *The Saturday Review*," with additional rebuttals by MacLeish, Winters, Mark Van Doren, Malcolm Cowley, and others.

Ironically, the last Bollingen grant was running out. Though not temperamentally suited to the task, Carruth tried diligently to find new funding. His efforts came to nothing. Dillon and Tate contacted the Bollingen trustees for a renewal. They replied they had problems of their own because of the Pound fiasco. Carruth then asked the University of Chicago to take over *Poetry*, and its $20,000 deficit. The University declined the invitation. By the end of November, the situation looked hopeless. Carruth, Strobel, and Geraldine Udell, the business manager, debated who should call the printers to tell them to stop the presses. Carruth prepared a statement that *Poetry* was closing. An hour later, a telegram arrived. The Bollingen trustees had decided, after all, to give the magazine an absolutely final grant.

Carruth felt he now deserved full editorial authority. But some of the older trustees and staff, particularly Marion Strobel, objected to his policies and wanted to keep control. After two meetings, the situation was still unresolved. Carruth threatened to resign. Strobel lined up her supporters and proposed Karl Shapiro for his replacement. At the full board meeting on 9 January 1950, they had their way. That evening, Shapiro got the call and accepted the editorship.

Poetry had "discovered" Shapiro in 1940, printed him often, and given him awards. He won the 1945 Pulitzer Prize for *V-Letter*, his book of war poems. In 1947, when he was Consultant in Poetry at the Library of Congress, the magazine brought him to Chicago for a lecture, and people had to be turned away. Shapiro began teaching at Johns Hopkins, but did not like the job. "I needed to escape the academy," Shapiro recalled at the 75th Anniversary celebration, "and Editor of *Poetry* seemed like a beautiful and exotic alternative." The board believed peace and prosperity had finally come to *Poetry*. Shapiro's five-year tenure turned out to be the rockiest in the magazine's history.

Always outspoken, Shapiro courted controversy. His acerbic articles, like his first assaults on literary dogma in his *Essay on Rime* (1944), created resentment among academic poets and critics. But his literary positions were often inconsistent. His policy at *Poetry*—or, as he boasted, his *lack* of a policy—was sometimes disconcerting. Upon arriving in Chicago, one of Shapiro's first decisions, after deleting the Whitman motto from the cover, was to dismiss Geraldine Udell. His wife, Evalyn, took over her duties, without pay. During her twenty-five years at *Poetry*, Udell had managed the business affairs devotedly and had befriended many trustees and poets. Several trustees resigned in protest. People with influence and expertise replaced them.

Editorially, too, Shapiro started with a clean slate, since there were few accepted poems in the files. Many of the younger poets Shapiro printed had already been "discovered" or presented in

Poetry in the forties. Among the more notable of those who eventually debuted under Shapiro were May Swenson, Frank O'Hara, James Dickey, Anthony Hecht, Philip Booth, Galway Kinnell, and Adrienne Rich. But throughout his term, Shapiro tilted heavily toward his contemporaries: Schwartz, Rukeyser, Wilbur, Roethke, William Jay Smith, Nims, Ciardi, and Jarrell. (Because Shapiro printed his poems exactly as written, Jarrell paid him the compliment, "You don't act like an editor at all.") Like Shapiro, these members of the "Middle Generation" were well-schooled in the Great Tradition. Nearly all of them taught, and in their own work they followed academic norms: compression, allusion, irony, "intellectual" content, and masterful technique displayed in forms polished to high finish—in short, the poetic values that would be abandoned by the rebels of the late fifties and sixties.

Following *Poetry* tradition, Shapiro arranged issues on single themes and devoted to foreign poets. The June 1951 number on modern Greek poetry presented George Seféris, Níkos Kazantzákis, Odysseus Elytis, and several others then unknown in the United States. St.-John Perse got star treatment in October 1951; September 1952 was devoted to other French poets. Creative writing courses were spreading, and one of the more publicized of Shapiro's special issues was the Workshop Number (February 1952), with student work from the programs directed by Paul Engle at Iowa and Theodore Roethke at Washington.

Shapiro's direction of the prose section often provoked negative reactions. Leslie Fiedler panned fifteen books in eleven pages with "Bad Poetry and the Tradition" in January 1951. Edward Dahlberg's bizarre assault on Conrad Aiken's *Ushant* in 1953 caused an uproar, and lost Shapiro Aiken's friendship. Hugh Kenner's several severe critiques also created hard feelings, starting with his demolition of Delmore Schwartz in 1951.

Shapiro discovered the financial side of his job was even more problematic. In 1950, *Poetry* had a projected deficit of $20,000, despite the Bollingen grant. Evalyn Shapiro lobbied the trustees to give another award. In January, the foundation pledged $7,500 for 1951 and $5,000 for 1952. Shapiro promised not to ask again. To balance his own budget, he had to take teaching jobs and give readings and workshops. In 1952, he also became editor of the Newberry Library's *Journal of Acquisitions*. He persuaded Stanley Pargellis, director of the Newberry, to join the board. The Library would eventually rescue the magazine.

In the spring of 1952, Evalyn Shapiro resigned. K.S. invited the wealthy Isabella Gardner to be first reader. She, too, served without pay, and became Shapiro's closest confidante. He then hired Nicholas Joost, a colleague at Loyola University, to handle prose. Joost also served as acting editor during Shapiro's several absences. Wallace Fowlie became foreign editor, remaining on the masthead until 1969.

Shapiro lectured at the Salzburg Seminar in January 1952. On his return, he discovered *Poetry* was losing $500 a month and would be out of business by September. The ten-year cycle was repeating itself, and it looked as though *Poetry* wouldn't make it to its 40th Anniversary. The board tried to get support from several foundations; as usual, it got nowhere. The only hope seemed to be to approach the Bollingen trustees yet again—rather awkward, given Shapiro's promise. Even so, they gave an award of $5,000 for 1953—and then another, *truly* final, grant in 1954.

Poetry squeaked into October. The well-publicized 40th Anniversary double number featured fifty well-known contributors, from Aiken and Auden to Williams and Marya Zaturensky. A special $500 prize for the "best" poem in the issue was awarded to Auden for "The Shield of Achilles." At this rare happy moment Shapiro fired the publicity director, who had just proved her effectiveness. She happened to be the wife of a trustee and was well liked by the board, who were very upset by Shapiro's abrupt action. From that point on, matters went from bad to near-bankruptcy.

Ellen Borden Stevenson, the ex-wife of the presidential candidate, became board president in January 1953. In May, when *Poetry* was evicted from its offices of over twenty years on Erie Street, she offered it space in the Borden family's mansion, which she was turning into an "Art Center." On the eve of the move, Shapiro announced he had received a Guggenheim Fellowship for 1953-54. The trustees had been annoyed by his 1952 trip, and relations with the board grew still more strained. As the magazine went deeper into the red, even the office's extra set of bound volumes had to be sold for quick cash. The rest of the *Poetry* archives followed. The University of Chicago got them for a pittance, but the magazine was desperate.

Mrs. Stevenson had promised to assume financial responsibility until the end of the year. Then she changed her mind. She thought income from her Center would cover expenses, but she soon learned otherwise. *Poetry* now had only $100 on hand. After much unpleasantness, the board met in emergency session. Mrs. Stevenson's letter of resignation was read. Since *Poetry* was no longer welcome in her house, Dr. Pargellis offered it rent-free space in the unheated attic of the Newberry Library.

After almost five years of turmoil, Shapiro wanted a change. He was offered a visiting professorship at Berkeley, starting in January 1955. In November, he informed the board and said he was willing to edit the magazine from California. He proposed Henry Rago as his stand-in. By early spring 1955, Shapiro had decided not to return, but asked that his resignation not be made official until September. Rago was already firmly in control well before the masthead was changed.

Ironically, almost as soon as Shapiro left Chicago, *Poetry*'s fortunes turned. Benefits were held, new donors were found, bankruptcy was averted. Drastic economizing had forced Shapiro to slash printing expenses. *Poetry* was put out with ugly typography on cheap paper bound with staples. It was in this low-budget format that Philip Levine, William Dickey, Donald Finkel, Thom Gunn, Donald Hall, Mona Van Duyn, James Wright, and other new talents made their first appearances in *Poetry*. Rago made it a priority to restore the magazine to its former elegance. The trustees had voted to make Rago "temporary" editor, adding that "his position was not to be regarded as a succession." Rago stayed fourteen years.

Rago visited Harriet Monroe when he was still in high school, and she first printed her "protégé" in 1931, when he was sixteen. Like the Founder, Rago would frequently offer encouraging words and detailed criticism to fledgling poets, including seventeen-year-old Billy Collins, the future Poet Laureate of the United States. After studying law at DePaul University, Rago took degrees in theology and philosophy at Notre Dame. He served in counterintelligence during the war—he met T. S. Eliot in London during the Blitz—and was among the first soldiers to enter Paris after the Liberation. In his three years there, Rago visited Alice B. Toklas and talked poetry with Gertrude Stein.

In 1947, Rago began teaching at the University of Chicago, where he and Hayden Carruth soon became close. When the University failed to reappoint him in 1954, he was delighted to accept Shapiro's invitation to join *Poetry*. Rago never practiced law, but his approach to the business and literary sides of the editorship was lawyer-like: meticulous in every detail. Probably no editor expended more energy than Rago on every aspect of running the magazine, or spent more time communicating with poets. Rago's detailed, gentle suggestions for changes made it difficult to argue with him. He was so courteous in returning manuscripts, he got letters of appreciation from poets he rejected.

Rago's tact and generosity helped him negotiate the quarrelsome sixties, and sustained his friendships with a wide variety of writers who were often not on speaking terms with each other. Many proponents of the new styles were antagonistic, carrying on disputes even more bitter than the theoretical and technical debates during the early days of Modernism. It is a measure of Rago's openness, and the magazine's prestige, that old practitioners and young experimentalists alike were happy to appear in *Poetry*.

Throughout his tenure, Rago made Monroe's Open Door wide enough to admit almost every literary innovator or trendsetter of note. As *Poetry* maintained a place for tradition, it mirrored what was developing into the second revolution in American poetry—a return to the radical ideas and methods of *Poetry*'s original Modernists, which had been tamed by the Academy in the thirties and codified in the New Criticism. By the late fifties and early sixties, an increasing number of emerging poets (and a few established ones) objected to or simply ignored academic strictures and pursued new directions in poetry. Many found inspiration in the example of Whitman and, above all, Dr. Williams, who received house calls from young disciples.

Rago was especially welcoming to the poets associated with Black Mountain College. By 1962, he published dozens of poems by Robert Creeley, Robert Duncan, and Denise Levertov. Charles Olson, the theorist of the Projectivist group, appeared more selectively in 1962 and after. Rago was extremely supportive to James Dickey, and had cordial relations with the combative Robert Bly. He regularly featured Bly and others sometimes labeled as the Deep Image "school," particularly Donald Hall and James Wright. Galway Kinnell, David Ignatow, and W. S. Merwin, among others loosely linked as surrealists, were also frequent contributors.

Most of poets in the "New York School" appeared in *Poetry* years before that misleading title was applied to those rather disparate individuals. John Ashbery, then living in France, sent many poems again beginning in the mid-fifties, as did Kenneth Koch. Frank O'Hara first appeared under Shapiro in 1951, and continued to receive eager acceptances from Rago. James Schuyler began to appear in the mid-sixties.

Although the assertion is often repeated that *Poetry* disregarded the Beats, the record indicates it was the other way around. In May 1957, Rago sent an eloquent letter of support to Lawrence Ferlinghetti for use by the defense at the *Howl* obscenity trial. The *Poetry* staff entertained Allen Ginsberg, Gregory Corso, and Peter Orlovsky at the office in 1959. Throughout his tenure, Rago welcomed and printed other counter-cultural and Eastern-influenced poets from both the East and West coasts — Lew Welch, William Everson (Brother Antoninus), Gary Snyder — and wanted to publish Ginsberg, too. But an editor cannot present work by authors who decline to submit any. Rago invited Ginsberg to send poems early in 1966, and immediately accepted "Wichita Vortex Sutra (I)" when it arrived in April. Unfortunately, *Poetry* couldn't present it: Ginsberg informed him that student pacifists in Omaha had already printed it in a mimeographed magazine.

Besides keeping up with the evolving American scene, Rago offered surveys of poetry abroad. Shapiro had initiated a number of foreign issues, but Rago completed the complicated work of assembling the Japanese (May 1956), Israeli (July 1958), and Indian (January 1959) issues. He regularly presented translations from French, Italian, Greek, and other European poets. Two years after Dylan Thomas died in New York City on 9 November 1953, Rago got a much-delayed special issue on the Welsh poet (now a Memorial Number) into print in November 1955.

In the year before the issue came out, *Poetry* had gone from what Rago later described as "the leanest and meanest time" in its history to unprecedented prosperity. Just as *Poetry* was near collapse in 1954, another angel stepped from the wings, the Chicago financier and art collector J. Patrick Lannan. Instead of several small programs and appeals to the usual sponsors, Lannan proposed one big annual event — to be called Poetry Day — featuring a reading, followed by a dinner and an auction. Robert Frost, one of *Poetry*'s earliest contributors and now

America's most famous poet, was invited to be the first guest of honor. Lannan got publishers, booksellers, and art dealers to donate first editions, paintings, and other items. Frost read to a packed house on 13 November. The auction attracted 168 high-bidding guests. When the evening was over, *Poetry* was well in the black.

So the pattern was set (although the auctions were dropped in later years), and Poetry Day continues as the longest-running reading series in the country. In 1956, Carl Sandburg drew an even bigger audience than Frost. John Crowe Ransom and Archibald MacLeish followed in 1957 and 1958. T. S. Eliot agreed to come in 1959, and the crowd that lined up could have filled Orchestra Hall twice over. W. H. Auden and Marianne Moore were only slightly less popular in 1960 and 1961. In 1962, Frost returned to give the reading, one of his last, in celebration of *Poetry*'s Golden Anniversary.

After two and a half years in the Newberry, *Poetry* was able to move to rented space at 1018 North State Street. Rago had the typography and layout of the magazine redesigned; the new format was introduced with the January 1957 issue. After the first Poetry Day, Rago was freer to concentrate on editing. But he worked tirelessly at promotion, and in each annual report the Editor announced steady increases in subscriptions, advertising, and national publicity. By 1961, monthly circulation had hit 5,500, making *Poetry* the largest of the little magazines.

Work on the 50th Anniversary issue and the year-long celebration began early in 1961. Rago also arranged *Poetry*'s third British number (May 1962), which included Donald Davie, R. S. Thomas, Austin Clarke, Ted Hughes, and several others. The entire July 1962 bilingual issue was devoted to Yves Bonnefoy. The Anniversary issue itself (October–November 1962) was the largest to date, at 160 pages, and featured work by almost sixty poets from both sides of the Atlantic. The most prominent of the postwar generation—Merrill, Merwin, Dickey, Gunn, Levertov, Lowell, Creeley, Sexton—mingled with several of *Poetry*'s long-time contributors—Aiken, Frost, Cummings, Graves, Jarrell, Rukeyser, Schwartz, Spender, Williams, Zukofsky.

Rago was even able to get a piece from the almost silent Ezra Pound. Along with a section from Canto CXIII, the issue printed facsimiles of the opening of the "Three Cantos" from 1917 and the manuscripts of "Prufrock," "Sunday Morning," and poems by Joyce, Williams, Frost, Moore, Crane, and Yeats. The number sold out quickly, and was reprinted as a paperback. By the fall of 1962, *Poetry*'s circulation was about 6,000; the magazine was now sent to every state in the Union and eighty-two foreign countries, seven behind the Iron Curtain.

To coincide with the Jubilee, the Library of Congress put on a three-day National Poetry Festival, 22–24 October, with the theme "Fifty Years of American Poetry." Rago gave the welcoming address, followed by Morton Dauwen Zabel, who offered pointed remarks about "The Poetry Journal in Our Time" and *Poetry*'s singular role. Eighty-five poets read. Frost, whose status as Grand Old Man was confirmed at the Kennedy inauguration, gave the longest address. He recalled Harriet Monroe as "a great little lady": "she wanted to be thought as good a poet as anyone, and she didn't get that recognition . . . she just hid her poetry by being such an editor."

Frost repeated most of his Festival recitations at Poetry Day, on 16 November. The crowds were so large that many had to be turned away. The gala was the high point of Rago's tenure. On the larger scene, the Golden Jubilee marked the end of an era. Frost died 29 January 1963; Williams was gone two months later. Hilda Doolittle had died in 1961, her fellow Imagiste, Richard Aldington, in 1962. Harriet Monroe's other original contributors and oldest collaborators soon followed: Zabel in 1964, Eliot in 1965, Sandburg in 1967, and Dillon in 1968. Pound and Moore lived until 1972, but their creative lives ended in the sixties.

From the sixties onward, Pound's call to "make it new" was heeded again, with gusto, as anti-Establishment poets defied the academic dogma they had been taught and identified with the iconoclasm of the old avant-garde. A second poetry renaissance was set in motion. It too became a revolution, in the primary sense: a return to the original principles and radical methods of Pound and the other experimentalists that *Poetry* first championed. By the late sixties, the notion of arbiters, orthodoxy, and a dominant style became unacceptable to the Now Generation. The diversity of approaches to poetry reflected the social and political upheavals of a culture again in rapid flux. The Generation Gap proclaimed by sociologists was expressed in the art world by a multiplicity of literary sectarians who segregated themselves in ideo-aesthetic subgroups. Rago was amicable to all camps, and printed the latest New Poetries sent in from the increasingly fragmented provinces of American poetry.

Amid the proliferation of new literary journals, *Poetry* maintained its leadership as the place where both established and emerging authors vied to appear, and circulation approached 9,000 by the end of the decade. But even with his stamina, Rago began to feel the strain of keeping *Poetry* going after fourteen years. He had begun teaching at the University of Chicago again, and asked for a year's leave of absence beginning October 1968. To fill in for him, he picked Daryl Hine, a young Canadian poet. By the spring of 1969, Rago and the board decided to make his leave permanent, and Hine was designated as his successor. Rago was about to depart for a summer on the Continent with his family when he had a heart attack. He died on 26 May 1969, eight months after leaving *Poetry*, at age fifty-three.

Hine was thirty-two when he came on board. After studying classics at McGill, he had taken his doctorate in comparative literature at the University of Chicago, and had already published five poetry collections and a novel. Like his good friend James Merrill, he was a formalist; and like him, he infused his finely crafted work with wit and wide cultural allusions during a period when those elements of style were being downgraded. But throughout his tenure, Hine was receptive to the new varieties of poetry, from the surreal to the confessional; he himself wrote much that was autobiographically inspired, including an epic in verse. Nonetheless, because his own style was formal, Hine was accused of favoring similar work in his editorial choices.

Such claims of bias were nothing new. Indeed, since Harriet Monroe's first issues—and no matter how active *Poetry*'s promotion of free verse and Imagism, as well as successive waves of innovative techniques in later decades—the editors have been reproached for presenting traditional types of verse. Early and late, allegations about *Poetry*'s supposed resistance to change have been retailed by aesthetic partisans. But during the increasingly acrimonious late sixties and early seventies, literary disputes became inextricably mixed with the divisive social and political issues of the day. Opposing sides were increasingly unwilling to give each other quarter. The modes of artistic works were taken as symptomatic of deeper philosophical issues or moral dispositions. The *free* in free verse was easily misconstrued, and given a political sense equating it with democracy, liberality, or liberation, of various kinds.

Because he chose to write in forms, many assumed and some charged that Hine was conservative. Perusals of the almost one hundred issues he edited prove otherwise. Although he was not enthusiastic about all the poets Rago favored, Hine adhered to the Open Door policy, and like all his predecessors he admitted accomplished work, "regardless of where, by whom, or under what theory of art it [was] written." He continued to publish many poets who had first appeared during H.R.'s tenure, including Adrienne Rich, May Swenson, Wendell Berry, Mark Strand, and Charles Wright. He also accepted early work by authors as diverse as Stephen Dobyns, Louise Glück, Erica Jong, Alfred Corn, Tom Disch, J. D. McClatchy, Lisel Mueller, Stephen Berg, Timothy Steele, Marilyn Hacker, Mark Jarman, Sandra McPherson, Sandra M. Gilbert, Margaret Atwood, Dave Smith, David Bottoms, and Robert Pinsky. Hine broke with *Poetry*'s generally non-political stance by publishing an anti–Vietnam War issue, with an all-black cover, in September 1972. He also printed a special translation issue featuring dissident underground Soviet poets in July 1974.

By the mid-seventies, *Poetry* began to have money problems, again. Like Carruth, Hine was not naturally inclined toward fundraising or publicity campaigns; and he had strained relations with the board, as well. He had been unhappy in the position for some time, but the additional burdens distracted him more and more from his own work, creating resentment. In the summer of 1977, he submitted his resignation, with a recommendation that John Nims succeed him.

Having served on staff in the dark days of the forties, Nims was well familiar with financial crises at *Poetry*. But no sooner had he taken over when a novel difficulty arose. *The Reader's Guide to Periodical Literature* decided to drop several literary magazines from its listings, *Poetry* included. Since many libraries subscribed only to journals listed in the *Guide*, the consequences were serious: sixty percent of subscriptions were institutional then. (Today sixty percent are individuals.) Within a year, the magazine lost hundreds of orders. As deficits rose, Nims took a salary cut. In February 1979, he was able to save rent by moving *Poetry*'s office, and extensive library, from 1228 North Dearborn Street to space provided by the University of Illinois at Chicago, where he taught.

Though subscriptions fell, submissions came in unabated, of course. Nims had taught literature and writing for almost forty years (his textbook, *Western Wind*, is still used widely), and he had many acquaintances in the literary world. They and their students were prompt to send work. Nims particularly welcomed fellow translators Richmond Lattimore and Richard Wilbur, as well as Donald Hall, Lisel Mueller, A. R. Ammons, Linda Pastan, Carolyn Kizer, Stephen Dunn, Gerald Stern, and Miller Williams. But poets of all varieties found a warm reception.

Even the rejected were encouraged to send again: not surprising, since Nims took considerable time to jot detailed, personal notes explaining his decisions and suggesting improvements. (These letters were usually far more interesting, and amusing, than the poems he sent back with them.) Among the younger poets published during his five years were Rita Dove, Mary Karr, Gary Soto, Alice Fulton, Albert Goldbarth, Pattiann Rogers, Carole Oles, and Edward Hirsch.

Although his tenure was relatively brief, Nims was able through his genial care to increase goodwill toward the magazine. And his personal sacrifices, as during his earliest service on the staff, made it easier for *Poetry* to weather another difficult period of stringent economy. In the summer of 1983, he was approaching seventy, and planned to retire from teaching. He wanted more time to work on his poetry and finish new editions of his books of translations, *Sappho to Valéry* and *The Poems of St. John of the Cross*. His resignation became official in September.

During our years at the magazine—twenty-six thus far, in my case, nineteen of them as editor-in-chief, and Stephen Young's fourteen as first reader and senior editor—we have observed probably every theme and variation in contemporary poetry, from formal verse to experiments beyond description, as expressed in numberless specimens received in the mail. Over the last two decades, however, there has been a growing re-emphasis on traditional craft—formalism never died, of course—doubtless stemming from practice in writing programs. Today's younger generations have not had to choose sides as in the literary battles of decades past.

By the same token, authentic avant-gardes—which once provided creative friction and useful opposition to convention—have dwindled and all but disappeared. Erstwhile iconoclasts have become the new Establishment. Poetry has been institutionalized, like "serious" music and the visual arts. "Outsiders" are welcomed and find refuge in the university, and become insiders; (mildly) dissident ideas are co-opted, assimilated, and copied very quickly, producing the homogenized species that constitute today's period styles. The term "academic" has a meaning quite other than what it was a half-century ago.

In any case, technical prowess by itself has never been a primary criterion in making choices at *Poetry*, which has always maintained its independence. To be sure, we appreciate solid workmanship, as well as truly imaginative innovations. But like most other readers, including readers of *Poetry*, we hope to find individual voices, fresh perspectives, interesting ideas—content, too, since it is not forbidden for works of art to be *about* something—as well as verbal panache, striking imagery, perceptive metaphor, and other poetic values that reward attention. Our selections from the issues we ourselves have edited are partial, in every sense; but we hope they represent fairly what is outstanding in recent poetry, as well as the continuing diversity and consistent quality that have characterized *Poetry* over its many years.

Time is the friend of anthologists; their enemy, too. The prodigious outpourings of poetry in the first half of the last century have already been thoroughly argued over by critics and winnowed by literary historians. Harriet Monroe's faith in her "experiment" was vindicated long ago, of course. The Poetry Renaissance and the modernism it fostered remained the most influential forces in twentieth-century literary history—and very hard acts to follow. No period since has proven as significant or produced so many masterworks in so short a space. But they were but few, as always, in comparison with the mass of material forming the general milieu. (Yvor Winters's estimate of the ratio of bad to good was generous.) Unlike most of the first revolutionaries, the mid-century counter-culture rebels had a genius for publicity (sometimes exceeding their actual writing ability). The changes in style they effected in the late fifties and sixties were in many ways recyclings of the basic disjunctive techniques invented by the intrepid artists of the teens and twenties.

Our selections from *Poetry*'s pages from mid-century onward, while reflective of a certain consensus and of the perspective that hindsight allows, are necessarily abridged. But it is sobering to reflect how many big names of the sixties and seventies have already been eclipsed. Robert Lowell, for example, enjoyed major attention throughout the different phases of his career, from arch-academic formalist to free-form confessionalist. Immediately after his death, the estimate of his work fell precipitously, and has continued to drop. (Meanwhile, in a countermovement by the wheel of fortune, the small, exquisite body of work by his good friend, the reticent Elizabeth Bishop, has been accorded ever-increasing esteem.) The nearer we approach our own time, the less certain we can be that what we find remarkable will leave a lasting impression. It is presumptuous at best to predict what portion of present-day work future readers will find to their taste and worthy of remembrance.

Contemporary poets share the benefits, and the burdens, of the efforts by artists and critics who preceded them. Editors do, as well. But the process of assembling an anthology is different from putting out a monthly publication. Practical realities— deadlines, the quality of offerings (or lack thereof) at any given moment—determine the character of a periodical, issue to issue, usually more than theoretical concerns. As magazine editors, we hope that future readers (and anthologists) may also find merit— and pleasure, too—in our selections for *Poetry*. In the meantime, we can only try to choose wisely from the best that is currently available—whatever the individual nature of its excellence—to support the genuine, and to encourage what seems most promising among the newest developments.

Poetry's circulation has risen to the highest point in its history (it is again the largest of the little magazines), and with it the number of submissions. At present, more than 90,000 poems are received each year, from around the world. And in keeping with the magazine's Open Door tradition, we have been particularly interested in finding and promoting untried talents. Over the last decade, about a third of the poets printed in *Poetry* each year have been first appearances, many of them still in school or recent graduates. For today's aspirants, Harriet Monroe's magazine remains, as Gwendolyn Brooks once called it, "The Goal." As authors young and older continually write us, *Poetry* is the place before all where they want to be printed. We hope that these selections from nine decades will indicate how the magazine has achieved its unique place in modern literature, as well as in the affections of poets.

— JOSEPH PARISI

NOTE

All poems in this collection are based on the original texts as they were first printed in *Poetry*. Some were retitled or revised in subsequent publication in books; most of the group titles in the magazine before 1937 were supplied by Harriet Monroe. The works are arranged here in chronological order, except for the last poem, which is taken from the September 1995 issue. Although a good number of the poets in this anthology made their earliest appearances in print in *Poetry*, we have not always chosen their debut offerings. Several authors went on to produce stronger, more distinctive work in later years, and we have tried to represent them with selections that indicate their more mature or characteristic styles.

We are deeply grateful to the many poets, heirs, executors, and publishers who allowed us to include work in this collection. Regrettably, some famous authors who appeared early and often in *Poetry*, as well as significant poems that were introduced in the magazine, could not be represented in this anthology, because permission was not granted or excessive fees were demanded by copyright holders. The Founder-Editor, who was very kind to a number of the writers missing here, tended to hold her silence and to forgive when her generosity was forgotten. The present Editor is not so inclined.

THE *POETRY* ANTHOLOGY

TO WHISTLER, AMERICAN

On the loan exhibit of his paintings at the Tate Gallery.

You also, our first great,
Had tried all ways;
Tested and pried and worked in many fashions,
And this much gives me heart to play the game.

Here is a part that's slight, and part gone wrong,
And much of little moment, and some few
Perfect as Dürer!

"In the Studio" and these two portraits,* if I had my choice!
And then these sketches in the mood of Greece?

You had your searches, your uncertainties,
And this is good to know—for us, I mean,
Who bear the brunt of our America
And try to wrench her impulse into art.

You were not always sure, not always set
To hiding night or tuning "symphonies";
Had not one style from birth, but tried and pried
And stretched and tampered with the media.

You and Abe Lincoln from that mass of dolts
Show us there's chance at least of winning through.

                                        EZRA POUND

* "Brown and Gold – de Race."
  "Grenat et Or – Le Petit Cardinal."

ΧΟΡΙΚΟΣ

The ancient songs
Pass deathward mournfully.

Cold lips that sing no more, and withered wreaths,
Regretful eyes, and drooping breasts and wing—
Symbols of ancient songs
Mournfully passing
Down to the great white surges,
Watched of none
Save the frail sea-birds
And the lithe pale girls,
Daughters of Okeanos.

And the songs pass
From the green land
Which lies upon the waves as a leaf
On the flowers of hyacinth;
And they pass from the waters,
The manifold winds and the dim moon,
And they come,
Silently winging through soft Kimmerian dusk,
To the quiet level lands
That she keeps for us all,
That she wrought for us all for sleep
In the silver days of the earth's dawning—
Proserpine, daughter of Zeus.

And we turn from the Kuprian's breasts,
And we turn from thee,
Phoibos Apollon,
And we turn from the music of old
And the hills that we loved and the meads,
And we turn from the fiery day,
And the lips that were over-sweet;
For silently
Brushing the fields with red-shod feet,
With purple robe
Searing the flowers as with a sudden flame,
Death,
Thou hast come upon us.

And of all the ancient songs
Passing to the swallow-blue halls
By the dark streams of Persephone,
This only remains:
That in the end we turn to thee,
Death,
That we turn to thee, singing
One last song.

O Death,
Thou art an healing wind
That blowest over white flowers
A-tremble with dew;
Thou art a wind flowing
Over long leagues of lonely sea;
Thou art the dusk and the fragrance;
Thou art the lips of love mournfully smiling;
Thou art the pale peace of one
Satiate with old desires;
Thou art the silence of beauty,
And we look no more for the morning;
We yearn no more for the sun,
Since with thy white hands,
Death,
Thou crownest us with the pallid chaplets,
The slim colorless poppies
Which in thy garden alone
Softly thou gatherest.

And silently;
And with slow feet approaching;
And with bowed head and unlit eyes,
We kneel before thee:
And thou, leaning towards us,
Caressingly layest upon us
Flowers from thy thin cold hands,
And, smiling as a chaste woman
Knowing love in her heart,
Thou sealest our eyes
And the illimitable quietude
Comes gently upon us.

RICHARD ALDINGTON

GENERAL WILLIAM BOOTH ENTERS INTO HEAVEN

(To be sung to the tune of "The Blood of the Lamb" *with indicated instruments.)*

Booth led boldly with his big bass drum.
Are you washed in the blood of the Lamb?
The saints smiled gravely, and they said, "He's come."

Bass drums   *Are you washed in the blood of the Lamb?*
Walking lepers followed, rank on rank,
Lurching bravos from the ditches dank,
Drabs from the alleyways and drug-fiends pale —
Minds still passion-ridden, soul-powers frail!
Vermin-eaten saints with mouldy breath,
Unwashed legions with the ways of death —
Are you washed in the blood of the Lamb?

Every slum had sent its half-a-score
The round world over — Booth had groaned for more.
Every banner that the wide world flies
Bloomed with glory and transcendent dyes.
Big-voiced lasses made their banjos bang!

Banjo   Tranced, fanatical, they shrieked and sang,
Are you washed in the blood of the Lamb?
Hallelujah! It was queer to see
Bull-necked convicts with that land make free!
Loons with bazoos blowing blare, blare, blare —
On, on, upward through the golden air.
Are you washed in the blood of the Lamb?

Booth died blind, and still by faith he trod,
Eyes still dazzled by the ways of God.

Bass drums
slower and
softer Booth led boldly and he looked the chief:
Eagle countenance in sharp relief,
Beard a-flying, air of high command
Unabated in that holy land.

Jesus came from out the Court-House door,
Stretched his hands above the passing poor.

Flutes   Booth saw not, but led his queer ones there
Round and round the mighty Court-House square.

Yet in an instant all that blear review
Marched on spotless, clad in raiment new.
The lame were straightened, withered limbs uncurled
And blind eyes opened on a new sweet world.

Drabs and vixens in a flash made whole!
Gone was the weasel-head, the snout, the jowl;
Sages and sibyls now, and athletes clean,
Rulers of empires, and of forests green!

Bass drums louder and faster

The hosts were sandalled and their wings were fire —
    Are you washed in the blood of the Lamb?
But their noise played havoc with the angel-choir.
    Are you washed in the blood of the Lamb?
Oh, shout Salvation! it was good to see
Kings and princes by the Lamb set free.
The banjos rattled, and the tambourines
Jing-jing-jingled in the hands of queens!

Grand chorus – tambourines – all instruments in full blast

And when Booth halted by the curb for prayer
He saw his Master through the flag-filled air.
Christ came gently with a robe and crown
For Booth the soldier while the throng knelt down.
He saw King Jesus — they were face to face,
And he knelt a-weeping in that holy place.
    Are you washed in the blood of the Lamb?

Reverently sung – no instruments

             NICHOLAS VACHEL LINDSAY

EPIGRAM

(After the Greek)

The golden one is gone from the banquets;
She, beloved of Atimetus,
The swallow, the bright Homonoea:
Gone the dear chatterer;
Death succeeds Atimetus.

             H. D.,
               "Imagiste."

From CONTEMPORANIA

TENZONE

Will people accept them?
                    (i.e. these songs).
As a timorous wench from a centaur
                    (or a centurian),
Already they flee, howling in terror.
Will they be touched with the truth?
                    Their virgin stupidity is untemptable.
I beg you, my friendly critics,
Do not set about to procure me an audience.

I mate with my free kind upon the crags;
                    the hidden recesses
Have heard the echo of my heels.
                    in the cool light,
                    in the darkness.

IN A STATION OF THE METRO

The apparition   of these faces   in the crowd :
Petals   on a wet, black   bough .

EZRA POUND

PROOF OF IMMORTALITY

For there is one thing braver than all flowers;
    Richer than clear gems; wider than the sky;
Immortal and unchangeable; whose powers
    Transcend reason, love and sanity!

And thou, beloved, art that godly thing!
    Marvelous and terrible! in glance
An injured Juno roused against Heaven's King!
    And thy name, lovely One, is Ignorance.

WILLIAM CARLOS WILLIAMS

TREES

I think that I shall never see
A poem lovely as a tree.

A tree whose hungry mouth is prest
Against the earth's sweet flowing breast;

A tree that looks at God all day,
And lifts her leafy arms to pray;

A tree that may in Summer wear
A nest of robins in her hair;

Upon whose bosom snow has lain;
Who intimately lives with rain.

Poems are made by fools like me,
But only God can make a tree.

JOYCE KILMER

From LUSTRA

I

O helpless few in my country,
O remnant enslaved!

Artists broken against her,
A-stray, lost in the villages,
Mistrusted, spoken-against,

Lovers of beauty, starved,
Thwarted with systems,
Helpless against the control;

You who can not wear yourselves out
By persisting to successes,
You who can only speak,
Who can not steel yourselves into reiteration;

You of the finer sense,
Broken against false knowledge,
You who can know at first hand,
Hated, shut in, mistrusted:

Take thought.
I have weathered the storm,
I have beaten out my exile.

III FURTHER INSTRUCTIONS

Come, my songs, let us express our baser passions.
Let us express our envy for the man with a steady job and no
worry about the future.

You are very idle, my songs,
I fear you will come to a bad end.

You stand about the streets. You loiter at the comers and
bus-stops,
You do next to nothing at all.
You do not even express our inner nobility,
You will come to a very bad end.

And I? I have gone half cracked.
I have talked to you so much
that I almost see you about me,
Insolent little beasts! Shameless! Devoid of clothing!

But you, newest song of the lot,
You are not old enough to have done much mischief.
I will get you a green coat out of China
With dragons worked upon it.
I will get you the scarlet silk trousers
From the statue of the infant Christ at Santa Maria Novella;

Lest they say we are lacking in taste,
Or that there is no caste in this family.

EZRA POUND

IRRADIATIONS

I

The iridescent vibrations of midsummer light
Dancing, dancing, suddenly flickering and quivering,
Like little feet or the movement of quick hands clapping,
Or the rustle of furbelows, or the clash of polished gems.
The sparkling mosaic of the mid-day light
Colliding, sliding, leaping and lingering:
Oh, I could lie on my back all day,
And mark the mad ballet of the midsummer sky.

II

Over the roof-tops race the shadows of clouds:
Like horses the shadows of clouds charge down the street.

Whirlpools of purple and gold,
Winds from the mountains of cinnabar,
Lacquered mandarin moments, palanquins swaying and balancing
Amid the vermilion pavilions, against the jade balustrades;
Glint of the glittering wings of dragon-flies in the light;
Silver filaments, golden flakes settling downwards;
Rippling, quivering flutters; repulse and surrender,
The sun broidered upon the rain,
The rain rustling with the sun.
Over the roof-tops race the shadows of clouds,
Like horses the shadows of clouds charge down the street.

VI

Not noisily, but solemnly and pale,
In a meditative ecstasy, you entered life,
As for some strange rite, to which you alone held the clue.
Child, life did not give rude strength to you;
From the beginning you would seem to have thrown away,
As something cold and cumbersome, that armor men use against death.
You would perchance look on death face to face and from him wrest
    the secret

Whether his face wears oftenest a smile or no?
Strange, old and silent being, there is something
Infinitely vast in your intense tininess:
I think you could point out with a smile some curious star
Far off in the heavens which no man has seen before.

X

Slowly along the lamp-emblazoned street,
Amid the last sad drifting crowds of midnight
Like lost souls wandering,
Comes marching by solemnly
As for some gem-bedecked ritual of old,
A monotonous procession of black carts
Full-crowded with blood-red blossom:
Scarlet geraniums
Unfolding their fiery globes upon the night.
These are the memories of day moulded in jagged flame:
Lust, joy, blood and death.
With crushed hands, weary eyes, and hoarse clamor,
We consecrate and acclaim them tumultuously
Ere they pass, contemptuous, beyond the unpierced veil of silence.

XI

The flag let loose for a day of festivity:
Free desperate symbol of battle and desire,
Leaping, lunging, tossing up the halliards:
Below it a tumult of music,
Above it the streaming wastes of the sky,
Pinnacles of clouds, pyres of dawn,
Infinite effort, everlasting day.
The immense flag waving
Aloft in glory:
Over seas and hilltops
Transmitting its lightnings.

JOHN GOULD FLETCHER

ILLICIT

In front of the sombre mountains, a faint, lost ribbon of rainbow,
And between us and it, the thunder;
And down below, in the green wheat, the laborers
Stand like dark stumps, still in the green wheat.

You are near to me, and your naked feet in their sandals,
And through the scent of the balcony's naked timber
I distinguish the scent of your hair; so now the limber
Lightning falls from heaven.

Adown the pale-green, glacier-river floats
A dark boat through the gloom—and whither?
The thunder roars. But still we have each other.
The naked lightnings in the heavens dither
And disappear. What have we but each other?
The boat has gone.

D. H. LAWRENCE

THE CODE—HEROICS

There were three in the meadow by the brook,
Gathering up windrows, piling haycocks up,
With an eye always lifted toward the west,
Where an irregular, sun-bordered cloud
Darkly advanced with a perpetual dagger
Flickering across its bosom. Suddenly
One helper, thrusting pitchfork in the ground,
Marched himself off the field and home. One stayed.
The town-bred farmer failed to understand.

What was there wrong?
                         Something you said just now.
What did I say?
                    About our taking pains.
To cock the hay?—because it's going to shower?
I said that nearly half an hour ago.
I said it to myself as much as you.

You didn't know. But James is one big fool.
He thought you meant to find fault with his work.
That's what the average farmer would have meant.
James had to take his time to chew it over
Before he acted; he's just got round to act.

He *is* a fool if that's the way he takes me.

Don't let it bother you. You've found out something.
The hand that knows his business won't be told
To do work faster or better—those two things.
I'm as particular as anyone:
Most likely I'd have served you just the same:
But I know you don't understand our ways.
You were just talking what was in your mind,
What was in all our minds, and you weren't hinting.
Tell you a story of what happened once.
I was up here in Salem, at a man's
Named Sanders, with a gang of four or five,
Doing the haying. No one liked the boss.
He was one of the kind sports call a spider,
All wiry arms and legs that spread out wavy
From a humped body nigh as big as a biscuit.
But work!—that man could work, especially
If by so doing he could get more work
Out of his hired help. I'm not denying
He was hard on himself: I couldn't find
That he kept any hours—not for himself.
Day-light and lantern-light were one to him:
I've heard him pounding in the barn all night.
But what he liked was someone to encourage.
Them that he couldn't lead he'd get behind
And drive, the way you can, you know, in mowing—
Keep at their heels and threaten to mow their legs off.
I'd seen about enough of his bulling tricks—
We call that bulling. I'd been watching him.
So when he paired off with me in the hayfield
To load the load, thinks I, look out for trouble!
I built the load and topped it off; old Sanders
Combed it down with the rake and said "O.K."
Everything went right till we reached the barn
With a big take to empty in a bay.

You understand that meant the easy job
For the man up on top of throwing down
The hay and rolling it off wholesale,
Where, on a mow, it would have been slow lifting.
You wouldn't think a fellow'd need much urging
Under those circumstances, would you now?
But the old fool seizes his fork in both hands,
And looking up bewhiskered out of the pit,
Shouts like an army captain, "Let her come!"
Thinks I, D'ye mean it? "What was that you said?"
I asked out loud so's there'd be no mistake.
"Did you say, let her come?" "Yes, let her come."
He said it over, but he said it softer.
Never you say a thing like that to a man,
Not if he values what he is. God, I'd as soon
Murdered him as left out his middle name.
I'd built the load and knew just where to find it.
Two or three forkfuls I picked lightly round for
Like meditating, and then I just dug in
And dumped the rackful on him in ten lots.
I looked over the side once in the dust
And caught sight of him treading-waterlike,
Keeping his head above. "Damn ye," I says,
"That gets ye!" He squeaked like a squeezed rat.

That was the last I saw or heard of him.
I cleaned the rack and drove out to cool off.
As I sat mopping the hayseed from my neck,
And sort of waiting to be asked about it,
One of the boys sings out, "Where's the old man?"
"I left him in the barn, under the hay.
If you want him you can go and dig him out."
They realized from the way I swobbed my neck
More than was needed, something must be up.
They headed for the barn—I stayed where I was.
They told me afterward: First they forked hay,
A lot of it, out into the barn floor.
Nothing! They listened for him. Not a rustle!
I guess they thought I'd spiked him in the temple
Before I buried him, else I couldn't have managed.
They excavated more. "Go keep his wife
Out of the barn."

> Some one looked in a window;
And curse me, if he wasn't in the kitchen,
Slumped way down in a chair, with both his feet
Stuck in the oven, the hottest day that summer.
He looked so mad in back, and so disgusted
There was no one that dared to stir him up
Or let him know that he was being looked at.
Apparently I hadn't buried him
(I may have knocked him down), but just my trying
To bury him had hurt his dignity.
He had gone to the house so's not to face me.
He kept away from us all afternoon.
We tended to his hay. We saw him out
After a while, picking peas in the garden;
He couldn't keep away from doing something.

Weren't you relieved to find he wasn't dead?

No!—and yet I can't say: it's hard to tell.
I went about to kill him fair enough.

You took an awkward way. Did he discharge you?

Discharge me? No! He knew I did just right.

ROBERT FROST

From CHICAGO POEMS

CHICAGO

Hog Butcher for the World,
Tool Maker, Stacker of Wheat,
Player with Railroads and the Nation's Freight Handler;
Stormy, husky, brawling,
City of the Big Shoulders:

They tell me you are wicked and I believe them, for I have seen
    your painted women under the gas lamps luring the farm
    boys.

And they tell me you are crooked and I answer: Yes, it is true
I have seen the gunman kill and go free to kill again.
And they tell me you are brutal and my reply is: On the faces
of women and children I have seen the marks of wanton
hunger.
And having answered so I turn once more to those who sneer
at this my city, and I give them back the sneer and say to
them:
Come and show me another city with lifted head singing so
proud to be alive and coarse and strong and cunning.
Flinging magnetic curses amid the toil of piling job on job, here
is a tall bold slugger set vivid against the little soft cities;
Fierce as a dog with tongue lapping for action, cunning as a
savage pitted against the wilderness,
Bareheaded,
Shoveling,
Wrecking,
Planning,
Building, breaking, rebuilding,
Under the smoke, dust all over his mouth, laughing with white
teeth,
Under the terrible burden of destiny laughing as a young man
laughs,
Laughing even as an ignorant fighter laughs who has never lost
a battle,
Bragging and laughing that under his wrist is the pulse, and
under his ribs the heart of the people,
                    Laughing!
Laughing the stormy, husky, brawling laughter of Youth, half-
naked, sweating, proud to be Hog Butcher, Tool Maker,
Stacker of Wheat, Player with Railroads and Freight Handler
to the Nation.

                                        CARL SANDBURG

EROS TURANNOS

She fears him, and will always ask
  What fated her to choose him;
She meets in his engaging mask
  All reasons to refuse him;
But what she meets and what she fears
Are less than are the downward years,
Drawn slowly to the foamless weirs
  Of age, were she to lose him.

Between a blurred sagacity
  That once had power to sound him,
And Love, that will not let him be
  The seeker that she found him,
Her pride assuages her, almost,
As if it were alone the cost.
He sees that he will not be lost,
  And waits, and looks around him.

A sense of ocean and old trees
  Envelops and allures him;
Tradition, touching all he sees
  Beguiles and reassures him;
And all her doubts of what he says
Are dimmed with what she knows of days,
Till even prejudice delays,
  And fades—and she secures him.

The falling leaf inaugurates
  The reign of her confusion;
The pounding wave reverberates
  The crash of her illusion;
And home, where passion lived and died,
Becomes a place where she can hide,—
While all the town and harbor side
  Vibrate with her seclusion.

We tell you, tapping on our brows,
  The story as it should be,—
As if the story of a house
  Were told, or ever could be;

We'll have no kindly veil between
Her visions and those we have seen, —
As if we guessed what hers have been
   Or what they are, or would be.

Meanwhile, we do no harm; for they
   That with a god have striven,
Not hearing much of what we say,
   Take what the god has given;
Though like waves breaking it may be,
Or like a changed familiar tree,
Or like a stairway to the sea,
   Where down the blind are driven.

EDWIN ARLINGTON ROBINSON

THE MAGI

Now as at all times I can see in the mind's eye,
In their stiff, painted clothes, the pale unsatisfied ones
Appear and disappear in the blue depths of the sky
With all their ancient faces like rain-beaten stones,
And all their helms of silver hovering side by side,
And all their eyes still fixed, hoping to find once more,
Being by Calvary's turbulence unsatisfied,
The uncontrollable mystery on the bestial floor.

WILLIAM BUTLER YEATS

ΤΟ ΚΑΛΌΝ

Even in my dreams you have denied yourself to me,
You have sent me only your handmaids.

EZRA POUND

THE COMING OF WAR: ACTAEON

An image of Lethe,
              and the fields
Full of faint light
              but golden,
Gray cliffs,
             and beneath them
A sea
Harsher than granite,
             unstill, never ceasing;
High forms
             with the movement of gods,
Perilous aspect;
             And one said:
"This is Actaeon."
             Actaeon of golden greaves!

Over fair meadows,
Over the cool face of that field,
Unstill, ever moving,
Host of an ancient people,
The silent cortège.

EZRA POUND

MOONRISE

Will you glimmer on the sea?
Will you fling your spear-head
on the shore?
What note shall we pitch?

We have a song,
on the bank we share our arrows—
the loosed string tells our note:

O flight,
bring her swiftly to our song.
She is great,
we measure her by the pine-trees.

H. D.

From NINETEEN-FOURTEEN

PEACE

Now, God be thanked who has matched us with his hour,
    And caught our youth, and wakened us from sleeping!
With hand made sure, clear eye, and sharpened power,
    To turn, as swimmers into cleanness leaping,

Glad from a world grown old and cold and weary,
    Leave the sick hearts that honor could not move,
And half-men, and their dirty songs and dreary,
    And all the little emptiness of love!
Oh! we, who have known shame, we have found release there,
    Where there's no ill, no grief, but sleep has mending,
        Naught broken save this body, lost but breath;
Nothing to shake the laughing heart's long peace there,
    But only agony, and that has ending;
        And the worst friend and enemy is but Death.

THE SOLDIER

If I should die, think only this of me:
    That there's some corner of a foreign field
That is for ever England. There shall be
    In that rich earth a richer dust concealed;
A dust whom England bore, shaped, made aware,
    Gave, once, her flowers to love, her ways to roam,
A body of England's, breathing English air,
    Washed by the rivers, blest by suns of home.
And think, this heart, all evil shed away,
    A pulse in the eternal mind, no less
        Gives somewhere back the thoughts by England given;
Her sights and sounds; dreams happy as her day;
    And laughter, learnt of friends; and gentleness,
        In hearts at peace, under an English heaven.

RUPERT BROOKE

THE LOVE SONG OF J. ALFRED PRUFROCK

S' io credessi che mia risposta fosse
A persona che mai tornasse al mondo,
Questa fiamma staria senza piu scosse.
Ma perciòcchè giammai di questo fondo
Non tornò vivo alcun, s' i' odo il vero,
senza tema d'infamia ti rispondo.

Let us go then, you and I,
When the evening is spread out against the sky
Like a patient etherized upon a table;
Let us go, through certain half-deserted streets,
The muttering retreats
Of restless nights in one-night cheap hotels
And sawdust restaurants with oyster-shells:
Streets that follow like a tedious argument
Of insidious intent
To lead you to an overwhelming question . . .

Oh, do not ask, "What is it?"
Let us go and make our visit.

In the room the women come and go
Talking of Michelangelo.

The yellow fog that rubs its back upon the window panes,
The yellow smoke that rubs its muzzle on the window panes,
Licked its tongue into the corners of the evening,
Lingered upon the pools that stand in drains,
Let fall upon its back the soot that falls from chimneys,
Slipped by the terrace, made a sudden leap,
And seeing that it was a soft October night,
Curled once about the house, and fell asleep.

And indeed there will be time
For the yellow smoke that slides along the street,
Rubbing its back upon the window panes;
There will be time, there will be time
To prepare a face to meet the faces that you meet;
There will be time to murder and create,
And time for all the works and days of hands
That lift and drop a question on your plate:

Time for you and time for me,
And time yet for a hundred indecisions,
And for a hundred visions and revisions,
Before the taking of a toast and tea.

In the room the women come and go
Talking of Michelangelo.

And indeed there will be time
To wonder, "Do I dare?" and, "Do I dare?" —
Time to turn back and descend the stair,
With a bald spot in the middle of my hair —
(They will say: "How his hair is growing thin!")
My morning coat, my collar mounting firmly to the chin,
My necktie rich and modest, but asserted by a simple pin —
(They will say: "But how his arms and legs are thin!")
Do I dare
Disturb the universe?
In a minute there is time
For decisions and revisions which a minute will reverse.

For I have known them already, known them all:
Have known the evenings, mornings, afternoons,
I have measured out my life with coffee spoons;
I know the voices dying with a dying fall
Beneath the music from a farther room.
        So how should I presume?

And I have known the eyes already, known them all —
The eyes that fix you in a formulated phrase.
And when I am formulated, sprawling on a pin,
When I am pinned and wriggling on the wall,
Then how should I begin
To spit out all the butt-ends of my days and ways?
        And how should I presume?

And I have known the arms already, known them all —
Arms that are braceleted and white and bare
(But in the lamplight, downed with light brown hair!)
        Is it perfume from a dress
        That makes me so digress?
Arms that lie along a table, or wrap about a shawl.
        And should I then presume?
        And how should I begin?

21

. . . . .

Shall I say, I have gone at dusk through narrow streets,
And watched the smoke that rises from the pipes
Of lonely men in shirtsleeves, leaning out of windows? . . .

I should have been a pair of ragged claws
Scuttling across the floors of silent seas.

. . . . . .

And the afternoon, the evening, sleeps so peacefully!
Smoothed by long fingers,
Asleep . . . tired . . . or it malingers,
Stretched on the floor, here beside you and me.
Should I, after tea and cakes and ices,
Have the strength to force the moment to its crisis?
But though I have wept and fasted, wept and prayed,
Though I have seen my head (grown slightly bald) brought in
        upon a platter,
I am no prophet—and here's no great matter;
I have seen the moment of my greatness flicker,
And I have seen the eternal Footman hold my coat, and
        snicker,
        And in short, I was afraid.

And would it have been worth it, after all,
After the cups, the marmalade, the tea,
Among the porcelain, among some talk of you and me,
Would it have been worth while
To have bitten off the matter with a smile,
To have squeezed the universe into a ball
To roll it toward some overwhelming question,
To say: "I am Lazarus, come from the dead,
Come back to tell you all, I shall tell you all"—
If one, settling a pillow by her head,
    Should say: "That is not what I meant at all;
        That is not it, at all."

And would it have been worth it, after all,
Would it have been worth while,

After the sunsets and the dooryards and the sprinkled streets,
After the novels, after the teacups, after the skirts that trail
     along the floor —
And this, and so much more? —
It is impossible to say just what I mean!
But as if a magic lantern threw the nerves in patterns on a
     screen:
Would it have been worth while
If one, settling a pillow or throwing off a shawl,
And turning toward the window, should say: "That is not it
     it at all,
     That is not what I meant, at all."

    . . . . . .

    No! I am not Prince Hamlet, nor was meant to be;
Am an attendant lord, one that will do
To swell a progress, start a scene or two,
Advise the prince: withal, an easy tool,
Deferential, glad to be of use,
Politic, cautious, and meticulous;
Full of high sentence, but a bit obtuse;
At times, indeed, almost ridiculous —
Almost, at times, the Fool.

I grow old . . . I grow old . . .
I shall wear the bottoms of my trousers rolled.

    Shall I part my hair behind? Do I dare to eat a peach?
I shall wear white flannel trousers, and walk upon the beach.
I have heard the mermaids singing, each to each.
I do not think that they will sing to me.

I have seen them riding seaward on the waves,
Combing the white hair of the waves blown back
When the wind blows the water white and black.

We have lingered in the chambers of the sea
By seagirls wreathed with seaweed red and brown,
Till human voices wake us, and we drown.

    . . . . . .

T. S. ELIOT

From DISCORDANTS

IV

Dead Cleopatra lies in a crystal casket,
Wrapped and spiced by the cunningest of hands.
Around her neck they have put a golden necklace,
Her tatbebs, it is said, are worn with sands.

Dead Cleopatra was once revered in Egypt—
Warm-eyed she was, this princess of the south.
Now she is very old and dry and faded,
With black bitumen they have sealed up her mouth.

Grave-robbers pulled the gold rings from her fingers,
Despite the holy symbols across her breast;
They scared the bats that quietly whirled above her.
Poor lady! she would have been long since at rest

If she had not been wrapped and spiced so shrewdly,
Preserved, obscene, to mock black flights of years.
What would her lover have said, had he foreseen it?
Had he been moved to ecstasy, or tears?

O sweet clean earth from whom the green blade cometh!—
When we are dead, my best-beloved and I,
Close well above us that we may rest forever,
Sending up grass and blossoms to the sky.

CONRAD AIKEN

THE ANSWER

When I go back to earth
And all my joyous body
Puts off the red and white
That once had been so proud,
If men should pass above
With false and feeble pity,
My dust will find a voice
To answer them aloud:

"Be still, I am content,
Take back your poor compassion—
Joy was a flame in me
Too steady to destroy.
Lithe as a bending reed
Loving the storm that sways her—
I found more joy in sorrow
Than you could find in joy."

SARA TEASDALE

BEETHOVEN

Behold the tormented and the fallen angel
  Wandering disconsolate the world along,
That seeks to atone with inconsolable anguish
  For some old grievance, some remembered wrong;
To storm heaven's iron gates with angry longing,
  And beat back homeward in a shower of song!

JOHN HALL WHEELOCK

SUNDAY MORNING

I

Complacencies of the peignoir, and late
Coffee and oranges in a sunny chair,
And the green freedom of a cockatoo
Upon a rug, mingle to dissipate
The holy hush of ancient sacrifice.
She dreams a little, and she feels the dark
Encroachment of that old catastrophe,
As a calm darkens among water-lights.
The pungent oranges and bright, green wings
Seem things in some procession of the dead,
Winding across wide water, without sound.
The day is like wide water, without sound,
Stilled for the passing of her dreaming feet
Over the seas, to silent Palestine,
Dominion of the blood and sepulcher.

II

She hears, upon that water without sound,
A voice that cries, "The tomb in Palestine
Is not the porch of spirits lingering;
It is the grave of Jesus, where he lay."
We live in an old chaos of the sun,
Or old dependency of day and night,
Or island solitude, unsponsored, free,
Of that wide water, inescapable.
Deer walk upon our mountains, and the quail
Whistle about us their spontaneous cries;
Sweet berries ripen in the wilderness;
And, in the isolation of the sky,
At evening, casual flocks of pigeons make
Ambiguous undulations as they sink,
Downward to darkness, on extended wings.

III

She says, "I am content when wakened birds,
Before they fly, test the reality
Of misty fields, by their sweet questionings;
But when the birds are gone, and their warm fields
Return no more, where, then, is paradise?"
There is not any haunt of prophecy,
Nor any old chimera of the grave,
Neither the golden underground, nor isle
Melodious, where spirits gat them home,
Nor visionary South, nor cloudy palm
Remote on heaven's hill, that has endured
As April's green endures; or will endure
Like her remembrance of awakened birds,
Or her desire for June and evening, tipped
By the consummation of the swallow's wings.

IV

She says, "But in contentment I still feel
The need of some imperishable bliss."
Death is the mother of beauty; hence from her,
Alone, shall come fulfilment to our dreams
And our desires. Although she strews the leaves
Of sure obliteration on our paths —
The path sick sorrow took, the many paths
Where triumph rang its brassy phrase, or love
Whispered a little out of tenderness —
She makes the willow shiver in the sun
For maidens who were wont to sit and gaze
Upon the grass, relinquished to their feet.
She causes boys to bring sweet-smelling pears
And plums in ponderous piles. The maidens taste
And stray impassioned in the littering leaves.

V

Supple and turbulent, a ring of men
Shall chant in orgy on a summer morn
Their boisterous devotion to the sun —
Not as a god, but as a god might be,
Naked among them, like a savage source.
Their chant shall be a chant of paradise,
Out of their blood, returning to the sky;
And in their chant shall enter, voice by voice,
The windy lake wherein their lord delights,
The trees, like seraphim, and echoing hills,
That choir among themselves long afterward.
They shall know well the heavenly fellowship
Of men that perish and of summer morn —
And whence they came and whither they shall go,
The dew upon their feet shall manifest.

WALLACE STEVENS

THE SCHOLARS

Bald heads forgetful of their sins,
Old, learned, respectable bald heads
Edit and annotate the lines
That young men, tossing on their beds,
Rhymed out in love's despair
To flatter beauty's ignorant ear.

They'll cough in the ink to the world's end;
Wear out the carpet with their shoes
Earning respect; have no strange friend;
If they have sinned nobody knows:
Lord, what would they say
Should their Catullus walk that way!

WILLIAM BUTLER YEATS

IN MEMORY OF BRYAN LATHROP

Who bequeathed to Chicago a School of Music

So in Pieria, from the wedded bliss
Of Time and Memory, the Muses came
To be the means of rich oblivion,
And rest from cares. And when the Thunderer
Took heaven, then the Titans warred on him
For pity of mankind. But the great law,
Which is the law of music, not of bread,
Set Atlas for a pillar, manacled
His brother to the rocks in Scythia,
And under Aetna fixed the furious Typhon.
So should thought rule, not force. And Amphion,
Pursuing justice, entered Thebes and slew
His mother's spouse; but when he would make sure
And fortify the city, then he took
The lyre that Hermes gave, and played, and watched
The stones move and assemble, till a wall
Engirded Thebes and kept the citadel
Beyond the reach of arrows and of fire.

What other power but harmony can build
A city, and what gift so magical
As that by which a city lifts its walls?
So men, in years to come, shall feel the power
Of this man moving through the high-ranged thought
Which plans for beauty, builds for larger life.
The stones shall rise in towers to answer him.

EDGAR LEE MASTERS

THE LAKE ISLE

O God, O Venus, O Mercury, patron of thieves,
Give me in due time, I beseech you, a little tobacco-shop,
With the little bright boxes
                piled up neatly upon the shelves
And the loose fragrant cavendish
                and the shag,
And the bright Virginia
                loose under the bright glass cases,
And a pair of scales
                not too greasy,
And the *volailles* dropping in for a word or two in passing,
For a flip word, and to tidy their hair a bit

O God, O Venus, O Mercury, patron of thieves,
Lend me a little tobacco-shop,
                or install me in any profession
Save this damn'd profession of writing,
                where one needs one's brains all the time.

EZRA POUND

From EPIGRAMS

The echo always mocks the sound—to conceal that she is his debtor.

The arrow thinks it is free, for it moves, and the bow is bound, for it is still. The bow says to the arrow, "Your freedom depends on me."

The world speaks truth. We take its meaning wrong and call it a liar.

The flute knows it is the breath that gives birth to its music. The breath knows it is nothing. And he who plays on the flute is not known.

Death threatens to take his son, the thief his wealth, and his detractors his reputation. "But who is there to take away my joy?" asks the poet.

Death belongs to life as birth does, even as walking contains the raising of the foot as much as the laying of it down.

RABINDRANATH TAGORE

From OBSERVATIONS

LA FIGLIA CHE PIANGE

Stand on the highest pavement of the stair—
Lean on a garden urn—
Weave, weave, weave the sunlight in your hair—
Clasp your flowers to you with a pained surprise—
Fling them to the ground and turn
With a fugitive resentment in your eyes:
But weave, weave the sunlight in your hair.

So I would have had him leave,
So I would have had her stand and grieve,
So he would have left
As the soul leaves the body torn and bruised,
As the mind deserts the body it has used.

I should find
Some way incomparably light and deft,
Some way we both should understand,
Simple and faithless as a smile and shake of the hand.

She turned away, but with the autumn weather
Compelled my imagination many days—
Many days and many hours:
Her hair over her arms and her arms full of flowers—
And I wonder how they should have been together!
I should have lost a gesture and a pose.
Sometimes these cogitations still amaze
The troubled midnight and the noon's repose.

MR. APOLLINAX

When Mr. Apollinax visited the United States
His laughter tinkled among the teacups.
I thought of Fragilion, that shy figure among the birch trees,
And of Priapus in the shrubbery
Gaping at the lady in the swing.
In the palace of Mrs. Phlaccus, at Professor Channing-Cheetah's,
His laughter was submarine and profound
Like the old man of the sea's
Hidden under coral islands
Where worried bodies of drowned men drift down in the
        green silence, dropping from fingers of surf.
I looked for the head of Mr. Apollinax rolling under a chair,
Or grinning over a screen
With seaweed in its hair.
I heard the beat of centaurs' hoofs over the hard turf
As his dry and passionate talk devoured the afternoon.
"He is a charming man," "But after all what did he mean?"
"His pointed ears—he must be unbalanced,"
"There was something he said which I might have challenged."
Of dowager Mrs. Phlaccus, and Professor and Mrs. Cheetah
I remember a slice of lemon, and a bitten macaroon.

MORNING AT THE WINDOW

They are rattling breakfast plates in basement kitchens,
And along the trampled edges of the street
I am aware of the damp souls of housemaids
Hanging despondently at area gates.

The brown waves of fog toss up to me
Twisted faces from the bottom of the street,
And tear from a passerby with muddy skirts
An aimless smile that hovers in the air
And vanishes along the level of the roofs.

T. R. ELIOT [SIC]

THE WAVE SYMPHONY

A Screen by Sotatsu

Around islands of jade and malachite
And lapis-lazuli and jasper,
Under golden clouds,
Struggle the grey-gold waves.

The waves are advancing,
Swirling, eddying; the pale waves
Are leaping into foam, and retreating—
And straining again until they seem not waves
But gigantic crawling hands.
The waves clutch at the clouds,
The near and golden clouds,
They rise in spires over the clouds,
And over the pine-branch set against the clouds.
And around the islands,
Jasper and jade,
Their rhythms circle and sweep and re-echo
With hollow and foam-crest,
Infinitely interlacing their orbits and cycles
That join and unravel, and battle and answer,
From tumult to tumult, from music to music,
Crest to trough, foam-height to hollow,
Peace drowning passion, and passion
Leaping from peace.

ARTHUR DAVISON FICKE

MARRIAGE

So different, this man
And this woman:
A stream flowing
In a field.

WILLIAM CARLOS WILLIAMS

From TRENCH POEMS

BREAK OF DAY IN THE TRENCHES

The darkness crumbles away—
It is the same old Druid Time as ever.
Only a live thing leaps my hand—
A queer sardonic rat—
As I pull the parapet's poppy
To stick behind my ear.
Droll rat, they would shoot you if they knew
Your cosmopolitan sympathies
(And God knows what antipathies).
Now you have touched this English hand
You will do the same to a German—
Soon, no doubt, if it be your pleasure
To cross the sleeping green between.
It seems you inwardly grin as you pass:
Strong eyes, fine limbs, haughty athletes,
Less chanced than you for life;
Bonds to the whims of murder,
Sprawled in the bowels of the earth,
The torn fields of France.
What do you see in our eyes
At the boom, the hiss, the swiftness,
The irrevocable earth buffet—
A shell's haphazard fury.
What rootless poppies dropping? . . .
But mine in my ear is safe,
Just a little white with the dust.

ISAAC ROSENBERG

From MY PEOPLE

IN TALL GRASS

Bees and a honeycomb in the dried head of a horse in a pasture
    corner—a skull in the tall grass and a buzz and a buzz of
    the yellow honey-hunters.

And I ask no better a winding sheet
                    over the earth and under the sun.

Let the bees go honey-hunting with yellow blur of wings in the
    dome of my head, in the rumbling, singing arch of my
    skull.

Let there be wings and yellow dust and the drone of dreams of
    honey—who loses and remembers?—who keeps and
    forgets?

In a blue sheen of moon over the bones and under the hanging
    honeycomb the bees come home and the bees sleep.

CARL SANDBURG

EVENING SONG

My song will rest while I rest. I struggle along. I'll get
    back to the corn and the open fields. Don't fret, love,
    I'll come out all right.
Back of Chicago the open fields. Were you ever there—
    trains coming toward you out of the West—streaks of
    light on the long gray plains? Many a song—aching
    to sing.
I've got a gray and ragged brother in my breast—that's a
    fact. Back of Chicago the open field—long trains go
    west too—in the silence. Don't fret, love. I'll come
    out all right.

SHERWOOD ANDERSON

RECIPROCITY

I do not think that skies and meadows are
Moral, or that the fixture of a star
Comes of a quiet spirit, or that trees
Have wisdom in their windless silences.
Yet these are things invested in my mood
With constancy, and peace, and fortitude;
That in my troubled season I can cry
Upon the wide composure of the sky,
And envy fields, and wish that I might be
As little daunted as a star or tree.

JOHN DRINKWATER

From FIGS FROM THISTLES

FIRST FIG

My candle burns at both ends;
    It will not last the night:
But ah, my foes, and oh, my friends—
    It gives a lovely light!

SECOND FIG

Safe upon the solid rock the ugly houses stand:
Come and see my shining palace built upon the sand!

THURSDAY

And if I loved you Wednesday,
    Well, what is that to you?
I do not love you Thursday—
    So much is true.

And why you come complaining
    Is more than I can see.
I loved you Wednesday—yes—but what
    Is that to me?

EDNA ST. VINCENT MILLAY

35

LE MÉDECIN MALGRÉ LUI

Oh I suppose I should
Wash the walls of my office,
Polish the rust from
My instruments and keep them
Definitely in order;
Build shelves in
The little laboratory;
Empty out the old stains,
Clean the bottles
And refill them; buy
Another lens; put
My journals on edge instead of
Letting them lie flat
In heaps—then begin
Ten years back and
Gradually
Read them to date,
Cataloguing important
Articles for ready reference.
I suppose I should
Read the new books.
If to this I added
A bill at the tailor's
And the cleaner's
And grew a decent beard
And cultivated a look
Of importance—
Who can tell? I might be
A credit to my Lady Happiness
And never think anything
But a white thought!

WILLIAM CARLOS WILLIAMS

NOSTALGIA

The waning moon looks upward, this grey night
Sheers round the heavens in one smooth curve
Of easy sailing. Odd red wicks serve
To show where the ships at sea move out of sight.

This place is palpable me, for here I was born
Of this self-same darkness. Yet the shadowy house below
Is out of bounds, and only the old ghosts know
I have come—they whimper about me, welcome and mourn.

My father suddenly died in the harvesting corn,
And the place is no longer ours. Watching, I hear
No sound from the strangers; the place is dark, and fear
Opens my eyes till the roots of my vision seem torn.

Can I go nearer, never towards the door?
The ghosts and I, we mourn together, and shrink
In the shadow of the cart-shed—hovering on the brink
For ever, to enter the homestead no more.

Is it irrevocable? Can I really not go
Through the open yard-way? Can I not pass the sheds
And through to the mowie? Only the dead in their beds
Can know the fearful anguish that this is so.

I kiss the stones. I kiss the moss on the wall,
And wish I could pass impregnate into the place.
I wish I could take it all in a last embrace.
I wish with my breast I could crush it, perish it all.

D. H. LAWRENCE

From PROPERTIUS

IV

When, when, and whenever death closes our eyelids,
Moving naked over Acheron
    Upon the one raft, victor and conquered together,
Marius and Jugurtha together,
            One tangle of shadows.

Caesar plots against India—
Tigris and Euphrates shall from now on flow at his bidding,
Tibet shall be full of Roman policemen,
The Parthians shall get used to our statuary
            and acquire a Roman religion;

One raft on the veiled flood of Acheron,
        Marius and Jugurtha together.

Nor at my funeral either will there be any long trail,
        bearing ancestral lares and images;
No trumpets filled with my emptiness;
Nor shall it be on an Attalic bed.
        The perfumed cloths shall be absent.
A small plebeian procession—
        Enough, enough, and in plenty.
There will be three books at my obsequies
Which I take, my not unworthy gift, to Persephone.

You will follow the bare scarified breast;
Nor will you be weary of calling my name, nor too weary
        To place the last kiss on my lips
When the Syrian onyx is broken.

        "He who is now vacant dust
        Was once the slave of one passion"—
Give that much inscription—
        "Death, why tardily come?"

You, sometime, will lament a lost friend,
        for it is a custom—
This care for past men—
Since Adonis was gored at Idalia, and the Cytherean
Ran crying with out-spread hair.
        In vain you call back the shade;
In vain, Cynthia, vain call to unanswering shadow—
        small talk comes from small bones.

EZRA POUND

WALT WHITMAN

Noon on the mountain!—
And all the crags are husky faces powerful with love for the sun;
All the shadows
Whisper of the sun.

EMANUEL CARNEVALI

RECUERDO

We were very tired, we were very merry—
We had gone back and forth all night on the ferry.
It was bare and bright, and smelled like a stable—
But we looked into a fire, we leaned across a table,
We lay on a hill-top underneath the moon;
And the whistles kept blowing, and the dawn came soon.

We were very tired, we were very merry—
We had gone back and forth all night on the ferry;
And you ate an apple, and I ate a pear,
From a dozen of each we had bought somewhere;
And the sky went wan, and the wind came cold,
And the sun rose dripping, a bucketful of gold.

We were very tired, we were very merry,
We had gone back and forth all night on the ferry.
We hailed, "Good-morrow, mother!" to a shawl-covered head,
And bought a morning-paper, which neither of us read;
And she wept, "God bless you!" for the apples and pears,
And we gave her all our money but our subway fares.

EDNA ST. VINCENT MILLAY

END OF THE COMEDY

Eleven o'clock, and the curtain falls.
The cold wind tears the strands of illusion;
The delicate music is lost
In the blare of home-going crowds
And a midnight paper.

The night has grown martial;
It meets us with blows and disaster.
Even the stars have turned shrapnel,
Fixed in silent explosions.
And here at our door
The moonlight is laid
Like a drawn sword.

LOUIS UNTERMEYER

THE HORRID VOICE OF SCIENCE

"There's machinery in the
    butterfly;
  There's a mainspring to the
    bee;
  There's hydraulics to a daisy,
    And contraptions to a tree.

"If we could see the birdie
      That makes the chirping sound
With x-ray, scientific eyes,
  We could see the wheels go
    round."

And I hope all men
Who think like this
Will soon lie
Underground.

                    VACHEL LINDSAY

SONG

Let it be forgotten, as a flower is forgotten,
  Forgotten as a fire that once was singing gold.
Let it be forgotten forever and ever—
  Time is a kind friend, he will make us old.

If anyone asks, say it was forgotten
  Long and long ago—
As a flower, as a fire, as a hushed footfall
  In a long forgotten snow.

                    SARA TEASDALE

From PECKSNIFFIANA

FABLIAU OF FLORIDA

Barque of phosphor
On the palmy beach,

Move outward into heaven,
Into the alabasters
And night blues.

Foam and cloud are one.
Sultry moon-monsters
Are dissolving.

Fill your black hull
With white moonlight.

There will never be an end
To this droning of the surf.

THE WEEPING BURGHER

It is with a strange malice
That I distort the world.

Ah! that ill humors
Should mask as white girls.
And ah! that Scaramouche
Should have a black barouche.

The sorry verities!
Yet in excess, continual,
There is cure of sorrow.

Permit that if as ghost I come
Among the people burning in me still,
I come as belle design
Of foppish line.

And I, then, tortured for old speech —
A white of wildly woven rings;
I, weeping in a calcined heart —
My hands such sharp, imagined things.

THE INDIGO GLASS IN THE GRASS

Which is real—
This bottle of indigo glass in the grass,
Or the bench with the pot of geraniums, the stained mattress
    and the washed overalls drying in the sun?
Which of these truly contains the world?

Neither one, nor the two together.

ANECDOTE OF THE JAR

I placed a jar in Tennessee,
And round it was, upon a hill.
It made the slovenly wilderness
Surround that hill.

The wilderness rose up to it,
And sprawled around, no longer wild.
The jar was round upon the ground
And tall and of a port in air.

It took dominion everywhere.
The jar was gray and bare.
It did not give of bird or bush,
Like nothing else in Tennessee.

THE CURTAINS IN THE HOUSE OF THE METAPHYSICIAN

It comes about that the drifting of these curtains
Is full of long motions; as the ponderous
Deflations of distance; or as clouds
Inseparable from their afternoons;
Or the changing of light, the dropping
Of the silence, wide sleep and solitude
Of night, in which all motion
Is beyond us, as the firmament,
Up-rising and down-falling, bares
The last largeness, bold to see.

THE PALTRY NUDE STARTS ON A SPRING VOYAGE

But not on a shell, she starts,
Archaic, for the sea.
But on the first-found weed
She scuds the glitters,
Noiselessly, like one more wave.

She too is discontent
And would have purple stuff upon her arms,
Tired of the salty harbors,
Eager for the brine and bellowing
Of the high interiors of the sea.

The wind speeds her,
Blowing upon her hands
And watery back.
She touches the clouds, where she goes,
In the circle of her traverse of the sea.

Yet this is meagre play
In the scurry and water-shine,
As her heels foam—
Not as when the goldener nude
Of a later day

Will go, like the centre of sea-green pomp,
In an intenser calm,
Scullion of fate,
Across the spick torrent, ceaselessly,
Upon her irretrievable way.

WALLACE STEVENS

DANNY

You marched off southward with the fire of twenty,
Proud of the uniform that you were wearing.
The girls made love to you, and that was plenty;
The drums were beating and the horns were blaring.

From town to town you fought, and bridge to bridge,
Thinking: "So this is Life; so this is Real."
And when you swept up Missionary Ridge,
Laughing at death, you were your own ideal.

But when you limped home, wounded and unsteady,
You found the world was new to you; your clutch
On life had slipped, and you were old already.
So who can blame you if you drink too much,

Or boast about your pride when no one sees,
Or mumble petulant inanities?

MALCOLM COWLEY

TO W. C. W. M.D.

There has been
Another death.
This time
I bring it to you.
You are kind,
Brutal,
You know
How to lower
Bodies.
I ask only
That the rope
Isn't silk,
(Silk doesn't break)
Nor thread,
(Thread does.)
If it lifts
And lowers
Common things,
It will do.

ALFRED KREYMBORG

ATAVISM

I always was afraid of Somes's Pond:
Not the little pond, by which the willow stands,
Where laughing boys catch alewives in their hands
In brown, bright shallows; but the one beyond.
There, when the frost makes all the birches burn
Yellow as cow-lilies, and the pale sky shines
Like a polished shell between black spruce and pines,
Some strange thing tracks us, turning where we turn.

You'll say I dream it, being the true daughter
Of those who in old times endured this dread.
Look! Where the lily-stems are showing red
A silent paddle moves below the water,
A sliding shape has stirred them like a breath;
Tall plumes surmount a painted mask of death.

ELINOR WYLIE

CUBIST PORTRAIT

She is purposeless as a cyclone; she must move
Either by chance or in a predestined groove,
Following a whim not her own, unable to shape
Her course. From chance or God even she cannot escape!

Think of a cyclone sitting far-off with its head in its hands,
Motionless, drearily longing for distant lands
Where every lonely hurricane may at last discover
Its own transcendent, implacable, indestructible lover!

What is a cyclone? Only thin air moving fast
From here to yonder, to become silent emptiness at last.

MARJORIE ALLEN SEIFFERT

THE GOLDEN FLEECE

I know that life is Jason,
And that beauty is the witch-maiden helping him.
I know that the soft, luminous night of stars
Is the golden fleece he is seeking.
I know that in the beginning

He sowed the boulders, the teeth of dead ages,
And the innumerable armored cities have arisen.
I know that he has thrown among them love and desire,
And they have warred and shall war with each other until the
    end.
And if you doubt the least word I have said,
Come out on the dark beach some strange summer night
And watch the huge quivering serpent of the ocean
Still coiled around the trunk of the tree of paradise.

OSCAR WILLIAMS

THE POET AT NIGHT-FALL

I see no equivalents
For that which I see,
Among words.

And sounds are nowhere repeated,
Vowel for vocal wind
Or shaking leaf.

Ah me, beauty does not enclose life,
But blows through it—
Like that idea, the wind,

Which is unseen and useless,
Even superseded upon
The scarred sea;

Which goes and comes
Altering every aspect—
The poplar, the splashing crest—

Altering all, in that moment
When it is not
Because we see it not.

But who would hang
Like a wind-bell
On a porch where no wind ever blows?

GLENWAY WESCOTT

From SUR MA GUZZLA GRACILE

THE SNOW MAN

One must have a mind of winter
To regard the frost and the boughs
Of the pine-trees crusted with snow;

And have been cold a long time
To behold the junipers shagged with ice,
The spruces rough in the distant glitter

Of the January sun; and not to think
Of any misery in the sound of the wind,
In the sound of a few leaves,

Which is the sound of the land
Full of the same wind
That is blowing in the same bare place

for the listener, who listens in the snow,
And, nothing himself, beholds
Nothing that is not there and the nothing that is.

TEA AT THE PALAZ OF HOON

Not less because in purple I descended
The western day through what you called
The loneliest air, not less was I myself.

What was the ointment sprinkled on my beard?
What were the hymns that buzzed beside my ears?
What was the sea whose tide swept through me there?

Out of my mind the golden ointment rained,
And my ears made the blowing hymns they heard.
I was myself the compass of that sea:

I was the world in which I walked, and what I saw
Or heard or felt came not but from myself;
And there I found myself more truly and more strange.

ANOTHER WEEPING WOMAN

Pour the unhappiness out
From your too bitter heart,
Which grieving will not sweeten.

Poison grows in this dark.
It is in the water of tears
Its black blooms rise.

The magnificent cause of being—
The imagination, the one reality
In this imagined world—

Leaves you
With him for whom no phantasy moves,
And you are pierced by a death.

OF THE MANNER OF ADDRESSING CLOUDS

Gloomy grammarians in golden gowns,
Meekly you keep the mortal rendezvous,
Eliciting the still sustaining pomps
Of speech which are like music so profound
They seem an exaltation without sound.
Funest philosophers and ponderers,
Their evocations are the speech of clouds.
So speech of your processionals returns
In the casual evocations of your tread
Across the stale, mysterious seasons. These
Are the music of meet resignation; these
The responsive, still sustaining pomps for you
To magnify, if in that drifting waste
You are to be accompanied by more
Than mute bare splendors of the sun and moon.

OF HEAVEN CONSIDERED AS A TOMB

What word have you, interpreters, of men
Who in the tomb of heaven walk by night,
The darkened ghosts of our old comedy?
Do they believe they range the gusty cold,
With lanterns borne aloft to light the way,
Freemen of death, about and still about
To find whatever it is they seek? Or does
That burial, pillared up each day as porte
And spiritous passage into nothingness,
Foretell each night the one abysmal night,
When the host shall no more wander, nor the light
Of the steadfast lanterns creep across the dark?
Make hue among the dark comedians,
Halloo them in the topmost distances
For answer from their icy Elysée.

WALLACE STEVENS

THE WITCH OF COOS

Circa 1922

I staid the night for shelter at a farm
Behind the mountain, with a mother and son,
Two old-believers. They did all the talking.

The Mother
    Folks think a witch who has familiar spirits
    She *could* call up to pass a winter evening,
    But *won't*, should be burned at the stake or something.
    Summoning spirits isn't "Button, button,
    Who's got the button," you're to understand.
The Son
    Mother can make a common table rear
    And kick with two legs like an army mule.
The Mother
    And when I've done it, what good have I done?
    Rather than tip a table for you, let me
    Tell you what Ralle the Sioux Control once told me.

He said the dead had souls, but when I asked him
How that could be—I thought the dead were souls,
He broke my trance. Don't that make you suspicious
That there's something the dead are keeping back?
Yes, there's something the dead are keeping back.
The Son
You wouldn't want to tell him what we have
Up attic, mother?
The Mother

Bones—a skeleton.
The Son
But the headboard of mother's bed is pushed
Against the attic door: the door is nailed.
It's harmless. Mother hears it in the night
Halting perplexed behind the barrier
Of door and headboard. Where it wants to get
Is back into the cellar where it came from.
The Mother
We'll never let them, will we, son? We'll never!
The Son
It left the cellar forty years ago
And carried itself like a pile of dishes
Up one flight from the cellar to the kitchen,
Another from the kitchen to the bedroom,
Another from the bedroom to the attic,
Right past both father and mother, and neither stopped it.
Father had gone upstairs; mother was downstairs.
I was a baby: I don't know where I was.
The Mother
The only fault my husband found with me—
I went to sleep before I went to bed,
Especially in winter when the bed
Might just as well be ice and the clothes snow.
The night the bones came up the cellar-stairs
Toffile had gone to bed alone and left me,
But left an open door to cool the room off
So as to sort of turn me out of it.
I was just coming to myself enough
To wonder where the cold was coming from,
When I heard Toffile upstairs in the bedroom
And thought I heard him downstairs in the cellar.

The board we had laid down to walk dry-shod on
When there was water in the cellar in spring
Struck the hard cellar bottom. And then someone
Began the stairs, two footsteps for each step,
The way a man with one leg and a crutch,
Or little child, comes up. It wasn't Toffile:
It wasn't anyone who could be there.
The bulkhead double-doors were double-locked
And swollen tight and buried under snow.
The cellar windows were banked up with sawdust
And swollen tight and buried under snow.
It was the bones. I knew them—and good reason.
My first impulse was to get to the knob
And hold the door. But the bones didn't try
The door; they halted helpless on the landing,
Waiting for things to happen in their favor.
The faintest restless rustling ran all through them.
I never could have done the thing I did
If the wish hadn't been too strong in me
To see how they were mounted for this walk.
I had a vision of them put together
Not like a man, but like a chandelier.
So suddenly I flung the door wide on him.
A moment he stood balancing with emotion,
And all but lost himself. (A tongue of fire
Flashed out and licked along his upper teeth.
Smoke rolled inside the sockets of his eyes.)
Then he came at me with one hand outstretched,
The way he did in life once; but this time
I struck the hand off brittle on the floor,
And fell back from him on the floor myself.
The finger-pieces slid in all directions.
(Where did I see one of those pieces lately?
Hand me my button-box—it must be there.)

I sat up on the floor and shouted, "Toffile,
It's coming up to you." It had its choice
Of the door to the cellar or the hall.
It took the hall door for the novelty,
And set off briskly for so slow a thing,
Still going every which way in the joints, though,

So that it looked like lightning or a scribble,
From the slap I had just now given its hand.
I listened till it almost climbed the stairs
From the hall to the only finished bedroom,
Before I got up to do anything;
Then ran and shouted, "Shut the bedroom door,
Toffile, for my sake!" "Company," he said,
"Don't make me get up; I'm too warm in bed."
So lying forward weakly on the handrail
I pushed myself upstairs, and in the light
(The kitchen had been dark) I had to own
I could see nothing. "Toffile, I don't see it.
It's with us in the room, though. It's the bones."
"What bones?" "The cellar bones—out of the grave."

That made him throw his bare legs out of bed
And sit up by me and take hold of me.
I wanted to put out the light and see
If I could see it, or else mow the room,
With our arms at the level of our knees,
And bring the chalk-pile down. "I'll tell you what—
It's looking for another door to try.
The uncommonly deep snow has made him think
Of his old song, *The Wild Colonial Boy*,
He always used to sing along the tote-road.

He's after an open door to get out-doors.
Let's trap him with an open door up attic."
Toffile agreed to that, and sure enough,
Almost the moment he was given an opening,
The steps began to climb the attic stairs.
I heard them. Toffile didn't seem to hear them.
"Quick!" I slammed to the door and held the knob.
"Toffile, get nails." I made him nail the door shut,
And push the headboard of the bed against it.

Then we asked was there anything
Up attic that we'd ever want again.
The attic was less to us than the cellar.
If the bones liked the attic, let them like it,
Let them *stay* in the attic. When they sometimes
Come down the stairs at night and stand perplexed

Behind the door and headboard of the bed,
Brushing their chalky skull with chalky fingers,
With sounds like the dry rattling of a shutter,
That's what I sit up in the dark to say—
To no one any more since Toffile died.
Let them stay in the attic since they went there.
I promised Toffile to be cruel to them
For helping them be cruel once to him.

The Son

We think they had a grave down in the cellar.

The Mother

We know they had a grave down in the cellar.

The Son

We never could find out whose bones they were.

The Mother

Yes, we could too, son. Tell the truth for once.
They were a man's his father killed for me.
I mean a man he killed instead of me.
The least I could do was help dig their grave.
We were about it one night in the cellar.
Son knows the story: but 'twas not for him
To tell the truth, suppose the time had come.
Son looks surprised to see me end a lie
We'd kept up all these years between ourselves
So as to have it ready for outsiders.
But tonight I don't care enough to lie—
I don't remember why I ever cared.
Toffile, if he were here, I don't believe
Could tell you why he ever cared himself. . . .

She hadn't found the finger-bone she wanted
Among the buttons poured out in her lap.

I verified the name next morning: Toffile.
The rural letter-box said Toffile Barre.

ROBERT FROST

WILD ORCHARD

It is a broken country,
the rugged land is
green from end to end;
the autumn has not come.

Embanked above the orchard
the hillside is a wall
of motionless green trees,
the grass is green and red.

Five days the bare sky
has stood there day and night.
No bird, no sound.
Between the trees

stillness
and the early morning light.
The apple trees
are laden down with fruit.

Among blue leaves
the apples green and red
upon one tree stand out
most enshrined.

Still, ripe, heavy,
spherical and close,
they mark the hillside.
It is a formal grandeur,

a stateliness,
a signal of finality
and perfect ease.
Among the savage

aristocracy of rocks
one, risen as a tree,
has turned
from his repose.

WILLIAM CARLOS WILLIAMS

IN HIGH PLACES

My mountains, God has company in heaven—
Crowned saints who sing to him the sun-long day.
He has no need of speech with you—with you,
Dust of his foot-stool! No, but I have need.
Oh, speak to me, for you are mine as well—
Drift of my soul. I built you long ago;
I reared your granite masonry to make
My house of peace, and spread your flowered carpets,
And set your blue-tiled roof, and in your courts
Made musical fountains play. Ah, give me now
Shelter and sustenance and liberty,
That I may mount your sky-assailing towers
And hear the winds communing, and give heed
To the large march of stars, and enter in
The spirit-crowded courts of solitude.

HARRIET MONROE

From BEGINNING AND END

KNOWLEDGE

Now that I know
That passion warms little
Of flesh in the mold,
And treasure is brittle,

I'll lie here and learn
How, over their ground,
Trees make a long shadow
And a light sound.

LOUISE BOGAN

MONODY TO THE SOUND OF ZITHERS

I have wanted other things more than lovers . . .
I have desired peace, intimately to know
The secret curves of deep-bosomed contentment,
To learn by heart things beautiful and slow.

55

Cities at night, and cloudful skies, I've wanted;
And open cottage doors, old colors and smells a part;
All dim things, layers of river-mist on river—
To capture Beauty's hands and lay them on my heart.

I have wanted clean rain to kiss my eyelids,
Sea-spray and silver foam to kiss my mouth.
I have wanted strong winds to flay me with passion;
And, to soothe me, tired winds from the south.

These things have I wanted more than lovers . . .
Jewels in my hands, and dew on morning grass—
Familiar things, while lovers have been strangers.
Friended thus, I have let nothing pass.

KAY BOYLE

From WANDERINGS

CHAMPS D'HONNEUR

Soldiers never do die well;
   Crosses mark the places—
Wooden crosses where they fell,
   Stuck above their faces.

Soldiers pitch and cough and twitch—
   All the world roars red and black;
Soldiers smother in a ditch,
   Choking through the whole attack.

CHAPTER HEADING

For we have thought the longer thoughts
   And gone the shorter way.
And we have danced to devils' tunes,
   Shivering home to pray;
To serve one master in the night,
   Another in the day.

ERNEST M. HEMINGWAY

PASTORAL

This is a place of ease:
Beauty has come to rest,
Color is gentle in the trees,
The willow leaves look
Timidly down, more timidly back from the brook.

Beauty has come to rest:
Sweet as a sleepy-bell
The breeze swings within the close-pressed
Shadows, and the sun
Falls in little sprays, to be picked by anyone!

MARION STROBEL

STATIC AUTUMN

Inimitably quick
To taut deceit, I
Note a bird
Amid the autumn

And my glossy bitch
Shatters leaves
Like water,
And the air

Is resonant
With pain.
I wait like one
Who has stood here before

With sunken head
In dropping leaves.

YVOR WINTERS

THE FLOWER-BOAT

The fisherman's swapping a yarn for a yarn
Under the hand of the village barber;
And here in the angle of house and barn
His deep-sea dory has found a harbor.

At anchor she rides the sunny sod
As full to the gunnel of flowers growing
As ever she turned her home with cod
From Georges Bank when winds were blowing.

And I judge from that Elysian freight
That all they ask is rougher weather,
And dory and master will sail by fate
To seek for the Happy Isles together.

ROBERT FROST

Written at the age of 20.
Published in *The Youth's Companion*.

CHICAGO

Your faith is in what you hold,
Monster, with your back against the lakes.
You gather the cities close, with iron reins
Knotted in your frozen grip.
But your sleepily savage eyes, like a white bull's,
Turn neither to the East nor West.
Sometimes a sickness takes you—
Convulsive movements pass along your length. . . .
I think there is a giant child that kicks in you,
Where your blood is running like a river under its ice.

LOLA RIDGE

From THREE SONGS

THESSALIAN

Bind your straight hair,
Thessalian,
For the winds pursue you
And the leaves.

The lake breeze would have you for a wrestler,
It would dust you with sand in the marshes,
Wash sedges and lilies to your feet;

Test your shoulders,
Whether they or the rushes were more supple,
Whether they or the larches were more sweet.

Bind back your hair,
Thessalian,
The fists of the wind are clenched.

WINIFRED BRYHER

From CONTRIBUTIONS

FOR INSTANCE

Vegetables

and jewelry, rightly displayed,
have an equal amount of fascination.

Carrots, for instance,
piled—
ferntops, bodies, and hair roots
so bound together in bunches—
bunches laid in rows
of oblong heaps with magnitude,
are sufficient to arrest any seeing eye.

Cabbages with a purplish tinge,
when of grandeur, with widespread petals,
as they rest in heaps
catching the dawn's first filtering of sunlight,
compare satisfyingly with roses enmassed,
with orchids, sunflowers, tulips,
or variegated flowers
extravagantly scattered.

While as to onions,
little can excel their decorative effect
when green tubes, white bulbs, and grey hair roots
rest in well arranged, paralleled piles
about which buxom women congregate,
laughing and chattering in wholesome vulgarity.

Crispness,
a cool indifference to the gash of knives,
to the crush of kind,
or to any destiny whatsoever,
has granted the vegetables an arrogance of identity
one would be foolhardy to strive after
with heated impressionable imagination.

Vegetables,
given their color,
scent and freshness,
too easily attain a cool supremacy of being
for our fumbling competition.

ROBERT MC ALMON

From BODY'S HEAD

HEAD ITSELF

If it were set anywhere else but so,
Rolling in its private exact socket
Like the sun set in a joint on a mountain,
I think I should not love it half as much.

But here, waving and blowing on my neck,
Of no particular kind of shape or geometry,
Its own original,
Flying my hair like a field of corn-silk
Tangled on the neglected side of a hill,
My head is at the top of me
Where my face turns an inner courage
Toward what's outside of me
And meets the challenge of difference in other things
Bravely, minutely,
By being what it is.

From this place of high preferment
I, the idol of the head,
Send all the streams of sense running down
To explore the savage half-awakened land,
Tremendous continent of this tiny isle,
And civilize it as well as they can.

                    LAURA RIDING GOTTSCHALK

ARS POETICA

A poem should be palpable and mute
As a globed fruit;

Dumb
As old medallions to the thumb;

Silent as the sleeve-worn stone
Of casement ledges where the moss has grown —

A poem should be wordless
As the flight of birds.

A poem should be motionless in time
As the moon climbs;

Leaving, as the moon releases
Twig by twig the night-entangled trees —

Leaving, as the moon behind the winter leaves,
Memory by memory the mind.

A poem should be motionless in time
As the moon climbs.

A poem should be equal to:
Not true.

For all the history of grief
An empty doorway and a maple leaf;

For love
The leaning grasses and two lights above the sea—

A poem should not mean,
But be.

ARCHIBALD MAC LEISH

CRIMSON TENT

The wind blows up the tent like a balloon.
The tent plunges tugging at pegged ropes,
About to wrench loose and soar
Above wormwood-carpeted canyons
And flinty saw-tooth hills
Up into the driven night
And the howling clouds.
Tight
As a worm curls wickedly
Round the stamen of a fuchsia,
A man curls his hands round a candle.
The flame totters in the wind,
Flares to lick his hands,
To crimson the swaying walls.
The hands cast shadows on the crimson walls.

The candle-light shrinks and flaps wide.
The shadows are full of old tenters—
Men curious as to the fashion of cities,

Men eager to taste new-tasting bread,
Men wise to the north star and to the moon's phases,
To whom East and West
Are cloaks pulled easily tight,
Worn jaunty about the shoulders:
Herodotus, Thales, Democritus,
Heraclitus who watched rivers.

Parian-browed tan-cheeked travellers,
Who sat late in wine-shops to listen,
Rose early to sniff the wind of harbors
And see the dawn kindle the desert places,
And went peering and tasting—
Through seas and wastes and cities,
Held up to the level of their grey cool eyes
Firm in untrembling fingers—
The slippery souls of men and of gods.

The candle has guttered out in darkness and wind.
The tent holds firm against the buffeting wind,
Pegged tight, weighted with stones.
My sleep is blown up with dreams
About to wrench loose and soar
Above wormwood-carpeted canyons
And flinty saw-tooth hills,
Up into the driven night
And the howling clouds.

Perhaps when the light clangs
Brass and scarlet cymbals in the east
With drone and jangle of great bells,
Loping white across the flint-strewn hills,
Will come the seeking tentless caravans
That Bilkis leads untired,
Nodding in her robes
On a roaring dromedary.

JOHN DOS PASSOS

AT MELVILLE'S TOMB

Often beneath the wave, wide from this ledge,
The dice of drowned men's bones he saw bequeath
An embassy. Their numbers, as he watched,
Beat on the dusty shore and were obscured.

And wrecks passed without sound of bells,
The calyx of death's bounty giving back
A scattered chapter, livid hieroglyph,
The portent wound in corridors of shells.

Then in the circuit calm of one vast coil,
Its lashings charmed and malice reconciled,
Frosted eyes there were that lifted altars:
And silent answers crept across the stars.

Compass, quadrant and sextant contrive
No farther tides. . . . High in the azure steeps
Monody shall not wake the mariner.
This fabulous shadow only the sea keeps.

HART CRANE

From BLUE JUNIATA

THE STREETS OF AIR

All night waiting, in an empty house
under dry electric moons, they cast
no shadow, a man striding impatiently
sucking a dry pipe, waiting
an empty sacrificial vessel waiting
without patience to be filled with God.

He said,
   —There was a scratching at my door
the noise of some one fingering the latch
once, but I opened and only found the night
empty of sound, empty—

The images of drouth
in a parched land growing, acacias in the sand
with thorns and thornlike leaves that cast no shadow,
dry leaves silently moving in the sun.

A wall rose there, of hewn enormous stones
laid without mortar and a gateway, barred
and skies closed in.
                 But you shall hear the thunder
of bursting walls, the gates of night swing wide,
and journeys will be set toward the thunder.

Your path shall be the empty streets of air.

MALCOLM COWLEY

TO A SEAMAN DEAD ON LAND

Bitten to dust are the savage feathers of fire,
And the foam lies in rusted chains on the sand.
The black weeds of the sea and the conch's spire
Are brittle as bird-claws upon my hand.

My ear on the drum of the dune is hollow
Under the sabres of clanging grass —
Stark for the thunder of sails to follow,
And the throb of wings when the dark gulls pass.

Ah, but the land has silenced you,
Your blood thinning down in dew on an inland plain.
Ah, but the loud sea would have rended you
On coral stalks and the straight white horns of rain.

The sea would have pierced you with the salt of its pace,
Boomed down your sails and the ribs of your bark on stones,
Given me touch of you in the bitter foam on my face
And the sea-mist coiled like silk about your bones.

KAY BOYLE

IN THE BEGINNING WAS A WORD

The difficulty was, it was
Simple, as simple as it seemed;
Needing no scrutinizing glass,
No intense light to be streamed

Upon it. It said what it said
Singly, without backthought or whim,
With all the strictness of the dead,
Past reason and past synonym.

But they, too dull to understand,
Laboriously improvised
A mystic allegory, and
A meaning at last recognized:

A revelation and a cause,
Crowding the cluttered stage again
With saints' and sinners' lies and laws
For a new everlasting reign.

ROBERT GRAVES

CONTEMPORARY

We shall be called harsh names by men unborn,
Since we have seen no glory in his face.
Our blindness shall not save us from the scorn
Of those who bend above the guarded case,
Where under glass his crowded note-book shines
(Pages we turn—dismiss with comment smug),
Become a thing a flaming dream enshrines,
The miracle we greeted with a shrug.

For now as always, tortured and alone,
Behind a paltry door he makes his fight;
Great thoughts sit down to dinner with a bone,
And beauty starves and sings and trims the light.
But no man comes—no man with praise for bread.
We shall be better friends when he is dead.

HORTENSE FLEXNER

O CARIB ISLE!

The tarantula rattling at the lily's foot,
Across the feet of the dead, laid in white sand
Near the coral beach; the small and ruddy crabs
Stilting out of sight, that reverse your name—

And above, the lyric palsy of eucalypti, seeping
A silver swash of something unvisited. . . . Suppose
I count these clean enamel frames of death,
Brutal necklaces of shells around each grave
Laid out so carefully. This pity can be told . . .

And in the white sand I can find a name, albeit
In another tongue. Tree-name, flower-name deliberate,
Gainsay the unknown death. . . . The wind,
Sweeping the scrub palms, also is almost kind.

But who is a Captain of this doubloon isle
Without a turnstile? Nought but catchword crabs
Plaguing the hot groins of the underbrush? Who
The commissioner of mildew throughout the senses?
His Carib mathematics dull the bright new lenses.

Under the poinciana, of a noon or afternoon
Let fiery blossoms clot the light, render my ghost,
Sieved upward, black and white along the air—
Until it joins the blue's comedian host.

Let not the pilgrim see himself again
Bound like the dozen turtles on the wharf
Each twilight—still undead, and brine caked in their eyes,
—Huge, overturned: such thunder in their strain!
And clenched beaks coughing for the surge again!

Slagged of the hurricane—I, cast within its flow,
Congeal by afternoons here, satin and vacant . . .
You have given me the shell, Satan—the ember,
Carbolic, of the sun exploded in the sea.

HART CRANE

From THINGS KNOWN

UNDER THE HILL

When darkness crept and grew
The hushed wide earth lay still.
I listened; I thought I knew
The vibrance under the hill.
If I were now just dead
I could not make less sound.
I slowly bent my head
Intently to the ground.
I listened again. My feet
Took root within the soil;
Earth grew within me, sweet
In my limbs. I knew the soil
Had claimed my body whole.
I listened. There came no sound
Across the darkening knoll
Or over the matted ground.

I had become a thing
Of earth. My face felt air
As leaves feel winds that bring
A sudden cool. My hair
Was grass, my flesh was sand—
Strange that it happened there
Upon the solid land!
My blood turned water. My bone
Took on the strength of stone.

Mixed with earth and sky,
I bore all things to die.
I caused the twig to sprout
And every flower come out.
Flaming the earth with spring
I made each robin sing,
Then sent the long heat down
Tinging green leaves with brown.
I made the summer old
With singing autumn gold,
And stilled all things that grow,
And covered the world with snow.

When darkness crept and grew
The hushed wide earth lay still.
Being earth, at last I knew
The vibrance under the hill.

RICHARD EBERHART

HOAR FROST

The last cold lilies cringed
Before this challenge hinted;
Our raptures have repented,
Death has been avenged.
Now beauty; stern as time
Usurps her rival beauty,
Effulgent, wild. No pity
Is scattered with her rime
Upon the earth's frail tide,
Inexorably sealing
Autumn's distilling
Of the summer's bright pride.
Bend before this chaste
Power, stark and subtle,
Now passion is effaced
And pride is futile.

MORTON DAUWEN ZABEL

BIRDS IN SNOW

See
how they trace,
across the very-marble
of this place,
bright sevens and printed fours,
elevens and careful eights,
abracadabra
of a mystic's lore
or symbol
outlined
on a wizard's gate.

Like plaques of ancient writ
our garden flags now name
the great and very-great;
our garden flags acclaim
in carven hieroglyph,
here king and kinglet lie,
here prince and lady rest,
mythical queens sleep here
and heroes that are slain

in holy righteous war.
Hieratic, slim and fair,
the tracery written here
proclaims what's left unsaid
in Egypt of her dead.

H. D.

From PUBLISHED CORRESPONDENCE

EPISTLE TO THE RAPALLOAN

Ezra, whom not with eye nor with ear have I ever
(But nevertheless as one by a rhyme-beat, one
By the break of his syllables, one by a slow breath) known,
By doubts that in common between us two deliver
Better your face to me than the photograph,
Which besides they say lies — they say, that is, you were never
The beautiful boy with the sullen mouth, the giver
Of ambiguous apples — Ezra, you that could laugh

When the rest of them followed your hearse in five-years-ago's
    mud,
When the rest of them talked of the promise of youth cut off
By a fever, a flush in the cheek, an ironical cough
(That did in truth, they were right enough there, bring blood),

Ezra, I've read again your Sixteen Cantos:
There's a word for my praise — if there's a rhyme for cantos!

ARCHIBALD MAC LEISH

MARCHING SONG

The foot cannot know
Whether marble or mire
The path it must go
Toward the mind's desire:

Then how shall the mind
Imagine its route?
It is brave. It is blind.
It is but a foot

Set free on the track
Of truth, if you will,
Where there's no turning back,
And no standing still,

But a long way to fare—
With mortality shod—
Maybe nowhere,
Maybe to God.

Be the shoe sheerest pain,
Or the obstacle stark,
It must stumble again
Like a foot in the dark.

GEORGE DILLON

SONNET

Women have loved before as I love now;
At least, in lively chronicles of the past—
Of Irish waters by a Cornish prow
Or Trojan waters by a Spartan mast
Much to their cost invaded—here and there,
Hunting the amorous line, skimming the rest,
I find some woman bearing as I bear
Love like a burning city in the breast.
I think however that of all alive
I only in such utter, ancient way
Do suffer love; in me alone survive
The unregenerate passions of a day
When treacherous queens, with death upon the tread,
Heedless and wilful, took their knights to bed.

EDNA ST. VINCENT MILLAY

From WORDS ON THE WIND

FRUIT OF LONELINESS

Now for a little I have fed on loneliness
As on some strange fruit from a frost-touched vine—
Persimmon in its yellow comeliness,
Or pomegranate-juice color of wine,
The pucker-mouth crab apple, or late plum—
On fruit of loneliness have I been fed.
But now after short absence I am come
Back from felicity to the wine and bread.
For, being mortal, this luxurious heart
Would starve for you, my dear, I must admit,
If it were held another hour apart
From that food which alone can comfort it—
I am come home to you, for at the end
I find I cannot live without you, friend.

MAY SARTON

KANSAS CITY WEST BOTTOMS

The nickelplate moon
Is low over the wires
Like a Queensboro
Electric lamp.
The lights along the street
Are fragments of
A shooting star.

The evening is a lonely wind
In my bones
And the sidewalks are
Thick fog inside me.
Down below
The lanterns at the
Railroad crossing
Are blue on my lips.
A caboose is stalled somewhere,
And the Long Island train
Rattles along the tracks
Like a talmudic student
In a chaider.

And after the night has
Rolled up into a piece of
Stage celluloid,
The Kansas City west bottoms

Returns and stirs up
The hossfly stockyards,
The strawy cool livery-stables,
The bluffs,
And the belly-stabbing
Hobo-pariah box-car '20's.

EDWARD DAHLBERG

HYPOCRITE SWIFT

After Reading Swift's Journal to Stella

Hypocrite Swift now takes an eldest daughter.
He lifts Vanessa's hand. *Cudsho, my dove!*
Drink Wexford Ale and quaff down Wexford water,
But never love.

He buys new caps; he and Lord Stanley ban
Hedge-fellows who have neither wit nor swords.
He turns his coat; Tories are in; Queen Anne
Makes twelve new lords.

The town mows hay in hell; he swims in the river;
His giddiness returns; his head is hot.
Berries are clean, while peaches damn the giver,
(Though grapes do not).

Mrs. Vanhomrigh keeps him safe from the weather.
Preferment pulls his periwig askew.
Pox take belittlers; do the willows feather?
God keep you.

Stella spells ill; Lords Peterborough and Fountain
Talk politics; the Florence wine went sour.
Midnight: two different clocks, here and in Dublin,
Give out the hour.

73

On walls at court, long gilded mirrors gaze.
The parquet shines; outside the snow falls deep.
Venus, the Muses stare above the maze.
Now sleep.

Dream the mixed, fearsome dream. The satiric word
Dies in its horror. Wake, and live by stealth.
The bitter quatrain forms, is here, is heard,
Is wealth.

What care I; what cares saucy Presto? Stir
The bed-clothes, hearten up the perishing fire.
Hypocrite Swift sent Stella a green apron
And dead desire.

LOUISE BOGAN

SAILOR

He sat upon the rolling deck
Half a world away from home,
And smoked a Capstan cigarette
And watched the blue waves tipped with foam.

He had a mermaid on his arm,
An anchor on his breast,
And tattooed on his back he had
A blue bird in a nest.

LANGSTON HUGHES

From SONNETS OF THE BLOOD

I

What is this flesh and blood compounded of
But water seething with convulsive lime?
This prowling strife of cells, sharp hate and love,
Wears the long claw of flesh-devouring time.
We who have seen the makers of our bone
Bemused with history, then make more dust
Pausing forever, and over their dust a stone,
We know the chastened look of men who must

74

Confess the canker gnawing the flesh flower
And are made brothers by mortality;
That is our treason to the murderous hour—
To think of brothers, hard identity
Not made of ash and lime by time undone
Nor poured out quite when the life-blood has run.

II

Near to me as my flesh, my flesh and blood,
And more mysterious, you are my brother;
The light vaulting within your solitude
Now studied burns lest you that rage should smother.
It is a flame obscure to mortal eyes
(Most like the fire that warms the deepest grave,
For the cold grave's the deepest of our lies)
Of which our blood's the long indentured slave.
The fire that burns most secretly in you
Does not expand you hidden and alone,
For the same blaze consumes not one, but two,
Me also, the same true marrow and bone
Contrived and seasoned in a house of strife
Built far back in the fundaments of life.

IV

The times have changed, there is not left to us
The vice of privilege, the law of form—
Who of our kin was pusillanimous
And took the world so easy, so by storm?
Why none, unless we count it arrogance
To cultivate humility in pride,
To look but blushingly and half-askance
On boots and spurs that went the devil's ride.
There was, remember, that Virginian
Who took himself to be brute nature's law
And cared not what men thought him, a tall man
Who meditated calmly what he saw
Until he freed his negroes, lest he be
Too strict with nature and then they less free.

VII

The fire I praise was once perduring flame
Till it snuffs with our generation, out—
No matter, it's all one, it's but a name
Not as late honeysuckle half so stout,
So think upon it how the fire burns blue
Its hottest, when the fury's all but spent;
Thank God the fuel is low, we'll not renew
Such length of flame into our firmament;
Think too the rooftree crackles and will fall
On us, who saw the sacred fury's height
Seated in her great chair with the black shawl
From head to feet, burning with motherly light
More spectral than November eve could mix
With sunset, to blaze on her pale crucifix.

IX

Not power nor the storied hand of God
Shall keep us whole in this dissevering air,
Which is a stink upon this pleasant sod
So foul, the hovering buzzard sees it fair.
I ask you therefore will it end tonight
And the moth tease again his windy flame,
Or spiders eating their loves hide in the night
At last, drowsy with self-devouring shame?
This is the house of Atreus where we live—
Which one of us the Greek, perplexed with crime,
Questions the future that with his lucid sieve
Strains off the appointed particles of time;
It is not spoken now, for time is slow,
Which brother, you or I, shall swiftly go.

ALLEN TATE

KANSAS BOY

This Kansas boy who never saw the sea
Walks through the young corn rippling at his knee
As sailors walk; and when the grain grows higher
Watches the dark waves leap with greener fire
Than ever oceans hold. He follows ships,
Tasting the bitter spray upon his lips,
For in his blood up-stirs the salty ghost
Of one who sailed a storm-bound English coast.
Across wide fields he hears the sea winds crying,
Shouts at the crows—and dreams of white gulls flying.

RUTH LECHLITNER

EXTRACT

Mica shines on the beach
and the frogs drone all night in the jungle.
In the valley the twigs clink under the falling snow.

The salamanders chant a pebble-song on the hill-road
and the storm advances between the mountains.
Astrea, convince me that resolution means
an elegy, and say but one word.

The night sky,
now white, now black,
performs a mute miracle
above the lowering sleet-storm.

The light-house sways at the edge of the farthest cliff,
and a crab crawls into a yellowed skull at low tide.
Give me your hand here on the sand dune
and explain to me the wisdom
of winter.

The gulls disappear into the north-east,
and the ocean groans darkly grey in the half-light.

PAUL FREDERIC BOWLES

WINTER NIGHT

For Charles Fenby

This evening holds her breath
And makes a crystal pause;
The streams of light are frozen,
Shining above their source.

Now if ever might one
Break through the sensual gate;
Seraph's wing glimpse far-glinting.
Is it, is it too late?

We look up at the sky.
Yes, it is mirror clear;
Too well we recognise
The physiognomy there.

Friend, let us look to earth,
Be stubborn, act and sleep.
Here at our feet the skull
Keeps a stiff upper lip;

Feeling the weight of winter,
Grimaces underground;
But does not need to know
Why spirit was flesh-bound.

CECIL DAY LEWIS

FEARFUL SYMMETRY

Muzzle and jowl and beastly brow,
bilious glaring eyes, tufted ears,
recidivous criminality in the slouch,
　　—This is not the latest absconding bankrupt
but a "beautiful" tiger imported at great expense from
　　Kuala Lumpur.

7 photographers, 4 black-and-white artists and an R. A.
are taking his profitable likeness;

28 reporters and an essayist
are writing him up.
Several ladies think he is a darling
especially at mealtimes, observing
that a firm near the Docks advertizes replicas
full-grown on approval for easy cash payments.

Felis Tigris (Straights Settlements) (Bobo) takes exercise
up and down his cage before feeding,
in a stench of excrements of great cats
indifferent to beauty or brutality.
He is said to have eaten several persons,
but of course you can never be quite sure of these things.

BASIL BUNTING

WATERSHED

From this high place all things flow:
Land of divided streams, of water spilled
Eastward, westward without memento;
Land where the morning mist is curled
Like smoke about the ridgepole of the world.
The mist is furled.

The sunset hawk now rides
The tall light up the climbing deep of air.
Beneath him swings the rooftree that divides
The east and west. His gold eyes scan
The crumpled shade on gorge and crest,
And streams that creep and disappear, appear,
Past fingered ridges and their shrivelling span.
Under the broken eaves men take their rest.

Forever, should they stir, their thought would keep
This place. Not love, happiness past, constrains,
But certitude. Enough, and it remains;
Though they who thread the flood and neap
Of earth itself have felt the earth creep,
In pastures hung against the rustling gorge
Have felt the shudder and the sweat of stone,
Knowing thereby no constant moon
Sustains the hill's lost granite surge.

ROBERT PENN WARREN

From PART OF A NOVEL, PART OF A POEM, PART OF A PLAY

THE STEEPLE-JACK

Dürer would have seen a reason for living
 in a town like this, with eight stranded whales
to look at; with the sweet sea air coming into your house
on a fine day, from water etched
 with waves as formal as the scales
on a fish.

One by one, in two's, in three's, the seagulls keep
 flying back and forth over the town clock,
or sailing around the lighthouse without moving the wings —
rising steadily with a slight
 quiver of the body — or flock
mewing where

a sea the purple of the peacock's neck is
 paled to greenish azure as Dürer changed
the pine green of the Tyrol to peacock blue and guinea
grey. You can see a twenty-five
 pound lobster; and fishnets arranged
to dry. The

whirlwind fifeanddrum of the storm bends the salt
 marsh grass, disturbs stars in the sky and the
star on the steeple; it is a privilege to see so
much confusion. Disguised by what
 might seem austerity, the sea-
side flowers and

trees are favored by the fog so that you have
 the tropics at first hand: the trumpet-vine,
fox-glove, giant snap-dragon, a salpaglossis that has
spots and stripes; morning-glories, gourds,
 or moon-vines trained on fishing-twine
at the back

door; cat-tails, flags, blueberries and spiderwort,
     striped grass, lichens, sunflowers, asters, daisies—
the yellow and the crab-claw blue ones with green bracts—
          toad-plant,
petunias, ferns; pink lilies, blue
     ones, tigers; poppies; black sweet-peas.
The climate

is not right for the banyan, frangipan, the
     jack-fruit tree; nor for exotic serpent
life. Ring lizard and snake-skin for the foot if you see fit,
but here they've cats not cobras to
     keep down the rats. The diffident
little newt

with white pin-dots on black horizontal spaced
     out bands lives here; yet there is nothing that
ambition can buy or take away. The college student
named Ambrose sits on the hill-side
     with his not-native books and hat
and sees boats

at sea progress white and rigid as if in
     a groove. Liking an elegance of which
the source is not bravado, he knows by heart the antique
sugar-bowl shaped summer-house of
     interlacing slats, and the pitch
of the church

spire, not true, from which a man in scarlet lets
     down a rope as a spider spins a thread;
he might be part of a novel, but on the sidewalk a
sign says C. J. Poole, Steeple-jack,
     in black and white; and one in red
and white says

Danger. The church portico has four fluted
     columns, each a single piece of stone, made
modester by white-wash. This would be a fit haven for
waifs, children, animals, prisoners,
     and presidents who have repaid
sin-driven

senators by not thinking about them. There
    are a school-house, a post-office in a
store, fish-houses, hen-houses, a three-masted schooner on
the stocks. The hero, the student,
    the steeple-jack, each in his way,
is at home.

It could not be dangerous to be living
    in a town like this, of simple people,
who have a steeple-jack placing danger signs by the church
while he is gilding the solid-
    pointed star, which on a steeple
stands for hope.

THE HERO

Where there is personal liking we go.
    Where the ground is sour; where there are
    weeds of beanstalk height,
    snakes' hyperdermic teeth, or
    the wind brings the "scarebabe voice"
    from the neglected yew set with
    the semi-precious cats' eyes of the owl —
awake, asleep, "raised ears extended to fine points," and so
on — love won't grow.

We do not like some things and the hero
    doesn't; deviating head-stones
    and uncertainty;
    going where one does not wish
    to go; suffering and not
    saying so; standing and listening where something
    is hiding. The hero shrinks
as what it is flies out on muffled wings, with twin yellow
eyes — to and fro —

    with quavering water-whistle note, low,
    high, in bass-falsetto chirps
    until the skin creeps.
    Jacob when a-dying, asked
    Joseph: Who are these? and blessed
    both sons, the younger most, vexing Joseph. And
    Joseph was vexing to some.

Cincinnatus was; Regulus; and some of our fellow
men have been, though

devout, like Pilgrim having to go slow
   to find his toll, tired but hopeful—
   hope not being hope
   until all ground for hope has
   vanished; and lenient, looking
   upon a fellow creature's error with the
   feelings of a mother—a
woman or a cat. The decorous frock-coated Negro
by the grotto

answers the fearless sightseeing hobo
   who asks the man she's with, what's this,
   what's that, where's Martha
   buried, "Gen-ral Washington
   there; his lady, here"; speaking
   as if in a play—not seeing her; with a
   sense of human dignity
and reverence for mystery, standing like the shadow
of the willow.

Moses would not be grandson to Pharaoh.
   It is not what I eat that is
   my natural meat,
   the hero says. He's not out
   seeing a sight but the rock
   crystal thing to see—the startling El Greco
   brimming with inner light—that
covets nothing that it has let go. This then you may know
as the hero.

MARIANNE MOORE

From THE URN

RELIQUARY

Tenderness and resolution!
What is our life without a sudden pillow,
What is death without a ditch?

The harvest laugh of bright Apollo
And the flint tooth of Sagitarius,
Rhyme from the same Tau (closing cinch by cinch)
And pocket us who, somehow, do not follow:
As though we know those who are variants,
Charms that each by each refuse the clinch
With desperate propriety, whose name is writ
In wider letters than the alphabet.
Who is now left to vary the Sanscrit
Pillowed by
My wrist in the vestibule of Time? Who
Will hold it — wear the keepsake, dear, of time —
Return the mirage on a coin that spells
Something of sand and sun the Nile defends?

PURGATORIO

My country, O my land, my friends —
Am I apart — here from you in a land
Where all your gas-lights, faces, sputum gleam
Like something left, forsaken? Here am I —
And are these stars, the high plateau, the scents
Of Eden, and the dangerous tree — are these
The landscape of confession, and if confession,
so absolution? Wake pines — but pines wake here.
I dream the too-keen cider, the too-soft snow.
Where are the bayonets, that the scorpion may not grow?
Here quakes of earth make houses fall,
And all my countrymen I see rush toward one stall.
Exile is thus purgatory — not such as Dante built,
But rather like a blanket than a quilt,
And I have no decision — is it green or brown
That I prefer to country or to town?

I am unraveled, umbilical anew,
As ring the church bells here in Mexico
(They ring too obdurately here to heed my call)—
And what hours they forget to chime I'll know,
As one whose altitude, at one time, was not so.

THE SAD INDIAN

Sad heart, the gymnast of inertia, does not count
Hours, days—and scarcely sun and moon.
The warp is in his woof, and his keen vision
Spells what his tongue has had, and only that—
How more? But the lash, lost vantage and the prison
His fathers took for granted ages since—and so he looms

Farther than his sun-shadow, farther than wings—
Their shadows even—now can't carry him.
He does not know the new hum in the sky
And—backwards—is it thus the eagles fly?

REPLY

Thou canst read nothing except through appetite,
And here we join eyes in that sanctity
Where brother passes brother without sight,
But finally knows conviviality.

Go then, unto thy turning and thy blame.
Seek bliss then, brother, in my moment's shame.
All this that balks delivery through words
Shall come to you through wounds prescribed by swords:

That hate is but the vengeance of a long caress,
And fame is pivotal to shame with every sun
That rises on eternity's long willingness.
So sleep, dear brother, in my fame, my shame undone.

ENRICH MY RESIGNATION

Enrich my resignation as I usurp those far
Feints of control, hear rifles blown out on the stag
Below the aeroplane, and see the fox's brush
Whisk silently beneath the red hill's crag—
Extinction stirred on either side
Because love wonders, keeps a certain mirth.

Die, O centuries, die, as Dionysus said,
Yet live in all my resignation.
It is the moment, now, when all
The heartstrings spring, unlaced.
Here is the peace of the fathers.

HART CRANE

WINTER SKETCHES

I

Now that black ground and bushes—
saplings, trees,
each twig and limb—are suddenly white with snow,
and earth becomes brighter than the sky,

that intricate shrub
of nerves, veins, arteries—
myself—uncurls
its knotted leaves
to the shining air.

Upon this wooded hillside,
pied with snow, I hear
only the melting snow
drop from the twigs.

II SUBWAY

In steel clouds
to the sound of thunder
like the ancient gods:
our sky, cement;
the earth, cement;
our trees, steel;
instead of sunshine,
a light that has no twilight,
neither morning nor evening,
only noon.

Coming up the subway stairs, I thought the moon
only another street-light—
a little crooked.

III

From the middle of the pool
in the concrete pavement a fountain
in neat jets; the wind scatters it
upon the water. The untidy trees
drop their leaves upon the pavement.

IV

Along the flat roofs beneath our window,
in the morning sunshine,
I read the signature of last night's rain.

V

The squads, platoons, and regiments
of lighted windows,
ephemeral under the evening star—

feast, you who cross the bridge
this cold twilight
on these honeycombs of light, the buildings of Manhattan.

CHARLES REZNIKOFF

From THE MAGNETIC MOUNTAIN

CONDEMNED

Tempt me no more; for I
Have known the lightning's hour,
The poet's inward pride,
The certainty of power.

Bayonets are closing round.
I shrink; yet I must wring
A living from despair
And out of steel a song.

Though song, though breath be short,
I'll share not the disgrace

Of those that ran away
Or never left the base.

Comrades, my tongue can speak
No comfortable words,
Calls to a forlorn hope,
Gives work and not rewards.

Oh keep the sickle sharp
And follow still the plough:
Others may reap, though we
See not the winter through.

Father, who endest all,
Pity our broken sleep;
For we lie down with tears
And waken but to weep.

And if our blood alone
Will melt this iron earth,
Take it. It is well spent
Easing a saviour's birth.

C. DAY LEWIS

From "THAT'S THE AMERICAN STYLE"

4TH OF JULY

I

The ship moves
but its smoke
moves with the wind
faster than the ship

—thick coils of it
through leafy trees
pressing
upon the river

II

The heat makes
this place of the woods
a room
in which two robins pain

crying
distractedly
over the plight of
their unhappy young

III

During the explosions
at dawn, the celebrations
I could hear
a native cuckoo

in the distance
as at dusk, before
I'd heard
a night hawk calling

WILLIAM CARLOS WILLIAMS

EMPTY DWELLING PLACES

Forever the little thud of names, falling,
Disappearing, baying at the moon for the last time—
Quiet obscure little names, leaving no trace
But the ash-flecked aroma of stale fragmentary careers.
Names that once clothed the pound of blood in a body,
That stood for lungs, and love-possible limbs,
And voices, voices rich in faith and friendly
To the sweep and surge of curious spying years.
In the brisk procession of sub-tunneled fame
The little names settle in the ooze of silent unhurried
          nothingness.

In the night the head on the pillow turns,
And a little changed hurt settles on the course
Of his dearest striving, a wrong music flooding
Forbidden chambers, with no semblance of comfort even
          in the words.
                    My name is . . .
                    (over and over)—
                    my name is . . .
I swear to you I knew it once.

KENNETH PATCHEN

From LOCAL HABITATION

ON INHABITING AN ORANGE

All our roads go nowhere.
Maps are curled
To keep the pavement definitely
On the world.

All our footsteps, set to make
Metric advance,
Lapse into arcs in deference
To circumstance.

All our journeys nearing Space
Skirt it with care,
Shying; at the distances
Present in air.

Blithely travel-stained and worn,
Erect and sure,
All our travelers go forth,
Making down the roads of Earth
Endless détour.

JOSEPHINE MILES

AT WOODWARD'S GARDENS

A boy, presuming on his intellect,
Once showed two little monkeys in a cage
A burning-glass they could not understand,
And never could be made to understand.
Words are no good: to say it was a lens
For gathering solar rays would not have helped.
But let him show them how the weapon worked.
He made the sun a pin-point on the nose
Of first one, then the other, till it brought
A look of puzzled dimness to their eyes
That blinking could not seem to blink away.
They stood, arms linked together, at the bars
And exchanged troubled glances over life.
One put a thoughtful hand up to his nose
As if reminded—or as if perhaps
Within a million years of an idea.
He got his purple little knuckles stung.
The already known had once more been confirmed
By psychological experiment;
And that were all the finding to announce
Had the boy not presumed too close and long.
There was a sudden flash, a monkey snatch,
And the glass was the monkey's, not the boy's.
Precipitately they retired back-cage
And instituted an investigation . . .
On their part, but without the needed insight.

They bit the glass and listened for the flavor,
They broke the handle and the binding off it;
Then, none the wiser, frankly gave it up,
And having hid it in their bedding straw
Against the day of prisoners' ennui,
Came dryly forward to the bars again
To answer for themselves.

                    Who said it mattered—
What monkeys did or didn't understand?
They might not understand a burning-glass.
They might not understand the sun itself.
It's knowing what to do with things that counts.

                              ROBERT FROST

NIGHT-MUSIC

When those who can never again forgive themselves
finish their dinners, rear up from the chair,
turning to movies, are caught in demonstrations
sweeping the avenues—Meet them there.

Watch how their faces change like traffic-light—
bold blood gone green as horses pound the street,
as the plates of sweated muscle push
them squarely back into retreat.

Notice their tremulous late overthrow,
caught irresponsible; as the first rank presses
up at the brown animal breast of law,
defying government by horses.

And after the quick night-flurry, the few jailed,
the march stampeded, the meeting stopped, go down
night-streets to unique rooms where horror ends,
strike-songs are sung, and the old songs remain.

Vaguely Ilonka draws her violin
along to Bach, greatest of trees, whereunder
earth is again familiar, grandmother,
and very god-music branches overhead.

Changeable spirit! build a newer music
rich enough to feed starvation on.
Course down the night, past scenes of horror, among
children awake, lands ruined, begging men.

Rebel against torment—
boats gone, night-battles, the sleepers up and shaking,
fear in the streets,
cruelty on awaking.

Make music out of night will change the night.

MURIEL RUKEYSER

"LONG LIVE THE WEEDS"

Hopkins

Long live the weeds that overwhelm
My narrow vegetable realm!—
The bitter rock, the barren soil
That force the son of man to toil;
All things unholy, marked by curse,
The ugly of the universe.
The rough, the wicked, and the wild
That keep the spirit undefiled.
With these I match my little wit
And earn the right to stand or sit,
Hope, look, create, or drink and die:
These shape the creature that is I.

THEODORE ROETHKE

A FAREWELL

Good-bye!—no, do not grieve that it is over,
   The perfect hour;
That the winged joy, sweet honey-loving rover,
   Flits from the flower.

Grieve not—it is the law. Love will be flying—
   Yes, love and all.
Glad was the living—blessed be the dying.
   Let the leaves fall.

HARRIET MONROE

JOURNEY TO ICELAND

And the traveller hopes: let me be far from any
Physician. And the ports have names for the sea,
   The citiless, the corroding, the sorrow.
   And North means to all Reject.

And the great plains are forever where the cold fish is hunted,
And everywhere. The light birds flicker and flaunt.
   Under the scolding flag the lover
   Of islands may see at last,

Faintly, his limited hope; and he nears the glitter
Of glaciers, the sterile immature mountains, intense
   In the abnormal day of this world, and a river's
   Fan-like polyp of sand.

Then let the good citizen here find marvels of nature:
The horse-shoe ravine, the issue of steam from a cleft
   In the rock, and rocks, and waterfalls brushing the
   Rocks, and among the rocks birds.

And the student of prose and conduct places to visit:
The site of the church where a bishop was put in a bog,
   The bath of a great historian, the rock where an
   Outlaw dreaded the dark.

Remember the doomed man thrown by his horse and crying
"Beautiful is the hill-side; I will not go":
    The old woman confessing: "He that I loved the
    Best, to him I was worst."

For Europe is absent. This is an island and therefore
Unreal. And the steadfast affections of its dead can be bought
    By those whose dreams accuse them of being
    Spitefully alive. And the pale

From too much passion of kissing feel pure in its deserts.
Can they? For the world is, and the present, and the lie.
    And the narrow bridge over the torrent, and the
    Small farm under the crag

Are the natural setting for the jealousies of a province;
And the weak vow of fidelity is formed by the cairn:
    And within the indigenous figure on horseback
    On the bridle-path down by the lake

The blood moves also by crooked and furtive inches,
Asks all your questions: "Where is the homage? When
    Shall justice be done? O who is against me?
    Why am I always alone?"

Present then the world to the world with its mendicant shadow:
Let the suits be flash, the minister of commerce insane:
    Let jazz be bestowed on the huts, and the beauty's
    Set cosmopolitan smile.

For our time has no favourite suburb. No local features
Are those of the young for whom all wish to care;
    The promise is only a promise, the fabulous
    Country impartially far.

Tears fall in all the rivers. Again the driver
Pulls on his gloves and in a blinding snowstorm starts
    On his deadly journey, and again the writer
    Runs howling to his art.

                W. H. AUDEN

WE LYING BY SEASAND

We lying by seasand, watching yellow
And the grave sea, mock who deride
Who follow the red rivers, hollow
Alcove of words out of cicada shade,
For in this yellow grave of sand and sea
A calling for color calls with the wind
That's grave and gay as grave and sea
Sleeping on either hand.
The lunar silences, the silent tide
Lapping the still canals, the dry tide-master
Ribbed between desert and water storm,
Should cure our ills of the water
With a one-colored calm;
The heavenly music over the sand
Sounds with the grains as they hurry
Hiding the golden mountains and mansions
Of the grave, gay seaside land.
Bound by a sovereign strip, we lie,
Watch yellow, wish for wind to blow away
The strata of the shore and leave red rock;
But wishes breed not, neither
Can we fend off the rock arrival,
Lie watching yellow until the golden weather
Breaks, O my heart's blood, like a heart and hill.

DYLAN THOMAS

POEM

You, my photographer, you, most aware,
Who climbed to the bridge when the iceberg struck,
Climbed with your camera when the ship's hull broke,
And lighted your flashes and, standing passionate there,
Wound the camera in the sudden burst's flare,
Shot the screaming women, and turned and took
Pictures of the iceberg (as the ship's deck shook)
Dreaming like the moon in the night's black air!

You, tiptoe on the rail to film a child!
The nude old woman swimming in the sea
Looked up from the dark water to watch you there;
Below, near the ballroom where the band still toiled,
The frightened, in their lifebelts, watched you bitterly—
You hypocrite! My brother! We are a pair!

DELMORE SCHWARTZ

MY LOVE WAS LIGHT

My love was light the old wives said—
Light was my love and better dead!

My love was of such little worth
Stones were but wasted on her tomb;
She left no kettle by the hearth,
No crying child nor silent loom.

My love drank wine the old wives said
And danced her empty days away;
She baked no bread, she spun no thread,
She shaped no vessels out of clay. . . .

But how should old wives understand
Eternally my heart must grieve,
The cup remembering in her hand,
The dance her ghostly feet still weave. . . .

My love was light the old wives said—
Light was my love and better dead!

THOMAS LANIER WILLIAMS

TWO MORNINGS AND TWO EVENINGS

PARIS, 7 A.M.

I make a trip to each clock in the apartment:
Some hands point histrionically one way
And some point others, from the ignorant faces.
Time is an Etoile; hours diverge
So much that days are journeys round their suburbs,
Circles surrounding stars, overlapping circles.
The short, half-tone scale of winter weathers
Is a spread pigeon's wing.
Winter lives under a pigeon's wing, a dead wing with damp
    feathers.

Look down into the courtyard. All the houses
Are built this way, with ornamental urns
Set on the mansard roof-tops where the pigeons
Take their walks. It is like introspection
To stare inside, or retrospection,
A star inside a rectangle, a recollection:
This hollow square could easily have been there
— The childish snow-forts, built in flashier winters,
Could have reached these proportions and been houses;
The mighty snow-forts, four, five, stories high,
Withstanding spring as sand-forts do the tide,
Their walls, their shape, could not dissolve and die,
Only be overlapping in a strong chain, only be stone,
Be grayed and yellowed now like these.

Where is the ammunition, the piled-up balls
With the star-splintered hearts of ice?

This sky is no carrier-warrior-pigeon
Escaping endless intersecting circles.
It is a dead one, or the sky from which a dead one fell.
The urns have caught his ashes or his feathers.
When did the star dissolve, or was it captured
By the sequence of squares and squares and circles, circles?
Can the clocks say: is it there below
About to tumble in snow.

A MIRACLE FOR BREAKFAST

*"Miracles enable us to judge of
doctrine, and doctrine enables us
to judge of miracles."*

At six o'clock we were waiting for coffee,
Waiting for coffee and the charitable crumb
That was going to be served from a certain balcony,
—Like kings of old, or like a miracle.
It was still dark. One foot of the sun
Steadied itself on a long ripple in the river.

The first ferry of the day had just crossed the river.
It was so cold we hoped the coffee
Would be very hot, seeing that the sun
Was not going to warm us; and that the crumb
Would be a loaf each buttered, by a miracle.
At seven a man stepped out on the balcony.

He stood for a minute alone on the balcony
Looking over our heads towards the river.
A servant handed him the makings of the miracle,
Consisting of one lone cup of coffee
And one roll, which he proceeded to crumb,
His head, so to speak, in the clouds—along with the sun.

Was the man crazy? What under the sun
Was he trying to do, up there on his balcony!
Each man received one rather hard crumb,
Which some flicked scornfully into the river,
And, in a cup, one drop of the coffee.
Some of us stood around, waiting for the miracle.

I can tell what I saw next; it was not a miracle.
A beautiful villa stood in the sun
And from its doors came the smell of hot coffee.
In front, a baroque white plaster balcony
Added by birds, who nest along the river,
—I saw it with one eye close to the crumb—

And galleries and marble chambers. My crumb
My mansion, made for me by a miracle,
Through ages, by insects, birds, and the river
Working the stone. Every day, in the sun,
At breakfast time I sit on my balcony
With my feet up, and drink gallons of coffee.

We licked up the crumb and swallowed the coffee.
A window across the river caught the sun
As if the miracle were working, on the wrong balcony.

FROM THE COUNTRY TO THE CITY

The long, long legs,
League-boots of land, that carry the city nowhere,
    Nowhere; the lines
That we drive on (the satin-stripes on harlequin's
    Trousers, tights);
His tough trunk dressed in tatters, scribbled over with
    Nonsensical signs;
His shadowy, tall dunce-cap; and best of all his
    Shows and sights,
His brain appears, throned in "fantastic triumph,"
    And shines through his hat
With jewelled works at work at intermeshing crowns,
    Lamé with lights.
As we approach, wickedest clown, your heart and head,
    We can see that
Glittering arrangement of your brain consists, now,
    Of mermaid-like,
Seated, ravishing sirens, each waving her hand-mirror;
    And we start at
Series of slight disturbances up in the telephone wires
    On the turnpike.
Flocks of short, shining wires seem to be flying sidewise.
    Are they birds?
They flash again. No. They are vibrations of the tuning-fork
    You hold and strike
Against the mirror-frames, then draw for miles, your dreams,
    Out country-wards.
We bring a message from the long black length of body:
    "Subside," it begs and begs.

SONG

Summer is over upon the sea.
The pleasure yacht, the social being,
That danced on the endless polished floor,
Stepped and side-stepped like Fred Astaire,
Is gone, is gone, docked somewhere ashore.

The friends have left, the sea is bare
That was strewn with floating, fresh green weeds.
Only the rusty-sided freighter
Goes past the moon's marketless craters
And the stars are the only ships of pleasure.

ELIZABETH BISHOP

PAST MIDNIGHT

After writing,
Reading late,
Too tired and tense
To take the author's sense,
My mind a metronome
That keeps its proper beat,
Always starting and alighting,
I strive to mark as if it were my own
The other's pulse too stuttering and slow,
To pull his periods straight,
To stretch them tighter than the vibrant bow
That speeds the arrow home.

EDMUND WILSON

BEARDED OAKS

The oaks, how subtle and marine!
Bearded, and all the layered light
Above them swims; and thus the scene,
Recessed, awaits the positive night.

So, waiting, we in the grass now lie
Beneath the langorous tread of light;
The grasses, kelp-like, satisfy
The nameless motions of the air.

Upon the floor of light, and time,
Unmurmuring, of polyp made,
We rest; we are, as light withdraws,
Twin atolls on a shelf of shade.

Ages to our construction went,
Dim architecture, hour by hour;
And violence, forgot now, lent
The present stillness all its power.

The storm of noon above us rolled,
Of light the fury, furious gold,
The long drag troubling us, the depth:
Unrocked is dark, unrippling, still.

Passion and slaughter, ruth, decay
Descended, whispered grain by grain,
Silted down swaying streams, to lay
Foundation for our voicelessness.

All our debate is voiceless here,
As all our rage is rage of stone;
If hopeless hope, fearless is fear,
And history is thus undone.

(Our feet once wrought the hollow street
With echo when the lamps were dead
At windows; once our headlight glare
Disturbed the doe that, leaping, fled.)

That caged hearts make iron stroke
I do not love you now the less,
Or less that all that light once gave
The graduate dark should now revoke

So little time we live in Time,
And we learn all so painfully,
That we may spare this hour's term
To practice for Eternity.

ROBERT PENN WARREN

AT CARMEL HIGHLANDS

Below the gardens and the darkening pines
The living water sinks among the stones,
Sinking yet foaming till the snowy tones
Merge with the fog drawn landward in dim lines.
The cloud dissolves among the flowering vines,
And now the definite mountain-side disowns
The fluid world, the immeasurable zones.
Then white oblivion swallows all designs.
But still the rich confusion of the sea,
Unceasing voice, sombre and solacing,
Rises through veils of silence past the trees;
In restless repetition bound, yet free,
Wave after wave in deluge fresh releasing
An ancient speech, hushed in tremendous ease.

JANET LEWIS

[IN THE NAKED BED, IN PLATO'S CAVE]

In the naked bed, in Plato's cave,
Reflected headlights slowly slid the wall,
Carpenters hammered beneath the shaded window,
Wind troubled the window curtains all night long.
A fleet of trucks strained uphill, grinding,
Their freights, as usual, hooded by tarpaulin.
The ceiling lightened again, the slanting diagram
Slid slowly off. Hearing the milkman's chop,
His striving up the stair, the bottle's chink,
I rose from bed, lit a cigarette,
And walked to the window. The stony street bestowed
The stillness in which buildings stand upon
The street-lamp's vigil, and the horse's patience.
The winter sky's pure capital
Turned me back to bed with exhausted eyes.

Strangeness grew in the motionless air. The loose
Film greyed. Shaking wagons, hooves' waterfalls
Sounded far off, increasing, louder and nearer.
A car coughed, starting up. Morning, softly
Melting the air, lifted the half-covered chair
From underseas, kindled the mirror
Upon the wall. The bird called tentatively, whistled,

Bubbled and whistled, so! Perplexed, still wet
With sleep, affectionate, hungry and cold. So, so,
O son of man, the ignorant night, the rumors
Of building and movement, the travail
Of early morning, the mystery of beginning
Again and again,
                    while history is unforgiven.

DELMORE SCHWARTZ

FOUR POEMS

I

When all my five and country senses see,
The fingers will forget green thumbs and mark
How through the halfmoon's vegetable eye
In the ten planted towers of their stalk
Love in the frost is pared and wintered by,
The whispering ears will watch love drummed away
Down wind and shell to a discordant beach,
And, lashed to syllables, the eyed tongue talk
How her sweet wounds are mended bitterly.
My nostrils see her breath burn like a bush.

My one and noble heart has witnesses
In all love's countries, that will watch awake;
And when blind sleep falls on the spying senses,
The heart is sensual, though five eyes break.

II

O make me a mask and a wall to shut from your spies
Of the sharp, enamelled eyes and the spectacled claws
Rape and rebellion in the nurseries of my face,
Gag of a dumbstruck tree to block from bare enemies
The bayonet tongue in this undefended prayerpiece,
The present mouth, and the sweetly blown trumpet of lies,
Shaped in old armor and oak the countenance of a dunce
To shield the glistening brain and blunt the examiners,

And a tear-stained widower grief drooped from the lashes
To veil belladonna and let the dry eyes perceive
Others betray the lamenting lies of their losses
By the curve of the nude mouth or the laugh up the sleeve.

III

Not from this anger, anticlimax after
Refusal struck her loins and the lame flower
Bent like a beast to lap the singular floods
In a land without weather,
Shall she receive a bellyfull of weeds
And bear those tendril hands I touch across
The agonised, two seas.

Behind my head a square of sky sags over
The circular smile tossed from lover to lover
And the golden ball spins out of the skies;
Not from this anger after
Refusal struck like a bell under water
Shall her smile breed that mouth, behind the mirror,
That burns along my eyes.

IV

The spire cranes. Its statue is an aviary.
From the stone nest it does not let the feathery
Carved birds blunt their striking throats on the salt gravel,
Pierce the spilt sky with diving wing in weed and heel
An inch in froth. Chimes cheat the prison spire, pelter
In time like outlaw rains on that priest, water,
Time for the swimmers' hands, music for silver lock
And mouth. Both note and plume plunge from the spire's hook.
Those craning birds are choice for you, songs that jump back
To the built voice, or fly with winter to the bells,
But do not travel down dumb wind like prodigals.

DYLAN THOMAS

THE MARGINAL FIELD

On the chalk cliff edge struggles the final field
Of barley smutted with tares and marbled
With veins of rusted poppy as though the plough had bled.
The sun is drowned in bird-wailing mist
The sea and sky meet outside distinction
The landscape glares and stares—white poverty
Of gaslight diffused through frosted glass.

This field was the farmer's extremest thought
And its flinty heart became his heart
When he drove below the return it yields
The wage of the labourer sheeted in sweat.
Here the price and the cost cross on a chart
At a point fixed on the margin of profit
Which opens out in the golden fields

Waving their grasses and virile beards
On the laps of the dripping valleys and flushing
Their pulsing ears against negative skies.
Their roots clutch into the flesh of the soil,
As they fall to the scythe they whisper of excess
Heaped high above the flat wavering scale
Near the sea, beyond the wind-scarred hill

Where loss is exactly equalled by gain
And the roots and the sinews wrestle with stone
On the margin of what can just be done
To eat back from the land the man the land eats.
Starved outpost of wealth and final soldier,
Your stretched-out bones are the frontier of power
With your mouth wide open to drink in lead.

STEPHEN SPENDER

THE SENSE OF THE SLEIGHT-OF-HAND MAN

One's grand flights, one's Sunday baths,
One's tootings at the weddings of the soul
Occur as they occur. So bluish clouds
Occurred above the empty house and the leaves
Of the rhododendrons rattled their gold,
As if some one lived there. Such floods of white
Came bursting from the clouds. So the wind
Threw its contorted strength around the sky.
Could you have said the bluejay suddenly
Would swoop to earth? It is a wheel, the rays
Around the sun. The wheel survives the myths.
The fire eye in the clouds survives the gods.
To think of a dove with an eye of grenadine
And pines that are comets, so it occurs,
And a little island full of geese and stars:
It may be that the ignorant man, alone,
Has any chance to mate his life with the life
That is the sensual, pearly spouse, the life
That is fluent in even the wintriest bronze.

WALLACE STEVENS

SONNET

The crumbled rock of London is dripping under
Clouds of mechanical rain, and other cities
Lie frozen round their rivers and the thunder:
For these new decades open of silent pities,
The poet dead by green enormous sculpture,
Roads sanded for expressionless invaders
And empty as flame the heavens for the vulture.
Here walk with open lips the pale persuaders
Of doom, over the concrete near the river,
Shadowed by trusts on whose retreating faces
The glassy light and crimson vapors quiver.
This town is full of ghosts: successive bases
Lost to the living send their last battalion.
There is no face tonight that is not alien.

ROY FULLER

From STANZAS IN MEDITATION

I

Full well I know that she is there
Much as she will she can be there
But which I know which I know when
Which is my way to be there then
Which she will know as I know here
That it is now that it is there
That rain is there and it is here
That it is here that they are there
They have been here to leave it now
But how foolish to ask them if they like it
Most certainly they like it because they like what they have
But they might easily like something else
And very probably just as well they will have it
Which they like as they are very likely not to be
Reminded that it is more than ever necessary
That they should never be surprised at any one time
At just what they have been given by taking what they have
Which they are very careful not to add with
And they may easily indulge in the fragrance
Not only of which but by which they know
That they tell them so.

IV

The whole of this last end is to say which of two.

V

Thank you for hurrying through.

VI

Why am I if I am uncertain reasons may inclose.
Remain remain propose repose chose.
I call carelessly that the door is open
Which if they can refuse to open
No one can rush to close.

Let them be mine therefor.
Everybody knows that I chose.
Therefor if therefor before I close.
I will therefor offer therefor I offer this.
Which if I refuse to miss can be miss is mine.
I will be well welcome when I come.
Because I am coming.
Certainly I come having come.

These stanzas are done.

GERTRUDE STEIN

PERDITA

The glamour of the end attic, the smell of old
Leather trunks — Perdita, where have you been
Hiding all these years? Somewhere or other a green
Flag is waving under an iron vault
And a brass bell is the herald of green country
And the wind is in the wires and the broom is gold.

Perdita, what became of all the things
We said that we should do? The cobwebs cover
The labels of Tyrol. The time is over-
Due and in some metropolitan station
Among the clank of cans and the roistering files
Of steam the caterpillars wait for wings.

LOUIS MAC NEICE

RALEIGH WAS RIGHT

We cannot go to the country
for the country will bring us
        no peace
What can the small violets
tell us that grow on furry stems
in the long grass among
lance-shaped leaves?

Though you praise us
and call to mind the poets
who sung of our loveliness it was
long ago!
long ago!
when country people
would plow and sow with
flowering minds and pockets
at ease—if ever this were true.

Not now. Love itself a flower
with roots in a parched ground.
Empty pockets
make empty heads. Cure it
if you can but do not believe
that we can live today
in the country
for the country will bring us
        no peace

WILLIAM CARLOS WILLIAMS

[ANYONE LIVED IN A PRETTY HOW TOWN]

anyone lived in a pretty how town
(with up so floating many bells down)
spring summer autumn winter
he sang his didn't he danced his did.

Women and men (both little and small)
cared for anyone not at all
they sowed their isn't they reaped their same
sun moon stars rain

children guessed (but only a few
and down they forgot as up they grew
autumn winter spring summer)
that noone loved him more by more

when by now and tree by leaf
she laughed his joy she cried his grief
bird by snow and stir by still
anyone's any was all to her

someones married their everyones
laughed their cryings and did their dance
(sleep wake hope and then) they
said their nevers they slept their dream

stars rain sun moon
(and only the snow can begin to explain
how children are apt to forget to remember
with up so floating many bells down)

one day anyone died i guess
(and noone stooped to kiss his face)
busy folk buried them side by side
little by little and was by was

all by all and deep by deep
and more by more they dream their sleep
noone and anyone earth by april
wish by spirit and if by yes.

Women and men (both dong and ding)
summer autumn winter spring
reaped their sowing and went their came
sun moon stars rain

E. E. CUMMINGS

THINGS

Things are the mind's mute looking-glass—
That vase of flowers, this work-box here,
When false love flattered me, alas,
Glowed with a beauty crystal clear.

Now they are hostile. The tulip's glow
Burns with the mockery of despair;
And when I open the box, I know
What kind of self awaits me there.

WALTER DE LA MARE

ANTIQUES

Those quaint old worn-out words!
Fashions in miniature:
Pious, amiable, reserved, serene,
Modest, sedate, demure!
Mental poke-bonnets, — and no less effete,
Why, even their meanings now are obsolete.

WALTER DE LA MARE

THEN ...

There were no men and women then at all,
But the flesh lying alone,
And angry shadows fighting on a wall
Which now and then sent out a groan
Stifled in lime and stone,
And sweated now and then like tortured wood
Big drops that looked yet did not look like blood.

And yet as each drop came a shadow faded
And left the wall.
There was a lull
Until another in its shadow arrayed it,
Came, fought and left a blood-mark on the wall.
And that was all; the blood was all.

If women had been there they might have wept
For the poor blood, unowned, unwanted,
Blank as forgotten script.
The wall was haunted
By mute maternal presences whose sighing
Fluttered the fighting shadows and shook the wall
As if that fury of death itself were dying.

EDWIN MUIR

UNIVERSITY

To hurt the Negro and avoid the Jew
Is the curriculum. In mid-September
The entering boys, identified by hats,
Wander in a maze of mannered brick
    Where boxwood and magnolia brood
    And columns with imperious stance
    Like rows of ante-bellum girls
        Eye them, outlanders.

In whited cells, on lawns equipped for peace,
Under the arch, and lofty banister
Equals shake hands, unequals blankly pass;
The exemplary weather whispers, "Quiet, quiet"
    And visitors on tiptoe leave
    For the raw North, the unfinished West,
    As the young, detecting an advantage,
        Practice a face.

Where, on their separate hill, the colleges,
Like manor houses of an older law,
Gaze down embankments on a land in fee,
The Deans, dry spinsters over family plate,
    Ring out the English name like coin,
    Humor the snob and lure the lout.
    Within the precincts of this world
        Poise is a dub;

But on the neighboring range, misty and high,
The past is absolute: some luckless race
Dull with inbreeding and conformity
Wears out its heart, and comes barefoot and bad
    For charity or jail. The scholar
    Sanctions their obsolete disease;
    The gentleman revolts with shame
        At his ancestor

And the true nobleman, once a democrat,
Sleeps on his private mountain. He was one
Whose thought was shapely and whose dream was broad;
This school he held his art and epitaph.

But now it takes from him his name,
Falls open like a dishonest look,
And shows us, rotted and endowed,
    Its senile pleasure.

KARL J. SHAPIRO

THE BLOODY SIRE

It is not bad. Let them play.
Let the guns bark and the bombing-plane
Speak his prodigious blasphemies.
It is not bad, it is high time,
Stark violence is still the sire of all the world's values.

What but the wolf's tooth chiseled so fine
The fleet limbs of the antelope?
What but fear winged the birds and hunger
Gemmed with such eyes the great goshawk's head?
Violence has been the sire of all the world's values.

Who would remember Helen's face
Lacking the terrible halo of spears?
Who formed Christ but Herod and Caesar,
The cruel and bloody victories of Caesar?
Violence has been the sire of all the world's values.

Never weep, let them play,
Old violence is not too old to beget new values.

ROBINSON JEFFERS

MEMORY

Cities are walled. It is a cruel land
And private as a dream. Nothing alive
Will grow there, yet great ghostly acres thrive
On a sound, an odor: one blown pinch of sand
Erects a cape, and soon the seas arrive.

But nothing alters there. Beyond return,
Joys lost, like meteors, cross the indifferent night
And fall away. While fixed, nailed to the sight,
Sharp as midsummer stars, that blind and burn,
More distant moments lend their chilling light.
Retired as the face of one who died,
The landscape lies. The structures, being old,
Keep griefs too awkward for one life to hold;
The rooms are many-mirrored, not for pride.
Yet there delight blooms in remorseless cold.

BABETTE DEUTSCH

IMMANENT

The drone of airplane neared, and dimmed away,
The child beyond high-tide mark still toiled on;
Salt water welled the trench that in his play
He'd dug to beleaguer his grey fortress stone.
Lovely as Eros, and half-naked too,
He heaped dried beach-drift, kindled it, and lo!
The furious furnace roared, the sea-winds blew—
Vengeance divine; and death to every foe!
Young god! and not ev'n Nature eyed askance
The fire-doomed Empire of a myriad Ants.

WALTER DE LA MARE

From CONSCRIPT

III

His mother sets the supper out,
Recalling what his father said;
He takes the curse his father bore,
The first horn of the dead.
The old darkness howling in our bones
Looses the creatures for their feast;
Nor shall he find his peace till they
Lie down together, man and beast.

He does not mouth deluded words
For glory and her blowzy kiss,
But something in him cries aloud
And what he says is this:
Time welds a brotherhood at last—
Tell me I know that this is true!
What little faith still lights the will
Is less for those I serve than those
They send me out to kill.
We cursed the fools who made the wrongs,
The criminals to right them,
And damned the knaves who make the wars
And damned the fools who fight them;
Reaping what I never sowed,
Answering for lies I never told,
I give my yard of bloody ground
And honor worth its weight in gold.

If villains forge the name of truth,
Thieves teach their blind to pray,
Tell me truth driven underground
Will bloom another day.
Not all the words I ever learned
could ever save my age;
But tell me once again the words
Survive the burning page.
Not swindled by the dulcet prayers
Nor practising the hero's voice
(Now no one good enough to fight
Has any but a victim's choice)
Not for the lies of murderers,
Whose death will be undone,
But lovers in the streets again,
Companions who will take the sun.
But a city they will call their own,
And who will build it fair,
Who see from this one brought to dust
Another written in the air.
In praises of the unarrived,
In lands where lies and guns have dinned,
Like seeds upon the doubtful air,
My faith entrusted to the wind.

Funeral Speech:

No love redeems the life of living men
But man the murderer extols the dead.
Summer will burn her skies away, and then
What dreams the leaf will kindle in his head.

Think what the arms that take us in farewell
Might fashion for the sick and living one,
And what in darkness all the dead would tell
The mortal begging in the squandered sun.

PETER DE VRIES

TO VIOLET

With prewar poems

These tracings from a world that's dead
Take for my dust-smothered Pyramid.
Count the sharp study and long toil
As pavements laid for worms to soil.
You, without knowing it, might tread
The grass where my foundation's laid;
Your, or another's, house be built
Where my mossed, weathered stones lie spilt;
And this unread memento be
The only lasting part of me.

BASIL BUNTING

HENRY JAMES AT NEWPORT

And shores and strands and naked piers,
Sunset on waves, orange laddering the blue,
White sails on headlands, cool
Wide curving bay, dim landward distances
Dissolving in the property of local air.

Viterbo, Bagdad, Carcassonne —
They play upon the mind, the eyes again,

Although these back verandas, resolutely prim,
Say *Quakers, Roger Williams*—murmurs of the past—
While special staircase ghosts return,
Known voices in the old brown rooms:
"People don't do those things."
The pictures huddle in the frames.

Removed from those blank days
In which the margin is consumed,
The palace sites stare seaward, pure, *blasé*,
Remember the detached, the casually disqualified,
The mild cosmopolites whose ivory dream
Found no successors, quietly embalmed.
They nursed nostalgia on the sun-warmed rocks,
Exquisite, sterile, easily distressed,
Thought much of Paris, died
While he lived out their deaths.

Shores, strands, white sails and naked piers,
Wide curving bay and landward distances.
Thoughts of the dispossessed on summer afternoons.
The sails are tattered and the shrubs are dead.
The stone-walled fields are featureless.

WELDON KEES

UPON THE HEAVENLY SCARP

I

And on that day, upon the heavenly scarp,
The hosannas ceased, the hallelujahs died,
And music trembled on the silenced harp.
An angel, doffing his seraphic pride,
Wept; and his tears so bitter were, and sharp,
That where they fell, the blossoms shriveled and died.

II

Another with such voice intoned the psalm
It sang forth blasphemy against the Lord.
O that was a very imp in angeldom
Who, thinking evil, said no evil word—
But only pointed, at each Te Deum,
Down to the earth, and its unspeakable horde.

III

The Lord looked down, and saw the cattle-cars:
Men ululating to a frozen land.
He saw a man tear at his flogged scars,
And saw a babe look for its blown-off hand.
Scholars, he saw, sniffing their bottled wars,
And doctors who had geniuses unmanned.

IV

The gentle violinist whose fingers played
Such godly music, washing a gutter, with lye,
He saw. He heard the priest who called his aid.
He heard the agnostic's undirected cry.
Unto him came the odor Hunger made,
And the odor of blood before it is quite dry.

V

The angel who wept looked into the eyes of God.
The angel who sang ceased pointing to the earth.
A little cherub who'd spied the earthly sod
Went mad, and flapped his wings in crazy mirth.
And the good Lord said nothing, but with a nod
Summoned the angels of Sodom down to earth.

A. M. KLEIN

THE DARK MORNING

This is the black day when
Fog rides the ugly air:
Water wades among the buildings
To the prisoner's curled ear.

Then rain, in thin sentences,
Slakes him like danger,
Whose heart is his Germany
Fevered with anger.

This is the dark day when
Locks let the enemy in
Through all the coiling passages of
(Curled ear) my prison!

THOMAS JAMES MERTON

THE SPRINGBOARD

He never made the dive—not while I watched.
High above London, naked in the night
Perched on a board. I peered up through the bars
Made by his fear and mine but it was more than fright
That kept him crucified among the budding stars.

Yes, it was unbelief. He knew only too well
That circumstances called for sacrifice
But, shivering there, spreadeagled above the town,
His blood began to haggle over the price
History would pay if he were to throw himself down.

If it would mend the world, that would be worth while
But he, quite rightly, long had ceased to believe
In any Utopia or in Peace-upon-Earth;
His friends would find in his death neither ransom nor reprieve
But only a grain of faith—for what it was worth.

And yet we know he knows what he must do.
There above London where the gargoyles grin
He will dive like a bomber past the broken steeple,
One man wiping out his own original sin
And, like ten million others, dying for the people.

LOUIS MAC NEICE

[WHAT IF A MUCH OF A WHICH OF A WIND]

what if a much of a which of a wind
gives the truth to summer's lie;
bloodies with dizzying leaves the sun
and yanks immortal stars awry?
Blow king to beggar and queen to seem
(blow friend to fiend: blow space to time)
—when skies are hanged and oceans drowned,
the single secret will still be man

what if a keen of a lean wind flays
screaming hills with sleet and snow:
strangles valleys by ropes of thing
and stifles forests in white ago?
Blow hope to terror; blow seeing to blind
(blow pity to envy and soul to mind)
—whose hearts are mountains, roots are trees,
it's they shall cry hello to the spring

what if a dawn of a doom of a dream
bites this universe in two,
peels forever out of his grave
and sprinkles nowhere with me and you?
Blow soon to never and never to twice
(blow life to isn't: blow death to was)
—all nothing's only our hugest home;
the most who die, the more we live

E. E. CUMMINGS

SIGMUND FREUD

Each house had its ghost. Graves opened to his voice,
The dead lived in him by his gray consent:
He was, by their constraint upon his choice,
Orpheus of all the lonesome, spent

His evenings charting out a private hell,
The spaceless realm that all the puzzled caught,
The swamps that made their frightful towns unwell:
He chained his life to theirs, was like them lost.

Perhaps unwillingly he did this, became
Laureate of those who were afraid.
For himself assumed them as a native guise,
Entered their warring lands as one of them,
Employed their rhetoric and blague to raid
The towers of their most strategic lies.

HOWARD NEMEROV

THE EMANCIPATORS

When you ground the lenses and the moons swam free
From that great wanderer; when the apple shone
Like a sea-shell through your prism, voyager;
When, dancing in pure flame, the Roman mercy,
Your doctrines blew like ashes from your bones;

Did you think, for an instant, past the numerals
Jellied in Latin like bacteria in broth,
Snatched for by holy Europe like a sign?
Past sombre tables inched out with the lives
Forgotten or clapped for by the wigged Societies?

You guessed this? The earth's face altering with iron,
The smoke ranged like a wall against the day?
The equations metamorphose into use: the free
Drag their slight bones from tenements to vote
To die with their children in your factories.

Man is born in chains; yet everywhere we see him dead.
On your earth they sell nothing but our lives.
You knew that what you died for was our deaths?
You learned, those years, that all men wish is Trade?
It was you who understood; it is we who change.

RANDALL JARRELL

TENNIS TROPHY

Back in boyhood, game was all
Loved to race the rabbit ball
Visor-crested; on my sweater
Shone like sun the blazoned letter.

Swart as Pawnee, hair like hay,
Sprinted on the plains of clay,
Rounded noon, and rash at seven
Cursed the light-forsaken heaven.

Loafer from the summer camp,
I upset the city champ.
Sharp attack and iron daring
Had the hot Achilles swearing.

Saw malacca banker stare,
Deb's Cellini-fluted hair.
With the cutie and the colonel
I was fêted in the *Journal*.

Player, never act again
Sagas of the centaur-men.
In the tombs of attic pack it—
Pewter loot and ribs of racquet.

Girl with golden-bolted knee,
Streamer-skirted, where is she?
Where is now the rich unreason,
Merlin nerve and angel season?

I in garret opus-lined
Cough and stoop and flicker blind,
In a topaz quarto nuzzle,
Annotate a printer's puzzle.

Morituri. Summer done,
Heroes ramble, leave the sun,
Bank to manage, book to garble;
Last, to catch in roots and marble.

JOHN FREDERICK NIMS

DOLOR

I have known the inexorable sadness of pencils,
Neat in their boxes, dolor of pad and paper-weight,
All the misery of manila folders and mucilage,
Desolation in immaculate public places,
Lonely reception room, lavatory, switchboard,
The unalterable pathos of basin and pitcher,
Ritual of multigraph, paper-clip, comma,
Endless duplication of lives and objects.
And I have seen dust from the walls of institutions,
Finer than flour, alive, more dangerous than silica,
Sift, almost invisible, through long afternoons of tedium,
Dropping a fine film on nails and delicate eyebrows,
Glazing the pale hair, the duplicate gray standard faces.

THEODORE ROETHKE

FABLE OF THE ANT AND THE WORD

Ink-black, but moving independently
Across the black and white parquet of print,
The ant cancels the author out. The page,
Translated to itself, bears hair-like legs
Disturbing the fine hairs of its fiber.
These are the feet of summer, pillaging meaning,
Despoiling Alexandria. Sunlight is silence
Laying waste all languages, until, thinly,
The fictional dialogue begins again:
The page goes on telling another story.

MARY BARNARD

FIRST SNOW ON AN AIRFIELD

A window's length beyond the Pleiades
Wintering Perseus grounds his bow on haze
And midnight thickens on the fall of snow.
Now on the sound of sleepers past their days
The barracks turns to myth, and none shall die
But widen and grow beautiful a while
And then be written on a Grecian sky.

Look, the burnt mountain whitens, and the trees
Grow cavernous. And the field's lights are spread
Spangling on the daubed and rushing air
That fills with drone of engines overhead.
And see: the constellations of the running-lights,
Crossed on the beacon's arm, bring home the planes
That almost layered the hills with trilobites.

As near as a chance: A winter's memory
Of seconds not too soon that might have been
Fossils at impact with the shrouded stone.
Here on the ground, the noise of a machine
Above the falling snow at season's turn—
Memory crossed with moment—and again
Tomorrow's manual of guns to learn.

JOHN CIARDI

LOSSES

It was not dying: everybody died.
It was not dying: we had died before
In the routine crashes—and our fields
Called up the papers, wrote home to our folks,
And the rates rose, all because of us.
We died on the wrong page of the almanac,
Scattered on mountains fifty miles away;
Diving on haystacks, fighting with a friend,
We blazed up on the lines we never saw.
We died like aunts or pets or foreigners.
(When we left high school nothing else had died
For us to figure we had died like.)

In our new planes, with our new crews, we bombed
The ranges by the desert or the shore,
Fired at towed targets, waited for our scores—
And turned into replacements and woke up
One morning, over England, operational.
It wasn't different: but if we died
It was not an accident but a mistake
(But an easy one for anyone to make).
We read our mail and counted up our missions—
In bombers named for girls, we burned
The cities we had learned about in school—
Till our lives wore out; our bodies lay among
The people we had killed and never seen.
When we lasted long enough they gave us medals;
When we died they said, "Our casualties were low."

They said, "Here are the maps"; we burned the cities.

It was not dying—no, not ever dying;
But the night I died I dreamed that I was dead,
And the cities said to me: "Why are you dying?
We are satisfied, if you are; but why did I die?"

RANDALL JARRELL

POEM IN OCTOBER

It was my thirtieth year to heaven
Woke to my hearing from harbor and neighbor wood
And the mussel pooled and the heron—
Priested shore
The morning beckon
With water praying and call of seagull and rook
And the knock of sailing boats on the net webbed wall
Myself to set foot
That second
In the still sleeping town and set forth.

My birthday began with the water—
Birds and the birds of the winged trees flying my name
Above the farms and the white horses
And I rose

In rainy autumn
And walked abroad in a shower of all my days.
High tide and the heron dived when I took the road
Over the border
And the gates
Of the town closed as the town awoke.

A springful of larks in a rolling
Cloud and the roadside bushes brimming with whistling
Blackbirds and the sun of October
Summery
On the hill's shoulder,
Here were fond climates and sweet singers suddenly
Come in the morning where I wandered and listened
To the rain wringing
Wind blow cold
In the wood faraway under me.

Pale rain over the dwindling harbor
And over the sea wet church the size of a snail
With its horns through mist and the castle
Brown as owls,
But all the gardens
Of spring and summer were blooming in the tall tales
Beyond the border and under the lark full cloud.
There could I marvel
My birthday
Away but the weather turned around.

It turned away from the blithe country
And down the other air and the blue altered sky
Streamed again a wonder of summer
With apples
Pears and red currants
And I saw in the turning so clearly a child's
Forgotten mornings when he walked with his mother
Through the parables
Of sun light
And the legends of the green chapels

And the twice told fields of infancy
That his tears burned my cheeks and his heart moved in mine.
These were the woods the river and sea
Where a boy
In the listening
Summertime of the dead whispered the truth of his joy
To the trees and the stones and the fish in the tide.
And the mystery
Sang alive
Still in the water and singing birds.

And there could I marvel my birthday
Away but the weather turned around. And the true
Joy of the long dead child sang burning
In the sun.
It was my thirtieth
Year to heaven stood there then in the summer noon
Though the town below lay leaved with October blood.
O may my heart's truth
Still be sung
On this high hill in a year's turning.

DYLAN THOMAS

JOURNAL

I grow accustomed to a new disguise:
Day after day with triggers at our thumb
We sit upon the calculated skies
Arranged upon the metal of a theorem.
Costumed in miracle we walk the wind,
Divide the sea, rain fire, but heal no blind.

Under the wing of omen Jericho
Falls in a blast of engines and we pass
Above the lame whose cure no engines know
Except to open craters in the grass,
Woven forever to the whistling graph
A bomb makes toward an epitaph.

Too nearly amateur at death by fire
We have our gift by borrowing, not by birth.
Yet we divine that we may mount still higher
And never be divided from the earth.
Opening whatever sky, the theorem turns:
We are the bomb, the crater, and what burns.

Compelled to our momentum which is Law,
We wait for mathematics to be right,
Improve our art, log what we did and saw,
And track the sun by day, the stars by night.
Yet though our engines master in our stead,
We fail the sick, but still may raise the dead.

                              JOHN CIARDI

PART FOR THE WHOLE

When others run to windows or out of doors
To catch the sunset whole, he is content
With any segment anywhere he sits.

From segment, fragment, he can reconstruct
The whole, prefers to reconstruct the whole,
As if to say, I see more seeing less.

A window to the east will serve as well
As window to the west, for eastern sky
Echoes the western sky. And even less —

A patch of light that picture-glass happens
To catch from window-glass, fragment of fragment,
Flawed, distorted, dulled, nevertheless

Gives something unglassed nature cannot give:
The old obliquity of art, and proves
Part may be more than whole, least may be best.

                              ROBERT FRANCIS

THE HIGHER EMPIRICISM

O Visionary who adjust your lens
Till it is focused on a wheel of fire,
What spotless lover would you find in space?
Let wisdom guide you to the market-place,
There to be broken on the wheel of sense
And burnt by adequate objects of desire.

FRANCIS C. GOLFFING

POEM FOR MY TWENTIETH BIRTHDAY

Passing the American graveyard, for my birthday
the crosses stuttering, white on tropical green,
the years' quick focus of faces I do not remember . . .

The palm trees stalking like deliberate giants
for my birthday, and all the hot adolescent memories
seen through a screen of water . . .

For my birthday thrust into the adult and actual:
expected to perform the action, not to ponder
the reality beyond the fact,
the man standing upright in the dream.

KENNETH KOCH

From "THEORY OF VISION"

THE GREEN EYE

Come child, and with your sunbeam gaze assign
Green to the garden as a metaphor
For contemplation, seeking to declare
Whether by green you specify the green
Of orchard sunlight, blossom, bark, or leaf,
Or green of an imaginary life.

A mosaic of all possible greens becomes
A premise in your eye, whereby the limes
Are green as limes faintly by midnight known,

As foliage in a thunderstorm, as dreams
Of fruit in barren countries; claims
The orchard as a metaphor of green.

Aware of change as no barometer
You may determine climates at your will;
Spectrums of feeling are accessible
If orchards in the mind will persevere
On their hillsides original with joy.
Enter the orchard differently today:

When here you bring your earliest tragedy,
Your goldfish, upside-down and rigidly
Floating on weeds in the aquarium,
Green is no panorama for your grief
Whose raindrop smile, dissolving and aloof,
Ordains an unusual brightness as you come:

The brightness of a change outside the eye,
A question on the brim of what may be,
Attended by a new, impersonal green.
The goldfish dead where limes hang yellowing
Is metaphor for more incredible things,
Things you shall live among, things seen, things known.

JAMES MERRILL

THE RETURN

I circled on leather paws
In the darkening corridor,
Crouched closer to the floor,
Then bristled like a dog.

As I turned for a backward look,
The muscles in one thigh
Sagged like a frightened lip.

A cold key let me in
That self-inflicted lair;
And I lay down with my life,
With the rags and rotting clothes,
With a stump of scraggy fang
Bared for a hunter's boot.

THEODORE ROETHKE

131

THE GHOST

(After Sextus Propertius)

A ghost is someone: death has left a hole
For the lead-colored soul to beat the fire:
    Cynthia leaves her dirty pyre
    And seems to coil herself and roll
      Under my canopy,
Love's stale and public playground, where I lie
And fill the run-down empire of my bed.
I see the street, her potter's field, is red
And lively with the ashes of the dead;

But she no longer sparkles off in smoke:
It is the body carted to the gate
    Last Friday, when the sizzling grate
    Left its charred furrows on her smock
      And ate into her hip.
A black nail dangles from her finger-tip
And Lethe oozes from her nether lip.
Her thumb-bones rattle on her brittle hands,
As Cynthia stamps and hisses and demands:

"Sextus, has sleep already washed away
Your manhood? You forget the window-sill
    My sliding wore to slivers? Day
    Would break before the Seven Hills
      Saw Cynthia retreat
And climb your shoulders to the knotted sheet.
You shouldered me and galloped on bare feet
To lay me by the crossroads. Have no fear:
Notus, who snatched your promise, has no ear.

"But why did no one call in my deaf ear?
Your calling would have gained me one more day.
    Sextus, although you ran away
    You might have called and stopped my bier
      A second by your door.
No tears drenched a black toga for your whore
When broken tilestones bruised her face before
The Capitol. Would it have strained your purse
To scatter ten cheap roses on my hearse?

"The State will make Pompilia's Chloris burn:
  I knew her secret when I kissed the skull
      Of Pluto in the tainted bowl.
      Let Nomas burn her books and turn
          Her poisons into gold;
The finger-prints upon the potsherd told
Her love. You let a slut, whose body sold
To Thracians, liquify my golden bust
In the coarse flame that crinkled me to dust.

"If Chloris' bed has left you with your head,
  Lover, I think you'll answer my arrears:
      My nurse is getting on in years,
      See that she gets a little bread—
          She never clutched your purse;
See that my little humpback hears no curse
From her close-fisted friend. But burn the verse
You bellowed half a lifetime in my name:
Why should you feed me to the fires of fame?

"I will not hound you, much as you have earned
  It, Sextus: I shall reign in your four books—
      I swear this by the Hag who looks
      Into my heart where it was burned:
          Propertius, I kept faith;
If not, may serpents suck my ghost to death
And spit it with their forked and killing breath
Into the Styx where Agamemnon's wife
Founders in the green circles of her life.

"Beat the sycophant ivy from my urn,
  That twists its binding shoots about my bones
      Where apple-sweetened Anio drones
      Through orchards that will never burn
          While honest Herakles,
My patron, watches. Anio, you will please
Me if you whisper upon sliding knees:
'Propertius, Cynthia is here:
She shakes her blossoms when my waters clear.'

"You cannot turn your back upon a dream
For phantoms have their reasons when they come:
    We wander midnights: then the numb
    Ghost wades from the Lethean stream;
        Even the foolish dog
Stops its hell-raising mouths and casts its clog;
At cock-crow Charon checks us in his log.
Others can have you, Sextus; I alone
Hold: and I grind your manhood bone on bone."

ROBERT LOWELL

NIGHT OF BATTLE

Europe: 1944
as considered from a great distance

Impersonal the aim
Where giant movements tend;
Each man appears the same;
Friend vanishes from friend

In the long path of lead
That changes place like light
No shape of hand or head
Means anything tonight.

Only the common will
For which explosion spoke
And stiff on field and hill
The dark blood of the folk.

YVOR WINTERS

MOTIVE

The motive of all of it was loneliness,
All the panic encounters and despair
Were bred in fear of the lost night, apart,
Outlined by pain, alone. Promiscuous
As mercy. Fear-led and led again to fear
At evening toward the cave where part fire, part
Pity lived in that voluptuousness
To end one and begin another loneliness.

This is the most intolerable motive: this
Must be given back to life again,
Made superhuman, made human, out of pain
Turned to the personal, the pure release:
The rings of Plato and Homer's golden chain
Or Lenin with his cry of Dare We Win.

MURIEL RUKEYSER

THE BROKEN BOWL

To say it once held daisies and bluebells
    Ignores, if nothing else,
Its diehard brilliance where crashed on the floor
The wide bowl lies that seemed to cup the sun,
Its green leaves curled, its constant blaze undone,
Spilled all its glass integrity everywhere;
    Spectrums, released, will speak
Of colder flowerings where cold crystal broke.

Glass fragments dropped from wholeness to hodgepodge
    Yet fasten to each edge
The opal signature of imperfection
Whose rays, though disarrayed, will postulate
More than a network of cross-angled light
When through the dusk they point unbruised directions
    And chart upon the room
Capacities of fire it must assume.

The splendid curvings of glass artifice
 Informed its flawlessness
With lucid unities. Freed from these now,
Like love it triumphs through inconsequence
And builds its harmony from dissonance
And lies somehow within us, broken, as though
 Time were a broken bowl
And our last joy knowing it shall not heal.

The splinters rainbowing ruin on the floor
 Cut structures in the air,
Mark off, like eyes or compasses, a space
Of mathematic fixity, spotlight
Within whose circumscription we may set
All solitudes of love, room for love's face,
 Love's projects green with leaves,
Love's monuments like tombstones on our lives.

JAMES MERRILL

LOVE POEM

My clumsiest dear, whose hands shipwreck vases,
At whose quick touch all glasses chip and ring,
Whose palms are bulls in china, burs in linen
And have no cunning with any soft thing

Except all ill-at-ease fidgeting people:
The refugee uncertain at the door
You make at home; deftly you steady
The drunkard clambering on his undulant floor.

Unpredictable dear, the taxi drivers' terror,
Shrinking from far headlights pale as a dime
Yet leaping before red apoplectic streetcars—
Misfit in any space. And never on time.

A wrench in clocks and the solar system. Only
With words and people and love you move at ease.
In traffic of wit expertly manoeuvre
And keep us, all devotion, at your knees,

Forgetting your coffee spreading on our flannel,
Your lipstick grinning on our coat,
So gayly in love's unbreakable heaven
Our souls on glory of spilt bourbon float.

Be with me, darling, early and late. Smash glasses—
I will study wry music for your sake.
For should your hands drop white and empty
All the toys of the world would break.

                    JOHN FREDERICK NIMS

NIAGARA FALLS

We saw it all. We saw the souvenir shops, and sitting
on the mist above the falls, the brilliant signs
saying hotels to love in, cigarettes to smoke,
souvenirs for proof; we give you anything you want,
even towels. Our disgust was as stylized as billboards,
and we suggested to ourselves that even our sympathy
for the ugly people of the off-season was outworn.
But here it was, nevertheless, the ferocious, spastic
enjoyment, the hotels like freight-yards or packing crates,
the lights that murder sight, and the community snicker.
The falls, of course, continued with great dignity.

                    ALAN DUGAN

SCHOOLYARD IN APRIL

Little girls smearing
the stolen lipstick
of overheard grown-up talk
into their conversation,
unconscious of the beauty
of their movements

like milkweed in the wind,
are beginning to drift
over by the drinking fountain
where they will skip rope

They speak in whispers
about the omnipotent teachers
while the little boys
scoff over their ball-mitts

The teachers themselves
stare out of windows,
remembering April.

KENNETH KOCH

"DREAMS ARE THE ROYAL ROAD TO THE UNCONSCIOUS"

— Freud

The King's Highway to the Dare-Not-Know
—but I beg my rides and oh I know
these boring roads where hundreds and hundreds
of cars fade by in hundred-hundreds
of flashing windows too bright too fast
to see my face. I am steadfast
long hours o' the morning, I am so sad.
An old-time trap, an ancient sad
horse and his farmer stop by the way,
they'll take me one mile on my way
—out of my way—is this the Way?
I used to think I used to be happy,
but is it possible to be happy?
What is it like?—like Plato oh
we'll copy it at large and oh
plan a city where all the distances
(where? where?) are walking distances.

PAUL GOODMAN

THE DIRTY WORD

The dirty word hops in the cage of the mind like the Pondicherry vulture, stomping with its heavy left claw on the sweet meat of the brain and tearing it with its vicious beak, ripping and chopping the flesh. Terrified, the small boy bears the big bird of the dirty word into the house, and grunting, puffing, carries it up the stairs to his own room in the skull. Bits of black feather cling to his clothes and his hair as he locks the staring creature in the dark closet.

All day the small boy returns to the closet to examine and feed the bird, to caress and kick the bird, that now snaps and flaps its wings savagely whenever the door is opened. How the boy trembles and delights at the sight of the white excrement of the bird! How the bird leaps and rushes against the walls of the skull, trying to escape from the zoo of the vocabulary! How wildly snaps the sweet meat of the brain in its rage.

And the bird outlives the man, being freed at the man's death-funeral by a word from the rabbi.

But I one morning went upstairs and opened the door and entered the closet and found in the cage of my mind the great bird dead. Softly I wept it and softly removed it and softly buried the body of the bird in the hollyhock garden of the house I lived in twenty years before. And out of the worn black feathers of the wing have I made these pens to write these elegies, for I have outlived the bird, and I have murdered it in my early manhood.

KARL SHAPIRO

THE FAT MAN IN THE MIRROR

What's filling up the mirror? O, it is not I;
Hair-belly like a beaver's house? An old dog's eye?
    The forenoon was blue
    In the mad King's zoo
Nurse was swinging me so high, so high!

The bullies wrestled on the royal bowling green;
Hammers and sickles on their hoods of black sateen . . .
    Smoking on my swing,
    The yellow-fingered King
Sliced apples with a pen-knife for his Queen.

This I, who used to mouse about the parafinned preserves,
And jammed a finger in the coffee-grinder, serves
    Time before the mirror.
    But this flabby terror . . .
Nurse, it is a person! It is nerves.

O where is Mother waltzing like a top to staunch
The blood of Rudolf, King of Faerie? Hip and haunch
    Lard the royal grotto;
    Straddling Rudolf's motto,
Time, the Turk, its sickle on its paunch . . .

Nurse, nurse, it rises on me . . . O, it starts to roll,
My apples, O, are charcoal in the meerschaum bowl . . .
    If you'd only come,
    If you'd only come,
Darling, if . . . The apples that I stole,

When nurse and I were swinging in the Old One's eye . . .
Only a fat man with his beaver on his eye,
    Only a fat man,
    Only a fat man
Breaks the mirror, O, it is not I!

ROBERT LOWELL

[IF(TOUCHED BY LOVE'S OWN SECRET)]

if(touched by love's own secret)we,like homing
through welcoming sweet miracles of air
(and joyfully all truths of wing resuming)
selves,into infinite tomorrow steer

—souls under whom flow(mountain valley forest)
a million wheres which never may become
one(wholly strange; familiar wholly)dearest
more than reality of more than dream—

how should contented fools of fact envision
the mystery of freedom?yet,among
their loud exactitudes of imprecision,
you'll(silently alighting)and i'll sing

while at us very deafly a most stares
colossal hoax of clocks and calendars

                                    E. E. CUMMINGS

THE PARTY

The standing guests, a grotesque glade
Dispensing microcosmic gloom,
Make artifice of light and shade
In an eternal drawingroom.

Each tubrous tree within this grove
Thinks itself other than a tree,
Impressed, from "somewhere else," to prove
A social personality.

So is some vanity appeased
Some bravoure made articulate,
Each in his anecdotage pleased
To find himself sophisticate.

80-watt stars in crystal cups
Keep all perspectives squat and square.
No alien unthought breath corrupts
This decorously airless air.

                                    MARGARET AVISON

1947

THE ULTIMATE POEM IS ABSTRACT

This day writhes with what? The lecturer
On This Beautiful World Of Ours composes himself
And hems the planet rose and haws it ripe,

And red, and right. The particular question—here
The particular answer to the particular question
Is not in point—the question is in point.

If the day writhes, it is not with revelations.
One goes on asking questions. That, then, is one
Of the categories. So said, this placid space

Is changed. It is not so blue as we thought. To be blue,
There must be no questions. It is an intellect
Of windings round and dodges to and fro,

Writhings in wrong obliques and distances,
Not an intellect in which we are fleet: present
Everywhere in space at once, cloud-pole

Of communication. It would be enough
If we were ever, just once, at the middle, fixed
In This Beautiful World Of Ours and not as now,

Helplessly at the edge, enough to be
Complete, because at the middle, if only in sense,
And in that enormous sense, merely enjoy.

WALLACE STEVENS

SMALL PRAYER

Change, move, dead clock, that this fresh day
May break with dazzling light to these sick eyes.
Burn, glare, old sun, so long unseen,
That time may find its sound again, and cleanse
Whatever it is that a wound remembers
After the healing ends.

WELDON KEES

RETURN OF THE GODDESS ARTEMIS

Under your Milky Way
    And slow-revolving Bear,
Frogs from the alder thicket pray
In terror of your judgment day,
    Loud with repentance there.

The log they crowned as king
    Grew sodden, lurched and sank:
An owl floats by on silent wing,
Dark water bubbles from the spring;
    They invoke you from each bank.

At dawn you shall appear,
    A gaunt red-leggèd crane,
You whom they know too well for fear,
Lunging your beak down like a spear
    To fetch them home again.

ROBERT GRAVES

THE DEATH OF A TOAD

A toad the power mower caught,
Chewed and clipped of a leg, with a hobbling hop has got
  To the garden verge, and sanctuaried him
  Under the cineraria leaves, in the shade
    Of the ashen heartshaped leaves, in a dim,
    Low, and a final glade.

The rare original heartsblood goes,
Spends on the earthen hide, in the folds and wizenings, flows
  In the gutters of the banked and staring eyes. He lies
  As still as if he would return to stone,
    And soundlessly attending, dies
    Toward some deep monotone,

Toward misted and ebullient seas
And cooling shores, toward lost Amphibia's emperies.
  Day dwindles, drowning, and at length is gone
  In the wide and antique eyes, which still appear
    To watch, across the castrate lawn,
    The haggard daylight steer.

RICHARD WILBUR

From THE METAPHOR

4. TERROR AND LOVE AS FUGITIVES

Terror sat knitting quietly. We waited,
Hiding in that room. Saphir and Thiel
Quarreled all night long, as though about ideas.
The small straight Jew against the nervous Swiss:
The one, conjuring Reason till it hissed
In the room like hate; the other tortured by
His terrible northern Christ. I waited as one
Impaled between the two. It was not pleasant.

Time clicked between the needles, but suddenly
There was no time. We left on the signal, but it was
Late. I remember Saphir screaming, shot,

Clown's face in blood, then shot again, and rolling
Meaninglessly down the long stairs;
And Thiel, only a moment's photograph:
Nerveless and unafraid at last, the blood a
Red slow flower on his mouth.

Terror and time exploded in my bowels:
Panic was freedom, walking was spasm of relief
Where war was the climate and the blackout stretched,
Unending everywhere, the cathartic moment
Ending all argument. Any doorway served
Lovers or fugitives, to hunch and couple
Or simply hide. Terror and love were safe
In the same refuge, looking so much alike.

HENRY RAGO

THE TRAVELER

They pointed me out on the highway, and they said
"That man has a curious way of holding his head."

They pointed me out on the beach; they said "That man
Will never become as we are, try as he can."

They pointed me out at the station, and the guard
Looked at me twice, thrice, thoughtfully & hard.

I took the same train that the others took,
To the same place. Were it not for that look
And those words, we were all of us the same.
I studied merely maps. I tried to name
The effects of motion on the travelers,
I watched the couple I could see, the curse
And blessings of that couple, their destination,
The deception practised on them at the station,
Their courage. When the train stopped and they knew
The end of their journey, I descended too.

JOHN BERRYMAN

LEAR

When the world takes over for us
and the storm in the trees
replaces our brittle consciences
(like ships, female to all seas)
when the few last yellow leaves
stand out like flags on tossed ships
at anchor—our minds are rested

Yesterday we sweated and dreamed
or sweated in our dreams walking
at a loss through the bulk of figures
that appeared solid, men or women,
but as we approached down the paved
corridor melted—Was it I?—like
smoke from bonfires blowing away

Today the storm, inescapable, has
taken the scene and we return
our hearts to it, however made, made
wives by it and though we secure
ourselves for a dry skin from the drench
of its passionate approaches we
yield and are made quiet by its fury

Pitiful Lear, not even you could
out-shout the storm—to make a fool
cry! Wife to its power might you not
better have yielded earlier? as on ships
facing the seas were carried once
the figures of women at repose to
signify the strength of the waves' lash.

WILLIAM CARLOS WILLIAMS

THE SLEEPING BEAUTY: VARIATION OF THE PRINCE

After the thorns I came to the first page.
He lay there grey in his fur of dust:
As I bent to open an eye, I sneezed.
But the ball looked by me, blue
As the sky it stared into . . .
And the sentry's cuirass is red with rust.

Children play inside: the dirty hand
Of the little mother, an inch from the child
That has worn out, burst, and blown away,
Uncurling to it—does not uncurl . . .
The bloom on the nap of their world
Is set with thousands of dawns of dew.

But at last, at the center of all the webs
Of the realm established in your blood,
I find you; and—look!—the drop of blood
Is there still, under the dust of your finger:
I force it, slowly, down from your finger—
And it falls and rolls away, as it should.

And I bend to touch—just under the dust
That was roses once—the steady lips
Parted between a breath and a breath
In love, for the kiss of the hunter, Death . . .
Then I stretch myself beside you, lay
Between us, there in the dust, His sword.

When the world ends—it will never end—
The dust at last will fall from your eyes
In judgment, and I shall whisper:
"For hundreds of thousands of years I have slept
Beside you, here in the last long world
That you had found—that I have kept."

When they come for us—no one will ever come—
I shall stir from my long light sleep,
I shall whisper, "Wait, wait! . . . She is asleep."
I shall whisper, gazing, up to the gaze of the hunter,
Death, and close with the tips of the dust of my hand
The lids of the steady—
                    Look, He is fast asleep!

RANDALL JARRELL

THE CHILDREN OF THE POOR

1

People who have no children can be hard:
Attain a mail of ice and insolence:
Need not pause in the fire, and in no sense
Hesitate in the hurricane to guard.
And when wide world is bitten and bewarred
They perish purely, waving their spirits hence
Without a trace of grace or of offense
To laugh or fail, diffident, wonder-starred.
While through a throttling dark we others hear
The little lifting helplessness, the queer
Whimper-whine; whose unridiculous
Lost softness softly makes a trap for us.
And makes a curse. And makes a sugar of
The malocclusions, the inconditions of love.

2

What shall I give my children? who are poor,
Who are adjudged the leastwise of the land,
Who are my sweetest lepers, who demand
No velvet and no velvety velour;
But who have begged me for a brisk contour,
Crying that they are quasi, contraband
Because unfinished, graven by a hand
Less than angelic, admirable or sure.
My hand is stuffed with mode, design, device.
But I lack access to my proper stone.
And plenitude of plan shall not suffice
Nor grief nor love shall be enough alone
To ratify my little halves who bear
Across an autumn freezing everywhere.

3

And shall I prime my children, pray, to pray?
Mites, come invade most frugal vestibules
Spectered with crusts of penitents' renewals
And all hysterics arrogant for a day.
Instruct yourselves here is no devil to pay.

Children, confine your lights in jellied rules;
Resemble graves; be metaphysical mules.
Learn Lord will not distort nor leave the fray.
Behind the scurryings of your neat motif
I shall wait, if you wish: revise the psalm
If that should frighten you: sew up belief
If that should tear: turn, singularly calm
At forehead and at fingers rather wise,
Holding the bandage ready for your eyes.

GWENDOLYN BROOKS

From THINGS OF AUGUST

I

These locusts by day, these crickets by night
Are the instruments on which to play
Of an old and disused ambit of the soul
Or of a new aspect, bright in discovery—

A disused ambit of the spirit's way,
The sort of thing that August crooners sing,
By a pure fountain, that was a ghost, and is,
Under the sun-slides of a sloping mountain;

Or else a new aspect, say the spirit's sex,
Its attitudes, its answers to attitudes
And the sex of its voices, as the voice of one
Meets nakedly another's naked voice.

Nothing is lost, loud locusts. No note fails.
These sounds are long in the living of the ear.
The honky-tonk out of the somnolent grasses
Is a memorizing, a trying out, to keep.

3

High poetry and low:
Experience in perihelion
Or in the penumbra of summer night—
The solemn sentences,

Like interior intonations,
The speech of truth in its true solitude,
A nature that is created in what it says,
The peace of the last intelligence;

Or the same thing without desire,
He that in this intelligence
Mistakes it for a world of objects,
Which, being green and blue, appease him,
By chance, or happy chance, or happiness,
According to his thought, in the Mediterranean
Of the quiet of the middle of the night,
With the broken statues standing on the shore.

8

When was it that the particles became
The whole man that tempers and beliefs became
Temper and belief and that differences lost
Difference and were one? It had to be
In the presence of a solitude of the self,
An expanse and the abstraction of an expanse,
A zone of time without the ticking of clocks,
A color that moved us with forgetfulness.
When was it that we heard the voice of union?

Was it as we sat in the park and the archaic form
Of a woman with a cloud on her shoulder, rose
Against the trees and then against the sky
And the sense of the archaic touched us at once
In a movement of the outlines of similarity?

We resembled one another at the sight.
The forgetful color of the autumn day
Was full of these archaic forms, giants
Of sense, evoking one thing in many men,
Evoking an archaic space, vanishing
In the space, leaving an outline of the size
Of the impersonal person, the wanderer,
The father, the ancestor, the bearded peer,
The total of human shadows bright as glass.

WALLACE STEVENS

THE CAGE

And the Americans put Pound in a cage
In the Italian summer coverless
On a hillside up from Pisa in his age
Roofless the old man with a blanket yes

On the ground. *Shih* in his pocket luck jammed there
When the partigiani with a tommy-gun
Broke in the villa door. Great authors fare
Well; for they fed him, the Americans

And after four weeks were afraid he'd die
So the Americans took him out of the cage
And tented him like others. He lay wry
To make the Pisan cantos with his courage

Sorrow and memory in a slowing drive
(And after five months they told Dorothy
Where Ezra was, and what, — i.e., alive)
Until from fingers such something twitcht free

. . . O years go bare, a madman lingered through
The hall-end where we talked and felt my book
Till he was waved away; Pound tapped his shoe
And pointed and digressed with an impatient look

"Bankers" and "Yids" and "a conspiracy"
And of himself no word, the second worst,
And "Who is seeryus now?" and then "J. C.
Thought he'd got something, yes, but Ari was first"

His body bettered. And the empty cage
Sings in the wringing winds where winds blow
Backward and forward one door in its age
And the great cage suffers nothing whatever no

                                        JOHN BERRYMAN

THE SELF UNSATISFIED RUNS EVERYWHERE

Sunday and sunlight ashen on the Square,
Hard wind, high blue, and clouded pennant sky,
Fifth Avenue empty in the autumn air,
As if a clear photograph of a dead day,
It was the Lord's day once, solemn and full
—Now I in an aftermath, desire spent,
Move with a will appeased and see a gull,
Then gulls drop from an arch—scythes of descent!—
Having (I guess) no wish beyond the foam
Toppling to them at each fresh exercise,
Knowing success like fountains, perhaps more wise
Than one who hesitantly writes a poem
—But who, being human, wishes to be a gull,
Knows nothing much, though birds are beautiful.

DELMORE SCHWARTZ

THE POEM

The painter of Dante's awful ferry-ride
Declared the world only a dictionary,
Words, words, whose separate meanings must go wide
Unless the visionary
Compose them, so his eyes are satisfied.

The saint from Africa called every thing
A word, the world being a poem by God,
Each evil tuned to make a splendor sing,
Ordered by God
With opposites that praise His fingering.

Was Delacroix a fool? Was Augustine?
The dictionary seems a poor appliance,
With venerable terms become obscene,
Too fertile science.
We try the poem, but what does it mean?

The rhymes are slant, of course, the rhythms free
Or sprung, the figures moving through the mind
Close as a caravan across country
Often unkind.
It is magnificent in its privacy.

And yet the words are there: fire, earth, ocean,
Sound, silence, odor, shape and shadow, fear,
Delight, animal, mineral, time, space, motion,
Lovely and queer,
The crystal's patience, the baboon's devotion.

The words are there; according to his powers,
The saint, the painter, gave the work a gloss,
Loving it. Anguish, as it scours, devours,
Discovering loss.
The logic of the poem is not ours.

BABETTE DEUTSCH

LITTLE ODE

What beasts and angels practice I ignore,
but the best of human use is careless love,
   and surely bravery and cunning merit
   the prize, they are the method of success.

Then crown us, friends, as on we speed
and play us music when the train arrives,
   for we, outwitting the obstacular world
   and forcing one another beyond fear,

to careless lust have won our way. Oh here
it is quiet—Friends! do you remember?
   Spinoza said, "Happiness, not only the reward
   of virtue, is itself the virtue"—is

effective, and we spread our satisfaction
whence there is much, disarming envy;
   the hours are not boring, they stand still;
   we deviate straight forward to immortal death.

PAUL GOODMAN

"A WORLD WITHOUT OBJECTS IS
A SENSIBLE EMPTINESS"

The tall camels of the spirit
Steer for their deserts, passing the last groves loud
With the sawmill shrill of the locust, to the whole honey of the arid
Sun. They are slow, proud,

And move with a stilted stride
To the land of sheer horizon, hunting Traherne's
Sensible emptiness, there where the brain's lantern-slide
Revels in vast returns.

O connoisseurs of thirst,
Beasts of my soul who long to learn to drink
Of pure mirage, those prosperous islands are accurst
That shimmer on the brink

Of absence; auras, lustres,
And all shinings need to be shaped and borne.
Think of those painted saints, capped by the early masters
With bright, jauntily-worn

Aureate plates, or even
Merry-go-round rings. Turn, O turn
From the fine sleights of the sand, from the long empty oven
Where flames in flamings burn,

Back to the trees arrayed
In bursts of glare, to the halo-dialling run
Of the country creeks, and the hills' bracken tiaras made
Gold in the sunken sun,

Wisely watch for the sight
Of the supernova burgeoning over the barn,
Lampshine blurred in the steam of beasts, the spirit's right
Oasis, light incarnate.

RICHARD WILBUR

ALCESTE IN THE WILDERNESS

(In Le Misanthrope *Alceste, having become disgusted with all
forms and manners of society, goes off into exile, leaving behind
Philinte, who shall now become his rival in love.)*

Evening is clogged with gnats as the light fails,
And branches bloom with gold and copper screams
Of birds with fancy prices on their tails
To plume a lady's gear; the motet wails
Through Africa upon dissimilar themes.

A little snuff-box whereon Daphnis sings
In pale enamels, touching love's defeat,
Calls up the color of her underthings
And plays upon the taut memorial strings,
Trailing her laces down into this heat.

One day he found, topped with a smutty grin,
The small corpse of a monkey, partly eaten.
Force of the sun had split the bluish skin,
Which, by their questioning and entering in,
A swarm of bees had been concerned to sweeten.

He could distill no essence out of this.
That yellow majesty and molten light
Should bless this carcass with a sticky kiss
Argued a brute and filthy emphasis.
The half-moons of the finger-nails were white,

And where the nostrils opened on the skies,
Issuing to the sinus, where the ant
Crawled swiftly down to undermine the eyes
Of cloudy aspic, nothing could disguise
How terribly the thing looked like Philinte.

Will-o'-the-wisp, on the scum laden water,
Burns in the night, a gaseous deceiver,
In the pale shade of France's foremost daughter.
Heat gives his thinking cavity no quarter,
For he is burning with the monkey's fever.

Before the bees have diagrammed their comb
Within the skull, before summer has cracked
The back of Daphnis, naked, polychrome,
Paris shall see the tempered exile home,
Peruked and stately for the final act.

ANTHONY HECHT

THE BEAUTY OF THINGS

To feel and speak the astonishing beauty of things—earth,
    stone and water,
Beast, man and woman, sun, moon and stars—
The blood-shot beauty of human nature, its thoughts, frenzies
    and passions,
And unhuman nature its towering reality—
For man's half dream; man, you might say, is nature
    dreaming, but rock
And water and sky are constant—to feel
Greatly, and understand greatly, and express greatly, the
    natural
Beauty, is the sole business of poetry.
The rest's diversion: those holy or noble sentiments, the
    intricate ideas,
The love, lust, longing: reasons, but not the reason.

ROBINSON JEFFERS

TO AN ANTHOLOGIST

Yes, even the Devil should have his due,
Though I've had all the praise that need he:
You don't like me; I don't like you,—
Still, I *do* wish that you'd read me!

THEODORE ROETHKE

HÔTEL DE L'UNIVERS ET PORTUGAL

The strange bed, whose recurrent dream we are,
Basin, and shutters guarding with their latch
The hour of arrivals, the reputed untouched Square.
Bleakly with ever fewer belongings we watch
And have never, it each time seems, so coldly before

Steeped the infant membrane of our clinging
In a strange city's clear grave acids;
Or thought how like a pledge the iron key-ring
Slid overboard, one weighty calm at Rhodes,
Down to the vats of its eventual rusting.

And letters moulting out of memory, lost
Seasons of the breast of a snowbird . . .
One morning on the pillow shall at last
Lie strands of age, and many a crease converge
Where the ambitious dreaming head has tossed

The world away and turned, and taken dwelling
Within the pillow's dense white dark, has heard
The lover's speech from cool walls peeling
To the white bed, whose dream they were.
Bare room, forever feeling and annulling,

Bare room, bleak problem set for space,
Fold us ever and over in less identity
Than six walls hold, the oval mirror face
Showing us vacantly how to become only
Bare room, mere air, no hour and no place,

Lodging of chance, and bleak as all beginning.
We had begun perhaps to lack a starlit Square.
But now our very poverties are dissolving,
Are swallowed up, strong powders to ensure
Sleep, by a strange bed in the dark of dreaming.

JAMES MERRILL

THE FOREBODING

Looking by chance in at the open window
  I saw my own self seated in his chair
With gaze abstracted, furrowed forehead,
    Unkempt hair.

I thought that I had suddenly come to die,
  That to a cold corpse this was my farewell,
Until the pen moved slowly on the paper
    And tears fell.

He had written a name, yours, in printed letters
  One word on which bemusedly to pore:
No protest, no desire, your naked name,
    Nothing more.

Would it be tomorrow, would it be next year?
  But the vision was not false, this much I knew;
And I turned angrily from the open window
    Aghast at you.

Why never a warning, either by speech or look,
  That the love you cruelly gave me could not last?
Already it was too late: the bait swallowed,
    The hook fast.

ROBERT GRAVES

THE INSTRUMENT

Death, and it is broken,
The delicate apparatus of the mind,
Tactile, sensitive to light, responsive to sound,
The soul's instrument, tuned to earth's music,
Vibrant to all the waves that break on the shores of the world.

Perhaps the soul only puts out a hand,
Antennae or pseudopodium, an extended touch
To receive the spectrum of colour, and the lower octave of pain,
Reaches down into the waves of nature
As a child dips an arm into the sea,

And death is a withdrawal of attention
That has discovered all it needs to know,
Or, if not all, enough for now,
If not enough, something to bear in mind.

And it may be that soul extends
Organs of sense
Tuned to waves here scarcely heard, or only
Heard distantly, in dreams,
Worlds other otherwise than as stars,
Asteroids, and suns are distant in natural space.
The supersonic voices of angels reach us
Even now, and we touch one another
Sometimes, in love, with hands that are not hands,
With immaterial substance, with a body
Of interfusing thought, a living eye,
Spirit that passes unhindered through walls of stone
And walks upon those waves that we call ocean.

KATHLEEN RAINE

NIJINSKY

The dive could come who was its fledgling first
Of wings that feathered ankles and stood up
And leapt and wide in the deep air immersed
The body that came down as soul went up
And taught the throat the foremost wind: and back
The living blood curved in the fluid hand
Whose fingers paused, and poised: the deadened slack
Was time's who stopped to see a dancer stand
Where sky was . . . There was God, where man was not
And heat in the heaving heart that moved alone
And left like a lover the still, praying spot
To surge where there were only air and bone
But once, as a mere odor comes and goes,
Dream: and the great anthropomorphic rose.

PARKER TYLER

THE SHIELD OF ACHILLES

She looked over his shoulder
　　For vines and olive trees,
Marble, well-governed cities
　　And ships upon wine-dark seas;

But there on the shining metal
　　His hands had put instead
An artificial wilderness
　　And a sky like lead.

A plain without a feature, bare and brown,
　　No blade of grass, no sign of neighborhood,
Nothing to eat and nowhere to sit down;
　　Yet, congregated on that blankness, stood
　　An unintelligible multitude,
A million eyes, a million boots, in line,
Without expression, waiting for a sign.

Out of the air a voice without a face
　　Proved by statistics that some cause was just
In tones as dry and level as the place;
　　No one was cheered and nothing was discussed,
　　Column by column, in a cloud of dust,
They marched away, enduring a belief
Whose logic brought them, somewhere else, to grief.

She looked over his shoulder
　　For ritual pieties,
White flower-garlanded heifers,
　　Libation and sacrifice:
But there on the shining metal
　　Where the altar should have been
She saw by his flickering forge-light
　　Quite another scene.

Barbed wire enclosed an arbitrary spot
　　Where bored officials lounged (one cracked a joke)
And sentries sweated for the day was hot;
　　A crowd of ordinary decent folk
　　Watched from outside and neither moved nor spoke
As three pale figures were led forth and bound
To three posts driven upright in the ground.

The mass and majesty of this world, all
   That carries weight and always weighs the same,
Lay in the hands of others; they were small
   And could not hope for help, and no help came;
   What their foes liked to do was done; their shame
Was all the worst could wish: they lost their pride
And died as men before their bodies died.

     She looked over his shoulder
       For athletes at their games,
     Men and women in a dance
       Moving their sweet limbs,
     Quick, quick, to music;
       But there on the shining shield
     His hands had set no dancing-floor
       But a weed-choked field.

A ragged urchin, aimless and alone,
   Loitered about that vacancy; a bird
Flew up to safety from his well-aimed stone:
   That girls are raped, that two boys knife a third,
   Were axioms to him, who'd never heard
Of any world where promises were kept
Or one could weep because another wept.

     The thin-lipped armorer
       Hephaestos hobbled away;
     Thetis of the shining breasts
       Cried out in dismay
     At what the God had wrought
       To please her son, the strong
     Iron-hearted man-slaying Achilles
       Who would not live long.

W. H. AUDEN

AFTER THE PERSIAN

1

I have wept with the spring storm;
Burned with the brutal summer.
Now, hearing the wind and the twanging bow-strings
I know what winter brings.

The hunt sweeps out upon the plain
And the garden darkens.
They will bring the trophies home
To bleed and perish
Beside the trellis and the lattices,
Beside the fountain, still flinging diamond water,
Beside the pool
(Which is eight-sided, like my heart).

2

All has been translated into treasure:
Weightless as amber,
Translucent as the currant on the branch,
Dark as the rose's thorn.

Where is the shimmer of evil?
This is the shell's iridescence
And the wild bird's wing.

3

Ignorant, I took up my burden in the wilderness.
Wise with great wisdom, I shall lay it down upon flowers.

4

Goodbye, goodbye!
There was so much to love, I could not love it all;
I could not love it enough.

Some things I overlooked, and some I could not find.
Let the crystal clasp them
When you drink your wine, in autumn.

LOUISE BOGAN

THEN THE ERMINE:

"Rather dead than spotted"; and believe it
      despite reason to think not,
I saw a bat by daylight;
hard to credit

But I know that I am right. It charmed me—
      wavering like a jack o' the green,
weaving about above me
insecurely.

Instead of hammerhanded bravado
      adopting force for fashion,
momentum with a motto:
non timeo

vel mutare—I don't change or frighten;
      though all it means is really,
am I craven?
Nothing's certain.

Fail, and Lavater's physiography
      has another admirer
of skill that axiomatically
flowers obscurely.

Both paler and purpler than azure, note marine
      uncompliance—bewarer
of the weak analogy—between
waves in motion.

Change? Of course, if the palisandre settee can express
      for us, "ebony violet"—
Master Corbo in full dress
and shepherdess

at once—exhilarating hoarse crownote
      and dignity with intimacy.
Our foiled explosiveness is yet
a kind of prophet,

a perfecter, and so a concealer—
      with the power of implosion—
like violets by Dürer;
even darker.

MARIANNE MOORE

From PATERSON, BOOK V

THE RIVER OF HEAVEN

Of asphodel, that greeny flower, the least,
        that is a simple flower
                like a buttercup upon its

branching stem, save
        that it's green and wooden.
                We've had a long life

and many things have happened in it.
        There are flowers also
                in hell. So today I've come

to talk to you about them, among
        other things, of flowers
                that we both love, even

of this poor, colorless
        thing which no one living
                prizes but the dead see

and ask among themselves,
        What do we remember that was shaped
                as this thing

is shaped? while their eyes
        fill
                with tears. By which

and by the weak wash of crimson
        colors it, the rose
                is predicated

                WILLIAM CARLOS WILLIAMS

SESTINA IN TIME OF WINTER

Walking towards the house, the terraces
where lords and ladies, feathers in their hands,
questioned the wind, I see the naked urns

silent and filled with snow like milky bells
rising abandoned, and deformed by ice
the marble cupids tightening in the ponds.

There are no deer, nor ducks upon the ponds
where the black reeds against the terraces
clack with their beaks and mandibles of ice,
nor do the wicked footmen, holding hands,
skate in the winter mornings blue as bells
and drink the whiskey hidden in the urns.

But, always, as I walk amongst the urns
or through the formal gardens to the ponds
in the white landscape where the jangling bells
of sleighs do not approach the terraces,
some dedication rustles in the hands
with which I pluck myself a rose of ice,

and through the tones of twilight and of ice
I feel my blood brocade me till, by urns
pacing and grave, the graces of my hands
dismiss the yew green vistas to the ponds,
conduct the silence of the terraces
and then at solemn doors knock and ring bells.

Deep in the house are dusty waves of bells
but no one answers and I break through ice
into those rooms behind the terraces
where mirrors darken like the reeded ponds
no birds alight on, chandeliers and urns
glitter obscurely at the clock's stopped hands.

But in the absence of all smiles and hands
I feel my heart flow back into that bell
whose voice still waits within the fluted urns:
then in the lovely negative of ice
pleasures alight in flocks upon the ponds,
peacocks and lovers crowd the terraces—

summer and winter strolling hand in hand
and chateau childhoods prisoned in the bell
of dark, held back excited by the urns.

PATRICK ANDERSON

FROM THE EMBASSY

I am Ambassador of Otherwhere
To the unfederated states of Here and There,
Enjoy (as the phrase is)
Extra-territorial privileges
With heres and theres I seldom come to blows
Or need, as once, to sandbag all my windows.
Then, though the Otherwhereish currency
Cannot be quoted yet officially,
I meet less hindrance now with the exchange,
Nor is my garb, even, considered strange,
And shy enquiries for literature
Come in by every post, and the side door.

ROBERT GRAVES

THE ILLITERATE

Touching your goodness, I am like a man
Who turns a letter over in his hand,
And you might think this was because the hand
Was unfamiliar, but truth is the man
Has never had a letter from anyone;
And now he is both afraid of what it means
And ashamed because he has no other means
To find out what it says than to ask someone.

His uncle could have left the store to him,
Or his parents died before he sent them word,
Or the dark girl changed and want him for her lover.
Afraid and letter-proud he keeps it with him.
What would you call his pleasure in the words
That keep him rich and orphaned and beloved?

WILLIAM MEREDITH

PRISON SONG

The skin ripples over my body like moon-wooed water,
rearing to escape me. Where could it find another
animal as naked as the one it hates to cover?
Once it told me what was happening outside,

who was attacking, who caressing, and what the air
was doing to feed or freeze me. Now I wake up
dark at night, in a textureless ocean of ignorance,
or fruit bites back and water bruises like a stone.
It's jealousy, because I look for other tools to know
with, and other armor, better girded to my wish.
So let it lie, turn off the clues or try to leave:
sewn on me seamless like those painful shirts
the body-hating saints wore, the sheath of hell
is pierced to my darkness nonetheless: what traitors
labor in my face, what hints they smuggle through
its arching guard! But even in the night it jails,
with nothing but its lies and silences to feed upon,
the jail itself can make a scenery, sing prison songs,
and set off fireworks to praise a homemade day.

ALAN DUGAN

THE WORD OF WATER

The word of water spoke a wavy line
To the Egyptians; we can also hear
Variations from the strict linear
In fall and faucet, pail and ice-pitcher.
Whether in fountain or in porcelain
It speaks a speech so crystal in its chime
We never think to question this cold
Transparent wanderer from the underworld
About the dead,—whose resurrection fills
More than half the earth uttering a word
That no man living has interpreted.

E. L. MAYO

MARGINALIA

Things concentrate at the edges; the pond-surface
Is bourne to fish and man and it is spread
In textile scum and damask light, on which
The lily-pads are set; and there are also
Inlaid ruddy twigs, becalmed pine-leaves,
Air-baubles, and the chain mail of froth.

Descending into sleep (as when the night-lift
Falls past a brilliant floor) we glimpse a sublime
Decor and hear, perhaps, a complete music,
But this evades us, as in the night meadows
    The crickets' million roundsong dies away
    From all advances, rising in every distance.

Our riches are centrifugal; men compose
Daily, unwittingly, their final dreams,
And those are our own voices whose remote
Consummate chorus rides on the whirlpool's rim,
    Past which we flog our sails, toward which we drift,
    Plying our trades, in hopes of a good drowning.

RICHARD WILBUR

THE ALPHABET

The letters of the Jews as strict as flames
Or little terrible flowers lean
Stubbornly upwards through the perfect ages,
Singing through solid stone the sacred names.
The letters of the Jews are black and clean
And lie in chain-line over Christian pages.
The chosen letters bristle like barbed wire
That hedge the flesh of man,
Twisting and tightening the book that warns.
These words, this burning bush, this flickering pyre
Unsacrifices the bled son of man
Yet plaits his crown of thorns.

Where go the tipsy idols of the Roman
Past synagogues of patient time,
Where go the sisters of the gothic rose,
Where go the blue eyes of the Polish women
Past the almost natural crime,
Past the still speaking embers of ghettoes,
There rise the tinder flowers of the Jews.
The letters of the Jews are dancing knives
That carve the heart of darkness seven ways.

These are the letters that all men refuse
And will refuse until the king arrives
And will refuse until the death of time
And all is rolled back in the book of days.

KARL SHAPIRO

HORATIAN ODE

Let the pines rock in torment of the storm
Of pressured weathers in the clouds contending
And the sheer slopes about us plunge headlong
Down to the waters' frantic rush and spending.

Our timbers morticed solid in the rock
And floor tiles in cement as firmly set
As if in molten lava petrified,
We keep the moveless center and can mock

At bedlam on the loose. Even the fire
In the chimney is menace broken to our will.
We are well at ease in our tight citadel.
Only if lightning strike or the earth yawn

Do we risk disruption . . . or even, say, extinction!
And how should accidents beyond control
Of mortal engineering now subvert
Our state with fears that do not touch the soul?

JOSEPH WARREN BEACH

AGING

I wake, but before I know it it is done,
The day, I sleep . . . And of days like these the years,
A life are made. I nod, consenting to my life.
—But who can live in these quick-passing hours?
I need to find again, to make a life,
A child's Sunday afternoon, the Pleasure Drive
Where everything went by but time — the Study Hour
Spent at a desk with folded hands, in waiting.

In those I could make. Did I not make in them
Myself? the Grown One whose time shortens,
Breath quickens, heart beats faster, till at last
It catches, skips? Yet those hours that seemed, were endless
Were still not long enough to have remade
My childish heart: the heart that must have, always,
To make anything of anything, not time,
Not time but—
           but, alas! eternity.

RANDALL JARRELL

CHEZ JANE

The white chocolate jar full of petals
swills odds and ends around in a dizzying eye
of four o'clocks now and to come. The tiger,
marvellously striped and irritable, leaps
on the table and without disturbing a hair
of the flowers' breathless attention, pisses
into the pot, right down its delicate spout.
A whisper of steam goes up from that porcelain
eurythra. "Saint-Saëns!" it seems to be whispering,
curling unerringly around the furry nuts
of the terrible puss, who is mentally flexing.
Ah be with me always, spirit of noisy
contemplation in the studio, the Garden
of Zoos, the eternally fixed afternoons!
There, while music scratches its scrofulous
stomach, the brute beast emerges and stands,
clear and careful, knowing always the exact peril
at this moment caressing his fangs with
a tongue given wholly to luxurious usages;
which only a moment before dropped aspirin
in this sunset of roses, and now throws a chair
in the air to aggravate the truly menacing.

FRANK O'HARA

THE ISLAND IN THE EVENING

At the gathered ends of rooty paths
The wharf attracts the playing children
Voices call across the water
Beginning games on a summer evening
A gull who drops on another island
Calls down the day below the sky

As the light rises into the sky
Softness comes to mossy paths
A breeze slides off the island
Against the faces of the children
Using the withering light of the evening
Reflected from the shadowless water

The games are new on the permanent water
And children under the yellow sky
Have no fear of the friendly evening
Who feel their way on darkening paths
Over roots that previous children
Knew as the shape of the sheltering island

Shadowed forests on the island
And beaches worn by tidal water
Keep some strangeness from the children
Under the candid giant sky
And all familiar forest paths
Are edged with strangeness in the evening

Yellow primroses of the evening
In bushy clearings on the island
And yellow mullein beside the paths
In rocky meadows with little water
Focus all the covering sky
In single blossoms for the children

Games invented by the children
Hold the light of the delicate evening
Before it is lost in the permanent sky

Starting again the life of the island
Eroded by the moving water
And running feet on rocky paths

Worn paths bring home the children
From tidal water on a summer evening
Across the island below the sky

FAIRFIELD PORTER

HIGH FIDELITY

I play your furies back to me at night,
The needle dances in the grooves they made,
For fury is passion like love, and fury's bite,
These grooves, no sooner than a love-mark fade;
Then all swings round to nightmare: from the rim,
To prove the guilt I don't admit by day,
I duck love as a witch to sink or swim
Till in the ringed and level I survey
The tuneless circles that succeed a voice.
They run, without distinction, passion, rage,
Around a soloist's merely printed name
That still turns, from the impetus not choice,
Surrounded in that played-out pose of age
By notes he was, but cannot be again.

THOM GUNN

LANDED: A VALENTINE

See how the brown kelp withers in air
          Gasping to its death
Upon the salty ice. A moment
          Only was enough
To banish the loveliness that made
          Of a few rather
Inexpressive weeds under water
          A lover's emblem
Of success — easy-moving, soft and
          In the heart's color.

Can simple air become so foul? Now
  After a short time
Parted from warm company we kept
  Together, I share
That condition, a gradual rot
  So far from the sea:
Absence of the proper element
  Will take effect, take
Soon the mouth out of my very words.

     RICHARD HOWARD

RADIO

Why do you play such dreary music
on Saturday afternoon, when tired
mortally tired I long for a little
reminder of immortal energy?
      All
week long while I trudge fatiguingly
from desk to desk in the museum
you spill your miracles of Grieg
and Honegger on shut-ins.
      Am I not
shut in too, and after a week
of work don't I deserve Prokofieff?

Well, I have my beautiful de Kooning
to aspire to. I think it has an orange
bed in it, more than the ear can hold.

     FRANK O'HARA

BACHELOR

A mystic in the morning, half asleep,
He is given a vision of the unity
That informs a small apartment, barefooted.
He takes the long view of toes in the bath-tub
And shaves a man whose destiny is mild.
He perceives hidden resemblances; particularly
He is struck by how breakfast equipment imitates her,
The object of his less than mystic dream.
Sunlight, orange-juice, newsprint, kitchenware:
Is it love's trick of doubling? Everywhere
Like those little dogs in Goya, objects show
A gift for mimicry. His coffee is morose.
A clock goes off next-door where probably
Someone has parodied his dream; and here
The solemn little mongrels of the day
Stare out at him, trying to look like her.
They leer and flirt. Let saints and painters deal
With the mystery of likeness. As for him
It scares him wide awake and dead alone.
A man of action dials the telephone.

WILLIAM MEREDITH

From CYCLE OF SIX LYRICS

V

O PEARL AND BREASTED WORLD

O Pearl and breasted World
At whose bright spring I slake
This bitterness of Ego,
And, a snivelling child,
Hush for its mother's sake,
Await my imago:

Let the natural causes
That unite us to
Our pearl and breasted mother
Exercise their forces
Till we are made to do
Justice by one another.

GEORGE BARKER

PERMANENTLY

One day the Nouns were clustered in the street.
An Adjective walked by, with her dark beauty.
The Nouns were struck, moved, changed.
The next day a Verb drove up, and created the Sentence.

Each Sentence says one thing—for example, "Although it was
    a dark rainy day when the Adjective walked by, I shall
    remember the pure and sweet expression on her face until
    the day I perish from the green, effective earth."
Or, "Will you please close the window, Andrew?"
Or, for example, "Thank you, the pink pot of flowers on the
    window sill has changed color recently to a light yellow,
    due to the heat from the boiler factory which exists
    nearby."

In the springtime the Sentences and the Nouns lay silently on
    the grass.
A lonely Conjunction here and there would call, "And! But!"
But the Adjective did not emerge.

As the adjective is lost in the sentence,
So I am lost in your eyes, ears, nose, and throat—
You have enchanted me with a single kiss
Which can never be undone
Until the destruction of language.

                                        KENNETH KOCH

BIRTH OF VENUS

What day was it she slid
Up from the innocent sea
Unstirred by tug of tide?
Under her feet the sand

Shifted. The waiting land
Enclosed her like a shell.
The stallions in the foam
Remarked her and were tame;

The chariot of flame
Stood still to see her come.
All nature felt the weight
Of her first faltering steps.

Time shifted, and the shapes
Of ordinary things
Altered beneath her touch;
There was no way to turn

Back. She must stay and learn
The role they had assigned:
To be their goddess, serve
The movable feasts of love.

CONSTANCE URDANG

METAMORPHOSIS

Haunched like a faun, he hooed
from grove of moon-glint and fen-frost
until all owls in the twigged forest
flapped black to look and brood
on the call this man made.

No sound but a drunken coot
lurching home along river bank;
stars hung water-sunk, so a rank
of double star-eyes lit
boughs where those owls sat.

An arena of yellow eyes
watched the changing shape he cut,
saw hoof harden from foot, saw sprout
goat-horns; marked how god rose
and galloped woodward in that guise.

SYLVIA PLATH

From INSCRIPTIONS ON CHINESE PAINTINGS

LINES TO DO WITH YOUTH

1

Willow-tassels grow in tremors of the spring wind
On this Festival of Peace in the Fourth Month,
And swallows guide their young close to the Women's Quarters
For a fluttering trial of new wings.

2

After I had brushed the floor, burned incense, shut myself in
    and slept,
The pattern of the mat looked like water and the gnats like a
    mist:
I had been waked as by winter and did not know where I was,
Till I opened the western window and saw mountains surging
    into heaven.

3

Though grass grow lowlier than the flowers
And be hidden by their laden stems,
Only happiness exists
For a handmaiden of the Ch'engs.

4

Having passed his government examinations,
He rides back home
Through ten miles radiant with almond blossoms
On a horse of air.

5

Past the water-crystal casement of her chamber
Butterflies fluttered under the eaves;
But the cats have wakened her from blissful dreaming
And her lover fades away.

6

Nothing is pleasanter than a cup of wine in the hand
And it is a surer thing than twelve moonrises.

7

Cockcrow in the moonlight, the roof of an inn,
A footprint in the frost on a wooden bridge.

8

Mountain-streams everywhere but no path,
Till under the dark willows blooms a village.

WITTER BYNNER

METAPHYSICAL

In festo Christi Regis

The level slope of colored sea
Rises degree upon degree
To hide the brazen ball of sun.
Ponderous is the planet side,
And nothing here but heart can slide,
And nothing but the day is done.

Glory the heavens here declare
Heavens in gloom deny elsewhere.
The jackal and the gaping shark
Possess the shambles of the night.
As upward eyries take the light
The downward longitudes are dark.

Eyes on the telluric rim
In tangent angles peering dim
Find shape and hour dark or down.
But centered lordship knows the art
Of bearing so toward every part
The studded sphere becomes his crown.

Rays of his mercy are besought
To magnetize my speck of thought.
Elated let the evening fall,
Abysmal be the golden day;
The ravaged carcass far away
Be supple in the life of all.

ROBERT FITZGERALD

THE APPROACH TO THEBES

In the zero of the night, in the lipping hour,
Skin-time, knocking-time, when the heart is pearled
And the moon squanders its uranian gold,
She taunted me, who was all music's tongue,
Philosophy's and wilderness's breed,
Of shifting shape, half jungle-cat, half-dancer,
Night's woman-petaled, lion-scented rose,
To whom I gave, out of a hero's need,
The dolor of my thrust, my riddling answer,
Whose force no lesser mortal knows. Dangerous?
Yes, as nervous oracles foretold
Who could not guess the secret taste of her:
Impossible wine! I came into the world
To fill a fate; am punished by my youth
No more. What if dog-faced logic howls,
Was it art or magic multiplied my joy?
Nature has reasons beyond true or false.
We played like metaphysic animals
Whose freedom made our knowledge bold
Before the tragic curtain of the day:
I can bear the dishonor now of growing old.
Blinded and old, exiled, diseased, and scorned—
The verdict's bitten on the brazen gates,
For the gods grant each of us his lot, his term.
Hail to the King of Thebes!—my self, ordained
To satisfy the impulse of the worm,
Bemummied in those famous incestuous sheets,
The bloodiest flags of nations of the curse,
To be hung from the balcony outside the room
Where I encounter my most flagrant source.

Children, grandchildren, my long posterity,
To whom I bequeath the spiders of my dust,
Believe me, whatever sordid tales you hear,
Told by physicians or mendacious scribes,
Of beardless folly, consanguineous lust,
Fomenting pestilence, rebellion, war,
I come prepared, unwanting what I see,
But tied to life. On the royal road to Thebes
I had my luck, I met a lovely monster,
And the story's this: I made the monster me.

STANLEY KUNITZ

THE UNSETTLED MOTORCYCLIST'S
VISION OF HIS DEATH

Across the open countryside,
Into the walls of rain I ride.
It beats my cheek, drenches my knees,
But I am being what I please.

The firm heath stops, and marsh begins.
Now we're at war: whichever wins
My human will cannot submit
To nature, though brought out of it.
The wheels sink deep; the clear sound blurs:
Still, bent on the handle-bars,
I urge my chosen instrument
Against the mere embodiment.
The front wheel wedges fast between
Two shrubs of glazed insensate green
—Gigantic order in the rim
Of each flat leaf. Black eddies brim
Around my heel which, pressing deep,
Accelerates the waiting sleep.

I used to live in sound, and lacked
Knowledge of still or creeping fact,
But now the stagnant strips my breath,
Leant on my cheek in weight of death.
Though so oppressed I find I may

Through substance move. I pick my way,
Where death and life in one combine,
Through the dark earth that is not mine,
Crowded with fragments, blunt, unformed;
While past my ear where noises swarmed
The marsh plant's white extremities,
Slow without patience, spread at ease
Invulnerable and soft, extend
With a quiet grasping toward their end.

And though the tubers, once I rot,
Reflesh my bones with pallid knot,
Till swelling out my clothes they feign
This dummy is a man again,
It is as servants they insist,
Without volition that they twist;
And habit does not leave them tired,
By men laboriously acquired.
Cell after cell the plants convert
My special richness in the dirt:
All that they get, they get by chance.

And multiply in ignorance.

THOM GUNN

From KING MIDAS

THE KING'S SPEECH

The palace clocks are stiff as coats of mail.
Time stopped; I flicked it with my fingernail.
My taste is shattered on these works of art
It fathers by a touch: My bread's too rich,
My butter much too golden, and my meat
A nugget on my plate as cold as ice;
Fresh water in my throat turns precious there,
Where every drop becomes a millionaire.

I rather would be blind than see this world
All affluent in yellow, bought and sold
By Kings that hammer roses into gold:
I did not know I loved their warring thorns
Until they flowered into spikes so hard
My blood made obdurate the rose's stem.
My God was generous. O much too much!
The nearest rose is now beyond my reach.

My furry cat is sculpture, my dog dead;
They stare at me with four wild sparkling eyes
That used to sparkle with dry wit; instead,
Having no wit that they can profit by,
They are pure profit, and their silences
Might make a King go mad, for it was I
Who made their lively muscles stiffly pose —
This jaundice is relentless, and it grows.

Princess, come no closer; my rigid kiss,
Though it is royal still, will make you this
Or that kind of a statue. And my Queen,
Be armed against this gold paralysis,
Or you will starve and thinly bed alone,
And when you dream, a gold mine in your brain
Will have both eyes release their golden ore
And cry for tears they could not cry before.

I would be nothing but the dirt made loud,
A ripeness of the weeds, a timid sun,
Or oppositely be entirely cloud,
Absolved of matter, dissolving in the rain,
Or any small, anonymous live thing
Than be the reigning King of this dominion
Where gold makes poor the richness of decay.
O Dionysus, change me back to clay!

HOWARD MOSS

WREATHS

I

Each day the tide withdraws; chills us; pastes
The sand with dead gulls, oranges, dead men . . .
Uttering love, that outlasts or outwastes
Time's attrition, exiles appear again,
But faintly altered in eyes and skin. . . .

II

Into what understanding all have grown!
(Setting aside a few things, the still faces,
Climbing the phosphorus tide, that none will own)
What paradises and watering-places!
What hurts appeased by the sea's handsomeness!

GEOFFREY HILL

A MARK OF RESISTANCE

Stone by stone I pile
this cairn of my intention
with the noon's weight on my back,
exposed and vulnerable
across the slanting fields
which I love but cannot save
from floods that are to come;
can only fasten down
with this work of my hands,
these painfully assembled
stones, in the shape of nothing
that has ever existed before.
A pile of stones: an assertion
that this piece of country matters
for large and simple reasons.
A mark of resistance, a sign.

ADRIENNE RICH

A MORNING LETTER

The various members of the hierarchy move,
early morning awakening of the world.
They are like the shuffling of doors,
eager and reluctant, two-faced, I suppose.
Eight o'clock carillons seem universal magic.

Now after hoping for magic,
I was an ordinary messenger to arrive.
Wake up, you are yourself the God of Love
asleep. Whom did you expect? you lay
eyes closed as if afloat.
Proud boy,
whom did you expect who did not wear
only your lesser face? someone from up there?
someone just stepped down from a throne,
smelling of majesty?
Poetry has gone straight to your head.
Your mind wanders.
There are no empty thrones in heaven.
This is early morning in a world without kings.
A small-time Don Juan knocks at your door.
I put on all my pride to climb the stairs.

I was only messenger of myself
to tell you you are yourself Love.
How do you arrange the young men in your dreams?
arranging and re-arranging youth's hierarchies.
Don't you hear the bells ringing,
starting the day out with common tunes?
Ta-ra-ra-boom-de-ay and *Auld Lang Syne*.
Waking up from your Imperial World,
you, for a moment, not I,
are Emperor of my world.
The hierarchies of powers move like doors
—this is a good dream figure.
I am not dreaming.

I came to praise Love, not you.
And the poor writhe.
Bringing spiteful wreathes to celebrate. . . .

I, being poor, brought my pride.
Wake up from your Empire. I am still dreaming.
This is early morning in a world of kings.

ROBERT DUNCAN

HOLDING THE MIRROR UP TO NATURE

Some shapes cannot be seen in a glass,
those are the ones the heart breaks at.
They will never become valentines
or crucifixes, never. Night clouds
go on insanely as themselves
though metaphors would be prettier;
and when I see them massed at the edge
of the globe, neither weasel nor whale,
as though this world were, after all,
non-representational, I know
a truth that cannot be told although
I try to tell you, "We are alone,
we know nothing, nothing, we shall die
frightened in our freedom, the one
who survives will change his name
to evade the vengeance for love . . ."
Meanwhile the clouds go on clowning
over our heads in the floodlight of
a moon who is known to be Artemis
and Cynthia but sails away anyhow
beyond the serious poets with their
crazy ladies and cloudy histories,
their heroes in whose idiot dreams
the buzzard circles like a clock.

HOWARD NEMEROV

IN TIME OF GOLD

Now there are gold reflections on the water,
how old am I and how have the years passed?

I do not know your age nor mine, nor when you died;
I only know your stark, hypnotic eyes

are different and other eyes meet mine, amber and fire,
in the changed content of the gazing-glass.

Oh, I am old, old, old and my cold hand
clutches the shawl about my shivering shoulders,

I have no power against this bitter cold,
this weakness and this trembling, I am old;

who am I, why do I wait here, what have I lost?
nothing or everything but I gain this,

an image in the sacred lotus pool,
a hand that hesitates to break

the lily from the lily-stalk and spoil
what may be vision of a Pharaoh's face.

H. D.

SHEPHERD

According to the silence, winter has arrived—
a special kind of winter. I, its inventor,
watch it freeze in calendars and stare
out of clocks. I do not feel its cold.

Across a certain farm evening crows go flying,
intervals of sky that I have seen before,
the bearing of a river: I advance, a wanderer
out of thought country, that serious, quiet place,

Till according to the silence all the light is gone
and according to the dark all wanderers are home.

WILLIAM STAFFORD

MIRROR

I grow old under an intensity
Of questioning looks. *Nonsense,*
I try to say, *I cannot teach you children
How to live. — If not you, who will?*
Cries one of them aloud, grasping my gilded
Frame till the world sways. *If not you, who will?*
Between their visits the table, its arrangement
Of Bible, fern and Paisley, all past change,
Does very nicely. If ever I feel curious
As to what others endure,
Across the parlor *you* provide examples,
Wide open, sunny, of everything I am
Not. You embrace a whole world without once caring
To set it in order. That takes thought. Out there
Something is being picked. The red-and-white bandannas
Go to my heart. A fine young man
Rides by on horseback. Now the door shuts. Hester
Confides in me her first unhappiness.
This much, you see, would never have been fitted
Together, but for me. Why then is it
They more and more neglect me? Late one sleepless
Midsummer night I strained to keep
Five tapers from your breathing. *No,* the widowed
Cousin said, *let them go out.* I did.
The room brimmed with gray sound, all the instreaming
Muslin of your dream.
Years later now, two of the grown grandchildren
Sit with novels face-down on the sill,
Content to muse upon your tall transparence,
Your clouds, brown fields, persimmon far
And cypress near. One speaks. *How superficial
Appearances are!* Since then, as if a fish
Had broken the perfect silver of my reflectiveness,
I have lapses. I suspect
Looks from behind, where nothing is, cool gazes
Through the blind flaws of my mind. As days,
As decades lengthen, this vision
Spreads and blackens. I do not know whose it is,
But I think it watches for my last silver
To blister, flake, float leaf by life, each milling-
Downward mild conceit, to a standstill
From which not even you strike any brilliant
Chord in me, and to a faceless will,
Echo of mine, I am amenable.

JAMES MERRILL

DEMANDS OF THE MUSE

I call up words that he may write them down.
My falling into labour gives him birth.
My sorrows are not sorrows till he weeps.
I learn from him as much as he from me
Who is my chosen and my tool in time.

I am dumb: my burden is not like another.
My lineaments are hid from him who knows me.
Great is my Earth with undelivered words.
It is my dead, my dead, that sing to him
This ancient moment; and their voice is he.

Born into time of love's perceptions, he
Is not of time. The acts of time to him
Are marginal. From the first hour he knows me
Until the last, he shall divine my words.
In his own solitude he hears another.

I make demands of him more than another.
He sets himself a labour built of words
Which, through my lips, brings sudden joy to him.
He has the illusion that at last he knows me.
When the toil ends, my confidant is he.

Vision makes wise at once. Why then must he
Wait through so many years before he knows me?
The bit is tempered to restrain his words
And make laborious all that's dear to him.
So he remains himself and not another.

Why is he slow to praise me when another
Falls at my feet? What conscience moves in him
To make a stubborn stand before he knows me?
It is reluctance that resolves his words.
I have been cursed, indeed, by such as he.

Yet, though a school invoke me, it is he
I choose, for opposition gives those words
Their strength; and there is none more near to him
In thought. It is by conflict that he knows me
And serves me in my way and not another.

VERNON WATKINS

TO THE SNAKE

Green Snake, when I hung you round my neck
and stroked your cold, pulsing throat
    as you hissed to me, glinting
arrowy gold scales, and I felt
    the weight of you on my shoulders,
and the whispering silver of your dryness
    sounded close at my ears—

Green Snake—I swore to my companions that certainly
    you were harmless! But truly
I had no certainty, and no hope, only desiring
    to hold you, for that joy,
                which left
a long wake of pleasure, as the leaves moved
and you faded into the pattern
of grass and shadows, and I returned
smiling and haunted, to a dark morning.

DENISE LEVERTOV

SKYKOMISH RIVER RUNNING

Aware that summer baked the water clear
Today I came to see a fleet of trout
But as I wade the salmon limp away,
Their dorsal fins like gravestones in the air,
On their sides the red that kills the leaves.
Only sun can beat a stream this thin.
The river Sky is humming in my ear.

Where this river empties in the sea
Trout are waiting for September rain
To sting their thirst alive. If they speed
Upstream behind the kings and eat the eggs
The silvers lay, I'll pound the drum for rain.
But sunlight drums, the river is the same
Running like old water in my ear.

I will cultivate the trout, teach their fins
To wave in water like the legs of girls
Tormented black in pools. I will swim

A week to be a witness to the spawning,
Be a trout, eat the eggs of salmon —
Anything to live until the trout and rain
Are running in the river in my ear.

The river Sky is running in my hair.
I am floating past the troutless pools
Learning water is the easy way to go.
I will reach the sea before December
When the Sky is turning grey and wild
And rolling heavy from the east to say
Late autumn was an oriental child.

RICHARD F. HUGO

CLOSE-UP

Are all these stones
    yours
I said
and the mountain
pleased

but reluctant to
admit my praise could move it much

shook a little
and rained a windrow ring of stones
to show
that it was so

Stonefelled I got
up addled with dust

and shook
    myself
without much consequence

Obviously I said it doesn't pay
to get too
close up to
    greatness

and the mountain friendless wept
   and said
it couldn't help
itself

A. R. AMMONS

DREAM

I see you displaced, condensed, within my dream,
Yet here before me in your daily shape.
And think, can my dream touch you any way
Or move you as in it you otherwise moved?

I prosper in the dream, yet may it not
Touch you in any way or make you move.
It is the splendour of the possible
Not to appear in actual shape and form.

It is the splendour of the actual
So to be still and still be satisfied,
That any else or more becomes a dream,
Displaced, condensed, as by my dreamed regard.

JOSEPHINE MILES

THE FIRE AT ALEXANDRIA

Imagine it, a Sophocles complete,
the lost epic of Homer, including no doubt
his notes, his journals, and his observations
on blindness. But what occupies me most,
with the greatest hurt of grandeur, are those
magnificent authors, kept in scholarly rows,
whose names we have no passing record of:
scrolls unrolling Aphrodite like Cleopatra
bundled in a rug, the spoils of love.

Crates of volumes on the wharves,
and never opened, somehow started first.
And then, as though by imitation, the library
took. One book seemed to inspire another,
to remind it of the flame enclosed
within its papyrus like a drowsy torch.
The fire, roused perhaps by what it read,
its reedy song, raged Dionysian, a band
of Corybantes, down the halls now headlong.

For all their tears the scribes,
unable to douse the witty conflagration—
spicy too as Sappho, coiling, melted
with her girls: the Nile no less, reflecting,
burned—saw splendor fled, a day consummate
in sunset ardencies. Troy at its climax
(towers finally topless) could not have been
more awesome, not though the aromatic house
of Priam mortised the passionate moment.

For here inside the holocaust
like a flock of phoenixes the luminaries
hand in hand composed a frantic dance.

Now whenever I look into a flame
I try to catch a single countenance:
Cleopatra, winking out from every joint;
Tiresias eye to eye; a magnitude, long lost,
restored to the sky and the stars he once
struck unsuspected parts of into words.

Fire, and I see them resurrected,
madly crackling perfect birds, the world
lit up as by a golden school, the flashings
of the fathoms of set eyes.

T. WEISS

THE DEATH OF MYTH-MAKING

Two virtues ride, by stallion, by nag,
　To grind our knives and scissors:
Lantern-jawed Reason, squat Common Sense,
One courting doctors of all sorts,
　One, housewives and shopkeepers.

The trees are lopped, the poodles trim,
　The laborer's nails pared level
Since those two civil servants set
Their whetstone to the blunted edge
　And minced the muddling devil

Whose owl-eyes in the scraggly wood
　Scared mothers to miscarry,
Drove the dogs to cringe and whine,
And turned the farmboy's temper wolfish,
　The housewife's, desultory.

SYLVIA PLATH

From THE BEAN EATERS

WE REAL COOL

The pool players.
Seven at the Golden Shovel.

　　We real cool. We
　　Left school. We

　　Lurk late. We
　　Strike straight. We

　　Sing sin. We
　　Thin gin. We

　　Jazz June. We
　　Die soon.

GWENDOLYN BROOKS

THE SPIDER

I

The spider expects the cold of winter.
When the shadows fall in long Autumn
He congeals in a nest of paper, prepares
The least and minimal existence,
Obedient to nature. No other course
Is his; no other availed him when
In high summer he spun and furled
The gaudy catches. I am that spider,
Caught in nature, summer and winter.
You are the symbol of the seasons too.

II

Now to expatiate and temporize
This artful brag. I never saw so quieting
A sight as the dawn, dew-clenched foot-
Wide web hung on summer barn-eaves, spangled.
It moves to zephyrs that is tough as steel.
I never saw so finely-legged a creature
Walk so accurate a stretch as he,
Proud, capable, patient, confident.
To the eye he gave close penetration
Into real myth, the myth of you and me.

III

Yet, by moving eyesight off from this
There is another dimension. Near the barn,
Down meadow to shingle, no place for spiders,
The sea in large blue breathes in brainstorm tides,
Pirates itself away to ancient Spain,
Pirouettes past Purgatory to Paradise.
Do I feed deeper on a spider,
A close-hauled view upon windless meaning,
Or deeper a day or dance or doom bestride
On ocean's long reach, on parables of God?

RICHARD EBERHART

RETURNING TO ROOTS OF FIRST FEELING

Feld, groes or *goers, hus, doeg, dung,*
in field, grass, house, day and dung we share
with those that in the forests went
   singers and dancers out of the dream;
for cradles, goods and hallows came
   long before Christendom,
wars and warblers-of-the-word where

me bifel a ferly, a fairy me thoughte:
and those early and those late saw
some of them poets
a faire felde ful of folke fonde I there bitwene,
for the vain and the humble go into one Man
and as best we can we make his song,

a simple like making of night and day
encumbered by vestiges and forebodings
in words of need and hope striving
to awaken the old keeper of the living
and restore lasting melodies of his desire.

ROBERT DUNCAN

NUDE DESCENDING A STAIRCASE

Toe after toe, a snowing flesh,
a gold of lemon, root and rind,
she sifts in sunlight down the stairs
with nothing on. Nor on her mind.

We spy beneath the banister
a constant thresh of thigh on thigh;
her lips imprint the swinging air
that parts to let her parts go by.

One-woman waterfall, she wears
her slow descent like any drape
and pausing on the final stair,
collects her motions into shape.

X. J. KENNEDY

SONG

What I took in my hand
grew in weight. You must
understand it
was not obscene.

Night comes. We sleep.
Then if you know what
say it.
Don't pretend.

Guises are
what enemies wear. You
and I live
in a prayer.

Helpless. Helpless,
should I speak.
Would you.
What do you think of me.

No woman ever was,
was wiser
than you. None is
more true.

But fate, love, fate
scares me. What
I took in my hand
grows in weight.

ROBERT CREELEY

IN FAVOR OF ONE'S TIME

The spent purpose of a perfectly marvellous
life suddenly glimmers and leaps into flame
it's more difficult than you think to make charcoal
it's also pretty hard to remember life's marvellous
but there it is guttering choking then soaring
in the mirrored room of this consciousness
it's practically a blaze of pure sensibility

and however exaggerated at least something's going on
and the quick oxygen in the air will not go neglected
will not sulk or fall into blackness and peat

an angel flying slowly, curiously singes its wings
and you diminish for a moment out of respect
for beauty then flare up after all that's the angel
that wrestled with Jacob and loves conflict
as an athlete loves the tape, and we're off into
an immortal contest of actuality and pride
which is love assuming the consciousness of itself
as sky over all, medium of finding and founding
not just resemblance but the magnetic otherness
that that that stands erect in the spirit's glare
and waits for the joining of an opposite force's breath

so come the winds into our lives and last
longer than despair's sharp snake, crushed before it conquered
so marvellous is not just a poet's greenish namesake
and we live outside his garden in pure tempestuous rights

                                        FRANK O'HARA

POPULATION

            Like a flat sea,
            Here is where we are, the empty reaches
            Empty of ourselves

            Where dark, light, sound
            Shatter the mind born
            Alone to ocean

            Save we are
            A crowd, a population, those
            Born, those not yet dead, the moment's

            Populace, sea-borne and violent, finding
            Incredibly under the sense the rough deck
            Inhabited, and what it always was.

                                        GEORGE OPPEN

GRAVELLY RUN

I don't know somehow it seems sufficient
to see and hear whatever coming and going is,
losing the self to the victory
　　of stones and trees,
of bending, sand pit lakes, crescent

round groves of dwarf pine;
for it is not so much to know the self
as to know it as it is known
　　by galaxy and cedar cone,
as if birth had never found it

and death could never end it:
the swamp's slow water comes
down Gravelly Run fanning the long,
　　stone-held algal
hair and narrowing roils between

the shoulders of the highway bridge:
holly grows on the banks in the woods there,
and the cedars' gothic-clustered
　　spires could make
green religion in winter bones: so I

look and reflect, but the air's glass
jail seals each thing in its entity: no
use to make any philosophies here:
　　I see no
god in the holly, hear no song from

the snowbroken weeds: Hegel is not the winter
yellow in the pines: the sunlight has never
heard of trees: surrendered self among
　　unwelcoming forms: stranger,
hoist your burdens, get on down the road

                              A. R. AMMONS

INSIDE THE RIVER

Dark, deeply. A red.
All levels moving
A given surface.
Break this. Step down.
Follow your right
Foot nakedly in
To another body.
Put on the river
Like a fleeing coat,
A garment of motion,
Tremendous, immortal.
Find a still root

To hold you in it.
Let flowing create
A new, inner being:
As the source in the mountain
Gives water in pulses,
These can be felt at
The heart of the current.
And here it is only
One wandering step
Forth, to the sea.
Your freed hair floating
Out of your brain,

Wait for a coming
And swimming idea.
Live like the dead
In their flying feeling.
Loom as a ghost
When life pours through it.
Crouch in the secret
Released underground
With the earth of the fields
All around you, gone
Into purposeful grains
That stream like dust

In a holy hallway.
Weight more changed
Than that of one
Now being born.
Let go the root.
Move with the world
As the deep dead move,
Opposed to nothing.
Release. Enter the sea
Like a winding wind.
No. Rise. Draw breath.
Sing. See no one.

JAMES DICKEY

[HOW MANY MOMENTS MUST(AMAZING EACH]

how many moments must(amazing each
how many centuries)these more than eyes
restroll and stroll some never deepening beach

locked in foreverish time's tide at poise,

love alone understands:only for whom
i'll keep my tryst until that tide shall turn;
and from all selfsubtracting hugely doom
treasures of reeking innocence are born.

Then, with not credible the anywhere
eclipsing of a spirit's ignorance
by every wisdom knowledge fears to dare,

how the(myself's own self who's)child will dance!

and when he's plucked such mysteries as men
do not conceive—let ocean grow again

E. E. CUMMINGS

THE ILLUSTRATION—A FOOTNOTE

Months after the Muse
had come and gone across the lake of vision,
arose out of childhood the long-familiar
briefly-forgotten presaging of her image—

"The Light of Truth"—frontispiece
to "Parables from Nature", 1894—a picture
intending another meaning than that which it gave
(for I never read the story until now)

intending to represent folly
sinking into a black bog, but for me having meant
a mystery, of darkness, of beauty, of serious
dreaming pause and intensity

where not a will o' the wisp but
a star come to earth burned before the
closed all-seeing eyes
of that figure later seen as the Muse.

By which I learn to affirm
Truth's light at strange turns of the mind's road,
wrong turns that lead
over the border into wonder,

mistaken directions, forgotten signs
all bringing the soul's travels to a place
of origin, a well
under the lake where the Muse moves.

DENISE LEVERTOV

THE BLESSING

Just off the highway to Rochester, Minnesota,
Twilight bounds softly forth on the grass.
And the eyes of those two Indian ponies
Darken with kindness.
They have come gladly out of the willows
To welcome my friend and me.
We step over the barbed wire into the pasture
Where they have been grazing all day, alone.

They ripple tensely, they can hardly contain their happiness
That we have come.
They bow shyly as wet swans. They love each other.
There is no loneliness like theirs.
At home once more,
They begin munching the young tuffs of spring in the darkness.
I would like to hold the slenderer one in my arms,
For she has walked over to me
And nuzzled my left hand.
She is black and white,
Her mane falls wild on her forehead,
And the light breeze moves me to caress her long ear
That is delicate as the skin over a girl's wrist.
Suddenly I realize
That if I stepped out of my body I would break
Into blossom.

JAMES WRIGHT

FOR THE PASSING OF GROUCHO'S PURSUER

PLAYED ALWAYS BY MARGARET DUMONT

*"Someone oughta tear you down and put
up a new building"* — Groucho Marx

Now that high, oft affronted bosom heaves
A final sigh, crushed by the wrecker's ball;
Like a definitive mansard, it leaves
Our view an empty lot. Before the fall
The game was to make sex grotesque, but when

Was anything more grave? For us, our grace
Was being the yoohooed-at, naughty men
Whose eyes would lower, finally, from that face.
Death, be not bowed by that solidity
But bear her ever upward, cloud by cloud,
To where she sits with vast solemnity
Enthroned; and may we, some day, be allowed
    If not a life of constant flight there, than a
    Glimpse of that fierce green land of mink and henna.

JOHN HOLLANDER

NOTES FOR A HISTORY OF POETRY

When Memory's Fabled Daughter
Descended to the Word,
The lapping sound of water
Was profitably heard.
Through language set in motion
By river, stream, or ocean
Men acted their devotion,
Both tragic and absurd.

Absurdity was troubling:
See now the poet's task:
Leave histrionic doubling
To don a simpler mask.
Winds of the world were nipping;
The bardic robe was slipping:
The poet wanders, sipping
The sad, hypnotic flask.

Now tipsy with suggestion
He staggers all alone,
Resolving every question
To solipsistic moan.
The voice was human; therefore
We credited its flaws:
Now it's the blanks we care for,
And listen for the pause.

Then crossed with this deflation
Came ironies of style,
Importing conversation,
The squint sardonic smile.
Then "Sir" declines to "Mister",
And "Mister" falls to "Bud";
The hail becomes a whisper,
The rocks dissolve to mud,
Which purify to water
In critical amend,
And memory's fabled daughter
Is Silence in the end.

DAVID DAICHES

THE ASTRONOMERS OF MONT BLANC

Who are you there that from your icy tower
Inspect the colder distances, the far
Escape of your whole universe to night;
That watch the moon's blue craters, shadowy crust,
And blunted mountains mildly drift and glare,
Ballooned in ghostly earnest on your sight;
Who are you, and what hope persuades your trust?

It is your hope that you will know the end
And compass of our ignorant restraint
In that lost time where what was done is done
Forever as a havoc overhead.
Aging, you search to master in the faint
Persistent fortune which you gaze upon
The perfect order trusted to the dead.

EDGAR BOWERS

STARS OVER THE DORDOGNE

Stars are dropping thick as stones into the twiggy
Picket of trees whose silhouette is darker
Than the dark of the sky because it is quite starless.
The woods are a well. The stars drop silently.
They seem large, yet they drop, and no gap is visible.
Nor do they send up fires where they fall
Or any signal of distress or anxiousness.
They are eaten immediately by the pines.

Where I am at home, only the sparsest stars
Arrive at twilight, and then after some effort.
And they are wan, dulled by much traveling.
The smaller and more timid never arrive at all
But stay, sitting far out, in their own dust.
They are orphans. I cannot see them. They are lost.
But tonight they have discovered this river with no trouble;
They are scrubbed and self-assured as the great planets.

The Big Dipper is my only familiar.
I miss Orion and Cassiopeia's Chair. Maybe they are

Hanging shyly under the studded horizon
Like a child's too-simple mathematical problem.
Infinite number seems to be the issue up there.
Or else they are present, and their disguise so bright
I am overlooking them by looking too hard.
Perhaps it is the season that is not right.

And what if the sky here is no different,
And it is my eyes that have been sharpening themselves?
Such a luxury of stars would embarrass me.
The few I am used to are plain and durable;
I think they would not wish for this dressy backcloth
Or much company, or the mildness of the south.
They are too puritan and solitary for that—
When one of them falls it leaves a space,

A sense of absence in its old shining place.
And where I lie now, back to my own dark star,
I see those constellations in my head,
Unwarmed by the sweet air of this peach orchard.
There is too much ease here; these stars treat me too well.
On this hill, with its view of lit castles, each swung bell
Is accounting for its cow. I shut my eyes
And drink the small night chill like news of home.

SYLVIA PLATH

THE BLACK ART

A woman who writes feels too much,
those trances and portents!
As if cycles and children and islands
weren't enough; as if mourners and gossips
and vegetables were never enough.
She thinks she can warn the stars.
A writer is essentially a spy.
Dear love, I am that girl.

A man who writes knows too much,
such spells and fetiches!
As if erections and congresses and products

weren't enough; as if machines and galleons
and wars were never enough.
With used furniture he makes a tree.
A writer is essentially a crook.
Dear love, you are that man.

Never loving ourselves,
hating even our shoes and our hats,
we love each other, *precious, precious.*
Our hands are light blue and gentle.
Our eyes are full of terrible confessions.
But when we marry,
the children leave in disgust.
There is too much food and no one left over
to eat up all the weird abundance.

ANNE SEXTON

From FOUR DREAM SONGS

III

To William Meredith

The high ones die, die. They die. You look up and who's there?
—Easy, easy, Mr. Bones. I is on your side.
I smell your grief
—I sent my grief away. I cannot care
forever. With them all again & again I died
and cried, and I have to live.

—Now there *you* exaggerate, Sah. We hafta *die.*
That is our 'pointed task. Love & die.
—Yes; that makes sense.
But what makes sense between, then? What if I
roiling & babbling & braining, brood on why and
just sat on the fence?

—I doubts you did or do. DC choice is lost.
—It's fool's gold. But I go in for that.

The boy & the bear
looked at each other. Man all is tossed
& lost with groin-wounds by the grand bulls, cat.
William Faulkner's where?

(Frost being still around.)

JOHN BERRYMAN

DEATH'S THE CLASSIC LOOK

Death's the classic look. It goes
down stoneworks carved with Latin Prose
and Poetry. And scholar's Greek
that no one now can really speak,
though it's all guessed at. The long view
contains bits of Etruscan, too,
(as guessed at as the Greek is, but
no one yet has figured out
more than a first few words, and those
the names for fish, bird, water, rose
painted beside the painting of
what a dead man kept to love
inside his tomb). In back of that
the view runs desert-rimmed and flat
past writings that were things, not words:
roses, water, fish, and birds.
The thing before the letters came,
the name before there was a name.
And back of things themselves? Who knows?
Jungle spells it as it grows
where the damp among the shoots
waterlogs the classic roots,
and the skulls and bones of things
last half as long as a bird sings,
as a fish swims, as a rose fills,
opens, lets out its breath, and spills
into the sockets where things crawl,
and death looks like no look at all.

JOHN CIARDI

FROM HERACLITUS

Matter is palsy: the land heaving, water
breaking against it, the planet whirling
days in night. Even at the still point
of night I hear the jockeying for place
and each thing wrestling with itself
to be a wrestler. Is the stress that holds
them, whirling in themselves, an ache?
If so strained to shape and aching for release,
explode to peace! But I am here poised
within this eddy, sentenced to a shape,
and have to wrestle through a gust of violence
before I sleep; so may I make or augment
all these lights at night, so as to give out
all the temporary ornaments I can to peace.

ALAN DUGAN

FOR HIS FATHER

When I was young I looked high and low for a father,
And what blond sons you must have tried on then!
But only your blood could give us our two men
And in the end we settled for one another.

Whatever death is, it sets pretenders free.
The secret loss or boy or self-defense
That won me your affectionate pretense
Is in a grave. Now you judge only me.

But like a living son I go on railing
A little, or praising under my breath,
Not knowing the generosity of death,
Fearing your judgment on my old failing.

Dear ghost, take pleasure in our good report,
And bully me no further with my blame.
You use my eyes at last; I sign your name
Deliberately beneath my life and art.

WILLIAM MEREDITH

THE MAD SCENE

Again last night I dreamed the dream called Laundry.
In it, the sheets and towels of a life we were going to share,
The milk-stiff bibs, the shroud, each rag to be ever
Trampled or soiled, bled on or groped for blindly,
Came swooning out of an enormous willow hamper
Onto moon-marbly boards. We had just met. I watched
From outer darkness. I had dressed myself in clothes
Of a new fiber that never stains or wrinkles, never
Wears thin. The opera house sparkled with tiers
And tiers of eyes, like mine enlarged by belladonna,
Trained inward. There I saw the cloud-clot, gust by gust,
Form, and the lightning bite, and the roan mane unloosen.
Fingers were running in panic over the flute's nine gates.
Why did I flinch? I loved you. And in the downpour laughed
To see us wrung white, gnarled together, one
Topmost mordent of wisteria,
As the lean tree burst into grief.

JAMES MERRILL

IF THE BIRDS KNEW

It is better this year.
And the clothes they wear
In the gray unweeded sky of our earth
There is no possibility of change
Because all of the true fragments are here.
So I was glad of the fog's
Taking me to you
Undetermined summer thing eaten
Of grief and passage—where you stay.
The wheel is ready to turn again.
When you have gone it will light up,
The shadow of the spokes to drown
Your departure where the summer knells
Speak to grown dawn.
There is after all a kind of promise
To the affair of the waiting weather.
We have learned not to be tired
Among the lanterns of this year of sleep
But someone pays—no transparency
Has ever hardened us before

209

To long piers of silence, and hedges
Of understanding, difficult passing
From one lesson to the next and the coldness
Of the consistency of our lives'
Devotion to immaculate danger.
A leaf would have settled the disturbance
Of the atmosphere, but at that high
Valley's point disbanded
Clouds that rocks smote newly
The person or persons involved
Parading slowly through the sunlit fields
Not only as though the danger did not exist
But as though the birds were in on the secret.

JOHN ASHBERY

FEVER 103°

Pure? What does it mean?
The tongues of hell
Are dull, dull as the triple

Tongues of dull, fat Cerberus
Who wheezes at the gate. Incapable
Of licking clean

The aguey tendon, the sin, the sin.
The tinder cries.
The indelible smell

Of a snuffed candle!
Love, love, the low smokes roll
From me like Isadora's scarves, I'm in a fright

One scarf will catch and anchor in the wheel,
Such yellow sullen smokes
Make their own element. They will not rise,

But trundle round the globe
Choking the aged and the meek,
The weak

Hothouse baby in its crib,
The ghastly orchid
Hanging its hanging garden in the air,

Devilish leopard!
Radiation turned it white
And killed it in an hour.

Greasing the bodies of adulterers
Like Hiroshima ash and eating in.
The sin. The sin.

Darling, all night
I have been flickering, off; on, off; on.
The sheets grow heavy as a lecher's kiss.

Three days. Three nights.
Lemon water, chicken
Water, water make me retch.

I am too pure for you or anyone.
Your body
Hurts me as the world hurts God. I am a lantern—

My head a moon
Of Japanese paper, my gold beaten skin
Infinitely delicate and infinitely expensive.

Does not my heat astound you! And my light!
All by myself I am a huge camellia
Glowing and coming and going, flush on flush.

I think I am going up,
I think I may rise—
The beads of hot metal fly, and I love, I

Am a pure acetylene
Virgin
Attended by roses,

By kisses, by cherubim,
By whatever these pink things mean!
Not you, nor him

Nor him, nor him
(My selves dissolving, old whore petticoats)—
To Paradise.

SYLVIA PLATH

From NINE DREAM SONGS

SNOW LINE

It was wet & white & swift and where I am
I don't know. It was dark and then
it isn't.
I wish the barker would come. There seems to be to eat
nothing. I am unusually tired.
I'm alone too.

If only the strange one with so few legs would come,
I'd say my prayers out of my mouth, as usual.
Where are his notes I loved?
There may be horribles; it's hard to tell.
The barker nips me but somehow I feel
he too is on my side.

I'm too alone. I see no end. If we could all
run, even that would be better. I am hungry.
The sun is not hot.
It's not a good position I am in.
If I had to do the whole thing over again
I wouldn't.

JOHN BERRYMAN

AFTER LORCA

The clock says "When will it be morning?"
The sun says "Noon hurt me."
The river cries with its mouthful of mud
And the sea moves every way without moving.

Out of my ear grew a reed
Never touched by mouth.
Paper yellows, even without flame,
But in words carbon has already become diamond.

A supple river of mirrors I run on
Where great shadows rise to the glance,
Flowing all forward and bringing
The world through my reflection.

A voice like a ghost that is not
Rustle the dead in passage
Leaving the living chilled,
Wipe clear the pure glass of stone.

Wipe clear the pure stone of flesh.
A song tickling God's ear
Till he laughs and catches it with his hand.
A song with a man's face
That God holds up in his fingers.

TED HUGHES

THE WORDS

Wind, bird, and tree,
Water, grass, and light:
In half of what I write
Roughly or smoothly
Year by impatient year,
The same six words recur.

I have as many floors
As meadows or rivers,
As much still air as wind
And as many cats in mind
As nests in the branches
To put an end to these.

Instead, I take what is:
The light beats on the stones,
And wind over water shines
Like long grass through the trees,
As I set loose, like birds
In a landscape, the old words.

DAVID WAGONER

SEEING AUDEN OFF

Ithaca last night, Syracuse at noon, Cedar Rapids tonight.
His face cracked like a dry salt flat, a line for every poem,
he tries two airport Gibsons, reserved (behind dark glasses)
for his flight. Sleet primes the runways, candlelight
preserves the bar. The jets suck air, burning their own feces.
Jakarta, Shannon, Idlewild, are everywhere the same.
Ithaca and Syracuse behind him, Iowa tonight.

He autographs deserted landing strips. In Iowa tonight
he'll sign five gins, whet his faults, and lust for limestone.
He has his autopilot on; who am I to name the pieces
into which a poet cracks? Fire and sleet and candlelight.
I gulp the beer he pays for, and see through his smeared glasses
the dark impossibility of home: we drink the price of being done
with Ithaca and Syracuse; I wave him off, toward Iowa, tonight.

PHILIP BOOTH

HERE LIES . . .

Here lies a poet who would not write
His soul runs screaming through the night,
"Oh give me paper, give me pen,
And I will very soon begin."

Poor Soul, keep silent. In Death's clime
There's no pen, paper, notion — and no Time.

STEVIE SMITH

LIKE ROUSSEAU

She stands beside me, stands away,
the vague indifference
of her dreams. Dreaming, to go on,
and go on there, like animals fleeing
the rise of the earth. But standing
intangible, my lust a worked anger
a sweating close covering, for the crudely salty soul.

Then back off, and where you go? Box of words
and pictures. Steel balloons tied to our mouths.
The room fills up, and the house. Street tilts.
City slides, and buildings slide into the river.
What is there left, to destroy? That is not close,
or closer. Leaning away in the angle of language.
Pumping and pumping, all our eyes criss cross
and flash. It is the lovers pulling down empty structures.
They wait and touch and watch their dreams
eat the morning.

LE ROI JONES

ABOUT MY POEMS

How fashionably sad my early poems are!
On their clipped lawns and hedges the snows fall;
Rains beat against the tarpaulins of their porches,
Where, Sunday mornings, the bored children sprawl,
Reading the comics, before the parents rise.
—The rhymes, the meters, how they paralyze!

Who walks out through their streets tonight? No one.
You know these small towns, how all traffic stops
At ten; the corner streetlamps gathering moths;
And the pale mannequins waiting in dark shops,
Undressed, and ready for the dreams of men.
—Now the long silence. Now the beginning again.

DONALD JUSTICE

METAPHYSIC OF SNOW

Tumbling, pausing, leaping, knocking together,
but always in ranks and serries, grimly in order,
herded by wind aslant the insentient trees,
the cold cattle of heaven come down, come down.

Now they are dancing, swinging in perfect figures,
in perfect time, with a thousand subtle kinds
of counter-point and turn and counter-turn;
stars trail from their horns, leap from their shoulders.

Arm in glittering arm, the galaxies
wheel like fat grandes-dames at the whim of air,
waltz after wheezing waltz, night after night,
or fling up their jewelled skirts and fall into bed.

The wind blows as he goes on his icy flute,
and numb, mindless, stumbling, willy nilly,
drunk on the stream of his music the cattle come,
reeling to left and right, and always, down.

DONALD FINKEL

THINGS WE DREAMT WE DIED FOR

Flags of all sorts.
The literary life.
Each time we dreamt we'd done
the gentlemanly thing,
covering our causes
in closets full of bones
to remove ourselves forever
from dearest possibilities,
the old weapons re-injured us,
the old armies conscripted us,
and we gave in to getting even,
a little less like us
if a lot less like others.
Many, thus, gained fame
in the way of great plunderers,
retiring to the university

to cultivate grand plunder-gardens
in the service of literature,
the young and no more wars.
Their continuing tributes
make them our greatest saviours,
whose many fortunes are followed
by the many who have not one.

MARVIN BELL

From THROUGH THE SMOKE HOLE

For Don Allen

I

There is another world above this one; or outside of this one;
the way to it is thru the smoke of this one, & the hole that
smoke goes through. The ladder is the way through the
smoke hole; the ladder holds up, some say, the world above;
it might have been a tree or pole; I think it is merely a way.

Fire is at the foot of the ladder. The fire is in the center. The
walls are round. There is also another world below or inside
this one. The way there is down thru smoke. It is not
necessary to think of a series.

Raven and Magpie do not need the ladder. They fly thru the
smoke holes shrieking and stealing. Coyote falls thru; we
recognize him only as a clumsy relative, a father in old clothes
we don't wish to see with our friends.

It is possible to cultivate the fields of our own world without
much thought for the others. When men emerge from below
we see them as the masked dancers of our magic dreams.
When men disappear down, we see them as plain men going
somewhere else. When men disappear up we see them as
great heroes shining through the smoke. When men come
back from above they fall thru and tumble; we don't really
know them; Coyote, as mentioned before.

GARY SNYDER

"THE WISH TO BE BELIEVED"

It is never enough to know what you want.
The brick in your hand, dampened but solid, crumbles,
and a boundary being built, in the midst of building,
stops. (Why shouldn't one say what it is like?
How would they ever know, otherwise?)

You find in your pocket a key, two keys,
one with a curlicued stem, heavy, absurd,
the other perfectly blank, anonymous.
Who knows what they open; you glance at keyholes.
It is like—you can't, after all, say exactly.

And the rooms, supposing you enter them calmly,
are different from your own; one is bare,
with a gilt-framed mirror facing the door.
Suppose you are tempted to insert your face—
you see a face, and the door closing.

And you go on past the half-built boundary,
clicking the keys together, entering.
And you reach, finally, a vivid, absolute place,
and stand in the center, saying to someone,
"Believe. Believe this is what I see."

                              MONA VAN DUYN

THE CORRESPONDENCE-SCHOOL INSTRUCTOR SAYS GOODBYE TO HIS POETRY STUDENTS

Goodbye, lady in Bangor,
who sent me snap
shots of yourself, after definitely hinting
you were beautiful;
goodbye, Miami Beach
urologist, who enclosed plain
brown envelopes for the return of your *very*
"Clinical Sonnets";
goodbye, manufacturer
of brassieres on the Coast, whose eclogues give
the fullest treatment in literature yet
to the sagging

breast *motif*; and
goodbye, you in San Quentin, who wrote,
"Being German my hero is Hitler!" instead of
"Sincerely Yours", at the end of
neat-scripted, scented letters demolishing
the Pre-Raphaelites.

I swear to you, it was
just my way of cheering myself up,
as I licked
all the stamped, self-addressed envelopes,
the game I had
of trying to guess which one of you, this time,
had poisoned his glue. I did care.
I did read each poem entire.
I did say what I thought was the truth
in the mildest words I knew. But I admit
I am relieved it is over.
Toward the last I could feel only pity
for that urge toward
more life
your poems kept smothering in words, the odor
of which, days later, would tingle
in your nostrils, as new, God-given impulses
to write.

Goodbye,
you who have become, for me, postmarks again
of unlikely towns—Burnt Cabins, Eureka, Hornell—
their loneliness
given away in poems, only their solitude
kept.

                    GALWAY KINNELL

SWAN AND SHADOW

```
                    Dusk
                  Above  the
              water hang the
                        loud
                       flies
                      Here
                      O so
                      gray
                      then
                      What                    A pale signal will   appear
                      When              Soon before  its shadow  fades
                     Where         Here in this pool of opened eye
                  In us        No Upon us As at    the very edges
                of where we take    shape in the dark air
                  this object hares its image awakening
                    ripples of recognition that will
                        brush darkness up into light
   even after this bird this hour both drift by atop the perfect sad instant now
                    already passing out of sight
                  toward yet-untroubled reflection
                this  image hears    its object darkening
                into memorial    shades Scattered bits of
                Light      No of water Or something across
                water          Breaking up No Being regathered
                Soon           Yet by then a swan will have
                gone                 Yes Out of mind into what
                vast
                pale
                hush
                of a
                place
                      past
            sudden dark as
              if a swan
                sang
```

JOHN HOLLANDER

THE BEAST IN THE SPACE

Shut up. Shut up. There's nobody here.
If you think you hear somebody knocking
On the other side of the words, pay
No attention. It will be only
The great creature that thumps its tail
On silence on the other side.
If you do not even hear that
I'll give the beast a quick skelp
And through Art you'll hear it yelp.

The beast that lives on silence takes
Its bite out of either side.
It pads and sniffs between us. Now
It comes and laps my meaning up.
Call it over. Call it across
This curious, necessary space.
Get off, you terrible inhabiter
Of silence. I'll not have it. Get
Away to whoever it is will have you.

W. S. GRAHAM

USES OF POETRY

Love poems they read
Were work of an aging man
Alone and celibate
Who published them in joy
Of his craftsman's skill,
How they folded into each other.

Many a lust-starched boy
Read them aloud to his girl
Till her widening eyes darkened
Till her breath trembled thin
Till the boy threw down the book
And they folded into each other.

WINFIELD TOWNLEY SCOTT

SLOWLY, SLOWLY WISDOM GATHERS

Slowly, slowly wisdom gathers:
Golden dust in the afternoon,
Somewhere between the sun and me,
Sometimes so near that I can see,
Yet never settling, late or soon.

Would that it did, and a rug of gold
Spread west of me a mile or more:
Not large, but so that I might lie
Face up, between the earth and sky,
And know what none has known before.

Then I would tell as best I could
The secrets of that shining place:
The web of the world, how thick, how thin,
How firm, with all things folded in;
How ancient, and how full of grace.

MARK VAN DOREN

CWMRHYDYCEIRW ELEGIACS*

Go, swallow, and tell, now that the summer is dying,
Spirits who loved him in time, where in the earth he is laid.
Dumb secrets are here, hard as the elm-roots in winter;
We who are left here confront words of inscrutable calm.
Life cuts into stone this that on earth is remembered,
How for the needs of the dead loving provision was made.
Strong words remain true, under the hammer of Babel:
Sleeps in the heart of the rock all that a god would restore.

Never shall time be stilled in the quarry of Cwmrhydyceirw,
Not while the boulder recoils under the force of the fuse.
Tablets imprisoned by rock, inert in the sleeping arena,
Quake in the shudder of air, knowing the swallow has passed.
One grief is enough, one tongue, to transfigure the ages:
Let our tears for the dead earn the forgiveness of dust.

VERNON WATKINS

*In a letter to *Poetry* just a few months before his death the poet told us that the
Welsh name in the title is pronounced Coomrheedercyroo. "It means 'Valley of the
Giants,' and in this quarry I found the memorial stone for Dylan Thomas, presented
by Caedmon, which is in Cwmdonkin Park in Swansea."

IMPLOSIONS

The world's
not wanton
only wild and wavering

I wanted to choose words that even you
would have to be changed by

Take the word
of my pulse, loving and ordinary
Send out your signals, hoist
your dark scribbled flags
but take
my hand

All wars are useless to the dead

My hands are knotted in the rope
and I cannot sound the bell
My hands are frozen to the switch
and I cannot throw it
The foot is in the wheel

When all is over and we're lying
in a stubble of blistered flowers
eyes gaping, mouths staring
dusted with crushed arterial blues
barred with tiger-lily reds

I'll have done nothing
even for you

ADRIENNE RICH

THE COWS AT NIGHT

The moon was like a full cup tonight,
too heavy, and sank in the mist
soon after dark, leaving for light

faint stars and the silver leaves
of milkweed beside the road,
gleaming before my car.

Yet I like driving at night
in summer and in Vermont:
the brown road through the mist

of mountain-dark, among farms
so quiet, and roadside willows
opening out where I saw

the cows. Always a shock
to think of them, those breathings
close to me in the great dark.

I stopped, taking my flashlight
to the pasture fence. They turned
to me where they lay, sad

and beautiful faces in the dark,
and I counted them—forty
near and far in the pasture,

turning to me, sad and beautiful
like girls very long ago
who were innocent, and sad

because they were innocent,
and beautiful because they were
sad. I switched off my light.

But I did not want to go,
not yet, nor knew what to do
if I should stay, for how

in that great darkness could I explain
anything, anything at all.
I stood by the fence. And then

very gently it began to rain.

HAYDEN CARRUTH

DEMONSTRATION

The loudspeaker repeating the same message
The children running on the grass
The people & the precise hexagons of the cobbles

From high up on the wall
Everything takes this quality of measure
The action of falling apart & together

It is a new thing with us
The game of death on the squares of this board
The calculation of moves & counters

The sleek cat on the ledge curled to an oblong
The bus noise & the park & the towers of the city
Or — We have known this before but differently

HUGH SEIDMAN

THE KING'S MEN

What is it, inside them and undeniable,
that mourns him? that drives them, searching
for the moon-shaped tracks of his horse,
a glint of armor within a maze of pines?

He'd know their barbarous need would never wane.
They will keep on to the next horizon
where he waits. They will keep on, lowering
their barred visors against the setting sun.

WILLIAM HEYEN

FIRE ISLAND

The Milky Way above,
the milky waves beside,
when the sand is night

the sea is galaxy.
The unseparate stars
mark a twining coast

with phosphorescent surf
in the black sky's trough.
Perhaps we walk on black

star ash, and watch
the milks of light
foam forward, swish and spill

while other watchers, out
walking in their white,
great swerve, gather

our low spark,
our little Way the dark
glitter in their sight.

MAY SWENSON

INVOCATION

Silent, about-to-be-parted-from house.
Wood creaking, trying to sigh, impatient.
Clicking of squirrel-teeth in the attic.
Denuded beds, couches stripped of serapes.

Deep snow shall block all entrances
and oppress the roof and darken
the windows. O Lares,
don't leave.
The house yawns like a bear.
Guard its profound dreams for us,
that it return to us when we return.

DENISE LEVERTOV

THE GAME

Let's spin the bottle
No I don't want to be kissed

Sometimes I feel my arm
Is turning into a tree

Or hardening to stone
Past memory of green

I've a long way to go
Who never learned to pray

O the night is coming on
And I am nobody's son

Father it's true
But only for a day

STANLEY KUNITZ

HANDBOOK OF VERSIFICATION

One thought the recurring "image" in the poet's song an
    instance of consciousness,

Clear, clear day, in sun, one's majority upon one, it
    is seen to be simple obsession, and helpless,

The mind careening through the infinite spaces of itself
    snags on some plain word:

Through and between whose familiar letters the true
    true image of what happened: of the blank world.

GILBERT SORRENTINO

COUNTERPARTS

There is no sky today. Echoes of birds
worry their way northward. They must have
everything repeated many times. You are here
and elsewhere, your face breeding like fear.
It is not for nothing that I keep my hands
raised for the fall. This is a country of smaller wars.

You have your office and ranch house, your foreign car
and family. You are still not necessary. I see
your face in a photograph from the war, surrounded
by soldiers convinced by their smiles. Later
there will be that look of faint surprise
as you meet the world and lie down to be counted.

The colors of blood are legion. Of necessity
your name must be also. Choose any direction
and it will lead to the heart. We call it a diamond.
Placed on the ground, we heap stones around it,
logs over it. What loss to a two car family?
We bring flowers. In error, people will call it a funeral.

Days pass, fires to be tended—their flames
like small fingers looking for your eyes. You have
already torn them from you. All things desire
to be surrounded by stone. There is rain on my hands.
There is the steady thud of birds falling into hills
sloping with sheep. We memorize the art of decay.

A swift and pervading grey slips through my fingers,
cloud covered and accustomed to war. A bone
is my weapon. It may not have been mine. Each end
is sharpened and carefully aimed. The ground
and pine boughs hiss a warning. There are rumours
of summer. There are seasons no longer acceptable.

                                        STEPHEN DOBYNS

THE MESSENGER

Is this man turning angel as he stares
At one red flower whose name he does not know,
    The velvet face the black-tipped hairs?

His eyes dilated like a cat's at night,
His lips move somewhat but he does not speak
    Of what completes him through his sight.

His body makes to imitate the flower,
Kneeling, with splayed toes pushing at the soil,
    The source, crude, granular, and sour.

His stillness answers like a looking glass
The flower's, it is repose of unblown flame
    That nests within the glow of grass.

Later the news, to branch from sense and sense,
Bringing their versions of the flower in small
    Outward into intelligence.

But meanwhile, quiet and reaching as a flame,
He bends, gazing not at but into it,
    Tough stalk, and face without a name.

                              THOM GUNN

HOMOSEXUALITY

So we are taking off our masks, are we, and keeping
our mouths shut? as if we'd been pierced by a glance!

The song of an old cow is not more full of judgment
than the vapors which escape one's soul when one is sick;

so I pull the shadows around me like a puff
and crinkle my eyes as if at the most exquisite moment

of a very long opera, and then we are off!
without reproach and without hope that our delicate feet

will touch the earth again, let alone "very soon."
It is the law of my own voice I shall investigate.

I start like ice, my finger to my ear, my ear
to my heart, that proud cur at the garbage can

in the rain. It's wonderful to admire oneself
with complete candor, tallying up the merits of each

of the latrines. 14th Street is drunken and credulous,
53rd tries to tremble but is too at rest. The good

love a park and the inept a railway station,
and there are the divine ones who drag themselves up

and down the lengthening shadow of an Abyssinian head
in the dust, trailing their long elegant heels of hot air

crying to confuse the brave "It's a summer day,
and I want to be wanted more than anything else in the world."

FRANK O'HARA

HOPE

On the avenue the faces change each day,
      washed like white pebbles on the sand.
    The undertow rolls them. Some must swim away

to form new coral islands. Some swarm, like bees,
      around a silver monarch building an empire
    from the mouth of the Amazon to the Hebrides.

But most, like friends, are turned by the water's care
      into smooth round stones that harden as they grow old,
    etched with error and excessive wear.

They bear their burdens sadly, for they bear them long.
      They barter scars of tragedies for fears
    although, like old religions, all prove wrong.

From this coarse commerce a lover picks by day
      what he can. His hand in his pocket smiles that one
    warm stone remains when the rest are washed away.

F. D. REEVE

BLACK MAPS

Not the attendance of stones,
nor the applauding wind,
shall let you know
you have arrived,

nor the sea that celebrates
only departures,
nor the mountains,
nor the dying cities.

Nothing will tell you
where you are.
Each moment is a place
you've never been.

You can walk
believing you cast
a light around you.
But how will you know?

The present is always dark.
Its maps are black,
rising from nothing,
describing,

in their slow ascent
into themselves,
their own voyage,
its emptiness,

the bleak, temperate
necessity of its completion.
As they rise into being
they are like breath.

And if they are studied at all
it is only to find,
too late, what you thought
were concerns of yours

do not exist.
Your house is not marked
on any of them,
nor are your friends,

waiting for you to appear,
nor are your enemies,
listing your faults.
Only you are there,

saying hello
to what you will be,
and the black grass
is holding up the black stars.

MARK STRAND

NIGHTLETTER

The night is a furrow, a queasy, insistent wound. Heavy the
flies hang, slow wheel the lingering birds. And the needle
between the fingers, stitching, stitching? Sutures, it wants to
say, O, sutures, but finds no edge.

When they fold your skin for a boutonniere, will it flower?
When they give your tongue to the flames, will the ashes
speak for themselves? The thing that is not left out always
is what is missing. Everything's certain.

CHARLES WRIGHT

PLAY

Nothing's going to become of anyone
except death:
    therefore: it's okay
to yearn
too high:
the grave accommodates
swell rambunctiousness &

ruin's not
compromised by magnificence:

the cut-off point
liberates us to the
common disaster: so
    pick a perch—
apple bough for example in bloom—
tune up
and if you like

drill imagination right through necessity:
it's all right:
it's been taken care of:

is allowed, considering

A. R. AMMONS

THE MAGI

Toward world's end, through the bare
Beginnings of winter, they are traveling again.
How many winters have we seen it happen,
Watched the same sign come forward as they pass
Cities sprung around this route their gold
Engraved on the desert, and yet
Held our peace, these
Being the Wise, come to see at the accustomed hour
Nothing changed: roofs, the barn
Blazing in darkness, all they wish to see.

LOUISE GLÜCK

CLIMBING YOU

I want to understand the steep thing
That climbs ladders in your throat.
I can't make sense of you.
Everywhere I look you're there—
a vast landmark, a volcano
poking its head through the clouds,
Gulliver sprawled across Lilliput.

I climb into your eyes, looking.
The pupils are black painted stage flats.
They can be pulled down like window shades.
I switch on a light in your iris.
Your brain ticks like a bomb.

In your offhand, mocking way
you've invited me into your chest.
Inside: the blur that poses as your heart.
I'm supposed to go in with a torch
or maybe hot-water bottles
& defrost it by hand
as one defrosts an old refrigerator.
It will shudder & sigh
(the icebox to the insomniac).

Oh there's nothing like love between us.
You're the mountain, I am climbing you.
If I fall, you won't be all to blame,
but you'll wait years maybe
for the next doomed expedition.

ERICA JONG

LOST

Stand still. The trees ahead and bushes beside you
Are not lost. Wherever you are is called Here,
And you must treat it as a powerful stranger,
Must ask permission to know it and be known.
The forest breathes. Listen. It answers,
I have made this place around you.

If you leave it, you may come back again, saying Here.
No two trees are the same to Raven.
No two branches are the same to Wren.
If what a tree or a bush does is lost on you,
You are surely lost. Stand still. The forest knows
Where you are. You must let it find you.

DAVID WAGONER

THE LIFE BESIDE THIS ONE

In the life you lead
Beside this one,
It is natural for you
To resemble America.
You require one woman;
You give her your name.

You work, you love;
You take satisfaction.
You are the president of something.
You are the same.

The children are clean,
They turn into lawyers.
They write long letters
And come home for Christmas.

It is a kind of Connecticut
Not to be twenty-five again.
Carefully in the evening
You do not think
Of the life you lead
Beside this one.

JOHN N. MORRIS

CREMATORIUM

Where laurel hedges hide the coal and coke
　　Our lawn-surrounded crematorium lies;
And every half-an-hour a puff of smoke
　　Shows what we loved dissolving in the skies—
　　Dear hands, dear feet, dear laughter-lighted eyes
And smiling lips which waited for a joke.

Now no one seems to know quite what to say:
　　Friends are so altered by the passing years—
Well anyhow it's not so cold today
　　And thus we try to dissipate our fears.
I am the Resurrection and the Life!
Strong, sly, and painful, doubt inserts its knife.

JOHN BETJEMAN

POETRY

The old forms are like birdhouses that
have been made homes so long they are
full of stuffing. Only the rarest birds
can squeeze in and out of the doorways. And
then they can't move around much inside, but
keep peeping the same sounds. Which the
stuffing almost entirely insulates. But
still they stay stuck, up on their poles.
And we keep listening hard for voices
to come out of them. And they do.

GREG KUZMA

THE VOWELS OF ANOTHER LANGUAGE

The road twisted through tongues of rock
And his mind kept changing yet he could not stop
To ask why he felt for these strangers
Feelings for which he had no name

TOM DISCH

DIDO: SWARMING

I am the ruined queen:
Imperious, go down, go down.
I cling to trees till the black
clotted bodies open me,

and one thick circle. Swarm in the air.
The rich round honey jar
is empty now. The husk sloughs off.
I go where no bees are.

Sting one last time! They say
stabbed swans disguise their throats
with song. How inadvised
to choke on the first note,

buzzing in misery, to vibrate
in the throng like any fly.
Remind me I am queen
and warm me while I die

wrapped in my stiffened wings:
I should have had the globe!
Vein in the rigid wrist instead;
I harden like a scab.

KATHLEEN SPIVACK

NEGATIVES

This is the light we dream in,
The milk light of midnight, the full moon
Reversing the balance like shapes on a negative:
The chalk lulls, the spectral sky,
The black rose in flame,
Its odors and glittery hooks
Waiting for something to snag.

The mulberries wink like dimes;
Fat sheep, the mesquite and chaparral
Graze at their own sweet speed,

The earth white sugar;
Two miles below, and out,
The surf has nothing to add.

Is this what awaits us, amorphous
Cobalt and zinc, a wide tide
Of brilliance we cannot define
Or use, and leafless, without guilt;
No guidelines or flutter, no
Cadence to pinpoint, no no?

Silence. As though the doorway behind
Us were liquid, were black water;
As though we might enter; as though
The ferry were there,
Ready to take us across
—Remembering now, unwatermarked,
The blackout like scarves in our new hair.

CHARLES WRIGHT

TO D—, DEAD BY HER OWN HAND

My dear, I wonder if before the end
You ever thought about a children's game—
I'm sure you must have played it too—in which
You ran along a narrow garden wall
Pretending it to be a mountain ledge
So steep a snowy darkness fell away
On either side to deeps invisible;
And when you felt your balance being lost
You jumped because you feared to fall, and thought
For only an instant: that was when I died.

That was a life ago. And now you've gone,
Who would no longer play the grown-ups' game
Where, balanced on the ledge above the dark,
You go on running and you don't look down,
Nor ever jump because you fear to fall.

HOWARD NEMEROV

THE POET'S FAREWELL TO HIS TEETH

Now you are going, what can I do but wish you
(as my wife used to say) "every success
in your chosen field".

What we have seen together! Doctor X,
having gagged us, hurling his forceps to the floor
and denouncing our adolescent politics,

or the time we caught trench-mouth in Iowa City
and had to drive west slowly and haltingly,
spitting in all the branches of the Missouri.

Cigar-stained and tired of cavities, you leave.
It is time to go back to the pure world of teeth
and rest, and compose yourselves for the last eruption.

As to those things in a glass by the bathroom sink
they will never communicate with me as you have done
fragile and paranoid, sensing the world around you

as wild drills and destructive caramel, getting even
for neglect by waking me into the pain of dawn,
that empty and intimate world of our bitter sharing.

Go, under that cool light. I will remember you:
the paper reports that people may still feel pain
in their missing teeth, as with any amputation.

I hope you relax by the shadowy root canals,
and thinking of me with kindness, but not regret,
toast me just once in the local anaesthetic.

WILLIAM DICKEY

PARABOLA

Year after year the princess lies asleep
Until the hundred years foretold are done,
Easily drawing her enchanted breath.
Caught on the monstrous thorns around the keep,
Bones of the youths who sought her, one by one
Rot loose and rattle to the ground beneath.

But when the Destined Lover at last shall come,
For whom alone Fortune reserves the prize,
The thorns give way; he mounts the cobwebbed stair;
Unerring he finds the tower, the door, the room,
The bed where, waking at his kiss she lies
Smiling in the loose fragrance of her hair.

That night, embracing on the bed of state,
He ravishes her century of sleep
And she repays the debt of that long dream;
Future and Past compose their vast debate;
His seed now sown, her harvest ripe to reap
Enact a variation on the theme.

For in her womb another princess waits,
A sleeping cell, a globule of bright dew.
Jostling their way up that mysterious stair,
A horde of lovers bursts between the gates,
All doomed but one, the destined suitor, who
By luck first reaches her and takes her there.

A parable of all we are or do!
The life of Nature is a formal dance
In which each step is ruled by what has been
And yet the pattern emerges always new:
The marriage of linked cause and random chance
Gives birth perpetually to the unforeseen.

One parable for the body and the mind:
With science and heredity to thank,
The heart is quite predictable as a pump,
But, let love change its beat, the choice is blind.
"Now" is a cross-roads where all maps prove blank,
And no-one knows which way the cat will jump.

So here stand I, by birth a cross between
Determined pattern and incredible chance,
Each with an equal share in what I am.
Though I should read the code stored in the gene,
Yet the blind lottery of circumstance
Mocks all solutions to its cryptogram.

As in my flesh, so in my spirit stand I
When does this hundred years draw to its close?
The hedge of thorns before me gives no clue.
My predecessor's carcass, shrunk and dry,
Stares at me through the spikes. O well, here goes!
I have this thing, and only this, to do.

A. D. HOPE

ON HEARING A NEW ESCALATION

From time one I've been reading slaughter,
seeing the same bewildered face of a child
staring at nothing beside his dead mother
in Egypt, the pyramid blueprints approved,
the phrases of national purpose streaming
from the mouth of some automated sphynx.
Day on day, the same photographed suffering,
the bitterness, the opportune hate handed down
from Xerxes to Nixon, a line strong
as transatlantic cable and stale ideals.
Killing's still in though glory is out of style.
And what does it come to, this blood cold
in the streets and a history book printed
and bound with such cost saving American
methods, the names and dates are soon bones?
Beware certain words: Enemy. Liberty. Freedom.
Believe those sounds and you're aiming a bomb.

RICHARD HUGO

MAY, 1972

Soft May mists are here again.
There, the war goes on.
Beside the privet the creamy
white tulips are extra
fine this year. There,
foliage curls blackened back:
it will, it must
return. But when?
A cardinal enchants me
with its song.
All war is wrong. The grass
here is green and buttoned
down with dandelions. A car
goes by. What peace. It—
the war—goes on. Fleeing
people. The parrot tulips
look like twisted guts.
Blood on green.
Here, a silent scream.
Can we, in simple justice,
desert our sought allies?
Draw out: I do not know.
I know the war is wrong.
We have it in us
to triumph over hate and
death, or so
the suburban spring suggests.
Here, the drive is wet
with mist. There,
the war goes on. Children
are more valuable than
flowers: what a choice
to make! The war
must end. It goes on.

JAMES SCHUYLER

WINTER DRIVE

Fallow fields, dark pewter sky,
Steely light on the wet plain,
Evening falls in freezing rain
With a promise and a lie.

Promise in the leaden sky,
In the sodden fields bleak shine,
In the slate vats full of wine,
In the knowledge that we die.

But the lie is in the soul,
And it rots the world we have
Till there's nothing left to save.

Dying world and deadened sky;
Traffic streams beyond control.
What is left to make us try?

JAMES MC AULEY

JULY 4TH

Gradual bud and bloom and seedfall speeded up
are these mute explosions in slow motion.
From vertical shoots above the sea, the fire
flowers open, shedding their petals. Black waves,
turned more than moonwhite, pink ice, lightning blue,
echo our gasps of admiration as they crash
and hush. Another bush ablaze snicks straight up.
A gap like heartstop between the last vanished
particle and the thuggish boom. And the thuggish
boom repeats in stutters from sandhill hollows
in the shore. We want more. A twirling sun,
or dismembered chrysanthemum bulleted up, leisurely
bursts, in an instant timestreak is suck swooped
back to its core. And we want more: red giant,
white dwarf, black hole dense, invisible, all in one.

MAY SWENSON

THE DESIRE OF WATER

Caught and composed, motionless blue, behind
the dam, the river and the rain appear
reserved, relying on a passing wind
to lick them back to life, that warps and moves
their welded surfaces against the sheer
wall with flowing room on its otherside.
But wavelets splashing cannot turn the tide
of emptiness enforced by concrete. Shove
as it might, surface water's only hope
is overflow, and that requires increasing
depth. Gradually, the billion rain drops
and bloated river combined, realizing
in their brooding blue depth the depth it takes,
rise toward the dam's lip too much for flood gates.

MARK JARMAN

DEATH & EMPEDOCLES 444 B.C.

Glittering, adroit, the Sicilian wonder
Stepped from the sea, spoke to the crowds:
"I was first a girl, then a blundering boy,
Then a briery bush (Ankh into Crucifix!),
Then a bird, a fish: and last of all,
Your friend, Empedocles.
                            I come to greet you."
Scattered applause, then groans and hisses:
A woman's voice: "He was my lover.
He taught my hands to conquer snakes."
And other voices: "Take him away. His face
Has the look of death."
                            "The distant west
Turns green, then violet. There are tremors
In the earth and menstrual heat. People are warned:
There are ashes falling."
                            Some saw him leap
Deep into Aetna:
                            a roar of smoke, slow lava pouring—

244

(We found his sandal near the crater's lip)—
Smell of psychosis, metempsychosis in the air:
Earth and its caverns towering over him;
His way was lost in flames, a Mandrake forest—
He could not unkindle fire, unwind the spell.
He was neither Herakles, nor Ganymedes
While madness (hope of fame) walked at his side.

Streets had turned treacherous, and crowds fell quiet—
Each waiting for a comet in the sky.

HORACE GREGORY

VERSE TRANSLATOR

Goethe, Racine, Neruda, Pushkin—next!
Some Choctaw? Aztec epic? Or Czech text?
Lo at his touch, as he invades *tromp tromp*,
Mountain on mountain, groaning, turns to swamp.

JOHN FREDERICK NIMS

LAST DAYS

You roar over the meadow and roar.
Silence purrs in the grass. In what
a hungry bum told you was larch, a parked hawk
keeps quiet. Silence. You roar again.
You remember the bum begged food and you
turned him away. You turned girls who loved you
away. One wept and said "cold" in July.
And so on. You roar each morning. Mute hawk
in the larch, bum on the road, girls
going away. Some mornings, words. You roar words
over the meadow. "Clambake" and "fracas."
The song of the creek dries up. Beavers
head for the sky. And so on. Hawk on larch.
Bum on road. Girls gone. Creek dry. Beavers
in flight. You roar editorials into the sun.
And so on. The silent, the indifferent sun.

RICHARD HUGO

From THE WAY DOWN

THEY RETURN

Long desired, the dead return.
—Saw our candle and were safe,
Bought from darkness by our care?
Light from ours has touched their eyes,
Blood of ours has filled their veins.
Absence, winter, shed like scales.

They return, but they are changed.
Armoured each in private shade,
Sullen, helmed against the light,
Their resentment fills our arms,
Sifting from their ribs like night.
Absence, winter, is their name.

Change comes slowly, where they were.
Pain, exclusion, long endured,
Ate their human places out,
Sold to darkness by our fear.
They, returning, bring us back
Absence, winter, what we gave.

                    JAY MACPHERSON

ELEGY FOR YARDS, POUNDS, AND GALLONS

An unduly elected body of our elders
Is turning you out of office and schoolroom
Through ten long years, is phasing you
Out of our mouths and lives forever.

Words have been lost before: some hounded
Nearly to death, and some transplanted
With roots dead set against stone,
And some let slide into obscure senescence,

   Some even murdered beyond recall like extinct animals—
(It would be cruel to rehearse their names:
They might stir from sleep on the dusty shelves
In pain for a moment).

Yet you, old emblems of distance and heaviness,
Solid and liquid companions, our good measures,
When have so many been forced to languish
For years through a deliberate deathwatch?

How can we name your colorless replacements
Or let them tell us for our time being
How much we weigh, how short we are,
Or how little we have left to drink?

Goodbye to Pounds by the Ton and all their Ounces,
To Gallons, Quarts, and Pints,
To Yards whose Feet are inching their last Mile,
Weighed down, poured out, written off,

And drifting slowly away from us
Like drams, like chains and gills,
To become as quaint as leagues and palms
In an old poem.

DAVID WAGONER

From SONGS OF THE TRANSFORMED

SIREN SONG

This is the one song everyone
would like to learn: the song
that is irresistible:

the song that forces men
to leap overboard in squadrons
even though they see the beached skulls

the song nobody knows
because anyone who has heard it
is dead, and the others can't remember.

Shall I tell you the secret
and if I do, will you get me
out of this bird suit?

I don't enjoy it here
squatting on this island
looking picturesque and mythical

with these two feathery maniacs,
I don't enjoy singing
this trio, fatal and valuable.

I will tell the secret to you,
to you, only to you.
Come closer. This song

is a cry for help: Help me!
Only you, only you can,
you are unique

at last. Alas
it is a boring song
but it works every time.

MARGARET ATWOOD

ODE TO PORNOGRAPHY

Hail mer-
ry, tricky, and clandestine
art! the schoolboy's peek at what might follow
first pubic hairs and acne, toy
for the worldly, secret vice
for the prim and proper, scorned

by priest,
proscribed by censor, you still
bear a socially redeeming message:
through photos, drawings, films, and books
you show jocund multitudes
eager, active (and passive),

going
at it in couples, threesomes,
and jampacked gangbangs, smooching and licking

whatever's in sight and rolling
around naked on beds, fur,
bearskin rugs, and haybarn floors

humping
non-stop any man, woman,
or friendly beast as fancy prompts, happy
to tempt us with, over here, some
curious devices and, there,
touch of lace or leather.

high heels
or creamy salves: the orgy
just keeps going—recoupling in every
known position while inventing
fresh ones, these people are as
simple and classic as those

in farce,
and their action is as com-
plicated, yet it all comes out all right—
Pornography! you make us want
to romp at large, consenting
adults where choice is free and

easy
and no one blushes, suffers
guilt, hurts, or gets hurt, and if your world can't
fit yet within our cramped confines
you prod us into gasping
for plenitudes ruddier than

our pinched
morality—I rise now,
I swell to climax!—as judges judge you
wanton, I praise you, knowing how
our species can be best and
blessed when we are most at play.

                              JACK ANDERSON

SIGNS

Threading the palm, a web of tiny lines
Spells out the lost money, the heart, the head,
The wagging tongues, the sudden deaths, in signs
We would smooth out like imprints on a bed,

In signs that can't be helped, geese heading south,
In signs read anxiously, like breath that clouds
A mirror held to a barely open mouth,
Like telegrams, the gathering of crowds —

The plane, an X in the sky spelling disaster:
Before the whistle and hit, a tracer flare;
Before rubble, a hairline crack in plaster
And a housefly's panicked scribbling on the air.

GJERTRUD SCHNACKENBERG

THE PLEASURE OF RUINS

We cannot walk like Byron among Ayasoluk's ruined
mosques, kicking the heads off yellow iris and eating
cold lamb, but still we never envy the Bedouin

for whom no city dies because any wall will brace
against a sand-struck wind. A heat rash or hotel dream,
with luck a capital's stone egg, or the rippled trace

of arches under water, perhaps a sketch, are all we take
back each week. If the statues were painted and the floors
were squared to scale, we would have no taste to make

the slow sacrifice to knowledge and learn the tomb
was always a gate, its prayers were only warnings
or directions for strangers towards the storeroom

we had made a court for our regret: that lizards
keep the place of lions in the garden, tracking
the sun across stones cut by history's haphazard

rearrangements, or the initials of a need to stay
beyond ourselves on columns. The prophets were right.
Babylon is "an astonishment and an hissing," afraid

to be seen in ropes and rails only guides dare cross.
So long quarried or fortified, the past is portioned now
to front the digs that sift what leaves us at a loss.

We frieze our hurts to watch them rubbed smooth
by tourists, and these reliefs are stunned in glass,
case studies scattered in city museums to approve

our pleasure at the site. Pleasure? The sight survives
its defeat and holds sea and cliff to a coast of pines
aligned like pillars to shade what gods may yet arrive.

J. D. MC CLATCHY

AN ASTRONOMER'S JOURNAL

Even in sleep my eyes are on the elements.
My eyes are pencils being perpetually resharpened
puzzling out the sky's connecting dots
one almost expects to be accompanied by numbers,
jig-saw animal shaped constellations,
bear, bent dipper, wed fish in repose,
crowding out the angels who I suppose
must be stacked up tier on tier
as in the horseshoe of the opera house.
Each night the sky splits open like a melon
its starry filaments
the astronomer examines with great intensity.
Caught in his expensive glass eye
more microscope than telescope,
it is his own eye he sees, reflected
and possessed, a moon-disc in a lake,
safe, even to himself, untouchable;
and so his notion of himself must be corrected:
"Actually, the universe is introspective".

JANE SHORE

From ESSAY ON PSYCHIATRISTS

XIV. THEIR SPEECH, COMPARED WITH WISDOM AND POETRY

Terms of all kinds mellow with time, growing
Arbitrary and rich as we call this man "neurotic"
Or that man "a peacock." The lore of psychiatrists—

"Paranoid", "Anal" and so on, if they still use
Such terms—also passes into the status of old sayings:
Water thinner than blood or under bridges; bridges

Crossed in the future or burnt in the past. Or the terms
Of myth, the phrases that well up in my mind:
Two blind women and a blind little boy, running—

Easier to cut thin air into planks with a saw
And then drive nails into those planks of air,
Than to evade those three, the blind harriers,

The tireless blind women and the blind boy, pursuing
For long years of my life, for long centuries of time.
Concerning Justice, Fortune and Love

There may be wisdom, but no science and few terms:
Blind, and blinding too. Hot in pursuit and flight,
Justice, Fortune and Love demand the arts

Of knowing and naming: and, yes, the psychiatrists, too,
Patiently naming them. But all in pursuit and flight, two
Blind women, tireless, and the blind little boy.

ROBERT PINSKY

A YOUNGER POET

No more exercises of style for him

He watches the energies that once fueled them
Dissolve in acids of self-suspicion

The tricks and glamors of favorite past masters
He has either assimilated or must discard now

His mode, for better and worse, seems set

He can now set about evading self-parody

How to be true to, though disappointed in, his art
Has become his major care
And actual subject matter, however couched

Should it bother him that those who read him
Understand things he didn't think he'd written?

It doesn't, he's grateful for any attention

But the more he tries to be clear, the more stupid
He seems to himself, the more stupid his readers seem

Stupidity coats the Earth like a vegetable invasion
In one of his inexpressible visions
— Or does it pour from the Earth itself, like lava?
In any case, it covers everything

He pokes at it obsessively
With the instrument of his chastened line

PETER SCHJELDAHL

WAITING ROOMS

What great genius invented the waiting room?
Every sublime idea no doubt is simple, but
Simplicity alone is never enough.
A cube sequestered in space and filled with time,
Pure time, refined, distilled, denatured time
Without qualities, without even dust . . .
Dust in a sunbeam between Venetian blinds
Where a boy and his mother wait . . . Eternity!
But I am straying from the subject: waiting rooms.

All over the globe, in the great terminals
And the tiny rooms of disbarred abortionists,
For transport, diagnosis, or divorce . . .
Alas! Maybe this mighty and terrible theme
Is too much for me. But wait! I have an idea.
You've heard it said, of course, that anything
May instantly turn into everything
In this world secreting figures of itself
forever and everywhere? How wonderful
That is, how horrible. Wherever you wait,
Between anticipation and regret,
Between the first desire and the second
Is but the razor of a moment, is
Not even time; and neither is motion more,
At sixty miles an hour or six hundred,
Than an illusion sent by devils to afford
Themselves illusory laughs at our expense
(we suffer, but they become no happier).

Think how even in heaven where they wait
The Resurrection, even in the graves
Of heaven with the harps, this law applies:
One waiting room will get you to the next.
Even your room, even your very own,
With the old magazines on the end tables,
The goldfish in the bowl below the window
Where the sunbeam falls between Venetian blinds . . .
And in the downstairs hall there is your mailbox,
One among many gathering paper and dust,
A waiting room in figure, summing up
Much in a little, the legendary box
Where hope only remains. You wait and see.

HOWARD NEMEROV

"CAN I TEMPT YOU TO A POND WALK?"

1

Tender fingers ran up my ankle
I was tempted and I fell
into a muddy stroll along
a field path of matted grass
to unreflecting water and
an unfinished, abandoned house
(cement blocks), a bombed-out building.

2

A hedgerow, trees grow in wild file.
Behind a scrim of cloud, a smudge
was mother, father, brother, sister sun.
A distant sound of shots: hunters.
I have nothing to say.

3

No, nothing to say. Tears
for my lost youth? Nope, not
even those. Soon a moon
full or almost full will rise
behind those clouds that hover,
forever, over Long Island. It
is almost New Year. May it
be better than the last. One
makes it so, of course, oneself.
Oh, I don't know about that,
nor why yesterday was sunny
and today was not. "Can I
tempt you to a pond walk?"
I have nothing to say, but, well, yes.

JAMES SCHUYLER

TRANSLATION

Lost: the Original, its Reason and its Rhyme,
Words whose meanings do not change through time,
"The soul in paraphrase", the heart in prose,
Strictures or structures, meter, *les mots justes*;
"The owlet umlaut" when the text was German,
Two hours of sleep each night, hapax legomenon,
A sense of self, fidelity, one's honor,
Authorized versions from a living donor.

Found in translation: someone else's voice:
Ringing and lucid, whispered, distant, true,
That in its rising accents falls to you,
Wahlverwandtschaft, a fortunate choice,
A call to answer, momentary grace,
Unbidden, yours; a way to praise.

RIKA LESSER

FRAGMENT I

O tender-heartedness right bitter grown
Because they knew thee not in all the world
Nor would, that gentleness thou hast to give.

•

And are chevaliers in the court of Him
Who reigneth ever where the stars grow dim
Beyond our sight.

•

Marble smooth by flowing waters grown.

EZRA POUND

THE ICE-CREAM WARS

Although I mean it, and project the meaning
As hard as I can into its brushed-metal surface,
It cannot, in this deteriorating climate, pick up
Where I leave off. It sees the Japanese text
(About two men making love on a foam-rubber bed)
As among the most massive secretions of the human spirit.
Its part is in the shade, beyond the iron spikes of the fence,
Mixing red with blue. As the day wears on
Those who come to seem reasonable are shouted down
(*Why you old goat!* Look who's talkin'. Let's see you
Climb off that tower—the waterworks architecture, both stupid
    and
Grandly humorous at the same time, is a kind of mask for him,
Like a seal's face. Time and the weather
Don't always go hand in hand, as here: sometimes
One is slanted sideways, disappears for awhile.
Then later it's forget-me-not time, and rapturous
Clouds appear above the lawn, and the rose tells
The old old story, the pearl of the orient, occluded
And still apt to rise at times).
                                A few black smudges
On the outer boulevards, like squashed midges
And the truth becomes a hole, something one has always
    known,
A heaviness in the trees, and no one can say
where it comes from, or how long it will stay—

A randomness, a darkness of one's own.

                                        JOHN ASHBERY

ASH

The substance that stirs in my palm
could well be a dead man; no need
to show surprise at the dizzy acts of wind.
My old father sitting uncertainly three feet away

is the slow cloud against the sky:
so my heart's beating makes of me a survivor
over here where the sun quietly sets.
The ways of freeing myself:

the glittering flowers, the immensity of rain for example,
which were limited to promises once
have had the lie to themselves. And the wind,
that had made simple revelation in the leaves,

plays upon the ascetic-faced vision of waters;
and without thinking
something makes me keep close to the walls
as though I was afraid of that justice in the shadows.

Now the world passes into my eye:
the birds flutter toward rest around the tree,
the clock jerks each memory towards the present
to become a past, floating away
like ash, over the bank.

My own stirrings like the wind's
keep hoping for the solace that would be me
in my father's eyes
to pour the good years back on me;

the dead man who licks my palms
is more likely to encourage my dark intolerance
rather than turn me
toward some strangely solemn charade:

the dumb order of the myth
lined up in the life-field,
the unconcerned wind perhaps truer than the rest,
rustling the empty, bodiless grains.

JAYANTA MAHAPATRA

POEM

Green things are flowers too
and we desire them more than
George Sand's blue rose not
that we don't shun poison oak

but if it's a question of loco
weed or marijuana why how
can we not rush glad and wild
eyes rolling nostrils flaring

towards ourselves in an unknown
pasture or public garden? it's
not the blue arc we achieve
nor the nervous orange poppy at

the base of Huysmans' neck
but the secret chlorophyll
and the celluloid ladder hid-
den beneath the idea of skin.

FRANK O'HARA

ON THE PIER

I'd like to walk out on ignorance like this,
long and brown like the ignorance of myself,
see the water shimmer and jump,
see the birds find something they could accept.

I would be voicelessly condemned, a bad
sailor walking the plank, hearing the boards
cry out like the boards of an old desk,
slightly gaping, wet with a collection of mornings.

At the end of the pier, at the end of this ignorance,
I'd celebrate. The sea, like many wine glasses
tipped, "Here's to you—you know nothing at all!"
And birds crashing—white gloves, in applause!

BRENDA HILLMAN

HOG HEAVEN

For NA & KP

In some dim sense he sees
it is already here
the field of delicate corn, the glittering
wallow where each rolls free
of the hill of flesh
of the jawless appetite
that inhales a world of garbage and shrieks *more*
(as if the skin didn't have a decent limit)
that tries to thrust himself upon himself
until all flesh balloons to one vast Pig—
on which he is the smile, satisfied.

Dozing on the warm cement he dreams
that the sun, puzzled, pauses in the heavens
that *first one at the trough for swill*
and *furthest from the draft at night*
are not enough
that the sun-warmed fly who now forgets to bite
buzzes another tongue and the lifting wind
sneaks glittering through the goldenrod
to whisper something else into his ear
before the whistle blows *it's time for slops.*

Like straw such dreams trouble the water's surface—
the pig's persistent business of stuffing, rutting
and grunting to his fellows his narrow will—
until the box pulls up and the ham-faced farmer
with hands like shovels and his sly-footed dogs
directs him into terror's dusty room
over something chumbling and shaking like a fly.
Too late: he cannot think for the squeals and bites
hunger, cold, and dust thick in his snout.

But after three days without water
sensing the golden sacrifice of bacon
the roast's crackling holocaust
he rises, hilarious as helium
arid, wingèd above the anonymous pen
a winter gaiety glazing his eye

a seraphic humor slimming his jowl
foresees and forgives all:
the rotating jaws, the dreamless fat and muscle
the bland pink hands which lift the plate for more.

ROBERT SIEGEL

THE RING

I carry it on my keychain, which itself
is a big brass ring
large enough for my wrist,
holding keys for safe deposit box,
friends' apartments,
My house, office and faithless car.

I would like to wear it,
the only ornament on my plain body,
but it is a relic,
the husband gone to other wives,
and it could never be a symbol of sharing,
but like the gold it's made of, stands for possession, power,
the security of a throne.

So, on my keyring,
dull from resting in my dark purse,
it hangs, reminding me of failures, of beauty I once had,
of more ancient searches for an enchanted ring.

I understand, now, what that enchantment is, though.
It is being loved.
Or, conversely, loving so much that you feel loved.
And the ring hangs there
with my keys,
reminding of failure.

This vain head full of roses,
crystal, bleeding lips,

a voice doomed to listen, forever,
to itself.

DIANE WAKOSKI

ANTIGUA

The heat standing tall as a door, you go outside
And drink from a tin dipper

Water so clear it holds the sky,
Mapping the blue and all that goes beyond.

It is dusk now.
It is the town with eyes of a sad mule.

You watch the dark become a back drop
To hunger, the streetlight

A moon that will not pull west,
Dragging its light under the rule of another heaven.

You think of the bus
And the dust that trailed it like a cape,

The slashed mountains rung pale
With roads that climbed through a fever of new air.

Below, streams twisted through the trees
And a mist balanced like scales

On the naked limbs,
While you rose even higher,

Your 24 years falling away,
With the language that had no reason to follow.

GARY SOTO

PHOTOGRAPHS OF OLD NEW YORK

They stare back into an increate future,
Dead stars, burning still. Air how choked with soot
One breathed then, the smudged grays and blacks impressed
In circles around East European eyes,
Top hats, a brougham, the laundry that hung
Like crowds of ghosts over common courtyards.
Dignity still knew how to thrust its hand
Into a waistcoat, bread plaited into shapes

How to dress a window, light under the El
Fall as negative to cast-iron shadows.
Assemble Liberty plate by plate—so
This giant dismembered arm still emerges
From folds of bronze and floats over the heads
of bearded workmen riveted in place
By an explosion of magnesium they've learned
To endure. Then, Union. Rally. March. Strike.

And still the wretched refugees swarming
Out from Ellis Island, the glittering door,
To prosper or perish. Or both. . . . The men
Don't see the women; or see how deftly hems
Can be lifted at curbs—well, any eye would
Be caught by that tilt of hat, profile, bearing.
Others strive to have mattered too, stolid
Forms that blush and crouch over sewing machines,
Haunt the libraries, speak on platforms.
Did they? And did this woman, who clearly still
Speaks no English, her head-scarf, say, Russian?
A son stands at her side, crop-haired, in clumpy
Shoes. She stares straight forward, reserved, aware,
Embattled. The deep-set eyes say something
About the emptiness of most wishes; and
About her hopes. She knows the odds are poor.

Or, the odds are zero, counted from here.
The past survives its population
And is unkind. Triumph no more than failure
In the longest run ever fails to fail.
Is that the argument against shuffling,
Dealing, and reshuffling these photographs?
They are not mementoes of death alone,
But of life lived variously, avatars
Energy, insight, cruelty took—and love.
Variousness: the great kaleidoscope
of time, its snowflake pictures, form after
Form, collapsing into the future, hours,
Days, seasons, generations that rise up
And fall like leaves, each one a hand inscribed
With the fragile calligraphy of selfhood;
The human fate given a human face.

ALFRED CORN

A VALENTINE FOR MATTHEW ARNOLD

The Seas of Faith are full again with vain
Philosophies, empty orders of gods,
Demons of the mind and heart supplanting
The slow angers of love with hollow stares
And rhetoric. These are not days to love,
When the rare expectations of morning
Will be blackened by the shoddy evening.
Let us be faithless to one another.
The monarch butterflies now copulate
In the kitchen, bats bare their teeth against
The screens, and throatless songbirds rasp all night.
At dawn, armies of toads and frogs litter
The walks. All animals act cruelly
Toward each other. We are no different.

WILLIAM LOGAN

From THREE NOTES TOWARD DEFINITIONS

II. OF FAITH

A puzzling topic, this. Should be filed under
Assurance, Things Unseen, Intimations. Yet
For all of its obscurities, it is
Expressed innumerably in objects — viz.,
A pencil, a French cigarette,
Suspension bridges, drawings of the sea,
Etchings of Japanese severity.

Which is to say that all of the above
(Pardon, dear reader, the didactic vein)
Imply convictions that our lives sustain.
Despite newspapers, bills, the efforts of
The politician, *Something real exists*;
And we in turn, by faith, produce
A further something for delight or use.

Granted, too smooth a formulation,
But it suggests a certain truth:
It is the incomplete and unexplored
That often offer the most true reward.

(See Hebrews 11.1-33,
St. Augustine's *Confessions*, Pascal's *Pensées*,
Darwin's *Autobiography*.)

So, too, by faith one may be led
To recognitions of a wealth of splendors:
The fine blond down on a child's wrist,
A dark field sheltered by an arm of mist,
The puddle in the driveway which reflects
A network of bare branches overhead.
Which brings us to the point that faith respects

Even the values of a fallen world.
Rimbaud discovered love in the bizarre,
Duccio an opulence in the austere.
So may we, in inauspicious weather
Or inauspicious labor, be aware
Of an angelic gift—though angels are
Another matter altogether.

TIMOTHY STEELE

ELEGY

The pages of history open. The dead enter.
It is winter in the spine of the book
where they land, inexplicable texts,
and a small rain falling, a mist of promises,
disjointed sentences, woes, failures.

The dead are puzzled:
was it for this they left
the land of grammar, the syntax of their skin?
We turn the pages. We read.
Sometimes, in moments of vertigo,

we notice that they are speaking.
Tiny whinings and murmurings arise,
as of insects urging their rights, their dissatisfactions,
invisible insects dwelling uncomfortably
in the margins, in the white spaces around words.

SANDRA M. GILBERT

AFTER THE SOLSTICE

The depths of winter copy those of age.
This artificial cosiness! Outside,
The ancient, cold, uncomfortable rage
Provoked by pity. Warmth has died
Of want, the spectre of impatient youth
Imperfect hedge against the steppe of death

Interminable as Siberia.
It seems we have been sentenced there for life,
Its infinite perspective drearier
Than any dream, and bleak as unbelief,
A whole generation frozen solid
That used to be spontaneous and squalid.

Evenings bereft before the fire,
Afternoons spent with foul weather friends,
Despair that dares to call itself desire,
The endless night that never the less ends:
Winter's pastimes pantomiming age's.
Immaculate the uninviting pages!

DARYL HINE

THE MUSE OF SATIRE

They put her together out of this and that.
Skins of tiny pears made up an elbow.
Often kissed, the silky arch of someone
else's brow. Laid like the narrow glove
rich relatives have fondled, a brown hand
of hair upon the knee, cast forward from
her bowed transparent head. A rumpled breast,
bricks showing through her half-completed navel,
a brace to keep her lavish sex in place
round out the sketch. Temporarily, a working draft
of pain. In time, perfected so she never
walks again, she'll burn your buildings down.

MARY KINZIE

MAN AND BOY

"You send us the boy; we return you the man."
A Military School advertisement

You will know that boy on sight.
In the advertisement
The same familiar gray
Half-inch face
Always arises
Out of its bell-hop collar —
The type of the boy
You are to send them
For the man in return.

They have kept that boy
In print these fifty years
In the back of the *Times*
Magazine section and the *Geographic.*
His head turned a bit to the right
And up, he stares at something
Serious a long way off.
You are the man
Returning that gaze. Unwearying,
He goes on
Being about fifteen
Forever, knowing
He will never return.

JOHN N. MORRIS

LOVE AND HOW IT BECOMES IMPORTANT
IN OUR DAY TO DAY LIVES

The man who tells you which is the whiter wash,
the woman who talks about her paper towels,
the woman whose coffee holds her home together,
the man who smells the air in his neighbor's house,

the man who sings a song about his socks,
the woman who tells how well her napkin fits,
the man who sells the four-way slicer-dicer,
the woman who crosses tape between her tits,

and scores besides trample my yard, a mob
demanding to be let in, like Sodomites
yelling to get at my guests but I have no guests.
I crawl across the floor and cut the lights.

"We know you're there," they say. "Open the door."
"Who are you?" I say. "What do you want with me?"
"What does it matter?" they say. "You'll let us in.
Everyone lets us in. You'll see. You'll see."

The chest against the door begins to give.
I settle against a wall. A window breaks.
I cradle a gun in the crook of my elbow.
I hear the porch collapse. The whole house shakes.

Then comes my wife as if to wake me up,
a box of ammunition in her arms.
She settles herself against the wall beside me.
"The towns are gone," she says. "They're taking the farms."

MILLER WILLIAMS

From THE VENETIAN VESPERS

III

   I am a person of inflexible habits
And comforting rigidities, and though
I am a twentieth-century infidel
From Lawrence, Massachusetts, twice a week
I visit the Cathedral of St. Mark's,
That splendid monument to the labors of
Grave robbers, body snatchers, those lawless two
Entrepreneurial Venetians who
In compliance with the wishes of the Doge
For the greater commercial and religious glory
Of Venice in the year 828
Kidnapped the corpse of the Evangelist
From Alexandria, a sacrilege
The saint seemed to approve. That ancient city
Was drugged and bewildered with an odor of sanctity,
Left powerless and mystified by oils,
Attars and essences of holiness

And roses during the midnight exhumation
And spiriting away of the dead saint
By Buono and his side-kick Rustico—
Goodness in concert with Simplicity
Effecting the major heist of Christendom.

I enter the obscure aquarium dimness,
The movie-palace dark, through which incline
Smoky diagonals and radiant bars
Of sunlight from the high southeastern crescents
Of windowed drums above. Like slow blind fingers
Finding their patient and unvarying way
Across the braille of pavement, edging along
The pavonine and lapidary walls,
Inching through silence as the earth revolves
To huge compulsions, as the turning spheres
Drift in their milky pale galactic light
Through endless quiet, gigantic vacancy,
Unpitying, inhuman, terrible.
In time the eye accommodates itself
To the dull phosphorescence. Gradually
Glories reveal themselves, grave mysteries
Of the faith cast off their shadows, assume their forms
Against a heaven of coined and sequined light,
A splatter of gilt cobblestones, flung grains
Or crumbs of brilliance, the vast open fields
Of the sky turned intimate and friendly. Patines
And laminae, a vermeil shimmering
Of fish-scaled, cataphracted golden plates.
Here are the saints and angels brought together
In studied reveries of happiness.
Enormous wings of seraphim uphold
The crowning domes where the convened apostles
Receive their fiery tongues from the Godhead
Descended to them as a floating dove,
patriarch and collateral ancestor
Of the pigeons out in the Square. Into those choirs
of lacquered Thrones, enamelled Archangels
And medalled Principalities rise up
A cool plantation of columns, marble shafts
Bearing their lifted pathways, viaducts
And catwalks through the middle realms of heaven.

Even as God descended into the mass
And thick of us, so is He borne aloft
As promise and precursor to us all,
Ascending in the central dome's vast hive
of honeyed luminosity. Behind
The altar He appears, two fingers raised
In benediction, in what seems two-thirds
of the Boy Scout salute, wishing us well.
And we are gathered here below the saints,
Virtues and martyrs, sheltered in their glow,
Soothed by the punk and incense, to rejoice
In the warm light of Gabrieli's horns,
And for a moment of unwonted grace
We are so blessed as to forget ourselves.
Perhaps. There is something selfish in the self,
The cell's craving for perpetuity,
The sperm's ignorant hope, the animal's rule
Of haunch and sinew, testicle and groin,
That refers all things whatever, near and far,
To one's own needs or fantasized desires.
Returning suddenly to the chalk-white sunlight
Of out-of-doors, one spots among the tourists
Those dissolute young with heavy-lidded gazes
of cool, clear-eyed, stony depravity
That in the course of only a few years
will fade into the terrifying boredom
In the faces of Carpaccio's prostitutes.
From motives that are anything but kindly
I ignore their indiscreet solicitations
And far more obvious poverty. The mind
Can scarcely cope with the world's sufferings,
Must blinker itself to much or else go mad.
And the bargain that we make for our sanity
Is the knowledge that when at length it comes our turn
To be numbered with the outcasts, the maimed, the poor
The injured and insulted, they will turn away,
The fortunate and healthy, as I turn now
(Though touched as much with compassion as with lust,
Knowing the smallest gift would reverse our roles,
Expose me as weak and thus exploitable.
There is more stamina, twenty times more hope
In the least of them than there is left in me.)
I take my loneliness as a vocation,

A policied exile from the human race,
A cultivated, earned misanthropy
After the fashion of the Miller of Dee.

It wasn't always so. I was an Aid Man,
A Medic with an infantry company,
Who because of my refusal to bear arms
Was constrained to hear the wounded and the dead
From under enemy fire, and to bear witness
To inconceivable pain, usually shot at
Though banded with Red Crosses and unarmed.
There was a corporal I knew in Heavy Weapons,
Someone who carried with him into combat
A book of etiquette by Emily Post.
Most brought with them some token of the past,
Some emblem of attachment or affection
Or coddled childhood—bibles and baby booties,
Harmonicas, love letters, photographs—
But this was different. I discovered later
That he had been brought up in an orphanage,
So the book was his fiction of kindliness,
A novel in which personages of wealth
Firmly secure domestic tranquility.
He'd cite me instances. It seems a boy
Will not put "Mr." on his calling cards
Till he leaves school, and may omit the "Mr."
Even while at college. Bread and butter plates
Are never placed on a formal dinner table.
At a simple dinner party one may serve
Claret instead of champagne with the meat.
The satin facings on a butler's lapels
Are narrower than a gentleman's and he wears
Black waistcoat with white tie, whereas the gentleman's
White waistcoat goes with both black tie and white.
When a lady lunches alone at her own home
In a formally kept house the table is set
For four. As if three Elijahs were expected.
This was to him a sort of *Corpus Juris*,
An ancient piety and governance
Worthy of constant dream and meditation.
He haunts me here, that seeker after law
In a lawless world, in rainsoaked combat boots,
Oil-stained fatigues and heavy bandoleers.

He was killed by enemy machine-gun fire.
His helmet had fallen off. They had sheared away
The top of his cranium like a soft-boiled egg,
And there he crouched, huddled over his weapon,
His brains wet in the chalice of his skull.

ANTHONY HECHT

THE GUILD

Every night, as my grandfather sat
in the darkened room in front of the fire,
the bourbon like fire in his hand, his eye
glittering meaninglessly in the light
from the flames, his glass eye baleful and stony,
a young man sat with him
in silence and darkness, a college boy with
white skin, unlined, a narrow
beautiful face, a broad domed
forehead, and eyes amber as the resin from
trees too young to be cut yet.
This was his son, who sat, an apprentice,
night after night, his glass of coals
next to the old man's glass of coals,
and he drank when the old man drank, and he learned
the craft of oblivion—that young man
not yet cruel, his hair dark as the
soil that feeds the tree's roots,
that son who would come to be in his turn
better at this than the teacher, the apprentice
who would pass his master in cruelty and oblivion,
drinking steadily by the flames in the blackness,
that young man my father.

SHARON OLDS

STROLLS

The brook gives me
sparkles plenty, an
abundance, but asks
nothing of me:
snow thickets
and scrawny
snowwork of hedgerows,
still gold weeds, and
snow-bent cedar gatherings
provide
feasts of disposition
(figure, color, weight, proportion)
and require
nothing of me,
not even that I notice: the near-winter
quartermoon
sliding high almost
into color at four-thirty—
the abundance of clarity
along the rose ridge line!
alone, I'm not alone:
a standoffishness and reasonableness
in things finds
me or I find that
in them: sand, fall,
furrow, bluff—
things one, speaking things
not words, would
have found to say

A. R. AMMONS

ONE PAGE IN
THE AMERICAN HERITAGE DICTIONARY

deathbed-Debs

Debridement is the word you want to check
having read last night how Nancy Sokol
in 3rd year of medical school at Bellevue
does it for Mr. McGowan, once strapping,
now lashed to the bedpost, gnashing
his teeth, sweating profusely. 'The surgical
excision of dead and devitalized tissue'
bluntly, cutting away on his 12-inch-square
bedsore. There is nothing debonair
about him. Life is the death-trap
he's caught in. No Deborah to lead him out
nor DeBakey to furnish a cure. He stares
at the death's head moth, loses the debate,
so will Simone DeBeauvoir.
He couldn't care less about presidents,
political parties. Socialism won't share
this. The debit side's too long for a rally.
He will not tour Debrecen in Hungary.
Debilitated, he couldn't walk if they
let him. Tall Mr. McGowan is becoming debris.

CAROLE OLES

POEMS

For Joyce Kilmer

I think that I shall never read
A tree of any shape or breed—
For all its xylem and its phloem—
As fascinating as a poem.
Trees must make themselves and so
They tend to seem a little slow
To those accustomed to the pace
Of poems that speed through time and space
As fast as thought. We shouldn't blame
The trees, of course: we'd be the same

If we had roots instead of brains.
While trees just grow, a poem explains,
By precept and example, how
Leaves develop on the bough
And new ideas in the mind.
A sensibility refined
By reading many poems will be
More able to admire a tree
Than lumberjacks and nesting birds
Who lack a poet's way with words
And tend to look at any tree
In terms of its utility.
And so before we give our praise
To pines and oaks and laurels and bays,
We ought to celebrate the poems
That made our human hearts their homes.

TOM DISCH

X RAY

Some prowl sea-beds, some hurtle to a star
and, mother, some obsessed turn over every stone
or open graves to let that starlight in.
There are men who would open anything.

Harvey, the circulation of the blood,
and Freud, the circulation of our dreams,
pried honourably and honoured are
like all explorers. Men who'd open men.

And those others, mother, with diseases
like great streets named after them: Addison,
Parkinson, Hodgkin—physicians who'd arrive
fast and first on any sour death-bed scene.

I am their slowcoach colleague—half afraid,
incurious. As a boy it was so: you know how
my small hand never teased to pieces
an alarm clock or flensed a perished mouse.

And this larger hand's the same. It stretches now
out from a white sleeve to hold up, mother,
your X ray to the glowing screen. My eyes look
but don't want to, I still don't want to know.

DANNIE ABSE

THE REST

You've tried the rest.
You've waited long enough.
Everything catches up with you.

And you're too old,
or too young.
Or you don't have the money

or you don't have the time.
Maybe you're shy, and maybe
you're just afraid.

How often have you heard it,
have you promised
yourself you'd try

something really different
if you had the chance?
Though you can't help but wonder

if all those people
know what they're doing, now
you're saying it with them:

Eventually everything
catches up with us,
and it starts to show.

We've waited all our lives, or as long
as we can remember, whichever
is long enough.

LAWRENCE RAAB

POEM BEGINNING WITH A LINE OF WITTGENSTEIN

The world is everything that is the case.
Now stop your blubbering and wash your face.

FOR AN EARLY RETIREMENT

Chinless and slouched, gray-faced, and slack of jaw,
Here plods depressed Professor Peckinpaugh,
Whose verse J. Donald Adams found "exciting."
This fitted him to teach Creative Writing.

DONALD HALL

EASTER MORNING

I have a life that did not become,
that turned aside and stopped,
astonished:
I hold it in me like a pregnancy or
as on my lap a child
not to grow or grow old but dwell on

it is to his grave I most
frequently return and return
to ask what is wrong, what was
wrong, to see it all by
the light of a different necessity
but the grave will not heal
and the child,
stirring, must share my grave
with me, an old man having
gotten by on what was left

when I go back to my home country in these
fresh far-away days, it's convenient to visit
everybody aunts and uncles, those who used to say
look how he's shooting up, and the
trinket aunts who always had a little
something in their pocketbooks, cinnamon bark
or a penny or nickel, and uncles who
were the rumored fathers of cousins

who whispered of them as of great, if
troubled, presences, and school
teachers, just about everybody older
(and some younger) collected in one place
waiting, particularly but not for
me, mother and father there, too, and others
close, close as burrowing
under skin, all in the graveyard
assembled, done for, the world they
used to wield, have trouble and joy
in, gone

the child in me that could not become
was not ready for others to go,
to go on into change, blessings and
horrors, but stands there by the road
where the mishap occurred, crying out for
help, come and fix this or we
can't get by, but the great ones who
were to return, they could not or did
not hear and went on in a flurry and
now, I say in the graveyard, here
lies the flurry, now it can't come
back with help or helpful asides, now
we all buy the bitter
incompletions, pick up the knots of
horror, silently raving, and go on
crashing into empty ends not
completions, not rondures the fullness
has come into and spent itself from

I stand on the stump
of a child, whether myself
or my little brother who died, and
yell as far as I can, I cannot leave this place, for
for me it is the dearest and the worst,
it is life nearest to life which is
life lost: it is my place where
I must stand and fail,
calling attention with tears
to the branches not lofting
boughs into space, to the barren
air that holds the world that was my world

though the incompletions
(& completions) burn out
standing in the flash high–burn
momentary structure of ash, still it
is a picture–book, letter–perfect
Easter morning: I have been for a
walk: the wind is tranquil: the brook
works without flashing in an abundant
tranquility: the birds are lively with
voice: I saw something I had
never seen before: two great birds,
maybe eagles, blackwinged, whitenecked
and –headed, came from the south oaring
the great wings steadily; they went
directly over me, high up, and kept on
due north: but then one bird,
the one behind, veered a little to the
left and the other bird kept on seeming
not to notice for a minute: the first
began to circle as if looking for
something, coasting, resting its wings
on the down side of some of the circles:
the other bird came back and they both
circled, looking perhaps for a draft;
they turned a few more times, possibly

rising—at least, clearly resting—
then flew on falling into distance till
they broke across the local bush and
trees: it was a sight of bountiful
majesty and integrity: the having
patterns and routes, breaking
from them to explore other patterns or
better ways to routes, and then the
return: a dance sacred as the sap in
the trees, permanent in its descriptions
as the ripples round the brook's
ripplestone: fresh as this particular
flood of burn breaking across us now
from the sun.

A. R. AMMONS

1979

LATE ECHO

Alone with our madness and favorite flower
We see that there really is nothing left to write about.
Or rather, it is necessary to write about the same old things
In the same way, repeating the same things over and over
For love to continue and be gradually different.

Beehives and ants have to be re-examined eternally
And the color of the day put in
Hundreds of times and varied from summer to winter
For it to get slowed down to the pace of an authentic
Saraband and huddle there, alive and resting.

Only then can the chronic inattention
Of our lives drape itself around us, conciliatory
And with one eye on those long tan plush shadows
That speak so deeply into our unprepared knowledge
Of ourselves, the talking engines of our day.

JOHN ASHBERY

WAVING GOODBYE

I wanted to know what it was like before we
had voices and before we had bare fingers and before we
had minds to move us through our actions
and tears to help us over our feelings
so I drove my daughter through the snow to meet her friend
and filled her car with suitcases and hugged her
as an animal would, pressing my forehead against her,
walking in circles, moaning, touching her cheek,
and turned my head after them as an animal would,
watching helplessly as they drove over the ruts,
her smiling face and her small hand just visible
over the giant pillows and coat hangers
as they made their turn into the empty highway

GERALD STERN

AFTER MINOR SURGERY

this is the dress rehearsal

when the body
like a constant lover
flirts for the first time
with faithlessness

when the body
like a passenger on a long journey
hears the conductor call out
the name
of the first stop

when the body
in all its fear and cunning
makes promises to me
it knows
it cannot keep

LINDA PASTAN

STATIC

Well, Old Flame, the fire's out.
I miss you most at the laundromat.
Folding sheets is awkward work
Without your help. My nip and tuck
Can't quite replace your hands,
And I miss that odd square dance
We did. Still, I'm glad to do without
Those gaudy arguments that wore us out.
I've gone over them so often
They've turned grey. You fade and soften
Like the hackles of my favorite winter shirt.
You've been a hard habit to break, Old Heart.
When I feel for you beside me in the dark,
The blankets crackle with bright blue sparks.

BARTON SUTTER

A SHAPE FOR IT

Sometimes when time goes by
I feel it bend.
The day becomes the same white room,
and the day won't end.

Its walls show no human scratch,
no useless wild attempt,
and echo neither curse nor cry,
but do not relent.

I wake amazed to be inside,
like an inmate slapped awake
while dreaming of an endless field
where the sun makes

festival of a girl's long yellow hair,
and she sways to gather
her dress as she waits,
and time seems clear as air.

MICHAEL RYAN

CLOSER

*If he spoke the words of invitation aright, the porpoise
would follow him with cries of joy to the surface.*
Colin Wilson, on native "callers"

"Lucifer," a student once wrote "fell
from God's thrown"—which is a little
true, about a long way down. The Garden must
have looked a little like Heaven—something,

maybe, of the distance fishes shimmied,
after Darwin, to lead into
mammal, then into Man. "And Satan
the bad angle saw them making love"—a,

er, little like Milton. I guess: they were closer
to panther's supple musculature, the great
ape-thrust of the buttocks, lioness
mothertongue licking, even the deep

indiscriminate milt-spawn fish pleasure
out of themselves then die — much closer
than we'll ever be, or might want to be,
though we sometimes try. The letters

of our friends / ". . . *our marriage splitting*
like the atom — kapow"; ". . . *& made of myself a*
wadded tissue of tears"; ". . . *back*
together, tho wobbly as loose teeth" / read

a little, though lesser, and profaned, like
the old myths of trial,
pain, redemption — carry the spark
of nerve and star into this evolved

scientific age. If the blood is a little
like the sea (and it is) I've put my lips
the singers against your lips the gates,
and called, and something of what

we were once — porpoise, narwhal,
angelfish — broke
surface, a long way up: to skin
from bottomsalt, to us two, through all fours.

ALBERT GOLDBARTH

JUNE FOURTH

Today as I ride down Twenty-fifth Street I smell honeysuckle
rising from Shell and Victor Balata and K-Diner.
The goddess of sweet memory is there
staggering over fruit and drinking old blossoms.
A man in white socks and a blue T-shirt
is sitting on the grass outside Bethlehem Steel
eating lunch and dreaming.
Before he walks back inside he will be changed.
He will remember when he stands again under the dirty windows
a moment of great misgiving and puzzlement
just before sweetness ruined him and thinking
tore him apart. He will remember lying
on his left elbow studying the sky,

and the loss he felt, and the sudden freedom,
the mixture of pain and pleasure — terror and hope —
what he calls "honeysuckle".

GERALD STERN

DYING

Nothing to be said about it, and everything —
The change of changes, closer or further away:
The Golden Retriever next door, Gussie, is dead,

Like Sandy, the Cocker Spaniel from three doors down
Who died when I was small; and every day
Things that were in my memory fade and die.

Phrases die out: first, everyone forgets
What doornails are; then after certain decades
As a dead metaphor, *dead as a doornail* flickers

And fades away. But someone I know is dying —
And though one might say glibly, "everyone is,"
The different pace makes the difference absolute.

The tiny invisible spores in the air we breathe,
That settle harmlessly on our drinking water
And on our skin, happen to come together

With certain conditions on the forest floor,
Or even a shady corner of the lawn —
And overnight the fleshy, pale stalks gather,

The colorless growth without a leaf or flower;
And around the stalks, the summer grass keeps growing
With steady pressure, like the insistent whiskers

That grow between shaves on a face, the nails
Growing and dying from the toes and fingers
At their own humble pace, oblivious

As the nerveless moths, that live their night or two —
Though like a moth a bright soul keeps on beating,
Bored and impatient in the monster's mouth.

ROBERT PINSKY

THE POETRY BUG

"Have your students really caught the poetry bug?"
Working Paper on Writing Teacher
evaluation at M.I.T.

If, driving home from the Russian poet's
Reading—he reads like a Russian, flailing
Eyes and arms, thus making the women
Listening, so they afterwards claim,
Want to run unclothed in the snow—she flails
An arm as she steers along icy roads
Crooning aloud in a kind of mock-Russian,
She's probably caught it; but if, as she drives,
She's jotting down notes with her Big Blue Marker,
Her poem about the Russian ("Take me,
Voznesensky") at 30 miles
Per hour to top a rise and see
A white-faced man in an orange parka,
Mittened, waving her down, and seven
Cars spread round at angles all over
The road, and applying the brakes, praying
They'll hold—sliding, pumping, steering
Into the skid—she's all the while thinking
Of how this image of losing oneself
At last in the hands of Chance as to hitting
Or coasting to a stop might actually
Fit in her Russian-poet-poem
(Or maybe better the one about easing
The laden mind into sleep) you *know*
Your student has caught the poetry bug.

                                    BARRY SPACKS

A POET OF OUR CLIMATE

History's gilt and grandiose opulence
he scorned from the start, that rose-and-gold-lit cloud
bashing itself perpetually overhead
to new fake marbles, spurious monuments—
and the smell of history: peonies and trenches.

Truth had no past. It was wordless as water, a fall
of shadow on stone. How he longed to approximate silence,
to see himself vanish into the hushed expanse
of snow in Ohio. Someday he would. Meanwhile,
he kept his lines short, and his vocabulary small.

KATHA POLLITT

SURVIVOR, WALKING

He knew the stories he could tell
  Like his own garden—well.
And then he knew the woods, could tame
  Each wildness with a name.
  Fondly he rapped the knees
  Of familiar, ancient trees

With his green beechwood hiking staff
  Their silence swelled his laugh
As he saluted those careers
  He'd followed forty years.
  Half rot, half youthful still,
  Growth was their only skill.

"Across this trunk note how the sun
  Shows burnished cinnamon.
(His loud, half-deaf discourse.) "The bark
  No longer looks just dark,
  It lives a hundred years
  Or so, till this appears.

Growling in anger once, he stopped
  Before some spruces lopped
(Years back) at the neck for Christmas trees.
  He cried, "Now look at these
  Some bastard has got at!
  Who'd do a thing like that?"

One birch, in a woodlot maples won,
  Leaned there, a veteran
Stripped naked, where its sun had failed.
  Even this one he hailed
  Like an impoverished friend
  Remembered to the end.

At home, on trees pulped down, he wrote
  Critique and anecdote.
Working out front, working back stage
  He chronicled his age
  And by this balanced act
  Delivered up the fact.

On walks he still hails trees recalled
  By name or stops, enthralled
By one no logger has cut down
  And lightning missed, whose crown
  Rails yet against the sky,
  Still at it, green and spry.

He will not hear us, not by half
  Silences make him laugh.
Beyond our powers to persuade
  He drops his hearing aid
  And marches to the woods
  To join his earthly goods.

STEPHEN SANDY

A CLOUD CREATES

A cloud creates the face of a man who, happening to look up, recognizes it as his own. The face under stress of the wind begins to disintegrate into wings, and the man sees in himself the ability to fly. He stretches forth his arms and raises them up and down as he begins to circle and dip as a birdman would in the currents of the wind, and then the face vanishes and the wings drift apart too, losing their forms in shreds and patches. By this, he foretells his aging, debility and eventual death; he can accept. The clouds darken, as they will; thunder rolls from their colliding with each other. Lightning flashes. He knows he is at war with himself, the reason for which he cannot go into at the moment; the war first must be fought for and against himself, and he stands in the pouring rain that has started at the first thunderclap. Though the face he had seen has disappeared, yet it is of the clouds that it was created and of which he feels himself a part, and so the rain is how he weeps at his loss among the clouds. There is no consolation, not until the rain ceases and the sun emerges and once more clouds arrive, white, brilliantly lit and so, for him, full of hope. He has not attempted to sort out his, as it seems, random feelings since sight of the face. There is no order to his feelings, he is certain, but he needs none, not while the sun rises and sets and weather prevails. It is from weather that he derives, and so he has no faults. He is without fault, he is of the weather.

DAVID IGNATOW

ON COMING TO NOTHING

Old friends, nearing senility,
we sit, every last prospect aim,
and think: The world was wrong about me . . .
but at least it was right about him.

RICHARD MOORE

A SCHEDULE OF BENEFITS

It is a part of the policy.
On this paper you find
How highly they value
Those things that may happen
To you in time. Before your eyes
Your eyes are written
Down at half a million.
They will replace each hand
With fifty thousand dollars.
Piecemeal you are worth a fortune.

But perhaps nothing
Of this will happen. Then
You will never receive them,
The benefits. Certain
Exclusions, too, are written in.
If you have lost your life
Without noticing it
Somewhere in your forties
Or misplaced it perhaps in childhood,
That casualty does not appear on the schedule.

Still, for years for every month that passes
You will have your salary
By way of compensation.
Over the door of your job
Is written *Arbeit Macht Frei.*
You are assured you will get
What is coming to you.
Though this is not a part of any policy.
That finally must be your consolation.

JOHN N. MORRIS

A HISTORY OF PHOTOGRAPHY

Prodigies flooded the market—the magnetic corset,
The one-twist tooth extractor, the camera.
At the exhibitions only the occasional
Yokel, up from the south, gaped in disbelief.

The church was not in principle opposed
To such a machine. Baudelaire granted its
Historical worth. Now, great-grandparents
Could be scrutinized, lost courtyards found,

Scenic postcards sent. Not great things
But something, nonetheless. A few professors
Hoped that the arrested moment might explain
To men mutability's shrewd devices.

Time would become richer, the human race
More meditative. Albums accumulated;
Robbers were apprehended by alert,
Newspaper-scanning citizens; rhetoric fizzled.

A sprinkling of adventuresome sons became
Photographers, another sort of profession,
Self-taught and self-employed. "I am not
A mechanic," more than one was forced to shout.

Reality, like a dumb beast, yawned.
You saw them with their apparatuses
Roaming the quays, the moors, the poor quarters,
The parliaments. There could be, the wits

Explained, no events without photographers.
Still, who could argue with modern life;
And for every locomotive there was
Relief to be found in some melancholic stroller,

Some Sunday morning wedding, some frolicsome
Roué. No photographer (the
Psychologists noted) had ever despaired
Although a few had to be artists and speak

of subtleties that embarrassed the unimproved
Eye. Yet everyone agreed even they
Were honest sorts, content to display their illuminations
On walls, content to lap up the world like so many

Warm-tongued cats. Mom smiled, Dad winked, the camera
Whose omnipotence the reviewers found "refreshing" blinked.

BARON WORMSER

DIOGENES TRIES TO FORGET

It's one of those days when everything is half-off,
half-on. My shirt, for example, which I notice
is buttoned wrong while staring in the diner window.
I think I want a slice of pecan pie, some life
sweeter than this, like my childhood in Texas.
There's no pie today, just you,
by accident again, bent over your coffee
like the "V" the geese fly south.

It's a fall day. Because we're melancholy,
we kick leaves, pick up rocks to consider
tossing them at dogs. *I only breathe with one lung
since you've gone*, you say. And I love you
with one hemisphere of my brain,
the dumb one, which forgets.

MARY KARR

FLESH TONES

What we got stuck with.
Housing for pains fevers phlegms cancers.
Endures incredibly
solid as statues, inwardly seething.

Devil's stronghold.
Matchless material for the torturer to work with.

Without breath (which is spirit)
or spirit (which is breath)
offal
or slab on the counter packaged in plastic
with by-products.

Resurrected? To be recycled?
Scary. Scared.
But speeds curves colors tastes and textures,
—look!—wonderful.

RICHMOND LATTIMORE

From IMAGES OF CHINA

TORTURE

Here torture was an art like landscape painting,
Bamboo beneath the nails, the body fainting.
The voice was marvelously trained for mingling
The craft of screaming and the art of singing.

CHINESE COURTESY

A courteous people. Executioners
Lifting their lovely swords have always said,
"Sorry, but this may hurt a little." Then
With graceful stroke cut off your aching head.

PAUL ENGLE

A DEATH

In the end you want the clean dimensions of it mentioned,
to know the thing adverbially — while asleep,
after long illness, tragically in a blaze —

as you would the word of any local weather:
where it gathered, when it got here, how it kept
the traffic at a standstill, slowed the pace,

closed the terminals. Lineage & Issue, Names &
Dates are facts you gain most confidence in facing,
histories and habitats and whereabouts.

Speak of it, if you speak of it at all, in parts.
The C.V.A. or insufficiency or growth
that grew indifferent to prayer and medication.

Better a tidy science for a heart that stops
than the round and witless horror of someone who
one dry night in perfect humor ceases measurably to be.

THOMAS P. LYNCH

I AM LEARNING TO ABANDON THE WORLD

I am learning to abandon the world
before it can abandon me.
Already I have given up the moon
and snow, closing my shades
against the claims of white.
And the world has taken
my father, my friends.
I have given up melodic lines of hills,
moving to a flat, tuneless landscape.
And every night I give my body up
limb by limb, working upwards
across bone, towards the heart.
But morning comes with small
reprieves of coffee and birdsong.
A tree outside the window
which was simply shadow moments ago
takes back its branches twig
by leafy twig.
And as I take my body back
the sun lays its warm muzzle on my lap
as if to make amends.

                         LINDA PASTAN

DUSTING

Every day a wilderness—no
shade in sight. Beulah
patient among knickknacks,
the solarium a rage
of light, a grainstorm
as her gray cloth brings
dark wood to life.

Under her hand scrolls
and crests gleam
darker still. What
was his name, that
silly boy at the fair with

the rifle booth? And his kiss and
the clear bowl with one bright
fish, rippling
wound!

Not Michael—
something finer. Each dust
stroke a deep breath and
the canary in bloom.
Wavery memory: home
from a dance, the front door
blown open and the parlor
in snow, she rushed
the bowl to the stove, watched
as the locket of ice
dissolved and he
swam free.

That was years before
Father gave her up
with her name, years before
her name grew to mean
Promise, then

Desert-in-Peace.
Long before the shadow and
sun's accomplice, the tree.

Maurice.

RITA DOVE

WHAT IS LEFT TO SAY

The self steps out of the circle;
it stops wanting to be
the farmer, the wife and the child.

It stops trying to please
by learning everyone's dialect;
it finds it can live, after all,
in a world of strangers.

It sends itself fewer flowers;
it stops preserving its tears in amber.

How splendidly arrogant it was
when it believed the gold-filled tomb
of language awaited its raids!
Now it frequents the junkyards,
knowing all words are second-hand.

It has not chosen its poverty,
this new miserliness.
It did not want to fall out of love
with itself. Young,
it celebrated itself
and richly sang itself,
seeing only itself
in the mirror of the world.

It cannot return. It assumes
its place in a universe of stars
that do not see it. Even the dead
no longer need it to be at peace.
Its function is to applaud.

LISEL MUELLER

FAILING IN THE PRESENCE OF ANTS

We live to some purpose, daughter.
Across the park, among
The trees that give the eye
Something to do, let's spread
A blanket on the ground
And examine the ants, loose
Thread to an old coat.
They're more human than we are.
They live for the female,
Raise their hurt, and fall earthward
For their small cause. And
Us? We live for our bellies,
The big O of our mouths.
Give me, give me, they say,

And many people, whole countries,
May go under because we desire TV
And chilled drinks, clothes
That hang well on our bodies—
Desire sofas and angled lamps,
Hair the sea may envy
On a slow day.
It is small to sweep
Ants into a frenzy, blow
Chemicals into their eyes—
Those austere marchers who will lift
Their heads to rumor—seed,
Wafer of leaf, dropped apple—
And start off, over this
And that, between sloppy feet
And staggered chairs, for no other
Purpose than that it might be good.

GARY SOTO

EDGEWATER HOSPITAL

keeps a different time. Across the street, Lake Michigan folds
and unfolds light. It's dawn. It doesn't stop. The light,
the water, meet at a line we know slips into another dimension:
call it forever. They call it that in poems. But in
the linen closets of Edgewater, no matter how intense
and satiated the gift flowers set in window sun, or how
resolutely well-meaning the orderly's smile, something
unfolds, a shadow kept in a deepest crease, and it's

inevitable: we walk from the ward to the radiant world
outside with a part of us dimmed by the visit, the looking
ahead to another visit: we're darkness's octaroons.
Pain is always outside of time. I know two hands across
a face is a clock; and so my father says it's half past
cardiac, and stuck. The doctors have books that call some
futures days. It all depends. The glucose is a note
in a bottle and so it cries for rescue. Writing easy

turns of language on a beach bench is a way of making morning
afternoon. The lake's a waiting. For miles the great
lake drums its fingers — dependable
wash and beat. Like what they call in poems a heart,
they use that simile over and over again, as if the over
and over were reason enough. I think so. A heart.

ALBERT GOLDBARTH

WINGS AND SEEDS: FOR MY BIRTH MOTHER

Hiking a levee through the salt marsh,
My new mother and I. She is not teaching
Me to read and write but to believe
The hummingbird mistrusts its feet,
Weak below its feisty wings.

We trample brass buttons and chamomile,
As if to concern ourselves no more
With clothing and tea.
We twine hands, we trade heavy binoculars.
The clouds are coming from far out on the sea
Where they'd only the fetch to ruffle.

Separately our lives have passed from earthy passion
To wilder highliving creatures with wings.
With our early expectancies
Did we come to think ourselves a part of nature?

Terns flash here, four dolled-up stilts in a pool,
Dozens of godwits a thick golden hem on the bay —
You'd think we too knew how to find
Our way back to this home ground.

I was a child of pleasure.
The strong pleasurable seeds of life
Found each other.
And I was created by passion's impatience
For the long wait till our meeting.

SANDRA MC PHERSON

HOW TO REGAIN YOUR SOUL

Come down Canyon Creek trail on a summer afternoon
that one place where the valley floor opens out. You will see
the white butterflies. Because of the way shadows
come off those vertical rocks in the west, there are
shafts of sunlight hitting the river and a deep
long purple gorge straight ahead. Put down your pack.

Above, air sighs the pines. It was this way
when Rome was clanging, when Troy was being built,
when campfires lighted caves. The white butterflies dance
by the thousands in the still sunshine. Suddenly, anything
could happen to you. Your soul pulls toward the canyon
and then shines back through the white wings to be you again.

WILLIAM STAFFORD

CORNERS

I've sought out corner bars, lived in corner houses:
    like everyone else I've reserved
corner tables, thinking they'd be sufficient.
    I've met at corners
perceived as crossroads, loved to find love
    leaning against a lamppost
but have known the abruptness of corners too,
    the pivot, the silence.
I've sat in corners at parties hoping for someone
    who knew the virtue
of both distance and close quarters, someone with a
    corner person's taste
for intimacy, hard won, rising out of shyness
    and desire.
And I've turned corners there was no going back to,
    corners
in the middle of a room that led
    to Spain or solitude.
And always the thin line between corner
    and cornered,

the good corners of bodies and those severe bodies
    that permit no repose,
the places we retreat to, the places we can't bear
    to be found.

STEPHEN DUNN

FLIRTATION

After all, there's no need
to say anything

at first. An orange, peeled
and quartered, flares

like a tulip on a wedgewood plate
Anything can happen.

Outside the sun
has rolled up her rugs

and night strewn salt
across the sky. My heart

is humming a tune
I haven't heard in years!

Quiet's cool flesh—
let's sniff and eat it.

There are ways
to make of the moment

a topiary
so the pleasure's in

walking through.

RITA DOVE

ANTHEM

These birds pursue their errands
    On curvatures of air;
Like swift and lyric gerunds
    Unfurling everywhere,
They lash the sky with ribbons,
    With wakes of wrinkled blue,
Chanting Orlando Gibbons
    And Mozart's *Non so più*.

Shall we not in all conscience
    And glittering major keys
Offer them fair responsions
    And reciprocities?
Fanfares and sound fulfillings
    Of melodies unheard:
Brave philharmonious Billings
    And airs of William Byrd.

ANTHONY HECHT

SAPPHICS

Usually late, the distinguished season
Apt to make us wait, is absurdly early;
Premature, intemperate buds deface the
    Marble of winter.

Green returns, a freshly invented colour
Like a recently rediscovered poem
In a strange but strictly familiar metre
    Palpably Sapphic.

Time's corrupted text: undeciphered blossoms
Scattered on the grass like discarded garments
Reminiscent of the abandoned body
    That they embarrassed;

Tantalizing glances at tattered stanzas
Fragmentary as an archaic statue
Damaged by the passage of feet and ruined
    By restoration,

Legible as Spring, that forgotten language
Conjugated annually with liquid
Consonants, irregular endings, florid
       Vigorous verb-stems:

Night . . . and maidens . . . singers . . . nocturnal friendship
(Love?) . . . a nymph with violet breasts . . . These doubtful
Readings satisfy the indecent human
       Weakness for meaning

Which appears an easy illusion. Each
Lacuna punctuating the fragrant fragments
Written in the spring of the world translates the
       Grammar of springtime.

DARYL HINE

THEIR BODIES

To the students of anatomy
at Indiana University

That gaunt old man came first, his hair as white
As your scoured tables. Maybe you'll recollect him
By the scars of steelmill burns on the backs of his hands,
On the nape of his neck, on his arms and sinewy legs,
And her by the enduring innocence
Of her face, as open to all of you in death
As it would have been in life: she would memorize
Your names and ages and pastimes and hometowns
If she could, but she can't now, so remember her.

They believed in doctors, listened to their advice,
And followed it faithfully. You should treat them
One last time as they would have treated you.
They had been kind to others all their lives
And believed in being useful. Remember somewhere
Their son is trying hard to believe you'll learn
As much as possible from them, as *he* did,
And will do your best to learn politely and truly.

They gave away the gift of those useful bodies
Against his wish. (They had their own ways
Of doing everything, always.) If you're not certain
Which ones are theirs, be gentle to everybody.

DAVID WAGONER

THE ORIGIN OF ORDER

Stellar dust has settled.
It is green underwater now in the leaves
Of the yellow crowfoot. Its vacancies are gathered together
Under pine litter as emerging flower of the pink arbutus.
It has gained the power to make itself again
In the bone-filled egg of osprey and teal.

One could say this toothpick grasshopper
Is a cloud of decayed nebula congealed and perching
On his female mating. The tortoise beetle,
Leaving the stripped veins of morning glory vines
Like licked bones, is a straw-colored swirl
Of clever gases.

At this moment there are dead stars seeing
Themselves as marsh and forest in the eyes
Of muskrat and shrew, disintegrated suns
Making songs all night long in the throats
Of crawfish frogs, in the rubbings and gratings
Of the red-legged locust. There are spirits of orbiting
Rock in the shells of pointed winkles
And apple snails, ghosts of extinct comets caught
In the leap of darting hare and bobcat, revolutions
Of rushing stone contained in the sound of these words.

The paths of the Pleiades and Coma clusters
Have been compelled to mathematics by the mind
Contemplating the nature of itself
In the motions of stars. The patterns
Of any starry summer night night be identical
To the summer heavens circling inside the skull.
I can feel time speeding now in all directions
Deeper and deeper into the black oblivion
Of the electrons directly behind my eyes.

Flesh of the sky, child of the sky, the mind
Has been obligated from the beginning
To create an ordered universe
As the only possible proof of its own inheritance.

PATTIANN ROGERS

THE BOY SHEPHERDS' SIMILE

Wind rose cold under our robes, and straw blew loose
from the stable roof.
We loved the cow tied to the oak, her breath rising
in the black air, and the two goats trucked
from the Snelling farm, the gray dog shaking with age
and weather.
            Over our scene a great star hung
its light, and we could see in the bleached night
a crowd of overcoats peopling the chairs.
A coat of black ice glazed the street.

This was not a child or a king,
but Mary Sosebee's Christmas doll of a year ago.
We knelt in that knowledge on the wide front lawn
of the First Baptist Church
while flashbulbs went off all around us
and a choir of angels caroled from their risers.
This was not a child wrapped in the straw
and the ragged sheet, but since believing was an easy thing
we believed it was like a child,
a king who lived in the stories we were told.
For this we shivered in adoration. We bore the cold.

DAVID BOTTOMS

INVERSE PROPORTIONS

Proverbs, aphorisms, epigrams
are designed to contain worlds
in solution: little goblets for
sampling whole seas and raging climates.

In this way would it not be good
to have one's life center upon something
private and small, such as
keys, names, sleeping tablets?

You could carry this secret
everywhere and fondle it like a lucky piece,
cool and heavy in the fingers . . .
perhaps like a coin minted in antiquity,
by some old Emperor blurred by
the rub of dead thumbs for centuries;
engraved with words nobody alive
can read. Here would be salvation
and all the wisdom you'd ever need.

JACK MATTHEWS

DOING THE EVOLUTION SHUFFLE

For Archie

Sometimes I feel I've shacked up
with low-life instincts: the apes
rise in my genes and call me sister.
Hate clogs my brainstem
like a bad drain.

On better days I edge toward
one of the shining
abstracts, love not least
among them, mind bobbing,
a white mum above
the body's rubble. Let's say

then I'm soaring above the next-door
neighbor's bray of fast
tans, bucks, bitches
out to get her
man, I'm sensing
the molecules' spark, the DNA's game
for change: how in ten millennia

such friction kindles
a new species, a being
that in the mean time,
like a halting dawn
consents to gentle the sting
of consciousness.

ALICE FULTON

From CHRONOMETRICS

IV. HOURGLASS

Belied at top and bottom, pinched at the waist,
I move this little desert I've encased
whichever way is down. Its thin descent
mounts to a dune by steady increment.
Once multitudes convened to see me perch
at preacher's hand in each conforming church,
and as he schooled this world to meet the next
I mimed his arid sifting of his text.
No sermon runs an hour now. Nor do I.
Shrunken in stature, wrested from on high,
I time a mere two minutes for your egg.
Nothing like time to take one down a peg.

ROBERT B. SHAW

CHANSON PHILOSOPHIQUE

The nominalist in me invents
A life devoid of precedents.
The realist takes a different view:
He claims that all I feel and do
Billions of others felt and did
In history's Pre-me period.

Arguing thus, both voices speak
A partial truth. I am unique,
Yet the old, ceaseless self-distress
Of desire buffets me no less
Than it has other sons of man
Who've come and gone since time began:

The meaning, then, of this dispute?
My life's a nominal/real pursuit,
Which leaves identity clear and blurred,
In which what happens has occurred
Often and never—which is to say,
Never to me, or quite this way.

TIMOTHY STEELE

NARCISSUS AND ECHO

Shall the water not remember   *Ember*
my hand's slow gesture, tracing above   *of*
its mirror my half-imaginary   *airy*
portrait? My only belonging   *longing;*
is my beauty, which I take   *ache*
away and then return, as love   *of*
of teasing playfully the one being   *unbeing.*
whose gratitude I treasure   *Is your*
moves me. I live apart   *heart*
from myself, yet cannot   *not*
live apart. In the water's tone,   *stone?*
that brilliant silence, a flower   *Hour,*
whispers my name with such slight   *light!*
moment, it seems filament of air,   *fare*
the world become cloudswell.   *well.*

FRED CHAPPELL

MY CONFESSIONAL SESTINA

Let me confess. I'm sick of these sestinas
written by youngsters in poetry workshops
for the delectation of their fellow students,
and then published in little magazines
that no one reads, not even the contributors
who at least in this omission show some taste.

Is this merely a matter of personal taste?
I don't think so. Most sestinas
are such dull affairs. Just ask the contributors
the last time they finished one outside of a workshop,
even the poignant one on herpes in that new little magazine
edited by their most brilliant fellow student.

Let's be honest. It has become a form for students,
an exercise to build technique rather than taste
and the official entry blank into the little magazines —
because despite its reputation, a passable sestina
isn't very hard to write, even for kids in workshops
who care less about being poets than contributors.

Granted nowadays everyone is a contributor.
My barber is currently a student
in a rigorous correspondence school workshop.
At lesson six he can already taste
success having just placed his own sestina
in a national tonsorial magazine.

Who really cares about most little magazines?
Eventually not even their own contributors
who having published a few preliminary sestinas
send their work East to prove they're no longer students.
They need to be recognized as the new arbiters of taste
so they can teach their own graduate workshops.

Where will it end? This grim cycle of workshops
churning out poems for little magazines
no one honestly finds to their taste?
This ever-lengthening column of contributors
scavenging the land for more students
teaching them to write their boot camp sestinas?

Perhaps there is an afterlife where all contributors
have two workshops, a tasteful little magazine, and sexy students
who worshipfully memorize their every sestina.

DANA GIOIA

BITCH

Now, when he and I meet, after all these years,
I say to the bitch inside me, don't start growling.
He isn't a trespasser any more,
Just an old acquaintance tipping his hat.
My voice says, "Nice to see you,"
As the bitch starts to bark hysterically.
He isn't an enemy now,
Where are your manners, I say, as I say,
"How are the children? They must be growing up."
At a kind word from him, a look like the old days,
The bitch changes her tone: she begins to whimper
She wants to snuggle up to him, to cringe.

Down, girl! Keep your distance
Or I'll give you a taste of the choke-chain.
"Fine, I'm just fine," I tell him.
She slobbers and grovels.
After all, I am her mistress. She is basically loyal.

It's just that she remembers how she came running
Each evening, when she heard his step;
How she lay at his fret and looked up adoringly
Though he was absorbed in his paper;
Or, bored with her devotion, ordered her to the kitchen
Until he was ready to play.
But the small careless kindnesses
When he'd had a good day, or a couple of drinks,
Come back to her now, seem more important
Than the casual cruelties, the ultimate dismissal.
"It's nice to know you are doing so well," I say.
He couldn't have taken you with him;
You were too demonstrative, too clumsy,
Not like the well-groomed pets of his new friends.
"Give my regards to your wife," I say. You gag
As I drag you off by the scruff,
Saying, "Goodbye! Goodbye! Nice to have seen you again."

CAROLYN KIZER

POOR ANGELS

At this hour the soul floats weightlessly
through the city streets, speechless and invisible,
astonished by the smoky blend of grays and golds
seeping out of the air, the dark half-tones

of dusk suddenly filling the urban sky
while the body sits listlessly by the window
sullen and heavy, too exhausted to move,
too weary to stand up or to lie down.

At this hour the soul is like a yellow wing
slipping through the treetops, a little ecstatic
cloud hovering over the sidewalks, calling out
to the approaching night, "Amaze me, amaze me,"

while the body sits glumly by the window
listening to the clear summons of the dead
transparent as glass, clairvoyant as crystal.
Some nights it is almost ready to join them.

Oh, this is a strange, unlikely tethering,
a furious grafting of the quick and the slow:
when the soul flies up, the body sinks down
and all night—locked in the same cramped room—

they go on quarreling, stubbornly threatening
to leave each other, wordlessly filling the air
with the sound of a low internal burning.
How long can this bewildering marriage last?

At midnight the soul dreams of a small fire
of stars flaming on the other side of the sky,
but the body stares into an empty night sheen,
a hollow-eyed darkness. Poor luckless angels,

feverish old loves: don't separate yet.
Let what rises live with what descends.

EDWARD HIRSCH

DODONA: ASKED OF THE ORACLE

The female body, its creases and declivities
leading to the sacred opening, the hollow
whose precincts, here, neither seduce nor threaten:
bee-hum, birdsong, side-oats' leaning awns,
the blowing grasses (one vivid
lizard flickers on gray stone,
is gone); the drifting
down of poplars; harebells,
convolvulus. The triumph-song,
far off, of strutting cocks
no threat, merely ridiculous. Olympus
a mountain range away: huge valleys
charged with gargantuan
foreshadowings, new-minted
laser glints of force.

What lustral commerce
might cleanse the consciousness, hallow the body,
and renew a broken trust? Before Dione,
the dim earlier consort, gave place
to nagging, bitchy Hera (who for her nagging
had, of course, good reason)
would there have been a time
the rustle of earth-nurtured
oaks had meaning—when doves in flight,
as yet unhackneyed by utopian

demagogueries old as Noah,
might prove oracular?
Or was there,
in the safety even of this
place, this hollow, the quaver
of that hovering melisma (heard now
from the taxicab cassette, or filtered
through the debate above the tric-trac),
the voice of a despair that finds no solace
in warfare or politics? Does the unease
lie deeper, even, than the
archetypal cleft of sex?

AMY CLAMPITT

BIG CARS

Ten years later
they arrive on the thruway,
pulling winged fenders and smiling
a lane wide—big cars,
old floats that took a wrong
corner somewhere and lost
the American dream parade. Around them

the strange, grilleless
cars of the future
hum at their tires—tiny aliens
of a planet out of gas.

To think of their long trip
just beginning—the irrepressible fuel
rising everywhere into their tanks!
For the first time, armrests
unfolded out of seats;
out of the armrests, ashtrays!
Maps fell open to the new roads

which led them, finally, here
to the right lanes of America—
the antiques of optimism
nobody understands or wants
except the poor. Or dictators

driving down boulevards in some country
where the poor do not have cars
and run alongside until it seems
that they themselves are riding
on soft shocks, under a sun roof,
toward the great plenty of the New World.

WESLEY MC NAIR

REARVIEW MIRROR

This little pool in the air is
not a spring but sink into which
trees and highway bank and fields are
sipped away to minuteness. All
split on the present then merge in
stretched perspective radiant in
reverse, the wide world guttering
back to one lit point, as our way
weeps away to the horizon
in this eye where the past flies ahead.

ROBERT MORGAN

THE DISAPPOINTMENTS OF CHILDHOOD

*Perhaps a bird was singing and for it I felt
a tiny affection, the same size as a bird.*
Borges

Imagine now, an affection the same size
as the thing it's felt for: for the seed,
seed-like emoluments of liking and,
for the rain, droplets of tenderness
clustered in puddles at your feet.

And now remember how, as a child,
someone is telling you they love you.
How much does daddy love you? they
ask and you, childlike, spread
your arms as wide as a child can.

Little do you know it then, but the rest
of your life will be spent measuring
the distance between "that much"
and what love, in fact, is capable of—

the narrow width of a man or a woman,
their terrible thinness,
their small bones
growing constantly inward
from your spreading arms.

MICHAEL BLUMENTHAL

JANUS

Janus writes books for women's liberation;
His wife types up the scripts from his dictation.

LIMERICK

The sex-life her husband dreamed of,
She considered herself far above.
   He craved osculation
   And *then* copulation!—
She wanted to kiss and make love.

LAURENCE PERRINE

CLOUD PAINTER

Suggested by the life and art of John Constable

At first, as you know, the sky is incidental—
a drape, a backdrop for trees and steeples.
Here an oak clutches a rock (already he works outdoors),
a wall buckles but does not break,
water pearls through a lock, a haywain trembles.

The pleasures of landscape are endless. What we see
around us should be enough.
Horizons are typically high and far away.

Still, clouds let us drift and remember. He is, after all,
a miller's son, used to trying
to read the future in the sky, seeing instead
ships, horses, instruments of flight.
Is that his mother's wash flapping on the line?
His schoolbook, smudged, illegible?

In this period the sky becomes significant.
Cloud forms are technically correct—mares' tails,
sheep-in-the-meadow, thunderheads.
You can almost tell which scenes have been interrupted
by summer showers.

Now his young wife dies.
His landscapes achieve belated success.
He is invited to join the Academy. I forget
whether he accepts or not.

In any case, the literal forms give way
to something spectral, nameless. His palette shrinks
to grey, blue, white—the colors of charity.
Horizons sink and fade,
trees draw back till they are little more than frames,
then they too disappear.

Finally the canvas itself begins to vibrate
with waning light,
as if the wind could paint.
And we too, at last, stare into a space
which tells us nothing,
except that the world can vanish along with our need for it.

JANE FLANDERS

313

READING THE WRITING

With his own hand he has given himself away.
"You are very secretive and fearful," she says
For twenty dollars, his mail-order explainer.
"You show no generosity to people
Or to yourself. Try not to be deceitful."
This is not palmistry. What she has read
Is something he has written.
Like everyone else he is a man of letters.

He thinks what she has read was written
Decades ago when first he was forming
His characters after the various models
His hand in its cunning
Always succeeded in failing
To be more than a variation on.
Only the *J* of his John Hancock is John Hancock's.
So he became himself, like everyone.

She has taught him a lesson, his accuser.
All this he had hidden in the open,
Showing everyone no generosity to himself.
Perhaps in the future he will send
Himself only to the printer, who will reform him.
For now, he is trying not to be deceitful.
He is giving himself away. Here. In his own hand.

JOHN N. MORRIS

PREPARING TO LIVE AMONG THE OLD

Go where there is music,
whether to parks and streets
with sun on flashing brass,
or darkened bars in jukebox glow.
This is your gentle beginning:
in the presence of song nearly all forgive
the wheezing voice and sagging heart.

Almost without your noticing,
allow no hand, year upon year,
to stroke or touch your skin.

Spend your days in a single room.
Imagine your walls as mirrors
reflecting mirrors behind you.
Wherever you look you will see —
past eyes and rounded shoulders —
your curving back, faceless.
A stranger you will not meet again.

STEPHEN COREY

FLIGHT

*In the early stages of epilepsy there occurs a characteristic
dream . . . One is somehow lifted free of one's own
body; looking back one sees oneself and feels a sudden,
maddening fear; another presence is entering one's own
person, and there is no avenue of return.*

George Steiner

Outside my window the wasps
are making their slow circle,
dizzy flights of forage and return,
hovering among azaleas
that bob in a sluggish breeze
this humid, sun-torn morning.

Yesterday my wife held me here
as I thrashed and moaned, her hand
in my foaming mouth, and my son
saw what he was warned he might.

That night dreams stormed my brain
in thick swirls of shame and fear.
Behind a white garage a locked shed
full of wide-eyed dolls burned,
yellow smoke boiling up in huge clumps
as I watched, feet nailed to the ground.
In dining cars white table cloths
unfolded wings and flew like gulls.
An old German in a green homburg
sang lieder, *Mein Herz ist müde.*
In a garden in Pasadena my father

posed in Navy whites while overhead
silver dirigibles moved like great whales.
And in the narrowing tunnel
of the dream's end I flew down
onto the iron red road
of my grandfather's farm.
There was a white rail fence.
In the green meadow beyond,
a small boy walked toward me.
His smile was the moon's rim.
Across his egg-shell eyes
ran scenes from my future life,
and he embraced me like a son
or father or my lost brother.

B. H. FAIRCHILD

THE POET AT EIGHTEEN

In the cab of a truck bound straight across Ohio,
      to earn my ride
and keep the driver sharp against the traffic flow,
      one night I tried

right out of my freshman textbooks to convince
      him of all things
to know thyself was best, and since
      to that iron string

each heart beats true, each man should undergo
      the search within
or with his dying gurgle will not know
      that he has been

alive. The driver was amused, and stayed awake
      but said he'd heard
those thoughts before. His large foot worked the brake
      to miss a furred

thing stumbling from the bushes. In the greenish light
      I saw him pop

a benny, swallow it with spit, then sight
    the first snowdrop

upon our windshield, rub it out. "Damn," he said,
    "it means we'll reach
Indiana like we're on a god-damn sled."
    He said that each

five miles slower was another half an hour
    from town to town—
more minutes when he could not sleep, nor wear
    a woman down.

It was a mighty snowstorm. At its end
    he slid the truck
beside a clapboard house, and left me there, went in
    to try his luck.

A soft loose woman's shadow met the curtains,
    then retreated.
I looked away. A stone deer sniffed the lawn
    for crusts of bread.

Freezing, wrapped in blankets, I began
    to draw my face
upon the frosted mirror. It took me until then
    to know my place.

DICK ALLEN

HAPPINESS

So early it's still almost dark out.
I'm near the window with coffee,
and the usual early morning stuff
that passes for thought.
When I see the boy and his friend
walking up the road
to deliver the newspaper.
They have on caps and sweaters,
and the one boy has a bag over his shoulder.
They are so happy
they aren't saying anything, these boys.

I think if they could, they would take
each other's arm.
It's early in the morning,
and they are doing this thing together.
They come on, slowly.
The sky is taking on light,
though the moon still hangs palely over the water.
Such beauty that for a minute
death and ambition, even love
doesn't enter into this.
Happiness. It comes on
unexpectedly. And goes beyond, really,
any early morning talk about it.

RAYMOND CARVER

SWEET WILL

The man who stood beside me
34 years ago this night fell
on to the concrete, oily floor
of Detroit Transmission, and we
stepped carefully over him until
he wakened and went back to his press.

It was Friday night, and the others
told me that every Friday he drank
more than he could hold and fell
and he wasn't any dumber for it
so just let him get up at his
own sweet will or he'll hit you.

"At his own sweet will," was just
what the old black man said to me,
and he smiled the smile of one
who is still surprised that dawn
graying the cracked and broken windows
could start us all to singing in the cold.

Stash rose and wiped the back of his head
with a crumpled handkerchief and looked
at his own blood as though it were
dirt and puzzled as to how
it got there and then wiped the ends
of his fingers carefully one at a time

the way the mother wipes the fingers
of a sleeping child, and climbed back
on his wooden soda-pop case to
his punch press and hollered at all
of us over the oceanic roar of work,
addressing us by our names and nations—

"Nigger, Kike, Hunky, River Rat,"
but he gave it a tune, an old tune,
like "America the Beautiful." And he danced
a little two-step and smiled showing
the four stained teeth left in the front
and took another suck of cherry brandy.

In truth it was no longer Friday,
for night had turned to day as it
often does for those who are patient,
so it was Saturday in the year of '48
in the very heart of the city of man
where your Cadillac cars get manufactured.

In truth all those people are dead,
they have gone up to heaven singing
"Time on My Hands" or "Begin the Beguine,"
and the Cadillacs have all gone back
to earth, and nothing that we made
that night is worth more than me.

And in truth I'm not worth a thing
what with my feet and my two bad eyes
and my one long nose and my breath
of old lies and my sad tales of men
who let the earth break them back,
each one, to dirty blood or bloody dirt.

Not worth a thing. Just like it was said
at my magic birth when the stars
collided and fire fell from great space
into great space, and people rose one
by one from cold beds to tend a world
that runs on and on at its own sweet will.

                          PHILIP LEVINE

ATHENE

Force of reason, who shut up the shrill
foul Furies in the dungeon of the Parthenon,
led whimpering to the cave they live in still,

beneath the rock your city foundered on:
who, equivocating, taught revenge to sing
(or seem to, or be about to) a kindlier tune:

mind that can make a scheme of anything—
a game, a grid, a system, a mere folder
in the universal file drawer: uncompromising

mediatrix, virgin married to the welfare
of the body politic: deific contradiction,
warbonnet-wearing olive-bearer, author

of the law's delays, you who as talisman
and totem still wear the aegis, baleful
with Medusa's scowl (though shrunken

and self-mummified, a Gorgon still): cool
guarantor of the averted look, the guide
of Perseus, who killed and could not kill

the thing he'd hounded to its source, the dread
thing-in-itself none can elude, whose counter-
feit we halfway hanker for: aware (half mad

with clarity) we have invented all you stand for,
though we despise the artifice—a space to savor
horror, to pre-enact our own undoing in—
living, we stare into the mirror of the Gorgon.

                                        AMY CLAMPITT

FIERCE GIRL PLAYING HOPSCOTCH

You sway like a crane to the tunes of tossed stones.
I am what you made to live in
from what you had: hair matted as kelp, bad schools.

Oh, you will never know me. I wave and you go
on playing in the clouds
boys clap from erasers. I am the pebble
you tossed on the chalked space and war-
danced toward, one-leg two-leg, arms treading air.

In this, your future, waves rechristen the sea
after its tiny jeweled lives
that hiss "Us Us" to the shore all day.
Where's the kid called Kateydid? The moonfaced
Kewpiedoll? The excitable pouting
Zookie? The somber O-Be-Joyful?

Lost girl, playing hopscotch, I will do what you could.
Name of father, son, ghost. Cross my heart and hope.
While the sea's jewels build shells and shells
change to chalk and chalk to loam and gold
wheat grows where oceans teetered.

ALICE FULTON

WHY FORTUNE IS THE EMPRESS OF THE WORLD

The insect born of royalty has Marx
And worker housing as a life; has sex
Or clover honey to his pleasure, as
Have we. The parrot speaks. All use: the ant
The aphid and the crocodile the bird.
What then is human wholly? Is it heart?
Fidelity exists in any dog.
Good Doctor who have found your Missing Link,
On your return what will you have him be?
Free agent or a tenant in a cage?

A simple test will serve. It more or less
Is this: can he be taught a game of chance?
It is not possible, you must agree,
To think of animals as gambling. Odds,
Except for us, do not exist. An ape
Assumes always his jump will reach the limb.
For all his skill, he cannot cut his loss.
We, on the other hand, at our most threatened
Turn instinctively . . . to Reason? No.
To Fortune, as a mindlessness of mind.
The random that we create creates us.
In overcrowded life boats, we draw lots.

TURNER CASSITY

CRUISING WITH THE BEACH BOYS

So strange to hear that song again tonight
Travelling on business in a rented car
Miles from anywhere I've been before.
And now a tune I haven't heard for years
Probably not since it last left the charts
Back in L.A. in 1969.
I can't believe I know the words by heart
And can't think of a girl to blame them on.

Every lovesick summer has its song,
And this one I pretended to despise.
But if I were alone when it came on,
I turned it up full-blast to sing along—
A primal scream in croaky baritone,
The notes all flat, the lyrics mostly slurred—
No wonder I spent so much time alone
Making the rounds in Dad's old Thunderbird.

Some nights I drove down to the beach to park
And walk along the railings of the pier.
The water down below was cold and dark,
The waves monotonous against the shore.
The darkness and the mist, the midnight sea,
The flickering lights reflected from the city—
A perfect setting for a boy like me,
The Cecil B. DeMille of my self-pity.

I thought by now I'd left those nights behind,
Lost like the girls that I could never get,
Gone with the years, junked with the old T-Bird.
But one old song, a stretch of empty road,
Can open up a door and let them fall
Tumbling like boxes from a dusty shelf
Tightening my throat for no reason at all
Bringing on tears shed only for myself.

DANA GIOIA

FOSSIL FUEL

Dark storms of the afternoon persist
until what little day there was has gone,
but she still lingers in his eyes
and seldom lets him sleep.
He has grown vulnerable —
a turtle with no shell,
a bird trapped in the cat's hypnotic eye.
Her shadow has left its imprint on the wall.

A scoop of coal revives the fireplace
and melts the chill that harbors in the bone
but soon releases ghosts of mastodons
and fish and flying reptiles
pressed in their carbon matrix since that day
when some upheaval trapped them in their bog.

He lives his life inert, compressed by time
growing steady in his orbit
and established in his ways
until somewhere on this journey
he is making to himself,
she returns to him to set his head afire
and all his million years of words
escape at last to keep her warm.

JOHN DICKSON

ACCORDING TO OVID

there is no future in virtue. A woman
who sews or weaves or quilts has little hope
if she has no family or proper place.

Like a spider blind to her own daring
this woman fills her house with movement
of only her hands, her domestic dance

full of allusion and longing.
One man alone watches the work, the needle
flashing in and out of the fleshy fabric

dragging its tail of thread, its thread
of a tale told in silence and flickering light.
A woman on the prairie a century ago wrote:

"I make them warm to keep my family
from freezing; I make them beautiful to keep
my heart from breaking."

So she sits like Arachne weaving,
as if a rival sits invisible across
the room and the competition

grows deadly. The colors bloom
as sudden as the sun after rain
which comes with its rainbow and fills

not the eye but the mind with the ghost
of lavender and violet-rose, a ribbon
to tie the package of her loneliness.

                              BIN RAMKE

HAWK HILL

August dusk. We rest on the green porch,
yellowjackets and ants at our knees—
You in from work, ready to cook
The dinner I can't; I three-fourths through
The eightieth sick-day, weaker still;
We cheering a milestone with smooth Glenlivet:
Eleven years of peace and war;
Our squalls and calms. The hidden thrush
In the big beech behind us pauses to play
His billionth variation on the five notes
Stamped in his throat. You face me and say
"*Real time*," then add with customary
Unbarked candor "Whether you make it
Or not, these days were real time"—

Twelve days in which you've fed me squarely,
Dried my bedsore, each night stripped
My slack legs for baby-sleep (that sound and brief);
No word or sign of balk or grievance.

Whether I make it or not, old struggler
(Treasured as any, with all our scars),
Feel it hereafter as all real time—
All one linked try to tread one void.

We pay for it now.

REYNOLDS PRICE

ILLINOIS: AT NIGHT,
BLACK HAWK'S STATUE BROODS

For Robt. D. Sutherland

The forests I believed in,
Where pathways were open,
Come to this:
Duck decoys,
Picnic tables,
Oak furniture,
Faces in mirrors.

Where is my father,
Who thrived
On a trickle of water,
Could feast
On skunk or buzzard?

My mother, whose hands,
Weaving like sand in the wind,
Took in birds
To mend their broken wings?

The land is old and tired,
It sleeps in its own shadow.

I cannot kneel
To touch the soil.
The wind in my ears
Makes everywhere
And nowhere
My home.

J. W. RIVERS

A CALLING

Over my desk Georgia O'Keeffe says
I have no theories to offer and then
takes refuge in the disembodied
third person singular: *One works
I suppose because it is the most
interesting thing one knows to do.*
O Georgia! Sashaying between
first base and shortstop as it were
drawing up a list of all the things
*one imagines one has to do . . .
You get the garden planted. You
take the dog to the vet. You
certainly have to do the shopping.*

Syntax, like sex, is intimate.
One doesn't lightly leap from person
to person. *The painting*, you said,
is like a thread that runs
through all the reasons for all the other
things that make one's life.
O awkward invisible third person,
come out, stand up, be heard!
Poetry is like farming. It's
a calling, it needs constancy,
the deep woods drumming of the grouse,
and long life, like Georgia's, who
is talking to one, talking to me,
talking to you.

MAXINE KUMIN

OH KEEP THE POET HENCE

Dante Gabriel Rossetti buried manuscript poems, bound in gray calf,
with his wife; seven years later he had them disinterred (in this
sonnet he does it himself) and then published them.

The Blessed Damozel was shocked. She fumed.
For, peering from the Realm of Lasting Life,
She saw that her Creator had exhumed
The coffin of his most beloved wife,
And there was fishing in the earthy vapors
For poems of which he had not kept a copy.
(This, for a man of many words and papers,
He now thought unprofessionally sloppy.)
The disillusioned Lady dropped a tear
As musically as in the Poet's verses,
Weeping that sentiment should disappear
Amid the mutterings and whispered curses—
That ended when he spied gray calf, that bound them:
"Oh bless my dearest Love. They're safe. I've found them!"

THOMAS CARPER

WRITTEN IN MY DREAM BY W. C. WILLIAMS

"As Is
you're bearing

a common
Truth

Commonly known
as desire

No need
to dress

it up
as beauty

No need
to distort

what's not
standard

to be
understandable.

Pick your
nose

eyes ears
tongue

sex and
brain

to show
the populace

Take your
chances

on
your accuracy

Listen to
yourself

talk to
yourself

and others
will also

gladly
relieved

of the burden—
their own

thought
and grief.

What began
as desire

will end
wiser."

Baoding, China
November 23, 1984

ALLEN GINSBERG

COLD QUILT

Our clear-eyed guide said it is the slick
Cotton that makes quilts cold. I wonder
if it isn't the enduring dowry of bitterness
stitched into them that makes us shiver,
as in that quilt (unfit for hanging) handed
down to me from my father's mother, begun
the day her husband died, a lifelong lament

composed of old suits and shirts he'd worn,
threaded to her leftover dresses, its design—
each pane a basket of memorial flowers,
a dozen loud triangles tipped on their sides—
a stiff pastiche of grief and the solitary
nights spent trying to transform their bad luck
into something useful, used. No busy bee

touched that quilt. Her life became a patchwork
of quilted plenty, her yard a dormitory
of vegetable beds, her table a dazzling pattern
of cakes and pies. But she stayed skinny
and wrapped herself in the plain handmade cocoon
of that death-quilt every night, even when
she began to fade in her children's used beds.

At the funeral home, my uncle the soldier
draped her coffin with it, prayed, then handed
her life's flag to me, compactly folded, her
crooked stitches and nearly-rotten panes still
tenacious after half a century, the sheep
I count now in the inherited dark, her cold quilt
a poultice I spread on my chest before sleep.

MICHAEL MC FEE

IN BED WITH A BOOK

In police procedurals they are dying all over town,
the life ripped out of them, by gun, bumper, knife,
hammer, dope, etcetera, and no clues at all.
All through the book the calls come in: body found
in bed, car, street, lake, park, garage, library,
and someone goes out to look and write it down.
Death begins life's whole routine to-do
in these stories of our fellow citizens.

Nobody saw it happen, or everyone saw,
but can't remember the car. What difference does it make
when the child will never fall in love, the girl will never
have a child, the man will never see a grandchild, the old maid
will never have another cup of hot cocoa at bedtime?
As in life, the dead are dead, their consciousness,
as dear to them as mine to me, snuffed out.
What has mind to do with this, when the earth is bereaved?

I lie, with my dear ones, holding a fictive umbrella,
while around us falls the real and acid rain.
The handle grows heavier and heavier in my hand.
Unlike life, tomorrow night under the bedlamp
by a quick link of thought someone will find out why,
and the policemen and their wives and I will feel better.
But all that's toward the end of the book. Meantime, tonight,
without a clue I enter sleep's little rehearsal.

MONA VAN DUYN

POSTSCRIPT TO AN ELEGY

What I forgot to mention was the desultory
Unremarkable tremor of the phone ringing
Late in the day, to say you were stopping by,
The door slung open on your breezy arrival,
Muffled car horns jamming in the neighborhood,

Our talk of nothing particular, nothing of note,
The flare of laughter in a tilted wineglass.
Or we would be watching a tavern softball game
And you would come short-cutting by, your last hard mile

Dissolving in chatter and beer on the sidelines.
How did that Yankee third baseman put it, tossing
His empty glove in the air, his old friend
Sheared off halfway home in an air crash? "I thought
I'd be talking to him for the rest of my life."

Talk as I may of quickness and charm, easy laughter,
The forms of love, the sudden glint off silverware
At midnight will get in my eyes again,
And when it goes the air will be redolent still

With garlic, a high note from Armstrong, little shards
That will not gather into anything,
Those nearly invisible flecks of marble
Stinging the bare soles of the curious
Long after the statue is polished and crated away.

GIBBONS RUARK

MY TWO LIVES

The life I could have lived,
that other, better one,
is also mine. Who else
can claim it? Each morning, stooping
down, I know that I'm not worthy
to tie my own showlaces.

ERNEST SANDEEN

ELEGY FOR JOHN, MY STUDENT DEAD OF AIDS

In my office, where you sat years ago and talked
Of Donne, of how you loved
His persona, the bravado he could muster
To cover love's uncertainties,
Books still line the shelves, centuries
Of writers who've tried to make a kind of sense
Of life and death and, failing that,
Found words to stand at least
Against the griefs we can't resolve.

Now you're dead. And what I've got to say
Comes now from that silence
When our talk last fouled up. I allowed you less,
As always, than you wanted to say.
We talked beside the Charles, a lunch hour reunion
Of sorts after years of your postcards
(New York, San Francisco, Greece),
Failed attempts to find a place to live.
The warm weather had come on

In a rush. You talked of being the first born,
Dark-haired, Italian son. How you rarely visited
The family you so clearly loved.
I shifted to books, to sunlight falling
Through sycamores and the idle play of underlying
Shadows. When we parted,
All that was really left was the feeling
You deserved better. And yet I was relieved
Our hour was up, that we had kept your confusion

To yourself. We shook hands, you drove off to Boston.
Now you're dead and I wonder
If your nobleness of living with no one
To turn to ended in dishonor,
Your family ashamed. Or if your death had
About it a frail dignity,
Each darkening bruise precise as a writer's word,
Saying, at last, who you were — exactly
And to anyone who would listen.

ROBERT CORDING

333

AND THE GRASS DID GROW

Nothing is happening,
and yet what is being acted-out
or proven right now, flamboyantly,
might just turn a corner
and become the real thing.

Mostly holed-up in a room
somewhere, or pacing the twi-lit
underworld of the neighborhood, another
honest display of emotion taking up
its fair share of available space,
and all the desire I can possibly
imagine, like a stone flung,
inscribing its arc of air.

But living is fickle, open-ended,
even the little myths break down.
Nobody thinks I'm very funny.
In fact, they're insulted.
They've exacted their portions
and now appear rather chipper,
scattering me over the hillsides

and into the night.
Like a pedestrian in a crosswalk
replaced by another man, I go with them.
And I don't go. The need remains
forever: to have, to get my hands on,
or to be taken, to lose myself
in a warmer, less urgent caress.

I open one eye, take a look around.
No pat answers, no permanence or rest.
Someone just happens to keep beginning,
and my life too, where I left it,
over there.

RALPH ANGEL

POLE VAULTING

Our thin, tough bodies were identical
And when we threw ourselves one at a time
Across the bamboo pole at chest level
Any of us could break the last record.
I was a girl, but had the longest legs.
One brother was the tallest, one the lightest,
And one afraid of nothing, though his knees
Were always bandaged, and his palms scraped raw.
We practiced in the field behind our house,
And at our tournaments, called our mother
To act as referee and audience.
We ran and flung ourselves into the air,
Vaulting on the metal clothesline prop,
Trying to make our bodies horizontal,
And keep our feet from touching the bamboo.
Sometimes I thought I had wings on my heels
And if I let go when I was highest,
I'd fly above the roof and disappear.

Is this the same light body I could toss
Or bend backwards, somersault or cartwheel?
My brothers' sons are what my brothers were.
I hold them on my lap, and realize
I did fly off above the roof one day
And no one noticed. But where did I go?
Into the clouds, which swirled across my face.
I liked the heady sensation of flight
Though I was dropping downward half the way
To this Memorial Day, this picnic.
My brothers fry hamburgers, call their sons
In fathers' voices, and now I see
How they, too, disappeared in the bright air
As they cleared the high pole, and kept going.

MAURA STANTON

COMING INTO HISTORY

While I sit in south light, suspecting nothing,
your cells begin to read the hidden code
which teaches your hand it must become the hand
and informs the foot of its own metatarsal.
Every minute, now, is hazardous.
Suppose your cells forget their language?
Suppose the language they know is monstrous?
But your tiny body lengthens, becomes a stalk.
The vertebrae bubble on your spine like pearls.
Your head begins to bulge. Your eyes appear
like flecks of pepper. Your nervous system spreads
its net. And then in the fourth week, your heart
starts beating. Careful and adroit, your cells
rehearse, trying to crowd out accident,
filling up the acquiescent water.
They copy their nature over and over like doom,
straining to make alternatives unthinkable,
practicing to grow inevitable,
to bring your body into history where
the midwife's hands are drawing on their gloves.

JEANNE MURRAY WALKER

MORNING JITTERS

And the storm re-established itself
As a hole in the sheet of time
And of the weariness of the world,
And all the old work that remains to be done on its surface.
Came morning and the husband was back on the shore
To ask another favor of the fish,
Leviathan now, patience wearing thin. Whose answer
Bubbled out of the waves' crenellations:

"*Too late!* Yet if you analyze
The abstract good fortune that has brought you
To this floor, you must also unpluck the bees
Immured in the hive of your mind and bring the nuisance
And the glory into sharper focus. Why,
Others too will have implored before forgetting
To remove a stick of night from the scrub-forest
That keeps us wondering about ourselves

Until luck or nepotism has run its course! Only I say,
Your uniqueness isn't that unique
And doors must close in the shaved head
Before they can spring ajar. Take this.
Its promise equals power." To be shaken thus
Vehemently back into one's trance doesn't promise
Any petitioner much, even the servile ones. But night in its singleness
Of motive rewards all equally for what cannot
Appear disinterested survival tactics from the vantage
Point of some rival planet. Things go on being the same,
As darkness and ships ruffle the sky.

JOHN ASHBERY

AVAILABLE NOW: ARCHAIC TORSOS OF BOTH SEXES

Though I'm modest as most,
I couldn't help noticing
certain parts of the statues
have been polished
to a high sheen
by passing hands
as the centuries passed.
If it's a form of worship
it's not much odder
or more perverse
than the saint's stone toe
kissed to a stub by fervent lips.

And even though Plato
suspected art almost as much
as he suspected the body's curves,
he did assert Desire
could lead to the True
and Beautiful.
                    Therefore
I choose to believe that mortals
pausing here to cup a marble
breast or buttock
were doing their best
to grasp the Ideal—
and their foolish gestures
made it shine more brightly.

GREGORY ORR

337

REFUGE

A stand of paper birches years & years
of lovers have tattooed with their black hearts
& initials shades the starved baby tapping
his mother's breast like a downy woodpecker.

In the marsh behind him, red-winged blackbirds
go down in flames to feed
cattail-sheltered nestlings, while bullfrogs
tune their bass instruments as if rehearsing

for the night ahead. Here, where generations
have come to leave their mark
in passing, the plus signs
still add up to something like desire:

all the letters of the alphabet
in love with each other to this day.

RANDY BLASING

TO MY MOTHER

I was your rebellious son,
do you remember? Sometimes
I wonder if you do remember,
so complete has your forgiveness been.

So complete has your forgiveness been
I wonder sometimes if it did not
precede my wrong, and I erred,
safe found, within your love,

prepared ahead of me, the way home,
or my bed at night, so that almost
I should forgive you, who perhaps
foresaw the worst that I might do,

and forgave before I could act,
causing me to smile now, looking back,
to see how paltry was my worst,
compared to your forgiveness of it

already given. And this, then,
is the vision of that Heaven of which
we have heard, where those who love
each other have forgiven each other,

where, for that, the leaves are green,
the light a music in the air,
and all is unentangled,
and all is undismayed.

WENDELL BERRY

PRAYER FOR MY FATHER

Your head is still
restless, rolling
east and west.
That body in you
insisting on living
is the old hawk
for whom the world
darkens.
If I am not
with you when you die,
that is just.

It is all right.
That part of you cleaned
my bones more
than once. But I
will meet you
in the young hawk
whom I see
inside both
you and me; he
will guide
you to the Lord of Night,
who will give you
the tenderness
you wanted here.

ROBERT BLY

ARMORED HEARTS

I'd been awakened before by hammers cracking across the pond,
but who'd be building at dawn? On a Sunday?

And I remembered the ducks, a loggerhead
must have eaten another duck. So I rolled into my jeans
and walked out onto the porch. Then the crack again,

and I saw through the fog dusting the banks and the pond
a man on the far bank, my neighbor
in the branches of a tree, his pistol
pecking at the water, and just the right angle
to catch my house with a ricochet.

Whatever new threat I shouted
must have worked. That afternoon he took to traps,
baiting his hooks with livers and fish heads,
floating them under milk jugs. All evening
I watched from my porch as he labored in his boat, knotting
his lines, tying his bait, easing out the jugs
like a rope of pearls,
and learned how much he cared for the ducks—

and how he must have hated what killed them, the snappers
with their ugly armored hearts, who wallow
like turnips in the muck of the bottom, clinging
to their stony solitude,
who refuse to sun, hiding like lost
fears, rising when they're least expected
into a panic of wings. This is what I thought about
as I rowed in the dark from one jug to the next, stripping
the bait from his hooks.

DAVID BOTTOMS

THE INVERSE SQUARE LAW OF THE PROPAGATION OF LIGHT

With apologies to Carl Sagan

Leaves are splitting free in the invisible,
random winds as the last of the daylight
wears down. We've walked to the bluff
where evening, by turns, is immense
with that deep and airy blue, where stars
begin to slide in and then come set,
sterling in their old, unsolved equations.

The scientist tells us there are a few
hundred billion stars in the Milky Way
alone—red giants, black, imploding holes.
But I like how the bushmen of Botswana have it—
the galaxy is simply the backbone of the night,
brilliantly holding up the sky.
                                        And just so,
Aquinas in his elaborate lock-step soul
would agree in so much as he saw that
all nature complements grace, and thus
went as far as you could go on Faith.
Just as abstract particles are not flung
into the sky to come down meshed cogs
and clocks, we might sift through
the velocity of Time and arrive at how
unlikely it is that we're just a splash,
haphazard in the cosmic pond—the stippled nebulae,
those scintillating bytes, may well add up,
connect like synapses in a mind.

The interstellar medium, then,
(read *dust*) sings brightly forth

in our bones, and the great, blind degree
and piecemeal of the void could well be still
swimming out from that initial spark.
And, given the unthinkable removes of light,
earth is as rare and predictable
a spot as any to be magnified against
the incoherent backdrop of the dark.

CHRISTOPHER BUCKLEY

THE BEARER

Like all his people he felt at home in the forest.
The silence beneath great trees, the dimness there,
The distant high rustling of foliage, the clumps
Of fern like little green fountains, patches of sunlight,
Patches of moss and lichen, the occasional
Undergrowth of hazel and holly, was he aware
Of all this? On the contrary his unawareness
Was a kind of gratification, a sense of comfort
And repose even in the strain of running day
After day. He had been aware of the prairies.
He had known he hated the sky so vast, the wind
Roaring in the grasses, and the brightness that
Hurt his eyes. Now he hated nothing; nor could he
Feel anything but the urgency that compelled him
Onward continually. "May I not forget, may I
Not forget," he said to himself over and over.
When he saw three ravens rise on their awkward
Wings from the forest floor perhaps seventy-five
Ells ahead of him, he said, "Three ravens,"
And immediately forgot them. "May I not forget,"
He said, and repeated again in his mind the exact
Words he had memorized, the message that was
Important and depressing, which made him feel
Worry and happiness at the same time, a peculiar
Elation. At last he came to his people far
In the darkness. He smiled and spoke his words,
And he looked intently into their eyes gleaming
In firelight. He cried when they cried. No rest
For his lungs. He flinched and lay down while they
Began to kill him with clubs and heavy stones.

HAYDEN CARRUTH

AGAINST POETRY

Suddenly I too see
why everybody hates it—
the manifestoes of metaphor, the mad
voice that mumbles all night
in the dark: *this is like that, that
is this*, the phosphorescent
flares of vision, the busyness
of words sweeping up
after all that sputter . . . .

When the princess spoke toads
everybody loathed her,
but when her mouth spouted jewels
it was hardly better:

Not much difference, muttered the courtiers,
*between a slide of slime, of jumpy
lumps on the table,
and a spurt of little glittering pellets
hitting you in the eye!*

*It would be more seemly all round
if that lady kept her shapely
lips
tightened on nothing.*

Although, as a matter of fact,
those marshals and admirals
kept on dreaming of things
that were—like what?
like *rubies*? like
emeralds?

                    SANDRA M. GILBERT

COORDINATING CONJUNCTION

And . . . and so it goes:
As the thread outlasts the spool,
 So the thorn, the rose.

Time observes its rule:
Each instant leaps back into
 The dark lilied pool

It sprang from. Each blue
Tile along the garden wall
 Ends where it has to

End, in a thin scrawl
Of grout that marks out its grave.
 Summer comes to fall.

Though breathing and brave,
The sentence stops, that must burn
 The air in its cave.

Thus our great concern—
Feeling shut in by the wall
 Of our own pattern—

Seems quite natural:
Even with some makeshift plan,
 How to keep it all

Going, how to fan
The embers of aftermath
 Up now into an

Even flame—not wrath
Nor sudden lust yielded to—
 But light on a path

That would continue
Until some kind of an end
 Crept up into view

From around some bend
Or straight toward us from the dark
    Who but would extend

That path, keep the spark
Still left glowing, nursed along
    A last walk through stark

Finality? (Strong
Last words will count more than fond
    Scraps of sometime song.)

Reaching out beyond
A last bit, we understand,
    Breaks some kind of bond:

Desperate, a hand
Trembling adds yet one more *and*
    And *and*, and *and*, and

                    JOHN HOLLANDER

WITNESS

We can't write ourselves into eternal life
and that is the sorrow and waste of writing,
but those who would write in this knowledge
have found a subterfuge by which to let
themselves be prompted, in heady confidence
of meaning: the wealth of self
spread among the readers who themselves
will read for reasons of earth:
that they have been witness
to their birth, growth and death
and shared the earth with earth.

                    DAVID IGNATOW

NURTURE

From a documentary on marsupials I learn
that a pillowcase makes a fine
substitute pouch for an orphaned kangaroo.

I am drawn to such dramas of animal rescue.
They are warm in the throat. I suffer, the critic proclaims,
from an overabundance of maternal genes.

Bring me your fallen fledgling, your bummer lamb,
lead the abused, the starvelings, into my barn.
Advise the hunted deer to leap into my corn.

And had there been a wild child—
filthy and fierce as a ferret, he is called
in one nineteenth-century account—

a wild child to love, it is safe to assume,
given my fireside inked with paw prints,
there would have been room.

Think of the language we two, same and not-same,
might have constructed from sign,
scratch, grimace, grunt, vowel:

Laughter our first noun, and our long verb, howl.

MAXINE KUMIN

MY AMBITION

For Wade Hall

is to become a footnote
in a learned work of the

22nd century not just a
"cf" or a "see" but a sol-

id note such as Raby gives
Walafrid Strabo in *Christ-*

ian Latin Poetry or Ernst
Robert Curtius (the most

erudite German who ever
lived) devotes to Alber-

tino Mussato in his *Euro-
päische Literatur und La-*

teinisches Mittelalter I
hope the scholar of the

22nd will lick his schol-
arly lips when he finds me

in some forgotten source
(perhaps the Obloquies of

Dreadful Edward Dahlberg)
and think here is an odd-

ball I would have liked,
immortalizing me in six

turgid lines of footnote.

JAMES LAUGHLIN

AFTER THE ALPHABETS

I am trying to decipher the language of insects
they are the tongues of the future
their vocabularies describe buildings as food
they can instruct of dark water and the veins of trees
they can convey what they do not know
and what is known at a distance
and what nobody knows
they have terms for making music with the legs
they can recount changing in a sleep like death
they can sing with wings
the speakers are their own meaning in a grammar without
    horizons
they are wholly articulate
they are never important they are everything

W. S. MERWIN

WHEN I AM ASKED

When I am asked
how I began writing poems,
I talk about the indifference of nature.

It was soon after my mother died,
a brilliant June day,
everything blooming.

I sat on a gray stone bench
in a lovingly planted garden,
but the daylilies were as deaf
as the ears of drunken sleepers,
and the roses curved inward.
Nothing was black or broken
and not a leaf fell,
and the sun blared endless commercials
for summer holidays.

I sat on a gray stone bench
ringed with the ingenue faces
of pink and white impatiens
and placed my grief
in the mouth of language,
the only thing that would grieve with me.

LISEL MUELLER

WAITING ON ELVIS, 1956

This place up in Charlotte called Chuck's where I
used to waitress and who came in one night
but Elvis and some of his friends before his concert
at the Arena, I was twenty-six married but still
waiting tables and we got to joking around like you
do, and he was fingering the lace edge of my slip
where it showed below my hemline and I hadn't even
seen it and I slapped at him a little saying, You
sure are the one aren't you feeling my face burn but
he was the kind of boy even meanness turned sweet in
his mouth.

Smiled at me and said, Yeah honey I guess I sure am.

JOYCE CAROL OATES

DREAMWOOD

In the old, scratched, cheap wood of the typing stand
there is a landscape, veined, which only a child can see
or the child's older self, a poet,
a woman dreaming when she should be typing
the last report of the day. If this were a map,
she thinks, a map laid down to memorize
because she might be walking it, it shows
ridge upon ridge fading into hazed desert
here and there a sign of aquifers
and one possible watering-hole. If this were a map
it would be the map of the last age of her life,
not a map of choices but a map of variations
on the one great choice. It would be the map by which
she could see the end of touristic choices,
of distances blued and purpled by romance,
by which she would recognize that poetry
isn't revolution but a way of knowing
why it must come. If this cheap, mass-produced
wooden stand from the Brooklyn Union Gas Co.,
mass-produced yet durable, being here now,
is what it is yet a dream-map
so obdurate, so plain,
she thinks, the material and the dream can join
and that is the poem and that is the late report.

ADRIENNE RICH

TO HIS PULSE

Taut, industrious little drum
tensed in the hollow of my wrist,
beating alert beneath my thumb,
nature ordains that you persist.

Even when sleep has swaddled half
the world and me with unconcern,
taps of your jungle telegraph
attend the planet's somber turn.

What's it about? — The steady throb
of traffic through your narrow sluice,
a rich monotony your job
of marking time must reproduce.

On the canal around the clock
you signal with your brisk tattoo
the level reached within the lock,
drumming the vital cargo through.

That ebb and flow that you denote
returns in circles to its source;
and I, no rebel yet to rote,
am pleased to leave it to its course,

and pleased to make your paces mine,
once more to the pump and back.
Your sudden halt will be the sign
that I have left the beaten track.

ROBERT B. SHAW

THE IMMORTAL

You're shivering my memory.
You went out early and coatless
To visit your old schoolmasters,
The cruel schoolmasters
And their pet monkeys.

You took a wrong turn somewhere.
You met an army of gray days,
A ghost army of years on the march.
It must have been the slop they ladled you,
The ditch-water they made you drink.

You found yourself again on that street,
Inside that narrow room
With a single dusty window.
Outside it was snowing as in a dream.
You were ill and in bed.
The whole world was absent at work.
The blind old woman next door
Whose sighs and shuffles you'd welcome
Had died mysteriously in the summer.

You had your own breath to listen to.
You were perfectly alone and anonymous.
It would have taken months for anyone
To begin to miss you. The chill
Made you pull the covers up to the chin.

You remembered the lost arctic voyagers,
The snow erasing their footprints.
You had no money and no prospects in sight.
Both of your lungs were hurting.
You had no intention of lifting a finger
To help yourself. You were immortal.

Outside the same darkening snowflake
Seemed to be falling over and over again.
You studied the cracked walls,
The many water-stains on the ceiling
Trying to fix in your mind each detail.

Time had stopped at dusk.
You were shivering at the thought
Of such great happiness.

                              CHARLES SIMIC

TO HIMSELF

So you've come to me now without knowing why;
Nor why you sit in the ruby plush of an ugly chair, the sly
Revealing angle of light turning your hair a silver gray;
Nor why you have chosen this moment to set the writing of years
Against the writing of nothing; you who narrowed your eyes,
Peering into the polished air of the hallway mirror, and said
You were mine, all mine; who begged me to write, but always
Of course to you, without ever saying what it was for;
Who used to whisper in my ear only the things
You wanted to hear; who comes to me now and says
That it's late, that the trees are bending under the wind,
That night will fall; as if there were something
You wanted to know, but for years had forgotten to ask,
Something to do with sunlight slanting over a table
And chair, an arm rising, a face turning, and far
In the distance a car disappearing over the hill.

MARK STRAND

TROLLING FOR BLUES

For John and Barbara

As with the dapper terns, or that sole cloud
Which like a slow-evolving embryo
Moils in the sky, we make of this keen fish
Whom fight and beauty have endeared to us
A mirror of our kind. Setting aside

His unreflectiveness, his flings in air,
The aberration of his flocking swerve
To spawning-grounds a hundred miles at sea,
How clearly, musing to the engine's thrum,
Do we conceive him as he waits below:

Blue in the water's blue, which is the shade
Of thought, and in that scintillating flux
Poised weightless, all attention, yet on edge
To lunge and seize with sure incisiveness,
He is a type of coolest intellect,

Or is so to the mind's blue eye until
He strikes and runs unseen beneath the rip,
Yanking imagination back and down
Past recognition to the unlit deep
Of the glass sponges, of Chiasmodon,

Of the old darkness of Devonian dream,
Phase of a meditation not our own,
That long mêlée where selves were not, that life
Merciless, painless, sleepless, unaware,
From which, in time, unthinkably we rose.

RICHARD WILBUR

WE ARE LISTENING

As our metal eyes wake
to absolute night,
where whispers fly
from the beginning of time,
we cup our ears to the heavens.
We are listening

on the volcanic lips of Flagstaff
and in the fields beyond Boston,
in a great array that blooms
like coral from the desert floor,
on highwire webs patrolled
by computer spiders in Puerto Rico.

We are listening for a sound
beyond us, beyond sound,

searching for a lighthouse
in the breakwaters of our uncertainty,
an electronic murmur,
a bright, fragile *I am.*

Small as tree frogs
staking out one end
of an endless swamp,

we are listening
through the longest night
we imagine, which dawns
between the life and times of stars.

DIANE ACKERMAN

READING THE FACTS ABOUT FROST IN
THE NORTON ANTHOLOGY

"Lover's quarrel" hah.
Little domestic
Eichmann in puttees
claiming he simply
had a taste for spats.

This was a real Scrooge.
His son killed himself.
Wait till you hear what
Mr. Thompson told
Mr. Ellmann. That's

all I know and all
I need to know. Frost
was a pig to his
wife, children, colleagues
and biographer.

So don't get suckered,
undergraduates.
Like by the poems.
Like by sycophants
or apologists.

We can instruct you
also about the
Galapagos: "an
island group in
the Caribbean."

GEORGE STARBUCK

OTHER-DIRECTED

Two roads diverge, each in a yellow smog.
It is the Freeway. I? I take the one
Most traveled by. It makes no difference,
Nor should it. Eight wide lanes and well-marked turns
Will get you there, without the waste and mud,
Ornate delays of detours. If you know—
Mind, really know—so late itinerant,
Where you are going, is there, now and then,
Some reason not to take the easy way?

TURNER CASSITY

THE LACE MAKERS

Their last pages are transparent,
they choose to see a world behind the words
not the words, tatting not stitching, an open page
of knots, never a closed fabric stitched by needles.
They see from the apples and pears on their plates
out to the orchard, from their tatting
to a bird with a piece of straw in his beak.
From combings transferred onto a running thread,
they make a row of rings resembling a reef,
a chain of knots, hammocks, fish nets,
things found in the hands of sailors.
Without looms, with their fingers,
they make bridal objects, knotted hair nets
seen in certain Roman bronze female portraits,
the twisted threads and knotted fringes of dusty
Egyptian wrappings, something for the cuff,
the lapel, the drawing room, nothing to wear in the cold.
They care about scrolls and variations,
a handkerchief, a design on a pillow,
a completed leaf, four ovals with connecting chains
becoming four peacocks, part of a second leaf,
as if they were promised the world would not
be destroyed, with or without paradise.
Noting the French for tatting is *frivolité*,
they make false chains, things obsolete, improper,
in search of new forms. They carry a thread

to a distant point, eight measured peacocks
of equal size with an additional thread
and the ends cut off. It has the heartless advantage
of being decorative in itself.
They sit and work in the aging light
like Achilles, hiding from his pursuers
in a dress, tatting among the women,
discovered by Odysseus offering gifts:
the women picked hammered gold leaves and bracelets;
deserted by his gods, Achilles chose a sword.
In any fabric there are constant beginnings
and endings with cut threads
to be finished off and cut out of sight.
The lacemakers read their yellow lace,
washing and ironing it is a fine art—
beautiful a straw basket filled with laundry
and language. But shall we call gossip prophecy?
Who will turn the hearts of the fathers to the children
and the hearts of the children to their fathers?
They are unworthy of undoing the laces of their own shoes.

STANLEY MOSS

FABERGÉ'S EGG

Switzerland, 1920

Dear Friend,   "Called away" from my country,
I square the egg and put it in a letter
that all may read, gilding each word a little
so that touched, it yields to a secret
stirring, a small gold bird on a spring
suddenly appearing to sing a small song
of regret, elation, that overspills all private
bounds, although you ask, as I do, what now
do we sing to, sing for? Before the Great War,
I made a diamond-studded coach three inches high
with rock crystal windows and platinum wheels
to ceremoniously convey a speechless egg to Court.
All for a bored Czarina! My version of history
fantastic and revolutionary as I reduced the scale
to the hand-held dimensions of a fairy tale,
hiding tiny Imperial portraits and cameos
in eggs of pearl and bone. Little bonbons, caskets!

The old riddle of the chicken and the egg
is answered thus: in the Belle Epoque
of the imagination, the egg came first, containing,
as it does, both history and uncertainty, my excesses
inducing unrest among those too hungry to see
the bitter joke of an egg one cannot eat.
Oblique oddity, an egg is the most beautiful of all
beautiful forms, a box without corners
in which anything can be contained, anything
except Time, that old jeweller who laughed
when he set me ticking. Here, among the clocks
and watches of a country precisely ordered
and dying, I am not sorry, I do not apologize.
Three times I kiss you in memory

of that first Easter, that first white rising,
and send this message as if it could save you:
Even the present is dead. We must live now
in the future.   Yours, Fabergé.

ELIZABETH SPIRES

THE BREATHING, THE ENDLESS NEWS

Every god is lonely, an exile
composed of parts: elk horn,
cloven hoof. Receptacle

for wishes, each god is empty
without us, penitent,
raking our yards into windblown piles. . . .

Children know this; they are
the trailings of gods. Their eyes
hold nothing at birth then fill slowly

with the myth of ourselves. Not so the dolls,
out for the count, each toe pouting from
the slumped-over toddler clothes:

no blossoming there. So we
give our children dolls, and
they know just what to do —

line them up and shoot them.
With every execution
doll and god grow stronger.

RITA DOVE

FIRST READER

I can see them standing politely on the wide pages
that I was still learning to turn,
Jane in a blue jumper, Dick with his crayon-brown hair,
playing with a ball or exploring the cosmos
of the backyard, unaware they are the first characters,
the boy and girl who begin fiction.

Beyond the simple illustration of their neighborhood
the other protagonists were waiting in a huddle:
frightening Heathcliff, frightened Pip, Nick Adams
carrying a fishing rod, Emma Bovary riding into Rouen.

But I would read about the perfect boy and his sister
even before I would read about Adam and Eve, garden and gate,
and before I heard the name Gutenberg, the type
of their simple talk was moving into my focusing eyes.

It was always Saturday and he and she
were always pointing at something and shouting "Look!"
pointing at the dog, the bicycle, or at their father
as he pushed a hand mower over the lawn,
waving at aproned mother framed in the kitchen doorway,
pointing toward the sky, pointing at each other.

They wanted us to look but we had looked already
and seen the shaded lawn, the wagon, the postman.
We had seen the dog, walked, watered and fed the animal,
and now it was time to discover the infinite, clicking
permutations of the alphabet's small and capital letters.
Alphabetical ourselves in the rows of classroom desks,
we were forgetting how to look, learning how to read.

BILLY COLLINS

SUN KING SULKING

In the park the peacocks
have made their own Versailles
but the sparrows prefer a universal slum.

We are classic because we live
so briefly: the ant tells the dung beetle,
"Labour on, Hercules."

Saint-Simon's entrails exploded
in their funerary bottle—more fun
than the levee of a constipated king

I said to Molière,
Virtue is above Morality
and my subjects are beneath it.

(I am not usually so easy to follow,
my oracles are tollgates
and arbitrary confiscations.)

We have always welcomed strangers—
André Breton introducing Henry Miller:
"Gentlemen, the Big Sur Realist"

Anachronism. I lift my cane
in time with Lully. Elliott Carter
beats down Boulez.

When asked for my reign's greatest
achievement, I've sometimes answered,
M. Perrault's *Puss-in-Boots*.

Port Royal never interested me
but the cannon fire at Oudenaarde
made sense of Protestantism.

Dutchmen, Dutchmen, no less,
have resisted my diplomacy,
but I am old, so paint me a victory.

A Mass is worth Paris,
as my grandfather didn't say.
He wasn't really an artist.

I recall my Chamberlain: "Sire,
a thousand musicians were born this year
but only one of them is Rameau."

A fire in the West,
the sun in my window,
I too am a spectacle.

PETER PORTER

HEADING OUT

Beyond here there's no map.
How you get there is where
you'll arrive; how, dawn by
dawn, you can see your way
clear: in ponds, sky, just as
woods you walk through give
to fields. And rivers: beyond
all burning, you'll cross on bridges
you've long lugged with you.
Whatever your route, go lightly,
toward light. Once you give away
all save necessity, all's
mostly well: what you used to
believe you owned is nothing,
nothing beside how you've come
to feel. You've no need now
to give in or give out: the way
you're going your body seems
willing. Slowly as it may
otherwise tell you, whatever
it comes to you're bound to know.

PHILIP BOOTH

FOR THE CALVINISTS

They shaped their souls on anvils of righteousness
and their houses out of doctrinal regard
for things less tangible than hand-hewn beams,
wattle and oaken buckets, pewter cups,
or the brick-and-fanlight grandeur of the streets,
where a straightened elegance declared their faith

in a now-denuded sacrament of labor,
a reverence eroded by their waste,
their dream-fed greed and God-infected hunger,
its ghost discredited, its slow cortège
winding through neighborhoods and onto highways
made straight by destinies we can't remember.

BEN HOWARD

INSPIRATION

About inspiration the Old Masters
Were never wrong. How well they understood
Its dependence on hard labor! As Maestro Segovia
Once said, they painted angels climbing up Jacob's
Ladder, rung by rung, though they had wings.

STEPHEN STEPANCHEV

I CAN'T SPEAK

*God is the Being . . . that may properly
only be addressed, not expressed.*
Buber, I AND THOU

It's hopeless. Our heads are full of television
But images fall apart when you enter a room.
And if not television, then words.
Poets, philosophers, intellectuals, theologians —
Can any of us truly love you?
And if not words, then equations.
I want to talk about kissing the small piece
Of nameless, edgeless geometry you've shown me
And how grateful I am. But should I say I'm the pond
A star fell into, or a rock? Should I talk to the homeless,
Or lovers, or new mothers? Or dying uncles
In their hospital beds?

Anyway, I can't speak about you,
Only to you, there's the whole trouble,
As if, when I tried to turn my body aside,
Some absolute force twisted it back around.
If I insist, *It's my body, my mind,*
My own mouth, I'll say what I want,
I have the right to,
You simply laugh.

ALICIA OSTRIKER

PEASANTS WAITING FOR RAIN

At dusk
they come back from their parched fields
dragging their ancient plow.
The untethered oxen dreaming
nose deep in a mirror of water.

They sit under the banyan,
arms bared against the sky,
frowns grown accustomed to doubt.

On the mud wall of the village,
the evening throws their turbaned shadows
lean like the helmets of knights,
slithering their heads into the roof.

The twilight swallows their stillness,
leaves on the banyan top ripple,
there's the sound of a stone skimming,
a hawk dives into the empty courtyard,
flutters awkwardly upwards
into a whittled cumulus.

They doze, ears cocked only
to sounds from above,
the sudden charge of wild horses.

G. S. SHARAT CHANDRA

SUMMER AT NORTH FARM

Finnish rural life, ca. 1910

Fires, always fires after midnight,
the sun depending in the purple birches

and gleaming like a copper kettle.
By the solstice they'd burned everything,

the bad-luck sleigh, a twisted rocker,
things "possessed" and not-quite-right.

The bonfire coils and lurches,
big as a house, and then it settles.

The dancers come, dressed like rainbows
(if rainbows could be spun),

and linking hands they turn
to the melancholy fiddles.

A red bird spreads its wings now
and in the darker days to come.

STEPHEN KUUSISTO

UTOPIAN MELODIES

As a stone has a sense of its hardness,
or steel of its hardness, so this man,
the department's most severe post structuralist,
feels all the world's books buffet against him
and fall away. Walking, he tilts forward
fully clenched as if fighting a stiff wind.
It forms his duty to the future to overturn
the lies of the past. And what lies:
the anger of Achilles, the madness of Lear;
rather fabrications patched together by minds
which had removed their attention from the plain
truths of the world, aspiring instead
to impotent godhood. But like a stone this man
is made of the world and the world is made
from his body and the world will tolerate
no lie. Even language has betrayed him, being
like smoke, not stone, and so he will reinvent it
just as he intends to remake all things.
His Eden will have a chainlink fence. Little
will grow there, nothing flower, for what is beauty
but the arch deceiver, something to snatch
one's heart for a few seconds, filling it
with light, before returning it to a world
which has grown darker. His ambition is for
a single emotion, a wintry one, and no lies,
a life focused like a microscope upon a virus,
and from his studies he will fashion a music
from metal being twisted and breaking glass.

STEPHEN DOBYNS

FOR THE BULLIES OF WEST MORRIS HIGH

Their childhoods must have come and gone
In a welter of manure smells and morning fog
And fistfights with their dads, tractor debris
Oiling their unseeded lawns
Like flotsam from destroyers lost at sea.
But this is speculation.

Loitering between classes where the corridor
Curved past the diorama
Of the Parthenon—on each side flanked
By school editions of Euripides, Aeschylus, and Homer—
They backed their dungarees against the glass,
Closed ranks as if to keep us from those myths

They weren't the heroes of.
Or fishing out a longhair from the shower stall,
They'd lather up his head
With hocks until the kid begged shamelessly
To be cast back. From homeroom to gym, shop to study hall,
These hydra-headed farmers' sons held sway.

Something about these Ralphs and Orens,
Dennises and Earls, has quietly turned timeless.
Like shame, the memory of them smolders
Half-hidden in the embers of cupped cigarettes.
On subways now one sometimes reawakens
Briefly in the nasal cough
Behind our backs, that stiffening in our shoulders

Before they flayed our shirts from loop to belt.
If to us they looked like avatars
Of Polyphemus, they weren't killed so easily.
Even those the government had dealt
Unlucky numbers in the Lottery
Would have joined up anyway,
Determined to refuel whatever wars

The likes of us had marched against.
And when one or two showed up each year
Between the hallway's lockered walls
In gauzy graduation photographs
Assembled in that same plate glass display,
Their violent grins, circled by wreaths,
Grew handsome in the afterglow of death.

STEVEN CRAMER

From THE SIX-CORNERED SNOWFLAKE

*

Not
above
a juggler's
way with words, as:
* in swank of scholastic Latin *nix* is *snow*; *
but, in his burlier German, *nichts* is *nothing*.
Ergo: this snow, like all the world, is
only a pale chemise on nothingness.
You doubt? He'll quote you Persius:
"O curas hominum, O quantum est in
rebus inane." Hollow hopes of men!
One solace though: "A living death
is life without philosophy." Or life
without its drollery: he'll wink at snow's
* raunchy role in folklore. "A snowflake *
got me with child,"
naughtier
ladies
say

*

*

All
primal
forms are
hieroglyph: *forma*
* means *soul* for the philosophers, as for *
John Dee, sometime astronomer in Prague,
who saw once in this mirror of a world
God as "the *Form* of forms." So Kepler
dreams. To find why forms from *Form*
scintillate, hover, hold in harmony
the universe — his passion's there,
his "only delight." Blear of eye, he
unriddled optics, made heaven an aviary
of singing planets, bizarre cage in cage,
* coped with his Starry Messenger, Galileo, *
but never rightly
solved the
why of
six

*

JOHN FREDERICK NIMS

WRITTEN IN BLOOD

What was blood
but a dream circulating,
so that the stars
would swing, and the

wind of the breath would
move, and the mind
would wake to a temporary
knowing that seemed endless?

Why was blood
spinning on course, if
not to make the body
and time seem endless,

to make gravity what
the heart was called to,
the in and out of the voice
itself, that calling

back to the world and
blood running to greet it?
Where was blood going
when it described those

orbits that a life is,
that perfect cycle that
a circle is, as pure as
the moon and as filled with

a light, the red glow
that the blood shines inside
us, so that every word
rising up is filled with it?

SUE OWEN

READING LAO TZU AGAIN IN THE NEW YEAR

Snub end of a dismal year,

                       deep in the dwarf orchard,

The sky with its undercoat of blackwash and point stars,

I stand in the dark and answer to

My life, this shirt I want to take off,

                  which is on fire . . .

Old year, new year, old song, new song,

                       nothing will change hands

Each time we change heart, each time

Like a hard cloud that has drifted all day through the sky

Toward the night's shrugged shoulder

                       with its epaulet of stars.

———

Prosodies rise and fall.

                    Structures rise in the mind and fall.

Failure reseeds the old ground.

Does the grass, with its inches in two worlds, love the dirt?

Does the snowflake the raindrop?

I've heard that those who know will never tell us,

                       and heard

That those who tell us will never know.

Words are wrong.

Structures are wrong.

              Even the questions are compromise.

Desire discriminates and language discriminates:

They form no part of the essence of all things:

                       each word

Is a failure, each object

We name and place

             leads us another step away from the light.

Loss is its own gain.

              Its secret is emptiness.

Our images lie in the flat pools of their dark selves

Like bodies of water the tide moves.

They move as the tide moves.

             Its secret is emptiness.

———

Four days into January,
                    the grass grows tiny, tiny
Under the peach trees.
Wind from the Blue Ridge tumbles the hat
Of daylight farther and farther
                    into the eastern counties.

Sunlight spray on the ash limbs.
                    Two birds
Whistle at something unseen, one black note and one interval.
We're placed between now and not-now,
                    held by affection,
Large rock balanced upon a small rock.

CHARLES WRIGHT

BRIEVES FROM THE BOOK OF KELLS

Hermeneutical as memory,
these symbols snarl and tangle,
spread wings or dance
in a pattern more ancient
than circled stones. One
creature with panther grace
extends a paw, while two more
entwine like vine and trellis.
A smiling fish flashes scales
like chain armor. A hawk-dog
sprawls, and red serpents
spiral. The inked colors
shimmer, as if to say secular
beasts thrive in the margins,
long to form new letters,
to wed the scripture's
sweet Latin, but something
must always guard the borders,
show symmetry and teeth
to any intruder whose heart
is not nourished in the right
church, archaic riddles,
the unabbreviated forest
and moth-eye of the soul.

R. T. SMITH

FORGETFULNESS

The name of the author is the first to go
followed obediently by the title, the plot,
the heartbreaking conclusion, the entire novel
which suddenly becomes one you have never read, never
   even heard of,

as if, one by one, the memories you used to harbor
decided to retire to the southern hemisphere of the brain,
to a little fishing village where there are no phones.

Long ago you kissed the names of the nine muses goodbye
and watched the quadratic equation pack its bag,
and even now as you memorize the order of the planets,

something else is slipping away, a state flower perhaps,
the address of an uncle, the capital of Paraguay.

Whatever it is you are struggling to remember,
it is not poised on the tip of your tongue
or even lurking in some obscure corner of your spleen.

It has floated away down a dark mythological river
whose name begins with an L as far as you can recall

on your own way to oblivion where you will join those
who have even forgotten how to swim and how to ride a
   bicycle.

No wonder you rise in the middle of the night
to look up the date of a famous battle in a book on war.
No wonder the moon in the window seems to have drifted
out of a love poem that you used to know by heart.

BILLY COLLINS

From AN ESSAY ON FRIENDSHIP

VII

Late one night, alone in bed, the book
Having slipped from my hands while I stared at the phrase
The lover's plaintive "Can't we just be friends?"

I must have dreamt you'd come back, and sat down
Beside my pillow. (I could also see myself
Asleep but in a different room by now —

A motel room to judge by the landscape I'd become,
Framed on the cinder-block wall behind.)
To start over, you were saying, requires too much,

And friendship in the aftermath is a dull
Affair, a rendezvous with second guesses,
Dining out on memories you can't send back

Because they've spoiled. And from where I sat,
Slumped like a cloud over the moon's tabletop,
Its wrinkled linen trailing across a lake,

I was worried. Another storm was brewing.
I ran a willowy hand over the lake to calm
The moonlight — or your feelings. Then woke

On the bed's empty side, the sheets as cool
As silence to my touch. The speechlessness
Of sex, or the fumble afterwards for something

To say about love, amount to the same. Words
Are what friends, not lovers, have between them,
Old saws and eloquent squawkings. We deceive

Our lovers by falling for someone we cannot love,
Then murmur sweet nothings we do not mean,
Half-fearing they'll turn out true. But to go back —

Come dawn, exhausted by the quiet dark,
I longed for the paper boy's shuffle on the stair,
The traffic report, the voices out there, out there.

J. D. MC CLATCHY

LITTLE ESSAY ON COMMUNICATION

Safe to say that most men who want
    to *communicate*,
who would use that word, are shameless

and their souls long ago have drifted
    out of their bodies
to faraway, unpolluted air.

Such men no doubt have learned women
    are starved
for communication, that it's the new way

to get new women, and admission of weakness
    works best of all.
Even some smart women are fooled,

though the smartest know that to communicate
    is a form of withholding,
a commercial for intimacy while the heart

hides in its little pocket of words.
    And women
use the word too, everyone uses it

who doesn't have the gift of communication;
    it's like the abused
asking for love, never having known

what it feels like, not trusting it
    if it lacks pain.
But let's say a good man and a good woman,

with no motives other than desire
    for greater closeness,
who've heard communication is the answer,

sign up for a course at the Y,
    seek counseling,
set aside two hours in the week

for significant talk. What hope for them?
    Should we tell them
very little, or none at all?

As little or none as there is for us,
    who've cut
right to the heart, and still conceal,

who've loved many times well into the night
    in good silence
and have awakened, strangely distant,

thinking thoughts no one should ever know?

STEPHEN DUNN

MRS. ADAM

I have lately come to the conclusion that I am Eve,
alias Mrs. Adam. You know, there is no account
of her death in the Bible, and why am I not Eve?
Emily Dickinson in a letter,
12 January, 1846

Wake up,
you'll need your wits about you.
This is not a dream,
but a woman who loves you, speaking.

She was there
when you cried out;
she brushed the terror away.
She knew
when it was time to sin.
You were wise
to let her handle it,
and leave that place.

We couldn't speak at first
for the bitter knowledge,
the sweet taste of memory
on our tongues.

Listen, it's time.
You were chosen too,
to put the world together.

KATHLEEN NORRIS

THE DEAD CARTESIAN

Part of me flies upward
or at least elsewhere,

thiswhere being the damp location
of newly separated body.

Thought is not going on
in my current neck of the woods,

my present nook of brown wood,
consciousness this blue afternoon

discreetly redistributed.
Mourners have chunks of it,

much has gone bobbing away
and settled like strings of lint

in unregarded corners.
A trickster god vacuums them up.

Words in their newspaper column
may have been what I am now,

an atomic thought in the mind
of overweening matter.

CHRIS WALLACE-CRABBE

THE DEATH OF ANTINOÜS

When the beautiful young man drowned—
accidentally, swimming at dawn
in a current too swift for him,
or obedient to some cult
of total immersion that promised
the bather would come up divine,

mortality rinsed from him—
Hadrian placed his image everywhere,
a marble Antinoüs staring across
the public squares where a few dogs
always scuffled, planted
in every squalid little crossroads

at the furthest corners of the Empire.
What do we want in any body
but the world? And if the lover's
inimitable form was nowhere,
then he would find it everywhere,
though the boy became simply more dead

as the sculptors embodied him.
Wherever Hadrian might travel,
the beloved figure would be there
first: the turn of his shoulders,
the exact marble nipples,
the drowned face not really lost

to the Nile—which has no appetite,
merely takes in anything
without judgment or expectation—
but lost into its own multiplication,
an artifice rubbed with oils and acid
so that the skin might shine.

Which of these did I love?
Here is his hair, here his hair
again. Here the chiseled liquid waist
I hold because I cannot hold it.
If only one of you, he might have said
to any of the thousand marble boys anywhere,

would speak. Or the statues might have been enough,
the drowned boy blurred as much by memory
as by water, molded toward an essential,
remote ideal. Longing, of course,
become its own object, the way
that desire can make anything into a god.

MARK DOTY

CORRESPONDENCE

The letter lies unanswered, thus free of lies.
The light all day has travelled the crowded pages,
Shifting the shadows, changing the hue of ink.
The truths, if truths there are, are stationary.

Now night comes on, from your time zone to mine.
The moon is tentative, not wholly herself,
And the owl bells, and the owl's mate bells back,
A dialogue of sorts, question and answer,

The answer being but the question asked.
East of your sleep, deep in the zodiac,
Tomorrow is already chronicled.
Oh, I shall write you what you want to hear.

HENRI COULETTE

EVENING WALK

You give the appearance of listening
To my thoughts, o trees,
Bent over the road I am walking
On a late summer evening
When every one of you is a steep staircase
The night is descending.

The leaves like my mother's lips
Forever trembling, unable to decide,
For there's a bit of wind,
And it's like hearing voices,
Or a mouth full of muffled laughter,
A huge dark mouth we can all fit in
Suddenly covered by a hand.

Everything quiet. Light
Of some other evening strolling ahead,
Long-ago evening of long dresses,
Pointy shoes, silver cigarette cases.
Happy heart, what heavy steps you take
As you hurry after them in the thickening
shadows.

The sky above still blue.
The nightbirds like children
Who won't come to dinner.
Lost children singing to themselves.

CHARLES SIMIC

TENTH-YEAR ELEGY

Careless man, my father,
always leaving me at rest-stops,
coffee shops, some wide spot in the road.
I come out, rubbing my hands on my pants
or levitating two foam cups of coffee,
and can't find him anywhere,
those banged-up fenders gone.

It's the trip itself that blinds him,
black highway like a chute
leading to the mesmerizing end,
his hands locked dead on the wheel
and following, until he misses me,
steers wide on the graveled shoulders,
turns around.

This time he's been gone so long
I've settled in here—married,
built a house, planted trees for shade,
stopped waiting to see him pull into the drive—
though the wind sometimes makes a highway roar
high up in the branches, and I stop
whatever I am doing and look up.

NEAL BOWERS

AS A CHILD, SLEEPLESS

The 'possum under the owl's claw,
The wet fawn huddled in the grass,
The soldier, hurt, in his lost trench
Clench the eyelid, clutch the breath
Till scavengers, till *coup de grâce*,
Death and the lurking terror pass.

Vice tight each muscle lest the pent
Tendon spasm, twitch; preserve
All rigor, silence, so the blood
Thuds slower, fainter through the vein
Till the chilled skin gives off no scent;
Drain all least current from the nerve.

Clamp the arm tight against the head
To hush that whisper in the nose,
The click if lips slip open. Cover
Over this face and form; disguise
Whose body's lying on the bed,
Eyes that still stare too wide to close.

W. D. SNODGRASS

DEFINING TIME

If it's like a river, the current is too much for us,
Sweeping us past a moment we're still not used to
Out to the void of the not-yet-come.
Should we resist, wherever we are,
Or be reconciled?
It seems to bring us gifts. Each day
Arrives as a fresh basket of bread.
Our right hand no longer can touch our left
Around the girth of our Buddha bellies.
How can that be if the minutes of the day are fish
Nibbling away at us till our bones show through,
Nibbling away at our friends, our houses?
Let's try to ignore it, whatever it is,
As we do the thin air of the Himalayas
When we climb, breathless, to pray for enlightenment.

Can we really ignore its earthy mass
As it lies between us and the thing we hope for?
A long wait till the train goes by
And we can cross the tracks into the evening,
Our favorite time. At last we're walking after dinner
On our ritual mile to the great magnolia.
There it is, glimmering at the end of the field.
Just a handful of whatever time is
And we'll be standing beneath its branches
Looking back at the poplars we're passing now.
How young we were back there, we'll say,
How confused and moody in that early era.
We need more time to consider it,
More than the dole allowed us at any moment,
The nickels and dimes.
We need to unfold time on the table like a map,
With the years gone and the years to come
Colored as vividly as the moment,
Proving how little it means to say
Time has gone by, passed through us
Or around us, and left us old.

CARL DENNIS

NOT RESPONSIBLE

The floodlights come on: look,
a Jewish girl without a permit for her bicycle
stands caught in Prague; it's 1938,
for the love of God!
Can't you *do* something?

Wait a minute. You're crazy;
that was fifty years ago; you weren't born;
turn the floodlights off,
go back to sleep, dream geese
carried under the arm of an old woman

walking in new shoes in 1938; she walks
in lavish twilight
toward a black mountain of shoes.

CAROLINE FINKELSTEIN

QUOTATIONS FOR A WINTER EVENING

*(Marie Luise Kaschnitz, Karl Kraus, Japanese
proverb, Valéry, Nietzsche, Marvell, Herman Hupfeld,
Santayana, Kafka, Shakespeare, Simone Weil)*

The unlived life is light, so light.
You don't even live once. Drink and sing,
an inch before us is black night.
God made everything out of nothing

but the nothingness shows through.
If you gaze long into an abyss
the abyss will gaze back into you.
Had we but world enough, and time . . . A kiss

is just a kiss, a sigh is just a sigh.
Having been born is a bad augury
for immortality. There is a goal
but no way to it; what we call the way
is hesitation. Ripeness is all.
Salvation is consenting to die.

DAVID JAUSS

TAKE A HIKE

I don't mind taking a hike in the woods.
There are stones like ellipses for crossing the creek.
I can abide the stuffy silence of owls

that spy from the branches without spectacles,
and like how their heads work. Plus, there are leaves
that are more like the rough drafts of leaves

and remind me the world is working
things through by gab and revision—like you,
like me—and knows when to edit, and knows

how to use, without showing off, its big
vocabulary. So what I can't name
the bush with thorns like fire on my cheek?

My flesh has the language for what happens next
and runs-on the sentence without skewing
the meaning and the blood's red penciling

is part of the text. The rest of the story
is a matter of stump rot, weather, hills,
and a lot of loose talk. How, anyway,

can you tell a flower from a weed
if both are comely? I'm beholden
to the author and the publisher, both.

JIM SIMMERMAN

OUT OF OUR HANDS

For Wing Tek Lum

Out of a hat
on a piece of paper
someone once gave me your name.

Your name flew
out of my hand,
the black letters

dismantling the air
above the school.
I watched the letters

form the bird
seeds of a language
I needed to know,

a language borrowed
from the children I taught
who shivered in borrowed coats.

Toward evening they scattered
outside the school,
red-bricked and torn

on the edge of Chinatown.
I watched them disappear
into their lives,

undisciplined like starlings,
they disappeared
in the broken shoes of the wind.

One day your name
came back
in a poem you were

writing in another city,
a poem you were determined
to write for the rest of your life.

The poem a subversive act.
The poem about being Chinese,
skin the glorious color of chicken fat.

CATHY SONG

THE THINGS OF THE WORLD

I would like to say something for things as they are, in themselves,
Not standing for anything else, multiform, legion
In their fleeting exactitude,

Fashioned in intricate and elusive ways, individual,
Each like nothing else precisely. I am speaking
Of observable things, this chair,

This leaf, that slab, the sun, dust, a fly,
Sometimes interacting, sometimes not, depending
On the nature of each, but always

And ever changing, coming into being, vanishing;
May be observed or not; beautiful or ugly
Only as someone's opinion;

Neither right nor wrong; neutral; concerned only with
Their presence here, enduring their given span:
The manifold things of the world

ROBERT SARGENT

CHICKAMAUGA

Dove-twirl in the tall grass.
                              End-of-summer glaze next door
On the gloves and split ends of the conked magnolia tree.
Work sounds: truck back-up beep, wood tin-hammer, cicada, fire horn.

History handles our past like spoiled fruit.
Mid-morning, late-century light
                              calicoed under the peach trees.
Fingers us here. Fingers us here and here.

The poem is a code with no message:
The point of the mask is not the mask but the face underneath,
Absolute, incommunicado,
                    unhoused and peregrine.

The gill net of history will pluck us soon enough
From the cold waters of self-contentment we drift in
One by one
              into its suffocating light and air.

Structure becomes an element of belief, syntax
And grammar a catechist,
Their words what the beads say,
                          words thumbed to our discontent.

CHARLES WRIGHT

WE HAVE NOT LONG TO LOVE

We have not long to love.
Light does not stay.
The tender things are those
we fold away.

Coarse fabrics are the ones
for common wear.
In silence I have watched you
comb your hair.

Intimate the silence,
dim and warm.
I could, but did not, reach
to touch your arm.

I could, but do not, break
that which is still.
(Almost the faintest whisper
would be shrill.)

So moments pass as though
they wished to stay.
We have not long to love.
A night. A day . . . .

TENNESSEE WILLIAMS

A FEW LAST LINES OF LAUNDRY

This ragged shining,
these embodied nothings
are the image of us:

full of ourselves
in every puff of air
and hanging on

for dear life. At mid-day,
when the wind picks up,
such dancing. Look at us:

washed and stretched
to the very limit,
almost touching one another.

EAMON GRENNAN

THE TREE OF LIFE

It's that time when grass begins growing its hair
long again, the little curled fists of leaf unfold
into sunshade, but Marjorie is not here to see it
except through your eyes, and my mother is still busy
in the Redding meadow, ash dissolving in rainwater,
drawn through narrow veinous halls into the trunk
and then straight up it—pure ascension in a dark body
a hundred years old, ashwater rising as sap in a well
of wood to the branching-out point, the variations
on a theme of open arms. Her death rose up through me
with unbearable bitterness, till I broke and broke
into leaf. All of my cells have died seven times,
seven trillion times, since I was just one of hers.
That's what the textbooks of embryology are all about,
division, complication, replacement of parts, the art
of outliving what intended us, hardly knowing how.

                              MARGARET HOLLEY

DEAD MAN INTERVIEW

Dead for twelve minutes, the plumber in Akron
has a tale to tell the newspapers,
of figures beckoning in a haze of light—
and he's never even heard of Blake or Dante.
Archetypes, the experts say, or the brain's
own chemistry, the final fireworks
before shutting down, like the great display
out over the harbor at the end of summer.

Knowing my father can settle this dispute,
I call him back for half an hour,
choosing twilight, the hinged sky almost shut,
and place him on the back steps smoking, studying
the space between himself and everything else,
something like a surf roaring between us
the way it always did those summer nights,
the minutes passing like limestone dripping
in a cave that will finally seal itself.

I want to know if the dying see more
than the poor brain guttering in a black cup,
and I want it straight from someone who didn't turn back;
but my father doesn't know he's dead,
inhabits just these moments willed for him;
and anyway, he can say only what I have him say,
so he tells me it's all right,
as he did years ago, standing in the open door
with the light pouring in behind him.

NEAL BOWERS

THE CAVE OF AIDS

It annoys him to speak,
and it hurts him not to.
Auden, "The Cave of Nakedness"

It was when you were dying and you
couldn't speak, that we loved you the most.

Mom and Dad were still doing
the wrong things the best they knew how.
Again you couldn't use the kind of
attention that they gave;
but all of us were out to annoy you,

because it hurt that you didn't speak.
Maybe there were forty words from you
in what was to be the last week
you breathed, sipping at the surface

like a trout when it feeds.
Drop by drop, the morphine
let us all go on. Into your arm
it went, and it held our tongues.

It got beyond what was healthy,
your keeping to yourself
our ancient live and let live,
each of us safekeeping. Your privacy's
blank as your diary now.
What annoyed you and hurt you,

you held until you couldn't eat,
you couldn't walk, you couldn't speak.
So we started talking. We left you
the room to die in, and went into the hall.
We said: he will die when he is ready.

And I think you did.
You yellowed and smelled
like the salamanders we used to catch
in the pool before we'd swim,
and then you went in.

In memory of Craig William Scott (1961–1984)

MARK SCOTT

TO A YOUNG DIVER

So long, silversides.
The lips of the sea
close over you.

I watch you shimmer
and vanish into
the inverted garden

where minnows flock
like sparrows
and tiny pods of air

sequin the powdered
shoulders of
the reef.

Deeper: obsidian walls
flicker with mystery—
fish are flame, coral sways

to the throb of
the young planet
in its skin.

Down there
you are only a fold
in the water, a mote

in time—yesterday spreads
beneath you, silent
as bedrock

while the future presses
upward: a helix rising
through Precambrian blue

brightening
to gem turquoise
as you break the surface

streaming gold, festooned
with your tangled cargo,
your frieze of stars.

MARILYN TAYLOR

WINGED TORSO OF EROS

You will never change, your life
suspended here, sealed off from the hush
of traffic and the weather, a twist of flesh
touched and wondered over by the likes
of me. Everything breakable in you
has been broken, but for those of us
who will not see, you take flight with a rustle
of ghost wings—your wings, too,

gone now, snapped off at the base,
even your sex—(a squeak of sole
on tile as Red Shirt leaves the hall)—
Oblivion beckons, you nod *Yes, yes* . . .
But he's coming back, we all do, to say *No,
I will never let you go.*

DANIEL HALL

FINAL NOTATIONS

it will not be simple, it will not be long
it will take little time, it will take all your thought
it will take all your heart, it will take all your breath
it will be short, it will not be simple

it will touch through your ribs, it will take all your heart
it will not be long, it will occupy your thought
as a city is occupied, as a bed is occupied
it will take all your flesh, it will not be simple

You are coming into us who cannot withstand you
you are coming into us who never wanted to withstand you
you are taking parts of us into places never planned
you are going far away with pieces of our lives

it will be short, it will take all your breath
it will not be simple, it will become your will

ADRIENNE RICH

MINGUS AT THE SHOWPLACE

I was miserable, of course, for I was seventeen,
and so I swung into action and wrote a poem,

and it was miserable, for that was how I thought
poetry worked: you digested experience and shat

literature. It was 1960 at The Showplace, long since
defunct, on West 4th St., and I sat at the bar,

casting beer money from a thin reel of ones,
the kid in the city, big ears like a puppy.

And I knew Mingus was a genius. I knew two
other things but they were wrong, as it happened.

So I made him look at the poem.
"There's a lot of that going around," he said,

and Sweet Baby Jesus he was right. He laughed
amiably. He didn't look as if he thought

bad poems were dangerous, the way some poets do.
If they were baseball executives they'd plot

to destroy sandlots everywhere so that the game
could be saved from children. Of course later

that night he fired his pianist in mid-number
and flurried him from the stand.

"We've suffered a diminuendo in personnel,"
he explained, and the band played on.

WILLIAM MATTHEWS

MEANER THAN A JUNKYARD DOG;
OR,
TURNER'S EVIL TWIN

Our genes have junk in them. Not all the messages
That DNA contains does RNA read out.
Inheritance has drastic editing. What, though,
Are unused possibilities the relic of?
A better us, or worse? Are we as we exist
Young Dr. Jekyll failed or full-blown Hyde avoided?
(If avoided.) As of now we cannot know.
All we can say is, both the shadow archetype
And Doppelgänger, and the succubus as well,
Hang near us. Life, genetic outcome of a code
That has its blind spots, parallels what it is not—
An endless replicase of what it has destroyed
To be. Dumb corpse one carries, Siamese dark self
Whose only life is to embarrass, in our joint
Past where did we in aim diverge? Is it that aim
Was in itself the agency of difference?
Ambition's never quite evaded progeny,
A shadow is by definition follower.
But in the hidden mirror of the goal suppressed,
What proud construct of junk discarded bides his time?

TURNER CASSITY

SEARCH PARTY

By now I know most of the faces
that will appear beside me as
long as there are still images
I know at last what I would choose
the next time if there ever was
a time again I know the days
that open in the dark like this
I do not know where Maoli is

I know the summer surfaces
of bodies and the tips of voices
like stars out of their distances
and where the music turns to noise
I know the bargains in the news
rules whole languages formulas
wisdom that I will never use
I do not know where Maoli is

I know whatever one may lose
somebody will be there who says
what it will be all right to miss
and what is verging on excess
I know the shadows of the house
routes that lead out to no traces
many of his empty places
I do not know where Maoli is

You that see now with your own eyes
all that there is as you suppose
though I could stare through broken glass
and show you where the morning goes
though I could follow to their close
the sparks of an exploding species
and see where the world ends in ice
I would not know where Maoli is

W. S. MERWIN

APOLLO

We pull off
to a road shack
in Massachusetts
to watch men walk

on the moon. We did
the same thing
for three two one
blast off, and now

we watch the same men
bounce in and out
of craters. I want
a Coke and a hamburger.

Because the men
are walking on the moon
which is now irrefutably
not green, not cheese,

not a shiny dime floating
in a cold blue,
the way I'd thought,
the road shack people don't

notice we are a black
family not from there,
the way it mostly goes.
This talking through

static, bounces in space-
boots, tethered
to cords is much
stranger, stranger

even than we are.

ELIZABETH ALEXANDER

THE DIGS IN ESCONDIDO CANYON

All summer under klieg lights
we stroke the dirt with trowels.
These digs would disappear; vandals
and idle boys playing plunder: an arrowhead
wedged in a faded Levi pocket, a jawbone mocked

and tossed away like a corncob,
a hand-smoothed bowl crushed to dust by a boot.
We unweave sand like castle tapestries,
thread by thread down to walls that breathe,
that need our touch to live.

We've found bronze kernels never baked,
seen golden ears hung up to dry
on Southwest porches, eaten tortillas
of such crushed corn. Here, people like us
lay down in darkness. We sift the dust

we're made of. What did they fear?
Near midnight on our knees,
we catalog clues for regional museums,
the signs of modest toil, evidence of hope
not seen, the kernels not consumed.

WALTER MC DONALD

YOU ARE RIGHT

In your super-logical,
analytical,
bumbling way,
with halting speech
and much digression,
you explain that male
mathematicians are rarely
verbal . . . .

"Oh by the way,
did I mention that this theory
is largely unproven, but
nevertheless, quite probable?"

because of a pre-natal
super-dose of testosterone
to the left side of the brain
which suppresses the right
side of the brain
where you are currently
trying to express
your lack of verbal agility

while at the same time
peeling an orange,
stroking your mustache,
pulling your ear,
and making little
finger-steeples.

And I am about to conclude
that you are right.

CATHRYN ESSINGER

ADIRONDACK MOOSEHEAD

The moose that once presided over games
of Monopoly and crazy eights,
that loomed above us, goofy and majestic,
into whose antlers we threw paper planes,
still hangs over the great stone fireplace
like the figurehead of a ship.

All these years he hasn't flicked an eyelash
in response to anything we've done,
and in that way resembles God,
whom, as children, we imagined looking down
but didn't know how to visualize. A moose
over the altar would have been

as good as anything—better than a cross—
staring down on us with kind dark eyes
that would have seemed, at least, to understand,
his antlers like gigantic, upturned hands
ready to lift us off the ground—
or like enormous wings outspread for flight.

JEFFREY HARRISON

HAVING IT OUT WITH MELANCHOLY

If many remedies are prescribed for an illness, you may
be certain that the illness has no cure.
      A.P. Chekhov, THE CHERRY ORCHARD

1. FROM THE NURSERY

When I was born, you waited
behind a pile of linen in the nursery,
and when we were alone, you lay down
on top of me, pressing
the bile of desolation into every pore.

And from that day on
everything under the sun and moon
made me sad—even the yellow
wooden beads that slid and spun
along a spindle on my crib.

You taught me to exist without gratitude.
You ruined my manners toward God:
"We're here simply to wait for death;
the pleasures of earth are overrated."

I only appeared to belong to my mother,
to live among blocks and cotton undershirts
with snaps; among red tin lunchboxes
and report cards in ugly brown slipcases.
I was already yours—the anti-urge,
the mutilator of souls.

2. BOTTLES

Elavil, Ludiomil, Doxepin,
Norpramin, Prozac, Lithium, Xanax,
Welibutrin, Parnate, Nardil.
The coated ones smell sweet or have
no smell; the powdery ones smell
like the chemistry lab at school
that made me hold my breath.

3. SUGGESTION FROM A FRIEND

You wouldn't be so depressed
if you really believed in God.

4. OFTEN

Often I go to bed as soon after dinner
as seems adult
(I mean I try to wait for dark)
in order to push away
from the massive pain in sleep's
frail wicker coracle.

5. ONCE THERE WAS LIGHT

Once, in my early thirties, I saw
that I was a speck of light in the great
river of light that undulates through time.

I was floating with the whole
human family; we were all colors — those
who are living now; those who have died,
those who are not yet born. For a few

moments I floated, completely calm,
and I no longer hated having to exist.

Like a crow who smells hot blood
on asphalt, you came flying
to pull me out of the glowing stream.
"I'll hold you up. I never let my dear
ones sink!" After that, I wept for days.

6. IN AND OUT

The dog searches until he finds me
upstairs, lies down with a clatter
of elbows, puts his head on my foot.

Sometimes the sound of his breathing
saves my life — in and out, in
and out; a pause, a long sigh . . . .

7. PARDON

A piece of burned meat
wears my clothes, speaks
in my voice, dispatches obligations
haltingly, or not at all.
It is tired of trying
to be stout-hearted, tired
beyond measure.

We move on to the monoamine
oxidase inhibitors. Day and night
I feel as if I had drunk six cups
of coffee, but the pain

stops abruptly. With the wonder
and bitterness of someone pardoned
for a crime she did not commit,
I come back to marriage and friends,
to pink fringed hollyhocks; come back
to my desk, my books, and my chair.

8. CREDO

Pharmaceutical wonders are at work
but I believe only in this moment
of well-being. Unholy ghost,
you are certain to come again.

Coarse, mean, you'll put your feet
on the coffee table, lean back,
and turn me into someone who can't
take the trouble to speak; someone
who can't sleep, or who does nothing
but sleep; can't read, or call
for an appointment for help.

There is nothing I can do
against your coming.
When I awake, I am still with thee.

9. WOOD THRUSH

High on Nardil and June light
I wake at four,
waiting greedily for the first
note of the wood thrush. Easeful air
presses through the screen
with the wild, complex song
of the bird, and I am overcome

with ordinary contentment.
What hurt me so terribly
all my life until this moment?
How I love the small, swiftly
beating heart of the bird
singing in the great maples;
its bright, unequivocal eye.

JANE KENYON

LAST WORDS

It wasn't Oscar Wilde who said, "Die, my dear
doctor, that's the last thing I shall do," but
Lord Palmerston. Wilde said, "Either this wall-

paper goes or I do." William Pitt said,
"Oh my country! How I leave my country!"
or, in an alternate version, "I think

I could eat one of Bellamy's veal pies.
Everyone dies alone, according to
the tough-guy swagger, though none who made it

into Bartlett's did. Gather witnesses.
Some may serve as straight men. "May God forgive
you," a French priest intoned, but the urbane

corpse-to-be waved him off: "Of course He will;
it's his *métier*." A last unsuffered fool
for old times' sake, but you can't count on that.

Someone lit a candle by Voltaire's bed
and he raised his eyelid: "Flames, already?"
Memorability comes by practice,

but you can be too ready, as Henry
James was. "Here it is," he said, "at last,
the distinguished thing," and then lived long

to think what a shapely phrase he'd spilled.
Study the masters is, as usual, the best
advice. Or you could try the worn nostrum

laconic nineteenth-century mothers
gave their daughters for wedding nights. "Relax.
You'll think of something. Let nature take its course.

WILLIAM MATTHEWS

A TELEGRAM FROM THE MUSE

CARO THOSE LAST FEW POEMS ARE DYNAMITE
STOP SOON THE SEVEN ENVIES WILL INVEST
YOUR FELLOW SCRIBBLERS STOP BUT DON'T IGNITE
BOTH ENDS OF YOUR STOUT CANDLE STOP TIME TO REST
TO READ SOME MYSTERY NOVELS TO GRILL
FAT TUNA STEAKS IN THAT WAVERY BLUE
GRAY ADIRONDACK LIGHT THAT STAINS THE HILLS
AT DUSK STOP I CONFESS THE RUMORS TRUE
I ONCE WROTE A LITTLE VERSE MYSELF STOP
SIT ON THOSE ADORABLE LAURELS AND UNSCREW
A FEW CORKS AND PLAY SOME TENNIS
STOP FELICIA SAYS YOU'RE PALE AS A DISH
OF HERRING IN FLUORESCENT LIGHT STOP DO
NOTHING TILL YOU HEAR FROM ME STOP

WILLIAM MATTHEWS

ANNIVERSARY

Soon I'll be the age you are
forever, the day you pulled
off the interstate, your heart
boiling like a cracked block,
to die in a phone booth
while everyone passed you by.

We'll be twins—
I see us coming in the amber of store windows.
The next day I'll be
the elder, you
tagging along to some
place you've already been.

Already you could be my mother's son.
Someday you could be mine.
Maybe then you'd listen
when I told you to stay
off the fatty foods and the interstates,
to slow down and stay well.
To grow old. To call.

WILLIAM GREENWAY

SOUL

If, as they always claim upon returning,
there's only radiance there, near death, and in
that radiance the brighter densities of all
their own beloved dead come out to greet them,
and they themselves now bodiless, rinsed clean
of eye or ear, can still somehow perceive them;
if it's the afterimage of the body
only, the thinning yet still sentient mist
of who they were, that keeps them only far
enough away from what they brighten towards
to know themselves as its auroral edge;—
why then do they return?

Couldn't it instead
be the body that rejoices there?
that radiance the body's radiance
of being only just aware enough
as body to know it is itself the star-
flung anonymity it's on the verge
of when the suddenly too quiet quiet
startles the soul awake, and soul comes rushing,
calling and rushing like a fearful and
ferocious mother to her only child?

ALAN SHAPIRO

THE PARENTS THEY WOULD BE

For M. and M.

wise in the ways of county fair judges
who could name us
the names of every apple
went into our sauces and butters and pies and cobblers
    and tarts and ciders
but don't

who pass slowly among
the fruits of our labor
as if there were all the time
and nothing better to do in the world than to praise
and to savor

JOE-ANNE MC LAUGHLIN-CARRUTH

THE RESURRECTION OF THE BODY

Do all who lie down expect to awake?
Long ago the worms abandoned this trough.
All they have left is a patch of leather
Where the skull hollows. Each vertebra,
Like an ancient fish with open mouth
And ragged fin, holds its place in line.

The pelvis could be a worn mortar
And the scattered finger bones, gimcrack.
But these are the remains of a woman
Buried in the gesture of sleep—
Her knees drawn up, one hand as a pillow.
Behold the kingdom that comes,
The earth the meek will inherit.

ERIC PANKEY

BALKAN

As if it were crisp onion skin
that might flake free, with every step
the stretcher bearers took, the char
that patched her grizzled arms curled back,
and knuckle bones broke through the snarl
of fingers shriveled into claws,
while from one nakedly dangling limb,
scraping the blacktop, dark drops fell.
And as the awkward litter drew
within the scope of the camera's lens,
because he couldn't bear his half
one-handed, one hand on her head,
nor fully block it with his sleeve,
the man who held the torso end
could not obscure the gaping chock
that the slit which crossed her throat became
each time the jostled head lolled back
as if on hinges. Throat thrown wide,
and vented like an organ pipe,
it seemed, if only lungs would gorge
and bellow, she still might sound a keen
so true that the world must break against it.

GABRIEL SPERA

A NOT SO GOOD NIGHT IN THE
SAN PEDRO OF THE WORLD

it's unlikely that a decent poem is in me
tonight
and I understand that this is strictly my
problem
and of no interest to you
that I sit here listening to a man playing
a piano on the radio
and it's bad piano, both the playing and
the composition
and again, this is of no interest to you
as one of my cats,
a beautiful white with strange markings,
sleeps in the bathroom.

I have no idea of what would be of
interest to you
but I doubt that you would be of
interest to me, so don't get
superior.
in fact, come to think of it, you can
kiss my ass.

I continue to listen to the piano.
this will not be a memorable night in my
life
or yours.

let us celebrate the stupidity of our
endurance.

CHARLES BUKOWSKI

MUSIC OF THE SPHERES

The first music we don't hear but
know, is inner, the rings around
atoms singing, the bright levels
in matter revealed by colors
through spectrum scales all up and down
the quantum ladder in fireworks
of the inner horizons, each
zone voicing its wavelength with
choirs in the tiny stadiums
of harmony of the deeper
galaxies, ancient octaves
and intervals, lit cities
within every speck of substance.

ROBERT MORGAN

IN THE AGE OF THE RADIO TELESCOPE

Because the universe, it seems,
is getting bigger,
because the space is deepening
between each star,
we listen now for light,
for murmurs from some fading sun.

The night sky's farther
than it was when we stood
hushed and hunched above a tripod
in the dark yard,
focusing the constellations
on their way away from us:

The gleam of galaxies an echo,
an ear for an eye,
the lens we squinted through
become a bowl of sound
tipped upward, open
as the black hole of a pupil.

JAMES SCRUTON

THE BOOK OF THE DEAD MAN (#33)

1. ABOUT THE DEAD MAN AND
A PARALLEL UNIVERSE

Perhaps it is not so important that the dead man lives.

After all, the dead man deserts the future.

He squints to better define the distance, a darkroom procedure.

He drops his jaw to hear better, he makes a fist around each
thing to gain a better purchase, he breathes with his mouth
open to better catch the odors of food and inhales as he
chews to better free its taste.

He walks downhill whenever possible.

Thus the dust where the dead man lies is fluffy, as if there were
a shadow shape within it, a more perfect dead man.

Hence the face of the earth wears an expression of beneficent
indifference, confirming that too much has been made of life
and death.

The dead man will be tears freed of eyes, laughter and moans
independent of any contraption, a soul without devices, a
spirit sans tricks.

The dead man is Darwin's resolution, an ultimate promise.

After the dead man, how can there be a body of myth, he is
the living truth.

The dead man seems smaller only because of where one stands
to see him, this is mental parallax.

2. MORE ABOUT THE DEAD MAN AND
A PARALLEL UNIVERSE

It is as if there were being woven a cloth shirt made of the
fibers of dead men, and of course it will be perfect.

People will take turns wearing it, each one imagining himself
to be its owner.

A true knowledge of it will banish weariness and ennui.

The feel of it will be like solace in the rain, its wearer will
shiver once and once only.

To the dead man the universe is a negative of a negative.

Thus the dead man's minuses combine to form the pluses of a
parallel universe.

When the dead man's effects have been fully distributed, his
  entropy come to fruition, then the imaginary numbers
  combine to pile up in reality, denial is replaced with
  permission, safelights with daylight and the fourth dimension
  with a greater three.
The dead man is over the top.

MARVIN BELL

THE ESSENTIAL STORY

We each wanted our own story, my father and I;
we were talkers, him first then me,
each wanted the other to listen until his heart broke.
It didn't matter where the story began,
or what it was about, each had a better one,
each had gone out farther, seen more,
each needed—this time—to be listened to;
each was ready to kill the other to get him to shut up.

Or so it seemed to me
until I hated him. He had the advantage,
years when I didn't exist; he knew war, marriage,
the birth of sons, decline; I knew dreams, agility,
desire, a boy's will. It was no wonder I got out of there,
no wonder I ran for my life
like a boy running at a sunset.

Everywhere I went, sons out on bail
yapped like maniacs. And every time a man stopped me
to pour out his heart, I understood why he did this.
And the whispers in theaters,
and the soft patter after lovemaking,
and the derelict explaining himself to a building
—I understood. A boy can't make his father listen to him,
and he can't make his father stop talking.
Even years later, when I returned,
my father wouldn't let me get a word in,
he had so much to say about how he missed me.

CHARLIE SMITH

TO REASON

Reason, I hope I never speak ill of you,
Dependable homely friend who prods me gently
To turn to the hour that's now arriving,
Not to the hour I let slip by
Twenty years back. No way now, you say,
To welcome a friend I failed to welcome
When she returned to town in sorrow;
Fresh from her discovery that the man
Who'd seemed to burn with the brightest flame
Could show a darker side as well.

You're right to label it magical thinking
When I say to a phantom what I never said
To flesh and blood, as if the words, repeated enough,
Could somehow work their way back to an old page
And nudge the silence aside and settle in,
A delusion not appropriate for a man no longer young
At the end of a century where many nations
Have set many things in motion they can't call back
Though the vote for reversal is unanimous.

I'm glad you ask, clear-sighted Reason,
Before what audience, if my speech can't reach her ears,
I imagine myself performing. Who is it
I want to convince I'd do things differently
This time around if the chance were offered.
You're right to say that half an hour a day is enough
For these gods or angels to get the point
If they're ever going to get it, which is doubtful.
Right again that if part of myself
After all my efforts still needs convincing
I should leave that dullard behind
With the empty dream of wholeness and move on.

I should move along the road that is not the road
I'd be moving along had I said what I didn't say
To someone who might have been ready to listen,
But a road as good, you assure me, Reason,
One that might lead to a life I can be proud of

So the man I might have been can't pity me.
Thanks for arguing I can solve the problems
He may have wanted to solve but hadn't the time for;
Being, as he was, preoccupied
With the life I would be living
Had I been ready long ago.

CARL DENNIS

PSYCHE AND EROS IN FLORIDA

In the subtropics it must be spring:
a flock of cedar waxwings, whispering,
has tethered the unswayed cabbage palm
to the last of the day's heat.

They devour the fruit no local bird wants.
Unswerving, they swerve through clotheslines.
Let their whispery cries be mine.
Their whisper of wings is yours.

But what good is sight?
In the dark, I thought, lay the struggle
of mind over body that kept Aquinas awake.
Whoever you were, you slept on.

By candlelight nothing is not beautiful.
The relief of your finely sculpted head;
The drop of wax that fell on your bare shoulder.
Why didn't you want me to see you?

The drop of red on each wing almost glows
this hour neither dark nor light.
Waxwings, forgive me. Fly away north.
What was the dark like?

I remember the mind fogged with something not dream.
And afterwards
what of the traitorous, languorous body?
It lies down. It begs.

DEBORA GREGER

TOOLS: AN ODE

The cheap
          screwdriver reams the cheap
                    screwhead,
and dull
        blades burn white oak
                and splinter cherry.
The bad wrench
        torques
              the bolt on crookedly
and strips the threads.
                 But underneath good tools,
the screw bites freely to its full depth,
                the board
rips cleanly
        and the hex nut weds its bolt.
Thin shavings rise in long unbroken curls,
each lovely in itself.
         The good tool
               smooths
rough lumber underneath an unforced hand,
unwarps
        the warped board,
             trues the untrue edge
before it chops the mortise, cuts
            the tenon,
and taps them home
        in happy marriage, snug
and nearly
        indestructible.
             With good tools
the edge falls
        plumb and all
           four corners square.
And there is order
        in the polity
and pleasure in
        each smile between old lovers.

ANDREW HUDGINS

WAYS OF TALKING

We used to like talking about grief
Our journals and letters were packed
with losses, complaints, and sorrows.
Even if there was no grief
we wouldn't stop lamenting
as though longing for the charm
of a distressed face.

Then we couldn't help expressing grief
So many things descended without warning:
labor wasted, loves lost, houses gone,
marriages broken, friends estranged,
ambitions worn away by immediate needs.
Words lined up in our throats
for a good whining.
Grief seemed like an endless river—
the only immortal flow of life.

After losing a land and then giving up a tongue,
we stopped talking of grief
Smiles began to brighten our faces.
We laugh a lot, at our own mess.
Things become beautiful,
even hailstones in the strawberry fields.

HA JIN

DEMOCRACY

Butare, Rwanda
November 3, 1992

Here it's the rainy season, but it still hasn't rained
so there's nothing for the dusty woman
in the roadside field to do
but lean on her hoe as if it's become a part of her body

and watch the bored checkpoint soldier
ask the suited and tied businessman
for the identity card he just can't seem to find.
Unconcerned, the Mercedes Benz pants in the heat,

the soldier just wants a cold beer;
the woman would rather be planting her beans,
and the businessman, who's obviously from the wrong tribe,
just keeps sweating and praying that the magic card

will materialize in some inside jacket pocket.
And if some tourist had snapped a photo of them all
like this, had in the instant stolen the souls
from this frightened man, this half-smiling woman,

the soldier just beginning to swing his gun around,
anybody with eyes in their head
would still swear years later that soon
something was bound to happen.

DERICK BURLESON

WATCHING DOGWOOD BLOSSOMS FALL
IN A PARKING LOT OFF ROUTE 46

Dogwood blossoms drift down at evening
    as semis pound past Phoenix Seafood

and the Savarin plant, west to the Turnpike,
    Paterson or hills beyond.

The adulterated, pearly light and bleak perfume
    of benzene and exhaust

make this solitary tree and the last of its bloom
    as stirring just now after another day

at the hospital with Mother and the ashen old ladies
    lost to TV reruns flickering overhead

as that shower of peach blossoms Tu Fu watched
    fall on the river bank

from the shadows of the Jade Pavilion,
    while ghosts and the music

of yellow orioles found out the seam of him
    and slowly cut along it.

AUGUST KLEINZAHLER

THE FAILURE OF SIMILES

In one image of the camps, the snow sifts down
like lime . . . or should it be the other way around?
Mere words now tumble like . . . corpses, like . . .
windy sacks in which the soul once sang.

You might have heard them somewhere
before they bloated in those earthen wombs.
And still we pile them higher and curse the stench
that rises from the cargohold of history.

Why can't we close that gash? *O Adonai,*
some shouted (it should have wrung the sky of color).
And now *Allah, Allah*—all the names empty
toward heaven—as tongues blister in the flames.

RICHARD FOERSTER

POEM ON THE FIRST DAY OF SCHOOL

All night the priestesses of wisdom have been practicing
the orders I remember of obedience,
silence and devotion to their measured tones,
index fingers hushed across their lips.
Consequently, it is pointless to inform them, half asleep
as I appear, arriving with my son,
how tiny I am in my own eyes, giving him up
to their language, a guide through second grade.
Now he must learn to mouth it as if it were a tongue
by which the world is formed. And he must take a second one
from such images as boys his age barter among themselves
that his words assume their sounds, therefore his own.
I remember. This is how it's done.
This is how I was given to the world.

PETER COOLEY

DUESENBERG, 1929

Speed and light, and what else is one to live for?
The edges rounded, smoothed, attenuated
to the point of imminent disappearance
(where shall speed end and light, at last, begin?),

the givens rearranged, less factual,
less obdurate, than one might have imagined,
once believed might obtain here, must obtain,
the walls guarding the factory abolished—

light, admit light here, let the weather in—,
cancelled, revoked, annulled, negated, shattered;
and the words pertaining to the mechanics
of the thing, crankshafts, pistons, axles, gears,

how it "works," unctuous methodologies
of assemblage, construction, piece work, "standards,"
words on the mouths of captain, foreman, workers,
bent at their tasks in narrow, airless places,

words still rancid from usage, common, parched,
stricken, at last, from the vocabularies
of those who, night to night, docile, compliant,
lacking the sense of where roads lead, all roads,

what, on certain evenings, they open out to,
work through the night to meet production schedules
(but for speed, but for light, what shall one live for?;
what, if not embarkation, does one dream of?);

the confines of the drawing-board subverted
in favor of—what to call it?—romance,
the utterly chrome-trimmed, the wholly sleek,
that which frees us to follow in its wake,

to improvise, to fill with splendor, grace,
turns, half-turns, cutoffs, dead ends, bends obscured
by all we seem not yet to know about them,
however far they lead, however deep,

the possible lying miles down the road
waiting for someone to have come upon it
late, in a small two-seater, both of us
drenched with the dark, things of pure speed, pure light,

where the road turns, the river, for the first time,
not without effort, each of us pronouncing
names for ourselves, the other, in the dark
names for the dark, for the things one might live for.

HERBERT MORRIS

ARCH OF TITUS

Disregarding the curse
that god will remove your name
from the list of the chosen people
for passing through the arch
families of tourists
from people not chosen
pass through blithely
as blithely conquering Romans
in the all-encircling frieze
destroy the Second Temple
and carry away their prize
menorah and chained slaves
as beautiful as themselves.
Though I've no god to lose
nor community of Jews
and never shared the need
for community of faith
I must not stray through
in my usual careless way
and deny what I have lost.

BARRY GOLDENSOHN

ON ME, THE IMPORTED SKIES

On me, the imported skies
    and the skin of local industry—
the detached, momentary
    meaning of millions,

tags leaping out of pockets
    or kissing my neck
anonymously affectionate:

   Checked by 107

   Assembled in Brazil with materials
       from outer space

   See other side of century
       for easy care instructions

I am the colored afterlife
    of Malaysian plants
another event in the petroleum
    evening, an international black
bottom line, puffing up
    from the Pacific rim.

I am an escapee
    from a mirror, the evolution
of Arabian sand and crumpled
    Spanish guitar strings
over slave-strummed voyages.

I am African music to an epileptic
    American beat, a convert
        to convenience, a contagious
            form of loneliness.

I am Anansi, the frequent-flyer spider,
a lover of Jewistinians and Sino-originals,
    Anglo-ricans, and Indo-shicksas—
        the conscience of Columbus
            watery and round.

                    WILLY CLAY

FERMI LAB: SISYPHUS OF QUARKS

What makes it all bearable,
                    participant/observer
in your underworld chute,
                    your circular tunnel,
they always return if only
                    in tracings.
                    Dwarf
                    boulders.
                    Emblems
of virtual order . . .
                    floaters
in the eye of the beholder.

PEARL ANDELSON SHERRY

GETTING THROUGH

Like a car stuck in gear,
a chicken too stupid to tell
its head is gone,
or sound ratcheting on
long after the film
has jumped the reel,
or a phone
ringing and ringing
in the house they have all
moved away from,
through rooms where dust
is a deepening skin,
and the locks unneeded,
so I go on loving you,
my heart blundering on,
a muscle spilling out
what is no longer wanted,
and my words hurtling past,
like a train off its track,
toward a boarded-up station,
closed for years,
like some last speaker
of a beautiful language
no one else can hear.

DEBORAH POPE

ANGLING

And I let the fish go.
Elizabeth Bishop

I let him go
as if he were
a fish I'd let
slip into water.

Cupping him in
my hands, his silver
wriggling and spit,
the sun had caught

his wet, flecked skin,
his breath, no breath,
the opening, closing
of gills, that grin.

I had removed
the hook from which
he'd swung with such
momentous grace.

But wasn't I snared?
That look, that flash
as I tossed him back,
alive, in air.

ELISE PASCHEN

GOGGLES AND HELMET

In her living room
we gather my mother's necessary
    or cherished objects for taking
north to the facility
    and care of nurses: caftans
and slippers; magnifying glass;
    checkbook and records; pretty
teacups and Dalton figurines;
    a photograph of my father

at college, grinning sideways
    into the camera seventy
years ago. Tonight she
    sleeps breathing oxygen
at Yale–New Haven, waking to fret
    over tomorrow's ambulance ride
of four sedated hours
    away from the house we moved into
when she was thirty-two
    and I was seven.

                I pace outside
the Ardmore Street house in
    darkness, on grass where I passed
a football with my young father
    back and forth for many autumns,
third grade to fourth, fourth to fifth,
    as if things never ended.
Here is the window-well in which
    I kept the turtles I caught
at Johnson's Pond, later finding
    scooped-out shells. The radio
stood by the living-room window
    so that I heard the good news
flash from the Philco: A Navy
    patrol plane had spotted
Amelia Earhart's Lockheed intact
    on a Pacific atoll near Wake
Island, and she was safe.

                                DONALD HALL

HAPPINESS

There's just no accounting for happiness,
or the way it turns up like a prodigal
who comes back to the dust at your feet
having squandered a fortune far away.

And how can you not forgive?
You make a feast in honor of what
was lost, and take from its place the finest
garment, which you saved for an occasion
you could not imagine, and you weep night and day

to know that you were not abandoned,
that happiness saved its most extreme form
for you alone.

No, happiness is the uncle you never
knew about, who flies a single-engine plane
onto the grassy landing strip, hitchhikes
into town, and inquires at every door
until he finds you asleep mid-afternoon
as you so often are during the unmerciful
hours of your despair.

It comes to the monk in his cell.
It comes to the woman sweeping the street
with a birch broom, to the child
whose mother has passed out from drink.
It comes to the lover, to the dog chewing
a sock, to the pusher, to the basketmaker,
and to the clerk stacking cans of carrots
in the night.   It even comes to the boulder
in the perpetual shade of pine barrens,
to rain falling on the open sea,
to the wineglass, weary of holding wine.

JANE KENYON

AFTER THE MISSIONARIES

We walk on lava,
solid of a liquid rock.

God is our rock.
Rocks were gods.

I say I am saved
but row far out,

too far to walk
even if they could

and say "Water
I still believe in you."

MICHAEL CHITWOOD

AT THE VIETNAM MEMORIAL

The last time I saw Paul Castle
it was printed in gold on the wall
above the showers in the boys'
locker room, next to the school
record for the mile. I don't recall
his time, but the year was 1968
and I can look across the infield
of memory to see him on the track,
legs flashing, body bending slightly
beyond the pack of runners at his back.

He couldn't spare a word for me,
two years younger, junior varsity,
and hardly worth the waste of breath.
He owned the hallways, a cool blonde
at his side, and aimed his interests
further down the line than we could guess.

Now, reading the name again,
I see us standing in the showers,
naked kids beneath his larger,
comprehensive force—the ones who trail
obscurely, in the wake of the swift,
like my shadow on this gleaming wall.

GEORGE BILGERE

FOR WILLIAM STAFFORD

30 August 1993

Someone we love, old friend, has telephoned
to let me know you're gone—and so you are.
I touch the steady books; my mind casts back,
then forth, and says, as you said once, *So long—*
I look toward seeing you everywhere.

HENRY TAYLOR

A POEM OF UNREST

Men duly understand the river of life,
misconstruing it, as it widens and its cities grow
dark and denser, always farther away.

And of course that remote denseness suits
us, as lambs and clover might have
if things had been built to order differently.

But since I don't understand myself, only segments
of myself that misunderstand each other, there's no
reason for you to want to, no way you could

even if we both wanted it. Do those towers even exist?
We must look at it that way, along those lines
so the thought can erect itself, like plywood battlements.

JOHN ASHBERY

TV MOVIE

This is true: it really happened. Honest.
Life is a movie based on a true story.
Doors open; faces glow in the hall.
There is the glint of the knife. It all ends
in court, or in the hospital where it started,
or in a ditch near some abandoned site,
or at a suburban bank that is being robbed.

There was a soft depression in the baby's head.
But he did well at school and never interfered
with his education, never questioned its creed.
He took care of dental hygiene, never lost his teeth.
His credit is A-OK. He could borrow tomorrow or now.
Still he has to die somehow. People have to sleep.
The thing has got to end in time for the local news.

JACK TURNER

DOES POETRY MATTER?

American poetry now belongs to a subculture; no longer part of the mainstream of artistic and intellectual life, it has become the specialized occupation of a relatively small and isolated group.

Dana Gioia

I am alone.
I lie next to stone

a man writes in the notebook he takes everywhere
in jail, a boy really
this shy, earnest twenty-two year old
who never seems comfortable
sitting—as if he's not yet used to the large, gangly body
that's grown around him.

You've got to believe me,
I never before lifted a hand to anyone. Never.

Now he goes nowhere without paper and pen,
rhymes everything. Everything
is a sonnet. He likes to hear the couplet
click shut like a door
only he has the keys for. He listens for the final word,
its prompt and perfect justice.

I am alone.
I lie down next to stone.

CHRISTOPHER BURSK

A DOG WAS CRYING TO-NIGHT
IN WICKLOW ALSO

In memory of Donatus Nwoga

When human beings found out about death
They sent the dog to Chukwu with a message:
They wanted to be let back to the house of life.
They didn't want to end up lost forever
Like burnt wood disappearing into smoke
Or ashes that get blown away to nothing.
Instead, they saw their souls in a flock at twilight
Cawing and headed back for the same old roosts
And the same bright airs and wing-stretchings each morning.
Death would be like a night spent in the wood:
At first light they'd be back in the house of life.
(The dog was meant to tell all this to Chukwu.)

But death and human beings took second place
When he trotted off the path and started barking
At another dog in broad daylight just barking
Back at him from the far bank of a river.

And that is how the toad reached Chukwu first,
The toad who'd overheard in the beginning
What the dog was meant to tell. "Human beings," he said
(And here the toad was trusted absolutely),
"Human beings want death to last forever."

Then Chukwu saw the people's souls in birds
Coming towards him like black spots off the sunset
To a place where there would be neither roosts nor trees
Nor any way back to the house of life.
And his mind reddened and darkened all at once
And nothing that the dog would tell him later
Could change that vision. Great chiefs and great loves
In obliterated light, the toad in mud,
The dog crying out all night behind the corpse house.

SEAMUS HEANEY

THE THROWBACK

Even I can't help but notice, my sweet,
that when you tuck your chin
into your chest, as if folding a sheet
while holding a clothes pin

between your teeth, or when, a small detail,
you put your hands like so
on your little pot-belly and twiddle
your thumbs like so, it's as if you're a throw-

back to the grandmother you never met,
the mother whom I sight
in this reddish patch of psoriasis

behind your ear that might
suddenly flare up into the helmet
she wore when she stood firm against Xerxes.

PAUL MULDOON

MOTHER IRELAND

At first
  I was land.
    I lay on my back to be fields
and when I turned
    on my side
       I was a hill
under freezing stars.
    I did not see.
       I was seen.
Night and day
    words fell on me.
         Seeds. Raindrops.
Chips of frost.
  From one of them
    I learned my name.
         I rose up. I remembered it.
Now I could tell my story.
  It was different
    from the story told about me.

And now also
    it was spring.
        I could see the wound I had left
in the land by leaving it.
        I travelled west.
                        Once there
    I looked with so much love
at every field
    as it unfolded
        its rusted wheel and its pram chassis
                        and at the gorse-
bright distances
    I had been
        that they misunderstood me.
Come back to us
    they said
        Trust me I whispered.

EAVAN BOLAND

THE ARRIVAL OF THE *TITANIC*

Gashed, from her long immobility on the sea-bed
gravid with the dreams of invertebrates, only half
here in the sense of consciousness, she pulls,
grey on a grey morning, into New York Harbor,
bearing all of the dead in their attitudes, the old dead
in dinner jackets, bare feet encrusted with barnacles,
their pearl eyes, their old assurance of conquest
over the negligent elements, and walking thin and
perplexed among them the new dead who
never realized on what crossing they had embarked.

We are the photograph's negative, made after
the color print, made after the abyssal waters
took color out of the Liberty scarves, the bright
upper atmosphere of tea dances, after the drift
downward, the pressures of winter. If it has been
abandoned, it is ours, it comes sailing silently
back with us. There were never enough
lifeboats, and never
enough gaiety to see us safely through past moonrise
and our monochrome exploration into the range of ice.

WILLIAM DICKEY

425

WITHOUT

we live in a small island stone nation
without color under gray clouds and wind
distant the unlimited ocean acute
lymphoblastic leukemia without seagulls
or palm trees without vegetation
or animal life only barnacles and lead
colored moss that darkens when months do

hours days weeks months weeks days hours
the year endures without punctuation
february without ice no winter sleet
snow melts and recovers but nothing
without thaw although cold streams hurtle
no snowdrop or crocus rises no yellow
no bright leaves of maple without autumn

no spring no summer no autumn no winter
no rain no peony thunder no woodthrush
the book is a thousand pages without commas
without mice or maple leaves windstorms
no castles no plazas no flags no parrots
without carnival or the procession of relics
intolerable without brackets or colons

silence without color sound without smell
without apples without pork to rupture gnash
unpunctuated without churches uninterrupted
no orioles ginger noses no opera no
without fingers or daffodils or cheekbones
the body is a nation tribe dug into stone
assaulted white blood broken to fragments

provinces that invade bomb shoot shell
execute rape retreat and attack
artillery sniper fire helicopter gunship
grenade burning murder landmine starvation
the ceasefire lasts forty-eight hours
then a shell explodes in a market
pain vomit neuropathy morphine nightmare

confusion terror the rack screw steroids
vincristine ara-c cytoxan vp-16
loss of memory loss of language losses
foamless uninterrupted sea without sea
delirium whipmarks of petechiae pcp
multiple blisters of herpes zoster
and how are you doing today I am doing

one afternoon say that the sun comes out
moss takes on greenishness leaves fall
the market opens a loaf of bread a sparrow
a bony dog wanders back sniffing a lath
it might be possible to take up a pencil
unwritten stanzas taken up and touched
beautiful terrible sentences unuttered

the sea unrelenting wave gray the sea
flotsam without islands broken crates
block after block the same house the mall
no cathedral no hobo jungle the same men
and women they long to drink hayfields
without dog or semicolon or village square
without hyena or lily without garlic

DONALD HALL

MARGINALIA

Sometimes the notes are ferocious,
skirmishes against the author
raging along the borders of every page
in tiny black script.
If I could just get my hands on you,
Kierkegaard, or Conor Cruise O'Brien,
they seem to say,
I would bolt the door and beat some logic into your head.

Other comments are more offhand, dismissive —
"Nonsense." "Please!" "HA!!" —
that kind of thing.
I remember once looking up from my reading,
my thumb as a bookmark,
trying to imagine what the person must look like
who wrote "Don't be a ninny"
alongside a paragraph in *The Life of Emily Dickinson*.

Students are more modest,
needing to leave only their splayed footprints
along the shore of the page.
One scrawls "Metaphor" next to a stanza of Eliot's.
Another notes the presence of "Irony"
fifty times outside the paragraphs of *A Modest Proposal*.

Or they are fans who cheer from the empty bleachers,
hands cupped around their mouths.
"Absolutely," they shout
to Duns Scotus and James Baldwin.
"Yes." "Bull's-eye." "My man!"
Check marks, asterisks, and exclamation points
rain down along the sidelines.

And if you have managed to graduate from college
without ever having written "Man vs. Nature"
in a margin, perhaps now
is the time to take one step forward.

We have all seized the white perimeter as our own
and reached for a pen if only to show
we did not just laze in an armchair turning pages;

we pressed a thought into the wayside,
planted an impression along the verge.

Even Irish monks in their cold scriptoria
jotted along the borders of the Gospels
brief asides about the pains of copying,
a bird singing near their window,
or the sunlight that illuminated their page—
anonymous men catching a ride into the future
on a vessel more lasting than themselves.

And you have not read Joshua Reynolds,
they say, until you have read him
enwreathed with Blake's furious scribbling.

Yet the one I think of most often,
the one that dangles from me like a locket,
was written in the copy of *Catcher in the Rye*
I borrowed from the local library
one slow, hot summer.
I was just beginning high school then,
reading books on a davenport in my parents' living room,
and I cannot tell you
how vastly my loneliness was deepened,
how poignant and amplified the world before me seemed,
when I found on one page
a few greasy-looking smears
and next to them, written in soft pencil—
by a beautiful girl, I could tell,
whom I would never meet—
"Pardon the egg salad stains, but I'm in love."

BILLY COLLINS

AFTER MAKING LOVE

No one should ask the other
"What were you thinking?"

No one, that is,
who doesn't want to hear about the past

and its inhabitants,
or the strange loneliness of the present

filled, even as it may be, with pleasure,
or those snapshots

of the future, different heads
on different bodies.

Some people actually desire honesty.
They must never have broken

into their own solitary houses
after having misplaced the key,

never seen with an intruder's eyes
what is theirs.

STEPHEN DUNN

HORSESHOES

Half my childhood my father carried in his dusty pocket
a miniature on a key chain, warm as a penny
when you rubbed it with your thumb.
Real ones lined a neighbor's drive, an uncle's flower bed,
and above the door of my grandfather's grocery
a parade shoe hung heels up
to keep what luck he had from spilling.

Wherever I looked there were horseshoes—
silver buckles, copper bracelets,
and dozens of pony shoes on the tack room floor,
strewn among the nails

you could throw like darts. Sometimes my cousin
rubbed a horseshoe before a test,
or carried it to school in her book bag.
A pharmacist at the Rexall, a man
I feared, wore a bright one of diamonds
in the hairs of a finger.
Everyone then seemed to need luck.

In that, at least, we're all old fashioned.
Just last year a woman in Montana
bought a horseshoe
from a blacksmith who'd hammered it into a heart.
She mailed it to my wife as a valentine.
Every few weeks it jars me awake,
clanging on the back porch, among the wind chimes.

DAVID BOTTOMS

A POSTCARD FROM GREECE

Hatched from sleep, as we slipped out of orbit
Round a clothespin curve new-watered with the rain,
I saw the sea, the sky, as bright as pain,
That outer space through which we were to plummet.
No guardrails hemmed the road, no way to stop it,
The only warning, here and there, a shrine:
Some tended still, some antique and forgotten,
Empty of oil, but all were consecrated
To those who lost their wild race with the road
And sliced the tedious sea once, like a knife.
Somehow we struck an olive tree instead.
Our car stopped on the cliff's brow. Suddenly safe,
We clung together, shade to pagan shade,
Surprised by sunlight, air, this afterlife.

A. E. STALLINGS

THE FRIDAY NIGHT FIGHTS

Every Friday night we watched the fights.
Me, ten years old and stretched out on the couch;
my father, in his wheelchair, looking on
as Rocky Marciano, Sonny Liston, Floyd Patterson
fought and won the battles we could not.
Him, twenty-nine, and beat up with disease;
me, counting God among my enemies
for what He'd done to us. We never touched.

But in between the rounds we'd sing how we'd
Look sharp! Feel sharp! & Be sharp! with Gillette
and Howard Cosell, the Bela Lugosi of boxing.
Out in the kitchen, my mother never understood
our need for blood, how this was as close as we'd get
to love — bobbing and weaving, feinting and sparring.

RONALD WALLACE

LOVER RELEASE AGREEMENT

Against his lip, whose service has been tendered
lavishly to me, I hold no lien.
Here's his heart, which finally has blundered
from my custody. Here's his spleen.
Hereafter let your hair and eyes and breasts
be venue for his daydreams and his nights.
Here are smart things I've said, and all the rest
you'll hear about. Here are all our fights.
Now, whereas I waive rights to his kiss,
the bed you've shared with him has rendered null
his privilege in mine. Know that, and this:
undying love was paid to me in full.
No matter how your pleasures with him shine,
you'll always be comparing them to mine.

J. ALLYN ROSSER

DROWNING IN WHEAT

They'd been warned
on every farm
that playing
in the silos
would lead to death.
You sink in wheat.
Slowly. And the more
you struggle the worse it gets.
"You'll see a rat sail past
your face, nimble on its turf,
and then you'll disappear."
In there, hard work
has no reward.
So it became a kind of test
to see how far you could sink
without needing a rope
to help you out.
But in the midst of play
rituals miss a beat—like both
leaping in to resolve
an argument
as to who'd go first
and forgetting
to attach the rope.
Up to the waist
and afraid to move.
That even a call for help
would see the wheat
trickle down.
The painful consolidation
of time. The grains
in the hourglass
grotesquely swollen.
And that acrid
chemical smell
of treated wheat
coaxing them into
a near dead sleep.

JOHN KINSELLA

THE OBLIGATION TO BE HAPPY

It is more onerous
than the rites of beauty
or housework, harder than love.
But you expect it of me casually,
the way you expect the sun
to come up, not in spite of rain
or clouds but because of them.

And so I smile, as if my own fidelity
to sadness were a hidden vice —
that downward tug on my mouth,
my old suspicion that health
and love are brief irrelevancies,
no more than laughter in the warm dark
strangled at dawn.

Happiness. I try to hoist it
on my narrow shoulders again —
a knapsack heavy with gold coins.
I stumble around the house,
bump into things.
Only Midas himself
would understand.

LINDA PASTAN

TWELFTH BIRTHDAY

As if because you lay
(*deeply embarrassing*) inside
my body, I could (*inconceivable*)
follow your swift thoughts into their blue
immersion even now,
stilettoes flickering, or schools of fish
maneuvering, first clear and then occluded,
though now and then a piercing gleam cuts through;

as if the snow reflections that glaze
the winter afternoon to porcelain
could penetrate the secrets of a skull
that happens to have lodged (*improbable*)

inside me once. Your liberation
twelve years ago today is the occasion
you and your friends are celebrating now
behind a door that's firmly shut.

The fantasy you've lately been devouring
features an evil mage with hourglass eyes.
Last week, when you were furious at me
(I must have thrown some precious thing away),
you swiftly slipped into your parents' room
and turned the bedside clock an hour ahead.
Discovered as the culprit, wickedly
you smiled. You knew time was my enemy.

RACHEL HADAS

VARIATION ON A THEME OF BAUDELAIRE

On sale at every English station
Bookshop: *Gray's Anatomy*,
Permanently remaindered—
Almost as embarrassing to be
Seen perusing as the configuration
Of bodies on a king-size bed

On that sex manual's cover: luminous
(Albeit remaindered) forms condemned
To permanent tumescence,
The bones and muscles limned
In Gray now seeming so laborious,
Losing the essence

Of those still figures which are full of arrows
Yet suffer nothing,
Wrapped in the decency of polysyllables,
Exempt from all that writhing
With strange flesh on positioned pillows,
Knowing no troubles.

DAVID RICKS

INTRODUCTION TO METHODS
OF MATHEMATICAL PHYSICS

You must develop a feeling for these symbols
that crawl across a page, for the text overrun

with scorpions. Like those books about insects
you read as a child, scared to touch the magnified photos,

this too will taunt you. It will become
your daily fare and meditation, your bedtime

reading, morning prayer. Soon a single Greek letter
makes your eyes smart. You find yourself flat

at the back of your skull, searching past daybreak
for the hidden path, the gilded key, a glimpse

of what those few must see at will, those few for whom
each equation is a playful catch, like bees into a jar.

LISA ROSENBERG

HOORAY FOR HOLLYWOOD

Tell me another, my dear Sheherazade:
The Tale the Tailor Told of God;
   The Voyage to the Isle of Gold;
   The Prince Who Could Not Feel the Cold.
Unscroll their names: Noah, Nimrod,

Nebuchadnezzar. All fiction's a fraud
Except for yours, which I applaud
   Reel upon reel. Invent, unfold,
      Tell me another.

The entire N.E.A. may be outlawed;
Orpheus may drone and Homer nod.
   You still enchant with tales not twice told
But once-and-a-thousandfold. Sheherazade,
   Tell me another!

TOM DISCH

FROM RUIN

Our guide is Turk-proud,
though he moved from Bosnia as a child.
During the winter he's an archaeology student
on a dig at Tyre—his dig, he smiles.

This morning, newspapers proclaim
the find of another Bosnian grave,
a scramble of the unidentified.

I ask if he has a picture of his girl.
Not with him, he says, and tells us goodbye.
They'll meet later and drive
through the night to his home in Ankara.
For him, there is only one day of rest
before another tour begins.
Pull over and sleep, I advise.

In the desolate steppes ahead,
they'll lie under a spread of stars,
only an occasional passing car,
miles of wheat swooning on all sides—

a long whisper across the land,
the promise of grains hanging on,
feeding them for a time,
their bodies close as flesh can get,
the heart, that bloody artifact,
sometimes more difficult to find.

JULIE SUK

THE SUIT

"I'll make you one," he said, "and balance it
Perfectly on you." And I could almost feel
The plumb line of the creased tweed hit my heel,

My shoulders like a spar or a riding scale
Under the jacket, my whole shape realigned
In ways that suited me down to the ground.

So although a suit was the last thing that I needed
I wore his words and told him that I'd take it
And told myself it was going for a song.

SEAMUS HEANEY

THE VOICE OF COL. VON STAUFFENBERG
RISING FROM PURGATORY

"Something fearful has happened . . . . The Führer is alive!"
Gen. Fellgiebel, July 20, 1944

That last night we passed quietly, my brother and I.
We sat talking of poems into the small hours;

And saw, at dawn, for the last time, through the beautiful tall
windows,
The smoke as of some great sacrifice suspended over the city.

And the little life remaining seemed very full.

And to turn away then, to turn one's back to God,
To cast one's self aside as simply as a child
Discards the doll he has grown weary of . . .

They led us out that evening into the courtyard.
There was a mound of earth there, left from the excavations,

Against which they posed us
And it was there that the lights of the parked trucks found us.

All it would ever come to now was grief and a little pride,
Grief, pride, and the overwhelming regret
That through failure one had been spared for heaven after all.

DONALD JUSTICE

MIDDLE PATH

To James Wright

Your foot would lift, as if levitating,
and move through the air and, like
the front strutting frond of a die rocker
stamp down—the awkward strut
of someone burning up inside—as if
you had been wound up elsewhere
and set going in a dangerous direction,
past things which open and show you their insides,
under a brilliant sky you wildly hoped
one day might flow from your pen,
the air-change of uncried tears; or
Middle Path could in reality go straight,
like Aristotle's radical Golden Mean the class
wouldn't have quite got the hang of yet,
into hell. What the hell. All
failures en route could be material
for the construction of speech out of trouble.
You would step along Middle Path
afire in the clear idea that it could be done
and it could not be done for long.
The drum majorettes of high school days
in Martins Ferry are all old,
in old bodies, now, or else dead.
But second clarity may have given some
a transfigured beauty—a beauty like that
which living weakened, in danger, with courage
in a second life clarified by love, gave you.
You of all of us were to be able
to sit down forever, almost without self,
with a notebook and pencil,
wherever life and death meet—
as today, this first day of spring,
you may have strayed off Middle Path
and stamp through the remains of snow
and hunker down before a gravestone
and peer at the letters time
and the chemical winds have spared:

ALFRED AND [effaced]
AGE 6   AGE 4
CHILDREN OF [effaced] AND ELIZABETH [effaced]
OF SUCH IS THE KINGDOM OF [effaced]

GALWAY KINNELL

ADD-WATER INSTANT BLUES

Got to get
over you, out of here,
through with this, real,
hold of me, back my soul,
by, with it, cool.

Got to get
up for it, down to it,
on with it, strong,
a grip, a life, past it,
clear, even, along.

Got to get
off of this, into it,
going, wise, done,
got to *get* it, get free of you:
Ready. Set. Gone.

ROBIN MORGAN

HOTWIRE

Some days I feel myself ravaged,
mercurial, and the future
open country around me; I will not
be your old slipper. I will not
have my words beaten into
shapes I never intended.
I will savor my mornings alone,
my thoughts clear as new rain.
Once my neighbor's red mare
ran straight through the single strand

of electric fence, its sting absorbed
in her body's explosion, her need
to be somewhere else. For a while
she was magnificent, all flame
and thunder, tearing the plowed acres.
Some days I barely feel the shock
of a future without you.
The mare, of course, was caught again,
and grazes quietly with the others
within the circle of that humming wire.

LESLIE ULLMAN

THE OBSOLESCENCE OF *THOU*

Last heard in a country church, in a prayer
That an elderly spinstress had decked out
In what manner she thought befitting
For heaven's immoderate ears, it seemed
All a Sunday rite and benediction

Except some grave care in its blurting-out
Made me think of the papa she'd tended
And kisses foregone for her all-mending,
Hands-on balm and alertness to afflictions
Just surrendered to the cemetery.

But also the way her prayer always ended
("Have thine own sweet way sweet Lord,
Have thine own sweet way") broadened the context
So I'd attach it to Pound wooing Keats
("O thou ivory sandaled woman of my dreams"),

And love that did get made, often sweetly
(But how soon antiqued and caricatured) —
Not that I'd managed it yet myself,
Just that it seemed prudent to have some sins
To repent, and that one in particular.

RODNEY JONES

VISITING HOURS ARE OVER

Down the hall past the half-
closed doors
a body
crumpled on every bed
striped pajamas three pills
in a pleated cup past the windows
double-glazed against
the rain past the waxy
sansevieria past the lead apron
of hospital drapes
down the front steps two blocks
to the car
I run
just to feel
my feet
hit the
pavement my hands
slap against my sides
cold wet
cold slippery wet
I don't
open the umbrella

CHANA BLOCH

THE BAOBAB TREE 1996

I hid in its wet hollowed trunk,
used it for liquid and shelter.
I called it *mother*.
It stood strong against the sun
with branches spread yards beyond
its bulging womb. I slept
beneath oblong fruit and knew the promise
of food. Somewhere else it was

cold, the air so dry my spirit had split
my skin. No balm could calm it.
I sat and wrote about it

in my room while she shivered
in her tomb — first winter

without her. I remembered
she told me how she wanted to come back
as a tree so I climbed

inside the oddest one,
where I knew I belonged.

SUSAN HAHN

THE PATIENT

At the end we prayed for death,
even phoned funeral homes
from his room for the best

cremation deal. But back
when he was tall, he once put
my ailing cat to sleep,

or helped the vet and me
hold it flat to the table
while we felt all muscles

tighten for escape
then freeze that way. Later
in my father's truck,

I held the heavy shoebox on my lap.
He said, I ever git like that
you do the same. I remember the slight

weight of my ten-year-old head
nodding without a pause. We peeled
from the gravel lot onto the rain-

blurred road. What did I know
of patience then? Or my dad
for that matter, shifting gears.

Each white second was knit
into a sheet that settled over his features
like a snowfield. Forgive me,

Father, this penitent face.
I was the patient one.
I got what I wanted.

MARY KARR

AT AN ISLAND FARM

If only the light might last,
    the mild sea-breeze hold steady,
I think perhaps I could soon be ready
    to relinquish a past

    that let go of *me* as surely
    as some stern wind last year
may have seized a wheat stem by the ear
    and shaken it, purely

    without a thought for
    whether the seeds were drowned
or whether, aloft, some few of them found
    another shore.

BRAD LEITHAUSER

THE DEVIL'S WORKSHOP

The master craftsman sits like Rodin's
Thinker, surrounded by his cosmic tools,
Experimenting with the greenhouse effect
& acid rain. A great uncertainty

Plagues him. Some hard questions
Wound the air. Yesterday afternoon
Children marched with a rainbow
Of placards. Perhaps he can create

A few suicides with his new computer
Virus. Something has gone wrong

In the shop, because the old gods
Of serpentine earthquakes & floods

Are having more fun than he is
In his laboratory of night sweats
& ethnic weapons. Lovers smile
As Cupid loads a blowgun with thorns.

YUSEF KOMUNYAKAA

AT THE POETRY READING

I can't keep my eyes off the poet's
wife's legs—they're so much more
beautiful than anything he might
be saying, though I'm no longer
in a position really to judge,
having stopped listening some time ago.
He's from the Iowa Writers Workshop
and can therefore get along fine
without my attention. He started in
reading poems about his childhood—
barns, cornsnakes, gradeschool, flowers,
that sort of stuff—the loss of
innocence he keeps talking about
between poems, which I can relate to,
especially under these circumstances.
Now he's on to science, a poem
about hydrogen, I think, he's trying
to imagine himself turning into hydrogen.
Maybe he'll succeed. I'm imagining
myself sliding up his wife's fluid,
rhythmic, lusciously curved, black-
stockinged legs, imagining them arched
around my shoulders, wrapped around my back.
My God, why doesn't he write poems about her!
He will, no doubt, once she leaves him,
leaves him for another poet, perhaps,
the observant, uninnocent one, who knows
a poem when it sits down in a room with him.

JOHN BREHM

FOR ALLEN GINSBERG

Ginsberg, Ginsberg, burning bright,
Taunter of the ultra right,
What blink of the Buddha's eye
Chose the day for you to die?

Queer pied piper, howling wild,
Mantra-minded flower child,
Queen of Maytime, misrule's lord
Bawling, *Drop out! All aboard!*

Finger-cymbaled, chanting *Om*,
Foe of fascist, bane of bomb,
Proper poets' thorn-in-side,
Turner of a whole time's tide,

Who can fill your sloppy shoes?
What a catch for Death. We lose
Glee and sweetness, freaky light,
Ginsberg, Ginsberg, burning bright.

X. J. KENNEDY

THE INVENTION OF SECRECY

The ancients were not able, save
for a few remarkable ones—
Alexander, Julius Caesar, Ambrose—

to read, or write, silently. *I would
have written to you sooner*, Cicero wrote
to a friend, *but I had a sore throat.*

Read to yourself, we say to children
still today. This they cannot do.
Saying the Latin answers at the Mass,

dressed in my white Sears shirt under
Medieval cassock and surplice,
Chuck Taylor Converse All-Stars—

to protect the sacristy carpet—
I heard some new music. The words
tasted nothing like Cleveland.

Ages ago, library, school, temple
were loud places where tongues flexed,
heart and lungs giving, taking,

the song and dance of subduing self
enough to put in our mouths words
of another body, words of our own.

Learning to read without even moving
our lips, we invented private life.
We created secrets of the dark hollows

of bone and flesh, a new selfishness,
deceiving ourselves into believing
that, alone, we could be complete,

silent, we would not grow too full.

DAVID CITINO

BECUNE POINT

Stunned heat of noon. In shade, tan, silken cows
hide in the thorned acacias. A butterfly staggers.

Stamping their hooves from thirst, small horses drowse
or whinny for water. On parched, ochre headlands, daggers

of agave bristle in primordial defense,
like a cornered monster backed up against the sea.

A mongoose charges dry grass and fades through a fence
faster than an afterthought. Dust rises easily.

Haze of the Harmattan, Sahara dust, memory's haze
from the dried well of Africa, the headland's desert

or riders in swirling burnooses, mixed with the greys
of hills veiled in Impressionist light. We inherit

two worlds of associations, or references, drought
that we heighten into Delacroix's North Africa,

veils, daggers, lances, herds the Harmattan brought
with a phantom inheritance, which the desperate seeker

of a well-spring staggers in the heat in search of—
heroic ancestors; the other that the dry season brings
is the gust of a European calendar, but it is the one love
that thirsts for confirmations in the circling rings

of the ground dove's cooing on stones, in the acacia's
thorns and the agave's daggers, that they are all ours,

the white horsemen of the Sahara, India's and Asia's
plumed mongoose and crested palmtree, Benin and Pontoise.

We are history's afterthought, as the mongoose races'
ahead of its time; in drought we discover our shadows,

our origins that range from the most disparate places,
from the dugouts of Guinea to the Nile's canted dhows.

II

The incredible blue with its bird-inviting cloud,
in which there are crumbling towers, banners and domes,

and the sliding Carthage of sunsets, the marble shroud
drawn over associations that are Greece's and Rome's

and rarely of Africa. They continue at sixty-seven
to echo in the corridors of the head, perspectives

of a corridor in the Vatican that led, not to heaven,
but to more paintings of heaven, ideas in lifted sieves

drained by satiety because great art can exhaust us,
and even the steadiest faith can be clogged by excess,

the self-assured Christs, the Madonnas' inflexible postures
without the mess of motherhood. With this blue I bless

emptiness where these hills are barren of tributes
and the repetitions of power, our sky's naive

ceiling without domes and spires, an earth whose roots
like the thorned acacia's deepen my belief.

DEREK WALCOTT

NATURAL SELECTION

proceeds by chance
and necessity

becomes nonrandom
through randomness

builds complexity
from simplicity

nurtures consciousness
unconsciously

evolves purposelessly
creatures who demand

purpose
and discover

natural selection

ALAN SHAPIRO

SONNET

All we need is fourteen lines, well, thirteen now,
and after this next one just a dozen
to launch a little ship on love's storm-tossed seas,
then only ten more left like rows of beans.
How easily it goes unless you get Elizabethan
and insist the iambic bongos must be played
and rhymes positioned at the ends of lines,
one for every station of the cross.
But hang on here while we make the turn
into the final six where all will be resolved,
where longing and heartache will find an end,
where Laura will tell Petrarch to put down his pen,
take off those crazy medieval tights,
blow out the lights, and come at last to bed.

BILLY COLLINS

THE DARK BETWEEN

the starry hush
& shadowy rust
in the wallpaper's bloom

the child's sofabed dreams
& warped room's well
in the echoing house

the collected escapes
& biblical hymns
in the whispering weeds

the long hungry weep
& suitcase shame
in the Diaspora sprawl

the scrap metal dead
& horses of rage
down kettledrum stones

the history of black sighs
& sway of great whys
in the stained glass rain

the miraculous wounds
& steerage eyes
of the enormous dead

the doing what we must
& stars diced to ice
in the boomeranging night

the nation of bells
& extravagant return
to the God no one judged

the oblivious shrug
& traveling so far
in the dark between

For Lillian Braude

PHILIP SCHULTZ

"FIND WORK"

I tie my Hat—I crease my Shawl—
Life's little duties do—precisely
As the very least
Were infinite—to me—
Emily Dickinson, #443

My mother's mother, widowed very young
of her first love, and of that love's first fruit,
moved through her father's farm, her country tongue
and country heart anaesthetized and mute
with labor. So her kind was taught to do—
"Find work," she would reply to every grief—
and her one dictum, whether false or true,
tolled heavy with her passionate belief.
Widowed again, with children, in her prime,
she spoke so little it was hard to bear
so much composure, such a truce with time
spent in the lifelong practice of despair.
But I recall her floors, scrubbed white as bone,
her dishes, and how painfully they shone.

RHINA P. ESPAILLAT

OLD MOVIES

Television is a hereafter
dead actors enter upon
wherein they are all spirit
and are become light.
Thus may you attend them
in your living rooms
and say to your wives:
They are gone, all gone.
And though the wives cringe,
asking not to be reminded,
yet it is a fortunate
reminder, a very blessing,
for even juveniles
are children eternally,
knowing neither age
nor early bedtimes, nor

the burdensome dignity
of leaving childish things.
Night upon night unreels
the familiar masks
of breathless ingenue,
narrow-eyed villain;
in their shadow kingdoms
beyond the burning glass
they are not like us.
They but pretend to die,
while their secret, actual
passing is to the realm
where the evil are scourged
and the good rewarded
because such is the way
the Code was handed down.

ROBLEY WILSON

DEAD LANGUAGE LESSON

They lift their half-closed eyes out of the grammar.

What is the object of love? *you,*
Singular. The subject? I.

Aeneas has nothing to say for himself.
Even the boys confess that he
Didn't intend to come back, the girls
Already know the tale by heart.

They wheedle me for tangents, for
Anything not in a book,
Even though it's all from books:
The many-wiled Penelope,
Orpheus struck dumb with hindsight.

I confiscate a note in which
The author writes, "Who do you love?,"
An agony past all correction.

I think, as they wait for the bell,
Blessed are the young for whom
All languages are dead: the girl
Who twines her golden hair, like Circe,
Turning glib boys into swine.

A. E. STALLINGS

THE OFFSPRING

More fertile than they think, or know,
beautiful women and men nightly beget hundreds —
some of them thousands — lying above or below
the face of the innocent spouse. In shame again
and one more time again the lover conjures up the ghost
of this delicious body, those famous blue eyes;
these children raked out of the fire
that burned in one partner's sighs.
And the lovely, how indifferent they are
to their unknown offspring, named for them —
the Dylans and Cindys, children of the far
cry, the perfect, the coming dream.
How startled the poor changelings must be
to find the real father or mother
looking down at them, loving and ugly.

LIZ ROSENBERG

PSALM FOR AN ANNIVERSARY

Praise to boredom: to the summer solstice;
to our long marriage, its minutes dissolving
into hours here on the roof at sunset
as we watch shadows print their towers on buildings

while impersonal windows blink and darken.
Praise to recurrences: rainfalls of laughter;
white roses you brought home; old Army talk
I want to hear again. Bless the ruptures

healed, faint as wire-dolls in the park below us—
the skiff I boarded once that coursed the bay
leaving your island: that was urgency,
not this, when voices fall, eased by the sky's

arc over a bridge. In lulls, the mind
can see another city above this one,
ironic, hybrid as a string of puns.
Cupolas and the pyramids cut the skyline;

a red-brick campanile shelters a watertank;
and nuns in their high habits sail in pairs
to a ruined chapel over a warehouse,
its empty sockets glaring salmon-pink.

A frieze of horses has survived, at least
in replica, as though it were eternal,
while we, flawed with mistakes, who thought the skins
we shed would be our last, survey a steeple,

a tower-clock, a dome. Praise to the sun
that flares and flares again in fierce explosions
even after sunset, to muddy rivers
that glow vermilion now, to second chances.

GRACE SCHULMAN

DRIVING WEST IN 1970

My dear children, do you remember the morning
When we climbed into the old Plymouth
And drove west straight toward the Pacific?

We were all the people there were.
We followed Dylan's songs all the way west.
It was Seventy; the war was over, almost;

And we were driving to the sea.
We had closed the farm, tucked in
The flap, and were eating the honey

Of distance and the word "there."
Oh whee, we're gonna fly
Down into the easy chair. We sang that

Over and over. That's what the early
Seventies were like. We weren't afraid.
And a hole had opened in the world.

We laughed at Las Vegas.
There was enough gaiety
For all of us, and ahead of us was

The ocean. *Tomorrow's*
The day my bride's gonna come.
And the war was over, almost.

ROBERT BLY

DETROIT, TOMORROW

Newspaper says the boy killed by someone,
don't say who. I know the mother, waking,
gets up as usual, washes her face
in cold water, and starts the coffee pot.

She stands by the window up there on floor
sixteen wondering why the street's so calm
with no cars going or coming, and then
she looks at the wall clock and sees the time.

Now she's too awake to go back to bed,
she's too awake not to remember him,
her one son, or to forget exactly
how long yesterday was, each moment dragged

into the next by the force of her will
until she thought this simply cannot be.
She sits at the scarred, white kitchen table,
the two black windows staring back at her,

wondering how she'll go back to work today.
The windows don't see anything: they're black,
eyeless, they give back only what's given;
sometimes, like now, even less than what's given,

yet she stares into their two black faces
moving her head from side to side, like this,
just like I'm doing now. Try it awhile,
go ahead, it's not going to kill you.

Now say something, it doesn't matter what
you say because all the words are useless:
"I'm sorry for your loss." "This too will pass."
"He was who he was." She won't hear you out

because she can only hear the torn words
she uses to pray to die. This afternoon
you and I will see her just before four
alight nimbly from the bus, her lunch box

of one sandwich, a thermos of coffee,
a navel orange secured under her arm,
and we'll look away. Under your breath make
her one promise and keep it forever:

in the little store-front church down the block,
the one with the front windows newspapered,
you won't come on Saturday or Sunday
to kneel down and pray for life eternal.

PHILIP LEVINE

RISK

Difficult to know whether humans are inordinately anxious
about crisis, calamity, disaster, or unknowingly crave them.
These horrific conditionals, these expected unexpecteds,
we dwell on them, flinch, feint, steel ourselves:
but mightn't our forebodings actually precede anxiety?
Isn't so much sheer heedfulness emblematic of *desire*?

How do we come to believe that wrenching ourselves to attention
is the most effective way for dealing with intimations of catastrophe?
Consciousness atremble: might what makes it so
not be the fear of what the future might or might not bring,
but the wish for fear, for concentration, vigilance?
As though life were more convincing resonating like a blade.

Of course, we're rarely swept into events, other than domestic tumult,
from which awful consequences will ensue. Fortunately rarely.
And yet we sweat as fervently
for the most insipid issues of honor and unrealized ambition.
Lost brothership. Lost lust. We engorge our little sorrows,
beat our drums, perform our dances of aversion.

Always, "These gigantic inconceivables."
Always, "What will have been done to me?"
And so we don our mental armor,
flex, thrill, pay the strict attention we always knew we should.
A violent alertness, the muscularity of risk,
though still the secret inward cry: What else, what more?

C. K. WILLIAMS

WIGHT

In the dark we disappear, pure being.
Our mirror images, impure being.

Being and becoming (Heidegger), being and
nothingness (Sartre) — which is purer being?

Being alone is no way to be: thus
loneliness is the test of pure being.

Nights in love I fell too far or not quite
far enough — one pure, one impure being.

Clouds, snow, mist, the dragon's breath on water,
smoke from fire — a metaphor's pure being.

Stillness and more stillness and the light locked
deep inside — both pure and impure being.

Is is the verb of being, I the noun —
or pronoun for the purists of being.

I was, I am, I looked within and saw
nothing very clearly: purest being.

STANLEY PLUMLY

CROW IS WALKING

Crow is walking
to see things at ground level,
the landscape as new under his feet
as the air is old under his wings.

He leaves the dead rabbit waiting —
it's a given; it'll always be there —
and walks on down the dirt road,

admires the pebbles,
how they sparkle in the sun;

checks out his reflection
in a puddle full of sky
which reminds him
of where he's supposed to be,

but he's beginning to like
the way the muscles move in his legs
and the way his wings feel so comfortable
folded back and resting.

He thinks he might be beautiful,
the sun lighting his back
with purple and green.

Faint voices from somewhere far ahead
roll like dust down the road towards him.
He hurries a little.

His tongue moves in his mouth;
legends of language move in his mind.

His beak opens.
He tries a word.

GRACE BUTCHER

IMMIGRANT PICNIC

It's the Fourth of July, the flags
are painting the town,
the plastic forks and knives
are laid out like a parade.

And I'm grilling, I've got my apron,
I've got potato salad, macaroni, relish,
I've got a hat shaped
like the state of Pennsylvania.

I ask my father what's his pleasure
and he says, "Hot dog, medium rare,"
and then, "Hamburger, sure,
what's the big difference,"
as if he's really asking.

I put on hamburgers *and* hot dogs,
slice up the sour pickles and Bermudas,
uncap the condiments. The paper napkins
are fluttering away like lost messages.

"You're running around," my mother says,
"like a chicken with its head loose."

"Ma," I say, "you mean *cut off*,
loose and *cut off* being as far apart
as, say, *son* and *daughter*."

She gives me a quizzical look as though
I've been caught in some impropriety.
"I love you and your sister just the same," she says,
"Sure," my grandmother pipes in,
"you're both our children, so why worry?"

That's not the point I begin telling them,
and I'm comparing words to fish now,
like the ones in the sea at Port Said,
or like birds among the date palms by the Nile,
unrepentantly elusive, wild.

"Sonia," my father says to my mother,
"what the hell is he talking about?"
"He's on a ball," my mother says.

"That's *roll!*" I say, throwing up my hands,
"as in hot dog, hamburger, dinner roll . . . ."

"And what about *roll out the barrels?*" my mother asks,
and my father claps his hands, "Why sure," he says,
"let's have some fun," and launches
into a polka, twirling my mother
around and around like the happiest top,

and my uncle is shaking his head, saying
"You could grow nuts listening to us,"

and I'm thinking of pistachios in the Sinai
burgeoning without end,

pecans in the South, the jumbled
flavor of them suddenly in my mouth,
wordless, confusing,
crowding out everything else.

GREGORY DJANIKIAN

TOMORROW

I

Tomorrow I will start to be happy.
The morning will light up like a celebratory cigar.
Sunbeams sprawling on the lawn will set
dew sparkling like a cut-glass tumbler of champagne.
Today will end the worst phase of my life.

I will put my shapeless days behind me,
fencing off the past, as a golden rind
of sand parts slipshod sea from solid land.
It is tomorrow I want to look back on, not today.
Tomorrow I start to be happy; today is almost yesterday.

II

Australia, how wise you are to get the day
over and done with first, out of the way.
You have eaten the fruit of knowledge, while
we are dithering about which main course to choose.
How liberated you must feel, how free from doubt:

the rise and fall of stocks, today's closing prices
are revealed to you before our bidding has begun.
Australia, you can gather in your accident statistics
like a harvest while our roads still have hours to kill.
When we are in the dark, you have sagely seen the light.

III

Cagily, presumptuously, I dare to write 2018.
A date without character or tone. 2018.
A year without interest rates or mean daily temperature.
Its hit songs have yet to be written, its new-year
babies yet to be induced, its truces to be signed.

Much too far off for prophecy, though one hazards
a tentative guess—a so-so year most likely,
vague in retrospect, fizzling out with the usual
end-of-season sales; everything slashed:
your last chance to salvage something of its style.

DENNIS O'DRISCOLL

From FIGURES IN THE CARPETS

[KAZAK]

Three sunbursts spin, enigmatic energies
    through golden latchhooks, surrounding
cloudbanks; three eagles, darting within
    their shifting images: they return him
to streets of lit porches in summer dark,
    a boy stuttering over random syllables,
a blindfolded man pleading for his life—
    whose fate is in the hands of some men
whose fate is in the hands of other men,
    whose fate . . . until the whole pattern
emerges, and the language becomes clear.
    On the floor lies his mother, moaning,
until he comes out, guilty, before her—
    amid the mud of his own frozen blood.

DAVID SCHLOSS

PRIDE

Crowned with a feathered helmet,
Not for disguise or courtship
Dance, he looks like something
Birthed by swallowing its tail,

Woven from a selfish design
& guesswork. As if masked
With a see-through caul
From breast to hipbone,

His cold breath silvers
Panes of his hilltop house
Into a double reflection.
Silhouetted almost into a woman,

He can beg forgiveness now
As he leans against a window
Overlooking Narcissus's pond
Choked with a memory of lilies.

YUSEF KOMUNYAKAA

From PARAGRAPHS FROM A DAY-BOOK

For Hayden Carruth

Thought thrusts up, homely as a hyacinth
wrapped in its bulb like a root-vegetable,
a ninth-month
belly, where the green indelible
pattern's inscribed into the labyrinth.
Thrust into light, it's air's inhabitant
with light and air as food and drink.
A hyacinth, tumescent pink
on the low wooden Mexican chest
confronts the wintry dusk
with informed self-interest.
Leaf-spears extravagantly ask
what idea, still gnarled up in a knot
of ganglions, will break through the husk
shaped at last, recognizable as thought.

MARILYN HACKER

TO MY OLD POEMS

You had no independence
From me, in, say, nineteen sixty-three
I was already thirty-eight years old
And you were eight years old
I wanted to take care of you
Make sure you were in the best books and magazines
Printed on good paper and in type that was clear. A couple of you
Became independent entrepreneurs
And laughed back at me from anthologies
While, with feet pained by ill-fitting shoes, I walked through France
Dying to find something new to go with you. In these years
You became almost my enemies, cruelly, I thought,
Showing me what I could no longer do. At this time
You seemed one and the same as my youth
Not separate from me
As I was then but as I was now.
But you were always separate from me.
You who are made out of words.
One thing you do is not respond
Which is all right, since what kind of poems would you be if you were
    capable of responding?
That's not what's meant by an "answerable style."
One wants a poem to be still.
But I'd like to know where you got your music—
From other poems, I know, but from where else?
And if the ability to make you is a gift that comes back—
One of you arriving, or being finished,
Like an ace or a king or a queen
In the hand of my otherwise foolish life. In any case
You're friendlier than you have been for a long while—
Things seem to be all right between us now.

                                        KENNETH KOCH

INDUSTRIAL TEFLON
COMES INTO DOMESTIC USE

After the wars were over, the ones people sang about,
things quit sticking. My grandparents, for instance,
shook the dirt from their shoes and moved to town,
drove the paved streets of Columbia, spurned
orange juice for astronaut Tang.
And what year exactly did I start shaking off hugs?

For a wedding gift, I got Teflon pans.
Teflon, if you'd like to know, is a long-chain polymer,
a fluorocarbon plastic, like Freon.
As good as gold and platinum at resisting things.
Eggs slide right off, as on TV.
Not to mention what came after, Reagan and Bush,
facts sliding across the screen, disappearing
out of memory.
Not to mention the literary canon: Pope, Richardson,
Dryden, Spenser. Who reads them now?

The private name he used to call me, what was it?
The last time, he came through snow, bringing
a bottle of Mateus, and we made love
on the floor, not looking at each other,
nothing left but flesh and bones.
It was 1973, still no news of the danger of Freon.
All summer, I kept the air conditioner on.
The kids opened and closed doors, hot and cold,
the hole in their hearts forming already.

Surely my own mother must have held me, early on,
before I recognized her broken heart and turned away.
Surely her own mother must have held her,
sometimes, in spite of garden-smudged hands,
just to hold her.

                                        FLEDA BROWN

THE PROBLEM WAS

The problem was a different sense of form.
He was all couplets, heroic and closed;
I always wanted to carry on, one line
into the next, never reaching an end,
or, if I did, imagining it might be
the possible beginning to a different train
of thought, which might lead to the exact
opposite of what I was saying now.

The problem was we rhymed in various ways:
he liked perfection; I preferred the wise
conjunction of nearly alike, almost
a match made in heaven, both of us most
certain we knew where to take the next line.
He loved his words the best, and I loved mine.

JOYCE SUTPHEN

PLATONIC LOVE

We dine at Adorno and return to my Beauvoir.
She compliments me on my Bachelard pad.
I pop in a Santayana CD and Saussure back to the couch.
On my way, I pull out two fine Kristeva wine glasses.
I pour some Merleau-Ponty and return the Aristotle to Descartes.
After pausing an Unamuno, I wrap my arm around her Hegel.
Her hair smells of wild Lukacs and Labriola.
Our small talk expands to include Dewey, Moore and Kant.
I confess to her what's in my Eckhart. We Locke.
By this point, we're totally Blavatsky.
We stretch out on the Schopenhauer.
She slips out of her Lyotard and I fumble with my Levi-Strauss.
She unhooks her Buber and I pull off my Spinoza.
I run my finger along her Heraclitus as she fondles my Bacon.
She stops to ask me if I brought any Kierkegaard. I nod.
We Foucault.
She lights a cigarette and compares Foucault to Lacan.
I roll over and Derrida.

CURT ANDERSON

467

THE CHARIOTEER

At Delphi

With most of the bronzes
melted down for weapons,

he stands, as though absorbed
in some deep thought,

reins dangling
empty as fame or victory

from his hand,
and doesn't seem to notice

the horses have since
wandered off with the chariot;

his dark eyes
disengaged as wilderness

from this room, these artifacts,
and all of us

saddled with passage and time.

FAYE GEORGE

BATTLEFIELD

Back when I used to be Indian
I am standing outside the
pool hall with my sister.
She strawberry blonde. Stale sweat
and beer through the
open door. A warrior leans on his stick,
fingers blue with chalk.
Another bends to shoot.
His braids brush the green
felt, swinging to the beat
of the jukebox. We move away.

Hank Williams falls again
in the backseat of a Cadillac.
I look back.
A wind off the distant hills lifts my shirt,
brings the scent
of wounded horses.

MARK TURCOTTE

SAYING GOODBYE TO
VERY YOUNG CHILDREN

They will not be the same next time. The sayings
so cute, just slightly off, will be corrected.
Their eyes will be more skeptical, plugged in
the more securely to the worldly buzz
of television, alphabet, and street talk,
culture polluting their gazes' pure blue.
It makes you see at last the value of
those boring aunts and neighbors (their smells
of summer sweat and cigarettes, their faces
like shapes of sky between shade-giving leaves)
who knew you from the start, when you were zero,
cooing their nothings before you could be bored
or knew a name, not even your own, or how
this world brave with hellos turns all goodbye.

JOHN UPDIKE

TEST

Imagine a surface
so still and vast
that it could test
exactly what
is set in motion
when a single stone
is cast into its ocean.
Possessed of a calm
so far superior
to people's, it alone
could be assessed
ideally irascible.
In such a case,
if ripples yawed
or circles wobbled
in their orbits
like spun plates,
it would be the *law*
and not so personal
that what drops warps
and what warps dissipates.

KAY RYAN

DUST

The dust motes float
and swerve in the sunbeam,
as lively as worlds,
and I remember my brother
saying, when we were boys,
"We may be living on an atom
in somebody's wallpaper."

WENDELL BERRY

AFTER FINDING A ONE HUNDRED DOLLAR BILL

On Bourbon Street. I changed it at a bank
into all ones—a wad like a green brick.
Might stuff it in a G-string at a strip

show, but I'd spend it right. I wouldn't plunk
it down on my broker's wish list. Wall Street
could wait and so could tires. Then here's a drunk

banker complete with gold tooth and tin cup,
eyes sprung ahead. He sways beside the kid
who's tap-dancing for tips, bottle-cap taps.

Mr. Goldtooth sees me and says, "Brother,
could you allow me to hold a quarter?"
Hold it, what luck, but I have no quarters.

I shucked ten bucks into the dancer's hat.
And I didn't forget Mr. Goldbreath. He got
to hold one bill. Big spender me—I let

him hold it although he'd broken Good Luck
Rule Number 100: DON'T EVER UNDERESTIMATE
GOOD LUCK. So, I felt good about myself

and so lucky I marched to the casino and
stopped at one of the dollar slot machines.
I just knew it wanted to shake my hand.

And I was right. It rolled its eyes
flattering and swooning, pumping my glad
hand exactly eighty-nine times.

DC BERRY

ZEN LIVING

Birdsongs that sound like the steady determined tapping
of a shoemaker's hammer,
or of a sculptor making tiny ball-peen dents in a silver plate,
wake me this morning. *Is it possible*
the world itself can be happy? The calico cat
stretches her long body out across the top of my computer
    monitor,
yawning, its little primitive head a cave of possibility.
And I'm ready again
to try and see accidents, the over and over patterns
of double-slit experiments a billionfold
repeated before me. If I had great patience,
I could try to count the poplar, birch and oak
leaves in their shifting welter outside my bedroom window
or the almost infinitesimal trails of thought that flash and flash
everywhere, as if decaying particles inside a bubble chamber,
windshield raindrops, lake ripples. However,
instead I go to fry some bacon, crack two eggs
into the cast-iron skillet that's even older than this house,
and on the calendar (each month another oriental fan
where the climbing solitary is dwarfed . . . or on dark blue
    oceans
minuscular fishing boats bob beneath gigantic waves)
X out the days, including those I've forgotten.

DICK ALLEN

LAND

For Christopher Merrill

Swear by the olive in the God-kissed land—
There is no sugar in the promised land.

Why must the bars turn neon now when, Love,
I'm already drunk in your capitalist land?

If home is found on both sides of the globe,
home is of course here—and always a missed land.

The hour's come to redeem the pledge (not wholly?)
in Fate's "Long years ago we made a tryst" land.

Clearly, these men were here only to destroy,
a mosque now the dust of a prejudiced land.

Will the Doomsayers die, bitten with envy,
when springtime returns to our dismissed land?

The prisons fill with the cries of children.
Then how do you subsist, how do you persist, Land?

"Is my love nothing for I've borne no children?"
I'm with you, Sappho, in that anarchist land.

A hurricane is born when the wings flutter . . .
Where will the butterfly, on my wrist, land?

You made me wait for one who wasn't even there
though summer had finished in that tourist land.

Do the blind hold temples close to their eyes
when we steal their gods for our atheist land?

Abandoned bride, Night throws down her jewels
so Rome—on our descent—is an amethyst land.

At the moment the heart turns terrorist,
are Shahid's arms broken, O Promised Land?

AGHA SHAHID ALI

ACADEMIC

I see straight through myself
and into the no mirror.

A frame stares back,
announcing the time: late.
And the temperature:
still warm.

I recognize the calm
bystander's snowy face,
the handwriting on the blackboard

where chalk dust
from the names of the present
falls to the ledge
toward those who have disappeared.

JOHN SKOYLES

WHAT BECAME

What became of the dear
strands of hair pressed
against the perspiration
of your lover's brow
after lovemaking as you gazed
into the world of those eyes,
now only yours?

What became of any afternoon
that was so vivid you forgot
the present was up to its old
trick of pretending
it would be there
always?

What became of the one
who believed so deeply
in this moment he memorized
everything in it and left
it for you?

WESLEY MC NAIR

HOW WE MADE A NEW ART ON OLD GROUND

A famous battle happened in this valley.
                You never understood the nature poem.
Till now. Till this moment — if these statements
                seem separate, unrelated, follow this

silence to its edge and you will hear
                the history of air: the crispness of a fern
or the upward cut and turn around of
                a fieldfare or thrush written on it.

The other history is silent: The estuary
                is over there. The issue was decided here:
Two kings prepared to give no quarter.
                Then one king and one dead tradition.

Now the humid dusk, the old wounds
                wait for language, for a different truth:
When you see the silk of the willow
                and the wider edge of the river turn

and grow dark and then darker, then
                you will know that the nature poem
is not the action nor its end: it is
                this rust on the gate beside the trees, on

the cattle grid underneath our feet,
                on the steering wheel shaft: it is
an aftermath, an overlay and even in
                its own modest way, an art of peace:

I try the word *distance* and it fills with
                sycamores, a summer's worth of pollen
And as I write *valley* straw, metal
                blood, oaths, armour are unwritten.

Silence spreads slowly from these words
                to those ilex trees half in, half out
of shadows falling on the shallow ford
                of the south bank beside Yellow Island

as twilight shows how this sweet corrosion
                 begins to be complete: what we see
is what the poem says:
                 evening coming—cattle, cattle-shadows—

and whin bushes and a change of weather
                 about to change them all: what we see is how
the place and the torment of the place are
                 for this moment free of one another.

EAVAN BOLAND

[HIS LIFE WAS THE PRACTICE]

His life was the practice of forming a single
sentence which, as he grew older, he tried to
simplify, reduce its compound-complex structure
into one statement ruled by the separate, inviolate
pronoun within which he attempted to live, always
engaged in revision and the act of becoming; as the
distilled statement gradually became a fleeting
inquiry, a mild interrogative, which he repeated and
refined, making it increasingly concise, almost, at
his conclusion, producing no more than a distinct
sound, not quite a word, less than a cry, which his
death erased leaving the question mark hanging in
the air, like a broken halo, emblem of his birth,
evolution and release: a full life.

STEPHEN DOBYNS

TO LUCK

In the cards and at the bend in the road
we never saw you
in the womb and in the crossfire
in the numbers
whatever you had your hand in
which was everything
we were told never to put
our faith in you
to bow to you humbly after all
because in the end there was nothing
else we could do
but not to believe in you

still we might coax you with pebbles
kept warm in the hand
or coins or the relics
of vanished animals
observances rituals
not binding upon you
who make no promises
we might do such things only
not to neglect you
and risk your disfavor
oh you who are never the same
who are secret as the day when it comes
you whom we explain
as often as we can
without understanding

W. S. MERWIN

HAN-SHAN FASHIONS A MYTH

The old poet loves peacock feathers
And gathers them as they fall, one
By one, from perches in the trees
Near his house.

First, he caresses
Them with a dry writing brush, oh, so
Carefully, lest he separate the delicate
Spines, knowing the colors are interlocked.

Then, he looks for a place to stand them
In his cramped, little house. Proper
Location, he says, is half of any art.
Near his bed he keeps a jarful of
These planetary perturbations.

In the egg-yolk light of his lamp,
He sees universes scintillating in blue
And gold like his beloved Saturn,
And hears, from close by roosts, the dry
Clattering of galaxies being re-arranged.

And then the cry of damnation comes:
He sleeps and dreams of starfalls
And all the rumpus of dragons.

GEORGE SCARBROUGH

TWO EVANGELISTS

1. THE DISCOUNTER

His too-Good News would strip the Scripture
of every inconvenient stricture.

2. THE EXTORTIONIST

Consumed with gall, this other one forgets
the News is Good at all, and just makes threats.

ROBERT WEST

IN GLASS

A photo for your album.

Floating in clear solution in a dish,
How beautiful they are, like cultured pearls,
Pale sequins of some iridescent fish,
Or cloudy globes in which we gaze, foreseeing
Your blue-eyed son, a daughter with my curls,
Frozen halfway from nothingness to being.

Here's the sublime of lab and microscope,
Their sacraments, invisible to sight.
Half trying, half afraid to summon hope,
We marvel at our colonies of cells—
Four perfect spheres, surrounded by the bright
Coronas of their still-unbroken shells,

Small stars, none more substantial than a wraith,
On which we wish with our agnostic faith.

CATHERINE TUFARIELLO

HOW TO WRITE A VILLANELLE

If you would write a villanelle
Choose two of your most brilliant lines,
Ones you should have jettisoned.

Repeat them till you're bored
And so's your reader if he's stuck
This far through your villanelle.

Do likewise if you find a perfect rhyme.
Have no illusions that you are the first:
Whoever was, he should have jettisoned

All his favorite rhymes and lines.
So should you. Try fancy foreign forms
If you would write a villanelle.

As with new lovers: you repeat a line
Till you are bored and so is he or she,
That line you should have jettisoned,

For soon you may suspect that he's or she's
A villain/villainess who does not care
if you would write a villanelle.
This one you should have jettisoned.

ELISAVIETTA RITCHIE

FOR MICHA'S MOTHER, WHO SIGNS

It is not poetry you fear, but poets,
their indelible brand
of words. How will your daughter
escape the mark men hanged
young women for in Salem?
I am nothing more than a teacher,
like you. See, I have removed
my shoes and socks. I am rolling
my trousers above my ankles.
No cloven hooves. Long feet and toes
like you and your beautiful daughter.

It is language that has won
her over, earth-bound words
walking orderly across the page
like children holding to
the rope attached to your wrist,
teacher and students
traversing the noisy street
at the crosswalk, with the light
of your fingers composing
the line your children read,
each syllable's afterimage trailing
your quick passage of hands
conducting the boys and girls
safely from one curb to the other.

ROBERT FINK

UPDATE ON THE LAST JUDGMENT

There will be no deafening noise. No hornblow of thunder.

The small plants of the earth will not tremble on the hillside as grace is prepared.

The sky will neither drown us in its plenty, nor the ground crack and consume feet in its hunger.

No, bodies will not, in their last rags of flesh, creep from under the earth, and with breath once torn from them, choke and expel the old mud of the world.

Adam and Eve, incredulous, will not embrace again in their poverty, not knowing whether to shield themselves, or to emerge shameless from the past's shadow, astonished to again greet *Terra Firma*.

The book of the world, encrusted with deep-sea pearls and the blood of the lamb, will not open up its pages in which all deeds have been inscribed.

And the totality of history will not roll back together, all events fusing, once and for all, into the great blazing sphere of time.

None will sit on the right hand. There will be no right hand.

And the figure of sorrow and grace, with his staff upright, its purple pennant caught in that final wind, will not be there to greet us, with the mercy of justice in his eyes.

No, never judgment. Just the abyss into which all acts are thrown down, and the terrible white silence in which judgment either endures or burns.

ELLEN HINSEY

LAMENT FOR THE MAKERS

I that all through my early days
I remember well was always
    the youngest of the company
    save for one sister after me

from the time when I was able
to walk under the dinner table
    and be punished for that promptly
    because its leaves could fall on me

father and mother overhead
who they talked with and what they said
    were mostly clouds that knew already
    directions far too old for me

at school I skipped a grade so that
whatever I did after that
    each year everyone would be
    older and hold it up to me

at college many of my friends
were returning veterans
    equipped with an authority
    I admired and they treated me

as the kid some years below them
so I married half to show them
    and listened with new vanity
    when I heard it said of me

how young I was and what a shock
I was the youngest on the block
    I thought I had it coming to me
    and I believe it mattered to me

and seemed my own and there to stay
for a while then came the day
    I was in another country
    other older friends around me

my youth by then taken for granted
and found that it had been supplanted
    the notes in some anthology
    listed persons born after me

how long had that been going on
how could I be not quite so young
    and not notice and nobody
    even bother to inform me

though my fond hopes were taking longer
than I had hoped when I was younger
    a phrase that came more frequently
    to suggest itself to me

but the secret was still there
safe in the unprotected air
    that breath that in its own words only
    sang when I was a child to me

and caught me helpless to convey it
with nothing but the words to say it
    though it was those words completely
    and they rang it was clear to me

with a changeless overtone
I have listened for since then
    hearing that note endlessly
    vary every time beyond me

trying to find where it comes from
and to what words it may come
    and forever after be
    present for the thought kept at me

that my mother and every day
of our lives would slip away
    like the summer and suddenly
    all would have been taken from me

but that presence I had known
sometimes in words would not be gone
        and if it spoke even once for me
        it would stay there and be me

however few might choose those words
for listening to afterwards
        there I would be awake to see
        a world that looked unchanged to me

I suppose that was what I thought
young as I was then and that note
        sang from the words of somebody
        in my twenties I looked around me

to all the poets who were then
living and whose lines had been
        sustenance and company
        and a light for years to me

I found the portraits of their faces
first in the rows of oval spaces
        in Oscar Williams' *Treasury*
        so they were settled long before me

and they would always be the same
in that distance of their fame
        affixed in immortality
        during their lifetimes while around me

all was woods seen from a train
no sooner glimpsed than gone again
        but those immortals constantly
        in some measure reassured me

then first there was Dylan Thomas
from the White Horse taken from us
        to the brick wall I woke to see
        for years across the street from me

then word of the death of Stevens
brought a new knowledge of silence
        the nothing not there finally
        the sparrow saying *Be thou me*

how long his long auroras had
played on the darkness overhead
    since I looked up from my Shelley
    and Arrowsmith first showed him to me

and not long from his death until
Edwin Muir had fallen still
    that fine bell of the latter day
    not well heard yet it seems to me

Sylvia Plath then took her own
direction into the unknown
    from her last stars and poetry
    in the house a few blocks from me

Williams a little afterwards
was carried off by the black rapids
    that flowed through Paterson as he
    said and their rushing sound is in me

that was the time that gathered Frost
into the dark where he was lost
    to us but from too far to see
    his voice keeps coming back to me

then the sudden news that Ted
Roethke had been found floating dead
    in someone's pool at night but he
    still rises from his lines for me

and on the rimless wheel in turn
Eliot spun and Jarrell was borne
    off by a car who had loved to see
    the racetrack then there came to me

one day the knocking at the garden
door and the news that Berryman
    from the bridge had leapt who twenty
    years before had quoted to me

the passage where *a jest* wrote Crane
falls from the speechless caravan
    with a wave to bones and Henry
    and to all that he had told me

I dreamed that Auden sat up in bed
but I could not catch what he said
    by that time he was already
    dead someone next morning told me

and Marianne Moore entered the ark
Pound would say no more from the dark
    who once had helped to set me free
    I thought of the prose around me

and David Jones would rest until
the turn of time under the hill
    but from the sleep of Arthur he
    wakes an echo that follows me

Lowell thought the shadow skyline
coming toward him was Manhattan
    but it blacked out in the taxi
    once he read his *Notebook* to me

at the number he had uttered
to the driver a last word
    then that watchful and most lonely
    wanderer whose words went with me

everywhere Elizabeth
Bishop lay alone in death
    they were leaving the party early
    our elders it came home to me

but the needle moved among us
taking always by surprise
    flicking by too fast to see
    to touch a friend born after me

and James Wright by his darkened river
heard the night heron pass over
    took his candle down the frosty
    road and disappeared before me

Howard Moss had felt the gnawing
at his name and found that nothing
    made it better he was funny
    even so about it to me

Graves in his nineties lost the score
forgot that he had died before
    found his way back innocently
    who once had been a guide to me

Nemerov sadder than his verse
said a new year could not be worse
    then the black flukes of agony
    went down leaving the words with me

Stafford watched his hand catch the light
seeing that it was time to write
    a memento of their story
    signed and is a plain before me

now Jimmy Merrill's voice is heard
like an aria afterward
    and we know he will never be
    old after all who spoke to me

on the cold street that last evening
of his heart that leapt at finding
    some yet unknown poetry
    then waved through the window to me

in that city we were born in
one by one they have all gone
    out of the time and language we
    had in common which have brought me

to this season after them
the best words did not keep them from
    leaving themselves finally
    as this day is going from me

and the clear note they were hearing
never promised anything
    but the true sound of brevity
    that will go on after me

W. S. MERWIN

EDITORS

1912–2002

HARRIET MONROE
October 1912–September 1936

MORTON DAUWEN ZABEL
October 1936–October 1937

GEORGE DILLON
November 1937–August 1942

PETER DE VRIES
(with Marion Strobel, Jessica Nelson North, and
John Frederick Nims)
September 1942–March 1946

GEORGE DILLON
April 1946–April 1949

HAYDEN CARRUTH
May 1949–December 1949

KARL SHAPIRO
January 1950–September 1955
(Henry Rago, Acting Editor,
January 1955–September 1955)

HENRY RAGO
October 1955–May 1969
(John Frederick Nims, Visiting Editor,
October 1960–September 1961)
(Daryl Hine, Visiting Editor,
October 1968–August 1969)

DARYL HINE
September 1969–December 1977

JOHN FREDERICK NIMS
January 1978–August 1983

JOSEPH PARISI
Acting Editor
September 1983–January 1985
Editor
February 1985–September 2003

PRINCIPAL STAFF
1912–2003

Alice Corbin Henderson, Ezra Pound,
Eunice Tietjens, Helen Hoyt, Emanuel Carnevali,
Jessica Nelson North, Marion Strobel, George Dillon,
Geraldine Udell, Morton Dauwen Zabel,
Peter De Vries, Katinka Loeser,
John Frederick Nims, Margedant Peters,
Hayden Carruth,
Evalyn Shapiro, Isabella Gardner, Nicholas Joost,
Robert Mueller, Joseph Wiley, Margaret Danner,
Wallace Fowlie, Hugh Kenner, Frederick Bock,
Helen Lothrop Klaviter, Nadine Cummings, Michael Mesic
Rob Colby Allen, Joseph Parisi,
Jim Elledge, Stephen Young, Drew Swinger,
Davis McCombs, Chad Gayle,
Damian Rogers, Aaron Fagan

CREDITS

Since 1960, *Poetry* has reserved the right to reprint poems first published in *Poetry* in any anthology consisting of at least 75 percent of material from its pages. For works published prior to 1960, every effort has been made to identify, locate, and secure permission wherever necessary from those who hold rights to the poems in this anthology. Any omitted acknowledgments brought to the editors' attention will be added to future editions. Although no specific credit is required, the editors are nonetheless grateful to the authors whose work has been included here under this policy.

Conrad Aiken: "Discordants." From the *Collected Poems Second Edition* by Conrad Aiken, copyright © 1953, 1970 by Conrad Aiken. Used by permission of Oxford University Press, Inc. Richard Aldington: "ΧΟΡΙΚΟΣ." Reprinted by permission of Catherine Aldington. A. R. Ammons: "Close-Up" and "Gravelly Run." Reprinted by permission of John Ammons. From *The Selected Poems, Expanded Edition* by A. R. Ammons. Copyright © 1987, 1977, 1975, 1974, 1972, 1971, 1970, 1966, 1965, 1964, 1955 by A. R. Ammons. Used by permission of W. W. Norton & Company, Inc. Sherwood Anderson: "Evening Song." Reprinted by permission of Harold Ober Associates as agents for Sherwood Anderson Literary Estate Trust. W. H. Auden: "Journey to Iceland" and "The Shield of Achilles." Copyright © 1956 by W. H. Auden, from *W. H. Auden: The Collected Poems* by W. H. Auden, copyright © 1976 by Edward Mendelson, William Meredith, and Monroe K. Spears, Executors of the Estate of W. H. Auden. Used by permission of Random House, Inc. and Edward Mendelson. Margaret Avison: "The Party." Reprinted by permission of the author.

George Barker: "O Pearl and Breasted World." Reprinted by permission of Elspeth Barker. Mary Barnard: "Fable of the Ant and the Word." Reprinted by permission of Elizabeth J. Bell, literary executor. Joseph Warren Beach: "Horatian Ode." Reprinted by permission of Joseph W. Beach. John Berryman: "The Traveler." Reprinted by permission of Kate Donahue, for the estate of John Berryman. From *Collected Poems: 1937–1971* by John Berryman. Copyright © 1989 by Kate Donahue Berryman, by permission of Farrar, Straus and Giroux, LLC. "The Cage." Reprinted by permission of Kate Donahue Berryman, for the estate of John Berryman. John Betjeman: "Crematorium." From *Collected Poems* by John Betjeman. Reprinted by permission of John Murray (Publishers) Ltd. Elizabeth Bishop: "Paris, 7 A.M.," "A Miracle for Breakfast," "From the Country to the City," "Song" ("Summer is over"), and "The Mountain" from *The Complete*

Heaven" and "The Horrid Voice of Science." Reprinted by permission of Nicholas C. Lindsay. Robert Lowell: "The Ghost (After Sextus Propertius)." From *Lord Weary's Castle,* copyright © 1946 and renewed 1974 by Robert Lowell, reprinted by permission of Harcourt, Inc. "The Fat Man in the Mirror." From *The Mills of the Kavanaughs,* copyright © 1947 and renewed 1975 by Robert Lowell, reprinted by permission of Harcourt, Inc.

Archibald MacLeish: "Ars Poetica" and "Epistle to the Rapalloan." From *Collected Poems 1917–1982* by Archibald MacLeish. Copyright © 1985 by The Estate of Archibald MacLeish. Reprinted by permission of Houghton Mifflin Company. All rights reserved. Louis MacNeice: "Perdita" and "The Springboard." From *The Collected Poems of Louis MacNeice* edited by E. R. Dodds, copyright © 1966 by The Estate of Louis MacNeice. Published by Faber and Faber Ltd. Reprinted by permission of David Higham Associates. E. L. Mayo: "The Word of Water." From *Collected Poems* by E. L. Mayo. Reprinted with permission of Swallow Press/Ohio University Press, Athens, Ohio. James McAuley: "Winter Drive." Reprinted courtesy of Curtis Brown Australia. William Meredith: "The Illiterate," "Bachelor," and "For His Father." Reprinted from *Effort at Speech: New and Selected Poems* by William Meredith, published by TriQuarterly Books/Northwestern University Press in 1997. Copyright © 1997 by William Meredith. All rights reserved; used by permission of Northwestern University Press and the author. James Merrill: "The Green Eye," "The Broken Bowl," "Hôtel de L'Univers et Portugal," and "Mirror." From *Collected Poems* edited by J. D. McClatchy and Stephen Yenser, copyright © 2001 by the Literary Estate of James Merrill at Washington University. Reprinted by permission of J. D. McClatchy, literary executor, and Alfred A. Knopf. Thomas James Merton: "The Dark Morning." From *The Collected Poems of Thomas Merton,* copyright ©1944 by Our Lady of Gethsemani Monastery. Reprinted by permission of New Directions Publishing Corp. Josephine Miles: "On Inhabiting an Orange." From *Collected Poems 1930–1983,* copyright © 1983 by Josephine Miles. Used with permission of the Estate of Josephine Miles and the University of Illinois Press. Edna St. Vincent Millay: "First Fig," "Second Fig," "Thursday," and "Recuerdo." Copyright © 1922, 1950 by Edna St. Vincent Millay; "Sonnet" ("Women have loved before"). Copyright © by Edna St. Vincent Millay and Norma Millay Ellis. All rights reserved. From *Collected Poems,* HarperCollins. Reprinted by permission of Elizabeth Barnett, literary executor. Harriet Monroe: "In High Places" and "A Farewell." Reprinted by permission of Ann Monroe. Marianne Moore: "The Steeple-Jack" and "The Hero." Reprinted with the permission of Scribner, an imprint of Simon & Schuster Adult Publishing Group, from *The Collected Poems of Marianne Moore.* Copyright © 1935 by Marianne Moore; copyright renewed © 1963 by Marianne Moore and T. S. Eliot. "Then the Ermine:." From *The Complete Poems of Marianne Moore* by Marianne Moore, copyright © 1981 by Clive E. Driver, Literary Executor of the Estate of Marianne Moore. Used by permission of Viking Penguin, a division of Penguin Putnam Inc. Edwin Muir: "Then . . . ." From *Collected Poems,* copyright © 1960 by Willa Muir. Reprinted by permission of Oxford University Press, Inc.

Howard Nemerov: "Sigmund Freud" and "Holding the Mirror Up to Nature." Reprinted by permission of Margaret Nemerov. John Frederick Nims: "Tennis Trophy." Reprinted by permission of Bonnie Larkin Nims, Literary Trustee. "Love Poem." From *The Powers of Heaven and Earth: New and Selected*

INDEX

A NOTE ON THE EDITORS

JOSEPH PARISI joined *Poetry* in 1976 and was Editor from 1983 to 2003, the longest tenure after that of founder Harriet Monroe. He also served as Executive Director of the magazine's parent organization, the Modern Poetry Association (now The Poetry Foundation). His books include *Marianne Moore: The Art of a Modernist* and, most recently, *Dear Editor: A History of* Poetry *in Letters: The First Fifty Years, 1912–1962* (W. W. Norton, 2002), co-edited with Stephen Young. A frequent lecturer on modernist literature and American poetry, he was awarded a Guggenheim Fellowship for 2000–2001 and was elected a By-Fellow of Churchill College, Cambridge, in 2002.

STEPHEN YOUNG began as an assistant at *Poetry* in 1988 and served as Senior Editor until 2003, when he was appointed Program Director of The Poetry Foundation. He attended Dartmouth College, where he held a Raible Scholarship, and did graduate work at the University of Chicago. In 2000, he received an Everett Helm Visiting Fellowship for work on *Dear Editor: A History of* Poetry *in Letters*.

MERIDIAN

Crossing Aesthetics

Werner Hamacher
& David E. Wellbery
Editors

Translated by
Rodger Friedman

*Stanford
University
Press*

*Stanford
California
1996*

POSTHUMOUS
PEOPLE

Vienna at the Turning Point

Massimo Cacciari

Posthumous People was originally published
in Italian in 1980 under the title *Dallo Steinhof*
© 1980 Adelphi Edizioni S.P.A. Milano

Stanford University Press
Stanford, California

© 1996 by the Board of Trustees
of the Leland Stanford Junior University

Printed in the United States of America

CIP data appear at the end of the book

Stanford University Press publications are
distributed exclusively by Stanford University
Press within the United States, Canada,
Mexico, and Central America; they are
distributed exclusively by
Cambridge University Press
throughout the rest of the world.

In memory of Ferruccio Masini

Preface

Parts of this book are adapted from articles originally published in *Laboratorio Musica*, edited by Luigi Nono, and in *Nuova Corrente*, edited by Giovanni Sechi, whose memory I honor here with affection and sorrow.

I hope this collection succeeds in breaking fresh ground after my earlier books on similar subjects, *Oikos* (1975), *Krisis* (1976), and *Intransitabili utopie* (1978). I would not have written it if I thought it a mere amplification of themes already covered.

The notes are solely to refer the reader to the body of criticism essential for understanding the text.

1980

Preface to the
American Edition

This American edition modifies somewhat the Italian edition of 1980 as well as the Spanish translation of 1989. In particular, I eliminated sections at odds with today's critical literature on Vienna around the turn of the last century. I have little interest in the amorphous "strudel" made of waltzes, decadence, a carefree apocalypse, and theatrical destinies that in the course of the last twenty years has come to be glorified as "Grand Vienna."

The last essay of the American edition, "Profane Attention," on Robert Musil, is not in either the Italian edition or the Spanish translation. It first appeared in 1979 in *Metaphorein*, the journal edited by my unforgettable friend, the great Italian Germanist Ferruccio Masini, to whose memory this new edition of my book is dedicated.

Attentive readers should recognize that this book is not simply a collection of scattered essays. Its diverse figures and various tempos form what I would rather call a *Liederzyklus*, a song cycle. This quality differentiates it from my subsequent books, *Icone della Legge* (1985), which will appear in English translation soon, and *L'Angelo necessario* (1986), already available as *The Necessary Angel*.

1995

Contents

Sixteen pages of figures follow page 96.

Translators' Note

Massimo Cacciari writes in a rich, allusive style that derives some of its fascination from highlighting Italian with German elements, indeed with German words. The English translation is necessarily plainer than the original and loses much of its Italo-German effect.

Where Cacciari translates from German sources, I have generally translated them anew, based on the original and on the Italian translations. An important exception includes all citations of Wittgenstein's *Tractatus Logico-Philosophicus*, which are taken from the standard English translation by D. F. Pears and B. F. McGuinness. Where references are available in English translations, I indicate so in a note.

It is only after death that we will enter *our* life and come alive, oh, very much alive, we posthumous people!

—Nietzsche, *The Gay Science* 365

Introduction:
The View from Steinhof

This book's epigraph might have been "Wer seiner Zeit nur voraus ist, den holt sie einmal ein" (Ludwig Wittgenstein, 1930), which means, "Those who are merely ahead of their time deserve to have it catch up."

Two symmetrical avenues along the edge of the Viennese woods lead to the church of Saint Leopold. Looking out from the top of Baumgartner Höhe, there must have been a brilliant view over Vienna, like a Bellotto landscape, the city shimmering and sparkling with light. Otto Wagner's church, crowning the grounds of Vienna's hospital for the mentally ill, stood out of the folds of green with its resplendent gold leaf cupola (see Figure 1). It is impossible to say what time this work was ahead of, and impossible to say what caught up.[1]

Four bronze angels stand at the vestibule. They are the *ermeneuti* [interpreters] of the interior and at the same time its custodians. The hieratic rhythm that scans them evidently quotes Ferdinand Hodler's figures. The principles of repetition and symmetry with which Hodler made "bitter and dangerous cracks in the world of impressionism,"[2] dominate the entire structure. Behind the four angels (by Othmar Schmikowitz) stands Kolo Moser's great semicircular stained glass window. The throne of the Father is in the middle, and at its sides are two angels draped in precious mantles, with their wings unfurled above them. Adam and Eve are on their knees at the extreme angles of the arch, practically enmeshed in the fronds of great curving plants. This window and two others on the transept cast white and gold, green and blue light over the interior of the church. Great angelic figures appear in their full glory in the transept windows. The two upper angels, hovering over saints that represent works of charity, have vast, magnificent peacock wings. For the main altar, decorated in majolica, stucco, and mosaic, Moser designed two other standing angels, facing front, exhibiting the symbols of Christ's martyrdom. The large panel between them shows the triumph of Christ surrounded by a chorus of saints, among them Dymphna, protector of fools.

The symmetrical, repetitive rhythm is accentuated from the outside by a revetment of thin marble blocks. The iron clamps and bolts that keep them in place, rimmed with copper leaf borders, give a sense of motion to these walls, yet without any monumental emphasis and without any concession to ornament. Inside, the building's perfect measure of basic forms is joined, without contrast, by the multicolored clarity of light that streams through the stained glass windows. Here is the meeting, never realized so well, of the principles of tradition and quotation on the one hand and the *Nervenleben* [vitality] of the Secession Movement's images and color on the other. *Nervenleben* illuminates the pure basic forms of the temple that constitute the space in which the oscillating Jugendstil tonalities find an order, a clear and comprehensible consistency, however ephemeral it may be. The interior space gathers this meeting into its center. A profound necessity moved Wagner, therefore, to "squeeze" the interior space of the cupola. While the exterior should be visible from far away and dominate the entire landscape, inside a centripetal force should prevail, a "gathering," since the forces that are found here give life to a difficult and brief unity. Perhaps the church at Steinhof can be understood only upon exiting and turning away from it. Then, while studying the various views that open out from the church, we understand the intimate weakness of its extreme theophanies. The infinite coming and going and the interminable crowds that inhabit this landscape began, perhaps, in the utopia that we just now left behind. Here all of them sought a final, impossible resting place. Woods straight out of Alfred Kubin's pictures embrace this church and block out its light. But the greatness of this church lies in its continuous, intentional crashing against the edges of the woods, on the beaches of the night, like one of those falling stars that Georg Trakl talks about.

Posthumous People

The view from this church looks out over a landscape of posthumous people. They haunt society. They go about in disguise, but they are recognized. They are objects of curiosity and interest. But in company—and not in contrast, as Nietzsche believed—they are ghosts. Nietzsche talks about them in *The Gay Science* (365) and later in *Twilight of the Idols*. They pass through closed doors when all the lights are out. Other people may reach out to them, but their hands pass right through them. This is not their only disguise. Indeed, they possess endless stores of masks and alibis. Posthumous people have too many alibis to be satisfied with simple truth. ("Every truth is simple—but isn't this a double lie?") Posthumous people go through an infinite number of masks without ever staying with any one of them. And "this causes fear," it is their *Unheimliches*, their uneasiness.

Since they have no substance, they are misunderstood more than others, more than actual people. And yet they are heard better. "Or more exactly, we are never understood," but the ghosts of posthumous people practically force themselves to be heard, practically cause the dimension of hearing to be rediscovered. Their "authority" is nothing but this solitary, mute invitation to be heard. "We, the subject," is converted into the form, "we, the posthumous people." The cogent force of a decree pronounced by the present and fully productive subject ("we, the subject") is transformed to the

4

dimension of an absence ("we, the posthumous people") that is clearly heard, while it criticizes, deconstructs, and shreds that idea of substance in which the kingdom of the subject resides. Therefore not only do posthumous people indicate the end of "we, the subject," but they are the only ones to survive, as mere phantasms, after the end of the subject. They are the only ones to initiate the hearing of the abyss, the *Ab-grund*, the dimension gaping beyond the foundation of the ground, the *fundamentum veritatis*. They are the hikers in Nietzsche's *Human, All Too Human* who seek to understand how things of the world proceed and who silently collect and maintain their multiple voices. In this way, posthumous people come alive. Only after the death of "we the subject"—and therefore only after death—will they have their lives.

Nevertheless, to call people posthumous is not to call them untimely. The term "untimely" carries, however unconsciously, the possibility of becoming timely. Untimely people can always look ahead to their own time. Not so for posthumous people; they are absolutely protected from the risk of expectation. They cannot be reached, they cannot be understood. Their own lives do not signify their actuality, that is, the establishment of their rationale. They have too many rationales to be able to confirm them. Untimely can still be a value that intends to realize itself on others, a potential subject. Posthumous people have traversed every subject to the end. The lives they protect do not confirm a subject, a presence, but rather confirm the insignificance, the superfluity of the actual (that in which the actual appears truly as "the indecent overvaluation" of itself and of its own language). Thus the dimension of posthumous people drowns out the dimension of the untimely (which many Nietzschean readings understand to be extreme).

Joseph Roth's "Invalid des Lebens" is posthumous. Ludwig von Janikowski is posthumous. He kept himself far from the lying life of writing, and he helped Karl Kraus to compose and revise the essays of his first collection, *Sittlichkeit und Kriminalität*. The most perfect interiors of Peter Altenberg and Adolf Loos are for these posthumous figures, for these strange ghosts. Hugo von Hofmannsthal's Sigismund tends to this very sort of posthumous life.

Hunted, expressed by silence, persecuted by the present and by research into the present, he wants to create a void in himself and around himself in order to listen to its sense, the imperceptible invitation. "We, the Posthumous People" must be the title of Robert Walser's entire opus.

It was Robert Musil, however, who more than anyone else understood the unheard of force of distance that being posthumous allows. The clarity and force of a Renaissance German engraving that underlies a piece like "The Flypaper"[3] comes from this distance. Being posthumous brings the most secret events into brilliant focus. Precisely because he is not only untimely, but posthumous, Musil's eye savors the unreachable gifts of distance, the *Entfernung*, the remoteness of remoteness. (Derrida gleans this notion from Nietzsche.) It is necessary to know how to survive in the most pure and rarified atmosphere so the eye may reach this point of clarity and may reflect images even in their most infinitesimal details—even, finally, to the point of becoming one with them. At the height of distance, in fact, the most profound sympathy opens up. That is why the power of Musil's language is so great. On the one hand, it submerges itself in the distance, but on the other, it captures the event in its most secret fibers. Musil's language "discovers" the event under the masks of truth that pretend to immobilize it and listens to its irreducible polyphony. If this is the poetry of "Pre Posthumous Papers and Other Prose," then Wittgenstein, from whom this work gets its initiative, wrote posthumous papers par excellence.

Sprachliches

In order to understand the crux of the *Tractatus*, it is necessary to consider the fault lines in the universe to which it belongs. If research on two or many Wittgensteins is as sterile as the scheme of a "seamless continuity,"[4] we must ask ourselves what body of problems is contained in the *Tractatus* and if these do not indicate theoretical fractures already existing in Wittgenstein's work. The first myth to dismantle, then, is that Gottlob Frege and Bertrand Russell together prepared its way. In reality, Frege's philosophy penetrates into the *Tractatus* and into its core in a much more organic fashion than does Russell's.

For Russell, there is no description without denotation. Description always has an ontological content, and logic is always ontology. There is no trace of this germ of neo-positivist philosophy in Frege. For Frege, descriptions can have meaning without denotation. I can name everything that I can think, but my thoughts cannot necessarily be reduced to denotations. "Good logico-syntactic forms of expression (in non-formalized languages) give no assurance that the expressions have an object."[5] The notation of "object" cannot be reduced to "direct denotation." Nor do we put names in univocal correspondences with single things. A single name for a single thing does not exist. That is why to Frege natural language never seems perfectly adaptable to logic. Wittgenstein rediscovers its intrinsic problematic nature in the *Tractatus*. Systems

of logic do not try to rationalize and remedy such language. There
are some languages of which it is senseless to ask if they are "true."
The idea of an essential logical framework of language, one that
would be the province of evidentiary logic, is not a metaphysical
idea, but is metaphysics itself. Profound, radical "irrationalism" is
to trust in such an idea and to repeat its failures infinitely, rather
than collect the fresh power that it confers upon *ratio*, upon logic,
rather than abandon it. Making logic a universal instrument of hy-
giene and development means to rigorously limit it to the discov-
ery of laws of being true, predictable only through pure thought.
Logic is good for much more than sublimating natural lan-
guages—or, according to Nietzsche's famous aphorism, reinforc-
ing faith in God with faith in grammar.

There is a fundamental perfection in creatures that in Frege has
as its symbol the insuperability of *Dichtung* [poetry]: the pseudo-
propositions of poetry cannot be idealistically surmounted. By de-
finition, creatures are beings endowed with fantasy. Logic gives this
faculty up, in its grand utopia of annihilation, in order to pursue
creatures who "lose themselves" in a fantasy world. Logic limits it-
self to the most rigorous and restrictive definition: the strong sense
of knowing the laws for being true, in the sense of a reality that is
independent of our recognizing it as such. This reality modifies
the subject whenever it is recognized, but it is not, in any sense,
produced by the subject.

The fact that logical propositions may not cover the range of the
term "true," as it is ordinarily used in speech, does not lead to the
conclusion that the sense of a proposition is supplied only from
the possible contexts of occurrence of the proposition itself. "On
the contrary, the *concept of proposition* itself should be limited" (De
Monticelli). Beyond the "fantastic" polymorphic capacities of nat-
ural languages, there is still a "third world," a context of justifica-
tion for the proposition itself, absolved from the status of the con-
sciousness and language of the speaker. Here perhaps is the most
significant connection between Frege and Edmund Husserl. It does
not seem that in Frege, contrary to Husserl, the same semantic in-
determinacy of natural language is assumed as a condition of open-

ness, of intentional charge. The "paucity" of natural language (compared to the logical precision of formalized language) underlies its intentionalizing power, its capacity to develop itself and enrich itself, constantly determining new ways to refer to the real. That is why the realism of these ways should not contradict the intentionality of the speaker, which is indeterminable a priori. Such manners embody themselves in language and represent human knowledge accumulated in language. Nothing can be expressed except through language and in language. The sense of a proposition is verified on the basis of language. Language is not invented—if it does not manifest a history, a tradition, at the same moment that it transforms history and tradition, then it cannot express anything or communicate anything.

Frege surrenders to a reconciliation of the pure formal language of thought with language in which we often "act against our will in poetry." This attempt at an answer to Frege's problem runs along a thread of paradox. In the semantic indeterminacy of natural language (and for Husserl philosophy was built, classically, upon and in natural language) there appear incarnate ideal ways to refer to the real. These ways have varied across history, due precisely to the formative receptiveness of natural language. Its variability is limited by the entire status of knowledge and by its forms of expression. This variability even presents itself as a kind of progress and development, to the extent that it is determined on the basis of a comprehensive test of inherited conditions. The problem of foundation is thus transformed in Husserl into one of the reciprocal limits, historically experienced, of variance and invariance in the dynamic of philosophical and scientific grammar.

What appears "paradoxical" in this response is, above all, the conversion of the paucity of natural language into the power of its intentionality (which is the perfect symbol of that paucity). The fact that natural language does not speak of simple things, that its meanings cannot be reduced to denotations, does not imply a production of ideal modes of reference to the real. The concept of intentionality establishes, in and of itself, that a meaning (signified) cannot be extracted from the intention of the subject in which it is expressed: the referent is constituted *only in language*. There is nothing else to derive from *intentio*. That may suffice to formulate as a problem Russell's neopositivism of derivation, but it does not constitute in any way a new foundation of Frege's "third world." For Frege, *concipere* means to take up a thought that already exists, independent of the fact that I think it. This thought certainly constitutes an ideal form of reference to reality, but is not at all a product of *intentio*. What schema can emerge between the poverty and indeterminacy of language (this language that *intentio* opens and transforms continually) and the independence and inalterability of the world of the thinking subject's thought? How can the forms of theory, which seize thought that already exists, determine the "range of variation of the concepts" (De Monticelli)? That the range of variability is not free—that it is historically determined by the status of knowledge and by the linguistic competence of the speakers—does not imply that its limits are frozen by fixed forms of theory, by ideal modes of reference. The problem can also be resolved (much more "economically") by establishing that these limits are made by the procedural nature and communicability of the range of play and by the bounty of their functions.

Affirming the innate forms and laws of the dynamic of knowledge does not resolve the problem of schematism, the Kantian legacy to the *cupio dissolvi* of subsequent philosophy. Even if we admit the procedural and self-regulating character of Husserl's ideal modes, there remains the problem of their proper language, of the foundation, the *Begründung*, without which, for Husserl as for Frege, there is no force behind scientific knowledge. This language appears embodied in natural language and its dynamics—even if, at the same time, it transcends natural language. The a priori conditions of the possibility of linguistic innovation consist in the "natural" openness to the intuition of ideal modes. Such modes establish the possibility of variation. They are the site of *Begründung*, and they transcend the operative dimension of scientific grammars. These modes describe wholly a priori the limits of variability, and no single "case" can be inscribed there.

This problem gives birth to the extreme teleology that dominates Husserl's *The Crisis of European Sciences* (the tragedy of which the armies of Husserl's scholastics have always attempted to convert to positivism and rationalism). Philosophical activity cannot concern itself with anything except the phenomenon of natural language. But chased back into the poverty of its semantic indeterminacy, philosophy discovers a new realm there. The realm of intentionality proper to natural language understands how to connect to the world of ideal forms, which describe the limits of variability of those same scientific grammars. Thus philosophy can be an activity that forms the basis of its own dynamics as expansion. Philosophy's gaze on science wants to be anything but "oblique." Not as "oblique" but rather as "interrupted" is how this activity intends to repropose itself as the language of foundation, as the transcendental language that, a priori, can describe possibilities and limits of transformation of play. Finally, either such possibilities and limits are actually inherent in the very dynamics of play, and nothing then can warrant the definition of an autonomous language and a specific scientific discipline (philosophy)—or the flexibility of play is etched a priori onto a horizon of invariance, absolutely objective, unchangeable on the speaker's part. And so it is necessary to deduce the forms of schematism between the speaker and such ideal modes. But how can such modes be "understood" by philosophy that is phenomenology of natural language? And how can such invariance belong to natural language, which is variation? If there is expression of invariance, it would be absolute logic (or knowledge), not philosophy. And if the field of possibilities and limits of variations are determined in the process of variation itself, multiple forms for their analysis and their calculation would emerge. And that is neither absolute logic nor philosophy.

Inquietum Cor Nostrum

It seems to me that Wittgenstein's research parts company with Husserl along these same lines. It is true that "fetishist" elements remain in Wittgenstein's respect for the rules of the game.[6] The manifest tension in his discourse, however, from the crisis of the *Tractatus* on, lies in his understanding all the rules of the game together as admitting the possibility of their transformation. The game is understood as the content of the participant's *intentio*, proportionately subject to willpower and therefore to the intrinsic indeterminacy of languages. As long as the game remains firmly aligned with its traditions and never destabilizes into mere invention and transformation, *ideal* modalities may not determine its limits unless those limits are understood in a weak sense and divested of any teleological weight—that is, unless their basic promise is not taken seriously. What counts is not so much the discord between Husserl and Wittgenstein over the fact that the processes of transforming the game are self-regulating, but that for Husserl they have a teleological disposition that is absent in Wittgenstein. In Husserl these processes can come autonomously, philosophically, which does not happen in Wittgenstein. Seen in this perspective, Husserl implements a powerful strategy of "reform" on the subject and its theory, conferring sense onto scientific grammar, a strategy Wittgenstein had already abandoned in the *Tractatus*.

The fault lines of the *Tractatus*, fundamental for understanding the later development of Wittgenstein's thought, correspond to the forms assumed by the critique of fundamental strategies.[7] The strategy of logical discourse no longer corresponds in the *Tractatus* to the objectives of making natural language logical or to the pretext of establishing scientific grammars. The strategy of logic is a "degenerate" proposition (Rosso), tautological, not descriptive, and unconditionally true only at great price. The strategy of scientific discourse is a mere image: scientific propositions (from the natural sciences) try "to provide a faithful image of the world, limiting themselves to the most relevant points on a single, homogeneous plane" (Rosso). This plane does not hearken back to any logical or philosophical basis, but to the "reckoning" of the denotative capacity of its propositions. Scientific propositions are wholly denotative. But how can denotations retreat from the absolute contingency of the facts they denote? The first, and fundamental, fault line of the *Tractatus* concerns, therefore, the statute of the scientific *image* as such. The critique of fundamental strategies, as it were, trails behind it.

The first proposition of the *Tractatus* may be translated as follows: "The world is the result of the choice wrought by the case in the realm of all that is possible" (Rosso). That is why whatever can be expressed is absolutely accidental and contingent. "Science reveals itself to be precisely the study of contingency" (Rosso), and that is why hierarchies of bodies cannot exist, every body being wholly and equally gratuitous. The significance of a proposition is the designated object—therefore, the accidental and gratuitous and contingent. But won't the meaning itself turn out to be contingent? The *Tractatus* turns—and *stops*—around this question. Wittgenstein means to withdraw scientific propositions from the radical contingency of their objects. He finds the logical and fundamental route blocked and interrupted. He tries to make an ontology of it: there is a world substance that cannot be further broken down, and every proposition is a function of it. The world is an accidental configuration—but of objects that are simply not accidental. That is why images of science contain not only the contingency of the configuration, but also the substantiality of the objects or simple entities that form the basis of the configuration. The theory of representation or of meaning native to the *Tractatus* makes an ontological question of *Begründung* [originating].

Is this ontological realism truly immune to the many aporias the establishment of unchanging reality encountered, independent of being true? Is it immune to the conviction that truth and falsehood *exist*, independently of our recognizing them? The ontological foundation of the *Tractatus*, in order to verify itself, ought to permit a reduction of the names of propositions, not to things that stand before it (*Gegen-stände*), but to simple objects that are *not* givens. Natural language, like scientific language, describes situations; it does not name objects. Even the most simple atom of language will end up always complex and contingent from the point of view of the demand for ontological foundations postulated in the *Tractatus*. It is impossible to name a simple object; it is impossible to describe the totality of the world. Language can only denote situations or construct tautologies—that is, logical propositions. All that can be sensibly expressed resides within these limits. Thus the ontological foundation's demand is established in the *Tractatus* with a fundamentality that condemns it to failure. Not for one moment, in the *Tractatus*, does *intentio* exhaust the intended or contain symbols of direct relation with it. *Intentio* is prefixed to an unreachable goal, and it does not depend for an instant on the reduction of meaning to simply-given, as will take place in the scholastic version of the Wiener Kreis, Vienna at the turning point.

If the problem of ontological *Begründung* is revealed clearly in *Philosophical Observations*, it was already present in the *Tractatus*. The images it speaks of cannot be analyzed as linear functions of simple objects or given data. The images (*Bilder*) of facts surely derive their inspiration from the work of Gustav Hertz and Ludwig Boltzmann much more than from Ernst Mach and the Wiener Kreis.[8] That is why every proposition endowed with sense is necessarily closed in by the inexpressible. The substance of the intended meaning is, in fact, *inexpressible*, along with the world in which the contingent situations that we intend take place. It is a myth that linguistic configurations contain signs of a direct relation with the objects they depict. The "substantial" necessarily evades the relationship of atom to totality. The expressible perseveres against its limits without being able to ever get through them.

Even through this line of reasoning we can see how the mystical (*das Mystische*) makes up, not an equivocal atmosphere in the *Tractatus*, but rather its necessary conclusion. It describes the limits of meaning for the propositions that come afterward. It is even their inherent law. It prescribes their rules, routines, and operative conditions. The mystical indicates how the world may simply show itself. "Let the world exist; let the possibility of the possible be given" (Rosso). That is the mystical. Facing the problem that comes before all problems, in the glow of all questions—"Why are there things rather than nothing?"—Wittgenstein does not flee into the passive voice of scientific equivalence or into visions about the totality of the world (*Weltanschauungen*). "To reawaken understanding of the sense of this question" (Heidegger) would be superfluous in comparison. But no discourse answers, except the ineffable showing itself. The problem becomes one of the meaning of the verb "to show," and we shall return to it. Is it not possible now to confirm that the parabola of Heideggerian thought intersects, in the end, with this "answer" of Wittgenstein's? Does not the history of metaphysics, which is Heidegger's subject (to the extent that it too is channeled by the space of history and criticism), also show, at its conclusion, the ineffability of being, the why of being?

In a note from 1931, collected in *Culture and Value*, Wittgenstein wrote, "The inexpressible (that which seems mysterious to me, *geheimnisvoll*, and that I am not capable of expressing) provides the ground upon which all that I am able to express acquires meaning."[9] The inexpressible exercises what amounts to a gravitational force on logical propositions and keeps them thus within the limits of "sensibility." This is its operative facet, merely self-evident. In terms of *Culture and Value*, we can say that the possibility of "liberating" the proposition from contingency has become in-

expressible, as have reconnecting the sign to the world and onto-
logically establishing the relationship between *intentio* and in-
tended. The problem of the inexpressible initiates the dissolution
of *Begründung* in the analysis of language's intrinsic limits and the
certainties they offer, and this dissolution will be completed in
Philosophical Investigations and, above all, in *On Certainty* (*Über
Gewissheit*). The foundation is convention. The inexorable tight-
ening of rules that we cannot logically refute is essential (Franck).
That is not the only reason why logical and mathematical formal-
ism is an "inexorable" game. Being certain means "to belong to a
community that is held together by knowledge and education."[10]
This certainty however has no psychological or sociological impli-
cations; it is composed of accumulated knowledge in language, in-
herently historical. "Certainty is not synonymous with a 'spiritual'
attitude; it is the articulation of a grammatical procedure"
(Wittgenstein). The "beginning" is not "*Ego cogito*," but the mass
of historical thoughts that are transmitted to us and that we know
how to engage and re-engage. Everyone postulates, decides, and
makes changes within the scope of these thoughts. They define the
limits of their grammar's variability. The operative nature of our
discourse has the fact of this action or play as a condition, as the
situation that it determines.

   This reasoning assumes the inexpressibility of the existence of
the world. If the existence of the world could declare itself, our
language would have the power to render it. The world would be
our phenomenon. Philosophy's madness, its rite, resides in this
pretext. Here is philosophy's vain attempt to deduce the existence
of the world, or rather to attack its manifestation in order to dis-
solve it, in order to substitute it with philosophy's own phantasms.
Philosophy appears either as the cutting off of the world, which is
absurd (*un-sinnig*) discourse, not meaningless (*sinnlos*), or as logical
tautology, or indeed as a radical calling into doubt of the world's
existence and its transformation and sublimation into a mere phe-
nomenon. Philosophy cannot resist the ineffability of the existence
of the world. The utopia of *Begründung* (whether logical or onto-
logical), the "empty ceremony of doubt" (Franck), the desperate

search for an answer to the Heideggerian question, are aspects of its "demented" rite.

Is it necessary to recur to this rite in order to avoid fetishism with regard to the world as it is? The mystical does not cut itself off from the world as it is. The mystical never speaks of an objective world, but limits itself rather to *showing* the world. The "fetishism" of verbalizing the world (as opposed to showing it) belongs to philosophical discourse and has nothing to do with the mystical, to the extent that the mystical indicates from within the limits of possible propositions (possible in the reductive sense of empirically possible). Propositions about the historicity and changing nature of action, of play, also belong to this field. The possibility of variation is inherent to play—otherwise the rules of the game would be replaced by new ideal forms, ideal invariance. But such possibilities cannot be described a priori. They proceed in the dynamics of the contingent language of the *intentio* of the speakers, *intentio* that appeals to accumulated knowledge, that tastes it, that experiences it, that plays with it and changes its rules. There is no metaphysics that can describe a priori the possible directions of change. But to be in an effectual sense practical and communicable, it has to be rooted in language and in knowledge accumulated in language. Only one general limit can be expressed a priori. Thus there is no "fetishism" in our game's linguistic situation, of which its *intentio* is a part. The awareness of limits of language is not fetishism. To be ignorant of them, rather, is consummate fetishism, since it signifies turning away, not from the world, but from the very contingency of situations of things as they are, preaching their dissolution, foundation, and sublimation. Wittgenstein's silence is not opposed to changing the game. It is opposed to preaching that comes from the realm of the expressible and with empty ceremonies proclaims its own powerlessness to be free.

The New Domain
of Trauerspiel

Behind the mirror of this thinking about language we find the problems we have confronted up to this point, along with more characters from the *serious* (as opposed to merely academic) Viennese turning point: "It is impossible to lead men to the good; it is only possible to lead men to some place. The good lies beyond the domain of facts and data [*Tatsachenraum*]."[11] This proposition from 1929 unfolds 6.4 of the *Tractatus*, "Alle Sätze sind gleichwertig"—all propositions are of equal value. All propositions endowed with sense have equal value, since they necessarily refer to that domain of facts and data. No hierarchy of them can be established. No value can be placed on the events of the world. If there were value, then it would be found outside of any event or development or state of being, since any event or development is a case (*Tractatus* 6.41). In Wittgenstein, the relationship between proposition and fact is transformed (and profoundly so in the *Tractatus*). The action or play of certainty is transformed, the norms are changed that define the utterable, but the axiom never fails that propositions endowed with sense, propositions on states of being, on cases, are of equal value. Such a "solution" arises with the force of ripping, irreversible experience. Whatever would render the world non-accidental—*nicht-zufällig*—cannot be found in the world, since, if it were found, it would be in its turn accidental—a case. The occurrence of the world, and the world is necessarily an occurrence, means that the world is like an accident. Reading the parts of *Nachlass* published so far bears witness to how deeply essential this thought was to Wittgenstein and to its continuity through Wittgenstein's work.

Finding the good through the accidentalness, the *casualness* of happening is inconceivable. If chance, through some hidden force, were to intend good, it would no longer be chance, but value. The force would have to come out of hiding and reveal itself as other than chance. If chance remains unutterable, the propositions continue to exist anyway in a state of perfect equivalence. If their forms take on meaning by chance, it is possible to lead only *irgendwohin*, to some place. From this case, here and now, I can foresee other possible cases, I can construct their possibilities, their intentions, and so on infinitely. None of these cases would be the home of the good, surmounting the *casualness* of happening. The leitmotif of the English Conference on Ethics was already in the *Tractatus*: the ineffability of Ethics. If language has chance occurrence as its contents, the possibility of new configurations of cases is implicit in its very definition. If a case were *the* case, that possibility would cease. The possibility of leading *irgendwohin* (of being unable to do anything but lead somewhere) is therefore written a priori into the confines of this language. The good exists beyond the domain of data and facts and beyond the limits of propositions of equal value, that try to express their configuration. To want to express the good is *Missbrauch* [abuse] of language. More than mere bad usage, it violates its form. Language can lead, but not to the end, to the goal. It can only lead from chance to chance, from event to event. What inexorable forms of understanding can analyze this chance and this inherent leading without resorting to impressionistic relativism? How do we know that the rules of the game do not appear less "inexorable" (in their rules of transformation) because they concern a game?

This radical surrender is the basis for meaningful language, for the equivalence of its propositions. Transferring it would not lead us beyond the limits of such a language, but to the abuse of its possibilities. Rather than learn to see the event clearly and to construct new cases, understanding the unutterable rapport between case and possible (a possibility that offers itself only because "the world is all that is the case"), we would build vain and contradictory rhetorics of the unutterable. Certainly one can always try to escape from the limits this surrender traces (specific, determined, not in the least "romantic") and from the despair (in the literal sense of the term) that indicates the experience of it. This is rather "evidence of a tendency in the human soul . . . that I really would not want, upon my life, to make fun of" (Wittgenstein). The ruin into which this tendency continually falls bears witness to its authenticity. The tendency and the ruin exist as evidence of an unsupressable component of language itself, enabled by the constant work of surrender. But is this enough to define it? Is this surrender, ever present, enough to make it a "master" of its limits?

What is the *Tatsachenraum* that precedes everything in Wittgenstein? *Tatsachenraum* is the space, the domain, of *Trauerspiel* [tragedy] in the pregnant symbolic acceptance that Walter Benjamin analyzed on the basis of German baroque drama.[12] This drama, with Hofmannsthal in particular, finds the limit of its metamorphosis in the *Tatsachenraum* of the *finis Austriae* [the end of Austria]. The Adolf Loos house in Michaelerplatz stands consciously before the Hofburg, as Hofmannsthal's *Der Turm* stands before Calderón de la Barca's *Life Is a Dream*. The consciousness of belonging to this Romania is shared by all the Viennese dialects of the turning point. Where the order of the *verum-bonum*—the true and the good—collapsed, there is the space of *Trauerspiel*. It is found in the area divided between signals, indications, traces, formation of personae, of the *entity* definitively emerged from its own "subjectivity" and from being a "translation" of substance, of the entity that is no longer a subject, and the area of chance crossed by the infinite passages from case to case, from form to form, the domain of the saying and leading of *irgendwohin*. This is not the domain of the pilgrim. Its personae happen like the things of the world, and these things want to see well. There is no light that can save the chance in value, but that does not mean chance is a fog, an indistinct opacity, which pilgrims must pass through until they come out on top. The equivalence of creaturely propositions is constructed according to rules and is changed in a clearly defined way. Cases have form. The desperation of resigning is fixed, almost frozen, on the scabrous terrain of facts in the logical domain of the utterable. Here the personae of *Trauerspiel* hold out.

To this domain belongs the "nihilism" in Loos's house at Michaelerplatz. Inhabitants surrender themselves to all allusivity or to every metaphor of the *verum-bonum* on the foundations of this nihilism. They do not "substitute" the absence of truth and the good, and that is why they can construct new linguistic possibilities, new combinations, from within their own history, within tradition, playing and replaying their game. Ornament is an extreme form of decadence in the metaphor of the *verum-bonum*. The tendency to render our propositions as propositions of value lives out a final, indecent day in ornament. This tendency, however, is no longer the tragic evidence of which Wittgenstein spoke. That is protected at all costs. It seeks to avoid ruin, to accommodate itself beside the propositions of sense (ornament and functionality, utility and beauty). As opposed to *Trauerspiel* that takes place in the *Tatsachenraum*, ornament is the light comedy of ruin, a homemade tendency to transcendence. It aspires to furnish the temples of the tragedy of ethics.

Peter Altenberg's *Extrakte des Lebens* also belongs to the new domain of *Trauerspiel*. The desperate holding out in surrender is founded in the *Extrakte des Lebens* with the perfect emergence of the subject, that is, with its radical critique, with its end as a subject. The subject transferred is no longer a subject—what is left of it speaks and transmits *irgendwohin*, it *happens*, and in happening it opens extraordinarily to all cases, its brothers, the things of this world. It loves them coming and going, and it heeds, in telling them, the limits of telling, since the *Missbrauch* of words would seem almost to harm their tone, their voices. Thus cases are chopped up very neatly in their language, harvested from a look that is part of them, that does not "comprehend" them, that does not judge them, that does not illuminate them. The cases are given to this look without fear. They believe in it.

But why should the new domain be that of *Trauerspiel?* Why is it impossible to settle in the absence of order established by the utterability of the *verum-bonum?* Wouldn't the language of equivalence, of equality of values, detached from any metaphysical pretext, disenchanted, be able to find its own place in this *Tatsachenraum,* in the measurability of its being present, right at hand—*Zuhandensein?* And why couldn't even Wittgenstein be read in this sense, in the sense of the totalizing destiny of technology, of its productivity, that knows nothing except phenomena compatible with its own ends? Wittgenstein's *Tatsachenraum* can be the scene of *Trauerspiel* because in tragedy words never exhaust deeds, names never exhaust things, and language never exhausts situations. If the idea of *adequatio* is already present in the *Tractatus* in a problematic and contradictory form, the idea emerges in the following works, in *On Certainty* and *Culture and Value* (which has the inflections of a diary), of certainty as construction and process. Not a utopian advancing over the world's contradictory being-thus in philosophies of foundation, it is a certainty of the present ability of rules that we do not succeed in refuting, of conventions that satisfy us because they work, a certainty of grammatical operations (which belong to tradition, community, laws of life) that succeed in seeing here and now, without pretending any invariance.

And yet the question comes up again: Isn't it possible to feel at home in this procedure? Precisely in this interminable building up of certainty? What could be less paradoxical and more domestic than convention? Of course, a similar practice of convention is always possible. But why do we believe that this one, far from representing the fulfillment of liberation of language from metaphysics, as its apologists claim, cheats with its own limits? Why do we believe that the expression of *Tatsachenraum* as *Trauerspiel* is the logical and necessary consequence? The *Gottlosigkeit* [godlessness] of language—language abandoned by *verum-bonum*—does not lead to a happy and unstoppable progress toward conquest and comprehension of the world, as if surrender were worthless except as a sort of strategic move to gain the absolute power of technology over and within *Tatsachenraum.* Nothing changes if we call the "search without end" the solution, if we establish that it answers all possible or anticipated questions, as long as no other utterable question remains. The disenchantment of interminably building up certainty is then mere publicity, since its practice is understood to be *effective* and it is the very idea of effect, of solution, that displaces that of substance: either the particular substance of fact or the substance of the subject that comprises it. One cheats with the meaning of convention whenever the limits of the assertable are traced down from above or, likewise, the limits of the arguable, of whatever it makes sense to ask, of whatever can be conceivably pronounced as a question. When operating thus in the building process, the process is in reality a solution, a domestication of the *verum-bonum* into *Tatsachenraum*, a domestication that falsifies both of them.

In the *Tatsachenraum* there is no language of solution. Any solution is structurally bound to the *casualness* of happening. This means that the new domain of factual data cannot present itself as the space where everything assertable and arguable is resolved— and this is so in spite of proclaiming research "without end." And it means, additionally, that language does not proceed in its quest progressively "recuperating" from its problems and finding its solution. Not only is it difficult to distinguish between "the cases in which I cannot, and the cases in which I can hardly make mistakes," not only must one always guard against the "spell" of word knowledge;[13] but it is necessary to argue against anyone thinking they have found the solution to this problem. It is enough to demonstrate that there was a time when that solution had not yet been discovered and that the solution discovered in that time now seems merely a case. And again: if someone were to predict that the next generation will learn to solve the problems that wear out the present, it is enough to show how the next generation will struggle with new problems and not solve the problems left unsolved by their parents. Roberto Bazlen seems almost to be thinking of these propositions from *Culture and Value* when he writes that there are only ways, and no way out; or where he says that we look for a way out only to build a new way, *irgendwohin*. We do not build this new way because we know where it will end, just as we do not know some things because everybody knows them. But the road is no less defined for this, and the rules of its construction are no easier.

The *Tatsachenraum* is the domain of *Trauerspiel* because that is where every solution takes shape in the questions of the here and now, in the questions formulated by this present entity. A solution could arise precisely in the measure in which this entity recognizes itself and accepts itself *wie ein Zufall* [like an accident]—does not pretend, that is, to go beyond its own world. A solution can only reveal, never unveil. From solution to solution is a matter of incessant revealing. Every generation lays its own veils on the problem, and none takes up the same problems as their predecessors, thus building what seems a sort of sacred chain wherever earlier solutions appear to have remained unfinished. But the pure despair over the limits of language negates the form of *Trauerspiel* as much as progressive metaphysics of the solution does. (Pure despair that not only does not belong to Wittgenstein, but does not even belong to Heidegger, despite what Hermann Weyl thought: radical perfection and pure despair are not analogous expressions, and Heidegerrian perfection does not at all exclude the interminable constructiveness of technology.) *Trauerspiel* does not mean to trace the limits of the utterable a priori in such a way as to impose or enjoin the domain of silence, but to understand language as a revealing ensemble of solutions and certainties. In the space of *Trauerspiel*, the annihilating confirmation of despair finds no place. It is rather the domain of revealing people interminably, of renewing problems profoundly (even as they seem to stay the same while time passes and people change) and, finally, of the showing of the other-than-utterable, and of the possibility of this showing, since an "endless quest" could never be authentic if it dressed itself in the logic of the solution.

"Wir stehen in Kampf mit der Sprache"—this struggle with language is endless. The new space of *Trauerspiel* is the field of this struggle. In the domain of facts and data, the limits of language are not providentially assigned to simplify internal order. We "frequently beat our heads" (Kraus) against the wall of language. Clarity of expression is not prepared for its limits. "The philosopher is a prisoner in the web of language" that Nietzsche spoke of, struggling with language to be able to constantly reveal, but in this struggle infinite documents are accumulated from that profound dedication to surpassing limits. Without that dedication, no revealing, no transforming game would be thinkable. To this same practice of linguistic revealing belongs our hurling ourselves "against the walls of our prison." Simultaneously quoting Nietzsche and Kraus, Wittgenstein can thus clarify that if language did not dash itself against its limits, we could not know what these limits were and therefore we could not even speak sensibly within them. This wreck is necessary to the very definition of the utterable, but, at the same time, the domain of the utterable appears thus absolutely foreign to that of dwelling.

There is no desire in this language—and nothing adorns it. It shows every intention of transcending the same limits as structural components of the same syntax, critical of the idea of solution and indefatigable revealing. The domain of *Trauerspiel* is that of our struggle with language and of language with itself, and not of the desire of language to surpass itself. It is the domain of words, perfectly defined and limpid in their despair, that know how to recognize the silence of ruin as essential to their uttering. The essential does not reside in avoiding it, in exorcising it, but in repeating it differently, ever in new places, since the answers are always different, since the problem is always different: "True life means: to invent new places where we can be ruined . . . ; every new work is only the invention of a new death."[14]

A Critique of
the Modern

The new domain of *Trauerspiel* is defined in the tension of a double antithesis: an opposition to the modern and the impossibility of the tragic.

The opposition to the "originality" of modernity appears in Wittgenstein as a radical separation, a metaphysical gap. In a draft of the preface to his *Philosophical Observations*, written before the published version and published separately in *Culture and Values*, Wittgenstein wrote, "This book is written for those who look kindly on the spirit in which it was written. This spirit, I think, is different from that of the mainstream of European and American *Zivilisation*," from the spirit that finds its expression in "industry, architecture, and music, in the fascism and the socialism of our age." That spirit is "completely alien and *unsympatisch* to the author." But this assessment, Wittgenstein warns, ought not to sound like a "value judgment" upon the age. The fact that *Zivilisation* is opposed to the idea of *Kultur*, where every element has its place, and where everyone can work in the spirit of all and measure their own success in the sense of the whole—the fact that these times are the age of *Un-kultur* ought not to lead to effete pessimism, but uniquely to the recognition of the radical transformation that humanity's means and forms of expression, and very existence, have undergone. Wittgenstein views *Zivilisation* without "sympathy."

He writes only for "friends scattered to the ends of the earth." In order to measure Wittgenstein's "ascents" out of the philosophical and cultural habitat of modernism, it is enough to compare his words with Rudolf Carnap's preface to the first Viennese edition of *The Logical Structure of the World,* dated May 1928: "We discern an intimate consonance between the basis of our philosophical work and the spiritual attitude that permeates every field of life today. . . . The conviction that the future belongs to this way of seeing supports our work." In a 1931 note we read the names of those in whom Wittgenstein recognized—sometimes sadly—the force of influence. Next to Boltzmann, Hertz, Frege, and Russell (not Mach), not only Kraus, Loos, and Piero Sraffa, but also Otto Weininger and Oswald Spengler. What "form" unifies these friends scattered to the ends of the earth? What is the essential difference between this diaspora and European and American *Zivilisation?*

Zivilisation, for Wittgenstein, rests upon a word and is bewitched by a word: *Fortschritt,* progress. It is nothing but the historicist secularization of the idea of a solution. Progress is the same as the idea of an ongoing, continuous, dedicated solution to problems. Its form is *typisch aufbauend: constructive* in its most intimate essence. This is realized by making structures that are ever more complex, in a constant growth and complication of the "perimeters" of the world. Therefore, Wittgenstein's disengagement from the idea of progress represents a disengagement from the reasoning behind it: from its essential constructivity or productivity. Already this definition is in itself alien to the varicolored traditions of European pessimism in the Age of Decadence. It does not oppose *Zivilisation* as something destructive and unorganic; on the contrary, it denounces precisely its constructive and productive aspects, its characteristic of reducing things into objects and objects into structures (structures that are ever more formalized and complex, noeses, mathematics). The essence of progress consists in building the world. Therefore scattered friends desire their own diaspora, not in order to flee presumed irrational and destructive forces of *Zivilisation* (a fatal destiny celebrated in the success of the

Faustian man), but in order to preserve their roles as the other, as foreign to the constructive essence of Western rationality, to the productive epos of its *Gedankenwelt* [ideal world].

What can "the friends" put up against this epos? They begin by asking themselves: The system of rationality represents itself necessarily as an *Aufbauen*, as a working edifice—but on what basis? The basis of this constructivity is the original "destructive intention" of the logos, whose dialectic can demonstrate that every sensitive or abstract object that can be expressed in a judgment can be proved to exist and not exist at one and the same time, possible and impossible.[15] This foundation returns as a *problem* in Wittgenstein, and it is its incessant return, its continuous reconsideration, that comes up against the epos of typically constructive reasoning (*typisch aufbauend ratio*). No amount of progress can ever resolve such a predicament. The path of history resembles the path of a cloud, says Musil—but of a cloud blown to *some place* by the incessant wind of this problem. It is *here* that things return. While the dialectical logos, believed to be resolved into constructive and productive forces, lines up its *Gebilde* or structures, one after another, almost like going from step to step, others remain where they are and insist on considering the same thing: the original problematic foundation of the destructive intent of this *ratio*. "The labyrinth of reason," writes Colli, "only seems an edifice." Already in Zeno "the cheerful aspect of dialectical reason" was transformed into "a harsh, hostile, dangerous, and devastating frown." Both of Parmenides' roads are passable by now, and the very heart of *aletheia* falls victim to the logos. But the world of representation, having reached this climactic moment, unveils its "inconsistency," so that "it betrays itself as self-destructive, in a nihilistic and at the same time cathartic push." "Reason's trust in being constructive" is brought into question and annihilated right from the start.[16] In building stairways toward determined objects (which constitutes progress), it is precisely this origin that must be sublimated. Nothing may ever go back there. But anything that can be "reached by a stairway does not interest me" (Wittgenstein). We should already be where we really must go.

The basis of dialectic's destructive intent shows the sense of the equivalence of the propositions in a perspective that cannot be reduced to a function or a construct. It demonstrates the unutterability, the impossibility of representing a content of propositions, a wisdom or a gnosis of them. The destructive intent radically demonstrates a metaphysical difference between the logos-that-speaks and the what-has-been-said. This ends up with dialectic turning against itself: it breaks down its own form, unveiling its unbridgeable distance from the thing in itself. The constructing and transforming of *ratio* rests upon complete comprehension of the thing in itself. In terms of "origins," the logos means something other than itself, a place, *aletheia*, whose form pitilessly contradicts the merely revealing form of dialectic. *Ratio typisch aufbauend* [constructive reasoning] of "mainstream" *Zivilisation* is nothing but the extraordinary sublimation of this original metaphysical difference. Constructivity and productivity do not occur without such sublimation: to surrender to it is impossible on the stairway that pretends to lead beyond "endless research" as a solution.[17] It is never possible to create authentic clarity in our language until it connects to considerations of this basic enigma of our *Gedankenwelt*, until it shows it can consist of *this same thing*, which comes back in every affirmation, every development of formalism latent in the logos.

Ratio typisch aufbauend sees this radical *Andenken* of the basis of its own intentionality as a disease to cure or "recuperate" from. Difference is itself a sign of sickness by its dialectic. In order to give up sublimating the basis it is necessary to place oneself under the sign of the fool. In order to understand something one must go mad while keeping one's head straight.[18] Madness embraces our thinking as death embraces life.[19] Clarity here means: to understand ever freshly our abiding in the sense of the basic problem, under the sign of its unresolvability.

But why do we say "clarity"? What word could seem more coherent with the idea of progress in our *Zivilisation*? Doesn't *Zivilisation* pit clarity victoriously against the dark background, against dialectic's obscure motives of destructive intent? *Zivilisation*'s clarity is not an end in itself, though. Its visibility and its brightness are only functional. It is the clarity of constructive calculation, production's necessary brightness. On the other hand, Wittgenstein's *Klarheit* is purely "in honor of God." The motto of *Zivilisation*'s own clarity sounds like this: *simplex sigillum veri* [simplicity is the seal of truth], where "simplex" does not at all contradict the complexity of the structure, of the construction, since this is precisely the result of the "simplicity" of calculations and logic with which the subject succeeds in reducing and governing the entity. While the "simplex" clarity of *ratio* is functional to the structure that it intends to produce, Wittgenstein's *Klarheit* means to render transparent the very foundation of construction, to constantly return to that same thing, constituted by its problem, to render its non-constructive foundation evident—the intrinsic, reciprocal affinity between nihilism and the metaphysical gap that is its sublimated content.

It is only the clarity of the simplex that dominates the modern. Certainly not the modern that Loos talks about, flinging itself against a nostalgic soft spot for the past, nor that of Klee, whose time belongs, as we shall see, to Rilke's magic marionettes. Their illusionless gaze on the modern derives (as Benjamin saw, and Stefan George before him) from that supreme moment of urban intellect that the lyric form intuited between Baudelaire and Mallarmé. Alongside and against the modern there is the "avant-garde" that, in the apparently disenchanted exaltation of the machine era, ignores the backward gaze of Benjamin's angel and the "eternal return" of its problem. Such an "avant-garde" is productive from the start: it is the utopia of the full resolution of any problem in building, in the "simply" constructive end that surpasses (perfect *Aufhebung*!) the original destructive intent, the utopia of the omni-mastery of language, of unending amplification, the unstoppable utterable. The aspects that are most clearly functionalistic and constructive are nothing but the most esoteric aspect of the whole matter of the avant-garde (at least of its public matter and of the "culture" that has flowered around it). It is rather exactly there, where it seems to excavate the dark background of the signified, the *Hintergrund der Bedeutung*, that its *ratio typisch aufbauend* appears with the most evidence. Everything can be produced, uttered, and made manifest. Everything can be made transparent. A feverish *horror vacui* torments it, a will to show all that it often interprets, nonsensically, as a direct affiliate of Nietzsche's *Wille zur Macht* (the will to power as art).

Wittgenstein's *Klarheit* is defined, on the contrary, precisely by confirming that the *Hintergrund der Bedeutung* is *un-aussprechbar*, unutterable, since it refers to the metaphysical difference between word and thing. And this difference brings with it a continuous return into our struggle with language and language's struggle with itself. *Klarheit* can emerge in Wittgenstein only by lacerating the certainty of the simplex, of construction as bringing every problem progressively into the evidence of the utterable. The "avant-garde" looks to the basis of meaning in order to discover the essential word, the word buried in the impersonal passive voice (in German, *man*), unconsumed root and content. *Klarheit* in Wittgenstein resides in the most pure surrender to this desire and thus preserves that basis as *un-aussprechbar*.

The clarity of *Trauerspiel* has the identical form. This is indeed the great form of the critique of constructive and productive rationalism. This reasoning becomes transparent in its dialectic. It argues with the semblance of progress, it slashes at its claims with pure crystal, until it reveals a dark, remote motive. The desperate analysis of this intention belongs to *Trauerspiel*: its place is defined by its metaphysical difference from the other, unutterable, unrevealed *aletheia*. The clarity of this form is essential. It is manifest in the perspicuity of relationships that are established in it, the evidence of its critique, the force with which it knows how to deny images of nostalgia, with which it knows how not to wander.

Klarheit is opposed, finally, to *Aufklären* [gloss]—and in order to elucidate this point it is very important to keep in mind Wittgenstein's critique of Freud (Wittgenstein's interior motives, rather than the direct pertinence of his critique to Freud). For Wittgenstein, the work of analysis tends fundamentally toward a "primal and essential sense" and a "latent thinking." At most, a "reality" is discovered that is completely different from appearance and is the reason that appearances are deceiving. The *Aufklären* of analysis—and *Erklären* [explanation] in general—always presupposes that objects signify something other than their appearance. But is this interpretation really necessary? Is it really necessary, in order to produce clarity, to "translate" these appearances into some other reality? And if the dream were nothing other than "a sort of game played by the dreamer"? Can we not produce clarity just by asking ourselves if by chance the dream that we now consider didn't inspire some of its images, without there being some causal connection between a "before" of the dream and the images that it now inspires in us? Or again, could it not be that only some images of a dream can be explained according to the methods of analysis? Wittgenstein viewed the form of *Erklären* as intimately involved with the solution, with a clarity that is essentially constructive and productive "simplicity." The *Klarheit* of *Trauerspiel* describes the revealing mechanisms that are part of the metaphysical gap between logos and *aletheia*—a gap whose continual reformulation as a problem is a critique of *ratio typisch aufbauend*.

Where Wittgenstein speaks of "order," it is unrelated to strategies of simple linguistic tidiness. It means to render clear—willfully and before God—every relationship in the tangle up to now: the basis of *ratio* as *the* problem to which there can never be *the* solution. Constructive and functional "simplicity" is reached through "clean" speech and the power of expression—*Klarheit*, the perfect analog of the most terse writings of Musil or Schoenberg, only reaching, and maintaining, their depth of meaning as an unutterable background. And it is against this background that language proceeds, amid the continuous course of events that its pure crystal reflects and recomposes in infinite ways.

The Impossibility
of the Tragic

The impossibility of the tragic is the other horn of the dilemma that defines the new domain of *Trauerspiel,* and it too is a leitmotif of *Culture and Value.* The equivalence of two propositions depends essentially on a surrender of the tragic form, and this surrender is suffered by no author in "Wittgenstein's" Vienna as deeply as it is by Wittgenstein himself.

There can be no tragic form in the new space of factual data, since tragedy is speculative and its development has been a circuitous return from the apparent multiplicity of a conflict to the conclusive unity of its metaphysical significance. Such a conclusion is denied to *Trauerspiel,* to its worldly aura. In this light, the speculative point of view could only reappear as *Werturteil,* as an assessment of value. Value judgment is nothing but an indecent substitution for tragic speculation in the world of the *Trauerspiel,* an ethical and constructive "translation" of the Tragic. But even more interesting is the explanation of the impossibility of a tragic form on the basis of its incongruity with the Judeo-Christian God. It is as if the metaphysical difference we explained above had returned here as the difference between Tragic and Romantic, in the Hegelian sense. A sense of names "archaically" conjoined to things belongs to tragedy, while the Judeo-Christian God imposes a difference between names and things as his law. He orders man never to make a tragedy of himself, for he has reserved heaven and hell

for him alone. Earth is the site of our labors: pure and insuperable
Tatsachenraum.

The infinite is unutterable. Earth is *eine wüste Gegend,* a desert
without images. Jews are prohibited by law from making images.
That is why tragedy, which is essentially symbol of the infinite, is
itself essentially non-Jewish (*un-judisch*). The contrast that rips
across Schoenberg's *Moses* and that appears in the same terms in
Wittgenstein's reflections develops in a direct form—opposed to
the circuitous form of tragedy—that concludes with the command
to hold out in the desert, since the unfocused mass of spirit can
only run *under* the desert. Nothing possesses this spirit, since noth-
ing can possess the name that it has as a thing. And Wittgenstein
quotes Goethe and Max Stirner, saying, "der Jude muss im
eigentleichen Sinn 'sein Sach auf nichts stellen' " (Jews have to base
their destiny on nothing, in the most radical sense of the term).

A bi-directional motion comes out of this condition of the Jew-
ish spirit. From one side, the centrality with which it insists on the
unrepresentability of the infinite, on the absence of a name, com-
pletely impedes its productivity; on the other, this very distance
from productivity permits it to understand more deeply the prod-
ucts of other people's creativity, to better analyze their limits and
their aporias. Wittgenstein characterizes the Jewish spirit as a peak
of analytical capability, of self-reflection. He discovers himself com-
pletely aligned to this power/powerlessness. Self-reflection is, for
him, absence of creativity, and capability is absence of "health."
And this is a disease that cannot be "analyzed," much less cured: a
radical otherness of character and of destiny.

One also needs to speak about Christianity in light of *Trauer-
spiel.* On this subject, too, Wittgenstein gives an important, ulte-
rior explanation on the theme of certainty. There is a sense of cer-
tainty at work in Christianity, in fact, that has a completely differ-
ent nature from the certainties before which "we are obligated to
bend our knees" (Wittgenstein) in the various activities of life.
This certainty has a *Glauben* for its content, a faith, a belief that is
radically opposed to every form of self-assurance as a component
of *Weisheit,* of wisdom. In *On Certainty,* the de-sublimation of

Logic does not lead anywhere except to the complexity of worldly conviction, to *Weltweisheit*. But Christianity establishes a certainty that divides itself *by the sword* from this *Weltweisheit*. The paradox consists in the fact that, while according to the logic of *On Certainty*, nothing can stop the ratification of certainty *even* of *Glauben* (it is not possible, that is, to prohibit such certainty), the "reasoning" behind this *Glauben* condemns all philosophy and all *Weltweisheit* to radical fallacy. This paradox cannot be resolved—but here too the essential consists in maintaining the form of this pure difference, without turning to edifying syntheses or compromises. The conciliation of the two forms of certainty belongs to the unutterable.

Christianity orders life to change, orders the completion of a global *metanoia*. Its belief is a scandal for the certainty of *Weisheit*. This change of life cannot be made rationally, but only *leidenschaftlich*, with passion and sorrow—or more precisely, with *enthusiasm*. *Weisheit*, adds Wittgenstein, does not know *Leidenschaft* (it is not enthusiastic, although it is worldly to a radical degree) while noting, "Kierkegaard calls faith *eine Leidenschaft*." Perhaps in no other passage is Kierkegaard's influence on Wittgenstein made apparent with such clarity, even if the Kierkegaardian concept of Christianity figures here in a cultural frame that is profoundly distinct: in Wittgenstein, in fact, contrary to Kierkegaard, this metanoia is absolutely unutterable; the fallacy of *Weisheit* that it confirms is unutterable; and this judgment is "senseless," as is any judgment of *Weisheit* upon faith.

Like Kierkegaard's, this concept of Christianity is opposed to Pauline synthesis. Wittgenstein believes he notices an irreducible difference between the Gospel of Christ and Pauline dogma. This difference, as is well known, had already been underlined by Nietzsche. Belief, with Paul, seems to want to confirm itself as positive certainty, like *scientia*. This dogmatic pretext makes it necessary to have hierarchies, honors, officers. The Gospel contains the scandalous, "senseless" obligation to change one's life. In Paul metanoia becomes method. And the method coincides with the Church. And the Church ends by opposing itself to the very *Richtung des*

Lebens [course of life], to the evangelical form of existence, to its "tents in the desert." The Church tends to dampen enthusiasm; this too, like worldly wisdom, becomes *leidenschaftlos*: in fact, the overcoming of "fear and trembling" constitutes its objective. Anguish derives from the reemergence of that unresolvable otherness between faith and wisdom that constitutes, for Kierkegaard as for Wittgenstein, its *own* Christianity. But the tradition of Christianity is the nationalizing of faith and wisdom in the form of Pauline doctrine.[20]

But why is this Christianity of Wittgenstein's essentially "Romantic" and anti-tragic? Because the imperative to change life means looking *directly* at the world, and looking at it directly means understanding that "absolute judgment is out of place before the facts of the world."[21] The gospel is self-assured—assured of its certainty—that value lies outside of the world and therefore outside of the propositions that describe it and construct it. That is why the Christian is prohibited from judging the world in the perspective of its value. The Christian does not judge, since "human language cannot express absolutes" (Vannini). The Christian's faith *never* changes into a foundation of knowledge, never betrays itself into judgment of value—even if it calls on wisdom and its judgments to change life. The contents of this metanoia consist in ceasing to betray the absolute into judgments of the world.

As Hegel had already seen, Christianity and *Trauerspiel* belong to each other reciprocally, since the *original* Christianity (the importance of seventeenth-century baroque drama, *post* Reformation, pertains here) recognizes the impossibility of value judgment for equivalent propositions and it reserves the contents of its faith in pure unutterability and unrepresentability, while *Trauerspiel*, against a background of the unutterable, expresses only the conflicts and the struggles that happen in language. The unutterable cannot however be "forgotten" in the space of the *Trauerspiel*, since the same equivalence of its propositions and the impossibility of Judgment begin to make sense only on its ground. Equivalent propositions have *nothing* to declare about the possibility of metanoia. But in the space of *Trauerspiel* the unutterable can nevertheless show itself. It does in fact show itself: but transcendence, the event of transcending equivalence, cannot ever find words there. This event is the Messiah of *Judentum* [Judaism]. (See "The Star of Narration" below.)

The final words of Schoenberg's *Moses* ("Oh you, you word, that eludes me") contain perhaps the secret reason for Mahler's farewells and for the silence of the unhappy Lord Chandos—they express without doubt the bidirectional motion of both the unutterability of the absolute and the equivalence of the powerless propositions on Judgment. This vision of evangelical *not judging* seems almost to reunite the Christian faith to the interminability of the Diaspora of *Judentum*, to the infinity of its *undichterisches Leben* [life without speech].²² But it also means that in the desert there are no victors, that in the desert we can recognize and love our limits and our anguish as our own character and destiny.

Visit the Serraglio!

Perfect figures of *Trauerspiel,* symbols much more than inhabitants of its new domain: Wozzeck and Lulu.

Pierre Boulez refers to the development of compositions like Alban Berg's as "novelistic development,"[23] continuous change without return. Extremely stable forms reclaimed from tradition are inextricably mixed, giving life to figures of extreme complexity and ambiguity. Such disquieting ambiguity derives from the fact that the various forms are themselves stabilized idioms, in and of themselves, and not material for a collage. There is thus a nonstop interaction between the intention of the compositional work and the autonomous sense of those forms that are reactivated or recalled in it. It is not at all a matter of the destruction of these forms, as Boulez seems sometimes to think, but a Nietzschean refusal to surrender to the "so it was," to "paying off" the past. Berg's work proceeds, in a way that recalls Walter Benjamin, to the discovery of the many pathways to the "beyond" that are hidden among the ruins, and to conferring upon the ruins the sense of such pathways. Mahler's compositional dialectic acts the same way toward traditional forms.

The labyrinthine qualities of Berg's work elude Boulez's definition of the "universe in perpetual motion" or "the ever-expanding universe." It eludes those commonplaces about the Viennese maestro's complex and contradictory variety of styles. The "severe logic," to use Berg's own phrase, that orders such variety is that of *Trauerspiel. Wozzeck* and *Lulu* are its models. The fact that Benjamin's notion is realized in the most finished way in a musical structure is deeply significant. The most authentic human sense is in fact the sense of hearing. To live is to listen, life is heard. But hearing cannot produce images. Nor can the sounds that it hears and constructs be described or replaced with images as consolation for lost nature.

Misunderstanding thus belongs to allegory, inasmuch as it is opposed to tragic seeing, to *theory*. But lies are exposed by severe logic. A being's self-contradiction, self-wounding, and confusion, its nothing-other-than-being-here is exposed, not as a root multiplicity, but as the actual form, available only as sound, of Hölderlin's no-more and not-yet. Allegory transposes, and in transposing, it necessarily destroys and betrays. It recognizes the no-more. At the same time, in this never-ending labor through tradition, the ways of the not-yet also emerge. Tradition is never available in the reassuring neoclassical framework of simple ruins. Allegory uproots tradition's no-more response to the not-yet. It turns that which has been heard into a herald of that which can be heard, of the purely possible. The sound of the not-yet seems able to manifest itself in this unending movement. Continual metamorphosis thus excludes either a return to origins (to the very principle of origin) or the discovery of new compositional orders leading to true peace. One order: the clarity of metamorphosis, the intelligibility of *Trauerspiel* as the essential musical architecture.

Ambiguity of form is the essential groundlessness of beings. This principle excludes all naturalism of the soul, to use Georg Simmel's expression. There is no "nature" where there is only translation and transportation of forms in their insuperable historicity. Berg is the negation of every *Urschrei* [primal scream] expressionist. Creaturely exsistence is intrinsically composed, irreducible to an origin. It is possible to enlarge, transform, and continually traverse the allegorical forest where creatures live speechless (*undichterisch*). Composition works it and re-works it, without ever being able to come to a conclusion, without ever being able to clear away the ambi-

guity. Even before Benjamin thought about it definitively—
roughly contemporary with *Wozzeck*—this compositional princi-
ple had already been in some way prefigured by the great Viennese
art critics, and in particular by Alois Reigl. For Reigl, the art of
decadence is not negatively defined as a loss or absence of the clas-
sical, but as an event apart from classical in a new severe logic of
essential historicity, of allegorical ambiguity. Berg's compositions
belong to this universe, not to seeking native forms of *Urschrei*
against it, which is characteristic of expressionism and modernism.
Decadence here expresses the conscious disenchantment of the twi-
light of the age of *Kultur*, and no vague sense of derivation. Deca-
dence is the non-representability of the whole, the elusiveness of
the symbol. It is knowing oneself apart from the symbol and thus
knowing the obligation to venture into composition, into saving
and transforming the fragments, sacred in themselves.

Here the deep influence of Nietzsche acts on the "language's
great Viennese," as Roberto Calasso has called them. Mario Bor-
tolotto has correctly understood how Nietzsche speaks of Wagner-
ian leitmotifs as a prefiguration of Berg. "Wagner, maestro of un-
stoppable speed, intangible nebula, crucial fibrillation, chromatic
collisions, microcosms suspended in a symphonic magma, resem-
bles Berg too closely, and is even closer to the Berg of Adorno's es-
says."[24] This affinity is rooted in an analogous decadence that as-
sumes its full meaning between Riegl's idea of expressionism and
Benjamin's notion of *Trauerspiel*. In light of what has been said, a
laughable reductionism ought to become evident in commonsense
interpretations of operas like *Wozzeck* and *Lulu*: social protest, con-
demnation of authority, and so forth. A tendency to reduce Berg's
allegories to expressionistic naturalism of the soul shows up again
in these categories. Not that such motives could be absolutely ab-
sent, but the true problem has less to do with the social criticism of
these operas than with their logical and compositive sense, in the
severe logic of the language of *Trauerspiel*.

Even insisting—mistakenly in my opinion—on the term mon-
tage (montage has as its transcendent condition the reduction of
material to semantic indifference, which should *not* happen in

Mahler's and Berg's assumption of the tradition), Bortolotto gave
us a splendid gloss of *Lulu.* "The parts build up, starting with the
Prologue, into impossible piles. Pieces on top of pieces." From the
illustrious as well as the plebeian topoi of musical theater to the
colors of the Prater, from Mozart to *Singspiel,* to the "inexhaustible
incarnations" of *Biedermeier* down to Brahms and Strauss, it de-
fines "an enormous structure, made of minutiae (Wagner's 'mini-
mal transitions'), a baroque volumetric made of cuts and *bibelots.*"
The grand form consists in composing this multiplicity of parts.
Grand form is not, however, a style, but an *excess* of style.[25] It is
impossible to reduce to categories of style the overabundance of
languages that strike us like "vagrant" quotations from Benjamin.
("Berg's quotations, like Benjamin's, reveal themselves to be va-
grants off the street that jump out with a weapon and demand the
lazy to form an opinion" [Bortolotto]). The grand form is the
enormous composition of minimal transitions. The excess of style
creates the compositional principle: the adventurous and prob-
lematic unity of composition, opposed to the static and formal
unity of style.

The grand form means "to comprehend" the world as the total-
ity of cases, as everything that is the case. In *Lulu* this principle
reaches perfect *Klarheit*: it lives in every fold of the opera, like a
presupposition, a precondition of its language. The scene of its
Trauerspiel is precisely that of *men without qualities,* of the purely
possible. But men of possibility are simultaneously absent. Pure
possibility causes all who encounter it to vanish, rendering them
liquid and spectral. As Bortolotto has already pointed out, it is this
quality of the absent that renders the characters of *Lulu* beyond
the reach of style. In *Lulu,* the domain of *Trauerspiel* combines it-
self, beyond style, with the logical space of the *Tractatus.* Lulu is
the angel of this combination. She is music beyond style; she re-
fuses the principle of style. She transcends it in the dimension of
pure possibility, and she finds grand form in this dimension, in its
compositional structure, and in the severe rules of the logic of her
game. That is why this figure of possibility can become the idea of
an aesthetic *intentio* at the same time that she reaches the bedrock

of profane vulgarity. This figure passes through *every* possibility, uncontrollable, irreducible. At the same time the language of equivalence, its premises radically questioned and applied, connects to the problem of manifesting the unutterable—to the problem of the limit that turns the composition into a grand form.

Lulu is the angel of possibility or, better, is the angel of the music of possibility. The angel is the face of unconsumable possibility. Without this, there can be no images or sounds. Lulu the angel is a divine vision captured in profane lights. A similar profane illumination agitates that most pure eros of Geschwitz. She knows that only Lulu's music can fulfill once again the dreams of the imagination, and it is to such dreams that her love tirelessly tends. But an angel that manifests the purely possible arouses an interminable love, attracts all the figures that she meets in a vortex that turns eternally in upon itself, like Geschwitz's waiting, beyond all jealousy and possession. This figure's peculiarity consists in having understood what Lulu says—not that Lulu is Music (everyone knows that), but that her music is an angel. It accompanies the facts as their insuperable limit. It expresses the ephemeral, and at the same time it expresses the illumination (the *Klarheit*) that issues from the ephemeral as *composition*: a paradoxically divine vision of possibility (far from the bourgeois "sublimation of sex" as Adorno, incredibly, misunderstood it).

As much as Lulu the Angel exceeds the stereotypes of the florid femme fatale, that is how much *Wozzeck* is irreducible to a category or metaphor of the unified organic world damaged by social oppression and by the authoritarian norms. The immense presentation of forms and motives makes the first act of *Wozzeck* an extraordinary universe of traditions and events. This same labyrinthine multiplicity rejects the myth of origin. It promises no methods for overcoming or getting beyond alienation, which is defined in terms of Nietzschean "decadence" as the logic of allegory. To such logic belongs the language of Wozzeck. To abstract him from the complex dialectics of the opera would be to place him in the glacial solitude of a tragic character, to make a tragic hero of him, turn him into a theory of the events that swirl around him.

The dramatic force of this most pure persona of *Trauerspiel* consists precisely in his desperate belonging to the allegorical ambiguity of the work. Wozzeck never penetrates his belonging, exploding into a naturalism of the *Ur-schrei*, of the primal scream of the soul. The persona's importance in this context does not derive from his being the bearer, to whatever extreme, of an origin or of a category that intends to reform him, but from the fact that his very existence, his very corporeality, expresses the creaturely nature of the work and its language with maximum tension and desperation. Wozzeck always hears the *Abgrund*, that point in the totality of cases where a vortex opens up and sucks everything in (the vortex that Hofmannsthal pictures in *Der Turm*). In Wozzeck, the multiplicity of voices and categories reaches an authentic sense of decadence: he shows how they pass through to the *Abendland* [land of twilight] and how they belong there inexorably. Wozzeck hears, already from the heart of the *Abgrund*, the voices of decadence, of the *Abendland*. As he hears them, those voices forgive their trite, quotidian surface, not in the sense that the music transfigures or redeems them, but in the sense that they lay bare the irreconcilable maze of their most secret and intimate nerves.

The importance of *Wozzeck* in context reaches its diapason in the second scene of Act I and in the extraordinary passage that accompanies the death of Wozzeck. Here the tension of that which cannot be heard (with hearing the voice that speaks in Wozzeck, with the sounding rod of the *Abgrund* where twilight occurs, with the intuition of the *Gebild am Himmel*") displaces the already-heard, crashes against the limits of the already-heard. But this breaking against the shoreline of tradition is the force that continually transforms it, is the crisis that changes its borders. Perhaps no other contemporary work portrays with more dramatic clarity the fact that the authentic nature of *Trauerspiel*'s persona, of all creatures, lies in being in constant struggle with the limits and history of language.

It would be a grave error, however, to assume dramatic *intentio* as an index of the solution or of the method for solution. Berg speaks of a "Piano-Oper mit Ausbrüchen"; the tone of the opera is "piano," which combines participation with estrangement. The intensity of participation is a condition of the acuity of intellectual understanding and vice versa. On the other hand, this tone is continually shattered. The entire architecture was reached by solutions of continuity, explosions. The principle of interruption dominates that of conclusion. There is no solution. Every motif is taken up again and varied, never followed through and developed in all of its possibilities. Every motif remains a possibility, holding out in the dimension of the possible. The metamorphosis renews itself by incessantly interrupting itself. The opera presents itself as an extraordinary universe of fragments: extraordinary because such fragments are not neutral shards in a collage, but entire traditions, forms, and languages. Every motif is continually revealed and reveiled; its surface and its sense are transformed—but never resolved, never presented as a whole that has finally been achieved. There is no method that can lead back from the fragment—from this idea of the fragment—to the symbol. Architecture-by-fracture in *Wozzeck* means precisely the impossibility of the symbol. This is the very language of nature, the logic of its allegorical nature. The disturbing passages from the second and third scenes of Act I and, above all, the screaming crescendo in A major that collides with the tavern dance in the interlude between the second and third scenes of Act III do not serve at all to isolate the various parts impressionistically. Instead, they clarify the logic of allegorical architecture as opposed to synthetic and symbolic architecture. Paraphrasing Heidegger: every pathway is interrupted, but these constant interruptions do not merely diverge through the forest, they lead to multiple centers, to multiple clearings, to innumerable discoveries. Multiplicity experienced, multiplicity interpreted, but never exhausted, is the source of *Wozzeck*'s sense of misunderstanding.

This is not aphoristic writing. Aphorism seeks definition, seeks to circumscribe microcosms with all the parts strictly and organically connected inside. The writing in Anton von Webern's *Six Bagatelles* Op. 9 is aphoristic, for example. The bagatelles are seeds of microcosms. The intuition of their *free* inner connection is *Er-*

lösung [redemption]. Aphorism in Webern defines the *necessity* of composition. Redemption consists of nothing other than embracing that necessity, in loving it, like Nietzsche. In Webern, the microcosm is finally the single sound itself in its purity, just as it echoes in the silence-within-us. As such, the aphorism is inseparable from the tragic form and the metaphysical opposite of the uncompromising movement of Berg's *Trauerspiel.*

Not that movement and transformation are missing in Webern, but his philosophy of time is different. Continuous variation attains, in Webern, a principle of non-repetition. The aphorism cannot be repeated precisely because it is complete, because its arrow has hit the bull's-eye (which is the silence-within-us, inasmuch as the target is the archer's heart). Any repetition would be ornamental. Continuous variation in Berg, on the other hand, derives from the opposite principle of the impossibility of tragic aphorism or, better, from the nonexistence of a center at which to direct the aphorism, from an inherent ontological poverty. While Webern's brevity is the symbol of the essential nature of the microcosm compressed to its limit, the compositional fracturing of Berg indicates allegorically the essential historicity of nature, its desperate productivity among the shifting facts of the world. Webern's intuition of the perfect annuls the linear dimension of time. In Webern, there returns with unequaled clarity the Nietzschean problem par excellence, which is the problem of liberation, of *Erlösung* of time. Webern's ascesis turns each fragment into a unique, unrepeatable microcosm. Certainly uniqueness can never be construed as a resolution, but it is in itself perfect and unequivocal. The *Abgrund* of Berg's *Trauerspiel,* on the other hand, grasps the same fragment, with its same intimate structure, in an unstoppable metamorphosis, where redemption is not possible or else appears like the light of a star extinguished since time immemorial.

For these metaphysical differences, there is much more significance in the sisterly relationship between these figures of the Viennese "school" and the names and motifs that together make up the culture: Trakl and Webern's Op. 14, for example. It is the song without words of one who has no country and who passes by the moribund city of *Abendland*. This song of Webern's is a mistake in Berg's terms, for *Abendland* is tinged with decadence and at the same time lit by raking sunlight. Trakl's poetry, that of a soul estranged from the world, is necessary to understand the very structure of *Wozzeck*. The motion toward the silence of this soul in Webern's Op. 14 finds its analogy in Berg's *Altenberg Lieder*. Here too, the structural function of silence in the composition, which is the deepest lesson of Mahler, seems to allude to the possible *Erlösung*. It is a matter of the tranquillity that follows snowstorms and long delays, of peace full of the gestures and pains resolved in that time. It is the silence of a long sigh, aware, beyond the reach of consolation, like the farewell at the end of Mahler's song-symphony *Das Lied von der Erde*. The snow that plays lightly on the lake of the heart (in Altenberg-Berg), the falling stars that inflame the rosy evening (in Trakl-Webern), the sea of the sky where the moon bobs in the waves (in Mahler) are voices brought together by differences. As productive as they are in developments and discoveries, they are that successful in justifying their diversity, as happens in the vocal and pianistic lines in Webern's Lieder Op. 12 or in Schoenberg's George Lieder. Moreover, to learn to hear the affinities among the diversity, like learning how languages develop and are transformed within family groups, is to learn how every family is a multiplicity of fragments wholly in themselves: this was the very principle of Schoenberg's teaching.

Music, Voice, Text

Since the order of musical composition cannot be "invented," but comes from an enriched transformation of inherited traditions within new, distinct configurations of signs, the relationship of music with text becomes a fresh problem, one of extraordinary complexity.

The way Schoenberg confronts it in his famous essay on "Der Blaue Reiter" could give it a reductive cast, with regard not only to Schoenberg's "philosophy" of composition, but also to those of Hugo Wolf and of Mahler. Schoenberg's essay brings a subtle equivocation into play: the text, as a denotative system, as discourse that directly signifies something, adds nothing to our understanding of Schubert's Lieder. The problem is even more radical: Why does the text exist? What structural function requires the presence of text? What compositional problems does it trigger in the entire Viennese "tradition" from Schubert to Webern? It is not possible to respond to this question as Schoenberg does in "Der Blaue Reiter" only by showing the ability of text to determine the formal articulation of a piece of music. That is true perhaps only at an elementary level of composition, where the text stands out against an extremely regular melodic structure, built of brief symmetrical phrases. It is evident that the procedure that results in maximum clarity and comprehension of the text in Schoenberg's or Webern's Lieder is completely different from the *radikale Re-*

47

produktion that Goethe praised in Carl Zelter. But the presence of
text as a structural element, one that participates as sound and
sense in the compositional form or, put more generally, the im-
portance of the *verbal* element in composition holds not only for
those forms that would seem to have a natural predisposition to
that relationship, but also for Beethoven's great romantic sym-
phonies.[26]

What is the meaning of the verbal element, as such, in compo-
sition? Why is it called a necessity? Because that is exactly what it
is: text is necessary in a Schubert Lied, but not to be better "in-
formed" about what the music "means," not to get the "program."
Rather, text is necessary in order to understand the entire compo-
sition clearly, within a framework that is not merely formal, indeed
is not even as formal as it is cultural and philosophical. A fresh di-
mension of the necessity emerges along the entire Schubertian line.
The problem is not "what is said," but the clarity of the emergence
of the voice. "What is said" could perhaps be entirely removed
without reducing the intelligibility of a Schubert Lied—but this
would certainly not remove the problem of the voice as the emer-
gence of a new compositional subject. The voice is not used up in
reciting a text; rather, the text appears as a mere material vehicle
for the voice. It sustains the voice's place as an uncontrollable force
within the entire instrumental composition. This force stands out
more and more sharply from the whole. It is not a simple instru-
ment among others in the language of composition. It contains in-
finite games, relationships of growing complexity. But it always
emerges as the specific subject, and for this reason its emergence
unfolds the indicated structural function. It actually points out the
whole of the composition as a problem that cannot be reduced di-
rectly to its coordinates. The *voice* breaks through this composi-
tion. And not the voice that is articulated in discourse, that ap-
pears directly as a simple means of communication and informa-
tion. Schoenberg was right not to pay attention to the words in
Schubert's Lieder. The words, in fact, were not essential to their
compositional structure; what mattered was the presence of the
voice. The usual approach has been notably reversed. While the

voice is usually understood as the mere medium of significant dis-
course (usually spent on verbal communication), here it is the text
that seems to serve as a vehicle for the appearance of the voice, and
the text that furnishes to the voice a mere means to manifest itself.

Schubert's Lieder are constructed around the utopian presence
of the voice. The location of the voice, in fact, is *no-where*. For us,
the sound of the voice is only the sound of the *signifying* voice.
Ever since Aristotle's *On Expression* (which remains too deep in
spite of Giorgio Colli's commentary), we disregard the voice as a
simple sound in favor of a true science of logos, in favor of expos-
itory discourse that connects us to the world only. It is as if this
discourse had no sound or the sound of the voice were completely
superfluous for it. Such a sound returns in Schubert as the pre-
ponderant problem facing the grammatical and syntactical line of
musical composition, and that is why it determines its entire sense
and structure. The composition pulsates in attendance of the un-
attainable sound of the voice. Surging from the head—indeed con-
fined to the head—the voice breaks out of the compositional fab-
ric as if in search of its native presence. The voice is intrinsic not
only to the text that embodies it, but to musical language itself.
True discourse here is that which the music develops, and this in
turn defines the voice. Beyond the verbal text and within musical
language, the problem of the voice imposes itself. That is, the voice
becomes a problem, after the long history of its sublimation, of its
"victory" in discursive structure. Indirectly, it is precisely this situ-
ation that Schoenberg underlines in his essay: the "what" of the
text of the Lied is truly and completely disinterested—but the
voice that manifests it is far from disinterested. The text is, literally,
the utopia of the voice.

All the subsequent literature of Lieder develops along this track.
But the problem of the voice and of its unattainable origin, which
confers authentic metaphysical content upon the *Sehnsucht* [long-
ing] of the Lied, is linked finally with the problem of text, in its
semantic value. To complete the preceding design, there is another
structural element: the clarity and intelligibility of the text as such.
If this is not the logos that "takes away" the voice, that removes its

problems, neither is it the simple pretext for a "heavenly" mani-
festation of the voice. The utopian attribute of the voice is clearly
recognized here. This attribute appears precisely with the manifes-
tation of the indomitable autonomy of the text from the voice,
with the irreversibility of the process that leads from the voice to
meaningful discourse, to the syntactic order of language. In order
to manifest the "body" of meaningful discourse, it is necessary to
put it in clear phonetic and semantic terms. The voice alone ap-
pears on this rugged terrain. It has no place of its own. But that is
exactly what it shows: that the place of the text does not use it up,
that the text is by no means its origin. The voice is not at home
in the text, but only in the text can it "go on."

All of which changes not merely the quality of the relationship
between text and voice, but also that of the whole relationship be-
tween text and musical composition. Diverse ways of rendering
come to light. Where the music reproduces or follows the text, or
where it turns back on itself as a disinterested vehicle of the voice,
this diversity cannot appear. There exists, then, only the order of
musical language, or the relationship between it and the utopia of
the voice. On the other hand, whenever the presence of the text
becomes a meaningful semantic presence, the relationship between
this presence and that of musical language is a relationship be-
tween two autonomous forms of connecting to the world. Con-
necting to the world is irreducibly complex. There is no idealistic
dialectic, no solution, that can resolve the complexity of it. It can
only be compiled: the order of composition is the order that re-
veals and renders comprehensible the diversity of elements. It is
the order that works on that diversity and transforms it, along with
the complex relationships of its elements. Various combinations
and configurations of signs appear in the composition. Metaphys-
ically, these take on the value of various possibilities of thinking or
of connecting to the world. None is a mere vehicle or pretext for
another—no one is the true sense of the other.

Thus even at this new level, it is not the "what" of the text, its
informative content, that really counts. Rather, it is the general
presence of another system beside the musical signs, of expressive

signs which are also thoughts. It follows that such a system has to be presented as fully organized in itself, fertile whether from an intrinsically musical point of view or from a truly semantic one. The inclusion of "babble" reveals the scope, which is to show a natural diversity of ways of connecting to the world. The presence of a particular text alongside the voice forbids musical language to delude itself with new universality, while it rigorously defines the borders of its possible domain. There is no clarity or intelligibility without defining limits, and the particular text becomes the symbol of the presence of limits that permit understanding and clarity. Between music and text a relationship happens: a relationship between two languages not dialectically surmountable in "higher" syntheses. The text poses a limit, but, in posing it, it questions. The relationship does not happen between two languages at peace with each other or on parallel tracks. The text is radically assumed as an interrogating presence, to which the response is—diverse, not neutral.

That is what happens between Hölderlin and Brahms in the *Schicksalslied,* and between Brahms and Goethe in the *Alto Rhapsody.* At the end of the *Schicksalslied,* the return of the conciliatory motif of the introduction is clearly an answer to the fall into *Ungewisse* [uncertainty], to the absolute loss of God on the part of Hölderlin's *leidender Mensch* [suffering humanity]. Likewise, the connection between poverty and utopia in Goethe's poem constitutes the unifying inspiration of the final section of the *Alto Rhapsody,* until it ends in silence, in *der Wüste* [the wilderness]. In both cases, the text is *presence*: a motif of order and articulation of the musical form. But much more, it is a problem for that form, the limit of its language, an interrogating *Gegen-stand* [subject].

Just as Peter Altenberg's essays are *Extrakte des Lebens,* Hugo Wolf's Lieder are "Extrakte der Seele." But how to manifest their distance from every late-Romantic *Zerrissenheit* [striving]? How to order and articulate the completed loss of ego? How to keep from getting lost in interminable allusive chains? If the problem of Wolf's musical language consists in rendering the *Extrakte der Seele* intelligible, this was also the profound intention of Eduard

Mörike's poetry. The relationship between music and text is truly essential here. Wolf captures definitively the problematic nature of the text, and he throws himself against it with abandon. He knows infinite ways "to go outside the stable structure of the strophe and bring out its most central nucleus." He "is the first to treat a poetic text with absolute indifference to its preexisting order,"[27] even while exalting every moment in it, so that it independently takes up and presents anew the most secret themes of the musical idea.

The autonomous text survives, even saturated with the problems that musical language confronts; not a text of music, but a question and answer directed at the articulation of musical form. After the "visionary" Wolf (Bortolotto), this relationship reaches its most complex expression in Mahler's *Rückert Lieder*. Ladislao Mittner criticizes too hastily this figure of an erudite poet. Friedrich Rückert's formal virtuosity, his historical and linguistic awareness of India and oriental civilizations in general put him in a precise cultural and aesthetic region: that which passes from Goethe's utopia of "universal literature" to the philosophical and artistic concepts of Schopenhauer. His language game is contemporary with Schopenhauer's pessimism about classical and romantic conceptions of art. That is, by now art can be nothing but cultural reworking, virtuoso philology, a linguistic game—despairing, finally, of any ethical or existential content ancillary to Nirvana. It is this *essential* despair that Mahler finds in Rückert's poetry. It is not by accident that Schoenberg speaks of Mahler "in the name of" Schopenhauer.

But here, too, the assumption of the text takes place in full freedom, criticizing its sense. In the five *Kindertotenlieder*, Mahler annihilates the elements of consolation present in Rückert's text. He dissolves their metrical assonance and their closed rhyme scheme to bring out of them two fundamental motifs: the simplicity of pain (withheld constantly in its pretense to declare itself) and reawakening (the impossible resurrection, powerless to sound here as in the finale of the Second Symphony, in spite of a mysteriously leavening utopia that embraces each word and each sound of abandonment and solitude). The slow rhythm, barely interrupted by brief cries of the voice against the limits of the form, indicates the irreversibility of time. The reawakening does not announce itself beyond such time, but appears rather as the experience of the eternal return *in the irreversible*, as "the joyous light of the world" that repeats itself in the irreversible. The farewell does not free one from the earth; it does not free one from its light. "Farewell" is bid to friends, to children, but not to the earth's light that illuminates irreversibility and poverty. The joyous light of the world turns the poverty of passing time into clarity (*Klarheit*).

An identical *itinerarium* is found in Mahler's *Five Lieder* with text by Rückert, composed almost at the same time as the *Kindertotenlieder*. From the springtime beauty and melancholic irony of the first three, it proceeds to the abandon of the fourth (which draws everything back "inside" the Lied). It then proceeds to the desperation of *Um Mitternacht*, where full defeat looms paradoxically and scandalously in the majestic passage from A minor to A major at the end ("in deine Hand gegeben . . . "). The finale links death and resurrection together, joins time to the final farewell and to repetition, joins the misery of time passing and the joy of the world's eternal light, the perfect void of Nirvana and the "sweet scent" of the first Lied. The multiplicity of language, the profound misunderstanding of the relationship between music and text, has perhaps never found a fuller expression than in the *musikalisches Denkmal* [musical memorial] that Mahler brought out of the words of the erudite poet—or rather, from their Schopenhauerian substance.

The text is a problem that musical form finds intrinsic to the compositional process. The text is a complex of signs, indices, memories, and facts that the music has to digest and rework; in turn, the text must manifest the *intentio* of the musical form. In this sense, a continuous thread connects Wolf and Mahler to Schoenberg. Not so much to Schoenberg's expressionistic reworking of Richard Dehmel as to his crash encounter with Stefan George.[28] Hofmannsthal said George subjugated life "to such a degree that he breathed an incredible calm and the freshness of a deep temple into our senses, which are used to confused noise."

Dehmel's position is far more complex than Schoenberg understands it to be, and the literary historians—even Mittner—have noticed as much. Not only is Dehmel's presence at Darmstadt colored by the original anti-Wagnerian intonations, but even his so-called "symbolic naturalism," above all in *Weib und Welt* (1896), enters into dialogue with motifs from Arthur Schnitzler to Otto Weininger, far from unknown to Schoenberg. Nor should we forget Dehmel's reading of Nietzsche—for example in *Nachruf an Nietzsche*—where he refutes the myth of a Nietzschean "school" and acutely captures the true sense of the *Wille zur Macht* [will to power] as the subduing of the True One: *I, God.* Dehmel, finally, is no "accident" for Schoenberg and cannot be reduced to the "spirit of '14" of his *Kriegs-Brevier*.

Only George's *Book of Hanging Gardens* could accompany Schoenberg in his approach to "an expressive and formal ideal that had already floated before me for several years." The extraordinary essence of George's poetic "music" recalls that of the piano literature, in which every note is stripped in its uniqueness, liberating it from all tonal *religio*. The voice, which preserves Schubert's secret intact, connects to the text in a more pregnant and incisive manner. The melodic construction lies, as Adorno noted, "in the use of minimal values, in the subdued declamation of legato notes detached from the conclusions of phrases, in the chromatic conversion of all central sounds."[29] The melodic construction transcends the space of floral imagery, of all the Jugendstil sensual sonority. But this transcendence is exactly George's problem, the roots of which are not to be found in any mythic Prussian esotericism, but rather in Mallarmé and in the great "metropolitan" French lyrics. Schoenberg's music confronts this whole aesthetic and philosophical problem in George's text. The dialogue between music and piano, "made of extreme subtleties, of subterranean connections, of projections at ever-recurrent intervals yet hardly noticeable at first,"[30] possesses nothing of the simple rapport between two players, two "instruments" in a cycle. It is rather a closed musical interrogation of George's text to extract the trace of the path from lyric naturalism of the soul to the absolute measure of an intellectual *imaginatio*, capable of plastic, objective strength.

The complex network of allusions, of cultural and formal meanings that constitute George's cycle of 1895 is not immediately recapitulated in the music. Only the fundamental metrical values— the text as a creator of order—are assumed in the music. For the rest, the music recomposes and reorganizes the sense or tendency of the text. In fact, the almost explicit objective of the rapport between the two players is that of rendering evident the idea that music and text do not form a totality, do not constitute a synthesis a priori. What is this fundamental textual tendency that the music must draw out and express? It is the tendency toward *form* that Hofmannsthal emphasized. The music's assumption of the text's metrical values is essentially a reading of the deep strata of George's work. The music freezes, in its own meter, the symbolist residues of the text, the flowery exuberance that shows through, and, above all, the exasperated, pale, and highly refined chromaticism. The fundamental tendency of the text (on which Schoenberg constructs his cycle) is death, the end of the brilliant insight, of the poetic possibility of voicing sentiment as nature, of expressing it as an object, a situation, a game of appearances. That which lives in the text as only an inaudible tendency becomes the explicit sense of the music. It is the collapse of the extreme naturalism of the soul, and finally the impossibility of poetry as a producer of images, of beautiful images in a brilliant intuition. "The images always flee . . . when the clear cold morning draws near." The morning of the music freezes the symbolic naturalism of which the text is already a contradictory witness. Read and listen to the eleventh poem in Schoenberg's cycle: "Ich erinnere, dass wie schwache rohre / Beide stumm zu beben wir begannen" (I remember, we both began to tremble silently like fragile reeds). What could be more clearly Jugendstil, or even more flowery, than these trembling reeds? But what logic can be more severe than the perfect meter that scans them? And here is how *this* tendency is comprised and is recomposed in Schoenberg, beyond any possible intuition or image, in the design of a unique line that voice and piano pursue independently, in "a solitude and a stillness full of continuous events of pure crystal" (Musil).

The text therefore is *other* material. It has its own strong principles of organization that the music assumes and considers as such, without reducing their complexity, without posing a solution to their problematic nature. But the presence of this other in the musical deed is destined to reconstitute its very form, since it defines, on the basis of this limit, its own non-universality and, at the same time, its own effectual "domain." As in the examples already cited, the relationship between music and text develops a complex logic of relationships, a network of intrinsically problematic relationships that are founded on the history of the respective languages, on the awareness incarnate in them, on their sense and their tendencies and their crises. Music and text constitute, relating to each other in this way, "prose" relationships, affinities, families of sense, conflicts, and contradictions. All of which prevents *a single* language from pretending universality, impedes an accord that presents itself as a synthesis, as *the* tonality. "Are dissolved patterns privileged in the structure of the accounts, in the formal systems, or in the theory of harmony, criteria that are proposed in order to choose the dissonance . . . ? For Wittgenstein, the formal proof is a paradigm, a harmonious figure. . . . Schoenberg—having rejected the formal responses of technique, the naturalistic privileging of tonality—assumed as his criterion of legitimacy of dissonance the perceptibility and perspicaciousness of the dissonant accords" (Gargani).

In this logic of relationships, every sign, every form, every movement consciously avoids the presence of the other. Within these limits they are organized, they are developed, they seek to become more powerful and more intelligible—within the silence that embraces them and that they need to demonstrate or allow to be demonstrated.

Wonders and Marvels

Equally complex is the composition of Musil's "Into the Millennium," the story he should have told but that escaped all his writings. In *The Man Without Qualities* Ulrich and Agathe begin from a premise of resignation.[31] They belong to that facet of desire that torments Margaret and Faust and whose motif runs from Goethe through all German literature. Severe rules of abstinence and self-imposed codes enforce separation, impede desire from being recognized, allow the lovers to be *pure*, and allow their quest to remain disembodied. Woman's beauty "evaporates" the obstacle of the human body, that "third thing" that Andreas-Salomé saw as the soul's tragedy in passion and that incites chastity.[32] Beauty attracts desire and keeps it from turning elsewhere. And yet, since it is ideal, it cannot be reached. It can only be contemplated in a platonic sense. This theme of passion crowned in resignation can express itself in the characteristics of incest that every couple ends up redressing.

This has little to do with generic asocial interactions or with philistine calculations intended to guarantee the survival of desire for the sake of continued abstinence, as Lemoine-Luccioni seems to believe. To the simple dialectics of the analyst nothing is more refracted than Musil's millennium. From the perspective of the finished novel, which sees the "wisdom" it expresses and communicates, the encounter of the two siblings happens at the peak of the

explosion of the subject as ego, beyond the limits of order and be-
yond the rule of ethical discourse. The *ekstatische Sozietät* of
brother and sister goes beyond those limits, and only its own in-
ternal sense can give it the force of sharing, of mutual assurance
about what to call their actions. As Emanuele Castrucci has dem-
onstrated,[33] Lord Chandos, who exceeds those very limits, finds
his exact double behind him in Benito Cereno (not by accident a
key figure for Carl Schmitt) and before him in Musil's couple. Ec-
stasy has therefore a precise foundation: it sends up the individu-
alistic and possessive sphere of the liberal age. In his relationship
with his sister, Ulrich attains the full absence of possession; he frees
himself from the category of possession.

This category is organized around the problem of property, of
appropriation. The history of truth, says Jacques Derrida, is "a pro-
cess of appropriation." To seek truth presupposes a fundamental
proper to which it belongs and supposes that "the value of belong-
ing has a unique sense and its own stability." Now it is exactly this
metaphysical stability that the man without qualities adulterates
and corrupts (without *Eigen-schaften* [qualities], and therefore for-
eign to the "family" of *Eigentlichkeit* [reality], and even to the Hei-
degerrian family of *Being and Time*). The man without qualities
always leads from the immutable preference for the proper "to the
abysmal structure of the proper," a non-fundamental structure, su-
perficial and bottomless at the same time, the structure of the abyss
that reveals the event detached from ontological consideration.[34]
Musil's novel connects to the most subtle games in Nietzsche's
thinking: the debasement of the basis, of the *Grund*, of the struc-
ture that constitutes the very possibility of appearance and appro-
priation. Any gesture or style opens onto the abyss (*Abgrund*) of
an event that can no longer be appropriated—onto the *marvel* of
the strange happenings of *Geschwisterliebe* [a love between brother
and sister].

The outer stillness of solitude that this resignation of the proper
is called upon to create ought to correspond to an internal
Gelassenheit, to an emptying in oneself, to an abandoning of one-
self. Only such a radical dispossession can fully show the meaning

of "without qualities." Ulrich is certainly the language of equivalence that dissolves value judgment into the facts of the world. But since Ulrich matures in the lunar light of his sister, he is the one "without propriety," he who seeks an interior dimension of emptiness in the surrounding stillness. There is a rapport between "without qualities" and *Gelassenheit*, but they are not identical. "Without qualities" remains within the limits of a critique of the possessive and acquisitive ego and its body, of the conservative power that it exercises. The idea of *Gelassenheit* indicates, rather, an *ecstasy* liberated from relations and conflicts with "property," an end to the very problem of possession. Language changes color from expository tones of irony and critical judgment to tones of enlightenment.

In the novel there is a double unwritten story. The first was not written because it already existed. It is the story of Lord Chandos. Many dare to interpret *The Man Without Qualities* as if the only story it contained were that of the unhappy scholar imagined by Hofmannsthal. The novel has more than just the desperation of Lord Chandos in its past—it also has the formation of syntax and language of equivalence that moves in that "common nutritive liquid" produced by dissolving the ego. From the first instant, Ulrich is language "without qualities," and it is absurd to imagine his route as a return to the original conditions from which he had detached himself. His route is rather to go beyond "without qualities." "Without qualities" is complicated by a radical "without property," and this figure, in turn, connects to the interior *Gelassenheit*—and still further beyond that dimension lies the story not narrated and impossible to narrate.

The opus that Ulrich wants to initiate with his forgotten sister turns out to be the redemption of time. The sacred dialogues that the couple embroider together tend imperceptibly, by minimal and musical transitions, to abstract her from the *mundus situalis* [the mundane], to vaporize her concerns, to refine and purify her material, as if in search of her invisible star. This star speaks in Agathe: "We have to break away from knowing and wanting, and free ourselves from reality and from the desire for reality. Draw into ourselves, until mind, heart, and body are all one silence." Brother and sister cultivate an extreme *attention*, sharpened against every sensation and thought. San Giovanni Climaco speaks of attention as an angel that stands guard at the gates of paradise. Everything that comes to the gates of the heart gets interrogated, in order to determine whether it comes as an enemy seeking to destroy the slow work of emptying, of *Gelassenheit*. The sacred dialogue tends evidently to a sort of interior prayer under the watchword of "attende tibi ipsi" [heed yourself].

The "arcane perception of something happening without anything happening," of "a solitude and an immobility full of continuous events of pure crystal," of time as the unending repetition of clouds in the sky, is a possible redemption of time that nevertheless takes place in time. This is due to the transforming of words *and their speakers* in the sacred dialogue, in the opus that it symbolizes. The dialogue has the rhythm of a slow and difficult decantation: Ulrich and Agathe raise themselves up, ever more pale and "dispossessed," from the critical and interpretive melancholy where their souls "hide." Here all the themes of the great novels return, as if in midflight, unable to be held. Critical judgment (Ulrich's native language and mother tongue) has dissolved, decomposed, and has demonstrated the groundlessness of vanity's attempted syntheses. It killed the mortal. That is why all of its themes must return. The dialogue between brother and sister would not even be conceivable without this dissolving of the stability and durability of appearances. The dialogue initiates another phase: nostalgia for the soul, which the material, dissolved at last, had kept prisoner. It is nostalgia for the "being that, behind appearances, thought and felt," and through which the "bodies transformed themselves into cruel prisons."

Meditatio and *imaginatio* are the terminal points of *Geschwisterliebe*. The conversation between brother and sister is above all an intimate conversation. It does not consist in an exterior dialectic, but in the attention that it develops and in the *Gelassenheit* that it produces and nourishes. As in the opus, here the value of the conversation lies in its speakers far more than in its results. It strips

brother and sister of their ephemeral bodies for the Millennium of
the immortal golden Eros. Behind the apparent dialogue, a true
metalogue, there lies the intimate conversation between spirit and
spirit, as with Hofmannsthal's Sigismund or, to use the words of
the *Lexicon Alchemiae* cited by Jung, a conversation with someone
"who remains invisible, even such as God, after having invoked
him, or with one's own self or with one's good angel." Behind the
apparent dialogue there lies, finally, "a living relationship with the
voice of the other."[35] *Imaginatio* blossoms out of the intimate con-
versation. It is the imaginative faculty of the soul, capable of con-
ceiving things that the world cannot conceive: the consonance be-
tween the star from which the *spiritus sydereum* emanates and our
own souls. Paracelsus says that when man succeeds in freeing him-
self from the body, as happens in dreams, then the soul can "*fabu-
lieren*," or converse with its star. In the solitude that they create
around themselves, it is as if brother and sister were searching their
sleep in order to dream the dream of God. If Ulrich and Agathe
are nihilistic and atavistic together, they are so under the sign of
imaginatio that flowers from *meditatio*. Their nihilism resides in
the intimate conversation with one's own good angel, which is the
symbol and image of the conversation between the soul and its
star. It was by imagining the universe that God created it. To
dream the dream of God means to dream a magic production, and
in the form of this dream, in its clarity, one is reborn from the dis-
solution of any quality or property, from the darkness of being
"without."

More than intermediary faculty of the soul, a bridge between
sensation and idea, *imaginatio* appears in "Into the Millennium"
as a point of arrival, the recurring and unattainable goal of intel-
lectual intuition. It guides the conversion from corporeal to spiri-
tual (a still shadowy movement toward stability and the light of
ideas). Its airy or fiery puff increasingly seems to be the only force,
the unique *spiritus*, that is capable of perceiving divine inspira-
tion.[36] It is as if the extraordinarily problematic nature of these re-
lationships were incarnate in Musil's "style." *Imaginatio* can no
longer be understood as an intuitive pass, a stairway that leads to

the contemplation of God, failing completely to define the love between brother and sister, or even its possibility, within such an "ascensive" scheme. *Imaginatio's umbra lucis* refines the corporeal and changes its colors in dreams. There is no light except in the *umbra lucis*. Brother and sister reciprocally transform their images into a continually changing chiaroscuro, as unpredictable as a dream. Like flashing wingbeats they fracture the darkness momentarily and reveal instants of light that are difficult to remember. Brother and sister are seen in waiting, ever ready to take hold of each other, to stop each other in memory, and ever in pain from the apparent vanity of this hope. Even in the repetitive pattern of "Into the Millennium," there is the constant and unstoppable change that results from this struggle between shadow and light, from which it is impossible to disengage. Clearly this moment consists of an infinity of colors, sounds, voices, and dreams. It is the irregular motion of the *spiritus phantasticus*.

Agathe is the mystical sister who, together with her brother, holds the key of this work. But the relationship between sister and *artifex* represents how much happens in the work itself. In their dialogue, it is as if brother and sister were animated by a nostalgia to blend together, to pass into each other—that is, to reproduce or reformulate their common single embryo. They are, it is true, separated and abandoned, but their unity has not been lost, and they seem drawn to it. Brother and sister need to *join* each other. In the marvelous vehicle of their dialogue, they tend to produce this conjunction. That is why calling each other brother and sister is not enough, nor is it enough to call each other twins, or even Siamese twins, in order to express the dream of "being two creatures and one," to express this quintessence of *imaginatio*, whose effect "was no different from that of a dream escaped from the confines of the night."

Only for a marvelous and strange instant does this dream of unification appear to be realized. "When Agathe had overcome her fright, . . . by one of those cases that no one can control, she found herself marvelously satisfied and indeed undisturbed by any earthly anxiety. He carried her, holding her sweetly close, across the darkening room to the window, and he placed her down next to him in the mild darkness of the evening that washed over her face like a flood of tears." Here it seems the *attention* succeeds in becoming truly free of disturbance and that the dialogue is transfigured into pure, interior prayer. This instant surprises the couple and reveals their love to them. It seems strangely distant from the pure force necessary to the development of the work. "They shared the fraternal figure of their own bodies, as both had grown from a single seed." Musil clarifies the symbolism even more directly with Ulrich's closing words: "Ulrich said foolishly, as if speaking into the void, 'You are the moon . . . ' Agathe understood. Ulrich said, 'You flew to the moon, and the moon gave you back to me.'" Silly lunar clichés? "Ulrich said, 'It is an *image*—we were outside of ourselves. We exchanged bodies without touching." What does *image* mean? To exaggerate reality? But reality here had been grand! Image is *fabulieren* with the star, and here the star indicates the twins' shared roots. "What brought us together from the very first could well be called a lunar lifetime of moonlit nights." Agathe resembles Pierrot Lunaire, who certainly has nothing to do with the romanticism of *Claire de lune*, but "must be the fragment of another life." Then Agathe truly understands—her attention opens the gates of her heart to the meaning of her brother's words: "he probably wanted to say, 'Why don't you know a spell that would keep all that from dividing us at the last moment?'"

The "last love story that could ever be" (Bazlen hits this nail on the head) ends on this note of disturbing proximity to the *coniunctio*. Even so, questions do not cease: "Toward what direction do our feelings turn? Toward what transformation and transfiguration of the real world and real people?" Does this questioning of attention sustain the heart and its *Gelassenheit*, or is it rather a discussion with the enemy, not knowing how to disengage from the struggle and passion of the dialectic? Does that strange and marvelous moment become truly "imagined" or, rather, pinned down anew in the vortex of the discussion? The "great truth" that is perhaps hidden behind the "common" truth remains an impossible question. The *imaginatio* that the conversation unfolds does not succeed in producing the Millennium. Making the dialogue deeper, opening the abyss to its common roots, emptying out the diabolical *Selbstheit* [selfhood], it seems to encounter ever renewed resistance or new points upon which it needs to rest and reflect. Infinite arguments appear, disappear, and reappear in the light of the sister's lunar beams. They seem to pour out interminably. The essay form returns, but as if in an atmosphere that ignores its critical arrogance. The opposite is also true. In conversations of love, agonistic forms of critical discourse return. The story is interrupted by the inseparability of the two dimensions. To conclude it would be to decide an ending, decide a solution that seems undecidable: either killing the voice of the twins, that singular language in which they had grown and in which they had found each other as the original One or—in the nihilistic negation of the *imaginatio*— dissolving that experience, the strange, marvelous event that happened in the mild darkness of the evening, in exaggeration, emphasis, and fantasy. The novel ends instead on a perfectly suspended note. On that note, it is definitive.

Every experience lives and becomes significant only upon the point of dissolving into the void, of being as if it had never been. But this experience, in its turn, dissolves ever anew the mere nihilism of reflecting and doing. We only have the endlessness of the relationship—therefore, not the perfect conjunction, and even less the child that it promises. We can ask what is the *imaginatio*, but the *imaginatio* remains sterile. The untold and untellable story is that of the conjunction and its creation. The image of *Geschwisterliebe*'s sterility transcends the space of mere dissolution of quality and of the typically constructive (*typisch aufbauend*) reason that emerges from it. The facile disenchantment and the simplex figure of "no illusions," are, once again, the distant past of Ulrich's story. His ruin is an absolutely new development: the symbolic creativity of *imaginatio*. The *Geschwisterliebe* is sterile when it comes to shedding light on an answer that touches all of life's problems, that combines the deepest forms of attention to every trifle with the feeling that "nothing is important." But *Geschwisterliebe* was able to plumb the depths of this problem. These two stances toward reality partake of each other reciprocally only once in a while, "in a propitious moment," secret and fundamentally incommunicable. The node that links brother and sister is the repetition of these moments and of the contradictory pathway that leads to them and forks off from them again toward the Millennium. The untellable story is the end of the story, where the end should be reconciled with the beginning. The untellable story is the point where the end reveals itself as the beginning. But it is this that constitutes the authentic sterility of *Geschwisterliebe*: that the circle is broken forever, that once broken it can never be critically or reflexively made whole again, that whoever has no home now can never have one. Many marvelous things can happen to Ulrich— troubled love, of course, "anything but simple." Profane illuminations can surprise him, coming out of the intricacies of facts and conjectures, like a flame that "dies down and droops, holds its breath, and then flares up even higher."

The Misfit

Hugo von Hofmannsthal's great *Lustspiel* [comedy] of 1920, *Der Schwierige*,[37] takes up the problem of language at the point where the *Chandosbrief* had left off. What happens to someone who snaps out of the illusion that words possess denotative ability? What happens to someone who stops believing the myth of the ontological foundation of language, or the pretext of the perfect transparency and communicability of all nouns? In other words, what happens to someone who emerges from the "war" of the *Chandosbrief*, from physical collapse, from *finis Austriae*? What happens to someone who "privately" keeps a memento of reconciliation and agreement among people?

In comedy no relevance is accorded to things; there is no "landscape." The protagonists are condemned to words—but words do not work as communication. They merely inform. To communicate is impossible, because where there is a failure of the ontological relationship between sign and world, communication can happen only through "tone." But the range of tones is infinite and infinitely varied—the length of a pause, the intensity of a single pronounced syllable, the context of a word, the sound of the voice. "Tone" is incommunicable: it is a gesture, whose connection to fact, plain to all, is a priori unexplainable.

So, if conversation, which is the beginning of comedy, is articulated only as information, which consists of signs and gestures that

are denotative only by convention, then misunderstandings are or-
ganically laid into its development. To speak (and it is necessary
to speak since we are fixed in a universe of *Konversation*) is "to pre-
sent images." But nothing attests to the descriptive and denotative
"truth" of these images, of these *Bilder*. Presenting images, as Emil
Staiger demonstrates, is inextricably connected to misunderstand-
ings and mistakes.[38] Comedy shows all the possible gradations of
misunderstanding, of *Missverständis*—tricks, slapstick, situations,
incomprehension. Even the blank page of silence, as the negative
side of language, is a source of error. Misunderstanding appears
with every line of speech or its opposite, reticence. The "ideologi-
cal," in other words, cannot be extricated from the very act of self-
expression. A perfectly transparent and perfectly communicable
language is an impossible utopia. The notion that natural language
could be logical or could be reduced to a logical unity is an im-
possible utopia. The will to be "definitive," the pretext of using
language in terms that are non-illusory and categorically univocal,
is implacably parodied in the figure of Stani, Hans Karl's nephew.
And it is not as if he had no memory or experience of fracture.

Misunderstanding has an even more essential foundation. It de-
rives from the primal tragic condition of speaking. As Staiger ex-
plains in his fundamental essay, speaking means *not* being unified
with things. Speaking is not, as it might appear to one with a naive
faith in language, the apex and synthesis of things, but on the con-
trary, departure from them, from their *Wesen* [essence]. Here is the
radical metaphysics of misunderstanding: it is impossible to speak
without "presenting images" of *Wesen*, without "giving the impres-
sion" of naming it—and even the very act of speaking demon-
strates the fallacy of the image and the impossibility of the name.
The character of Hans Karl connects to this stinging contradic-
tion. He recognizes it and he *lives by* it. It remains hidden to the
others, and they merely *live in* it. Hans Karl recognizes the inde-
cency of faith in words as an expression of *Wesen*. That kind of
faith is possible only to those who are dominated by an *indezente
Selbstüberschätzung* [arrogance]—to those who believe their own
linguistic conventions to be the Name of the Spirit of Time. There

are no *sacred* words. It is indecent to presume that one's own words can be torches to light others' deeds and inevitable "conversations."

If words cannot possess things, they are even less able to possess the essence, the soul, of the speaker. Hans Karl cannot "explain himself." Not a misfit, but a man for whom nothing fits (Mittner), Hans Karl does not succeed in explaining and understanding the factual situation in which he finds himself, the *Gegen-stand,* or in explaining and understanding himself. "But really you do *not* see the eye" (*Tractatus*, 5.663); "The subject does not belong to the world: rather, it is a limit of the world" (5.632); "The self of solipsism shrinks to a point without extension, and there remains the reality coordinated with it" (5.64). *De nobis ipsis silemus. De re agitur.* [We say nothing of ourselves; we stir things up.] But which reality? And how coordinated with our signs? Can only propositions in the natural sciences be utterable? But then, wouldn't they be illusory, *Konversation* dreams? Isn't natural language perhaps connected to the conventionality of conversation? No decree can ever remedy it. Its misunderstanding cannot be eliminated. Its fault is independent of my willing what-the-world-is. That is why Hans Karl must speak, independently of his will, knowing that he brings to consciousness only misunderstandings, "in spite of all and everything." Speaking is hesitation, silence, gesture, and tone, with the burden of possible, inevitable, desired misunderstandings, with floods of senseless words. Hans Karl is condemned to speak. And the deep, tragic paradox of Hofmannsthal's work consists in its being a comedy—a *Lustspiel,* a work "made to be spoken" and even structured around a persona that points to speech as a disgrace and silence as the only (yet impossible) decency (Staiger).

But this is exactly where a miracle seems to happen. The universe of mere signs and blunders, where all is *Konversation* and *Konvention,* seems finally to "redeem" itself. The conclusion of Hofmannsthal's paradoxical *Lustspiel* diverges profoundly from the negative closure of the *Chandosbrief* and from the unnavigable labyrinth of *Andreas* as well. With no explanation, the misfit suddenly succeeds at something—and it is something that concerns "our vital problems." The possibility arises of being understood, of being revealed, of a relationship that arches beyond misunderstanding. Nor does this relationship resemble Musil's *Geschwisterliebe*, since the latter presents itself as the possibility of real, everyday communication, aesthetic even prior to being ethical. The last scene between Hans Karl and Helene indicates, in Hofmannsthal, the outermost edge of a radically contradictory utopia: to find a place in the world, within *Konversation* and *Konvention*, to succeed in communicating—to find the essence of the relationship in common words. This utopia has no foundation in the severe logic of the work. Certainly, it is not Hans Karl directly who converts the meaning of it. It is Helene. Hans Karl wants with all of his power to find himself in his friend's words. "Do you understand everything?" "Do you know all this?" And then, "You knew it all . . . " "How well you say it!" But neither does this moment come near the case, which practically delivers itself from all distress, from *Geschwisterliebe*. The tragic paradox of *Lustspiel* is betrayed in this conclusion. Hofmannsthal will no longer have the "courage" of such conclusions. Inaccessible, *Der Turm* and *Andreas* will resist the "indecency" of lighting pointless candles of hope at the end. *Der Schwierige* truly ends not in a marriage ceremony, but in a spoken marriage in the stupendous scene of Hans Karl with Toinette. Hans Karl speaks about marriage as a case where timing and necessity converge, as a case of reconciliation, forgiveness, and resistance all together. He *must* speak of marriage as the unspeakable paradox that Thomas Mann also described in the same period, although without Hofmannsthal's sad awareness. "It is a matter not only of locating the flesh in spirit, but also vice versa, locating the spirit in flesh: Indeed, this above all, given that there is nothing sacred that is purely spiritual." How can Toinette understand him? She interrupts him, misunderstanding him completely. In the words of Hans Karl, marriage (which in Mann is still, however paradoxically, an institution) is represented in the farewell, which is the very essence of the term "sacred": separated, distinct, divided off, alone. In the end, however, Helene's courage and force of desire seem to be enough to get him back, as if Hans Karl's refusal were the result only of his existential condition and not of the metaphysical complex of relationships between words and world. Certainly the others—Stani and Crescence—see only convention in marriage, but that is not how it is. Hidden behind this aspect, protected from misunderstanding like Kierkegaardian knights of faith, Hans Karl and Helene are *pledged* to each other. They *believe* they are pledged to each other, to have quieted their own silence. And this faith consumes the most extreme, deep, and painful *Missverständis*, so essential that not even Hans Karl can admit it, from which Hofmannsthal himself pulls away. But for the last time: the "sacred" of *Der Schwierige* is represented in *Die Frau ohne Schatten* only as a perfect utopia, to be lost, finally, in the labyrinthine sign of *Andreas*. The misfit is the bridge between the immediate negative of the *Chandosbrief* and the awareness, already implicit in *Andreas* and in *Der Turm* and total only in Musil's novel, that the story does not function to say (which would be impossible) or even to hide, but to demonstrate that which cannot be said.

Acheronta Movebo

I shall stir up hell: "Acheronta movebo." Freud used this epi-
graph (the fury's oath from *Aeneid* VII) to seal his own work, and
Hofmannsthal has the Doctor swear it to Julian at the end of Act
II of *Der Turm*.[39] "I shall unclose the gates of hell and shall em-
ploy the lowest of the low. . . . Mighty is the age that wishes to re-
new itself through nobility." *Acheronta movebo* is an oath "to free
the forces." This falls to the Doctor: "in the end there is a higher
judge." At the beginning of Act IV, in the first version of 1925, Ju-
lian, in a stupendous dialogue with Sigismund played entirely
upon misunderstandings, now becomes a full dramatic figure and
takes up the Doctor's words: "It is true what someone said, that
we need to uncap hell." And again when he begins to understand
Olivier's betrayal and when the revolt of the *Namenlosen*, the No
Names, begins to spread, "I unchained hell and now hell has free
passage. So I must look it in the face."

The motif has a double personality, and this indicates the spe-
cifically equivocal nature of Hofmannsthal's late work. Julian mis-
represents the hermetic figure of the Doctor. The Doctor is a psy-
chopomp: he wants to ferry Sigismund's soul toward the light of
awareness and the dignity of man. But Julian wants to free him in
order to have him and put him into action. The Doctor leads to
complete dispossession of the sacred dialogue between spirit and
spirit; Julian, to the renewal of the terrestrial realm. Both of them

71

lead, both assume in a certain way the figure of the psychopomp—but their alliance is a hybrid, a diabolical amalgam between two forces of the soul that inhibits the success of the work just as it will inhibit John Dee, as imagined by Gustave Meyrink in *The Angel of the Western Window*. The misunderstanding, in fact, is not Julian's alone. The Doctor joins Julian and consents to his plans. He speaks of spiritual rebirth and of a new Adam, but he never opposes Julian's profane designs. He limits himself to recognizing them, which is what takes place in the dialogue in Act I, without impeding or combatting them (as the Beggar, by contrast, does with King Basilio in *Life Is a Dream*). Julian and the Doctor accept misunderstanding, and they pursue their own works along its fault lines. The figure of the psychopomp becomes a double figure, and its two faces seek in vain to reconcile themselves. The Doctor himself, in fact, is a strange and disquieting hermit: he does not guide beyond the material realm to a symbolic death that promises resurrection into a divine state, nor does he approach the divine, but he causes one to wake up in the world. He is the magician who puts Sigismund to sleep, who closes him into a hermetic dream, but only until he is carried into the presence of the King and into a vortex of power games. It would be possible to say that the Doctor tends dangerously close to the profane in mistaking his mission and that Julian (as Sigismund constantly reminds him) also misrepresents his own most intimate and hidden vocation in following the mirage of power.

To which of the two figures, or to which of the contradictory tendencies that they express, does Sigismund belong? He confirms that Julian is his teacher. But his teaching was involuntary, or rather, Sigismund deluded himself about what it meant. Julian taught Sigismund that "wir sind aus solchem Zeug, wie das zu Träumen," that we are such stuff as dreams are made on, but he meant, in reality, to mold him into "no illusions," ready for orders and for action. In the first version of the play, it seems in some way that this teaching is realized. Sigismund assumes power and learns "in haste the language of the world," even if he is only an *interré*. And yet, he still wants the Doctor beside him, whose wisdom he loves. ("Wisdom isn't merely renting space in you; in you it lives in its own house.") In the first version, Sigismund seems to collect himself at the point where the Doctor's and Julian's paths of destiny cross. But in reality it is nothing other than a crossing of misunderstandings, which renders Sigismund's material extremely weak, too mortal, and makes the conclusion of the work "unacceptable" to Hofmannsthal. It is no accident that, in the last acts of the 1925 version, the figure of the Doctor appears faded and insignificant, while in the final version he holds the key dialogue with Olivier.

In the final version, Sigismund does not belong to either of the two faces of the psychopomp. He remains uncollapsable before Julian's misunderstandings, and he alone recites that prayer that the others refuse to say, right to the end. Not even the Doctor, who had procured a symbolic death for him only to bring him back before his earthly father, can "comprehend" his horizon anymore. Both give Sigismund "words of comfort in this desert of life," and now these words flow in him with no obstacles. He is *alone*, freed from both of them—from Julian's "nothing" and from the Doctor's imposing speeches to Olivier. He knows what neither Julian nor the Doctor knows, that "the tongue is too thick" to say what is truly worth saying. He has taken a lesson from both of them that they gave involuntarily. A reversal therefore takes place: Sigismund becomes the psychopomp. It is he who carries Julian's hidden soul to light, and the Doctor's as well. He carries souls with him on his way to his own destiny, while he abandons the "body" of his teachers to the "cold and sober" daytime of the No Names.

The Doctor is never on the same plane as Julian, even if, in the final and (in my opinion) truly definitive version, Sigismund disentangles himself from the misunderstandings underlying his relationship with the Doctor and Julian and between the two of them with each other. What underworld does the Doctor want to stir up? The first act gives no cause to doubt the intentions of this hermetic figure. He rises up against the monstrous crime "that cries to heaven," committed in the person of Sigismund in name of the interests of the state. Wherever these crimes are committed, they open a vortex that carries everything down, because "everything holds together," and it is not possible to fix a part without renewing the whole. Only charlatans, he says, responding to Julian, can pretend to heal the body while the soul of the world is sick. The Doctor announces the need for a *renovatio*, the very stamp of which is on Sigismund, on Sigismund the victim. This idea of the whole, this ideal of a consonant universe composed of different worlds and disparate elements, is evidently derived from hermetic and Neoplatonic traditions. Strains of Paracelsus and of Pico's *De dignitate hominis* can be discerned in the figure of the Doctor. In other words, the Doctor is the image of the "unfinished dawn"[40] destined for ruin in Olivier's here-and-now, in this "naked reality" that holds many prisoners. With an extraordinarily keen cultural sense, Hofmannsthal captures in *Der Turm* (in the final version) the complex image of that utopia and the cause of its impotence.

The symbols are easily decipherable and send us back to the ones we already saw in the analysis of Musil's married couple. Raw material is locked in the "oven," where no artifice may free its soul. The Doctor bears light into the midst of this material, and he discovers that a ray must have already penetrated there and roused its "most profound essence." In the depths of dejection, the Doctor discovers this imprisoned ray and learns that his task is to free it, purify it, and pour it forth. Even in the midst of filth the possibility of a quintessence is hidden, and the entire work appeals to quintessence. A "gold" that is formed slowly, through nature's design, is hidden in the depth of misery, just as "alcohol appears in our muscles as soon as putrefaction emits its first breath. From mortal poison the energy of health." (This, of course, is the basic principle of Paracelsian medicine.) The Doctor discovers Sigismund the animal, pure material, abiding in his lair, and the Doctor needs to flush him out of this "abiding," and make the material volatile. This is also Julian's objective. But Julian seeks fool's gold; his intentions are evil. The Doctor, consenting to Julian's plan, becomes an accomplice. He catches the disease of the tower guard. He can succeed in no undertaking where the *intentio* is not perfectly direct. He must fail—for reasons that are different from, and yet secretly complementary to, those that render the distress in Agathe and Ulrich's love insurmountable.

Let us say that impure *artifex* is the flip side of the figure of the Doctor and that it reveals itself precisely in the motto, *Acheronta movebo*. This slogan expresses the aspect of hermeticism that comes closest to *hubris prometeica*, a gesture of challenging the Olympians (in Virgil, the fury's "flectere si nequeo superos, Acheronta movebo"—if I cannot sway the heavens, I shall rouse up hell). The price of this gesture consists in ignoring the end of the work. It does not end in the hands of the Doctor. He penetrates into Sigismund's lair and is able to bring him out; but that is the extent of his science. The possibility of misunderstanding everyone and everything rests on this essential ignorance, from which Sigismund is freed only in silence and in a death that is nothing more than a symbolic voyage. The Doctor's Paracelsian magic is, in effect, interrupted. *De dignitate hominis* is seen from the standpoint of its failure. The "fallen" psychopomp brings Sigismund out of his past, from the dark forces that imprison him there. He wants to heal him of the insupportable weight of his relationship with a father who did not know—because of the blow that paralyzed him (he cannot even move in his cell)—that the son had killed his mother coming into the world. But this cannot be understood as *renovatio*, nor can it hide the vortex that "carries everything down." Doesn't Sigismund give the Doctor's work back to the King? Or to Julian's designs? Or to the nameless power of Olivier? The figure of the Doctor is torn and his most profound calling seems incomprehensible and incommunicable in Olivier's world. In their dialogue with the No Names, the Doctor cannot even pronounce it. He seeks in vain to demonstrate to the new power the height, the purity, and innocence of the creature that he has raised up out of the muck. His language appears to Olivier a mixture of doctor and priest and his world "a truckload of walking clowns." The intrinsic groundlessness and negativity of the "Olivierian Principle" is not revealed—as I have already demonstrated in "Intransitabili utopie"—through the words of the Doctor. It is revealed in the solitary figure of Sigismund, who finally overtakes his teachers.

This is also what happens in the utopia of the children who are called upon to make new laws (clearly modeled on the esoteric accents of Shakespeare's later plays).[41]

There is no *symbol* that can hold together the hermetic magic of Paracelsus, the unfinished utopia of consonance, and the Freudian analysis of dreams; Pico's *De dignitate* and "the language of the world"; the meeting of youths in Shakespeare's *The Tempest*, the *Kinderkönig* of *Der Turm*, the utopia and the earthly *renovatio* that Julian pursues and that the Doctor, torn within, should sustain. All of these unresolvable contradictions intersect in the image of the Doctor. Hofmannsthal infused him with his most erudite and disparate knowledge. The "Doctor of Dreams" knows better than anyone that "the powerful bosom of a man who dreams, who creates his own world," is a candidate for the stars, beyond the reach of the torments and overpowering forces that bring down "obscure" men. And yet, it is he who leads Sigismund to his reawakening, into the cold light of the dawning day that dissolves dreams, that reveals the impotence, finally, of *imaginatio*. The memory of the hermetic psychopomp may be kept in the here and now only in a figure that inverts its *itinerarium*.

The Private Adolf Loos

Another misfit, in those same years, experienced Hans Karl's contradictions. Another master of the German language, Adolf Loos, could not resist the perfect measure of the sign and the perfect ineffability of the sacred. He let himself be tempted by the indecent self-love (*Selbstüberschätzung*) of believing, in spite of everything, his own signs to be *more* than signs and their power to be the expression of laws based in aesthetic, ethical, and ontological foundations. Temptation erupted in him, not merely to show, but to *speak* das Mystische, and he could not stop it.

In order to understand the extent to which Loos's temptation ran counter to the artists of the period, it is enough to observe his smile when he visits the "invented" artist colony on Mathildenhöhe in Darmstadt. "Of Behrens's house Loos said, 'It would make a nice design for a necktie,' and broke into a laugh."[42] It was modern, certainly. But the modern is contingent, current, quotidian. There is no value in the modern: its aim is far from the necessary or the good or the more "advanced," as the self-styled avant-garde's nineteenth-century rhetoric of progress would have it. Change? You want to put a *modern* face on this antique building? Ask Loos and his bunch. You want new marble and wood walls to mess up the marvelous landscape that you see from this window? Don't you understand that it is precisely the simplicity of these walls that reinforces a hundred times the impression made by this interior?

Love of materials is one expression of this culture. It expresses the impossibility of conceiving material egocentrically as a simple medium at the disposition of the artist. Moreover, it expresses the impossibility of assuming the perspective of the ego as the only organizing language, as the only word of power. Note the relationship of Loos with the marble of Casa Müller: he uses imperfect marble that he found in storage, forgotten, set aside. Note his work on the ceiling of the American Bar: the Italian artisan whose job was to mount the slabs of marble was certain they would fall down, and Loos answered him calmly, "Just put up the ceiling." "And the ceiling is still in place, after more than twenty years." And once, interrupting his wife in the bath, "You want to be my wife? You, who care nothing for material? You have no idea how I fought my entire life against senselessness (*Sinnlosigkeit*), against *das Ornament*, against squandering forces, against wasting material? And you, my wife, you don't care at all if that excellent soap comes to ruin *sinnlos* in the water?" Loos's care for material and struggle against the principles of ornament is accompanied by a veneration for tidiness. It permeated him to the point of mania for the smallest details, even of his posture. This aspect could not be preserved by the "modern" historians of constructive functionality and transparent simplicity. Loos would have replied to their laughable and persistent progressivism with the story about Reb Hirsch the Servant. Rabbi Mendel's son was surprised to see Zvi Hirsch the servant cleaning the shul with his customary enthusiasm the very morning after his wedding. Disturbed by this, he went to his father and said, "It is not right that your servant neglects his wedding celebration and busies himself with such vile work during the seven-day feast." Rabbi Mendel of Rymanov answered, "My son, with this news you bring me great joy. I was very worried, wondering how we might be able to pray today if the servant Zvi Hirsch had not cleaned the shul, since cleanliness chases all the demons away and brings in pure air, so we can pray."

Loos's difficulties emerge, as we shall see, in the relationship between the image of the building and its interior, between Hans Karl's *Konversation-Konvention* and his holy ineffable. Function is the architect's business, simple functions, those that are possible to classify, according to the *Tractatus*, as the poverty of the utterable. The kitchen is utterable: the little kitchen in Casa Müller, for instance, small, narrow, practically a dining car. The staircase is utterable: like a stepladder on a boat. ("The ship is the model for a modern house.") The exterior, the façade, is utterable: its language should be the language of the street, of the square, of the city, in that infinite and variable chain of elements that no serious architect can ever dream of reinventing, constructing, defining, or reforming (that immortal, indecent *Selbstüberschätzung* of the architect/artist). But the house is not merely the utterable. With no dialectical bridge, it nevertheless exists and *becomes* the *intérieur*. It is pointless to pretend that the language of architecture is complete, that its word is definitive. Its word is powerless to measure experience, to foresee the future, to represent tone and gesture. All of which is concealed to the utterable in the utopian space of the *intérieur*. "The head of the household has an entire life ahead," in order to grow within and together with the house, and to put everything pleasing into place for the future. The architect should "make an empty space" within the house, in its interior. There is an article of faith about houses that will never be spoken in architecture, much less "resolved," that composition is powerless and the majesty of the artist is silence. "The bedroom, Lerle, is private and holy—no stranger can defile it."

And yet even this private Loos, a misfit, composed of quick jabs and unheard one-liners (the veins of the imperfect marble, its minimal, invisible depth, the classic quote about Haus Rufer) seeks finally to go beyond the limits of his own language. Hans Karl's marriage celebration is "haphazard" (in comparison with the paradoxical logic of the *Lustspiel*). Loos's urban pretension, his later projects for systematizing and ordering life according to values, is "haphazard" (in comparison with *Nihilismus-Haus*, with the unresolvable tension of interior with exterior). And the fall of Loos is far more strident and painful than Hofmannsthal's ephemeral decline. "Every man ought to have his own little house and his own garden. Rentals ought to be for commercial activity only. In England there are entire commercial neighborhoods, and the people live in cottages outside of town." Incredibly, the blind philistinism of an intellectual faced with a crowd reappears, a thousand miles this side of Nietzsche. It is philistinism that brought Wittgenstein to the point of disgust. It is the impossibility of any great intellectual of crisis, of any misfit who has ever known how to manage his life, seeing it through to the point of having it in retrospect, to tolerate the logic of the *Tractatus*. But to have foreseen it, and to have begun to write it down, is too much. "Wer gross denkt muss gross irren"—whoever thinks grandly must make grand mistakes.

Lou's Buttons

The reflective "stroll" that Lou Andreas-Salomé proposes in "Zum Typus Weib" begins with a story of buttons.[43] The buttons represent the quintessence of all that is "not given away but rather collected," the quintessence of the inalienable, of the non-equivalent. In this sense buttons are the opposite of coins: they oppose division, circulation, and exchange with the principle of the secret and the hidden. Coins exist exclusively in an external and public dimension. Buttons, on the other hand, are an unattainable maternal relic, kept in the innermost part of a virgin mountain. (Lou makes the association with the Jungfrau.) Coins are collected as values to be spent, and spending brings about in turn an acquisition, a possession. Buttons are put away as *unicum*, as treasure. Coins are intrinsically productive. They are never left out in the open, but they open things up in the sense that they carry everything into the domain of the merely acquirable. Coins turn all things into possessions. Buttons jealously guard their own unproductivity. They flee from sight and hide themselves as much as possible in a "box of wonders." It is easy to see how Lou connects univocal masculine aggressivity to the coin's productivity, as well as the unhappiness of man's "hurried step." The peculiar lingering of women at the original communion of spirit and sense (to whatever extent this image is increasingly "obscured" by the very progress of the spiritual, by the *Geist* considered in opposition to the *Seele*) seems to rest in the marginal, apparently derelict and in-significant figure of the button. Buttons represent the rest of pro-ductivity, all that remains and resists its typically constructive (*typ-isch aufbauend*) language. Resistance to the universe of equivalence takes on the form of reduction to the margins of insignificance.

How to collect buttons? And where to find them? Does the pos-sibility still exist for a "collection zone" removed from the market of visible things? This zone is interior, but not every interior can be a collection zone for that which survives in the unproductive. The difficulty of defining such a zone results from the fact that it must appear in relationship with the unhappiness of the productive, with the sacrifice that it entails. If this dimension were ignored or removed, the figure of the button would have to be relegated to a simply chronological past, to absolutely lost time, of which it would be false even to speak. If the childhood of buttons exists and works, it ought to appear in the here-and-now, in connection with the domain of coins, the market that trades and exchanges money, the street where it circulates. The "collection zone" should exist *in* the productivity of the metropolis. But how is this possible?

Lou does not get the most out of this problem, since the details of her buttons' childhood are unclear. She appears to believe that childhood can be preserved as such, that a "box of wonders" can protect childhood as childhood. But if buttons are not marginal-ized into small change by the metropolis, they are fetishistically transformed into closely guarded treasure, and they cease to exist as an authentic childhood. They return to being a possession, albeit an unproductive one. Unproductivity is not enough to "go be-yond" the language of the metropolis. Childhood must find its own interior within its relationship to the metropolis.

Not every interior is a "collection zone." Bad poetry (*Hei-matkunst*), for instance, that exalts home as protection from the metropolis is the opposite of a collection zone. The home wants to be seen as a treasure chest, but that very desire exhibits its own interior and makes it visible. What is brought out and made visible while pretending to be a place of non-equivalence is a travesty of the coin, not its opposite. And vice versa, the perfectly metropolitan home has no interior. It assumes programmatically that internal structure and arrangement are transparent, that they are clearly and simply understood in the vision of the whole. Between interior and exterior there is nothing but an insoluble functional bond. The metropolitan home (the building) correctly criticizes false childhood in the "box of wonders," while unknowingly representing its simple reverse, its exact counterpoint, in the space of *Modernität*. Even in that box, there is nothing hidden or secret. Its plan tends to the same pure visibility of the metropolitan home. That is why the treasure chest is truly nothing other than a tattoo image of the metropolis. Nothing more than its presence in the metropolitan fabric can render evident its intrinsic tendency to liquidate any possible collection zone.

An interior that protects buttons can only exist in a metropolis, and in absolute contrast with its exterior. The exterior should not betray the things collected in its interior. The exterior resides in the same dimension and sense as coins, should, in fact, be worth pure and perfect money, should *function* in the universe of circulation and trade. This universe should not be adorned, it should just work. If there is an authentic "collection zone," it can only be found within such a language, the unproductive flip side of the perfect coin. This is not to say that the exterior may be treated as a sort of obstacle or material impediment to *Seele*. On the contrary, the reified purity of the exterior is the very factor that permits an authentic interior. If the exterior were to be treated in allusive forms or were to be forced to indicate its interior metaphorically or, again, were to be understood as an obstacle, as not-I—if, that is, the awful late-Romantic ideology of the purpose of building were to prevail again, we would necessarily sink into ornament (which has its own a priori conditions in the dialectic of allusiveness). We would then conceive interiors as imperfect unless expressed, turned into language. It would be impossible to conceive any interior as childhood. There can be no interiors except where the exterior is felt purely and perfectly—studied, analyzed, calculated, and realized with maximum rigor in its own rhythm and relative to the rhythm of the metropolis. Only where the exterior is

adored the way Kraus adored language can another dimension of it
show up, as inalienable as it is unproductive, an *internal* childhood
of language. That is why the "collection zone" is not exactly the
"poetic ensemble" of interior and exterior (the "box of wonders")
or the harmony of the two, but neither is it simply the interior in
and of itself. The "collection zone" is the *difference* between interior
and exterior—this impalpable *utopia* that separates them meta-
physically at the same time that it renders them inseparable.

It is so difficult to understand these rambles that Loos can still
pass for a pioneer and prophet of modernity, while the calculated
perfection of his exteriors is a Krausian *pietas* for language, stripped
of the totalizing and patriarchal ethics of *Die Fackel,* intent upon
reducing things to the transparence of linguistic order. The exterior
of the possible "collection zone" is pure language, charged with its
history, with its difficult links, with its inertia that requires such
tireless patience, but not transparence. Certainly there is nothing
(like a shop sign) to indicate from the exterior that there is an in-
terior to this language. But neither should anything indicate that
there is not, as happens with the treasure chest, with allusive or-
nament, or with the "virile statements" of happily metropolitan
buildings. This exterior does not express, does not produce, has no
transparence. And for these very reasons it can perhaps safeguard
an interior, an authentic "collection zone." It "leaves room," so to
speak, for the possibility of an interior.

This matter of Loos "leaving room" for a "collection zone" in
the midst of (coolly recognized) "metropolis" conditions and his
concern for the possibility of such a place, without nostalgia for
the impossible negation of the exterior—this could be called Loos's
deeply feminine side. In the interior of his house (now, alas, "visi-
ble" only at the Museum of the City of Vienna) all of this is made
clear, even formally. But this is not the essence. The essence is the
gulf of difference carved out between exterior and interior, not the
formal solution discovered in the composition of one or the other.
This gulf is the secret of Loos's house: the measure of this differ-
ence is the measure of Loos's concern for Lou's buttons, that they
should have a place outside of the treasure chest.

In a fine passage, Eugénie Lemoine-Luccioni writes of the "intimate bond between a woman and her things." Without things, women are lost. Their things inhabit an interior, and they cannot be transformed into coins. The house where they are collected should be inhabitable, not visible from the exterior. The act of seeing a house is fundamentally different from dwelling in it. To define the possibility of dwelling in a house by this difference and not abstractly in and of itself, as if dealing with a question of style or furniture, is, I would say, Loos's feminine greatness. He is concerned with a space where things are safe in their intimate associations with our experience, where things are infused with those *Extrakte des Lebens* that form life's experience. To continue in Altenberg's line, such things are invalid for going out and producing, but they are not therefore a literary protest against metropolis, technology, and *Zivilisation*. In fact, the retreat into the interior means perhaps that the world is by now "simply full of things (an indefinite plural"; Lemoine-Luccioni) or, in other words, that things are by now only perfectly manipulable, alienable, destitute of any consistency, and separated from Being. These things merely exist, are seen, are spoken about. The things that Andreas-Salomé mentions hearken, rather, to a forgotten dimension of dwelling and of experience connected to dwelling. The difference in Loos between seeing and dwelling, between exterior and interior, seeks to provide a space where this dimension can be collected. This difference is the *extreme interior*.

Rilke's dolls stand metaphysically opposite the soul of Lou's things.[44] Impenetrable, rumpled, damaged, impure, "privy to the earliest unutterable experiences of their owners," and even mistreated in some of those first unquiet moments of solitude, the dolls surrender to every tenderness, yet they remember none and are grateful for none. If now we take up a doll "from the cumulus of things that have become part of us," it practically revolts us with its "crass dearth of memory," its disproportionate lack of imagination. We are disconcerted by the sight of this "horrifying alien body, to whom we have given over our most genuine warmth." We wouldn't have traded that senseless bundle of material for anything, heavy and dumb, "stupid as a peasant Danae who is insignificant except for the golden rain of our unending inventions." Lou's buttons resemble rather "things that are part of us"—not only the flash of gems, but also domestic linens, the fingering of a violin, the most simple things that sink their roots in humanity: the "simple and condescending" soul of a ball, the inexhaustible soul of a picture book, the "surd, funnel-shaped soul of a bold tin horn." These are the things that aspire to the otherness of the interior and that render an interior necessary. The doll inhabits places of oblivion, remote hiding places, and when it re-emerges by chance, then our hatred for it erupts, unconsciously developed in the long hours in which we sat with it and pointlessly waited for a response.

The unresponsive doll still does not pass by in vain. Not only and not so much because "we had to have things like that, things which put up no resistance," but because the doll teaches us silence, "life's greatest silence, that always reappeared in our breathing, every time and in every place where we came to the edges of our existence" (*unseres Daseins*). The doll teaches us to recognize the soul's inclination, left over from childhood, toward all that is impossible and hopeless. The doll's absolute lack of imagination points out the silence that envelops us. And in this perspective, the doll's affinities with Lou's buttons emerge once again. The objects without which women seem lost are at once "things that are part of us" and dolls: Lou's buttons respond to the overflowing affection that cares for them, defines a dwelling. That affection points out the silence that this dwelling embraces and points out the soul's unstoppable inclination toward its own abyss. That is why the space of Lou's buttons resembles the hidden and forgotten space of the dolls. Something like the essence of the dolls is preserved in Lou's buttons.

At the crossroads where a doll's silence brings on an awareness of language in the dimension of "things that are part of us" and where those "things that are part of us" not only return our affections but also reveal their metaphysical tendency to silence—that is where the soul of the marionette appears to take shape. "Dolls are as inferior to things as marionettes are superior to them." "A poet can fall under the spell of a marionette, because a marionette has nothing but imagination." But a marionette's imagination is not simply the quintessence of "things that are part of us." It compels us to pose our inclination "beyond hope." The marionette is not the pure and simple negation of the doll, just as Lou's buttons were not.

This quality "beyond hoping" had already been indicated by Kleist: to find the "brightest and most majestic" grace after having traversed infinite consciousness, infinite reflection. The totally unconscious grace of marionettes seemed to Kleist characteristic of a utopian grace available only after having tasted anew the fruit of the tree of knowledge. This no-place is where the marionette is hooked. The strings that animate it are like the long staircase the gods used to descend in order to speak with humans. A bridge that to us seems rickety is mysteriously solid for the marionette. Kleist's nostalgia for marionettes is the nostalgia of the figure Plato speaks of in the *Laws*, who is still "intertwined" with the cosmos, an ensemble of threads and interior strands that the gods use to pull him and drive him. Marionettes keep the memory of the golden chain that unified the universe with insoluble bonds.[45] Dolls have lost this memory completely. Dolls, in fact, are characterized precisely by their state of dejection, of collapse, of radical historicity. But since the marionette is a utopia today, to rediscover its figure is possible only by filling up the absolute void of the doll's silence with nostalgia. If such a void were not formed in us since childhood, the marionette's quality "beyond hoping" would not have been able to appear.

Klee's work is interlaced with these fleeting relationships between coin, "things that are part of us," buttons, dolls, and marionettes. Difficult affinities, paradoxical theophanies, ephemeral orders of movement and flight express themselves in these relationships. The figure of the Angel seems to sum them up and keep them within itself. Its gaze is turned upon these things. It has to compose them and put them in order so that it can save their essence from imminent fragmentation and contradiction. The angel of *things* intuits the necessity of the process that leads from the soul in simple conversation with "things that are part of us" to naming, finally, the empty silence of the doll and from there to the divine figure of the marionette. The angel prevents the marionette from collapsing, as Hofmannsthal understood on that December evening in 1918 of which Burckhardt tells us. It prevents the marionette from retreating into an unutterable past. Klee's figures, Benjamin wrote, "are, so to speak, projected onto the drawing surface, and as a good car, even in the factory, obeys the necessity of the motor above all, so Klee's figures obey, in the expression of their forms, their 'interior' above all." So, these figures are essentially marionettes. The angel is the prince of marionettes. Loos's interiors would seem to be designed for such figures. In the compositional clarity and economy of these interiors, everything achieved through greatest exercise is made to appear natural and necessary. At the end of the road that brought us from coins to marionettes, we must try to imagine the pose of the latter, as if we had discovered it by good luck.

The Glass Chain

At the beginning of *Infanzia e storia*—a work I frequently refer to—Giorgio Agamben analyzes Walter Benjamin's extraordinary short essay of 1933, "Experience and Poverty."[46] The decline of experience or its current poverty (which, according to Agamben, the various philosophies of life affirm rather than refute) finds its exemplum in the presence of the "modern movement" in architecture. Functional architecture of "glass and steel" represents the programmatic liquidation of the very conditions of experience. Its stated goal is to make it impossible to leave a trace, to produce a hidden place, to macro-visualize the house as a mere edifice—not only its individual physical structure, but its relationship with the entire urban organization. For this idea of "pure transparence," glass is the building material par excellence, the prince of materials. Glass is the very principle of transparence. Benjamin quotes Paul Scheerbart, saying, "we can well speak of a *Glaskultur*. The new environment of glass will completely transform humanity. And one can only hope that the new civilization of glass will not run into too much opposition."

But glass is not merely, as Benjamin seems to believe, the enemy of all "auras." It attacks the very idea of interior. That is why Loos can never be confused, from any perspective, with Scheerbart's *Glaskultur*. Glass is only indirectly opposed to ownership. The essential objective of its *Kultur* consists in opposing whatever underlies a place where a "collection" becomes one's own inalienable experience. Glass is not opposed to ownership per se, but to the idea of an *inalienable* ownership. Displaying every possession, glass wants to turn it all to coin, to put it all on the market. *Glaskultur*'s critique of ownership follows the lines of circulation and exchange exclusively. The uninterrupted flow of stimuli and insights in the glass and steel metropolis, the continuous "enrichment" of "spiritual" life,[47] profanes more than the ancient "aura." It desecrates the very possibility of experience. It brings out the poverty of experience. In a universal transparence, all things are assumed to be equivalent. The transparence of glass bares every interior, betraying it and delivering it to the equivalence of the passerby whose mourning dress Baudelaire sang about (in "A une passante"). This is the source of the names with no past in Scheerbart's novels, his "completely new creatures" (Benjamin), with their radical lack of an interior. These characters live in the open, but like Hofmannsthal's No Names, they are prisoners of Olivier's disenchantment.

We know that Loos's interiors are far from that plush furniture that even Benjamin seems to foist on him. An interior by Loos expresses a principle contrary to a nostalgic resistance to current developments, on the grounds of his energetic acceptance of the age, the visible sign in any society of its "best and brightest." From this point of departure, though, it is possible to render transparent the "aura" that is still dominant in *Glaskultur* and in its rhetoric of modernity. *Glaskultur* passes a death sentence over past experience. Its windows *reflect* current poverty. In spite of its gesture toward the avant-garde, which rejects inherited language and remains aware of its arbitrary (and not organic) structure, *Glaskultur* belongs to a perfectly logocentric civilization. Its will to bare, "demystify," and render everything transparent expresses a utopia of full, progressive identification between human and linguistic realms: every secret is told, every interior shown, every childhood exposed. Here language, and the power of language, is absolute. Its new ability to form free constructions is precisely what permits it to take full command of the subject/self. Freed finally even from the *intentio* of subject, language speaks, grows, and transforms itself. Man is the animal that language possesses, but it is a language of transparence, exposition, and production. It is a language of technology. It means concluding the very metaphysics of the self that says, "I think . . . " *Glaskultur* is only one of the forms such a conclusion may assume.

To *criticize* the limits of this power fails to express the powerlessness to endure it, but expresses rather the desire to traverse it and to manifest its organic ties to current poverty. *Glaskultur* uses every means it can to mystify its part in the current poverty. Consider Bruno Taut, who is broadly influenced by Scheerbart. When he illustrates his *Glashaus*, a model or platonic form of the glass house exhibited at Cologne in 1914, he speaks of a kaleidoscopically rich architecture, varied and fascinating. The principle of glass is here embellished and gilt with every word. Even the connection between intensity of urban stimulation and poverty of experience, highly present in Georg Simmel, vanishes. Every effort is made to harmonize the irresistible surge of *Glaskultur* with nostalgia for the soul and *Erlebnis*. Loss of experience is cosmogonically sublimated in that ingenuous facsimile of an alchemical experiment, the collection of drawings, dedicated to the spirit of Scheerbart, of *Der Weltbaumeister* (1920). Through successive operations of *separatio* and *coniunctio*, the perfect crystal for a house gleams in the light of the summer sun and to the singing of children, *das leuchtende Kristalhaus* [the glowing house of crystal]. The stone reveals its wonders. Here the principle of glass, far from being treated (as Benjamin believed) completely without illusions, presumes to disclose the quintessence of an interior. But the glass does not possess an interior to exhibit and therefore has none to negate in the absolute command of language. The interior that its word seems to magically produce is nothing but, again, "*blitzendes Glas*": the glass that reproduces its own sterile image. It reflects its own reflection. Lost experience is replaced with every wretched pan-cosmic *cupio dissolvi* of the individual and finite form. This is nothing but a road traveled in order to reach the point of departure: a chain of glass.

It must be added that glass has a totally different value in Mies van der Rohe, and that Benjamin should have turned to Mies, not to Scheerbart. Mies's transparence is total because it is born from the exact and truly desperate awareness that there is nothing left to "collect" and, therefore, nothing to make manifest. Glass no longer violates the interior, but appears, now, as a ghost of itself. Its function has become as "archaic" as the very thing it helped to destroy. Is this decree, which finally finds an exact definition in Mies, also applicable to the problem that captivates Loos? Where glass plays a fundamentally structural role, as in the American Bar for example, it reflects and multiplies an interior. It doesn't disclose an interior. It is as un-transparent as a smooth and precious plate of marble. Loos's tireless efforts to find ever more delicate and subtle marble plate clearly demonstrate how he was inclined to replace the principle of glass. The glass interior of the American Bar does not say that experience takes place there, and it does not emphasize the surrounding space as if it were a rediscovered treasure chest. Nor does it produce it in language—although it holds back its possible development. Glass dilates the interior into a long pause, into an enduring delay. In this delay the interior reflects itself in its *otherness* and reflects upon a possible zone for experience in a possible not-yet. It is indecent to pursue in reverse the no-more of experience, but it is just as indecent to declare that everything is just glass and steel. The possible does not advertise itself, does not shout, does not even leak a rumor. But perhaps it gives a meaning to silence and collection while waiting.

Invalid des Todes

Joseph Roth hated *Glaskultur* and understood the current poverty of experience. The complete uprooting of the very possibility of a zone of experience is Roth's great theme.

Roth's *Heimat* [native land] is a vast interior, an unconfined zone of experience, where the Hapsburg Viennese interior extends without breaking continuity through the line of Czechs, Slovenians, and Poles, to find its alter-ego in the shtetl of *Ostjudentum* [East European Jewish culture]. *Heimat* is feminine, as is interior. Its surrender (Claudio Magris insists on this "category")[48] is, basically, a surrender of any possible return (*Heimkehr*) to conditions of experience.

This zone of experience is not German. German experience is *Glaskultur* and avant-garde. "Only our Germans, the ethnic majority, betrayed Alpine dolts and Sudeten Bohemians and Nibelungen cretins," exclaimed Count Chojnicki in *The Emperor's Tomb*.[49] They razed Sipolje, empire and shtetl, every *Heimat*, to the ground. Austria's soul stayed at the outskirts. Loos believed God is in the details, and that is why there are *no* details. The soul of Austria was "collected" by the Jews in Boryslav caftans, by the horse dealers of Baksha, by the Muslims from Sarajevo, by chestnut vendors from Mostar. It was loud hillbillies from the Alps that sang "Watch on the Rhine." And they won. The empire was an enormous interior with extraordinary detail, an infinite number of people capable of having possessions, bound to the inalienable right to possess their own things. But these things were destroyed forever—and the details, now, are fragments, meaningless shards, neutral material for collage.

Thus fade the Viennese nights, leaving us in cruel play between surrender and unquenchable desire. In the wake of the old capital city comes the essence of metropolis, that "turns the earth into asphalt, walls, and bricks," that "without doubt" raises a province around itself "only to devour it in a day." There are places for passersby and for coins: theater, market, art, commerce, cinema, subway. The world is already consolidated "to the point that even editorial pages could be revolutionary." This is the world where the lost and superfluous end up, as well as everyone who survived the death of experience. The act of holding nostalgia for ransom sometimes tears through Roth. It is precisely this awareness of having survived, inflexible against oneself in speaking nothing about the no-longer and hoping nothing for the not-yet. Franz Tunda goes all over Europe, has meetings, speaks many languages; even Trotta in *The Emperor's Tomb* is full of events; and Mendel Singer is assaulted by the same weakened destiny. None of this is experience, though. It is the negation of experience. Their world is everything that is the case. That these characters take part in it does not change nature. *Flight Without End* is an endless flight from experience, not through experiences but through mere cases that negate the very possibility of experience. Experience takes place before the story begins. The story (or narrative) is singularly the account of the death of experience. It is the account of cases that drag the survivors (that have been judged *unfit unto death*) into experience. Peter Altenberg's "Invalid des Lebens" finds its fundamental sense in the "Invalid des Todes."

Read in this way, the conclusion of *Job* does not appear consolatory in the least. Whoever has been judged unfit to die (together with their interior at their own *Heimat*) is obliged to be swirled through events persecuted by the case and by things (in the indefinite plural). Only by "greatness of miracles" can everything be regained. The conclusion of *Job* is the rigorous negation of all happy endings. Far from home, the shtetl gone, *only by a miracle* can the child conceivably be found. No story, no narration can emerge from this encounter. The story is only about the diaspora and about exile from the very sites of the diaspora. The miracle that connects to experience shows only itself. Seen in the equivocal light of the biggest metropolis, it is unutterable. That is why not even the most painful nostalgia reveals itself in language. Experience is not to be spoken. It was before, and it can come back again, but only by *striking* like a miracle. Certainly it can only come back to overwhelm those who had lived it before. And therefore the disappearance of these inhabitants (which already do not include Tunda or Trotta or Kargan) is the disappearance of the very possibility of miracles.

Chojnicki appears to maintain ties to experience. He is a profoundly good and spiritual figure, like the figure of that friend of Loos and Kraus, Ludwig von Janikowski, who left no written work, but is known through the impressive portrait of him by Oscar Kokoschka. The "young friends" are too fragile in their modernity to recognize the cavernous wealth of these figures. Trotta's mother, too, has certainly passed through experience, but without being able at all to communicate it to her son, except as nostalgia and surrender. "What a great deal this mother must have undergone and read," thinks Trotta. His interior cannot even resist the transparence, and his house is turned into a pension. Among the guests, there is a typical exponent of *Glaskultur*, Elisabeth, Trotta's fortuitous wife. She works in the "applied arts" with a "new" woman whose name Trotta's mother cannot pronounce (her name is "inhuman," like those of Scheerbart's heroes). The art of *Modernität*, of the original and functional, of simplicity opposed to Wittgenstein's *Klarheit*, inexorably occupies every interior. Both Loos and Roth are too far from Mendel Singer to be able to wait for miracles.

Roth's characters are incapable of experience and incapable of sharing death. They fruitlessly reflect on their demise or search in vain to exceed it by mistaken or interrupted pathways (like Kargan). Does this circle enclose them in a "perfect" way? Or can survival itself, in its apparent superfluousness, preserve the possible, collect a meaning? Can one listen to an unpossessed silence that is not experience but that is open to the possibility of experience, by living with its death? Can this be done without betraying it into ornaments and images and by repeating the radical difference between interior and exterior? Can this be done by forbidding the exterior from assuming the value of a unique Logos, by going into exile without wanting to "co-exist" in the various countries and languages? The souls of those whose throats were slit in the name of the Gospel are dressed in white and are told to wait "for the quota of their families and comrades who must be put to death with them." It is an unpossessed silence that is not experience, but a condition, today, of an extreme possibility of experience. The last pages of Musil's novel are alive to this concern. So, perhaps, are the last pages of the *Tractatus*, sober as they are on the surface.

Figure 1 The Church of St. Leopold at Steinhof, Vienna.

Figure 2 Alfred Kubin, *Unglücks Vögel* [Birds of bad luck].

Figure 3 Alfred Kubin, *Madame Mors*.

Figure 4 Alfred Kubin, *Sumpfpflanzen* [Swamp flowers].

Figure 5 Alfred Kubin, *Rübezahl II*.

Figure 6 Max Klinger, *Centaur mit Wäscherinnen*
[Centaur with launderers].

Figure 7 Max Klinger, *Verfolgter Centaur*
[Centaur pursued].

Figure 9 Max Klinger, *Gesandschaft* [The ambassador].

Figure 8 *(left)* Max Klinger, *Bär und Elfe* [Bear and fairy].

Figure 10 Arnold Böcklin, *Melancholia.*

Figure 11 Alfred Kubin, *Die Haarschleppe* [The train of hair].

Figure 12 Alfred Kubin, *Das Gezücht* [The brood].

Figure 13 Alfred Kubin, *Die Spinne* [The spider].

Figure 14 Max Klinger, *Tote Mutter* [Dead mother].

Figure 15 Egon Schiele, *Liebespaar* [Loving couple].

Figure 16 Egon Schiele, *Häuser und Föhren* [Houses and pines].

On the Mystical
Again

Giorgio Agamben writes, "Experience is this: people are born without speech. They were once and are ever in-fants (from Latin, 'without speech')." Infancy is the arch-limit of language. Its expropriation by language is never complete and must be repeated constantly. For Agamben, the mystical in Wittgenstein would be such an arch-limit, permitting a correct definition of language. For others, though (such as for Gianni Baget-Bozzo, who confronts the problem in the strictly theological frame of the speech or silence of God), the ineffable in Wittgenstein would itself be seen as an effect of language, defined as a cardinal function of a decree that, developed, might sound like this: "I say: I (here) am silent."[50] The possibility of transgression is in the very essence of the decree. How might the possibility of transgression be conceived?

Let us look again at the final propositions of the *Tractatus*. Nothing can be spoken but *Sätze der Naturwissenschaft*, "propositions of natural science—that is, something that has nothing to do with philosophy" (*Tractatus* 6.53). The "true method" of philosophy would consist in making it vanish, just as the problem of life is resolved when it vanishes (when one understands that formulating it is impossible, that it is not a question). Yet we feel (*wir fühlen*), even when every possible question has an answer, that the problems of life remain untouched. The ineffable belongs to this dimension, where the problem cannot be articulated in the lin-

97

guistic domain of the question. Baget-Bozzo calls this concept of the ineffable "ingenuous." Agamben, however, calls it an image of infant speechlessness that transcendentally accompanies language (because of which humans cannot be reduced to a glass chain of questions and answers). One sees in the ineffable the simple negative of language; the other sees its transcendental origin. In both cases, Wittgenstein's last propositions would become perfectly clear, and the problem gripping us would vanish.

Wittgenstein's text confirms without a doubt that: (1) since there can be in language only what there is in the world, the limits of language are not an enigma; (2) the true method of philosophy consists in demonstrating how certain meanings correspond to certain sounds and in making the rest vanish (that is, "the problems of life"); (3) all that can be spoken are "propositions of natural science"—but it establishes that, at the same time, (4) none of this takes an Enlightenment form of progress capable of slowly abolishing the ineffable. The ineffable *remains*. "Es gibt allerdings Unaussprechlices." The "allerdings" presupposes an adversative that must be made clear in the translation: "There are, *indeed*, things that cannot be put into words." The ineffable cannot be said, cannot be shown (which is perfectly obvious); the form of its expression cannot be linguistic—and yet there it is. It happens. The mystical is the form of its being there. Put more precisely, ineffable things appear: "They make themselves manifest." The accent falls here, and not on the "trivial" fact that the unutterable cannot be spoken or that there is a dimension of human existence that cannot be reached or penetrated by the language of equivalent propositions. Wittgenstein does not characterize the ineffable as negative—not at all. He says that things that cannot be put into words make themselves manifest. Theirs is the plane of epiphany, which is the mystical.

Epiphany is recognizable. To understand it requires a true "intensity of recognition" that Baget-Bozzo and Benvenuto find in Saint Augustine. (Not by chance is Augustine a primary influence on Wittgenstein.) This recognition cannot be communicated or demonstrated in language. It can, however, be shown. Wittgenstein does not deny that after a long period of doubt, "the sense of life" may become clear. He, like Roth, does not proclaim miracles to be impossible. He limits himself, rather, to asserting that there is no way to say it. For Augustine, too, the ineffable is that which cannot be expressed or said, but of which one must nevertheless forever speak. Wittgenstein glosses Augustine listening to silence: the only possible way to unsilence the ineffable is to recognize its manifestation. This is the *implicit* "transgression" in Wittgenstein's declaration (apparently contained in the final proposition) that gives him complete mastery over his limits.

There is no room in Wittgenstein for an ingenuous and all-encompassing idea of what can be spoken. But neither does Wittgenstein balance what can be spoken against silence "for the sake of symmetry and negation" (Baget-Bozzo and Benvenuto). The ineffable cannot be understood simply as the silence that accompanies and transcendentally limits every proposition, the silence that binds speechlessness, truth, and language in a "founding relationship" (Agamben). This reading, if it cancels all "mysticism," does not capture the *autonomy* of Wittgenstein's dimension of the ineffable or the problematic possibility that it can exceed the limits of that relationship. A linear connection between the dimension of the mystical and the questions that we feel we cannot "sensibly" ask, the doubts that persist even where there are no questions, the enigma "*outside* space and time," is far from evident. The mystical is the dimension of self-manifestation and of the "intensity of recognition" that invests it.

So the mystical is not understood as an otherworldly dimension, above the plane of the utterable and its propositions. Having thrown out the scale we used to measure the "correct method in philosophy" (in Wittgenstein's paradoxical philosophy), a new Kingdom of the Mystical does not appear. Had it been so, we would still understand the mystical in terms of the ex-static, the sublime, as the way over the poverty of experience. Agamben is right. The mystical inexorably accompanies the utterable. But it does so in a dimension other than that of the utterable itself, in contrast with it: as manifestation. That which manifests itself is not spoken, is not produced by saying. It is the premise of speech. As speakers, we are ever mere in-fants. We exist prior to the dimension of manifestation, before that which manifests itself, before the premise, the presupposed. The premise is not the "sublime." It means: that the world exists, and the world is a defined, limited whole.

The mystical in Wittgenstein cannot be understood in a generally esoteric or gnostic sense. It does not indicate a plane of occult knowledge—as if most of the *Tractatus* had addressed the profane and it now alluded to the initiate's silence. The mystical manifests itself. Therefore, it is not obscure. The ineffable is a presence, and it is the premise of speech. It is an open area: it manifests itself. We cannot indicate any hidden parts: it manifests itself simply and entirely. Not by accident does this self-manifestation remind us so much of *aletheia* [unconcealment]. The language of equivalence radically obscures the problem of *aletheia*, since it essentially pursues the cancellation of the premise. Wittgenstein reactivates the problem with a gesture of classical *Klarheit* destined to leave its mark on every new, authentic thought. He defines the metaphysical limits and essential historicity of the language of equivalence. On the one hand, there are equivalent propositions, where *aletheia* is not a factor; on the other hand, there is self-manifestation as an area of unconcealing, not reducible to speech. It is an area that is not "beyond" the utterable, nor is it an object of all-knowing awareness or a negative of language or its mere transcendental arch-limit. It is an area about which there can be no declaration at all, about which it is necessary to be silent—yet its existence is certain because it manifests itself. It manifests itself; it does *not* declare itself. The utterable cannot reach any premise or unconcealedness, because the utterable is merely productive. It cannot negate the premise and its unconcealedness, because, if it could, these things would become fully utterable, since negation is nothing other than a form of the utterable. Therefore the mystical holds out as absolute difference along with language. It is as powerless to exhaust or go beyond language as language is able to declare its absence.

If the dimension of the mystical as self-manifestation resembles the problem of *aletheia*, then it recalls Franz Rosenzweig's *Offenbarung*.[51] Self-manifestation, as a premise, is revelation—becoming clear and open. There is what is shown, what shows itself. Philosophy's mission and destiny is to eliminate this premise, *das Gesetz*. To represent the problem of *aletheia* means to take account of philosophy's entire mission and destiny as the problem: to define its metaphysical limits. Yet it is absurd to wait for the philosophical logos to "naturally" encounter the "problem" par excellence, which is the manifestation of the prelinguistic premise—because it exceeds the limits of productivity of the logos. It would no longer be a manifestation if it were to derive dialectically from the rungs of philosophy or if it were to wait for its culmination. The manifestation can come as a surprise anywhere, because the problem (*aletheia*, the prelinguistic premise) can return anywhere, in spite of any prior declaration and any *Selbstüberschätzung* of language. Language that sustains such *faith* in itself as to make believe it has resolved every premise is intrinsically contradictory. It turns its own equivalence into a value: idolatry.

Is there a possibility of experience in the labyrinth of these relationships? In the pauses, perhaps, that divide and interconnect the crossing of the philosophical ladder with the manifestation of the unutterable; in language radically critiqued in all the instances declaring the speechlessness that accompanies language, yet open to the problem of the prelinguistic premise, *Offenbarung*'s "surprise" of the premise. In this circle there is perhaps the word that "exceeds" the chain of glass, the place where the possibility of experience has withdrawn. Neither the when nor the how of the not-yet can ever be spoken. But in the manifestation of the mystical there lives the near-memory of the premise, and the intensity of its recognition for a moment seems truly to interrupt the nihilism of the logos.

Abendland

The intersection of the lines of Rosenzweig and Heidegger at their point of origin, in Wittgenstein, leads to that area of Georg Trakl's poetry about which Heidegger wrote a definitive essay.[52]

In his Opus 22, Schoenberg resumes a dialogue with Rilke that he had begun with Stefan George. But he never met Trakl, who instead became Webern's favorite poet. The territory where the manifestation of the unutterable is already a first step toward the not-yet-said, where the thought of the crisis attains complete *Klarheit*, seeking new possible orders of language not only internally but also in the very speechlessness of language and the words that surpass it—this is Trakl's territory and the zone of Heidegger's *Erörterung* [discussion] of Wittgenstein's "too deep" and distant friend.

Heidegger's essay is definitive because the "site" that it indicates for Trakl's poetry is the same for the problem of the general condition of contemporary humanity. It casts a direct light on the entire Heideggerian interpretation of contemporary fate. The discussion focuses on the poem "Frühling der Seele." The soul is called *ein Fremdes* on the earth: a stranger. But being strange implies being a stranger in transit, passing through on the way to somewhere else. The word has the same etymological derivation as the English "pilgrim": one who journeys in foreign lands. Being a stranger means to seek one's own place, a homeland. It means going to a calm, secure home. "The soul seeks the earth, it does not flee it." The soul wants to spend time on earth, to save the earth as earth. In Rilke the journeying soul, the stranger, describes things by name; in Trakl it describes the continuous metamorphoses of nature, the play of its colors, and the sounds that surprise us and take hold of us—the foundational Being, independent of our "measures," of the premise. To feel the thing itself anew in the name as foundational Being, to free it from its common dailiness, to rediscover in it the magic relationship with the world—this is the poetry of the soul, *ein Fremdes* on earth.

The soul shows its own going, its own state of being away from home, to the "rational animal," to the human who is not yet "fixed" in the security of true being, to the "blue wild game" of the last stanza of Trakl's poem, "Summer's End." The "blue wild game" can become aware of being away from home only by listening to the voice of the estranged soul. Then, the very person becomes *ein Fremdes, ein Einsames,* a solitary loner who abandons his own already decomposed form and is changed into the form of the departed (*der Abgeschiedene*). The blue game animal who is open to listening reaches the place of departure, and this site signals the unity, for Heidegger, of Trakl's poem. But where is it departing to? The soul calls out to abandon its earlier form, calls out to death that divides it off but does not signify the end. "The dead one lives in his grave": "The end—being the end of the decaying kind—precedes the beginning of the unborn kind." Heraclitus assumes the departure is all spirit and fire, "burning flame of the spirit," which leaps off the stump consumed in fire. In Nietzsche's eternal return, the "dark wandering of the soul" takes mortals back to their origin, to that which has been, to the "primordial dawn of day." Thus Heidegger interprets the death of Elis as preparing the "future awakening," "der sanfte Gesang des Bruders am Abendhügel" ("the gentle song of the brother by the evening hill"),

> die kühle Blaue und die leuchtende Neige des Herbstes,
> das stille Haus und die Sagen des Waldes,

Mass und Gesetz und die mondenen Pfade der
   Abgeschiedenen

the frozen blue and the shining descent of autumn
the motionless house and the legends of the woods,
Measure and Law and the lunar paths of the departed

that revolve around the "patience" at the end of the "Song of the
Departed." The death of Elis, the blue wild game kept apart and
departed, connects to the speechless measure of the prelinguistic
premise, of *Gesetz.*

   The one who tends-toward, who sets oneself apart and gathers
all the pain aroused by the spirit-flame leaping to its death off the
stock (" 'flaming' pain tears away"), is a *Wahnsinnige*, a madman.
He listens to the soul, the stranger, and feeds on "a mighty agony,
the grandsons yet unborn" ("Grodek"). Through his own death,
his own departure, the madman passes to the dawning of the ori-
gin and invites his brother to follow him. This motif of Heideg-
ger's *Erörterung* harks back to Wagner's *Parsifal.* That hero's name,
Parsi-fal, also signifies *pure madness*, and he inhabits a realm of
apartness. From his very first appearance, he has no shared memo-
ries. He comes from "caverns of silence." He is the unborn. More
than abstention (the plane of Parsifal in the mystifying interpreta-
tions à la Bayreuth is not apartness, but abstention), his is the
realm of strangeness. Parsifal is *ein Fremdes auf Erde.* The way of
the unborn does not pass *through* "gloomy towns, . . . lonely sum-
mers" ("Stundenlied"), but only *past* them. And like Trakl's soul,
Parsifal also calls mortals to follow him, and he carries them, upon
"the sweet wings" of his madness, to the fatherland, to the "home"
that Wagner intends in the sense of "sublime" redemption, of an
inside knowledge. Heidegger, in the style of Nietzsche, intends
"home" in the sense of the earth and of the redemption of the
earth—of the foundational ground, the earth of Heraclitus, that
perhaps breaks through in the finale of Mahler's Second Sym-
phony.

   Heidegger names this earth *Abendland* (the land of twilight, the
west), this earth that "consents to be lived in," to which the soul

calls, to which madness holds us, this earth that the death of Elis keeps for the unborn. It is an older western world, "which is to say, earlier and therefore more promising than the Platonic-Christian land, or indeed than a land conceived in terms of the European West. . . . The land of descent is the transition into the beginning of the dawn concealed within it": going toward the twilight of the soul is not therefore a simple self-dissolving, but a return to the yet unrevealed land, not simple decline or ruin (*Decline of the West!*), but "der süsse Gesang der Auferstandenen" ("Abendländisches Lied"), "the gentle song of the revived." Only in the twilight (on earth, which is the land of twilight) is the possible still unrevealed, that is, the possible revelation, its manifestation, which is now unrevealed. That is why the madman heads toward twilight. He seems mad because he tears away toward death. But only where the sun shines can there be a way through to the sweet song of the dawning day, of the revived. Through the silence of Parsifal's road, in the dark caverns of the more silent people, these lines are composed: "aus harten Metallen das erlösende Haupt," "the captain is called to redemption from strong metals" ("To the Silenced").

Why is Heidegger's *Erörterung* crucial? Because it reinterprets the entire course of Trakl's lyrics as the destiny of contemporary lyric poetry. Lyric cannot be understood only in Benjamin's terms of urban dilation of intellect, much less as thinking of decline and ruin, but rather as the plane in which the road through a radical poverty of experience intersects thinking on the eternal return. This interpretation unhinges the traditional "pessimistic" visions of contemporary lyric and captures the epochal meaning of its "hermetic" spirituality. This interpretation is also crucial because it locates the home of the *Wahnsinnige* in thinking about the *Abendland.* Here the madman can speak to the angel again, be surprised at it and at peace with it. Contemporary lyric takes the form, therefore, of language on humanity's *historical* condition (*Geschichte,* not *Historie*). It takes the form of language on a time that does not know the future as a "simple extension of the present," the only future, in fact, that Europe knows (Europe, not *Abendland*). Trakl's lyrics would be the place for a reversal of Western metaphysics, or better, for its going mad, a reversal that could create the void in us for hearing "the gentle song of the revived."

Is Trakl the only one to say this? Heidegger's Trakl is articulate under the sign of Heidegger's reading of the rapport between Heraclitus and Nietzsche, which assumes here the appearance of a Parsifal revisited and even, as we shall see, of Otto Weininger. Heidegger re-systematizes Trakl; he turns him into discourse. Trakl's deep and fundamental enigma passes through Heidegger's interpretive net. Heidegger takes on what the lyrics *say* as a problem, not the relationship between this "what" and the song itself, the "who" of the song.

The song is not, indeed, the song of the soul, of the stranger, nor is it the song of the *Wahnsinnige* dying to follow it. It is the song of the soul's brother, of its friend. The soul takes its leave, as in Mahler's *Der Abschied*, but it creates silence in this leave-taking. The music that is still heard is the song of those who are left behind. The brother and friend of the stranger are left behind. They do not know how to detach themselves. This is Trakl's tragic aporia, as it is Rilke's, and it seems to have escaped Heidegger's notice: the poem or song is not the word of the departed, the word that names foundational Being, that intuits its return, that saves the earth. The language of the Heraclitean poem is impossible for Trakl. Its singer is none other than the friend. But the friend is precisely the plane from which *ein Fremdes* takes leave and departs. The friend sings of this departure, but can only be its witness. The friend knows that departure, this twilight, is neither ruin nor pessimistic decadence, but a going-toward, a seeking. Yet, what is sought cannot be intuited through song. Poetry will never be in its presence, because poetry flows from the friend who remains behind, not from the stranger who tends-toward. The poet hears and re-states "the spirit's euphoria in departure." The poet participates in departure, but can only hear it and translate it, nothing more. He "translates" the stranger's steps, he does not create them. The departure does not speak poetically, nor does the departed. The soul does not sing. We have, perhaps, a record of its song, the words on record. So how is it possible to say what the soul sees and, even before that, how the soul sings this song? We have "translations" only. Never direct intuitions, unconcealment of Being—never again will this poetry be *poesis*.

The great utopia of Heideggerian thinking about art, as it appears in the essays on Trakl and Rilke, is rooted in the idea of poetry as *Wahnsinnigkeit* [the stuff of madness] that seeks unconcealment, *aletheia*, in the place of foundational *Abendland*. This "system" is a bit narrow for both Trakl and Rilke. The tragedy of their lyric poetry consists in the full awareness of the impossibility of speaking the utopia's name. The utopia is neither absent nor overlooked. Lyric intersects its territory, but it is not where lyric lands. Lyric lands at the recognition of the soul's silence, at the silent farewell of the stranger, and at the song's being merely the song of the friend left behind, a broken symbol. The intuition of departure is retraced in this song. The meaning of departure is kept in the interior of whoever is powerless in the face of separation, in the mortal disease of everything that exists.

The stranger in the dying crowd is *sprachlos* [speechless] and nationless among broken families, "falling stars" that live in "great cities built of stone on the plains" ("Abendland"). The madman is dead, "the stranger is in his grave" ("Psalm," second version). This death and burial are not "images." The one who is buried begins his cycle, is *sprachlos*, "exceeds" all possible language. He can hear his poet-friend only at the first step of his quest. He does not, however, possess the name of resurrection or return. At the end of "Helian," after the description (and language is enough for this) of the "horrifying twilight" of the ancient stock, there begins an interminable pause. A song commemorates the boy's madness. A song recalls his departure. But faced with thinking about return, poetry is silent: "our silence is a black cavern." Song retraces and sustains only this: "lasset das Lied auch des Knaben gedenken, / Seines Wahnsinns, und weisser Brauen und seines Hingangs . . . ": "Let the song recall the child, too, / His madness, his white eyelashes and his departure . . . " The poet who must remain behind remembers the exact time and place of separation. The site of separation is not the same as that of unconcealment.

O, wie lange bist, Elis, du verstorben.
Dein Leib ist eine Hyazinthe,
In die ein Mönch die wächsernen Finger taucht.
Eine schwarze Höhle ist unser Schweigen,

Daraus bisweilen ein sanftes Tier tritt
Und langsam die schweren Lider senkt.
Auf deine Schläfen tropft schwarzer Tau,
Das letzte Gold verfallener Sterne.

("An den Knaben Elis")

Oh, Elis, how long have you been dead.
Your body is a hyacinth,
In which a monk digs his wax finger.
Our silence is a black cavern,

where a gentle creature comes out
and slowly lowers its heavy lids.
A black dew lies on your temples,
the last gold of the fallen stars.

And in "Rondel": "Verflossen ist das Gold der Tage . . . Des Hirten sanfte Flöten starben": "Flown the gold of day . . . the gentle shepherd's flute is dead."

On Cliffs
and Swamps

Alfred Kubin was obsessed with picturing the land of decaying tree trunks and fallen stars, where the soul, *ein Fremdes*, climbed over the horizon. Ernst Jünger saved detailed maps of Kubin's woods, where "splendor and rot, proud wickedness and nauseating putrefaction, the cult of sublime and unfocused pain" manifest "universal life operating so mysteriously in humanity, in animals, in plants, in every rock."[53] The old sage of Zwickledt, Jünger says in *Strahlungen*,[54] belonged to that troubling "pack of Eastern authors" who knew how to describe our decadence more profoundly. Kafka calls out its demons, Trakl gets its putrefaction (and only by way of putrefaction did he arrive at the *Abendland*). Kubin *sees* its dust and mold, and like Horst Lange, whose work he illustrated, he sees the expanding swamps, the unstoppable spread of brush and swamp. Our world has gotten old. Kubin documents its catastrophe. His images, pulled out of the rubble, translate no words but see this world as *Todessymbolik*, a grand astral theater where the powerful breath of Saturn expresses the hieroglyphs of death.[55] Universal life is described here at the end of its cycle. When a cycle nears its end and comes to its questionable *Abendland*, in the gray color of the swamp, the realms are confused. The line does not contain forms in flight, but it splits them open, it chops them up and mixes the pieces together. Girls fly like birds over the swamp. Fish-men and toad-men hunt weird beasts together. A death arrow hits a farmer from a tree, or the bird of evil omen crashes into his house from a leaden sky (*Unglücks Vögel*; see Figure 2). The sun remains ever hidden behind thick clouds that rise up from a sour earth. Universal life is expressed here decomposing the forms of its old cycle. But decomposition is also *irony*. Irony is a powerful caustic philter, the subtle work of the diabolical smile, resulting in a deliberate confusion of realms, not an unforeseen catastrophe. Irony produces an unceasing exchange between forms—testimony to their tremendously illusory nature. That is why universal life is ironic whenever it produces a catastrophe. Its smile disperses the apparent gathering of forms, their specificity and distinction. It "dissolves" them.

Irony and the disintegration that it produces are *hybrid*, like the demiurge of Pearl, the capital of Kubin's fantasy novel, *The Other Side*.[56] Disintegration leads to pure possibility: future realms and future forms are given as purely possible. The swamp festers with germs. Its most troubling aspect is not the decaying of what has already been, but its exhibiting this decay as an unexpected, unpredictable growth. New forms and new orders will be born, slowly, from this lacustrine realm of the indistinct and uncomposed, but we cannot foresee their outline. The irony is twofold: on the one hand, it demonstrates the illusory nature of the idea of a universal life peacefully progressing from form to form, through continuous improvements canceling out every archetypal swamp; and on the other hand, it smiles over the absolute image of death produced by catastrophe. The face of death jumps out from the thicket of reeds wearing a student's cap and points a finger adorned with a fake grasshopper. In another apparition, Madame Mors dances among the tombs like a skeletal courtesan. She tries in vain to hide her decadence behind a mask and a blond wig (*Madame Mors*; see Figure 3). The swamp's disintegration is a kind of decadence. Madame Mors is one of the many apparitions that flash among the will-o'-the-wisps of disintegration. Disintegration is represented as a hybrid of decomposition and germination. In a 1905 drawing, fantastic swamp-born flowers blossom out of the corpse of Ophelia (*Sumpfpflanzen*; see Figure 4). The perennial endurance of life, in the metamorphosis of its realms, plays dead.

The swamp is a "disintegrated" realm of play, where not even death is sacred. Sometimes there is a Shakespearean Fool to describe it (as in some of Kubin's drawings of the *böhmisches Land* [Bohemia]), and sometimes there are the genies of the hills, whose figures are made of crazed roots. The light of the woods is lunar, or rather, it comes from the diamond that Rübezahl brought out of the earth (*Rübezahl II*; see Figure 5). An illusory brightness emanates from the moon. "It is—how shall I say—a slow convergence that, like a magic lantern, reverses the action of that damned arrogant sun's creative life-giving rays. It bewitches the human mind, projecting every kind of concrete form into a seeming reality, and causes the poisonous liquid of death and putrefaction to spread and breathe under the most diverse forms and shapes." Gustav Meyrink, whom Jünger forgot in his "pack of Eastern authors," seems to have presented the precise image of the Old Magician of Zwickledt in *The Four Brothers of the Moon* [*Die vier Mondbrüder*]. For these brothers, forms are simply dreams, and bodies "convulsions of ether." Kubin, unlike Meyrink's lunar brothers, does not declare "I am, I remain" when the entire universe goes to pieces. Nor is his house what Meyrink imagines—"then, to distract myself, I lean my curious ears toward the wild howling that reaches me across the surrounding silence from a nearby castle of bandits, in which the wild painter Kubin now lives, who celebrates decadent orgies in the circle of his seven children until the first light of dawn." Nothing can last, nothing can remain entire until the return of *Urschlamm*, the primeval swamp, and the decadent orgy that takes hold of things, plants and animals, takes hold of the ego and its very death. Only possibility, the infinite swarm of possibilities, can fill this halfway world, this equivocal plane, this *Zwischenwelt*. Irony itself belongs to the halfway world, suspended between putrefaction and possibility, where only possibility is real. Infinite worlds carry this swamp within, and, as Kubin's friend Paul Klee recognized, very few figures emerge from it. (Klee's illustrations for *Candide* fully reveal his "exchange" with Kubin.)[57] The swamp, then, is not only the putrefaction of the has-been, but also the death of many possibilities. The tragic peak of irony does not consist in simply dissolving the illusory nature of given forms, but in shadowing the work of death upon possibility itself, in allowing for a notion of the disintegration of infinite, invisible possibilities.

In Kubin's novel, Pearl lies beyond deserted swamplands. Vast reaches of forest and swamp stop the sun from shining. An opaque olive green, a greenish gray, wipes out even the memory of the "damned arrogant sun." The entire disintegration of forms ripens in the melancholic hue of Pearl, in the shadow of bureaucratic practices collected from all over the world "to promote a special kind of homo sapiens." A mountain made completely of iron rises up in the center of the realm (Trakl's fallen stars!) protected by powerful magnetic charges from the wanderers and vagabonds who want to visit it. The swamp with its demons laps the edges of the sidereal iron. Its discharges of electricity pervade the realm of Pearl, saturating its atmosphere and producing continuous metamorphoses. Kubin's style, fragmented, contorted, multiplying itself in every direction, expresses this impalpable, fecund, and disintegrating *energheia*.

Like the damp folds of the land, Patera encloses infinite faces. Its sovereign is Proteus, seen the way another authentic citizen of Prague, Arcimboldo, had portrayed him.[58] Quick as a lightning bolt he is a young woman, a child, an old man, fat, skinny, kind, wicked. A theatrical magic incessantly transforms his appearance: his and that of all men together, and all animals, jackal and stallion, serpent and bird. Kubin remembered the revelation of the "sovereign form" of Krishna on the field of battle at Arjuna in his description of the metamorphosis of Patera: "I see you with multiple arms, multiple bodies, and your faces, and your eyes, with your shape everywhere unlimited" (*Bhagavad Gita* XI) that, later, Hesse recalled in the transfiguration of Siddhartha in the eyes of Govinda. But while Krishna is time that makes the world waste away and then absorbs it again into himself, into his completely developed perfection, and Siddhartha appears as a unity of Nirvana and Samsara, Patera participates in the confusion of elements. Not only did he produce the swamp where the corrupt elements reciprocally dissolve themselves, but he participates in their degeneration. From the wild regions that surround Pearl and that were considered sacred, numberless animals come and finish the work of decay. "A morbid and irresistible dream" annuls the endurance of the ancient cycle. But to that cycle, apparently, belongs also that ancient citizen of Prague, Patera.

The finale of *The Other Side* is not a cosmogonic sacrifice. Doubt and equivocation form "the sun, the great sun" that, "like the brilliant sound of a fanfare," dissolves the clouds of the realm of dreams, appearing from behind the snow clouds at the conclusion of the grandiose *polemos* between Patera and his double, his Lucifer, the American. Patera was tired and probably "weaker than everyone else." "Perhaps the true sovereigns were the blue-eyed men that galvanize an inanimate puppet with their magic powers." Perhaps Patera is none other than Meyrink's golem that wants the brothers of the moon, and the great sun is not enough to close the abyss of dreams "where I sank." In the days following the apparent triumph of the sun, or rather, "in the nights following, full of moonlight, . . . I thought about my death as a great, heavenly joy, as the beginning of an eternal wedding night." The "dissolute" realm of play has no end here. The work has no conclusion. His teachers ignore the *I Am* and live in that perennial *Zwischenwelt*, a chiaroscuro where "the most sublime moments are subject to the ridiculous, to mocking, to irony," and where General Rudinoff's operetta-style occupation succeeds the great myth that narrates the collapse of the realm of dreams. The teacher is too tired. Subject to the rituals of the wild regions, he knows the formulas of metamorphosis and degeneration, but is powerless to produce the forms that will survive Madame Mors's barbarian toss of dice. The secret of possibility is perhaps in the hands of bizarre elves, swamp demons, or impenetrable blue-eyed figures that impassively assist the workings of the realm of dreams. For us, "the demiurge is a hybrid."

A closely woven net of affinities, reflections, and allusions binds works apparently so far apart as Jünger's *The Other Side* and his *On the Marble Cliffs*.[59] The Chief Ranger can see from the dark

swamps that border the Campagna all the way to the forest that
extends its wooded arms into the grazing meadows. "In the deep
recesses of the forest" lives a gang of wild bandits from Poland and
the lower Rhine, "in Nibelungen caves," beyond any law, outcasts
from heretical sects, wizards and witches. "A river of foul blood
wound its way from here through the veins of the world." This
oppressive atmosphere of horror, made of swamp and unpassable
forest, of animated desolation and bubbling clouds, is a vision
straight out of Kubin. The Chief Ranger is this realm's master: a
sinister magician who is regarded with repugnance and terror by
legitimate alchemists. The pure alchemists of the Marina seek "the
immutable element encased in a box of appearances," and they
seek it according to the ancient spiritual orders, beginning with
"breathing exercises and a strict diet." The end of this work con-
sists in the salvation of whoever practices it, in a capacity to com-
mand, "like holding the reins of a charger," the powers of life that
the Chief Ranger would rather savagely liberate. The severe logic
of forms answers whatever is "solved" and perfect in itself,
"Olivierian," understood only by the profane power of the Chief
Ranger. The severe logic of forms neither ignores nor scorns ap-
pearances (a box), but helps them to manifest the gold of the
spirit.

Here too, as in Kubin, disintegration comes from the slow but
unstoppable penetration of the swamp demons into the cultivated
Campagna and into the Great Marina's culture. The opposite prin-
ciple—at its moment of twilight—also appears in Jünger: the
magic that preserves elements from destruction. In the scope of
this magic, disintegration, like fog, is only "at the surface of
things." Magic preserves things by naming them according to their
true essence. Kubin's visions come after the sack of the Marina: *On
the Marble Cliffs* constitutes a kind of secret prologue to it. Brother
Otho and the Narrator live in the last days of the Marina with des-
perate awareness. Unspeakable melancholy is their lot. They are
intent upon distilling things in the eternal, as they learned from
the aged master Nigromontanus. Whatever burns in the magic
mirror turns invisible and is preserved there "as if it had been
closed and hidden behind armored gates." To spare themselves the

hour of their annihilation, they can only take refuge in the security of nothingness. The beautiful coastal landscape, their fine erudition, cannot endure and be saved except in the invisible, and in absence.

The Marina's landscape pertains to absence, and that is the root of its fascination. The mirror of Nigromontanus purified it in the Rilkean invisible. The symbolic shining of its details resembles the vision of a memory that still observes the most minute details of the past, while desperately aware of it being past. The image of *dichterisch wohnen*, of dwelling poetically, is perfect, therefore, in every sense, where the providential gods of wine and bread are venerated, where the dead "gather invisibly around us," where mythic correspondences unite vine, human, and animal, the cultivator of the field with the cultivator of the word. The Chief Ranger profanes the ancient meters, since he scorns the cultivation of vineyards and grain fields. His hunters "crossed the rich earth as if it were desert, barren and unused," and his blind guitarists return "to the vulgar iambs of hatred and revenge, hissing in the mud." A wild Diana gleams monstrously between the magician's forest and the swamp, while the divine in the Marina is none other than the perfect consonance between various works and various steps of existence. Heideggerian *Geviert* [square] is divine in the Marina, the harmony of *dichterisch wohnen* with earth, sky, god, and mortal. In the woods, however, the dissonance of idols prevails, announced by the deities of the shepherds, "roughly shaped in stone or ancient oak," at the crossroads in the Campagna. At the Marina and in the Rue-Garden Hermitage observance is expressed in working. Work does not transform nature except to liberate its name, its essence. For the Chief Ranger this is oppression, violence, a change for the sake of control. The sense of this work is manifested in the wild charge of his bloodhounds, led by Chiffon Rouge. The beasts and idols of the swamp and the woods, as imagined by Kubin, even hurl themselves against the mirror of Nigromontanus. Here the serpents of Erius—of the hermit child, son of work—destroy "the entire forest crew." The idol cannot touch the eternal. By now, anyway, eternity belongs only to memory.

The Marina's dwelling poetically carries the seed of its own demise. It rotates powerlessly toward the death of its cycle, as if its decline carried down the Chief Ranger. (The desert that he imposes participates in the present good times.) *On the Marble Cliffs* cannot be reduced to the fatal contrast between culture and an anarchic will to power. Any interpretation of the kind would lose the extraordinary wealth of relationships, details, and variations that make up the work. At its center is the bloodless fragility of the dwelling place, the inner wavering of the ancient meter, and weariness even with living happily. The reasons for the Marina's slow weakening flow out of Jünger's writings almost without notice, since memory tends to remove them. The Marina itself is a *hybrid*. The saturation of its colors and the metaphysical wholeness of its landscape can only hide that fact with great effort. Even Marina, its symbol, is full of vacillating contradiction: her certainty that destruction is not real, that it is an illusion and not happening, seems too weak to the eyes of Braquemart's "definitive nihilism" as well as to the Chief Ranger's "wild anarchy." What Brother Otho and the Narrator think—that the crown of gardens shines more brightly from the Rue-Garden Hermitage "before the sun goes down past the horizon"—has traces all through the Marina's life and in its very *humanitas*. The evening light of sundown is necessary to see the Marina—because the Marina is *Abendland*, its *hybrid*.

The *consonantiae* of the Marina are in reality composed of elements that tend to disintegrate into each other and dissolve. The work that brings out their accord and the harmony that makes them resonate in the here and now are ephemeral. Work and harmony are utopian. The most profound content of this utopia is the perfect symbiosis between pagan and romantic, classic and Christian. Look at the description of the festival at the Marina, in the days of its "wild abundance," when in the autumn the guardians of the vineyards go masked through the fields hunting birds or when in spring "we celebrated like mad." Even the two inhabitants of the Rue-Garden Hermitage participate in the festival ("at the hilltops of the vineyard . . . I found her, exhausted, and I took her trembling in my arms and I lowered my red mask onto her face"). Brother Otho, too, whose discourse on humanity comes out of Pico's *De dignitate*, goes to the Woodpecker group, "which plays its march beating ladles and spoons against a wooden barrel." The game here reveals anew its ancient ritual sense. The "orgy" permits man to participate in the eternal cosmogonic event. It periodically reestablishes the original chaos in order to permit *renovatio*. The festival and its license have symbolic value. That is why Brother Otho and the Narrator take part: the proceedings of the festival "imitate divine gestures or certain episodes of the holy drama of the cosmos" (Eliade). Regeneration can only occur by reconnecting the sphere of play and the sphere of the sacred in this way, and by hearing the "archetypes" that are common to the various religious traditions, tending toward that foundational unity where the ascetic humanists of the Marina fix their gaze.

The figure of Father Lampro, practically the tutelary spirit of the Marina, repeats this nostalgia. The very name of his cloister is a transparent symbol of it: St. Mary of the Moon. The pagan goddess who carries a scythe and the Virgin who is "ruler of all that changes" both inhabit Father Lampro's priesthood. Father Lampro, in fact, "didn't like contradictions." Therefore he liked neither the dialectical struggle nor the decision implicit in Christian metanoia. The "double" of the Mauretanians is equally irresolute, the defined order that the lives of the Marina depend upon. If the exercise of power wants to take form through their doctrine of *semper victrix* and no compassion can adulterate it, then it is inevitable that violence and tyranny will cling to its "definitive nihilism" like a poisonous vine. The mortal struggle between forest and Marina appears, in the double light of the story of the Mauretanians, to be the catastrophe of a single organism, the fruit of its secret disagreements and fissures. Brother Otho and the Narrator understand that Braquemart is powerless to oppose the Chief Ranger, and they also see the bloodless decadence of the prince who goes with him. The severe logic of the Chief Ranger embraces Braquemart's utopia of order's original *intentio* and its *renovatio*. In this light, the image that closes the novel may appear all that much weaker: the amphora containing Braquemart's head, resting on the first stone laid in the foundation of the Marina's great cathedral, the great work's cornerstone. This distant and unreliable promise of *renovatio* is reversible, however. It can mean that "definitive nihilism" lies at the foundation of the Marina's Christian resurrection. The rock that should have been the foundation takes on aspects of diabolical imagery—the "rock of shame." It is not the Marina of *Geviert* that rises; it is not the utopia of a pagan and Christian synthesis that emerges, but the cathedral of Christianity qua "definitive nihilism." The rock on which the Church is built is only the rock of nihilism.

In the "rich life of studious leisure" that takes place in the Rue-Garden Hermitage, "we followed the lofty example of Linnaeus." The order that he confers on things is one of names and language; the immutable standard is the standard of discourse. Even Father Lampro teaches how to name things. Naming expresses dominion of the spirit "over the fields in flower and over the innumerable legions of insects." However, even this dominion appears unfounded in the end. When things capture us in their light and surprise us with it, then words are detached from appearance and will no longer serve in the usual way. The glory of things makes process and destruction seem illusory, but that is exactly what constitutes the ineffable. Our words, Linnaeus's words, name appearances and put them in order. Appearances do not exist except by the light of words. "The dazzling new splendor of things" seems to lead to the edge of silence. The highest authority of the Marina, that of the word, falls short before this splendor, since even such an authority is an unresolvable *hybrid* made of "definitive nihilism" ordering phenomena in the presence of discourse, mixed with "saving" the world, freeing its very essence.

However different the design of Pearl might seem at first glance from that of the Marina, the asphyxia that seizes both landscapes is the sign of an incurable, internal illness. The sun that shines on the Marina is as melancholic as the atmosphere of Pearl. If one looks closely, the greatness of the opening pages of *On the Marble Cliffs* does not depend on colors, but on the contrast of black and white. We stand before an engraving, not a painting. Linnaeus's terms are not adequate to name the sun, no matter how they may try. The art of drawing can do it, as in Kubin—and as in one of his teachers, Max Klinger. Can one think of Patera as a lost Mauretanian? And of the blue-eyed men, who seem to judge him in the end, as the order that can by now only serve in the game of destruction and becoming? History knows nothing but the downward path of disintegration, and the description of the forces that afflict it are identical in Kubin and Jünger. To whatever extent the description in *On the Marble Cliffs* may resemble Kubin, that is how much the initial landscape, from the spreading sea to the orchards and vineyards, from the Campagna to the icy Alta Plana, belongs to Klinger's drawings.

Blanchot's writings about Jünger and De Chirico's about Klinger are—not by accident—interchangeable.[60] The landscape of the Rue-Garden Hermitage is perfectly described, and anyway it's beauty cannot be captured "the way you might capture a land of enigmas" (Blanchot). The festivals of the Marina are enigmatic. The encounters with the primordial genies of the land that animate the festivals are enigmatic. The very images of the Rue-Garden Hermitage, of Brother Otho and Little Erio, lords of snakes, are enigmatic. And yet the things dreamed in thought are expressed here as figures. The admirable cool and cruel dignity (Blanchot) of their language leaves no room for facile evocations of fantasy. Not fantasy, but *imaginatio*. Thus in Klinger the neatness of contour, the perfection of the image, is a gift of distance (the patience of Father Lampro). The landscape opens its own interior only to those who observe it from afar. Only melancholy born of detachment can lend reality to the things dreamed in thought dreaming about itself. Then nothing is abandoned to impression or chance. Thus the centaur that talks with the washerwoman from behind a wall and reaches out to finger the white sheets hung out in the sun is an *image*; the centaur that flees across the field and spins around to shoot an arrow into the throat of his pursuer's horse is an *image* (*Centaur mit Wäscherinnen* and *Verfolgter Centaur*; see Figures 6 and 7). The "realism" of *Eine Mutter, Op. 9*, is found again in the pure dream of the other cycle, *Brahmsphantasie*,

Op. 12. The neoclassical pessimism that assigns "every contemporary work to the glossorist," that holds "that nothing is left for us contemporaries except games of assembly," is here happily and "ingenuously" abandoned for another "method," thanks to which "the ancient myths, in their reappearance, will offer us their enigmas and their exorcisms with an unrecognized face. The fiction of the myths consists in new fatigue and new terrors."[61]

The intellectual art of assembly and the reappearance of myth have rarely been so fully realized as in Klinger's glove cycle, *Paraphrasen über den Fund eines Handschuhs, Op. 6.* The "banal" event of the first two plates is transformed, through the springtime nostalgia of the third, into the dreams and nightmares of those that follow: from the Marina's demons of *Ängste* to the monster bird that steals the glove off the outstretched hands of the dreamer during the night. From the glove that lies "so bourgeois" on the track, to the goddess of love in triumph on the foaming sea, to the glove, finally, on the last table that the winged child observes with an ironic smile—the figure and its sign are identical. As in Jünger, the game of assembly, even carried to the peak of complexity and sophistication, is foreign to all allusivity, to all ornamental likeness. Myths can be fabricated.

Kubin discovered Klinger's glove cycle in Munich at the beginning of the century, and he found it enlightening. "A completely new art was revealed to me here that offered the possibility of expressing in quick suggestive strokes all possible emotions. . . . I was suddenly brimming with a torrent of visions and images in black and white." Kubin's predilection for the glove cycle, like that of Giorgio De Chirico, Max Ernst, and the symbolists, is well understood: it presents a fabricated myth in combination with an airy note of Romantic irony. It is the same element of distance that we saw in regard to the landscape. Irony prevents any possibility of becoming one with the fabrication, with the fiction—and that permits the fiction to reach a perfect, definite *image.* The same intricate game can be noticed in Klinger's other masterpieces: *The Swing, Bear and Fairy* (*Bär und Elfe*; see Figure 8), the *Titelblatt* of the *Radierte Skizzen.* A vast, luminous Mediterranean gulf provides the background for the fairy's feathery game with the bear. (It is humor's game with the spirit of gravity; Kubin also portrays it frequently.) These are the passages that most recall Jünger (like the high plain in the background of *Akkorde* in the *Brahmsphantasie*). They stand in the splendor of the Mediterranean (De Chirico), like blessed islands. Splendor is, however, a principle of distinction and clarity. The sun appears, but it does not burn. A cloudless light allows things to appear, but at the same time it cancels out their colors. De Chirico notes that Arnold Böcklin's landscape is completely different. The same Mediterranean sea is here swollen with its own deities, sensed through intense chromatic contrasts: a Nordic, continental dramatic force. Klinger's themes are here, too (and everywhere the influence of the painter from Basel—city of Nietzsche, Burckhardt, *and Böcklin*, as Hermann Hesse had to say), but as if tormented "by north winds and Nordic demons." Satyrs and nymphs are mixed in the oceanic element. The very silence of the sea is figured as a siren, a temptress, in the drowned man's monstrous reflex. In *Gesandschaft*, however, where Klinger's graphic genius more fully informs the quality of the painting, the lovely sphinx of silence on a boundless and deserted beach queries the hero-bird who dares to approach her (see Figure 9). No gesture, no dramatization disturbs this moment.

Böcklin and the portrait that Alberto Savinio made of him in *Men, Tell Your Story* and his fabrication of myth all inhabit *On the Marble Cliffs*. The sudden apparition that surprises the Narrator and Brother Otho on the way back from the Rue-Garden Hermitage ("thus images broke into our dark drunkenness then, perhaps one of those goat horns on a long pole that farmers plant down in their gardens, or perhaps. . . . Certainly we remained still as rocks and a sudden fright took hold of our hearts") seems taken from "Pan and the Pastor." Böcklin's chromaticism sometimes breaks into Jünger's Klingerian drawings, and this constitutes the bridge to the Kubinian visionary crescendo that traverses the collapse of the Marina. All of these threads come together under the sign of *Melancholia*. Its season is autumn. Its element is the wetness of the sea, of the shore, of the swamp. Its line is the horizon. In the monumental figure of a woman with a black-veiled mirror in her hand that Böcklin finished in 1900, his last work and the last work of the century, we find the figure of *Herbstgedanken*, she who contemplates the slow-moving currents of the stream under the shadow of autumn branches (*Melancholia*; see Figure 10). She sits in the landscape of *Heiliger Hain*. She is the woman who gazes at the beach in the distance in *Villa am Meer*. She is Iphigeneia forgotten against the background of a classical villa, prey to the encroaching wild. We find the famous, funereal cypress trees of the *Island of the Dead*. We recognize these, in fact, in the mirror's black veil. The vast beaches, the moors, the Campagna (so admired already by the German Romantic painters who lived in Italy or "through" Italy—it would be possible to trace the elements of imaginative continuity from them to Böcklin),[62] furrowed by brooks moving slowly among autumnal trees until they arrive at the swamp, the lacustrine landscape, the silence beneath the woods: all these images, variously accentuated and experienced, are also found in the Jugendstil. As Ernst Bloch was to say,[63] the land of the Jugendstil is *Sumpfmoor* and *Heide*, swamp, marsh, and moor. The landscape is built on the horizon line, horizon by horizon. The tree in its emerging does not indicate anything except the caesurae of this broad meter. The very lines that make up Jugendstil ornaments are derived from "*flacher Sumpfmythos*" (Bloch): complications and "scrambling" of the horizon. Loos does not notice this origin. They are details, fragments of *Melancholia*, bits of mosaic in the fiction of the myth, broken into pieces by now, shards that survived the smashing of the images of death (the images of war and plague, recurring obsessively in Böcklin and Klinger and Kubin). The line is ever the unreachable horizon. In Jugendstil it curves, circles back on itself, seeks new rhythms—but remains the line that indicates the horizon, the impassable limit. And even the colors, however much they may seem to be freed from any descriptive purpose, remain the colors of autumn or of uncertain springs.

Centaurs

In those years, Basel was also the city of Johann Jakob Bachofen. Arnold Böcklin's fabricated myth is directed at mourning, at *threnos*. It is a Lycian rhythm—whose twofold nature was discovered by Bachofen. The required horizon line expresses the idea of repose. *Melancholia* seems to reflect on the motto "that the oracle recalled to the inhabitants of Camarina, in Sicily, as the supreme principle of the sacred," *akineta me kinein,* do not move the unmovable.[64] The way Böcklin's *The Island of the Dead* reproduces a Lycian necropolis has escaped notice, along with the way it describes "a sepulchral and grandiose world, solid as a rock, destined to endure through eternity" (Bachofen), monotonous as the flat sea that surrounds it and the silence that inhabits it. The Lycian cities of the dead command the most beautiful sites, "at the heights of cliffs struck by the first rays of the sun in the morning and lit by the last rays of the sun in the evening." They participate variously in the lives of the living, visible from amphitheaters, halls, and stadiums. The Lycian cult of the dead, Bachofen explains, is associated with the idea of awakening, with the worship of the sun, whose nature is expressed by the very name of the people. This element is completely missing in Böcklin's *Toteninsel.* It shows a desperate Lycia that appears in the figure of Glaucus, when Diomedes encounters him in the tumult of battle: "Men are like leaves shaking at the stem." (The identical comparison appears in the Brahms

Requiem.) The solid cliffs of the Toteninsel do not yield the birth of spring (*ver sacrum*). The *ver sacrum* will be nothing, really, but an autumn of broken horizons, fragments of woods and country-side.

The landscape of the Great Marina is perhaps closer to the Lycia imagined by Bachofen. Kore approaches Apollo's rites, and the tel-lurian presence sits beside the luminous power and shines. (The Marina's hierophants are double, like Böcklin's and Klinger's.) Yet the physical structure itself seems drawn from Bachofen's en-thralled description of Lycia: the glance of the traveler "rests now on the snowy fields or on the dark wooded slopes of the high mountains, now on the dark blue mirror of the sea. And in an il-lusion created by the incomparably limpid sky, the contours of woods and sea frequently join in what seems an unbroken line." The ancient culture of the fertile valleys, the very character of the people who live their lives there without feeling the need to travel to foreign lands, belongs to the myth of the Marina. As the har-mony of the Marina is destined to shatter into its various parts, so Bachofen's *Land of Dawn* breaks down into its constituent ele-ments. The fortunate symbiosis between Lycian Apollo and Kore cannot endure. In Lycia and at the Marina, night and day are still united in the light of dawn. But the successive development's des-tiny will be to "progress to the idea of an unchanging source of light" (Bachofen), uncontaminated by night, *ignis non urens* [un-scathed by fire], as the Delphic nature of Apollo.[65] The catastro-phe of the Marina seems analogous to that of the impossible Ly-cian symbiosis. Bachofen's "progressive" idea of evolution rests in Apollo's superiority. Yet the swollen night of hurricanes that ap-proaches Böcklin's necropolis is far more menacing. The horns of the forest that threaten to contaminate Junger's Campagna are far more disturbing. Böcklin's deserted Lycia becomes merely a necropolis, as the dark demons of the Chief Ranger follow the col-lapse of the "happy case" of the Lycian utopia. Bachofen's Delphic Apollo merely expresses the other side, the symbol, of this collapse.

The Lycian utopia is too complex a game for Otto Weininger's pale, juvenile enthusiasm. Here Apollo reveals the hybrid quality of his light, the equivocal source of his Delphic splendor. Even in

Evola's analysis[66] (which brings out several obstacles in the older Bachofen), the Lycian motif is left in the background, while the foreground looms with mortal, absolute disagreement between all the tellurian forces below and the great Olympian mysteries, between Samsarian existence "conceived as an eternal and meaningless wheel of birth" (Evola) and the "true" Hellas, the Apollonian, Olympic Hellas. Even Weininger (with less erudition but with more inventive force) denies this absolute contrast that confines the "civilization of the Mother" to the pure, dynamic appearance of the Pelasgian figure of Gaia. Weininger tries to adapt Kant in a "paradoxical" sense to this mythic scheme. (Kant delivered the "academic philosophy" of his time.)

The most surprising and disturbing aspect of Lycian experience is the fact that the dominion of light preserves "the pre-eminence of the maternal principle." Furthermore, Apollo remains variously associated with the Pelasgian element and "in perfect correspondence with the ideal of the most ancient Orphism" (Bachofen). The god still appears a child of Leto, the surging genetrix of Aurora. We have seen the positivistic and progressivist schematicism Bachofen uses to resolve the paradox: Lycia would not be "elevated" again to the level of a Delphic religion. Lycia would "never have reached this superior level, the Hellenic idea of the divine." "Progressively," the child of Leto frees himself from earth's lap, *gremium matris terrae*, cancels his Thracian Orphic traces, and pronounces his plain affirmation: the *is* of being. Lycian Apollo would be, finally, incomplete, and his incompleteness would consist in the ambiguity of his actions. "Progress," therefore, is simplicity, good form, "economy."

Weininger is limited to "resolution" of Bachofen's Lycian Utopia (whose polemical groundlessness Giovanni Colli demonstrated in other terms, incorrectly, in Nietzsche):[67] on one hand Apollo and on the other his opposite, the "femininity" of Dionysius. As Bachofen confirmed in *Mutterrecht*, the relationship between Dionysius and Kore passes to a new plane in the relationship between Dionysius and Aphrodite. The Lycian Utopia founders under symbols from the "well-ordered" mother of grain harvests to the Bacchic bunch of grapes and voluptuous fruits, from milk and honey to "wine, bearer of drunkenness and of sensual excitement" (Bachofen), from the lofty symbols of Demeter to the tellurian weight of the swamp with all its creatures and flora. The harmony of bread and wine, which is celebrated in the happy temples of the Marina and Lycia, collapses when the swamp and forest surge. Wine accelerates into drugs (not by chance did Ernst Jünger dedicate one of his best books to drugs),[68] and bread becomes the fruit of *Abgrund*, of the abyss. Jünger, too, still resists the idea of utopian harmony. In Weininger, this idea needs to be struck. The hand that strikes it proclaims itself Olympian. The target, however, is the same one that the Chief Ranger's mute wild woman pursues. We wait for the paradoxical exchange of roles that renders Klinger's centaurs so enigmatic. Who defends the Marina? Who are its inhabitants? Who can gaze upon the splendor of things in the Mediterranean light? Perhaps Klinger's centaur in flight (see Figure 7) is the inhabitant of the Marina that defends its land from the Chief Ranger's hunters. The centaur has a double nature—he preserves in his figure the doubleness that constitutes the Lycian utopia. The men who pitilessly hunt him want to resolve, define, divide him. He cannot rest in peace between divine and human, man and animal, Apollo and Kore. Is he not Chiron, who passes his knowledge on to men, drawing down upon himself the hatred of the new gods? Does he not sing along with Orpheus? And do not the centaurs live "where the banks are rich with cliffs and grottos," in the regions where "the river had to wind before finding its way?" Glossing Pindar, Hölderlin sees the centaur that lives in the in-between time when the earth tries to give its own elements form, when the dry things congeal and the rivers find their direction through "strong rooted trees." The Lycian utopia also exists in this in-between time, whose wisdom still knows how to reconcile opposites. It sings "the true songs of Centaurs, sung with the spirit of the river." But the centaurs embody the earth when the new regime of the hunter breaks out in it: man and horse divided. And the honeyed wine that they experienced for the first time served only to make them lose the way.

Weibliches

Arnold Böcklin's oceanic creatures embody the tradition that ends with ignoring Apollo's Lycian relatives (Nietzsche's Dionysius is in fact very close to them) and with imagining women only in the figure of Io tormented by desire. Bachofen remembers that Io is driven by passion all the way to Cilicia and Panfilia, but she never reaches Lycia. A painting like *Ulysses and Calypso* could illustrate Weininger: Calypso, who holds the harp of seduction, gazes toward the figure of a man, upright on the cliff, sick with unbound nostalgia. The man turns his back to the woman, who wants to hold onto him. He is all longing and strife, *Sehnsucht* and *Streben*, a figure of the transcendent. While the woman is not the Iphigeneia in Taurus of the *Villa am Meer* or *Melancholia*, she is the appearance and enchantment of becoming. This Pelasgian image of woman continues down to Gustav Klimt's streaming goddesses (and Egon Schiele's, following Klimt's example). She evidently operates in Kubin, too. In one of his most beautiful drawings, an immense wave of hair falls from a proud figure shown in profile (*Die Haarschleppe*; see Figure 11). Elsewhere, the myth of Gaia comes up oppressive. Gaia in her tellurian obscurity (*Unser aller Mutter Erde*) or in her animal generation (*Das Gezücht*; see Figure 12), even transforms herself into the incubus of the *Temptation of Saint Anthony* or of *Die Spinne* (see Figure 13). In Klinger the female's belonging to the marine element is taken for granted.

In *Die Quelle* or *Die blaue Stunde* or *Am Strande*, her figure is contemplated as such by whomever must be detached or by those for whom detachment means pain, for whom loss is anguish. In Böcklin, in addition to the Siren, there is Flora, who sows the earth with flowers and the Elysian Fields with the love games of the blessed.

Otto Weininger's exasperated univocality might seem a wretched desperation indeed compared to the complexity and wealth of these motifs, but even the young Viennese knew how to fabricate myths, and these remain crucial for explaining the verses of Trakl, and Schiele, and the Heideggerian *Eröterung*.

The myth of Poros and Penia is found in Plato (*Symposium*, XX). Drunken Poros, failing in his role as the son of Metis, embraces Penia's endless thirst, embraces the non-being of illusory, ephemeral satisfaction, the privation and poverty that follow every apparent satisfaction. Eros is born from this submerging of the power and fullness of Being. Pandora is the fruit of this derailment of Being, the female embodiment of cupidity for whose sake, according to Hesiod, death entered the world. Women are an abyss for *viryâ* (energy), the figure that siphons off the magic virility of Being and determines its fall. Weininger's vision of the embrace is obsessed with this myth. The expression *viryâ* indicates arresting the flow of becoming or stopping the wheel of appearances, the way of high ascesis. Women are made of desire. "She darkens the sun." They are the eternal sorceresses that fascinate, that *seduce* the ascetic. They deflect the ascetic from the straight path onto the path of error. Women, who can give life, bar access or tend to bar access to all that lies beyond life. They reduce man to mere bearer of the phallus.[69] Weininger's war between the sexes cannot be reduced to paradoxically rendering Kant's ethics into absolutes. As in Meyrink, this is born of a great capacity to feel the myth nearby, as part of experience. (Briganti has noted the same intensity in Böcklin.)

In Weininger the ascetic and transcendental traditions of *viryâ* are continuously betrayed in ethical and moral terms. The reason for *viryâ*'s presence, insurmountable although embarrassing, in the entire Viennese "apocalypse series," lies in its imaginative force, in the imposing mystical background of Weininger's (evil) "metaphysics of gender." Running through the whole "apocalypse series" is Weininger's idea of the pure lover, the absolute unfurling of Eros, placing women in a superior order. He renders women aware of the void that contradistinguishes their essence, aware of the inexhaustibility of their thirst. At the peak of their erotic potential, women can finally comprehend all their misery and intuit the possibility of and the conditions for achieving a superior existence. The fact that this argument changes its form in Kraus, for example, does not for one moment alter its inner structure. What is Olympian for Weininger becomes for Kraus the cross of his condemnation. For both, however, the subject is the same. Kraus falls into curious "sociologistic" errors whenever he sees in "the struggle for pleasure" nothing other than a superstitious manifestation of bourgeois morality. For Kraus, feminine amorality takes an offset print, uniquely reversing the appearance of Weininger's terms for feminine *kâminî* (she who is made of desire, Pandora). Kraus sees women symbolized in Lulu, eternally pursued, confined to the bed of Procrustes. Such women remain the centripetal force of Weininger's mythology. Morality wants to crucify Lulu and take revenge on her (Jack is none other than Lulu's ultimate torturer), because she flees morality and does not allow herself to be possessed, and remains an elusive virgin. The elusiveness of the "absolute" woman is a central idea in Weininger: as much as men fall for her and lose themselves over her, they will never succeed in possessing her ideal. Man may not possess if he embraces Penia. This "reversal" of appearance that Kraus effects is even more evident when considering his interpretation of Lulu as an "angel" to the extent that she is delivered from the will to procreate. Weininger's female lover, the *Typus-Weib*, is free from all reproductive instinct. She loves without producing and finds desire complete in the act. This is Penia's true, paradoxical nature. The feminine lover gives herself eternally. She knows how to lose herself and so she is able to lose. Kraus's critique of the productive (that is the center of his *Eröterung* of the text of Frank Wedekind), however "prophetic" of

crucial moments in contemporary thinking, is substantially ex-
pressed by avenging the heroic character. This is the same figure
that for Weininger prevents any heroic *Streben* and masculine nos-
talgia. The critique of aggressive male productivity registered in
Salomé shares with Weininger an analogous relationship. Lou An-
dreas-Salomé reflects Weininger in her analysis of the "great pres-
ence" of the body in love, of its power to preserve, of its tragedy for
the soul.

Weininger's reversed presence in later "immoralism" and in
many later examinations of "values" makes him that much more
important. Wittgenstein confirmed that Weininger's greatness con-
sisted of his "enormous error," "which on the whole means that if
one answers 'no' to his entire work, he is speaking an important
truth." And what of Kraus's "no" or of Andreas-Salomé's even
weaker "no"? And what of the simple examination of eclectic mix-
tures of traditional thought and morality? Or is it necessary to con-
clude, with Freud, that women hold the place of an impenetrable
enigma, decipherable only in fragments and pieces? ("If you want
to know more about femininity, look into your own experience.")
Freud's conclusion turns out to be not very far from Weininger's.
Because what is woman if not becoming and flowing, and thus de-
cipherable only in pieces? What expresses her figure if not absolute
opposition to the *standing* of law, to which man aspires? And fi-
nally, would the truth that Weininger indicates as a very "bour-
geois truth" be a "no" were it appended to his entire work? That
"no" would necessitate advocating a complete legal parity of gen-
ders. (It could just as well happen on the basis of reconfirming a
metaphysical difference between them: Weininger is *apertis verbis*
for legal parity, and he cares deeply about differentiating himself
from the intentions of the "banal" Möbius.) Weininger's truth can
emerge only by negating it, not by merely reversing it. No critique
carried out in the name of "values" that he repudiates and disowns
will ever be able to touch him. Such a critique persists in the fun-
damental opposition of the two principles: the transparence of the
norm on one hand and the way of non-being, of desire and of its
constitutive misery, on the other. The transcendental nostalgia of
Olympian man is in absolute disagreement with the "exclusive"

woman of the hour. Woman embodies man's obligation, straps him down, and keeps him down by the force of her body, blinding him to the idea. The "no" that opposes Weininger can only look upon the refusal to decide in terms of this recurrent discord. (There are infinite secular bastard varieties of this myth.) This discord ignores the "double" of the Lycian Utopia, the Nietzschean game between the masks of Apollo and Dionysius, between redemption from time and ruthless critique of every metaphysics of Being. Its unilateral nature is demonstrated in the very questions to which it yields. On one hand, women receive their own existence from the sexualization of men, from men's guilt and fall, and therefore women are not a true entity. (Women exist uniquely as an expression of Don Juan.) On the other hand, one wants to find out how to abandon this specter, to become the active force that helps men to realize themselves according to their supposed being. Women are the ones capable of disturbing the seers sent by the king to *seduce* the boy "born to Enlightenment," born to study the ascetic and to save the Buddha! Gender and character seem to end in this invocation that finds new accents in Lou Andreas-Salomé (the abandonment of women to productivity, her custody of a self-enclosed "happiness," complete and pure in the sexual impulse).

Andreas-Salomé is just the right figure to help us make a final pass at discovering Weininger's "truth." Her abandonment is a nostalgia for the idea. She wants to provide a form, in and of itself, to Weininger's idea. In wanting to assume man's nostalgia for herself, she reveals the basis of her desperation: an authentic *desperatio de viro*. Man is by now, in reality, driven into an indistinguishable chiaroscuro of Poros and Penia. A pale memory of the Olympian can live only in women, since only women suffer its absence. Whether women attempt to express Weininger's idea in and of itself or whether they rise up against it (thus regenerating it continually, denouncing it as law, as the norm, as moral suffocation of desire), they do not succeed in naturalizing themselves in its absence, in the void that its absence leaves. Either women try to substitute themselves there, or they reproduce the specter incessantly, in order to hurl themselves against it.

All this indicates Weininger's "truth": the man of his myth does not exist. The hero immersed in gardens of Kundry must go back, across abandonment, to the heavens of logic, of values, of law. The hero that goes beyond any *doxa* (even Lukács in those years delineated his tragic solitude) is the specter of a tradition interrupted forever, a hallucination that Weininger forces himself to grasp in vain. Man exists only in becoming and in desire, against which his idea should struggle encompassing intelligence, wandering, and metropolitan prose. Nostalgia for his idea belongs to women. The downfall of the idea provokes in woman an insufferable delusion. The *viryâ* remains as a specter of women, and never so clearly as when women hurl themselves against a nonexistent *viryâ*. Man forces himself to adopt the illusion for himself (as in *Lulu*, for instance), but he only becomes more foolish and strained in that role. As man disappears little by little, as his cycle declines, the more forcefully must he produce a nostalgia for woman, and so the more violent is his assault on the idea. Feminism is the supreme act in which women seek to embody the declining myth of man. "Marfisa is a feminist. Bradamante is a feminist. All the women warriors are feminists who shudder with anger and shame at the very notion of being beaten by a knight. Hedda Gabler enacts a superior feminism when she compensates for the lack of pride, dignity, and courage in the man she loves."[70]

It is clear why Weininger cannot understand Nietzsche. "Human, All Too Human" is already an act of reciprocal nonexistence, so to speak, between man and woman and points to something beyond their metaphysical disagreement. And here Nietzsche finds himself in agreement with Trakl and Schiele, in radical negation not only of Weininger, but of his very "reversals." In Trakl, men and women are a unified family stock. The ancient family, cloven and exiled, embraces both. They form a unified family stock of their own even through discord—since discord is precisely the family's destiny. This curse cannot be surmounted through an ascetic stance toward the world of things and senses. Wagner's Parsifal (even Nietzsche refused to find charm in its libretto) does not have at its core the destruction of the idea of "redemption by means of love," as Weininger resolves in *On Supreme Things*. Instead, Parsifal stands for *parting* from this idea, in the sense of Trakl's Heideggerian *Erörterung*: in favor of seeking the earth, the possibility of which is established in the singing.

Men and women are a *unified* family stock, consigned by destiny to discord, but also open to *parting*, to splitting apart. In its fundamental sense, this means abandoning metaphysical discourse, for which every "doubling," every otherness, seems wrong. The place from which men and women, a unified family stock, become estranged in their ruined cycle is not the unity of Being of metaphysics, but peaceful otherness, otherness that happens on earth and under the heavens, that declares itself as discordant harmony rather than transgression. The parting can be reached only after demolishing Weininger's myth. Colette Peignot, Georges Bataille's Laura, makes a partial attempt when she says, "To declare yourself free you have to imagine the chain that I would be. Then you have something to break, a fixed order to transgress. I, a girl, treating you the way my mother treats me. I must deny what you want because you want it times ten."[71] Vasilii Rozanov also assists this demolition by uncovering Weininger's preference for the "strong sex," the "feminine eye," "his envy of women."[72] But in this Weininger only evokes the specter of man reproduced by woman. Men must "transgress" women and women men. Each becomes the other's norm. Two poles, each fantasizing the other as an obstacle or chain. Each continues to live with the dead myth of the other. And when the vision of this nonexistence can no longer be held back, then hopeless discord breaks out, where "the lacerating discord of the sexes" (Heidegger) seems complete or close to it. What is completed here is, once again, the structure of "appropriation" at the basis of eroticism's will to power. This motif shows up continually in Nietzsche: love between the sexes as an impulse to ownership (*Eigentum*), as an appropriative instinct, as greed. This powerful impulse is based on otherness—on the otherness felt as a contradiction to be removed, to be surmounted, or to be liquidated. Therefore, it is based on man and woman each being a reciprocal norm to the other, a norm that is transgressed in order to obtain unity. Weininger is completely subject to this pattern, and so are

all of his possible "reversals." The disabling of the terms of rapport
is the first step toward the negation of Weininger, already dis-
cernible in Nietzsche. This negation strips away the old posses-
sions, disabling them completely. The breaking open of the *Grund*
[ground] leads immediately to the mere *Ab-grund* [abyss], whose
first images cannot but seem specters of Schiele. They still belong
to the appearance of the war between the sexes, of its completed
cycle. Yet in this war they are no longer capable of any settled own-
ership. A hopeless stupor signifies relationships that stifle and are
confused, and to these belong a body still capable of suffering.

Beyond this curse, where men and women desire to be over-
whelmed and are reflected in reciprocal discord, is there a depar-
ture for the *Abendland* of discordant harmony and a rest at home
in otherness?

The Eternal Child

Is such a harmony thinkable, if the singing belongs only to the friend who remains, if the singing does not come from parting, but from that "lacerating discord" where men and women have fallen and where they are *nothing* to each other? All the Traklian tones of undoing are present in Schiele. The road of the departed, that which lives in the tomb of the *Wahnsinnige* [the madman] remains rigorously unutterable. Surmounting the curse of otherness, for those who remain alive, is unutterable. The state of otherness disintegrates, exposing its sinews, betraying its ephemeral nature. But, for men and women, it is possible to reach nothing more than the common recognition of the damnation of that state. There is no embrace then, but rather men and women gripping each other, as in Schiele's great canvass of 1917, embracing separation, a death (the monk with his eyes wide open, that shows up frequently in Schiele: for example, in *Death and the Maiden*, 1915). And when the embrace gets tired, because it takes place in disintegration, they remain absent organisms, coupled in a single misery (*The Family*, 1918).

It is the world that Trakl describes thus in "Allerseelen":

> Das Seufzen Liebender haucht in Gezweigen
> Und dort verwest die Mutter mit dem Kind.
> Unwirklich scheinet der Lebendigen Reigen
> Und wunderlich zerstreut im Abendwind.

A cry of lovers trembles in the branches
and there the mother and child spoil.
The dance of the living seems unreal,
strangely scattered in the evening wind.

Bodily flesh cannot be redeemed in the sense of ethics or
Weininger's myth or (although palpitating elsewhere in Trakl) in
the sense of the "lunar voice" of the "sister" across the "spiritual
night" (*Spiritual Sunset,* second version), of an extreme *Geschwis-
terliebe.* Schiele's bodily flesh is already marked in the gaze of chil-
dren. It weighs like an insurmountable obstacle on solitary figures,
in spite of their solitude. (Even in extreme solitude one is alone
with one's own sex.) Death here seems to ignore the tone that Hei-
degger finds in Trakl, almost a preservation of the not-born in or-
der to announce the *Abendland.*

The not-born is already wrapped in the black mantle of death.
In fact, he lives in a dead mother, powerless to give birth to
him (*Tote Mutter,* 1910, see Figure 14; the motif was present in
Klinger). "Alles ist lebend tot," writes Schiele that same year:
everything living is seen in its ruin, the pregnant woman stands
next to death (*Schwangere und Tod,* 1911) and the very lymph that
carries things into presence decrees their undoing. "Where are the
living?" cries the "eternal child" (*ich ewiges Kind*) to Arthur
Roessler. "To live means to cast seed, sow seed, to be prodigal."
But for whom? For eternal scholars? For the dead who masquer-
ade as the living? For the eternal states where life is money? The
child who counts only gifts, who despises school and money, who
opposes his own radical recklessness to productivity, does not
know where to find the living so he can disseminate himself
among them. He is "chosen." (That is why there is no new art,
only new artists. Art is singular, and basically ever the same, the
art that the "chosen" know how to express.)[73] But art has no one
to choose.

In man's vision there is no peace. The same line that in Klimt
indicated the fleeting nature of form is reversed here into a pitiless
analysis of the sinews that hold a body up. The living is already

dead, and the drawing reveals the masquerade. The autumn and winter trees, Schiele's landscapes, resemble the body (*Winterbaüme* and *Herbstbaum in bewegter Luft*, 1912). Even the houses show an affinity to it. Foreign to any idea of dwelling, they seem to be awful refuges (*Tote Stadt*, 1911), blank windows opened wide, like the eyes of *The Blind Mother* (1914). Houses and windows cling to each other, dominated by high, silent bell towers (*Stein's Views over the Danube*, 1913). Even the flowers, like people and trees, are stripped down to the sinews.[74] The stupendous sunflower of 1909–10 is at once straight and withered, "*und lacht und weint*"—it laughs and it cries, like the figures in the self portraits.

Trakl provides words to Schiele's landscapes:

> Häuser dräu'n aus stummen Nähen;
> Helle im Theatersaal.
>
> Kirchen, Brücken und Spital
> Grauenvoll im Zwielicht stehen.
> Blutbefleckte Linnen blähen
> Segel sich auf dem Kanal.
>   ("Winterdämmerung")

> Menacing houses, huddled close in silence;
> Light in the theater.
>
> Churches, bridges, hospitals
> loom horribly in the dark.
> Swollen sheets, red with blood,
> are the sails on the canal

But "the lunar pathways of the departed" cannot reach in Schiele "das stille Haus und die Sagen des Waldes, / Mass und Gesetz." This image is prohibited to him. (In Franz Marc the woodland animals take charge in their wisdom.) The extent to which it was left an unresolved problem in Trakl was discussed in Heidegger's *Erörterung*. This is unutterable.

The unutterable, nevertheless, manifests itself. The image has weight. The soul that is a stranger on earth carries it along. It constitutes the "too deep" that Wittgenstein suffered in Trakl. Schiele, too, in a poem published in *Die Aktion* in 1916, exhibits it as the *Abendland*:

> Ich roch die Sonne.
> Jetzt war der blaue Abend da,
> sang und zeigte mir erst die Felder.
> Einen blauen Berg umfloss noch roter Schein.
> Ich war von all dem Vielduftigen umträumt.
>   ("Abendland")
> I sensed the aroma of the sun.
> The blue hour of twilight now sang
> and first showed me the fields.
> A red glow embraced a blue mountain,
> and all the perfumes dreamed around me.

In "Empfindung," published in *Die Aktion* the previous year, the wanderer travels the earth, without ever noticing the weight of his body, he had become so light. The wanderer travels toward the horizon that shows up in Schiele's *Vier Bäume* of 1917. Also through the harmonic articulation of space, recalling Hodler, the landscape transfigures any naturalistic tonality. The reality that opens up, through the curtain of the four trees, before the eyes of the wanderer or whoever begins to wander over the grounds of separation, is the spiritual *Abendland*. Colors are suspended between dawn and dusk. The sky has the sunrise colors that Heidegger speaks of when he says, "*Dämmerung* is also the rising." The blue takes on qualities of brown and red. In the background appear the blue mountains, again mantled in red splendor. Hidden in darkness, they now call out and choose. An earth calls out near the pale red sun. They are the colors of an ultimate summer, lasting not even long enough to be seen, which is why memory fails to capture them on canvas. It is a screaming self-portrait like Klinger's last work, *Enfant perdu*. The "chosen" is the departed, the *Wahnsinnige*, "I, the eternal child." Trakl says, "Thus, spiritually, the oaks on the forgotten path of the dead turn green, the clouds turn gold, suspended over the lake" ("In Hellbrunn"). And it happens, then, as if the disease that seems to take hold of everything that exists, the non-living of life, revealed by Trakl, were transfigured by the voice of the Angel of the *Duino Elegies*: "But to have been one time, even only one time, to have been on the earth, seems irrevocable."

What couple on this earth rises up, almost imperceptibly? Perhaps the *Liebespaar* (see Figure 15), a pastel of 1909. Their arms are interwoven in a prayer-like dream. In perfect reciprocal trust, their lines present mysterious memories of the foundational discordant harmony.

Songs of the Departed

Closely related to the idea of departing is the idea of hiking or wandering. In Robert Walser's prose, wandering is to departing what, in Mahler, the Lied is to the symphony. The poet gets a "sacred, golden education"[75] from living outdoors. The idea of wandering is "high and noble." Benjamin was the first to fully understand how "difficult" wandering might be and how resistant to Romantic idling. The idea comes "out of night at its darkest, out of the Venetian night." Let us remember Simon's nighttime journey to visit his brother in the provincial town where they "were supposed to decorate a ballroom." And the other, even more enigmatic and labyrinthine ramble to the place where his sister Hedwig was a teacher, marked by the meeting with the poet Sebastian, who had frozen to death. The force that makes this meeting an occasion for joy goes unnoticed: " 'Your death under the open sky is beautiful. I shall not be able to forget it for a long time. . . . ' He should have been able to scream for joy in the freezing night pierced with stars." Only a "sacred, golden education" could render its faithful capable of finding in this death no less than "an exhortation to life." "He felt a profound joy for having seen once more, for having met in such a mysterious way, that poor unhappy being." Whence springs this "flame of life" that sweeps away images of death, that transforms the rigid body of the poet lying in the snow into "splendid repose," that embroiders marvelous flowers

over the coldest winter night? An irresistible, disturbing force of
"yes" emerges from Walser's hike. Wandering is a way of saying
"yes" to every image of life and death, of opening oneself com-
pletely to the infinite possibility of meeting.

Wandering reveals the facts of the world. It bears silent witness
that the world is all that is the case. Wandering brims over with
directions, situations, meetings, and impressions. It is beyond any
possibility of discourse. Cases that constitute experience make up
the whole world. No superior wisdom can redeem manifold coin-
cidence from it. Agony comes of such experience, which stops a
Romantic idler such as Knut Hamsun's nomad. In Walser, an ab-
solute sense of decency about language does not let agony express
itself. The reality is made manifest, the *fact* of agony, not agony. It
is necessary to speak of things, not of words. Marvelously, every-
thing that is utterable is said whenever one simply states the case.
Wittgenstein should have spoken about Walser, not about Johann
Ludwig Uhland. But to reach such a simplicity constitutes the cul-
mination of the "sacred, golden teaching" that Walser "initiates."

This simplicity cannot be reduced to the opening passages of
the *Tractatus* (to the case, the way it appears there) or to knowing
how to demonstrate agony with silence. It is even further from "de-
finitive understanding of the provisional and dissonant nature of
life."[76] In Walser, the intent of the compact grandiosity of the ego
is self-evident. The intent of the Romantic ego as wanderer is like-
wise self-evident. (Nothing is more "grandiose" than Caspar David
Friedrich's pilgrim on the misty sea.) The miracle is that the sort of
agony that comes from such an intention is not the essence of the
work, nor does a sense of decency (the authentic *aidos*) cause us to
remain silent about it. The case is not seen as mere dissolution of
the ego, as absolute and definitive dissonance. That the world is
the totality of facts does not suggest a radical devaluation. No phi-
losophy of value, no idea about the measure of the world can shed
light on Walser's facts—and yet these facts shine with unnoticed
energy. They are like miracles.

An unforseeable abyss seems to crack open the surface of the
most radical nihilism. There is no value, since there can be no val-

ues among the facts of the world. There are only equivalent propositions, only the utterable. And even this does not mean a desperate glimpse of caducity. Walser ignores the assumed virility of such a glimpse. He gives up all hope of value, but then the very form of his despair is seductive and enchanting. His necessary acceptance of the propositions of nihilism opens miraculously onto enchantment and onto the splendor of the case, a mysterious joy in the apparently provisional and fleeting nature of the world. This world, a world without values, shines with its own new light. It is no longer the light emanating from judgment, whether it be the wanderer's Romantic agony or the "virile" judgment of a rational disavowal of a home or dwelling. Wandering does not simply consume the *Entwertung* (devaluation) of the world; it celebrates the transformation of fact into miracle. It is a miracle that the thing shines precisely as a fact. It is a miracle that there are facts that surprise us, that impress us, that stand and remain as fleeting and ephemeral, in a divine fullness, autonomous, ignorant of our reflecting and judging. A moment of grace, inexpressible in itself, takes place when the same, direct, "simple" description of the fact demonstrates its divine fullness. Thus in Walser the ineffable manifests itself continually.

A fact is unique. Its singularity makes it solitary, extraordinary, and not capable of being repeated. "And they want you to exalt these things that live among the fallen. Fleeting, they throw an anchor to us, the most fleeting." Martin Buber says, "Not to repeat oneself is an eternity of the single."[77] The same applies to Walser's pursuit of the wanderer: the light of the event that captures it is that of its singularity. The wanderer is capable of aspiring to the extraordinary singularity of every fact: the rustle of the woods, the welcoming inn, the local artist's song. The "flood of gratitude that breaks forth from a contented soul" that impresses him in these encounters turns out to be incommunicable to others: it is his relationship with the fact as an autonomous and unique existence that others find incomprehensible. They don't know how to see with the eyes of a wanderer. Each case, for them, emerges in sudden apparent caducity. They do not know how to submit to

Walser's song sung before every fact in the world, before pure events: "Eternity, I love you." However, the wanderer teaches them nothing. He only sees that "here it ought to be divinely beautiful to love, to kiss," and to lie "discreetly buried in the fresh woodland ground, . . . to have a tomb in the forest." In this glimpse he meets the gaze of things. ("Es käme jetzt zur Geltung und träte hervor ein reizendes, feines Wirtshaus"—the house where we joyously meet is released from the realm of infinite possibility.)

Walser's journey takes place over the scabrous terrain of Nietzsche's most secret subjects. Only by remaining on their surface is it possible to plumb their depths. Appearance is deep: the eternal singularity of the fact within its eternal self-repetition. There is nothing beyond the "bona fide earth." Everything is here and "I'll have nothing anywhere else." Walser loves this destiny of belonging to earth and to the cases that flourish here. The "sacred, golden teaching" of wandering is a gay science. This is also the source of Walser's special ironic tonality that Roberto Calasso isolated,[78] so different from the Romantic assertion of laughter over the equivalence of the world, not a diabolical irony, but a cheerful one. Irony dissociates an event from the discursive and metaphysical forms that had made it logical. Cheerfulness demonstrates its intrinsic depth and gratefully accepts its eternal singularity. There can be no cheerfulness without irony. There can always be, however, malicious irony.

What makes up this gay science? Certainly it is not a critique of repetition alone (a critique of Kierkegaard's subtle ascendancy—yet another connection between Walser and Kafka). It is not even a Nietzschean critique of the *Grund*, of the study of origins and foundations that the wheel of appearances would celebrate and that would touch the sage through asceticism's methods of self-denial. The true problem of the gay science lies in the relationship between the "yes" and "amen" to life and time, and redeeming time. The profound melancholy that comes from "so it was" confuses the glimpse that takes in the miracle of an event. Is this fortunate fact destined to pass away? Does its singularity equal an eternal absence? Does saying it is never repeated mean it will be lost forever? At the end of the journey, Walser's wanderer has certainly collected many colorful flowers, but now he must ask himself if they should be strewn over his own sorrow. He is occupied "by a disturbing and irrepressible thought. . . . Life is so florid, with all the delightful colors and the joy of living . . . , and one day you disappear and die." The facts that flourish for him along his walk seem to recede definitively into the dark night, to abandon him. Was that divine nature that they expressed, then, a fantastic illusion? In Simon's final enigmatic words, the unresolved Nietzschean connection reappears between becoming (vanishing while becoming) and the idea of the eternal return (as opposed to mere repetition). He speaks of the marvelous face of the earth, saying he is in love with it but that it is offended and requires expiation. Simon must repay "all that I neglected, all that I lost playing and dreaming, all that I left out and all that I got away with." Why is earth offended and why does it require expiation? Weren't they earth's facts that summoned him to play and to dream? Isn't knowing how to see life as a game, free of foundations, chains, and *religio*, the greatest praise it can be given? Earth did not require a denial of the game, but rather that the game should not have passed from nothing to nothing. In the end, earth does not want the flowers picked on a journey that proceeds from departure to be strewn over the unhappiness and melancholy of "so it was." Earth asks the paradoxical redemption from time, *in* time of nihilism. It asks for a quest for which there is no name. In the time of nihilism, the "glory" of things is nothing but unstoppable lightning that for an instant rends the course of time. Earth wants expiation for our powerlessness to halt the quest and to name it. Simon becomes, then, the tragic hero who recognizes this fault and assumes it radically upon himself. That is why "he will not be lost."

The musical *Stimmung* of Walser's wandering is purely from Schubert. It belongs to a tradition that concludes "with implacable exactness" in Webern's ceremonial "syllabification, in his Lied that shuns the impulse to salvation in order to listen to the truth of the sound-symbol, in the silence of the internal man" (Bortolotto).

Such a tradition is founded on the "endless attempt to silence agony" that Elias Canetti recognizes in Walser. "The great meditation on the foreigner, wanderer, or derelict" that is "the compulsory gate into Schubertian liederism" and that continues to Wolf and Mahler (Bortolotto) is dominated by the problem of silencing agony. Manifest in the agony of the departed are frugality, moderation, avoidance of frenzy, avoidance of novelty, attraction to the traditional elements, regret over *Modernität*, simplicity that stems from the most ardent engagements, and a decency about language. An inexorable connection unites, in the Webern of Op. 14 and in Trakl's verse, the conditions of being *heimatlos* and *sprachlos* (homeless and speechless). If one lacks a dwelling, one's speech betrays it. Words belong to the experience of dwelling, in the Heideggerian sense. This is clear in the silent splendor of the lovers in Webern's Op. 8, after Rilke.

Nothing is conceded to the *trauriges Lied* (sad song) from the pressing, repeated condemnation of the fugitive in "In der Ferne," from the "I'm not sorry" that the fugitive intones in "Abschied" and from the symbolic journey in "Winterreise." Irony and pleasure jealously guard the secret of composition: a place to linger, the "muss ich vorbei," resounds in the clarity of the deed, in the actuality of going. These same principles are carried by Wolf to their radical consequences. He rediscovers "musically the Pythagorean formula that regulates the rhythms of the world: the march, the serenade, and the dance" (Bortolotto). He is the first to rediscover Walser's rhythm of the step that treads the roads, that cuts furrows in the brow of Mother Earth. The step takes pleasure in friction, resistance, and resonance. In a cardinal passage, Bortolotto explains the characteristics of the music that Nietzsche could not hear, music of deep appearance or, as noted, of the eternal singularity of the case. In a few texts like Eduard Mörike's "Fussreise" or "Auf eine Wanderung," the soul that is a stranger on the earth is very near to a morningtide *renovatio* and to the *Liebeshauch* [breath of love] that blows from the woods at the first light of sunrise. The song has flowers waving in the breeze (the very life in the air). It is sung with extraordinary freedom and invention, and without anything to concede to "the florid goddesses of love" (Bortolotto). It is the happy moment, the *kairos* [crisis], when the soul of the world opens up, when "the marvelous tableau of the present moment" becomes the only sensation: "the days of the future became dim, the past vanished. I, too, was burning in the blaze of that moment." The climactic experience of Walser's wandering already appears in Wolf's "madness," when in every direction there stands out "everything that is great and good, luminous, in shining gesture of blessing." The moment is "divinely beautiful" in its accidental quality. There is no ecstasy, no dream of transcendence. The same "little things" cited in the opening Lied of the *Italienisches Liederbuch* appear renewed, and with them the glimpse of the world appears renewed. "Madness" is the wanderer's intuition of the divine oneness of the case. The wanderer's detachment does not reach beyond the world. It stops at this worldly light, this worldly eternal lighting of the "smallest things." Walser says, "I looked around attentively at how many of the smallest, most modest things there were, while the sky seemed to arch high above and plunge into the deep. The earth was a dream. I myself had become an interiority and I went along as if I were inside the interior. Every exterior form dissolved, comprehended before but now incomprehensible." There is a profound and ineffable encounter in the midst of the extra-ordinary ordinary: that the world exists and is not nothing, and that it resists nothingness.

The departed, the "madman," knows neither *trauriges Lied* nor *klagendes Lied*: he neither complains nor accuses. He has learned calm and silence from the forest. The forest is quiet, and yet its color and motion reveal its secret suffering. "Whoever suffers can learn from the madman how unpleasant it is to prematurely embitter the lives of others with one's own sullen and complaining presence." In Walser's woods the genre of happiness coincides with that of sorrow, just as it does in the Schubert song, and in Wolf and Mahler. "Happiness and sorrow are intimate friends." This woods is not simply the opposite of Kubin's forest, since it also suffers profoundly; it also is a damp, running, overwhelming wave that dissolves forms, a "tumult" of colors that "awakens in hu-

manity only sentiment, not reason." It also, ultimately, is sublime.
The gaze that passes through it is renewed. The gaze that takes in
Sebastian dead and frozen is renewed, a gaze fascinated by the pres-
ent that belongs to one who knows how to listen. Simon says (with
accents that seem reborn from the spirit of Sigismund), "I am
nothing if not one who listens and waits, and in this I am perfect,
because I have learned to dream while I wait." Whoever is perfect
in listening and waiting cannot fear the demons of Kubin's forest.
Agony and delight marry each other there while passing through.
Agony is not sorrow. Sorrow is enduring melancholy, self-ab-
sorbed, trapped, and enclosed. *Melancholia* can never be the fig-
ure of the departed. Rather, agony is the ancient *penthos* [grief] of
the earliest hermits, a repentance for their own sins that coincides
with a renewed attraction to serve God by force of pleasure: *servite
Domino in laetitia.*

Another "perfected being" loved the woods and wandered in
them fearlessly, heedless of the monster that lived there. Martin
Buber tells how the young Israel ben Eliezer, the future Baal Shem
Tov, went to school every day leading the other Jewish children of
his muddy village, "taking a wide detour through meadow and for-
est." The children were happy, picking flowers and green boughs
to carry along the way. In the forest there lived a charcoal maker
who turned into a monster at night, a werewolf who attacked an-
imals and terrified people there (but who never harmed a human
being). One day the Adversary took the charcoal maker by the
throat, tore out his heart, and replaced it with his own, a heart out
of the heart of darkness. At dawn, the monster, livid and terrible,
attacked the children of Israel and terrified them with his mouth
foaming. But Israel knew how to listen and wait. He implored the
parents to trust him with their children once again, so he could
confront the monster in the forest. He led the children to the place
by the forest. The werewolf appeared and grew huge before their
eyes. Israel penetrated the monster's chest and grasped the heart,
dripping with "the infinite suffering that was within it from the
beginning." The monster is sorrow imprisoned in the realm of
Melancholia. Israel is the power of prayer and of the cheerfulness

that goes with it. Israel is called upon to demonstrate this, even if the children soon forget and end up like "grown-ups," going through the countryside with their heads bowed, seeing nothing. Only "perfected" beings know how to wander.

Those who listen and wait do not judge. The very essence of the "sacred, golden teaching" of the wanderer, of Simon, of the helper, consists in not judging. Wittgenstein's theories and Hassidic *pietas* and *humilitas* seem based in this commandment. If judgment is value, it is outside of the world, outside of the case; in the world judgment is impossible. If we judge, our judgment is intrinsically groundless, because if one were to make a grounded judgment, it would be according to Truth, it would have Value, that is, it would exist outside of the world. Therefore, it would not exist. The abandonment of *Grund* (and of the "*religio*" of *Grund*, as Magris and Calasso have explained) carries with it the abandonment of judgment. This abandonment, in Walser, is a source of new affection and not simple "virile" despair. It is a *metanoia* that unexpectedly impresses, that takes hold in the happiest moments, beyond any possible method. Walser's labyrinthine chatter (Calasso) intends to rescind every connection between the discursive nature of method and the way of awakening, the way that mysteriously leads to the "divine beauty" of the case. Not judging is, then, an exaltation of the creation and sanctification of living things, a self-emptying in order to yield to the fullness of what is manifest. What is manifest is certainly not, for Walser, God *signified* by the world or, as in Hassidic tradition, the world as the evidence of God.[79] In Walser, irony itself assumes the function of insuring that his "cheerful" abandonment to things does not seem a yielding to the fullness of the divine. Irony here shows that being a wanderer is a fundamental condition. Since being a wanderer means that one listens and waits, the condition is open also to the possibility of an inscrutable offering, like the existence of Mendel Singer. Walser's idiot declares himself unworthy of this miracle: whoever has no home now can never live in one. But his "madness" has separated him already from the old building. Already this is a cheerful fact, a fact that is praised through the entire scale in the gay science of Wolf's Lieder.

Walser's idiot, like the Hassidic fool, shuns confrontation and avoids any dialectical contest. ("He who weighs and measures becomes empty and unreal like weights and measures.") His ancient wisdom urges him not to condemn and never to think of himself as other than a sinner. (Walser ignores the real meaning of the word.) He is urged to live in peace and to sustain love in spite of the long distances (the relationship between Klara, Simon, and Kaspar seems to be a memory of an earlier life, of a joyful closeness past, that the labyrinths of exile have not been able to erase). Even Simon can confirm that, for him, no one is "the other," that there is nothing in the world that is not touched with life. (Every creature knows it, in unknowing omniscience.) The humble Hassid, however, "ends up on the edge of the cliffs of solitude, perfecting an alliance with the infinite" (Buber). His affinity with terrestrial things and his sympathy for animals are nothing other than the symbol of his alliance with the infinite. They prepare it and they announce it. The kind of wandering that Walser proposes changes its mood like the sky, according to the line in a key poem from *Kleine Dichtungen* (1914).[80] His style of wandering does not know the mystery of the soul straining for *the* end (the only thing that never lies and never gets lost). The soul stretches to the point of identifying with the end and living for it. The Hassidim call this intention *kavanah*. This intention is missing in Walser, because the idea of redemption is missing, the idea of returning from exile into *shekinah* [presence], of participating in the divine glory of the Creator. In Walser, the countless sparks of souls fallen and strewn among creation make no pilgrimage to their source. Instead, they end up contradicting themselves in their joy and suffering, in their guilt and innocence. Walser does not discuss simple absence of faith, but rather an infallible instinct directed against any possible form of dualism. Walser has never been able to say, like the zaddik introduced by Buber, that he awaits redemption as he opens the window, and looks about, and declares, "There is no renewal." Walser's waiting corresponds to the continuous renewal of the landscape and sky. In his eyes the world has no need of redemption, but his eyes need to recover from loving the world's singularity that eternally renews itself. How is it possible to think about redemption and not see, at the same time, the world as shell or mere appearance, or as an obstacle to the divine? How is it possible, through this faith, to surmount dualism?

The dialogue between Klara and Simon in *The Tanners* is unforgettable. As for the young Baal Shem, nowhere is more pleasing to his God than the woods. ("God seems to have created the woods to pray there as in a holy temple.") Like a zaddik, God remains in ecstasy whenever he is thanked, "even just a little, even superficially." God is *grateful.* He is "happy if his creatures remember him somewhat." He is *humble.* He confines himself in a realm of silence, of soft modesty, of apparent "indolence." He is *otiosus*, idle, but not because humanity forgets him or replaces him with other names, but rather because "he doesn't insist on anything, doesn't want anything, doesn't need anything." Perhaps he has "forgotten" his creation. When humanity adores him, "they pray in the woods without meaning to." It is as if God had remembered for an instant and were content with that memory, even though it is nothing to him. The absence of God has never been explained in more mysteriously simple terms. God is silence, but a secret current of affection binds this silence to the prayers of the heart that prays to him (and praying is the same as "becoming lost in thought"). The exile of God from the world is interrupted, at times, along the sudden arch of this memory. The painful awareness of this exile and of that silence can yield up cases of happiness. God does not want "people to be believe too much in him." God "wants to be forgotten," wants to be *otiosus.* He does not intervene, does not enlighten, and does not guide. He is the opposite of infinite production that characterizes his "official" image. He does not want to be called back from exile and oblivion—which is what the Hassidim seek in their excessive faith through unceasing prayer. The blind pride of man believed God's idleness was the result of his gaze and judgment! He, amenable, retreated, "delighted," before the injuries that would batter him and declare him dead. He "permits all thoughts." Where does his extraordinary richness reside? It resides only in the "lower regions"[81] of the profane, of the quotidian, of babble, only in the regions rejected by the arrogant pride of producing, only in the particular and in the humble sympathy for things and their events, only where faith is "little" and silent. Only there can a new and secret connection light up, forgotten, between creation and an "incautious" God. The greatness and goodness of the image of God rests in his desire to be forgotten and in his pliancy. The truth about God in this world lies in his not appearing here and his not producing here.

Klara feels herself beautiful when she says, "Whoever I caress with my hands can be happy." The perfect statement about listening and waiting is hers, however much suffering and "madness" it requires. It is madness in the manner of Hölderlin, according to a likeness that Walser perceived exactly, and it casts new light upon his entire doctrine of wandering. Hölderlin is "the hero in chains," a "royal Greek" obliged to move about within the narrow, horribly papered walls of a bourgeois room.[82] Hölderlin is a spirit who is capable only of living free. Freedom, however, is now a dying dream, and his song uncovers the empty squalor of life. "The hands that hold destiny pull it out of this world." They free it in madness, in the noble, good, and luminous abyss of *Wahnsinn*. For him, everything becomes "an abyss, an unbounded," free and open space. This is the madness of the solitary wanderer, of Simon, hardly masked by Klara's words. For Walser, the wanderer is the extreme figure of Hölderlin's kind of madness.

Hölderlin intones his highest and most regal song at the waning of the dream of being free in the world, of being here and now in the world in the light of the infinite. His tragic *threnos* accuses the world of the absence of God. In Walser, the tragic word is absent. Rather, continuous vigilance obstinately impedes any minimal hint of it. It is not simply modesty, not simply a sign of our poverty; it is the quest for a new way of looking at the time of the no-more and the not-yet. It is the attempt to see this time with love. Its desert is the only place where our destinies may cross, where one may listen and wait. Its singularity is loved and served. The desert of crossed destinies provides a foundation to our going—and journeys can have secret destinations that not even travelers know. Poverty is bitter, and the desert also means preserving, caring for this secret possibility. Its image is reached through tragedy, even if tragedy is an impossible measure of it. If asked, it would respond that tragedy is too high and noble for its "lower regions," but in reality the despair that lives there is a different song, a different quest: a highly fragile word, merely possible, evanescent in its possibility, almost negligible, too discrete, in near perfect silence, but as such cut off from all that can be weighed, handled, and judged—a word apart, departed, "mad."

The act of serving manifests this madness above all. It is found in the *Dieneridee* [idea of service] that dominates Walser's entire work. The theme of submission, of obedience performed with joy and conviction, is on the face of things tied to the theme of humility. It is tied to the tragic form's pure hopelessness and to how it prevails over free existence. One does not often notice the contradiction between the themes of the *Un-grund*, the absence of foundation, and of *Dieneridee*. Why must flight from *religio* express itself in the figure of the assistant, the clerk, the waiter? Too often we are constrained to repeat Walser's words, which appear to be so simple, "*ich bin noch nichts*" [I am still nothing]. ("I am a man, you should know, who does not deserve to be known"; "I am poor, and everything I say sounds impoverished.") Simon does not attach humility to service. The motifs of submission and obedience appear in various contexts, with the themes of abandonment and departure ("A Painter"), with themes of wandering and the woods. What upsets their quiet appearance is that the "servant" is a seducer. The "servant" knows how to execute a detour. That is, the "servant" knows how to take the lead down unfamiliar roads, along a thread of words whose secret he alone, almost unaware, seems to possess. There are people who defend themselves from seduction and others who, like Klara, abandon themselves to it. But service always indicates—or rather lets itself show—the possibility of a radical detour. That is how the servant seduces: because the servant already seems fundamentally, wholly, absolutely seduced. He is the most easily seduced, the ingenue par excellence. His condition pro-

claims how simple seduction is: how imminent, how close the pos-
sibility for our method to drive someone crazy, to seduce some-
one. That is why the servant is the other side of pure madness.

A work that can be linked to Walser only as its opposite can help
to understand this nexus in which the figure of the servant directs.
It would seem that nothing contrasts with Walser's *wandering* more
than Herman Hesse's *pilgrimage*.[83] Pilgrims have a destination, and
the destination continues to speak to pilgrims in their exile, as they
resolutely inhabit their intention. Even if they moved without con-
cern, pilgrims would still be directed. Their journeys stretch out
in time, through impenetrable twists, toward the destination that
has always existed. The star of redemption guides them, whether
their path turns to "the East, land of light," land of esoteric tradi-
tions that Hesse brings together, or whether they answer the voices
of the antique land that call them from their extreme poverty, as
with the Baal Shem Tov. "Where are we going? Ever home." In
Hofmannsthal, too, the journey is toward home. It is a pilgrim-
age, except in his last works, *Andreas* and *Der Turm*, where the pil-
grim wakes up suddenly a pure traveler, and the landscapes no
longer come to meet his soul, which had always lived in expecta-
tion of this happy visit. Hofmannsthal, in his last works, truly does
not deserve Walser's fierce dig that Canetti so enjoyed: "Can't he
forget being so famous for just a little while?"

It is in the course of a pilgrimage that a character of Hesse's re-
veals the hidden side of the servant in Walser. The account of the
journey to the homeland is well known, "the soul's youth" that
takes place in the magic circle of the unification of time and place.
In that story, we meet names we already know, from the restless
Hugo Wolf to the painter Paul Klee, whose Bible was *Don Quixote*.
All the characters rotate around the servant Leo, whose sudden dis-
appearance down the throat of Morbio makes them lose their faith
in the journey and breaks up their group. They cannot endure the
trial, and "a thousand tangled threads that a hundred hands would
take years to sort out" hold them prisoners in exile. With Leo's dis-
appearance, the journey animated by a pilgrim's clear intention is
superseded by stumbling about in the labyrinth. Pilgrims of the

League turn into solitary vagabonds (whom Hesse had already softly sung in *Eine Fussreise im Herbst*: "To live is solitude. No one knows the other. Everyone is alone"). How can the disappearance of a simple servant determine such a downfall? What secret is hidden in serving?

Leo is a perfect servant. Whenever he presents himself to H.H. to drive him up to the cathedral, they cannot help but notice his "elastic, patient stride, all driver, completely dedicated to the task at hand, all function." During the happy days of pilgrimage, Leo had spoken to H.H. about the law by which an artist's image seems more alive than the artist, just as a mother passes her own beauty and energy to her children. "'The law?' I asked with curiosity. 'What law is that, Leo?'" The law of serving, Leo answered. Whoever wants to live a long life must serve. Whoever wants to rule does not live long. Only the servant endures, whoever loves serving endures. The others, those who want to become bosses, "all end up in nothing." They are sick. "'In what nothing, Leo?' 'In rest homes, for example.'" The need to rule signifies an essential void, a fundamental poverty. Penia is a ruler. Whoever wants to become a boss is empty, lacking, woefully imperfect, weakened by their incompleteness, and destined to vanish (the pointless war of Basilius, in the words of Ignatius). Serving, rather, is inexhaustible. It is Poros, fullness of being, a well whose source never dries up. It is unending *dépense* [expense]. Whoever commands must use other people, imprison them, and transform them in order to survive. Whoever obeys the law gives life, expends endlessly, is consumed for other people, is renewed by this, and so endures. The boss, who merely acquires and produces, gets sick and dies.

In these words we rediscover intact the dialogue between Simon and Klara: "I do not place great value on my life, but only on the lives of others, and nevertheless I love life, but I love it because I hope it gives me the chance to dispose of it decently . . . , and so I give myself to you because I know no better gift. . . . This gift that I give you is unstable and eternal: because even the simplest person is eternal. I shall belong to you still when in a short while I will no longer be anything, not even a speck of dust: because the gift always survives as long as the one who receives it can mourn the loss of its possessor." Life is given to Simon to be spent; in fact, to be given as a gift, since only the gift is eternal. Through giving, the memory of those who know how to give also survives, since those who know how to give, give themselves. "I was born to give. I have always belonged to someone. I was disappointed if I went an entire day without finding anyone to whom I could offer myself." Wandering consists in seeking someone to whom to give oneself, in consuming oneself by giving oneself. Those who know how to serve are in search of those who know how to listen to the law of serving. The servant puts the law to the test and with it seduces. That is the source of the uneasiness of the characters around Simon's crystalline *Klarheit.* He literally hates to receive gifts! "You shouldn't love those who want to love, otherwise they would be disturbed in their devotion." The utopia of a relationship where one only gives, without ever "acquiring," emerges from the words of the perfect servant. And it is the same motif as in Musil's *Geschwisterliebe.*

Certainly, Simon is unlikely in the role of the supreme leader of the League, "in solemn and magnificent attire." The transformation is impossible for him, no less than the faith of the zaddik is impossible for him. But he, too, is one of the masks of the servant, one of the forms in which the foolish wisdom of giving is refracted. He is perhaps its most profanely enlightened form, without any miraculous gleam, far from any ex-static initiation (and further from any burst of literary decadence, which thrives in Hesse's theme concerning the relationship between character and author). Simon is also one of the cured, one of the awakened. Like Leo, he can go along singing and whistling, playing with animals and things, learning their languages. His madness is the sign of reawakening, and of healing, that follows the dark Venetian night. This night is not madness, as Benjamin said, but rather despair. Despair does not ever appear directly in Walser's works, since he assembles his characters after they have reawakened. We learn with bitter distinction about their past, about this memory of theirs. But the story speaks only of the madness of the reawakening and of its relationship with the cases of the world in the light of the golden teaching of wandering and serving. On this side of despair,

Leo explains, live the children, and beyond it live the reawakened. The way to despair traverses "every serious attempt to comprehend and justify human life," every search dedicated to judging cases according to value. H.H. is in the middle of the realm of despair. The work that he desires to write testifies to this. Works of despair are worth nothing. They suffer only from their own poverty. They do not know how to give themselves. Simon is not desperate. Nor is the child. Simon has crossed through despair, and he is finally able to feel the joy of serving and giving. The brother, a painter, is still a child. (Coincidentally, the art of Karl Walser, who illustrated a few of his brother Robert's works, partially to help stimulate their distribution, is an art of simplicity that renders interpretation superfluous. It is a playful art without system or law, a gently ironic art with flashes of Rococo and Biedermeier.)[84] The brother is a child who resists despair. Simon, on the other hand, confronted despair and traversed it. But this decisive experience is not utterable. Simon manifests it only in the two great forms of existence, his wandering and his serving: his opening up to receive the case as a divine singularity and the giving of himself. This double form merely indicates the possibility of a healthy permanence, of not ending up in the void, of not passing from nothing to nothing.

Simon does not teach this possibility. Simon is never the teacher, unlike Leo the servant, who in the end becomes one. Like his infinite capacity to give, Simon's enigma sustains itself and remains. However well he knows how to seduce (just as Leo the servant is a seducer), this seduction does not ever transform itself for him into power, into art. This is the peculiarity of Walser's style (which recalls Wittgenstein). The reawakened one is not a teacher; that experience cannot be taught. To teach is impossible. Only those who have undergone the experience understand it. This madness lets itself be understood by those who hold out their hand to it. In some way, like Klara's God, the madness is content with this gesture—it is content whenever people listen to it and attempt to utter it, because it is in that instant that they give themselves.

The Art
of Archery

The impossibility of teaching is connected with Wittgenstein's response to the idea of solution[85] and with Schoenberg's "didactic principle." Teaching is an indefatigable act of re-covery that ought to clarify the infinite complexity of languages and traditions that constitute their specific *Tatsachenraum*, an act never at home and never in pilgrimage. This is equally true of Walser's writing.

The cultural coordinates of the grand form have been up to now only partially investigated. Its radical difference from the "style" of contemporary European culture, from American-European civilization, is usually assimilated into the problem of an internal discord whose terms would never exceed the sphere of that civilization except in elusive motifs. But to the extent that this discord is never explicitly acknowledged, to the extent that the discretion and modesty of misfits is stronger and more refined than ever for the possibility of their own language, such an "excess" takes place. A possible path has already been indicated (we will return there) in the matter of the critical presence of *Ostjudentum* in the culture of the *Donaumonarchie*. Another is represented by the peculiar nostalgia for the East that runs through the sphere of American-European civilization almost continuously, even if it only reveals itself fully in sudden moments.

This attraction, which has solid and well-known roots in German culture, received a new impulse with the translations of Bud-

dhist writings by K. E. Neumann for Piper Verlag (not acciden-
tally the publisher of Wilhelm Worringer and the "Blaue Reiter"
group, of Schopenhauer's works, and of deluxe books in homage to
Mahler in 1910 and to Schoenberg in 1912). While the German
"pilgrimage to the East" was clearly influenced by Schopenhauer
and focused on the most "systematic" aspects of Hindu and Bud-
dhist mysticism, Vienna at the turning point was galvanized by the
"undogmatization" that runs through the Chinese and Japanese
Zen Buddhist traditions.[86] The German Orient appears as a Tao, a
Way, both logical and ascetic, involving painful sacrifice and de-
nial of the world of appearances in search of the full light of the
nullification of being. The Viennese eternal travelers do not dare
utter the Way. On the Way, everything happens as a function of
the destination. Everything aims toward the end. The value of each
step is measured only by its progress toward separation from be-
ing. This in-tending to separate, this relationship between Way
and destination by which every being along the Way is nullified as
a function of the end, which is itself the condition of non-exis-
tence, constitutes a profound motif of the Viennese critique of the
subject-object relationship and of the concept of substance or es-
sence. The history of this critique cannot be encompassed within
the "internal" limits of contemporary European culture, and even
less by reducing the relationship with *this* Orient to an exotic fas-
cination. Such a relationship happens by fixing on and measuring
the abyss that opens out from the eye of the Zen monk, the eye
that sees the solution. (They asked Joshu, "What is my essence?"
And he responded, "The tree bends, the bird flies, the fish leaps,
the water is muddy." And again, "What is my self?" And he, "The
oak in the yard. *Look at it!*"). A critical and nostalgic comparison,
inextricably entwined, follows the direct look, the gesture of Chu
Hsi that Hesse praised. ("About enlightenment or about the be-
ginning and end of the world, he kept silent. He only raised his
finger and lightly pointed. And the wisdom of that silent-speak-
ing finger became ever more eloquent and profound: it spoke, it
taught, it praised, it punished, and it guided thus uniquely to the
heart of the world and of the truth.") Siddhartha's ascesis is also

completely imbued with it. It leads to the veneration of the Buddha who enlightens every rock, every plant, and every animal to the perfection of every instant, to the sanctity of every being. *Love* is the force that compels us toward this destination, love as the quintessence of the *person*, of seeking, of in-tending—of metaphysical separation from being, since "the moment you aim toward something, you have already lost it." To express in terms of love and seeking the direct look at the divine value of the self is intrinsically contradictory. The very awareness of it—of the otherness of that look as opposed to reflection—renders the Viennese "seeker" like Hesse's Siddhartha in every other aspect, a coarse figure, not disposed to giving literary consolation. Zen motifs, common in Viennese Central Europe, are distributed within well-defined limits of critical and nostalgic consciousness.

This also happens to the figure of the teacher. We have already seen how, in Walser, reawakening is the living negation of teaching, and we find an identical repudiation of it in Wittgenstein, in Schoenberg, and in Freud's confession that teaching is impossible. The Viennese non-teachers do not preach, do not judge, and do not show the way. There are profound echoes of Zenjitsu in their counsel, of the ancient T'ang dynasty master: "to live in the world and yet not join the world's dust . . . ; a noble heart never shows itself . . . ; criticize yourself, no one else. Do not discuss truth and error." The idea that judging (as if one were in possession of values) is indecent belongs not only to a radical and paradoxical perspective on evangelism (Vannini) but also to *this* Orient. "I consider judgment of good and evil like the serpentine dance of a dragon, and the coming and going of beliefs like nothing other than the traces left by the four seasons." Zen masters wait for those who know how to listen to them, they do not ever seek them out. They "do not preach models to follow, do not believe in the edifying power of words" (Herrigel). The teachers never explain, but only point. Their relationship with those who listen to them is never discursive or agonistic; they are not out to convince. As the image of steps in the *Tractatus* undoubtedly alludes to a discourse of the Buddha, so it is impossible not to discern the Zen "style" in the first line of the Preface. ("Perhaps this book will be understood only by someone who has himself already had the thoughts that are expressed in it—or at least similar thoughts.") A Zen style runs through Wittgenstein's writing in general: in its attempt to render the problem plastically intelligible, to reduce it to a *case* for meditation, to articulate the argument in dialogue. The very roots of Wittgenstein's critique of Western *ratio typisch aufbauend* should also be seen in this perspective.

What all this is getting at is precisely the transcendence of the dual notion of reflection, of the a priori condition of constructive reasoning that consists in separating the thing from the self and in attributing substance to the self. It is perfectly clear to Wittgenstein, when he declares himself alien to the spirit of this civilization, that nihilism and the constructive power of nihilism reside precisely in this metaphysical separation. To tend, to in-tend, to ex-press, and to pro-duce all belong to such constructiveness and to its nihilism. Their action presupposes a fundamental separateness and, at the same time, the readiness of the thing, reduced to a phenomenon, to be reached, joined, transformed, and consumed. There is no *intentio* where "the perceiver is beyond the subjective and objective . . . , has the impression not of being the one to perceive things but of being perceived by them, has the sensation that they take advantage of the perceiver's senses in order to be and in order to reach the maximum fullness of being" (Herrigel). The text of *Zen in der Kunst des Bogenschiessens*[87] is throughout a limpid sign of this critique of intentionality as the key category of nihilism. The practice of archery does not help to develop attention to the "other," to the target (to learn to see the target, the "enemy"), but exactly the opposite, to reach a state that is free of intention, to become empty of the constructive and intending self. It is a doctrine that denies the presence of "a self-substance in the spiritual life of humanity" (Suzuki). The right shot at the right moment only happens when the archer is removed from any attachment to the old self, whether spiritual or physical, and remains surprised by the shot itself. "To the extent that she reveals herself more willing to learn to shoot a sure arrow and to hit the target,"

Herrigel's archery teacher explains, "she will be that much less able to succeed in the one thing and that much farther from the other. The obstacle is her will, which is too eager." One can never be one with the target where will controls the archer's hand (and will hangs upon power over the target). Thus the readiness should not be understood as intentional waiting and not as a simple absence of seeking, but as perfect presence: living in the present, in the moment, ready for enlightenment, just as without looking the archer hits the center of the target. The technical Mahayana term to define this state of illumination (satori) is *paravrittis*, which means to turn back or re-turn (Suzuki). It is a looking into oneself as remembering (*anamnesis*), a fundamental identity between the one who hits and the one who is hit.

Regardless of how useful the way of Zen may be for understanding the critique of Western civilization by the great Central European Viennese, that is not why it was proposed as a model. It is, in fact, practically never explicated. The impossibility of even discussing its Westernization is widely admitted. No one can traverse the inexorable lexicon of metaphysics by simply ignoring it. The Zen Way remains a great metaphor for this fundamental "ignorance," for ignoring the lexicon of metaphysics, and the caducity, the transience of nihilism that composes it. By this comparison (which remains critical) constructive reasoning is deprived of its "obviousness," stripped of the teleological and progressive basis that had legitimized its prevalence. Criticizing it does not by any means amount to traversing it and perhaps does not even constitute a first step. This is made very clear by a passage in Herrigel (even though he does not seem to realize its importance). To his archery teacher, who wants to show him how the bowstring is hung in the same way that an *infant* pulls the finger of someone who offers it, Herrigel asks, "Should I then intentionally do away with my intentions?" The master cannot understand this compound question-confirmation and does not know "the right answer." To typical Western sophism, the Zen way cannot answer. Non-intentionality is intentional for the West. What Herrigel is up against isn't the problem the Zen archer cannot answer, but the very life that problem reveals. For the West, any interior void is examined, attended with intention. Any ecstasy is pro-duced, brought forward. This condition precedes any dual-reflective self-articulation of thought. Thought can reach a point of seeing the other by itself, but never of being struck by it. It can reach a point of having a reflective idea of satori, of enlightenment—an idea, that is, that negates the very essence of enlightenment. Herrigel himself explains Zen in relative terms—by negation with respect to the reflecting *intentio*. This takes us to the paradox of a discursive explanation of satori. Precisely because of its intrinsic baselessness, such an explanation helps us understand which aspects of the Zen Way had a signficant influence in Central European culture around the time of the First World War: a vision of things as having the seal of the absolute, a vision of the origin of things as being without form and inaccessible, an intimate contact with them, to the point of having the sensation that "the thing is directed not toward the one who sees it, but toward itself" (Herrigel). The explanation of satori is wholly relative to the typically Western problem of traversing and surmounting nihilism. The term "satori" is used to mean the equivalent of non-discursive, non-logical experience, of a perfect liberation from reflection, and of immersion in the center beyond all contrasting. Thus Pai Chang responded to a question on enlightenment, "Once confirmation and negation, pleasure and displeasure, approval and disapproval, all the various opinions and the various feelings reach a terminus and cannot bind, then one is free wherever one may go; that person is called bodhisattva, with a new awakened mind that rises immediately to the arena of Buddha-hood." The idea of this enlightenment acts, in Herrigel, as the idea-limit of evident Kantian ascendance. Thus even in Viennese culture the Zen Way is an object of nostalgia. It involves an awareness of detachment, of unresolvable difference, and yet an attempt to utter it, to live it—an attempt that is bound to relapse into "unredeemable" intention. This gives way to an extraordinary, labyrinthine reflection on language. Zen teaches that experience is superior to thought by as much as thought is superior to language. Experience, however, has here become an idea-limit that is continually renewed, as such, in reflective thought. Thought inclines toward experience, but it is structurally impossible to reach it and define it. The limit of language here means much more than the reassuring image of an "endless search," of a generic and judicious task of disestablishing dogma. It shows the poverty of reflection at the peak of its civilization, in comparison with experience as experience.

It does not seem that this aspect of the Viennese critique of language can be found in Karl Kraus. His linguistic hygiene is mastery, and the magic of language *compos sui* consists in pitting it against the corrosive effect of time. Language emerges as "the true enemy of time." Kraus believes in the word, and specifically in the word as an instrument by which one can immerse oneself in the center of Being. "I can always count on words, / they know how to take me from appearance to essence." The correct words express the correct concept. Kraus finds himself in the correctness of language. He teaches it and he is its custodian. Beyond language thus defined there is nothing but "journalistic" events, the day to day *samsarian* life! No one reduces the real to the correctly utterable more completely than Kraus does, and no one therefore makes the utterable so completely real. His effort is entirely dedicated to restoring an ontological dignity to language, liberating it of any conventionality and artificiality. He wants to get himself "out" of this world of relativity, within whose limits, by contrast, Zen seeks nirvana. "Whatever may be your effort, nirvana should be sought in the middle of *samsara* (the transpiring world)" (Suzuki).

There is a distinct contrast between Kraus's position and the development both of Wittgenstein's intellectual perspective and of Fritz Mauthner's, whose reflections on language certainly influenced Wittgenstein. Mauthner considered incredible the idea "that language reflects and represents the constituent elements of a unique and universal reality, and that therefore from the existence of words can be inferred the existence of corresponding extra-linguistic entities."[88] Language is nothing but *bildliche Darstellung* (Wittgenstein's *Bild*)—a conventional form—even if the desire to become substance lies in the depths of the convention, the desire to hypostatize the *Bilder* that constitute it. By making language the enemy of time, Kraus reveals this desire, the superstitious need to possess, in language, Being itself, *Wesen*, and to use language (which is an instrument of nihilistic reflection) as a means of prevailing over events. Thus he would remove the unresolvable tension between words, thought, and experience—that is, between words and their silence.

At the peak of this tension stands Webern's music. Chinese texts develop, in Mahler's Lieder, in Berg, and in Webern, an essential function, precisely because they disclose the value of silence in compositional structure, which every interpreter has maintained. In Webern the pursuit of this value is programmatic. The musical propositions, abbreviated to spasms, scanned from lull to lull, isolated in their singularity, radiate with crystalline purity from the silence that encircles words and that words cannot subsume. The perfectly isolated sound that cannot be repeated (since the case is unrepeatable and since every being in its singularity is unrepeatable and eternal) is fixed in the silence within us, the void within us, that we made in ourselves in order to listen to it and take it in. To make silence within us is also the final key of Mahler's *Das Lied von der Erde*. Mahler's cycle seems to conclude with a gesture like that of Haku-in, who used to hold his hand up high and invite his disciples to listen to the sound of it. The power of this void appears great. Infinite sounds of exquisite purity emanate from it, and it receives infinite sounds in return. Entire orchestral scores are invaded by its might (Boulez). It is a generative void, but not in the productive and constructive sense of the term. The cases that break out from it, like forms of listening, are not fixed on a scale of evolutionary and progressive coordinates, by which the one completes the other or expresses its meaning, its destiny. Every sound is unique and unrepeatable. The composition demonstrates that sounds are unrepeatable. Their purity is exalted by not repeating them. "When Kakua went back to Japan, the emperor heard about him and asked him to teach him Zen. Kakua remained in silence before the emperor for a long while. Then he pulled a flute from the folds of his robes and he played a single, brief note. Bowing deeply, he left."

The principle of brevity and of absolute clarity concentrates the content of the utterable into a single point of unheard tension. When *Klarheit* is complete, a white, perfect serenity prevails. A Zen master named Seikyo, during the Sung dynasty, illustrated the states of spiritual purification through the symbol of the gradual "whitening" of an ox (Suzuki). One of the pictures is *white on white*. "Everything is empty: the whip, the yoke, the man, the ox. . . . When this state prevails, the spirit of the ancient master is manifest." The same tension without in-tention in the *white on white* (one of the most esoteric and yet traditional aspects, therefore, of contemporary avant-garde art) dominates in the silent art of Japanese theater, "frozen dance, dance without dance" (Herrigel), and above all in Zen painting. In Zen landscapes, unmoving space full of infinite breath encircles the observer "who is at the center without being the center; who is within, at one with the pulse of things" (Herrigel). "One lets nature draw its own images without reference to people. It has its own moods, expressed through rocks, mountains, rivers, tree trunks, birds, human beings, and plants" (Suzuki). The relationship between drawing and void is here as critical as that between words and silence or between sound and pause or lull. All senses of the landscape are comprehensible only to the extent that they are woven with void and silence. The void unites the isolated images and permeates them. It does not express them in their immediate isolation, which any perspective could measure. The void makes every image leap into presence, into its own space without foundation and without tonality. The problem of this void obsessed Viennese thinking about design and architecture. Klimt struggled throughout his entire work with the relationship between void and image, but his background remained too "rich" and resonant to be truly detached from the West's *horror vacui*. A landscape by Schiele, on the other hand, one of his last, *Häuser und Föhren* (see Figure 16), seems truly dedicated to clarity without an atmosphere of Zen seeing. The void invades this brief sketch, as it does Webern's. Unique and eternal cases unlock themselves there into existence, cases that a profane enlightenment succeeds in grasping as such. I am reminded of the little painting that Hesse's character Klingsor wanted to give to his friend Louis, "the most Chinese painting ever painted, with the pagoda, the red pathway, the jagged trees in pale green." Wherever it is possible to see and clearly describe the visible, there the void that encircles it, its foundation of silence, becomes manifest—and nothing is lost.

Zen poetry is based on the same principles that continually return in Wittgenstein's "aesthetic" judgments. Responding to Basho's haiku, "Old marsh! The frog jumps! Splash of water!" Herrigel comments, "That is all. And yet, does it not contain the entire universe?" Conversely, the in-tending toward essence, the shouting at the unutterable, the romantic and expressionistic *Streben* does not merely have the effect of producing compositions dominated by *horror vacui*, that is, by fear of silence, of a pause, of a lull, and powerlessness to stand the void. It also has the effect of reducing any single existence to details, to *a* detail. For the tired eyes of seekers after essence and the "most profound," of those who in-tend toward the beyond, all that exists is nothing but *a* detail. On the other hand nothing is detail, *a* detail, for the great Viennese thinkers on language. In other words, for them, God is in the details. Details must emerge the way mountains, woods, trees, flowers, and animals emerge in a Zen landscape, with absolute *Klarheit*, without ornament. Loos's critique, on the contrary, which is still interpreted as a sort of functionalistic ascesis, practically as an epigone of nineteenth-century progressiveness or a fetishist image of technology,[89] confirms precisely the essential nature of details, the deep aspect of appearance. It is possible to "decorate" only what is held to be insignificant. The "tattoo" quality of ornament would lend harmony and form to a mere particle, to the marginal, and would redeem the supposed vulgarity of detail. But when details are seen with *Klarheit* and heard in the utmost concentration of the void per se, then that is all, or all is manifest in that. The Zen story of Rikyu is literally identical with Loos's and Wittgenstein's behavior with the craftsmen (when Wittgenstein built his sister's house). Rikyu, a master of the tea ceremony, asked a carpenter to help him hang a flower pot, and he advised him during the job ("higher, lower, more to the right, more to the left") until he found the right spot. The carpenter, just to make sure, marked the spot and then pretended to have forgotten it. "Was it here," he asked, "or rather here?" But the master indicated exactly the spot he had chosen before. So too the story of Loos's soap exhibits exact correspondence with the anecdote of the young student who brings a pail of water to Master Gisan and spills a few splashes. "Idiot," screams the master, "what right do you have to spill a single drop inside this temple?" Thanks to this reprimand, the disciple attains satori and from that moment on is known as Splash.

Love of details and care for material are in Loos, as we have seen, one and the same. The figure of the craftsman is exalted through this motif, whose metaphysical roots necessarily elude aesthetic and literary, as well as historical and sociological, interpretation. Loos's craftsman is an expression of the point at which technical capacity becomes spiritual, at which concentration on material and tools is already part of the work. Thus for a painter using india ink the act of drawing the image on rice paper, all the work that went into preparing the stylus and colors, and the hours of concentration and marshaling forces during which the artist is unreachable, all this "precipitates" as if from afar. Thus a master of flower arranging begins his lesson "cautiously choosing the string" that ties them and, "after carefully rolling it up, puts it aside" (Herrigel). This is not a matter of simply putting "small things" in order; it is a matter of essential moments in the work itself, since the work is a metaphysical consonance of art and craft, material and spiritual, subjective and objective.

Walser's idler knows the art of Zen painting and flower arranging very well. From his first work, *The Themes of Fritz Kocher*, the method of an authentic "small" master is described with minute attention, along with "reverential respect for everything that exists" (and with the profound nostalgia that necessarily results from this in the *Abendland* that ignores it). Consider the praise of calligraphy in "The Class Theme Paper," the recommendations on how to sit quietly in your seat and on what paper to use. Consider the recurrent motif of *courtesy*, of fascination with the norm that prevents "originality," and the imperceptible changes in the ceremony. Consider, finally, the part on winter that combines, again, Webern with Kakua's flute: "I like things that are one color, one tone. Snow is a single song on a single tone."

Master of this brevity, of this simplicity which is *Klarheit*, Peter Altenberg could be called in to tie together all the motifs analyzed to this point. Like Fritz Kocher, Altenberg is incapable of those flaming colors that are like "a song of too many voices singing too high." In the extreme discretion of his language it is as if all the others were retracted into a dimension of pure memory, into a perfect no-place. This distinction takes the form of irony, but it is the irony that follows awakening—the awakening that, in its turn, followed despair. It is the irony of the awakened, of those who know that the idea of their waking is a perfect no-place in the *Abendland*—that this idea is only "interior." Altenberg's *kleines Leben* [ordinary life] is encountered not only after despair, like Walser's, but also after the awakening. Its impulse to see is not a tenacious refusal of judgment. It is the condition of full awakening, of a daytime without emphasis, without blinding light, that thus permits every single tone to exist and be seen. Their *Ansichtskarten* [picture postcards] are perfect examples of this impulse, and thus Berg and Webern understood the truly Wolfian "little things" of his genius *ohne Fähigkeiten* [without technique]. The concentration of style, in some of his pieces, is next to enlightenment, and the suspended tonality that vibrates there is comparable only to the waiting without intention of Zen poetry.

Those who recognize essence as a property of such waiting also feel its absence. Altenberg's irony clarifies the intention that dominates this form in spite of everything. It explains how intention prevents any fullness of the present, how it subdivides time into memory and future, and makes the moment volatile. The moment's flight is the sound that Altenberg transcribes in its singularity. This pursuit, which amounts to a pursuit of self, always returns anew to the forms of recollection, of passing away.[90] The torment of the interminable quality of this pursuit does not recognize the "fallen" of Hofmannsthal's misfits. This torment too is *seen*, is one of the facts of life, one of the cases that it is necessary to learn to see with unencumbered eye. It is one of the cases in life where seeing is actually an attempt to see, where speaking is nothing but an effort to speak. It is one of the cases in life whose awakening cannot be experienced except in reflection and otherness. And still, the "miracle" to be achieved consists in understanding all of this in the form of *Klarheit*. It is not the "miracle" of the priest who succeeded in writing the holy name of Amida in the air or of the monk who walked on the waves of a river and to whom Huang Po turned and said, "If I had known you would invent miracles, I'd have cut off your legs." Neither can it be the full miracle of Bakei, who eats when he is hungry and drinks when he is thirsty, since we are powerless to become one with the target, to immerse ourselves in ourselves free of any intention. It is a matter of a "miracle" for our interminable intending, discovering all of its poverty, the perfect form of that eating and drinking. Since this and no more manageable object is the scope, Peter Altenberg is one who pursues himself without ever being able to find himself. Nor does he have Govinda's gift ("'I am old, it's true,' said Govinda, 'but I have never paused in my pursuit, which seems to be my destiny.'") of deluding himself at the end on the perfect smile of Siddhartha.

A Dark Alley
in the Old City

Peter Altenberg's Ersucher shares nothing with diffident Ulysses, who fears "that Calypso may be a trap," who lacks tact and suffers from a persecution complex typical of intellectuals, who tries to eliminate risk. Bazlen drew a ruthless portrait of him.[91] Altenberg's Ersucher represents Bazlen himself, in his novel, in his readings. Viennese Central Europe is completely at home in the Trieste of Bazlen and Saba. Indeed, Trieste at times took Vienna's enigma into account with even more sobriety and detachment, if that is possible, and with greater intelligence. On Trieste, Bazlen's *Intervista* is unequaled. A bourgeoisie "that believes they milk the wolf in Rome to feed the family" and whose thought takes on golden wings when they show *Nabucco* at the theater collides with impartial Austria, full of the tolerance and dignity "of the dying snobs." At home this bourgeoisie encounters a bureaucracy more liberal than the irredentists, obliged to prohibit something every so often, but ready to sack the telephone operator who had incautiously "intercepted" a patriotic conversation of Svevo's daughter. This bourgeoisie, if it had to escape, would have broken the ghetto book stalls under the weight of Carduccis, D'Annunzios, and Sem Benellis, while the Germans departed "leaving a great unofficial culture behind them, important and hardly known." Yet this bourgeoisie gave birth to Italo Svevo and Umberto Saba, Scipio Slataper, Roberto Bazlen, and Carlo Michelstaedter, and took Ferrucio

Busoni on his first steps. It could happen (and it did to Ladislao Mittner in another Babel not far away) that the father could be a Hungarian with a German name, but fascinated with Italian culture, and the mother could be an Italian whose ancestors were Croatian, with an irredentist uncle wearing German insignia, and another uncle a Bohemian but loyal to the Emperor.[92] "I am anything but a melting pot," Bazlen justifiably observes. "I am a crossroads." At the crossroads, the different roads do not fuse into a single highway, but all possible directions remain open. The impulse to learn them and travel them all arises from here, an unused restlessness, that impresses whoever is born at the crossroads and whoever celebrates their epos in Theodore Däubler.

Among these diverse, possible directions, alongside Ibsen's Nordic and expressionistic direction, alongside Michelstaedter's tragic and classical direction, alongside Svevo's protagonist of European decadence (decadence, according to Bazlen: "the last European movement in which literature might have made a living contribution to European culture"), there is the Vienna that is defined by Hofmannsthal's misfits and Altenberg's and Musil's man without qualities, that lives in Loos's "details" and in Webern's pauses. Bazlen and Saba are deeply connected to Vienna, and every attempt to understand them solely within the scope of twentieth-century Italian culture is a priori destined to fail. Nor are they connected to the empire as peripherals. Saba takes the problem of compositional clarity, brevity, and comprehensibility to a level of exceptional prominence. Bazlen advances a new critical perspective of *Einfühlung* [empathy], alien to the intentional and reflective paradigm, and far from the pseudo-creativity of homogenizing the work under consideration.

Bazlen's critical perspective involves reading, not interpretive teaching. It does not furnish the key to mastery of the work, but it shows the work, indicates it, and reveals it. These are glosses, comments, and footnotes. "Almost all books are footnotes swollen into volumes (*volumina*). I only write footnotes." It is a genre to which the best things of Altenberg and Kraus also belong, as well as Saba's *Scorciatoie*. Nietzsche's influence is evident throughout Bazlen's

Note. He considers Nietzsche's first and most important creative renewal (along with Saba's, as discussed below). Goethe's criticism is Nietzschean. "Goethe's perfection: not in the statuary clarity (what does it mean?) but in the rhythmic equilibrium between clarity and madness." And again, "The harmony of Goethe's life: not Apollonian, but the most beautiful, the most rhythmic alternation of form and chaos." His "genealogy" of morals is Nietzschean. "Socrates is the West's first plebeian. . . . Drinking the hemlock in that satisfied manner with no edge of agony, like a businessman, with the sure conviction that 'up there' all is still happier." He also considers a Nietzsche rewritten in the "low" measure of the footnote, in which motifs remain hardly mentioned, stripped of any evangelical or prophetic pretense. The *measure* of Bazlen's Nietzsche (who comes from a bitter experience of submission and linguistic asceticism) is not, however, in Kraus's sanctification of language, but rather in the "profane" awareness that language is a precious and irreplaceable gift and at the same time limited, weak, always on the point of vanishing, delicate in its mechanisms. One turns to this Nietzsche, however, with patient irony. He is not a new idol, nor should he believe himself to be so. It is necessary to teach him to distance himself from his misery, to see it critically. It is necessary to educate him about this, not to lose him to the despair and anguish that, as we know, precedes the awakening. In irony, language finds an affinity with its limits, learns to recognize them and become, *in* them, self-possessed.

The "philosophy" of the footnote, of submission to the *volumina,* is not a matter of falling to ones knees before fetishized language, but of preserving it as a weak and precious gift before the attack of the great intentions, the visions of the world, the judgments. ("Teach nothing to people: they are capable of learning on their own"; "the exaggerated veneration of intelligence is left over from the age when it was difficult to be intelligent," which could be, literally, an aphorism of Wittgenstein or a phrase from Musil's *On Stupidity.*) The footnote is also an adventure, a risk. It gives itself over to the text entirely. It is listening, ready for surprises, profoundly curious. It loves temptation, yet it is difficult to please. Apparently adventure is centrifugal, as Calasso has noticed, and it turns about an empty point, a pause, a silence. Because listening is full, it must create the void within itself. It must always return to this "interior" adventure, the kind most alien to Ulysses' "prudence." The adventure is essentially concentration and immersion: to put all content (to tempt it) to the test of the interior void, to see if it can manage the silence. The arrow of the footnote is shot at that target, at the heart of the archer himself.

One comes alive when this exercise succeeds. ("Born dead, some succeed, little by little, in becoming alive.") Saba is a great and subtle master of this. He flings his shortcuts (*Scorciatoie*) like a shot from a sling. His writing is full "of parentheses, dashes, quotation marks, and italics. . . . I do not know anymore how to speak without abbreviating; and I could not abbreviate otherwise." The telegraphic style of the soul invented by Altenberg finds, in footnotes, in souvenirs, in Saba's short stories, one of its most perfect realizations. Shortcuts save no time. Brevity is difficult, impervious ("paths for goats"), when one seeks *Klarheit* with every step "in God's honor." Shortcuts are not the shortest path, but the path of concentration and of maximum density, of radical *dépense*, without Penelope in waiting. Not even a path, but a crossroads again, a contrasting complex of voices that never join, but that are compound, that require composition of their rigid differences.

Bazlen, in a fragment of his unfinished *Capitano*, defines the principle of this composition thus: "I could tell you that you are still very young, and that the great sorrow is small sorrow, and the great happiness is small happiness. Perhaps, though, I am as young as you, and I believe in a time in which voices remain equally clear in happiness and sorrow." In *Parole*, Saba had imagined this principle in the same terms. He seeks "a corner of the world" where words could be cleansed "of the falsehood" that blinds them. Tears (the divine value of tears) can restore the word to a clarity "where the heart of humanity was reflected, / naked and surprised, in its origins." The voice of awakening does not ignore despair and is not an ecstatic dismemberment. It remains limpid and clear in exhibiting the same sorrow. The voice should always remain limpid and clear, as in one of Wolf's Lieder, as if tense without intention in composing the differences between words and silence, between sound and pause. It is not yet time for this voice. The footnotes, the shortcut, Altenberg's *Extrakte*, all clearly indicate a void here, show a no-place. Saba points it out in Nietzsche, too, in "my good Nietzsche (not the other Nietzsche of others)," who is capable of speaking of the soul and of things of the soul "the way Carmen spoke of love to Don José." In his "poor and dear Nietzsche," Saba finds "a nearly complete sublimation of Eros," that would have rejected the soul if it had been found with Doctor Rosenberg and would have strangled his dirty sister with his own hands (and Saba wrote these things in 1945!). Saba points out the possible Nietzsche of the dance who attempts to traverse nihilism, who tries to utter its problem, and whose rhythm Bortolotto heard again in Wolf. It is the same Nietzsche found in Savinio's *Encyclopedia*, lyric and "generous," astonished, in pain and despair finally, when confronted by the "darkness people" who inquire about his purposes, his supposed hidden sense, his practical responsibility. "Do not let the darkness people mix with the people of light, and do not let them use their 'incomprehensible' words." It is the Nietzsche who sings "my simplicity" over "learned" texts, whose innocent "little tricks" would weave "pants for the spirit."

Even if a voice such as the one Nietzsche dreamed about, so eternally clear, cold, and concise, could never be; even if the voices "become hoarse . . . because they still have an entire life ahead of them, with heavens and hells and purgatories" (Bazlen), it is necessary to be prepared every day for that clarity, to fling words into the center of it. The fact that we are bound to in-tend this clarity lends credence to our critique of everything that arises in our time like an indestructible idol. We are therefore always infinitely distant from it. This fact has not even reached the bottom level of despair—indeed, it strives to remove it. The things of the past that do not want to die are liquidated, and the most fleeting fruits of time that would redeem us from time are liquidated. "The danger here is not in the solution, but in the palliatives that slow it down." In the end, Saba "the conservative" invites a parricide. It is Bazlen: "whatever does not wish to die must fall apart." This not wanting to die is the perfect sign of the world of the dead.

The Star
of Narration

Claudio Magris has pointed out the development of a Hassidic *pietas* in storytelling that informs not only contemporary Yiddish literature, but Joseph Roth himself. I think, however, this development is not so "remote," and an examination of its cultural terms may help to understand the motifs of Vienna at the turning point in a new perspective.

It could not have happened otherwise, since the dissolution of Eastern European Jewish culture, *Ostjudentum*, is an integral part of the *finis Austriae*. Its *Heimat* is both the shtetl *and* Vienna. I doubt that anyone experiences Vienna as a "familiar synthesis of a harmonious multiplicity" (Magris). I would repeat rather Bazlen's statement about Trieste: neither melting pot nor harmonious synthesis, but crossroads, a dramatic intersection of various events and different directions. The crossroads consists of a multiplicity of directions that mysteriously and momentarily meet and combine. The *Vaterland* is one route, the master avenue, designated as destiny in the rhetoric of solution. *Heimat* remains only at the crossroads: the realm without qualities of possibility, the place where possibilities meet and cross and blend and become one another. The real does not come out of this meeting of possibilities. Other, new directions emerge from it and leave those crossroads behind, venture out to find others. Narrative narrates the past, the absence, exhausted by now, of the crossroads of *Heimat*.

The *pietas* of narrative consists in preserving the past. Preservation is possible only through and in narrative. Narrative takes on the color of what it preserves, and so narrative and *Heimat* blend (a crossroads of possibilities that still know how to resist their *reductio ad unum*, yet they live in full awareness of their final day). Narrative becomes the only possible homeland. Narrative narrates itself, and what counts in the end is not its object, but the fact of its existence. The great collections of Martin Buber, Samuel A. Horodetzski, and others bear witness to the extraordinary fabulistic energy of the Hassidim. For them, it is a blessing to *narrate* the stories of the blessed and the events of their lives, even if not everything they tell really happened. The "what" of the story is not the blessed and true, but the intention of the narrator who narrates his spiritual *Heimat*, an intention that assumes the unblendable, very real matters of *Ostjudentum*.

The power of the book also reveals *pietas* through the power of narrative per se. No one can sit on a bench if a book is resting on it. Never leave books upside down. "If a book falls to the ground, we pick it up and kiss it."[93] When a book becomes completely worn out and unreadable, or ruined by fire in a pogrom, then the sextant buries it in the cemetery, running a risk like Shemarja in Roth's *Tarabas*. Certainly it is a matter here of veneration for Hebrew script, whose every letter is a name of God. In addition, there is the resonance of praising the symbol that permits the protection of the *Heimat*, the possession in some way of the tragedy of existence. The object of veneration in the book is its *words*. It is that the book can be read continuously. It can be experienced and transformed into stories, and into stories about anyone. Whoever knows something good about a righteous person (and it does not matter if it is not all "true") should tell it without delay, even if the story is already familiar to the audience. It is therefore the opposite of a logocentric sanctification of books. Words are real here in a sense distinct from a univocal correspondence to the reality of facts. Words are reality, are "things" in themselves. This sense of reality is available through hearing. One must prepare oneself to hear it. Words produce themselves magically as reality does, and humanity must become all-hearing in order to understand them. Perfect all-hearing individuals appear as the zaddikim in their stories.

This strong symbolic quality of Hassidic narrative (which is coded in the noun *d'var*, meaning both word and thing) comes apart in Roth, just as it does, in spite of linguistic continuity and a certain formal resemblance, in Isaac Bashevis Singer. *Heimat* here is only past and absence. The narrative narrates an absence. The narrative preserves things and words in the invisible. In *Shosha*, Singer warns about the radical groundlessness of the passing away of things into absence. "The history of the world was a book that man could read only going forward. He could never turn the pages of this world book backward. But everything that had ever been still existed. Yppe lived somewhere. The hens, geese, and ducks the butchers in Yanash's Court slaughtered each day still lived, clucked, quacked, and crowed on the other pages of the world book."[94] Would this "intuition" make sense if it were spoken to someone other than Shosha, the "idiot," the "pure fool," a fundamental figure in the Hassidic tradition? Shosha is the last survivor of those who know how to listen to tales. She is the last all-hearing figure. Her extraordinary powers of listening characterize her as the "fool." Her faith is seated, physically, in her sense of hearing. Without listening, without its power, narrative is meaningless. No one can narrate except to Shosha. At the center of narrative form is the form of listening. An identical *pietas* involves both dimensions. Those who know the language of stories listen. Those who already know the story listen. Those who can participate in it, correcting it, enriching it, reliving it, those who live in it listen. Shosha is a survivor of listening, and Tsutsik has not finished listening yet, because his roots are in narrating, in the Hassidic *pietas* that accompanies it. These roots are buried now, and the city where Tsutsik lives has no "circle" that listens.

In Roth, this process is complete, and listening completely disappears. His peculiar language would itself prevent listening. Narrative folds in on itself and tends to change into soliloquy. The silence of listening expresses the irreversible loss of *Heimat* and the impossibility of going home again. An attention to words as an end remains, since they are forever "the abyss over which every speaker treads" (Buber), but this attention is a desperate exercise. It is still necessary "to speak as if words opened the heavens: to speak as if words did not come from inside your mouth, but as if you went inside the words." The "as if" that appears in the Hassidic text with the immediacy of a symbolic relationship "falls" in Roth under the principle of Hans Vaihinger. (Feitelzohn, the extraordinary character in Singer's *Shosha*, would edify his entire mock temple with ideas in the name of Vaihinger.) It is necessary to continue to narrate *as if* there were still listeners, with the same simplicity and the same absence of "special" pathos, with the same *pietas* for words, even if they have nothing left of *d'var*.

If in reality narrative narrates *Heimat*, if narrators are narrated by *Heimat* (which is land, language, and legend), then now that *Heimat* has been transcended, narrative itself becomes an absence, a no-place. If narrative no longer has the foundation of *Heimat*, its words launch into a mad dance where they tear off their own limbs and throw them into the air, as happened to Rabbi Jacob Joseph, when he refused to recognize the sanctity of the Baal Shem Tov. "The propositions stood up saying they no longer wished to serve an unknown end overarching them, but rather they wanted to live by themselves for themselves." The discipline of *as if* would prevent this final diaspora: the narrative must have the same simplicity and clarity it would possess if that end still existed. It would be a false nostalgia to ignore the decline of discipline and therefore to pretend that language itself was not now an absence. Words must be forced to name it with the same clarity with which they narrated the *Heimat*.

Even in Hassidic narrative the motifs of home and of listening do not appear in terms of a happy synthesis or of a realized truth. A parable obsessed the Rabbi of Kotzk. When God was about to create Adam, Love got into a quarrel with Truth. Love said, "Let him be created, because he will perform many acts of mercy." Truth said, "Let him not be created, since he will be a liar." To listen to Love, God must bury Truth underground. Truth, then, abides in the tomb, or, as the Baal Shem said, Truth "is driven from place to place, and it is compelled to wander the earth." The vagabond of the Eastern lands that Roth mentions is, in his folly, a living symbol of Truth. The world, its creatures, their beauty—all of it is possible because Truth is not there. God would have destroyed our world, too—as he destroyed innumerable others before ours—if he had listened to Truth. In the interregnum, in the time that separates us from the coming of the Messiah, Truth is inaccessible. The impossibility of going home again (of *Heimkehr*) appears as the symbol of inaccessibility. At home, too, speaking and narrating are other than Truth. At home, too, truth lies entombed. In this sense, the nation of Israel has been *heimatlos* from its very beginning. There has never been a home for it. Its exile began with its origin in Egypt. That first, foundational, and essential laceration constitutes the dominant theme of Rosenzweig's great work, *The Star of Redemption*. It involves the loss of the motherland, fleeting and transient, of *Ostjudentum*, of the Hassidic shtetl. Then a second laceration divides us from words that live and renew themselves in listening. The characters in Roth and Singer represent both of these lacerations. They have ancestral knowledge of the abyssal difference between words and truth. They are children of the diaspora and exile. They can never adore words as a new idol, but at the same time they must wander to where language is everything, since earth is no more and since home has become nothing. It lives only in the pages of the book of the world.

Words are authentic when they know themselves within their limits, that is, when they know that Truth is underground. Every story is thus wrapped in the silence of Truth. The silence of listening is the last figure of the diaspora, whose roots are the silence of truth. Since nothing is comparable to the possession of truth and since truth is now silence, the greatest secret will definitely reside in silence. The silent foundation of words, the pauses that distinguish them, the void from which figures emerge, count more than any story. The most lofty secret "is submerged in the white sea that surrounds the letters on every side. The secret of the blank

parchment around the letters is so immense, that all the world is
not broad enough to contain it. . . . No one knows how to read it.
No one penetrates it. Only the future world will understand it.
And then what is written in the Torah will no longer be read, but
what is not written in it, the blank parchment" (Langer). The
blank parchment that embraces the letters (again the relationship
between life and death, reason and folly) represents the silence of
Truth. A time will come, though, of apocalyptic beauty in which it
will be possible to understand it and read it. When the Messiah
comes, the truth that the blank area of the book now preserves in
the invisible will shine forth. It will be the time in which the Torah
can be forgotten, in which the law will be put aside.

The struggle against law that renders Roth's writing so dramatic
is the struggle against a kind of law that endeavors to phagocytize
the sacred "white letters," the blank area of the book, and thus
eliminate all space that preserves the possibility of redemption. To
invade every page of it, prevent the repetition of words, mark every
one of them with an appropriate pause, abbreviate their breath,
this is what binds Roth to the great Viennese thinkers on language
with their supreme indifference to *horror vacui*. It is his desperate
exercise to keep words in the presence of the possibility of that
time or, better, to keep words as purely within their limits as if this
possibility were still open. The book's logocentric dominance is
doubly overcome: by words that live only in listening and by the
white letters, the blank space where truth is buried and where its
secret is kept.

We find these relationships again in Canetti, not in Kraus. For
Canetti as for Kraus, the integrity of words is sacred. ("I don't like
to let myself get involved with words in perverse adventures. . . .
There is enough to trouble me contained *in* words, in their hearts,
and I do not wish to extract it from them as if I were an Aztec high
priest. I despise such gory ways.") No amount of integrity, how-
ever, can ever make of words a perfect image of truth. Kraus's asce-
sis turns to integrity and *seems* to end there. (We shall see the "se-
cret" hidden in that integrity.) Canetti's ascesis begins in such in-
tegrity, but turns immediately to listen to the silence embracing it

and carrying it forward. ("Every one ought to reach their funda-
mental ascesis. Mine would be the discipline of silence.") In Kraus,
words struggle against the blank area of the book in order to engulf
it, and they do not feel themselves integral outside of this strug-
gle. Canetti is too keen a reader of Kafka not to abandon this pre-
text. For Canetti, words are too "modest" to presume to maintain
essence as opposed to appearance, to represent the immortal and
defend it from time. Integrity of words consists for Canetti, as for
Kafka, in clearly expressing the problematic nature of a world that
survives and renews itself thanks to the burial of truth. Doubt is
"natural" in this world, and no philosophical game of words is
qualified to resolve it. The philosophical "rite" of doubt does noth-
ing but re-dress it continually. There is no answer to a question if
the answer is not already implicit in the question itself. It is there-
fore pointless to ask if asking is not already superfluous per se.
Kafka in his *Diary* cites the paradox of Rabbi Nachman, and this
can perhaps constitute a secret basis for Wittgenstein's tautology
as well.

The burial of truth in Hassidic narrative does not become in-
difference or hatred for life. It is here that the principles of this
narrative incline more towards Walser than towards Roth. The
Jewish will to live and the desperate attachment to life even at the
peak of suffering that we find in Canetti and Kraus, and that so
fundamentally separate both from Heidegger, spring from a vision
of the substantially unfinished quality of the world. The work of
creation is not over. It will end only in the time of redemption. In
waiting for its completion, Jews must preserve their essence in any
way they can. Jews must fight to survive by any means (Rosen-
zweig). Every moment of life, for them, is a blessing.

The Baal Shem praises God because God has buried truth and
thus has rendered the world possible. It is impossible to praise the
creator and despise his creatures. It is a sin to hide oneself from
one's own flesh (Isaiah 58:7). Those who despair over the burial of
truth and suffer from their own flesh preach death. The "modesty"
of Canetti's language is, ironically, a strenuous resistance to death,
the absolute master. Language that is less than modest strives for

and desires truth, so it desires to surmount and negate all appearances, everything finite. The truth of the finite resides, for this reason, in its vanishing. Such strong language causes the death of appearance, of life as a changing totality of appearance. "Philosophers who want to give us a dowry of death" embody power, whose utopia has always resided in reducing every life to a *state* and in liquidating any "resistance" to the state. Canetti responds to this "philosophy" with Kafka's typical figure of the animal. Swallowed, digested, assimilated, and thus bound to an unending conflict with death, the animal rises to the order of symbol of the resistance. Not by chance are dialogues with animals a recurrent motif in Hassidic tales, along with preaching to birds. All material is full of spiritual sparks of divine holiness that are heard and redeemed. Buber explains that ponds, rocks, plants, and animals are alive with waiting for the redemptive hour. To listen to the "spirituality" of material, however, also means to know how to enjoy it, to love life and cherish it, in whatever mask it presents itself. The pure simplicity of the Baal Shem's constant emphasis on joy is not in Canetti or Roth. For them, the earth can no longer be a cradle, or the sky a mirror and an echo. The power of death has closed the gaps and silences of *Heimat*. Life's resistance to death is refigured in the undefended "modesty" of narrative, and in the image of writing uncontaminated by power. This writing (for Canetti, it was in Kafka and Walser) preserves the past of Hassidic joy, as it preserves the blank area of the book of Truth. Even if the time of redemption has become the object of an impossible faith, it is necessary to narrate *as if* we were waiting for it, with infinite care and patience. All of which frustrates the tone of lament, of accusation and of resentment, since the vain mortification of the flesh (De Menasce) and sins against the body generate sorrow.

The irony in Hassidic stories comes from the tension balanced between joy transformed into blank silence and the *as if* of waiting. It is the opposite of Kraus's irony, which derived, inexorably, from judgment of opinions and appearances that senselessly stimulate daily life. Canetti's irony comes, rather, from communion with life. It does not sentimentalize, but it lives the life of the other. It lives the sorrow of its characters and succeeds in demonstrating to them the deep roots of their contradicting themselves and their passing away. Pursuit of a spark of the common soul is in every gesture and in every word. The idler leads this basic pursuit, unaware and almost speechless. Irony informs its interminability and the complex, limpid reserve of its words. It is the negation of sermons preaching ascesis and silence. The ego *judges*. Kraus's irony is the product of the absolute contrast between the values of the ego's honest *logos* and the debased values of the sick chatter of the masses. The ego is also the subject of philosophy. The ego swallows, digests, and assimilates the animal. Canetti's resistance to death contradicts, therefore, the entire framework of Kraus's discourse. How would it be possible to live the life of the other, outside Schopenhauer's compassion (which is critical in Kraus), if one were to confirm the full identity of one's ego? One day the Jewish community of a town came out to follow the carriage of Rabbi Reb Melech, to gain merit for honoring his wisdom. The zaddik thought about this a great deal and suddenly said, "If this is the case, I, too, want to follow their example." He got out and joined the throng behind his now-empty carriage. Another story tells how one evening a student felt a great desire to hear Rabbi Aaron recite the Book of Lamentations. He knocked on the teacher's window, saying, "Aaron! Open up! Open the door for me!" The teacher said, "Who's there?" "It is I," said the student, but Aaron neither answered nor opened. The student cried and called, "Aaron, why don't you open the door for me?" Then the Rabbi said, "Who is it who dares to say 'I,' as God himself said on the day he gave us the Law in the midst of thunder and lightning? No one born of a woman has the right to call himself so!" To show the unpronounceable nature of "I" is also the focus of irony. The meaning of characters like the fool, whose blithe humor unseats grave sobriety, resides in non-modesty of the ego. According to the Baal Shem, the only people who have already earned their places in the next life are two fools. "When people are depressed, we restore their good humor." The fool shows that "My very own I, with nothing in its way, was taken away by a little child, and it looks back at me disturbed, silent and alien as a dog" (Hofmannsthal, *Terzinen*). With a truly Hassidic gesture, Canetti transforms what Hofmannsthal expresses in the forms of *Trauerspiel* (in this passage, that reminds us of Rilke, that seems to come straight out of the *Duino Elegies*) into the very reason for putting up resistance to the subjugating subject of philosophy.

That is not the only reason why we ought to invoke the figure of the fool (and of his inseparable friend, the animal). God participates in the misadventures of his exile. When Jews suffer in their fundamental alienation, God takes part in their suffering. The Hassidim need to know how to console him. The greater their misery, the more their blessings on life should soar, and their happiness for life. In the midst of the most atrocious suffering, they need to show themselves *happy* before God, to sing and dance for him. Earth's melancholy has no hold on them. The force that allows them to experience the suffering of the other is the same one that makes them participate in God's suffering, in divinity's very exile. This is their highest "office": to console God for the diaspora that he cannot prevent and joyfully to assume the burden of it; to free God of it. One must turn into a fool in the presence of a suffering God.

Ostjudentum does not know the ghetto. The shtetl is in a certain sense the opposite of the ghetto, of its "totally unnatural" quality (Mandel). Hassidic tales overflow with colors and landscapes. The Hassidim wander "the beautiful roads that lead through this land of a thousand colors," and even more vividly they announce the cry of the land of the Messiah in waiting. These descriptions seem to contrast fundamentally with the desert that spreads out before Jiri Langer. "Far and wide, there is not a tree or hill, only an endless plain. On the horizon a small bridge leads to a sparse field, the only parcel of nature, my only relief in this desert." The only thing the two passages have in common is the absence of the ghetto. The extraordinary journeys of the Hassidim, which in a few moments traverse infinite distances, express how their existence cannot be confined within the limits of the ghetto.

If, however, the desert is without limits, then the eternal fountain of creation that the Baal Shem praised as "a river that never ends" cannot be announced there. The paradox is easy to explain. The multicolored riches of the desert are, to Hassidic eyes, the embodiment of the blank area on the page. All the forces of the living, all secrets from creation to redemption, are told in that blank area. The desert is animated by creation's "river that never ends." Hassidic landscapes abound with objects, animals, and villages beyond any spatial or temporal "coherence," like air full of burgeoning seeds. The vivid colors are not descriptive, but they capture the sparks of the universal soul inhabiting the desert. In the desert, no visible color acts as an obstacle or screen to the splendor of sparks, just as in the infinite plains no border hinders the lightning voyages of the Baal Shem from shtetl to shtetl and from town to town. The figure of the eternal wanderer floats out from the chimneys on the roofs of the shtetl, shrouded in white. Around him fly the sparks of the souls of objects, animals, and houses. Every hour of the day in every season of the year has its own spark. Sparks renew the struggle against the darkness of night and bring forth the light of the living. This is the meaning of the rooster, the rooster crowing at daybreak, the day's first caller, who praises the palingenesis of light, the splendor of the landscape of the living.

The figures in Hassidic landscapes turn out to be Chagall's. Even in Chagall they are already filtered through the narrative of memory. In no other artist is memory capable of such visionary force, finding itself so securely among the symbols of the past and recognizing them, intuiting them, reliving them. In others, nothing remains of the complex Hassidic landscape except for the steppes, the desert, the absence. Only Chagall still knows the secret that animates the desert with colors, that makes the hidden sparks fly, and that seeds the air with figures. Roth joins shtetl and ghetto. The shtetl takes on the colorlessness of the ghetto. The infinity of its landscape represents the infinite abjection of the ghetto. In Chagall, however, the shtetl is a living no-place, a utopia of Hassidic springtime. He permits the festival of one moment in the *Heimat*, pictured in memory, in the invisible, in pure story. At the rooster's

crowing, all the beggars, merchants, clowns, fools, and animals
gather as simple implements and objects charged with history and
memory. They meet on the roofs, in the sky, on the streets. With
the last sparks of the soul they shine through misery, and they light
up whatever exists there again in the splendor of ephemeral and
eternal singularity.

The doubleness of the Hassidic landscape matches the double-
ness of *galuth* (diaspora, exile, persecution). It means not only the
time of damnation, but the space necessary to prepare oneself for
redemption. The method of redemption is in *galuth*. Its road sup-
ports our steps for as long as the end is deferred. The Jews are a
naked and wandering mass.[95] The exodus from Egypt repeats it-
self for them with inexorable regularity. In the desert, as Schoen-
berg bears out in his *Moses*, the Jews are invincible. It is in the
desert that "the people see themselves united" (Canetti) and con-
centrated. There they receive the laws and define the goal. If re-
demption is not conceivable except by means of exodus and desert,
then the desert itself is home. The desert becomes transfigured, as
in Chagall the immense steppes and the muddy villages are trans-
figured. This transfiguration of the desert is the strength of the
Hassidism, but that does not mean one can dismiss and eradicate
messianism. Such a dismissal takes place wherever this tradition
comes alive in a solely critical sense, as it does in contemporary
Yiddish literature and in Roth. Certainly, Hassidism reacts to the
great messianic hope that the Kabbalah nourished in Hebrew mys-
ticism down to the seventeenth century, and "eliminates" its cen-
trality (as Scholem explains)[96] in religious life. But the idea of re-
demption remains fundamental in it, a redemption that is pre-
pared daily and deferred in the precarious state of exile. Thus it is
not a simple "peace" with exile, and even less a resigned peace or
the simple end of messianic hoping. It is, rather, a new vision of
the desert of *galuth*, exempt from any mortifying lament or vain
sorrow. One can say that in Hassidism the theme of traversing is
privileged over that of transcending. The great messianic hope of
the preceding ages sought forms of transcending the desert. For

the Hassidim this is a vain presumption. Since we have not yet learned to walk, we are infinitely distant from learning even the right steps that would allow us to begin to cross it.

No zaddik calls himself "Messiah" or defines the time of the Messiah's coming. Yet the Messiah lives, "who knows where, isolated, unrecognized by anyone" (Langer). It is because of our guilt that he cannot reveal himself. He comes to every generation, but we have not even begun to cross the desert of exile. If the world were to finally recognize him, then the devil would oppose him, which is what happened to the Messiah of Belz. The devil changed into a beautiful woman and, disputing with the Messiah, succeeded in provoking him into such a state of fervor that he forgot the words of the Talmud that forbid men to remain alone even for a moment with a strange woman. Was not the Baal Shem bound to flee just as he came into sight of the Land of the Lord that had called to him so powerfully? He called out to the ancient land, where he would want at that point to lie down and die, raising his voice to a volume that covered the territory, saying, "No, my dear friend, I will not die. Do not be angry with him whom you have called. He is born to return, and the hand of God is on his roots, to lead him in his time, to lead him to his time, O my dear friend." In the end, the Messiah's earthly wandering repeats itself, only renewing the strength of waiting and listening. This renewal overturns any failure.

A Messiah that actually comes will come too late. Earth will already be a cemetery, and everyday language "a continuous, involuntary, funereal metaphor" (Magris), expressing desolate despair over Hassidic *kavanah*, over its possible resistance and survival. Even at their most somber, the words of Hertz Yanovar under Nazi bombs turn Hassidic faith upside down: "Death is the Messiah. That's the truth. . . . Only the old tomb in the cemetery bears witness that the Messiah, Reb Aaron Messiah, once lived in Belz." The tomb of the Messiah is again the blank part of the book, and things still swell from the parts of its secret. Even if the element of faith is not missing, in Yiddish literature stories are constructed around it in negative. Stories narrate loss and the absence of faith. Extreme silence is the silence of faith; the extreme desert is none other than the nothing of the hope that established it.

Only Canetti's "resistance" still preserves, perhaps, the possibility of hope. Canetti also speaks of and in the desert of pure crossing. No messianic prophecy could limit it, not even that which overturns the Messiah in death. He reveals himself in the minute analysis of forms of crossing, in their "modesty," and in their structural powerlessness. There is nothing but crossing. Canetti recognizes no power, state, or god ("and whoever has him is his prophet") who may be a power in the desert. "That which is merely *recorded* still contains a grain of hope, however grand the despair from which it comes." The Hassidic god is accompanied through uninterrupted wandering narrative, because he is not a power. The Hassidic god fails with his Messiah. He suffers endlessly with his people. For the Hassidim, the sorrow that comes of the idea of God's suffering is terrible, and it would be even more terrible if his people were to accuse him. An extraordinary and overwhelming *generosity* toward God in exile spans Hassidic wandering narrative. "All the sorrows of humanity are also the sorrows of *shekhinah*." Heschel adds that the consolation of knowing the divine presence shares the burden of one's own agony is total consolation. The emphasis is not so much on demanding consolation as on giving it. The negation of any triumphalistic theology is basic here, but the secret of negation lies in rupturing the binomial power-divinity, the fundamental theological symbol of power. Wandering is not the only aspect characterized by powerlessness of the divine. Powerlessness is a thing to be preserved and cared for. Even if God were able to break forth miraculously in the middle of suffering and exile and decree the end of it, this intervention would only be possible if his zaddikim called for it, if they forced God into it. One day a disciple came to the Rabbi of Kotzk asking him to bless a Hassid who had fallen into poverty. The Kotzker replied, "How can I contradict the will of heaven?" Yet this God who cannot work miracles (and miracles are, as we know, the quintessence of power), suffering in his exile, consoled by the songs and dances of the Hassidim, perhaps stricken (as Feitelzohn believed) by a kind of amnesia "that made him lose the sense of his creation," this God is not at all *otiosus*. His figure concentrates in itself, at the peak of tension, every sense and every direction of exile. Not his "otiosity" or indifference, but his nearness, his sympathy for every aspect of exile is disturbing. Essential, not otiose, is the symbol of powerlessness that expresses itself in him.

Rosenzweig explains the sense of the "eradication" of messianism that ends—inverted—in Roth's and Singer's despair. The Messiah cannot express the idea of becoming, of developing toward redemption. Christians develop; Christians *become* Christian. Jews think of themselves as eternal. One enters into Christianity; one is Jewish. Jews are eternal in their present, and eternal from the beginning, from Genesis. Their language is the language God spoke.[97] Waiting for the Messianic hour should not suffocate this present eternity, this ability to see in the present none other than the denunciation of the non-fullness, of the emptiness and silence of God. The wandering of the Jews is doubled, since in their wandering the waiting plunges into the eternal roots of their body and blood. "This matter of taking root in us and only in us guarantees our eternity" (Rosenzweig). Wandering is not mere movement, a development from years of condemnation to the fullness of time. Jews have no roots in the earth, but nevertheless they are "profoundly rooted in themselves." This eternal root expresses itself precisely in their wandering. "Die Macht der Weltgeschichte"— the force of world history, of becoming, of things coming to be and passing away into nothing—shatters against it. Jews exist in time, but they have been in time *eternally*. Time and eternity are confused in their eternal wandering. The Messiah is expressed in this symbol, in its currency, and not in the future of a redemption that removes the present condemnation. The aim of the Jews is, rather, as distant as it is present: "was *immer* ist, ist nicht zeitlos; was sich immer *bleibt*, ist nicht zeitlich"[98] (whatever has been *eternally* may wander on eternally in time, but whatever remains eternally fixed in its roots cannot be consumed by time).

These last considerations shed new light on the structure of narrative. It is not the failure of messianic hope, already "eradicated" in Hassidic mysticism, or the loss and absence of *Heimat,* of the seat of *Ostjudentum,* which had played such a large part in the crossroads of the Empire, that resulted in the despair of Roth and Singer. It is rather the sterilization of the eternal roots of Jewish selfhood. Not having roots on earth and the eternity of wandering per se could not provoke despair. The agony is the silence of roots in self, the silence of one's body and blood. When the agony becomes aware of itself, then wandering will be transformed into becoming, will exist only in time, and time will not consume it. Narrative must follow destiny. It is no longer possible to show the eternity of the roots that sustained it. The symbol is shattered and only one part of it remains, solitary: the interminable absence of dwelling on earth. This means no longer being able to be at home with oneself.

To try to express all of this with the clarity of Hassidic tales, to say it without lament, without pointless accusations against agony, is a grand form. Roth did it in his last days, in "The Legend of the Holy Drinker." It is a story of the repetition of disaster on the path of restitution. This path, which leads to those who know how to give, is closed off until death. In life, the voice that calls us back to it is repeated incessantly together with voices that "seduce," that lead elsewhere, and that get confused with it. Yet no other way is presented. An irony that comes up whole forms the most profound communion with the suffering, forms a language that has its equal only in the finest Hassidic tales. Roth's "Legend" is modeled on tales like that of Rabbi Nachman's "The Seven Beggars," whose end we will not be worthy to hear until the Messiah comes, "may God speed that day and make us its witnesses."

Kraus's Ideogram

There is another form of nostalgia for the East in Vienna at the turning point. I have already commented what a reductionist mistake it is to concentrate all the multiple perspectives from Steinhof into Karl Kraus's "juridical mode" of discourse. In March 1907, Schnitzler and Hofmannsthal, Schoenberg and Freud, Klimt and Moser signed the manifesto inviting Mahler to remain in Europe, but Kraus did not. Later, around the time of his collaboration with the *Blauer Reiter* almanac, Schoenberg wrote in his diary: "Kraus knows perfectly well that he belongs to hated journalism, even though he does everything he can to make people think he is an artist. . . . He intends to impose the idea that he is not only an artist, but he is *the* artist, the only true artist of our times. To a journalist without scruples, nothing is impossible."

In the beginning, but only in the beginning, Kraus had faith in language. He placed it under close examination then, studying the meaning of the subjective genitive, developing an idea of thought embodied in language, and articulating language's self-reflexive nature. Like all beginnings, Kraus's was profoundly tied to the past and baffled by the new. What remains essential in Kraus's work, though, lies in the ethical and discursive basis that he lends to the critique of artistic facts and to the analysis of language. The unity of ethics and aesthetics rests in a still more basic origin, such as nature and language. Language is the basis of ethics and aesthetics, just as nature is the basis of all creation. Kraus produces no critique of the idea of origin, although that is the center of the Viennese turning point (around a "Nietzschean core.")

From *Sittlichkeit und Kriminaltät*, a collection of essays written between 1902 and 1907, Kraus attacks the quotidian (idealized in the daily press) and the times (summarized as too *wienerisch*, too Viennese). Both charges are leveled in name of a morality that Kraus hardly subjects to even a minimal dialectic consideration. Kraus is ethical in exactly the same way as Weininger, whose influence pervades the work of the eruptive author of *Die Fackel* without ever being acknowledged. Take this fragment from "The Persecution of Women" for example: "Whoever has come to recognize the ethical indifference of women's souls will break up in laughter over the indignation of the petit bourgeois who calls for police protection and involves the aid of psychiatry against his lover for lying."

Kraus's critique of Heine and appreciation of Johan Nepomuk Nestroy demonstrate definitively that this ethical and aesthetic attitude represents the past (the necessary past) of Wittgenstein's Vienna. The theoretical impossibility of wholly embracing the European tendencies of nineteenth-century German literature combines here with a repugnance (like Weininger's) for Jewish *Heimatlosigkeit*, for the Jewish culture of exile. Consequently not Heine, but Nestroy: the *Burgtheater* of the healthy Viennese tradition that fills Kraus's *Schauspielkunst* (plays). That also explains his attacks on Max Reinhardt: actor and word, not direction and action.[99]

Kraus's attitude to Dollfuss goes back to previous conditions. It has deep roots in his life and work. "He would talk about the polar ice caps to anyone who felt a little cold." He "tried to prove how good counts for nothing without understanding it, or how desire is incapable of truth without knowing what is true" (Brecht). Again in *Sittlichkeit und Kriminaltät* Kraus presents himself "as the one who struggles for the survival of conservative forces against an erupting horde with no traditions; as the one who prefers the police state included, not only for aesthetic reasons, in supporting a despotism of journalists." In spite of such pronouncements, Kraus was a great celebrity to critics who made him the embodiment of "grand Vienna." In contrast to them, he knew how to recognize his historical and spiritual situation. He knew that it was not possible to stem the tide of the age. He was the first to decide against everything that broke with tradition. "I am not an imitator living in the crumbling old slum of language," he wrote in one of his best poems, adding, as a true protagonist of the Viennese turning point: "mein Grab ist leer"—"my grave is empty."

Kraus's later defenders can hardly imagine how far back his case on language may reach. Calasso laments it,[100] in the tradition of Heller and Benjamin. Benjamin called Kraus's work "a war dance over the crypt of the German language." But in 1931, in both a conference and an essay, two critics found in Kraus the drama, rhythm, and style of classical Chinese. Kraus kept this secret hidden even from himself. Awareness of this affinity with Chinese was unavailable to a criticism that exalts only the most fleeting aspects, yet it saves his work in an authentic dimension of timelessness. What seemed a mixture of ethics and aesthetics is transformed in this very dimension into a utopian harmony between words and things, between words and actions. The order of words acquires a cosmic significance, transcending the linguistic dimension of its formal relationship with the universe of situations and facts. Words should define thoughts with precision and sincerity, so right actions may follow, so justice may reign in the land. "Heaven hates disorder," it says in the *Shih Ching* [The classic of songs],[101] and for Kraus, disorder in language is a sign of great disorder in the cosmos.

The first emblem of Kraus is the ideogram of man attached to word and faithful to it. The word appears at his lips, but has its roots in his entire being. The sense of belonging to a tradition (more powerful when more dedicated) transcends historical and linguistic dimensions. The continuous exercise of a reanimating memory that can salute the dead as if they were living and listen to their music as if it were being played here and now looks to the center, to the invariable. What seemed the true, unmoving axis of discourse is transformed into the utopian mixture of foundational harmony between words and being, between human and divine Tao. Classical Chinese education orients itself directly toward this center. A close study of the *Shih Ching* is necessary for learning how to use words well. Using words well means centering oneself in the invariable. The *Shih Ching* says, "This is my sorrow: that there are men who have no desire to understand the beauty of ancient things." The book continually cites this beauty, as it incessantly repeats the ceremonies and rituals of justice "that govern a monarch as if he were enlightened." Kraus's principle of quotation belongs to this time of ritual and public prayer.

Kraus's integrity of words (something that should "surge from the ground in harmony with earth and sky") is also direction, process, and energy, even when it seems to flee before any originality, seeking refuge in the soil of its tradition, of its classicism. Kraus's second emblem could be the sign of footprints leading to intelligence or one on the virtue of work after having gazed directly into the heart, or knowing oneself. For this, Kraus's Confucian brushstrokes can seem, as they did to Benjamin, motivated by "mad laughter." The mask of whoever seeks the classical rhythm of quotation is obligated to struggle against quotidian profanity, though the end result may be the disfiguring of one's own brushstrokes. What are we still capable of quoting? *Die Fackel* is a dead sea, almost a document for paraphrasing what Theodore Adorno said of Berg, that it is impossible to abandon the already-said and that one must assimilate it and get nourishment from it. In Kraus's style of quotation the standard of classicism that provides words with order is inseparable from the demons that destroy tradition and memory. Kraus gazes too directly to have missed this struggle and to have turned away from the adversary's pressing force. The principle of quotation expresses unvarying humanity, and that is why it lives in language, while it testifies to the dissolution of classical beauty. The principle of quotation admits no exceptions. The classical tradition endures indirectly in the voices that deny it and negate it. Quotation turns into a reflection of disorder that "flows like water coursing in spring toward the valley, overflowing its channels, lost in pools." This dramatic change is seen straight on, without illusion or nostalgia, in *Die letzten Tage der Menschheit*.[102] It shows an apocalypse in which "the most incredible things were said, and the most macabre things were quotations. The specters and ghosts that haunt us have the names of living people" (Kraus). Quotation is condemned to repeat the tragedy that destroys humanity. The protagonists in this tragedy are "characters from operetta." The destruction of humanity is a laughing matter. It is comedy. "Life dies, and the killers dance a tango"—"Das Leben starb. Die Mörder tanzen Tango"—Kraus wrote in a poem in 1913, during a night awake over Musil. It is necessary to learn to laugh at the killers. Kraus in his authentic mask (his Chinese mask) protests the difficulty of this art, and since he continues to carry it, with fatigue, he protests the necessity of weeping.

Profane Attention

Almost at the end of *The Man Without Qualities* appear the chapters on "the expression of the idea of emotion." They are among the last parts Musil revised before his death. The reassuring image of a "tangible likeness between reality and the idea we make of it" had collapsed. It was no longer possible to assume that "emotions discolor the exact image of the world, that they deform it and misrepresent it." Gone was the myth of the "original" to which the idea of possessing a "true" reality would have conformed. The unreality of the "subjective" opposes "true" reality. Subjective reality is an unreality that analyzes the world in diverse images composed of emotion's various grades. Ulrich certainly "did not have the least intention of mistaking awareness for an error or the world for an illusion." The predominant force that causes us to better adapt ourselves to reality appears as a grade of emotion, confused with representations of various depths. This passage, in which Musil brings Mach and Nietzsche into critical confrontation, introduces the problem of an "unfounded" reality. Through infinite procedures, we clarify its image "under the urgency of life," a problem specified and developed in "Ulrich und die zwei Welten des Gefühls." It is not a matter here of a broad "division of labor" between emotions, but of the possibilities of development within every emotion.

Emotions appear to Ulrich in two fundamental types: those that develop in an exterior sense and those of an interior sense. Certainty—*Bestimmtheit*—characterizes the former. Exterior development (*äussere Entfaltung*) of emotion always directs itself toward something, has something in sight, leads to an action or a reasonably univocal resolution (*Beschluss*). The interior mood (*Stimmung*) seems, by contrast, inactive, as if it were limited to witnessing events "from behind tinted glass." Yet, fixed emotions, emotions that tend toward resolve and that behave like imprisoned energy, restrict their destinations one by one until they are gone. They discharge their strength at their targets. On the other hand, the *Stimmung* that flows over every object "without any effect on anything," transmutes the world incessantly "with the same indifference and disinterest with which the sky changes colors. In this way things and events are transformed like clouds in the sky."

Defined emotions are like a substance with outstretched arms—"ein Wesen mit greifenden Armen." They pass from object to object, from destination to destination, without power to stop. Defined emotions have an indefinable need to change allegiance, while emotions that remain indeterminate, that have nothing in their sights, seem to endure "like a family or species."

Emotions may develop, therefore, into voracious and acquisitive elements. Emotions approach things to know them, possess them, and dominate them. Their resolve always leads into blind alleys. The thing possessed and dominated turns out to be nothing, and the intention is bound to feel loss and approach something else. It is an interminable interval, composed of intention, waiting, satisfaction, and loss, studded as it may be with attempts to "radiate," with nostalgia for the interior development of emotion, for its "indifference." People in whom the exterior development predominates "voraciously seize everything that they meet and are ever on the attack." Their passions are as strong as they are mutable. Against this "Faustian" type we can juxtapose the contemplative, whose emotions are, indeed, introverted, turned inward. Musil calls this type "oriental," capable of "concentrating oneself within, to the point that mind, heart, and body are all one silence."

Ulrich warns that such definitions may be unfounded. These

"affected, stylish phrases" only deliver a tiny part of the thoughts and "deep respirations of a summer day." Certainly "he saw a great difference" between the two described types, between those who put their entire beings "at peace" and concentrate themselves in a place where things "happen without anything happening"; and the wandering thought that leaps from problem to problem, that, as Evagrio said, "leads the mind from city to city, from village to village, from home to home," engaged in long discourses. "A fundamental difference in life" seems to express itself between these two types, developed to their extreme limits. Musil flees, though, from a distilled phenomenology of emotions or from limiting himself to macro-classifications of visions of the world. The last part of the novel certainly constitutes a powerful re-cognition of the transcendental conditions, so to speak, of nihilism. The analysis of acquisitive emotions is an essay in Nietzschean psychology on the foundations of nihilism. Ulrich tries to probe these foundations in the "sacred dialogues" with his sister. This is not, however, the proper place for the last part of the novel. It is not an awareness that detachment from nihilism should be arrested upon its re-cognition. Nor is it a realization that ex-stasis from the foundations of nihilism is an extirpation and cannot attain that brimming silence, radiant, capable of burning in itself any acquisitive intention, whose every word is a reminder that utopia is unattainable. The extraordinary *Klarheit* of silence is a story that by definition cannot be told. The story that is told is the infinite probing of nihilistic emotions—a story that is necessarily unfinished.

Musil's essay touches all these elements without drawing a circle around them. If his tour had a center, it would be the essential impossibility of deciding between the two worlds of emotions. Musil's essay is not motivated by the analysis of the two worlds as such or by the unattainable nature of what we can define as hesychastic. This drama motivates it: in the state of being "without qualities," we cannot decide between the two worlds of emotions, in spite of their radical differences. They fall into reciprocal equivalence, constantly exchanging places and reversing themselves. This does not deny recognition of the conditions of nihilism or the idea of a possible turning of emotions toward the diaphanous clarity of the gratuitous. It denies rather the possibility of an exclusive choice between the two worlds. These worlds do not fall within the realm of choice. In the state of being "without qualities," these emotions come, become, from time to time, as the case may be. They happen, they fall on man. Thus he does not have a sense of nostalgia for the contemplative, and he apparently lacks a virile acceptance of Faustian destiny. Our world exists in the insurmountable indifference of this difference. The metaphysical quintessence of the "man without qualities" is a recognition of undecidable differences that are therefore indifferent or equivalent.

The twofold essence of all emotions furnishes a "possible explanation that is too simple." Its "pretentious and arrogant" concepts can give "great satisfaction" to Ulrich, but the two-fold essence remains a tight knot. It is as if the concept did not give way to judgment, to *Ur-teil* (separation, distinction, fundamental decision). The essay does not lack a concept, but it lacks a capacity for judgment, a power to decide—*Urteils-kraft*. The "man without qualities" expresses, in fact, a superabundance of concepts. He seems to offer several means to penetrate into the most secret "types," but he cannot pass judgment among them. Thus all the manners of emotion that he discovers signify only one kind of man, the kind that understands in himself the most radical differences without being able to decide upon the "quality" of any of them. He is a nihilist who nevertheless "dreams dreams of God." He is an impatient activist, who is far from taking any pragmatic action in spite of his impatience. Ulrich and Agathe recognize each other as nihilists and activists (and, we might add, as hopelessly contemplative and acquisitive): "und bald das eine bald das andere, je nachdem wie es kam"—"now as one and now the other, as it happened, as the case may be." This is their key. The relationship between twins belongs to that constellation of indivisible things that can nonetheless never be united. The twins (Gemini) are indivisible in their insuperable difference. This is not a sign of synthesis or harmony, but a sign of the unreconcilable and double, in which projects are planned "like pure unreality" and one tries to act in a spirit "that was the magic spirit of inactivity." In this constellation the ways of emotions follow each other and cross over each other, happy/unhappy, as the case may be. The time of conversation between the twins is the time of the case.

This awareness of time derives almost necessarily from the "expression of the concept of emotions." It is the secret "gift" of the man without qualities and the structure of the utopia of "essayism." Where emotions happen, and only the idea of them appears, then *Ur-teil*, the divisible linearity of time, remains clean and unbroken. When emotions take place in the constellation of the twins (Gemini), they do not congeal into a point on the line that leads from a beginning to an end. No temporal absolute underlies them. Musil underscores the *case* of the beginning ("Über dem Atlantik . . . ") with all the force of his irony. The *Stimmung* of "Into the Millennium" fathoms a silence that is never perfectly attainable, as in certain of Mahler's finales. Musil's *Erlebnis* of time resides in his concentration on the case at hand throughout the narrative, down to the most intimate fibers of narrative material, and his ability to incarnate himself in it. Every instant of the novel, every mood, every gesture reaches fulfillment and has its moment in time. These are not moments that express various isolated situations that, in turn, can be measured and analyzed interchangeably. This is a matter of an undefinable multiplicity of moments, each with its independent fact. They are moments/facts that collect together in bunches, that make and unmake "families," and that form unrepeatable events.

Through an *Erlebnis* of time Musil expresses the crisis of narrative. Narration is possible where time develops an "explanation" for events, determining their relationships, indicating a beginning and an end. Time here maintains a secret idea of self-redemption stemming from an ancient and nearly always forgotten eschatological beginning. In secularized eschatology, human relationships in their diverse languages develop according to a plan and manifest a sense of direction. The fundamental structure of this concept of time remains unchanged even if the direction leads to nothing, to the abyss, and not to the good. Even if eschatology reverses its promise, its form still dominates the narrative. The current possibility of sending such a form into crisis, however, constitutes the unique, decipherable "sense" of Musil's novel. Time explodes into a myriad of moments that accompany, upon complete disenchantment with any eschatological perpective, maximum attention to the *fact*, the event, the moment: maximum attention to this singularity. The perfect form of attention clothes every word, mood, thought, and gesture in diaphanous clarity. It breaks every continuum, every simple linearity, and repeats itself in various forms, *wie es kam*, as the various facts present themselves.

Musil "smilingly" presents this feeling of time through a long quotation from Swedenborg. The quotation creates an effect of distance, almost of resigned irony, as if this feeling of time should necessarily flee any attempt at a precise definition and as if it were possible to register it only through the "extravagant" words of a visionary. The motto of the meditations that Ulrich develops is a contemplative's dream, and it could not be otherwise: that only the absolute time of narration can be judged systematically. Essay time, on the other hand, declares itself only in the manifestation of the cases that incarnate it. It cannot be extracted from the *Stimmung* of the moment. The image indicates its possible place, registers its character, without attempting its solution.

Angels "do not know what time is, because in heaven there are no days or years. There are only changing moods." Angels "have no notion of time, unlike humans. . . . If they hear someone speaking about time (God has always supplied angels to keep humans company), they understand it in terms of moods and the determination of moods. . . . In the spiritual world, angels appear as soon as they feel a need for their presence, because then they are transported to that mood; and inversely, if they feel aversion they go away." Ulrich "felt true delight" in evoking these images out of "old metaphysics," in the capacity to speak of angels with the accuracy and precision of an "engineer," in a dry and dispassionate manner. The explosion of time into moments and moods is fundamentally distant from turning completely away from the exterior emotions, from the acquisitive, for the voracious resolve of the Faustian. The "setting sights" of the acquisitive would be inconceivable apart from a basis of linear and eschatological time, however secularized the eschatology may appear. A concept of time that abstractly excludes the acquisitive, however, is unsuitable to the infinite variations of mood. Such variations fit the constellation of facts at the crossroads between nihilist and activist, between contemplative and acquisitive.

God has always supplied angels to keep humans company, so that they may speak of these possible times and moods. They are the no-place that attends humanity's actual space and time. *Essayistically*, a *decision* between the two dimensions is impossible. It would mean either living in heaven or idolatrously endorsing time as the only conceivable reality. That is why Musil/Ulrich can only speak "smilingly" about the "angelic ingenuity" of the old metaphysics, so dear to Goethe and Kant (who actually believed in its vision of a correspondence between time and interior state and who spoke of it "as if it were a matter of Stockholm and its inhabitants"). Yet "angelic ingenuity" exposes how unfounded is the pretext of time as an absolute, with its spaces and distances. It reveals the character that would become the absolute and utter master because it rules over absolute time: the acquisitive, omnidetermined, and nihilistic. The collapse of this vision connects to the entire infinite complex of possibilities of living, to the difficult *ars combinatoria* that knows how to seize the quality and moment of every possibility and how to make it resonate. Thus the problem of time, rediscovered at the end of the analysis of emotions, passes into the problem of "heuristic ethics." This is "an ethics endowed with real growth power," not subject to "periodical catastrophic defeat." It rests "not on a hierarchy fixed for all eternity but rather on the uninterrupted activity of a creative imagination."[103] This problematic ethics corresponds in Musil to the problematic appearance of a moment that bunches single moods, that illuminates them and embraces them as, in a hundred places in Hieronymus Bosch, great glass halos both separate and hold together the enchantment of lovers who cannot unite, yet are never divided.

It is not possible here to fully investigate the problem of the essay in Musil. It would be enough to have pointed out its incorporation into the pattern of analysis that we are attempting to identify. The essay is certainly not the expression of an age in which "insecurity" comes back into fashion, in which people from "slightly uncertain professions: poets, critics, women, and 'junior' professionals" loudly demand new faiths and basic values. The essay holds suspect any pretense of center, of order, of unshakable foundations. Its prohibition against "believing things finished" is not in itself provisional or accessory, as if it were a matter of "discarding" lost *Weltanschauungen*. The essay form appears rather as a definitive life style and style of thinking, a broad assumption of responsibility over any decadent insecurity and any perennial philosophy. The essay is not a free-roaming intelligence, impressionistic writing, or merely a form of suspended judgment, as if it were lying in wait for new systems. It is truly the writing of interior moments and states as something removed from the continuum and from narrative. These are things that cannot be reduced to a system, but are no less capable of being described analytically, precisely, *microscopically* in their distinctions. The polarity of irony and utopia[104] (the essay's elements of style) is also the polarity between dissolving the continuum (the turning point of narrative) and the no-place of the angelic state, "ironically" described through Swedenborg. The infinite grades of reality's participation in utopian nature (the novel's very content) also express infinite possible relationships between time and fact, infinite possible meanings of events. This is no allegory, "where everything means more than what it can honestly claim," but, nonetheless, there is the greatest *attention* to all of these possibilities. There is also *surrender*—exempt from any hesitant pessimism—to the inability to finish the itinerary, resolve the utopia, make of the world of facts a spiritual world where no distance impedes the transformation of emotions.

The essay form, according to Musil, neither gravitates around a center nor announces nor alludes to a future system.[105] Thus its moment is not repeated in orbit after orbit around a center that attracts it and that always retreats from it. Nor does it charge eschatologically toward the new message, the new order. Rather, the moments of the facts are what captures its attention. That is what essayistic attention considers. The essay writes out these moments and considers them, with greatest attention to the world as a whole, a protean "totality of facts." Attention is critical distance, *irony*, the opposite of impressionism or any vitalistic *Einfühlung*. Irony is transfigured when it crystallizes the utopia of the twilight of time onto the rugged, hard, profane surface of the case. Irony has the ability to manifest the utopia of the immediate and perfect transpiring into space of the interior state.[106]

The final part of *The Man Without Qualities*, dominated by infinitesimal attention to moods, is also where Musil's idea of the essay finds fuller expression. The essay appears as attention's own form. For such a form there are no "details." There are only irreducible singularities. Every "detail" connects, as soon as attention focuses on it, to unforeseen and bottomless abysses of singularity. The tone of the final part brings out the extraordinary tension that unites brother and sister, as if they could be united only on the edge of the most fundamental separation. The uninterrupted meditation (not stream of consciousness, but stream of meditations!) generated by such a state is its proper form of attention. The tone resembles the mystical *prosoché* [attention] of those who seek silence. Ulrich shows himself to be aware of this, even if there is no method, no technique to teach it. Ulrich's attention cannot be pure in the sense of being free of thought or imagination, free of intention or will. Attention is not a perfect method for contemplation. Its purity belongs to the moments of its own essayism. It is paradoxical from the mystical point of view inasmuch as it is attention turned to "profane" moods, attention that is developed along a non-liberating *ex-stasis*, but that leads back with more force and passion to these moods, to their "details." The paradox of Musil's attention lies in its turning toward the profane, to infinite grades of reality's participation in utopian nature, *as if* it suffered from divine things (*theia pathein*), *as if* it were a matter of describing changes of mood in a purely spiritual world. The dissolving magic of *ironic* recognition still returns for that "as if" at the outer limit of the novel's contemplative and meditative force, the inflexible protector of that force.

Simone Weil says, in *La connaisance surnaturelle*, "God is attention without distraction."[107] The great mystical theme of an inexhaustible force of intuition, of reaching a dimension of ecstasy that renders oblivion impossible (thus the opposite of the common currency of the term "mystical"), returns therefore in the *cases* of Musil's novel—that is, in the situation most abandoned by God: the state of being "without qualities." To construct the essay form as attention without distraction, to make the essay into an unseducible intuition, is the great *complexio oppositorum* that ties together the novel's events and its *Erlebnisse*. The wandering thinking of the essay succeeds in acquiring, in an inexhaustible traversing of cases, the tone of *prosoché*. None of the cases is so removed, so forgotten. Attention penetrates to each and reveals of each an *abyssal* dimension. The essay form's thinking wanders abyssally, and not from surface to surface anymore or from moment to moment.

There is even greater evidence of the paradoxical nature of attention according to Musil if we reflect on the essay as a fundamentally non-predicating form of writing. To preach is to judge *divisio primaeva*, to possess or want to possess the essence of a thing as a priori distinguishable from its "appearance." The case of Musil does not tolerate such differentiation. The essay that waits for moments that are named for the different facts that happen in them does not have their true names. Essays are dispossessed writing.[108] The greatest force of attention that this writing can develop requires not excluding or forgetting the impossibility of judgment and not allowing oneself to be seduced by *preaching*. And if the essence of preaching lies in the verb "to be," essayistic writing is disconnected from "being" or confirms "being" only by ironizing its groundlessness. The most profound connection between Musil and Nietzsche lies in their critique of the category of "being," of any pretense of confirming a distinction between essence and appearance through preaching.[109]

Derrida's comments about Levinas could easily, at this point, be repeated about Musil. For Musil, too, a "non-violent" language would be a language deprived of the verb "to be." "Since the verb to be and the predicating act are implied in every other verb and every common noun, non-violent language would be, at most, a language of pure invocation, of pure adoration. It would utter only proper nouns to invoke the other from far away."[110] The dialogue between brother and sister comes to realize a similar language unintentionally. Ulrich and Agathe "invoke" each other from afar. They are, *so far apart*, the indivisible one who can never be united. This language is the most extreme utopia conceivable. It is the last dimension of the reality's participation in utopian nature. Precisely because a perfectly non-violent language would be, at most, pure invocation (it would speak the mystical language of the heart's silent prayers), the dimension of distance is natural to it. This language can do nothing but call from afar. It is distant. The essay form corrodes and criticizes the violence of preaching to the point of calling from afar the utopia of language dispossessed of all "being." It can reach this point, not beyond. This language would be, in reality, a form of listening, as happens for Kierkegaard in true prayer, in which pure attention to conversation with God is freed from any seduction, from any pretense, and from any question, and stands in pure listening.[111] The essay reaches the point of making "a gesture" toward this form of listening. The divine state of it, though, is necessarily denied.

The pinnacle of attention would be, therefore, a language deprived of "being," resolved in listening. Musil's essayistic attention demonstrates this utopia, with irony and surrender. A language that speaks without "being" would be the equivalent of an ethics that acts as a "creative imagination," without obligation, to a love that neither demands nor possesses, but is free, non-exclusive, non-acquisitive, only giving, pure *dépense*. This is, perhaps, an attempt to give voice to the silence that embraces all preaching, all *Ur-teil* of the language of "being," irreducible to preaching, whose road Wittgenstein prohibited at the end of the *Tractatus*.

Notes

Notes

1. Foolish things have been written about Otto Wagner's St. Leopold am Steinhof. It seems that starting with J. A. Lux and H. Tietze, whose monographs (1914 and 1922 respectively) spoke of a "blessed delight" at the sight of the church, of the interior as a "festival chamber," "a kind of church for non-practicing people," and so forth, the only things that attracted the attention of historians and architects were the comfortable footstools and the hygenic fonts for holy water.

2. W. Jollos, *Arte tedesca fra le due guerre* (Milan: Mondadori, 1955), p. 65.

3. See Robert Musil, *Selected Writings*, ed. Burton Pike (N.Y.: Continuum, 1986), pp. 315–16.—TRANS.

4. See M. Rosso, "Introduction," in L. Wittgenstein, *Osservazioni filosofiche* (Turin: Einaudi, 1976), p. lxxii. [All citations from the *Tractatus* are from *Tractatus Logico-Philosphicus*, new ed., trans. D. F. Pears and B. F. McGuinness, Introduction by Bertrand Russell (London: Routledge and Kegan Paul, 1971).—TRANS.]

5. R. De Monticelli, "Frege, Husserl, Wittgenstein," *Nuova Corrente* 72–73 (1977). I am grateful to Roberta De Monticelli for numerous ideas and suggestions.

6. See my *Krisis: Saggio sulla crisi del pensiero negative da Nietzsche a Wittgenstein* (Milan: Feltrinelli, 1976), pp. 85 ff.

7. Regarding this critique, I base my remarks on G. Franck, "Fondazione della conoscenza e fondamenti dell'operare," *Nuova Corrente* 72–73 (1977), and on many recent studies by A. Gargani, from his "Scienza e forme di vita," also in *Nuova Corrente* 72–73, which is entirely

dedicated to Wittgenstein, to *Il sapere senza fondamenti* (Turin: Einaudi, 1975); from "Tecniche descrittive e procedure costruttive," in U. Curi, ed., *La razionalità scientifica* (Abano Terme: Francisci, 1978), to *Wittgenstein tra Austria e Inghilterra* (Turin: Einaudi, 1979).

8. See on these themes, in addition to the "encyclopedic" work of A. Janik and S. Toulmin, *Wittgenstein's Vienna* (New York: Simon and Schuster, 1973), W. M. Johnston, *The Austrian Mind* (Berkeley: University of California Press, 1972); and the important studies by Enrico Bellone, *I modelli e la concezione del mondo nella fisica moderna da Laplace a Bohr* (Milan: Feltrinelli, 1973), and *Il mondo di carta: Ricerche sulla seconda rivoluzione scientifica* (Milan: Mondadori, 1976) [in English, *A World on Paper: Studies in the Second Scientific Revolution*, trans. Mirella and Riccardo Giacone (Cambridge, Mass.: MIT Press, 1980)].

9. L. Wittgenstein, *Vermischte Bemerkungen* [in English, *Culture and Value*, ed. G. H. von Wright with Heikki Nyman, trans. Peter Winch (Chicago: University of Chicago Press, 1980)].

10. L. Wittgenstein, *Über Gewissheit* [in English, *On Certainty*, trans. Denis Paul (Oxford: Blackwell, 1969)].

11. Wittgenstein, *Culture and Value*.

12. The scope of this essay does not permit me to develop Benjamin's concept of *Trauerspiel*, but I have analyzed it in "Di alcuni motivi in Walter Benjamin," *Nuova Corrente* 67 (1975) and in "Intransitabili utopie," in H. von Hofmannsthal, *La Torre* [*Der Turm*], trans. S. Bortoli Cappelletto (Milan: 1978).

13. L. Wittgenstein, *Della Certezza* [*Über Gewissheit* / On Certainty], trans. M. Trinchero (Turin: Einaudi, 1978), pp. 110, 70.

14. R. Bazlen, *Il capitano di lungo corso* (Milan: Adelphi, 1973), p. 208.

15. G. Colli, *La nascita della filosofia* (Milan: Adelphi, 1975), pp. 85 ff.

16. G. Colli, *Filosofia dell'espressione* (Milan: Adelphi, 1969), pp. 191–92.

17. I have relied for this discussion on ideas contained in the essays of E. Severino, from *Essenza del nichilismo* (Milan: Adelphi, 1982) to *Gli abitatori del tempo* (Rome: A. Armando 1978) and *Legge e caso* (Milan: Adelphi, 1979).

18. From a letter from Roberto Bazlen to Eugenio Montale, used as an epigraph in O. Manoni, *Fictions freudiennes* (Paris: Seuil, 1978).

19. Wittgenstein, *Culture and Value*; the "aphorism" is taken up again in his *Remarks on the Foundations of Mathematics* [English translation, rev. ed. (Chicago: University of Chicago Press, 1986)].

20. Thus also S. Quinzio, *La fede sepolta* (Milan: Adelphi, 1978), p. 92.

21. M. Vannini, *Lontani dal segno: Saggio sul cristianesimo* (Florence: La Nuova Italia, 1971), p. 14.

22. To understand this "reversal" of a Heideggerian concept, formed on a famous text of Hölderlin, see my essays "Eupalino o l'architettura" and "Die Christenheit oder Europa," both in *Nuova Corrente* 76–77 (1978), an issue entirely devoted to Heidegger.

23. P. Boulez, *Par volonté et par hasard: Entretiens avec Celestin Deliege* (Paris: Editions du Seuil, 1975).

24. M. Bortolotto, "Altra Aurora," in F. Nietzsche, *Scritti su Wagner* (Milan: Adelphi, 1979), p. 55.

25. M. Bortolotto, "Le vin du voyant," in *Adelphiana 1971* (Milan: Adelphi, 1971).

26. L. Nono, "Text-Musik-Gesang" (1960), in J. Stenzl, *Luigi Nono: Texte Studien zu seiner Musik* (Zurich-Freiburg: Atlantis, 1975), p. 44.

27. M. Bortolotto, *Introduzione al Lied romantico* (Milan: Adelphi, 1984), pp. 162–63.

28. See A. Schoenberg, *Fünfzehn Gedichte aus dem Buch der hangenden Gärten für eine Singstimme und Klavier, Op. 15; Texte von Stefan George* (Vienna: Universal Edition, 1914).—TRANS.

29. T. W. Adorno, *Impromptus: Zweite Folge neu gedrückter musikalischer Aufsätze* (Frankfurt: Suhrkamp, 1968). In this passage Adorno retraces, on the same basis, a parallel between Berg and Schoenberg.

30. G. Manzoni, *Arnold Schoenberg: L'uomo, l'opera, i testi musicali* (Milan: Feltrinelli, 1975), p. 42.

31. R. Musil, *Mann ohne Eigenschaften*; in English, *The Man Without Qualities*, trans. Sophie Wilkins, editorial consultant Burton Pike (New York: Knopf, 1995).—TRANS.

32. E. Lemoine-Luccioni, *Partage des femmes* (Paris: Seuil, 1976), pp. 125 ff.

33. E. Castrucci, "Ekstatische Sozietät: Note filosofico-politiche su Robert Musil," *Rivista Internazionale di Filosofia del Diritto* 2 (1977): 4.

34. J. Derrida. *Eperons: Les styles de Nietzsche* (Paris: Flammarion, 1978), pp. 86–92.

35. C. G. Jung, *Psychology and Alchemy*, trans. R. F. C. Hull, 2nd ed. rev. (London: Routledge, 1992 [1968]).—TRANS.

36. For this section see the fundamental essays of R. Klein, "Spirito Peregrino" and "L'immaginazione come veste dell'anima in Marsilio Fi-

cino and Giordano Bruno," in *La forma e l'intelligibile* (Turin: Einaudi, 1975). [In English, *Form and Meaning: Essays on the Renaissance and Modern Art,* trans. Madeline Jay and Leon Wieseltier (New York: Viking, 1979).]

37. H. von Hofmannsthal, *Der Schwierige,* ed. W. E. Yates (Cambridge, Eng.: Cambridge University Press, 1966).—TRANS.

38. E. Staiger, "*Der Schwierige,*" in *Meisterwerke deutscher Sprache,* 2nd ed. (Zurich: Atlantis-Verlag, 1948).

39. H. von Hofmannsthal, *Der Turm: Ein Trauerspiel* (Frankfurt: Fischer, 1992).—TRANS.

40. Cf. H. De Lubac, *L'alba incompiuta del Rinascimento* (Milan: Jaca Book, 1977).

41. F. A. Yates, *Shakespeare's Last Plays: A New Approach* (London: Routledge and Kegan Paul, 1975). After one has arrived at an understanding of this part of my work, it is recommended that a comparison be made with Yates's other books, *Giordano Bruno and the Hermetic Tradition* (Chicago: University of Chicago Press, 1964), as well as *Theatre of the World* (Chicago: University of Chicago Press, 1969), which treats John Dee, protagonist of Meyrink's *The Angel of the Western Window.* About Dee, see also F. Jesi, "John Dee e il suo sapere," *Communità* 166 (1972).

42. C. Loos, *Adolf Loos Privat* (Vienna: W. Bohlau, 1985), pp. 103–4.

43. L. Andreas-Salomé, "Zum Typus Weib," in *Das "zweideutige" Lacheln der Erotik: Texte zur Psychoanalyse* (Freiburg: Kore, 1990).

44. R. M. Rilke, "Puppen," in *Gesammelte Werke,* vol. 4 (Leipzig: Insel-Verlag, 1927).

45. M. Eliade, *Mephistopheles and the Androgyne: Studies in Religious Myth and Symbol,* trans. J. M. Cohen (New York: Sheed and Ward, 1965).

46. G. Agamben, *Infanzia e storia: Distruzione dell'esperienza e origine della storia,* 2nd ed. (Turin: Einaudi, 1971 [in English, *Infancy and History: The Destruction of Experience,* trans. Liz Heron (London, New York: Verso, 1993)]. Walter Benjamin, "Erfahrung und Armut," in *Gesammelte Schriften* unter Mitwirkung von Theodor W. Adorno und Gershom Scholem, herausgegeben von Rolf Tiedemann und Hermann Schweppenhauser (Frankfurt, 1980) vol. 2, part I, p. 218.

47. On Simmel's influence on Benjamin, see my *Metropolis* (Rome: Officina, 1973).

48. C. Magris, *Il mito absburgico nella letteratura autriaca contempo-*

ranea (Turin: Einaudi, 1963), and *Lontano da dove: Joseph Roth e la tradizione ebraico-orientale* (Turin: Einaudi, 1971).

49. J. Roth, *Werke*, 4 vols. (Cologne: Kiepenheuer und Witsch, 1975–76). The Overlook Press, Woodstock, N.Y., has undertaken the project of publishing Roth in English translation. See *Confession of a Murderer Told in One Night* (1985), *The Emperor's Tomb* (1984), '*Hotel Savoy*,' '*Fallmerayer the Stationmaster*,' and '*The Bust of the Emperor*' (1986), *Job: The Story of a Simple Man* (1982), *The Legend of the Holy Drinker* (1991), *The Radetsky March* (1994), *Right and Left* (1992), *The Silent Prophet* (1980), '*The Spider's Web*' and '*Zipper and His Father*' (1989), and *Tarabas, a Guest on Earth* (1987). TRANS.

50. G. Baget-Bozzo and E. Benvenuto, *La conoscenza di Dio* (Rome: Borla, 1978), p. 98.

51. F. Rosenzweig, *Der Stern der Erlösung* (Frankfurt: Kauffmann, 1921) [in English, *The Star of Redemption*, trans. William W. Hallo (Notre Dame, Ind.: Notre Dame University Press, 1985)]. High-quality studies of Rosenzweig are not common; see N. N. Glatzer, *Franz Rosenzweig: His Life and Thought* (New York: Farrar, Straus and Young, 1953). For the relationship between Rosenzweig's Jewish mysticism and Christian concepts, it is interesting to regard the letters between Rosenzweig and Eugen Rosenstock-Huessey, in E. Rosenstock-Huessy, ed., *Judaism Despite Christianity: The Letters on Christianity and Judaism Between Eugen Rosenstock-Huessy and Franz Rosenzweig* (Tuscaloosa: University of Alabama Press, 1969).

52. M. Heidegger, "Language in the Poem: A Discussion of Georg Trakl's Poetic Work," in *On the Way to Language* [in English, trans. Peter D. Hertz (San Francisco: Harper & Row, 1971), pp. 159–98].

53. See A. Kubin, *Mappenwerke, Bücher, Einzelblätter aus der Sammlung Hedwig und Helmut Goedeckemeyer* (Göttingen: Kunstgeschichtliches Seminar der Universität Göttingen, 1980). See also Kubin's autobiography, *Dämonen und Nachtgesichte* (Munich: R. Piper, 1959), and the catalogue raisonée, A. Marks, *Alfred Kubin* (New York: Praeger, 1969).— TRANS.

54. E. Jünger, *Strahlungen* (Tübingen: Heliopolis-Verlag, 1949) [in English, *The Paris Diaries, 1941–1944*, trans. Michael Hulse (New York: Farrar Straus Giroux, 1989)].

55. E. Jünger, "Die Staubdämonen," in *Alfred Kubin: Weltgeflecht, Schriften und Bilder zu Leben und Werk* (Salzburg: Galerie Welz, 1978).

56. A. Kubin, *Die Andere Seite*; in English, *The Other Side: A Fantastic Novel* (New York: Crown, 1967).—TRANS.

57. W. Schmied, *Der Zeichner Alfred Kubin* (Salzburg: 1967), p. 36 [in English, *Alfred Kubin* (New York: Praeger, 1969)].

58. On this resemblance see A. M. Ripellino, *Praga magica* (Turin: Einaudi, 1973), and R. Barthes, *Arcimboldo* [English translation, New York: Rizzoli, 1980].

59. E. Jünger, *Auf den Marmorklippen* [in English, *On the Marble Cliffs: A Novel*, trans. Stuart Hood (New York: New Directions, 1947)]. The book, whose first copy reached Jünger October 6, 1939, reflects in a very transparent way the cultural and political positions of the author with regard to the Nazi regime, positions of almost desperate detachment that seem to plunge roots into the most aristocratic and esoteric aspects of the "conservative revolution" of the 1920's. In his diary of 1939–40, *Gärten und Strassen*, it is possible to follow the draft of the novel and see the importance that Jünger attributed to it: "I think I have succeeded, in this work of fantasy, in writing pieces that can sustain comparison with the best that has been produced in our language."

60. M. Blanchot, "Un oeuvre d'Ernst Jünger," in *Faux pas* (Paris: Gallimard, 1943). G. De Chirico, "Betrachtungen über eine Ausstellung deutscher Kunst" and "Max Klinger (1920)," in *Wir Metaphysiker: Gesammelte Schriften* (Berlin: Propylaen Verlag, 1973). On Klinger, and in particular on the *Glove* cycle, see A. A. Dückers, *Max Klinger* (Berlin: Rembrandt-Verlag, 1976).

61. J. Lezama Lima, "Classical Myths and Fatigue," in *Las eras imaginarias* (Madrid: Editorial Fundamentos, 1971).

62. Cf. G. Briganti, *I pittori dell'immaginario* (Milan: Electa, 1977), pp. 248–49.

63. E. Bloch, "Herbst, Sumpf, Heide, und Sezession," in *Literarische Aufsätze* (Frankfurt: Suhrkamp, 1965), pp. 439 ff [in English, *Literary Essays*, trans. Andrew Joron and Helga Wild (Stanford, Calif.: Stanford University Press, forthcoming)].

64. J. J. Bachofen, *Il popolo licio* (Florence: G. C. Sansoni, 1944). (See also Bachofen, *Gesammelte Werke* [Basel: Schwabe, 1943–67].—TRANS.)

65. On this passage, see J. Lezama Lima, *Introduccion a los vasos orficos* (Barcelona: Barral Editores, 1971).

66. J. Evola, "Introduction" to the collection Bachofen, *Le madri e la virilità olimpica* (Milan, 1949).

67. G. Colli, *Dopo Nietzsche* (Milan: Adelphi, 1974).

68. E. Jünger, *Annäherungen: Drogen und Rausch* (Stuttgart: Klett, 1970).

69. J. Evola, *The Metaphysics of Sex* (New York: Inner Traditions International, 1983).—TRANS.

70. A. Savinio, *Vita di Enrico Ibsen* (Milan: Adelphi, 1979), p. 51.

71. G. Bataille, *Laura: Storia di una ragazzina e altri scritti* (Rome, 1976), p. 119.

72. V. Rozanov, *Foglie cadute* (Milan: Adelphi, 1976), p. 136 [in English, *Fallen Leaves*, trans. S. S. Kotcliansky (London: The Mandrake Press, 1929–)].

73. This is how Schiele expresses himself in his "manifesto" *Neukünstler*, now collected with his other writings in C. M. Nebehay, ed., *Egon Schiele, 1890–1918: Leben, Briefe, Gedichte* (Salzburg: Residenz, 1979).

74. Dylan Thomas's line comes to mind: "My hero bares his nerves along my wrist . . . ' "—a line that could serve to explain not only Schiele's self-portraits, but also those disturbing self-portraits of another *ewiges Kind*, Richard Gerstl, one showing a standing nude (1908), streaked, screaming, fatigue *expressed* in every fiber, and with the most desperate "I must." [See D. Thomas, "My Hero Bares His Nerves," in *Collected Poems, 1934–1953*, ed. Walford Davies and Ralph Maud (London: Dent, 1988).—TRANS.]

75. R. Walser, *Der Spaziergang* (Herrliberg-Zurich: Buhl, 1944), *Geschwister Tanner* (Frankfurt: Suhrkamp, 1967), and *Fritz Kochers Aufsätze* (Zurich: Suhrkamp, 1986).

76. C. Magris, "Davanti alla porta della vita," in R. Walser, *L'assistente*, trans. E. Pocar (Turin: Einaudi, 1978).

77. M. Buber, *Legend of the Baal Shem* [English translation, New York: Harper, 1955]. I will also refer to Buber's other book, *Die Erzählungen der Chassidim* (Zurich: Manesse Verlag, 1949) [in English, *Tales of the Hassidim*, trans. Olga Marx (New York: Schocken, 1947–48)].

78. R. Calasso, "Il sonno del calligrafo," in R. Walser, *Jakob von Gunten*, trans. E. Castellani (Milan: Adelphi, 1970).

79. J. De Menasce, *Quand Israel aime Dieu* (Paris: Plon, 1931), pp. 139 ff.

80. R. Walser, *Kleine Dichtungen* (1914) in *Das Gesamtwerk*, (Geneva: Kossodo, 1967–75), vol. 2, p. 6.

81. E. Canetti, *La provincia dell'uomo* (Milan: Bompiani, 1978), pp. 304–5.

82. R. Walser, "Hölderlin," in *Poetenleben* (1918), in *Das Gesamtwerk* (Geneva: Kossodo, 1978), vol. 3, pp. 116 ff.

83. I cite Hesse, *Morgenlandfahrt* (Berlin: S. Fischer, 1932) [in English, *Journey to the East,* trans. Hilda Rosner (New York: Farrar Straus Giroux, 1956)]; *Siddharta: Eine indische Dichtung* (Berlin: S. Fischer, 1923) [in English, trans. Hilda Rosner (New York: New Directions, 1951)]; and *Klingsors letzter Sommer* (Zurich: Fetz & Warmuth, 1958 [in English, *Klingsor's Last Summer,* trans. Richard and Clara Winston (New York: Farrar Straus Giroux, 1970)].

84. K. Scheffer, "Karl Walser," in *Talente* (Berlin: B. Cassirer, 1921).

85. *Tractatus* 6.521: "The solution of the problem of life is seen in the vanishing of the problem."—TRANS.

86. The citations that appear in this part of the book are taken, essentially, from the following works: D. T. Suzuki, *Mysticism: Christian and Buddhist* (New York: Harper, 1957), and *Essays in Zen Buddhism* (London: Luzak, 1927); E. Herrigel, *Der Zenweg* [in English, *The Method of Zen,* trans. R. F. C. Hull (New York: Pantheon, 1960)]; Yuan-wu, *Pen yen lu* [in English, *The Blue Cliff Record,* trans. Thomas and J. C. Cleary (New York: Random House, 1977)]; Shih Chao-shu, *Radical Zen: The Sayings of Master Joshu,* trans. Yoel Hoffman (New York: Random House, 1974); and P. Reps, *101 Zen Stories* (Philadelphia: David McKay, 1940).

87. E. Herrigel, *Zen in der Kunst des Bogenschiessens* (Weilheim: O. W. Barth, 1981) [in English, *Zen in the Art of Archery,* trans. R. F. C. Hull (New York: Pantheon, 1953)].

88. F. Bellino, "Wittgenstein e Mauthner: la filosofia come Sprachkritik," in *Studi e ricerche dell'Istituto di Filosofia* (Bari: L'Istituto, 1977).

89. Thus M. Müller, *Die Verdrängung des Ornaments: Zum Verhältnis von Architektur und Lebenspraxis* (Frankfurt: Suhrkamp, 1977), pp. 99 ff.

90. See M. Gelsi, "Peter Altenberg e la sacralità del quotidiano," *Nuova Corrente* 79–80 (1979).

91. R. Bazlen, *Note senza testo* (Milan: Adelphi, 1970), pp. 79 ff.

92. L. Mittner, "Appunti autobiografici," *Belfagor* 4 (1975), and "Randglossen zur Kulturgeschichte der Donaumonarchie," in *Jahrbuch der deutschen Akademie für Sprache und Dichtung* (Heidelberg-Darmstadt: Edward Roether, 1973).

93. J. Langer, *Nine Gates to the Chassidic Mysteries* (New York: Behrman House, 1961). Apart from works of Buber, De Menasce, and Langer cited above, I refer here to A. J. Heschel, *A Passion for Truth* (New York: Farrar Straus Giroux, 1973); A. Mandel, *La voie du hassidisme* (Paris: Calmann-Levy, 1963); M. Buber, *Schriften zum Chassidismus,* in

Gesammelte Werke, vol. 3 (Frankfurt: Fischer, 1963); and G. Scholem, *Judaica* (Frankfurt: Suhrkamp, 1963), pp. 165–206.

94. I. B. Singer, *Shosha* (New York: Farrar Straus Giroux, 1978).

95. E. Canetti, *Massa e potere* (Milan: Adelphi, 1972), p. 192. We have already seen how Wittgenstein might express the identical judgment in *Culture and Value*.

96. G. Scholem, *Major Trends in Jewish Mysticism* (New York: Schocken, 1946), pp. 329 ff. Scholem also dedicated his great work on Sabbatai Zevi to the theme of Messianism, *Sabbatai Zevi, the Mystical Messiah* (Princeton, N.J.: Princeton University Press, 1973).

97. See J. Habermas, "Der deutsche Idealismus und die judischen Philosophen," in *Philosophisch-politische Profile* (Frankfurt: Suhrkamp, 1971), p. 49.

98. K. Löwith, "M. Heidegger und F. Rosenzweig, ein Nachtrag zu 'Sein und Zeit,'" in *Gesammelte Abhandlungen* (Stuttgart: W. Kohlhammer, 1960).

99. H. Kohn, *Karl Kraus, Arthur Schnitzler, Otto Weininger: Aus dem judischen Wien der Jahrhundertwende* (Tübingen: Mohr, 1962), p. 59.

100. R. Calasso, "Una muraglia cinese," in K. Kraus, *Detti e contradetti* (Milan: Adelphi, 1972).

101. I extract Kraus's emblems from the explication of basic ideograms in Confucian texts by Ezra Pound. Pound prepared poems from the *Shih Ching* for Italian readers in the 1950's, including *Confucio: Studio integrale & l'asse che non vacilla* (Milan: All'Insegna del pesce d'oro, 1955; 2nd ed., 1960).

102. K. Kraus, *Die letzten Tage der Menschheit: Tragodie in fünf Akten mit Vorspiel und Epilog* (Munich: Kosel-Verlag, 1957) [in English, *The Last Days of Mankind: A Tragedy in Five Acts* (New York: F. Ungar, 1974)]. Kraus's supreme mastery in rousing the horror that Canetti so splendidly analyzed in *Potere e sopravivenza* (Milan: Adelphi, 1974) bursts into flame in this work, precisely through the device of quotation. Quotation became a means to stir horror. Unfortunately, now we can only quote horrors.

103. P. Zellini, *Breve storia dell'infinito* (Milan: Adelphi, 1980), p. 29.

104. See, in this regard, B. Allemann, "Robert Musil," in *Ironie und Dichtung* (Pfullingen: Neske, 1956).

105. In this, Musil's essay form is metaphysically distinct from Lukács's in *The Soul and Forms* (just as his irony is distinct from Mann's). It appears, rather, to hold a stricter affinity with that of Benjamin. See G.

Schiavoni, *Walter Benjamin: Sopravivere alla cultura* (Palermo: Sellerio, 1980), p. 35.

106. On the subject of moments, see my essay and others collected in M. Bertaggia, et al., *Crucialità del tempo: Saggi sulla concezione nietzchiana del tempo* (Naples: Liguori, 1980).

107. Quoted in A. Del Noce, "Simone Weil interprete del monde d'oggi," in *L'epoca della secolarizzazione* (Milan: Giuffre, 1970), p. 141; I have this essay in mind for this and other points in my work, in spite of (or perhaps as a result of) my enormous distance from its "conclusions."

108. Castrucci's interesting observations in "Ekstatische Sozietät: Note filosofico-politiche su Robert Musil" should be developed in this direction.

109. On the relationship between Musil and Nietzsche, an intelligent "summary" can be found in I. Seidler, "Das Nietzschebild Robert Musils," in *Nietzsche und die deutsche Literatur*, B,2 (Tübingen: Niemeyer, 1978).

110. J. Derrida, "Violence and Metaphysics," in *Writing and Difference* (Chicago: University of Chicago Press, 1978). F. Desideri rightly refers to this passage with regard to Benjamin, in his volume, *Walter Benjamin: Il tempo e le forme* (Rome: Riuniti, 1980), p. 91.

111. S. Kierkegaard, *Dagboger*, vol. 1 [in English, *Diary*, ed. Peter P. Rohde (New York: Philosophical Library, 1960)].

Figure Sources

Figures 2–5, 11–13, by Alfred Kubin, © 1996 Artist Rights Society, (ARS), New York / VG Bild-Kunst, Bonn

Figure 8, by Max Klinger, Kupferstichkabinett, Staatliche Museen zu Berlin PK

Figure 9, by Max Klinger, Museum der bildenen Künste Leipzig

Figure 10, by Arnold Böcklin, Oeffentlich Kunstsammlung Basel, Kunstmuseum, Gift of the Carlo Markees Family, Basel, 1970; photo: Oeffentliche Kunstsammlung Basel, Martin Bühler

Figure 15, by Egon Schiele, Historisches Museum der Stadt Wien

Figure 1; Figures 6, 7, 14, by Max Klinger; and Figure 16, by Egon Schiele, courtesy Adelphi Edizione S. P., Milan

M E R I D I A N

Crossing Aesthetics

Library of Congress
Cataloging-in-Publication Data

Cacciari, Massimo.
[Dallo Steinhof.   English]
Posthumous people : Vienna at the turning point / Massimo
Cacciari; translated by Rodger Friedman.
         p.   cm. — (Meridian, Stanford, Calif.)
Translation of: Dallo Steinhof. Milano : Adelphi, 1980.
ISBN 0-8047-2709-0 (cloth : alk. paper). —
ISBN 0-8047-2710-4 (paper : alk. paper)
    1. Vienna (Austria)—Intellectual life.   2. Politics and culture—
Austria—Vienna.   3. Vienna (Austria)—Social life and customs.
4. Vienna (Austria)—Biography.   5. Intellectuals—Austria—
Vienna.   6. Vienna (Austria)—Civilization.   I. Title.
II. Series.
DB851.C3213   1996
943.6'13—dc20   96-14952   CIP

Original printing 1996

Last figure below indicates year of this printing

05   04   03   02   01   00   99   98   97   96